Death, Dominance, and State-Building

Death, Dominance, and State-Building

The US in Iraq and the Future of American Military Intervention

ROGER D. PETERSEN

OXFORD
UNIVERSITY PRESS

OXFORD
UNIVERSITY PRESS

Oxford University Press is a department of the University of Oxford. It furthers
the University's objective of excellence in research, scholarship, and education
by publishing worldwide. Oxford is a registered trade mark of Oxford University
Press in the UK and certain other countries.

Published in the United States of America by Oxford University Press
198 Madison Avenue, New York, NY 10016, United States of America.

© Oxford University Press 2024

Library of Congress Cataloging-in-Publication Data
Names: Petersen, Roger Dale, 1959– author.
Title: Death, dominance, and state-building : the US in Iraq and the future
of American military intervention / Roger D. Petersen.
Other titles: US in Iraq and the future of American military intervention
Description: New York, NY : Oxford University Press, [2024] |
Includes bibliographical references and index.
Identifiers: LCCN 2023049372 (print) | LCCN 2023049373 (ebook) |
ISBN 9780197760741 (hardback) | ISBN 9780197760765 (epub)
Subjects: LCSH: Postwar reconstruction—Iraq—Evaluation. | Iraq War,
2003-2011. | Nation-building—Iraq—History—21st century. |
Internal security—Iraq—Evaluation. | Iraq—Politics and government—2003– |
United States—Relations—Iraq. | Iraq—Relations—United States. |
Nation-building—United States—History—21st century. | Intervention
(International law)—Government policy—United States.
Classification: LCC DS79.769 .P48 2024 (print) | LCC DS79.769 (ebook) |
DDC 956.7044/3—dc23/eng/20231206 '
LC record available at https://lccn.loc.gov/2023049372
LC ebook record available at https://lccn.loc.gov/2023049373

DOI: 10.1093/oso/9780197760741.001.0001

Printed by Integrated Books International, United States of America

For Daniela, always

CONTENTS

LIST OF ACRONYM

AAH	Asaib Ahl al-Haq
ADM	Assyrian Democratic Movement
AO	area of operation
APP	Assyrian Patriotic Party
AQI	al-Qaeda in Iraq
ATAK	Android Team Awareness Kit
BCT	brigade combat team
CDE	collateral damage estimators
CENTCOM	US Central Command
CERP	Commanders' Emergency Response Program
CF	Coalition Forces
CHB	clear, hold, build
CIA	Central Intelligence Agency
CJSOTF	Combined Joint Special Operations Task Force
CJTF-7	Combined Joint Task Force-7
CO	commanding officer
COIN	counterinsurgency
COIST	company intelligence support team
COL	colonel
COP	command outpost
CPA	Coalition Provisional Authority
CTC	Counter-Terrorism Command
CTJF-7	Combined Joint Task Force 7
CTS	Counter-Terrorism Service
DIA	Defense Intelligence Agency
DoD	Department of Defense
EFP	explosively formed penetrator
FBI	Federal Bureau of Investigation

FM	field manual
FOB	Forward Operating Base
FPS	Facilities Protection Service
GEN	general
GG	Ghazaliyah Guardians
GMCIR	General Military Council of Iraqi Revolutionaries
GMLRS	Guided Multiple-Launch Rocket System
GOI	Government of Iraq
GPS	global positioning system
GWOT	Global War on Terror
HMMWV	High Mobility Multipurpose Wheeled Vehicle (aka "Humvee")
HQ	headquarters
HUMINT	human intelligence
HVT	high-value target
I MEF	I Marine Expeditionary Force
IA	Iraqi Army
IAF	Iraqi Armed Forces
ICDC	Iraqi Civil Defense Corps
IED	improvised explosive device
IGC	Iraqi Governing Council
INA	Iraqi National Accord
INC	Iraqi National Congress
IO	Information Operations
IP	Iraqi Police
IRGC	Islamic Revolutionary Guard Corps of Iran
ISF	Iraqi security forces
ISG	Iraq Survey Group
ISI	Islamic State of Iraq
ISIS	Islamic State of Iraq and Syria
ISOF	Iraqi Special Operations Forces
ISR	intelligence, surveillance, and reconnaissance
JAM	Jaysh al-Mahdi (aka Mahdi Army)
JCS	Joint Chiefs of Staff
JOC	Joint Operations Center
JRTN	Jaysh Rijal al-Tariqah a-Naqshabandia
JSOC	Joint Special Operations Command
JSOTF	Joint Special Operations Task Force
JSS	joint security stations
JTAC	joint terminal attack controller
JTJ	Jamiat al-Tahwid wal-Jihad

KDP	Kurdistan Democratic Party
KH	Kataeb Hezbollah
KIA	killed in action
KRG	Kurdistan Regional Government
KRSC	Kurdistan Regional Security Council
KRSI	Kurdistan Regional Security Institution
LT GEN	lieutenant general (also LGEN and LT. GEN.)
LTC	lieutenant colonel
MCOO	Modified Combined Obstacle Overlay
MCWP	Marine Corps Warfighting Publication
MEF	Marine Expeditionary Force
MiTT	Military Transition Team
MNB-NW	Multi-National Brigade–Northwest
MNC-I	Multi-National Corps–Iraq
MND-N	Multi-National Division–North
MNFI	Multi-National Force–Iraq
MNF-W	Multi-National Force–West
MNSTC-I	Multi-National Security Transition Command–Iraq
MOD	Ministry of Defense
MOI	Ministry of the Interior
MRAP	Mine-resistant Ambush-protected Vehicles
NATO	North Atlantic Treaty Organization
NCO	noncommissioned officer
NGO	nongovernmental organization
NP	National Police
NPF	Nineveh Plains Forces
NPG	Nineveh Plains Guards
NPU	Nineveh Plains Protection Units
NSA	National Security Agency
NSC	National Security Council
ODA	Operational Detachment Alpha
OMS	Organization / Office of the Martyr Sadr
ORHA	Office of Reconstruction and Humanitarian Assistance
PKK	Kurdistan Workers Party
PM	prime minister
PMC	Popular Mobilization Commission
PMF	Popular Mobilization Forces
PRT	provincial reconstruction team
PSF	Provisional Security Forces
PUK	Patriotic Union of Kurdistan
ROE	rules of engagement

RPA	remotely piloted aircraft
RPG	rocket-propelled grenade
SAS	Special Air Service
SCIRI	Supreme Council for the Islamic Revolution in Iraq
SEAL	Sea, Air, and Land Teams
SIGACT	Significant Acts of Violencesignificant activity
SIGINT	signals intelligence
SOCOM	Special Operations Command
SOF	Special Operations Forces
SOI	Sons of Iraq
SOTF-W	Special Operations Task Force West
SVBIED	suicide vehicle-borne improvised explosive device
SWEAT-MSO	sewer, water, electricity, academics, trash, medical, safety, and other
TF	Task Force
TOC	Tactical Operations Center
TRADOC	US Army Training and Doctrine Command
TSU	tactical support unit
UAV	unmanned aerial vehicle
UIA	United Iraqi Alliance
UK	United Kingdom
UN	United Nations
USAID	US Agency for International Development
USIP	US Institute of Peace
USMC	US Marine Corps
VBIED	vehicle-borne improvised explosive device
WERV	Western Euphrates River Valley
WMD	weapons of mass destruction
YPG	Yekîneyên Parastina Gel / Kurdish People's Protection Units

SECTION I

FRAMEWORK

Death, Dominance, and State-Building

*The United States in Iraq and the Future of
American Intervention*

1.1. Introduction

The Iraq invasion and war were hugely consequential for the United States. Although the Iraq war is almost universally derided as one of the biggest foreign policy blunders of the post–Cold War era, the course and conduct of the conflict are actually poorly understood. Above all, the "lessons" taken from the Iraq case are unhelpful overgeneralizations. From a general policymaking standpoint, the lesson is that the United States cannot do "nation-building." From the US military side, the lesson is that the military should not do counterinsurgency. Indeed, as US policymakers and military leaders turn toward "near-peer" competition, "counterinsurgency" is something of a dirty word. Correspondingly, few wish to hear more about Iraq because it is seen as a quintessential case of nation-building and counterinsurgency. These dismissals are unfortunate. The United States cannot simply wish away insurgencies. They are going to occur. The question is what the United States and other great powers might do about them.

Furthermore, these lessons are not just overgeneralizations: they are oversimplifications, not connected with what actually happened. Two misunderstandings stand out above all others. The first has to do with US strategy and conduct in Iraq. There was no single counterinsurgency strategy in Iraq. The United States instituted at least five different strategies: clear, hold, build (CHB); decapitation; community mobilization; homogenization; and warfighting. These strategies, and combinations of these strategies, were employed at

different times and in different regions in Iraq. Insurgents confronted US efforts
with their own counterstrategies. These interactions among opponents sometimes favored the United States and the Coalition; other times those interactions
favored the insurgents. In effect, there was not one single war in Iraq, there were
many. The Iraq war produced a multitudinous number of interactions with tremendous variation in outcomes.

To fail to consider this variation in favor of gross generalization is an ab-
dication of critical thinking. For any social scientist dedicated to explaining
variation in violence and state-building, the Iraq conflict provides an incred-
ibly rich and valuable recent history. To say that the United States lost, won
at a high cost, or drew is not particularly helpful. Indeed, the US military
often succeeded in reducing violence. US forces succeeded less in the realm
of state-building. Even in the realm of state-building, the reality is complicated. In its 2018 evaluations, Freedom House gave Iraq a 32/100 score, far
better than many other Middle Eastern states. Also in 2018, Polity, a database assessing levels of democracy, gave Iraq a score of 6, a high score by
regional standards. As of this writing in 2023, Iraq stumbles along. Iraq is
not Afghanistan.

There is a failure to appreciate variation in US strategy in Iraq and how it
produced different types of conflicts over space and time. A second major failure
is in understanding the overarching environment where strategies played out. At
a most fundamental level, the war and political battles in Iraq from 2003 until the
end of the Islamic State (ISIS) war have been a struggle for group dominance. As
the reader will note—death and state-building are two of the words in the title of
the book. Dominance is the third. While the Iraq war and related conflicts were
highly decentralized on the one hand, identity master cleavages often played an
overarching and decisive part in explaining key outcomes. We cannot fully understand variation in violence, state-building, or the general contours of the Iraq
conflict without understanding the underlying identity contests for dominance
among Shias, Sunnis, and Kurds.

This book is composed of four sections. The middle two sections are empirical. The 16 chapters that comprise these sections consist mostly of case studies.
Section II covers 2003–2011, the years from the invasion to the end of the official US presence. Section III addresses the impact and legacy of the 2003–2011
US intervention and counterinsurgency policies through an examination of Iraq
from 2011 up to the time of writing (2023). Based on the work's findings and
conclusions about the entire period from the time of invasion to the present, the
fourth and final section speculates about the future of U.S. military intervention.
These three interconnected sections require an analytical framework that can be
consistently and coherently applied across time and region. Section I provides
that framework.

1.2. A Brief Overview of Iraq from 2003 to 2020

This is a long and detailed book that will tell a complicated and sometimes nuanced story about the Iraq war and its legacy. Yet, a focus on two basic phenomena—violence and state-building—underlie most of the book. I address each in turn.

Two of the most commonly referred to sources of data on the Iraq wars are US Significant Acts of Violence (SIGACTS) and the Iraq Body Count. Many readers may be familiar with the two figures below. Figure 1.1 captures variation in SIGACTS across time and Iraqi region from 2003 until 2008. The figure illustrates violence against Coalition forces during the height of the US presence. SIGACTS numbers are compiled from patrol, intelligence, and artillery counter-battery reports (and thus they undercount Iraqi-on-Iraqi violence where US troops are not present). Despite such issues, the figure usefully depicts broad trends. The primary axis on the left measures the monthly level of significant activity of violence recorded by Coalition forces between February 2004 and December 2008, disaggregated by region.[1] The graph breaks down the numbers by six regions—Baghdad, a "central" region around Baghdad, the Sunni-dominated Western provinces of Anbar, the Kurdish "north," the ethnically and religiously mixed northern region of Ninewa, and the largely Shia "south." The secondary axis on the right measures the overall level of international troops stationed in Iraq, with US troops figures separated from international forces.

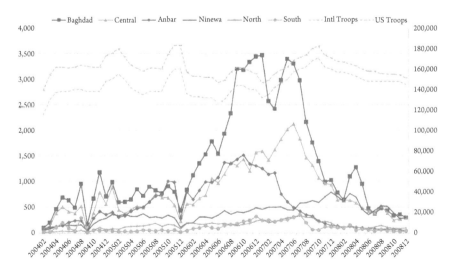

Figure 1.1. Significant acts of violence. Source: SIGACT data derived from Multi-National Forces Iraq SIGACT-III database as reported by Berman et al (2008); Troop data from O'Hanlon and Livingston, "Iraq Index," 16.

Figure 1.1 highlights three notable characteristics of the post-invasion period. First, the levels of violence were often shockingly high. In the second half of 2006, Baghdad alone was recording over 3,000 significant acts of violence per month. This violence in turn created large numbers of internally displaced people fleeing uncertainty and brutality.

Second, levels of violence vacillated wildly over time. The very contours of the conflict have been defined by stunning and unpredicted peaks and declines in violence. Baghdad saw dramatic changes over the course of a few short years. In December 2005, the number of SIGACTS totaled just 500. This number skyrocketed to 3,500, a seven-fold increase, by January 2007. The figure then plummeted as dramatically as it rose, returning to a level of approximately 600 SIGACTS by February 2008. The Iraq conflict is characterized by dramatic rises in violence and then reactions to quell that violence.

Third, violence varied dramatically by region. Baghdad's explosions of violence stand in stark contrast to the near absence of violence in both the northern region (essentially the Kurdistan Region of Iraq) and the southern region. Regions also experienced different peak periods of violence. Violence in the north evolved differently than in any other region. Note that SIGACTS numbers in Anbar Province begin their fall before the Surge of US troops, while Baghdad numbers fall during the Coalition troop increase. Violence levels in all regions did finally come down together by the end of 2008.

The empirical cases in Section II will explain the reasons for these sharp increases and declines in violence over time, especially as they played out in the capital city of Baghdad. How was it possible for violence to reach such high levels given the presence of US troops? What caused the incredible decline of violence in 2007? Why did levels of violence vary so dramatically across time and region?

Section III will continue to address variation in violence in Iraq in the period 2011–2020, the period after US withdrawal. Figure 1.2, from Iraq Body Count (IBC), presents numbers of civilian casualties from the time of invasion in 2003 until 2018 with the defeat of ISIS.[2] IBC's public database is compiled from crosschecked media reports supplemented by morgue, hospital, nongovernmental organization (NGO), and other records. As the reader will note, in many key respects, the overall pattern of civilian deaths during the years of US presence resembles that of SIGACTS recorded in Figure 1.1. The dramatic rise and fall in civilian deaths in 2006–2008 mirrors that in attacks against Coalition forces. Figure 1.2 takes the story further, documenting another dramatic rise of killing with the coming of ISIS in 2014. Civilian deaths persisted until the defeat of ISIS.

Why did the state-building and counterinsurgency efforts of the 2003–2011 period fail to prevent the violence and state collapse seen with the coming of ISIS? How was ISIS eventually defeated? Section III will address this question, among others, including the strategies used to defeat ISIS, the creation of new forms of Iraqi security forces, and the strategic calculations of minority groups. Figures 1.1 and 1.2 capture variation in violence through different but often-cited data sources. The other outcome of interest in this book concerns state-building. There are many ways to talk about the strength or weakness of a state. International organizations devoted to strengthening and rebuilding fragile states often refer to five goals: (1) legitimate politics (citizens accepting the rule of state organs and elected leaders); (2) security; (3) justice; (4) economic foundations; and (5) revenues and services.[3]

US political leaders had their own list of state-building goals and criteria. Regime change meant replacing Saddam's defective and dangerous state with a new type of state, hopefully a democratic one observing the rule of law and human rights, but at minimum a state that could at least control its own borders and ally with the United States against terrorism. In his remarks at Camp Lejeune in 2009, President Obama stated:

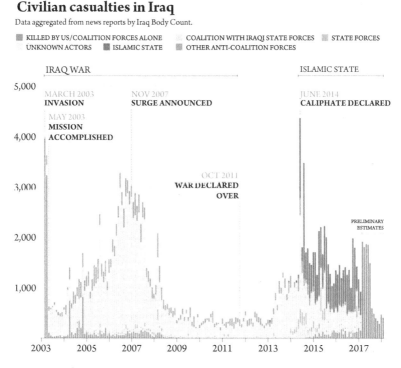

Figure 1.2. Civilian casualties in Iraq.
Source: https://www.iraqbodycount.org/

Today, I can announce that our review is complete, and that the United States will pursue a new strategy to end the war in Iraq through a transition to full Iraqi responsibility. This strategy is grounded in a clear and achievable goal shared by the Iraqi people and the American people: an Iraq that is sovereign, stable, and self-reliant. To achieve that goal, we will work to promote an Iraqi government that is just, representative, and accountable, and that provides neither support nor safe-haven to terrorists.

At the core of these passages is his three-element phrase— "sovereign, stable, and self-reliant."

By either the five-pronged international organizational rating or President Obama's three characteristics, Iraq has demonstrated state weakness since the 2003 invasion and in many ways has remained a dysfunctional state as of 2023. Despite its enormous oil resources, Iraq's economic foundations and services have been weak. The 2019 Tishreen demonstrations railed against poor public services, high unemployment, and a lack of electricity; these protests questioned the very legitimacy of the government, working to bring it down and force new elections. On the rule of law, justice, and transparency, Iraq ranked 157th out 180 countries surveyed in the Transparency International 2022 index. If sovereignty has any meaning, it involves a measure of control over territory. The Iraqi state lost control of one-third of Iraq's territory to ISIS in 2014, not long after the US departure. The Kurdish territories voted overwhelmingly for independence in a 2017 referendum, and Kurdish territories are still under dispute at the time of writing. In 2023, both Turkey and Iran make regular incursions onto Iraqi territory. Regarding stability, political factions fought a pitched battle in the Green Zone in August 2023. While oil income provides a measure of self-reliance, as late as February 2018, in the wake of ISIS, donors pledged $30 billion for reconstruction, a number far short of the $88 billion that Iraqi leaders were seeking.[4]

In some ways, Iraq possesses characteristics that could help build a strong state. Unlike Lebanon, Iraq possesses a legacy of strong state; in the era before the First Gulf War in 1991, citizens looked to the state for jobs and services. Iraq's oil reserves may feed the dynamics of "the oil curse," but they also provide the state considerable resources for infrastructure projects. The question then becomes why, despite these advantages, despite US goals and efforts, Iraq remains a weak state. Relatedly, why has the Kurdistan Regional Government, a quasi-state with many opportunities and advantages, failed to develop a coherent and functioning state?

Violence and state-building are separate phenomena. In fact, this book will illustrate how US strategies were often effective in reducing violence despite failing to build the basis for a strong state. At a fundamental level, however, violence and state-building are inextricably linked. If violence rages and the government cannot control its own territory, creating effective institutions is impossible. If institutions do not provide for bargaining between societal and political groups, if they cannot produce honest police and judges, if they cannot execute basic functions in public services, if they are not seen as legitimate, then non-state violent actors are likely to persist and thrive.

1.3. The Method of the Book and Preview of Chapters

The answers to both questions of violence and state-building require a detailed understanding of the contests between state and counterinsurgent on one side, and the state opponents and insurgents on the other. Accordingly, the first order of business is to develop an analytical framework able to break down these contests into understandable and comparable parts. This task is the focus of Section I. This framework will then be applied to most of the cases found in the 16 chapters of Sections II and III. This approach is inductive. As the framework is consistently applied to a wide variety of cases, findings and lessons will emerge. While Section I will specify and justify the elements of the analytical framework, the following paragraphs provide a preview. A short summary of the book's sections and chapters follows.

A primary focus of the analytical framework is to develop a way to analyze the matchup of strategies between the state/counterinsurgent and insurgents.[5] A first assumption is that individuals come to occupy and often move among identifiable roles during insurgency. These roles can be aligned on a spectrum. "Neutrals" occupy the middle position. For both the state and the insurgents, roles of nonviolent supporter, armed and locally organized supporter, and mobile fighter form the other nodes on this spectrum.

The second assumption is that there are reasons why individuals move into different roles on this spectrum. There are reasons why neutrals move into roles of unarmed support, or join local militias. These reasons can be linked to what social scientists term "mechanisms"—fine-grained forces behind actions. The

Figure 1.3. Spectrum of roles.

social sciences have identified many such mechanisms, which can be categorized into four broad groups: rational choice, norms, emotions, and psychological phenomena. For our purposes, only a relatively small number of these mechanisms are highly relevant to insurgency and violent domestic conflict.

The third fundamental assumption is that both the counterinsurgents and insurgents develop strategies intended to trigger specific mechanisms and in turn move individuals into desired roles. As the empirical chapters will lay out, the United States implemented no less than five identifiable counterinsurgency/state-building strategies during the 2003–2011 period. These strategies included (1) war-fighting; (2) clear, hold, build (CHB); (3) decapitation; (4) community mobilization; and (5) tacit homogenization. Each of these strategies was built on explicit or implicit ideas about the best means to trigger mechanisms and shift individuals into new roles. On the other side, the insurgents and state opponents developed strategies of their own, using their comparative advantages to blunt the US strategy and take advantage of its deficiencies.

These three concepts—roles, mechanisms, and strategies—are the building blocks of the book's analytical framework and are discussed and described in detail over the next three chapters, which form the first section of the book. This framework allows the analysis of the logic, or lack of logic, of the various strategies used by competing actors. Through its identification and concentration on mechanisms and processes, the framework can help provide an understanding of why these strategies accomplished or failed to attain their intended results, as well as how the interaction of competing strategies produced unforeseen outcomes.

Section I chapters include:

Chapter 2: Analytical Framework I: Roles and Strategy
Chapter 3: Analytical Framework II: Mechanisms and Strategy
Chapter 4: US Counterinsurgency Strategy and Practice

The second and third sections of the book apply the framework in the course of 16 chapters. Many chapters in Section II are case studies of how the war played out in different neighborhoods of Baghdad, the decisive locus of the war. There are also chapters on Anbar and the Kurdistan region. One chapter is topical, covering the difficulties of establishing local security. There is a reason why this study requires so many empirical chapters. Because of the fragmentation of the insurgency and the de facto decentralization of the US effort, there were in fact many distinct dynamics playing out in different places and different times.

Section II chapters include:

Chapter 5: Violence, State-Building, and the Sunni-Shia Cleavage

To emphasize from above, the application of the framework will show how US strategies and insurgent strategies matched up in terms of their abilities to trigger specific mechanisms able to move individuals in and out of desired roles. These chapters will produce a fine-grained explanation of US success and failure in specific places and times that will allow us to get away from overly broad generalizations.

All of the cases will bring in the role of identity and master cleavages and the effect of changes in group power and hierarchy in driving decision-making and outcomes. Some of the cases concentrate more directly on state-building than others. Chapter 9, "The Failure to Establish Local Security," will focus mainly on how sectarian militias captured many state security organs. Chapter 14, on Iraqi Kurdistan, will show how a political master cleavage dividing the Kurdistan Democratic Party (KDP) and the Patriotic Union of Kurdistan (PUK) negatively affected state-building, even in favorable conditions.

Great power military interventions are meant not only to quell violence in the short run, but also to change the nature of the target state and its longer-term trajectory. This point brings us to Section III. Figure 1.2 shows two peaks of high civilian casualties, the first during the US presence and the second largely corresponding to the incursion and attacks of ISIS. These two peaks in violence are not unrelated. This work will illustrate how the nature of strategies implemented in the earlier period (the focus of Section II), combined with a general failure in state-building, helped lead to the eruption of later violence covered in Section III.

Critically, the Iraqi state failed to build effective state institutions during the years of low violence. Even though violence receded from 2008 forward, little was done to create an effective state able to resist a future incursion of a Sunni insurgent organization. The Iraq state failed to develop a competent and minimally cohesive military that could put up a fight, let alone win a fight, against ISIS insurgents. More generally, the Iraqi state's failure to build functional governing institutions did little to give citizens incentives to support the center versus ISIS. On many scores, lack of state-building led to later violence and collapse.

Section III chapters include:

Chapter 15: Hawija: Explaining Sunni Resurgence

Chapter 16: The Third Iraq War

Chapter 17: Hybrid Actors: The Emergence and Persistence of the Popular Mobilization Forces

Chapter 18: How Minorities Make Their Way: The Case of Christian Militias in the Nineveh Plains (co-written with Matt Cancian)

Chapter 19: The Kurdistan Regional Government Revisited: Death, War, Machinations, and Little Change

Chapter 20: The Decline of Dominance? Emotions and Institutions in Iraq 10 Years after the US Withdrawal.

Section III pursues multiple related goals. First, it will again apply the analytical framework to cases. As with Section II, the application of our framework will try to identify the strategies, mechanisms, and movement among roles that help us understand outcomes in level of violence and state-building. The reader will note the continued salience of master cleavages, the persistent fears of domination, and reactions to perceived changes in the status hierarchy.

The Hawija case of Chapter 15 serves as a bridge between Section II and Section III, showing how the power of Sunni resentment against the Shia-dominated state helped maintain the potential for violence and state breakdown across more than a decade. Chapter 16 on the Third Iraq War, better known as the war against ISIS, provides a view of the transformation of US military intervention policy and practice from the first period. The war against ISIS was fought with a different relationship to the Iraqi state and Iraqi military. The fourth section returns to this chapter to argue that US practices and capabilities in the ISIS war may become a watershed in the evolution of US military intervention. Chapter 17 covers the emergence of the Popular Mobilization Forces (PMF)—non-state security forces who draw on state resources. The PMF phenomenon has major ramifications for state-building. The emergence of hybrid actors suggests ways in which practitioners must reconceptualize the state in future conflicts and interventions. Chapter 18 on the Christian minority explains how and why sections of a minority group moved from relative pacifism to the creation of militias. Chapter 19 revisits the Kurdistan Regional Government (KRG) with a chapter centered on the disastrous independence referendum of 2017. Again, we examine the role and intersection of two master cleavages— Kurd versus Arab, and KDP versus PUK. Finally, the last chapter of the section will again focus on the power and persistence of master cleavages in Iraq, although with a consideration of their decline with the clear establishment and acceptance of Shia ascendance.

Section IV starts out by summarizing the findings from the empirical chapters. Chapter 21 ends with a list of lessons that not only relate to Iraq, but can also be applied to great power military intervention in general. Not all lessons will be learned, and some will likely be forgotten. Chapter 22 considers the forces, both international and domestic, that work to shape learning, and forgetting, for US policymakers. Chapter 23 takes into account both lessons and learning to speculate on the future of American military intervention.

Section IV chapters include:

Chapter 21: Findings and Lessons
Chapter 22: Constraints on Learning: The Influence of the Changing International System and US Domestic Politics
Chapter 23: The Future of American Military Intervention.

As mentioned, Chapter 21 begins the section by summarizing findings. What were those findings?

1.4. Preview of Findings: Lists, Arguments, and Variables

The conclusions of this book can be presented in three different ways. As mentioned above, the application of the analytical framework across cases will identify patterns and general findings about the key dynamics driving the contests which took place across Iraq. These findings can be presented in the form of a list. The book also presents and supports some broad arguments. The method and findings of the book can also be discussed in terms of variables and processes. We address each way of previewing the findings of the book below, starting with a list of findings from Iraq, then laying out central arguments, and finally displaying the book's approach through a flow chart and reference to variables.

1.4.1. List of Findings

1.4.1.1. Iraq's conflicts have been pervaded by concerns over group dominance/subordination. In the contest among Shia, Sunni, and Kurds, Shia emerged as dominant.

One of the most general findings of this study is that the conflict in Iraq has been driven by competition by sectarian and ethnic groups for dominance. Historically, the Sunni minority occupied most positions of authority in Iraq. Even in the 1990s, Shia groups in exile were preparing to return and change that reality. In short, the majority Shia population was not going to be denied ascendance. The coming of democracy would certainly propel that goal. In response, Sunnis would find it difficult to accept a status reversal.

With the coming of a changing and uncertain new ethnic hierarchy,[6] both groups acted on their perceptions of unjust hierarchy: Shias looking to change the past hierarchy, Sunnis resenting what they perceived as an unjust Shia rise. The flow of events illustrated the dynamics. In the 2005 elections, Shias combined to form a dominant coalition, while Sunnis boycotted the election. A sectarian-based civil war broke out and erupted in massive violence. Shia militias "cleansed" neighborhood after neighborhood of Sunni residents, resulting in the incredible rise of deaths seen in the figures above. The decrease in violence seen in those figures in 2007–2008 comes at a time where Shia dominance in Baghdad had been established. The rise of ISIS and its rapid drive through the Sunni areas of northern and western Iraq was fueled by remaining Sunni resentment against the Shia-dominated government.

In the north, the Kurds as a group struggled to enhance their position versus the Iraqi Arab-dominated state, expanding their control over disputed territories throughout the post-2003 era. Within Iraqi Kurdistan, KDP and the PUK competed for dominance, or at least the avoidance of subordination.

After the end of the ISIS war, and the failed 2017 Kurdish independence referendum, Shia political organizations came to essentially "own" the Iraqi state. Many Sunnis had retained hope of regaining their former dominant status on the eve of the ISIS invasion. Any remaining belief in such a recovery was destroyed by the ISIS war. In this war, a Sunni organization—the Islamic State—produced nothing but the destruction of Sunni cities and lives. On the other hand, Shia militias in the form of the Hash'd al Shabi (Popular Mobilization Forces, or PMF) had been a key force in driving ISIS out of Iraq. The war produced desolation among Sunnis, pride and confidence among Shias.

For the Kurds, the outcome of the Independence Referendum of 2017 clarified the subordinate position of Kurds within the Iraq state. Since 2003, Kurds had taken control over much of the so-called disputed territory. After the referendum, a combination of government and Arab forces, aided by the PUK, rolled back Kurdish control to the 2003 lines. Despite the overwhelming vote for independence, the post-referendum moves on the ground by the Shia-dominated central government, combined with international indifference to the outcome, showed that independence would again have to be put on a back burner. Today, the KRG remains politically divided and troubled.

With a new clear ethnic hierarchy in place in Iraq, the era of sectarian violence in Iraq came to end. In the Shia-dominated state, Sunni and Kurds became renters or junior partners. Iraq still saw violent clashes, but only between Shia factions.

1.4.1.2. Shia ascendance was aided by superior political and military organization.

Beyond their majority numbers and motivating status resentments, Shia organizations had strong potential for mobilization. The Badr Organization had trained for years in Iran. Moqtada al-Sadr could easily mobilize mass protests and raise fighters from his base in the giant Shia slums of Sadr City; he could build off the reputation and organizations left by his uncle and father. The so-called special groups, off-shoots of the Sadrist Jaysh al-Mahdi (JAM), operated with effective logistical support through Iran. Moreover, the nature of Shia religious practice produced focal points and centralized communication.

In comparison, while Sunnis were motivated by a perception of status reversal, their internal base for mobilization relied on former Baathist networks. While some of these networks were effective, particularly those of military veterans, others were weak. In terms of outside support, Sunnis depended on extremist groups such as al-Qaeda. In Anbar, Sunni organization was tribal, and at least before the Awakening, highly decentralized and locally focused.

Meanwhile, Kurds squandered their opportunity to construct a unified quasi-state in the north through internal divisions.

1.4.1.3. Economic/rational-choice-based mechanisms are overrated; emotional mechanisms are underrated.

Chapter 3's subtitle is "Mechanisms and Strategy." As defined above, mechanisms are the fine-grained forces behind actions. Strategies possess theories about triggering specific mechanisms in order to shift individuals into new desirable roles. As outlined in detail in the following chapters of Section I, some strategies are based on using "sticks and carrots," often economic in nature, as the primary mechanisms. The logic is that providing jobs and increasing incomes will move individuals into roles on the right, pro-state side of Figure 1.3 above. The empirical chapters will show that these types of mechanisms were not as powerful in Iraq as often assumed. Rather, in a struggle involving group dominance, the emotions of resentment, anger, and humiliation (discussed and defined in Chapter 3) are often more compelling.

1.4.1.4. In the contests between counterinsurgent and insurgent, what explains who wins?

The analytical framework is designed to systematically compare the strategies of competing forces. One of its primary tools is the spectrum of roles seen in Figure 1.3. Strategies are designed to concentrate on some of these roles/nodes rather than others. These strategies aim to trigger mechanisms to move individuals from one role to another or to eliminate the individuals occupying certain nodes. By matching up the strategies, it is often possible to identify why one side gains an advantage (see especially Chapters 6, 7, 10, and 15). As the empirical chapters demonstrate, the US efforts either concentrated on the population-centric middle nodes (winning "hearts and minds" to move individuals from unarmed insurgent support (at −1) to unarmed government support (at +1) or went after mobile insurgents at the −3 node. On the other side, insurgent groups often successfully countered with their abilities at the armed local level (−2).

The application of the framework can also help explain the resiliency and long-term success of certain organizations. One of the major puzzles in Iraq has been the survival and ascendance of the Sadrists. The United States and allied forces routed the Sadrists in 2004 and again in 2008. Yet, the Sadrists made a comeback. In fact, only two years after their 2004 defeat, the Jaysh al-Mahdi (JAM) was winning the Battle of Baghdad while systematically cleansing many of Baghdad's neighborhoods of their Sunni population. Indeed, the Sadrists remained the most powerful political force in Iraq in 2023. As several of the empirical chapters demonstrate, the Sadrist resiliency comes from being able to fill all the roles on the left side of the spectrum. They can move the general population to −1 roles of support through social service networks; they can recruit locals into −2 militias at the neighborhood level; they can develop a mobile force able to fight across Iraq at the −3 level. They were also able to infiltrate or capture local police stations at the +2 level. Even when the United States was able to crush mobile Sadrist insurgents (−3), the Sadrists could use their demographic base and long-term networks in the Sadr City neighborhood of Baghdad to regenerate resistance.

1.4.1.5. The weakness of the Iraq state was not fully understood.

We also need an understanding of ethnic and sectarian politics and dominance to address one of the central questions of the Iraq case and US military intervention: after all the blood and treasure spent, why is Iraq in 2023 such a weak state? Contrary to Western and US assumptions, many actors in Iraq have not been driven by sovereignty concerns. The goal of a fully independent and sovereign state may exist, but it is superseded by the goal of preventing the domination of another group within the state.

If actors are worried about being dominated, and come to believe they cannot become dominant themselves, then a weak state becomes an attractive outcome. A strong state can become a vehicle for domination. If no strong state exists, there will be no such vehicle for opponents to capture. One of the questions to be pursued later in this work asks why militia groups directed by political parties or Iran, such as the PMF, are funded by the Iraqi state. The answer may be that key actors like this outcome. While a fully sovereign and functioning state has benefits, actors also want to retain security forces that guarantee freedom of action and prevention of domination (as outlined in Section III). Iraq's weak state perpetuates its weakness by actually funding and giving legitimacy to non-state violent actors.

Related, there is another more specific connection between dominance concerns and strategy. As the state is the locus of power, status, and domination, strategies involving capture of parts of the state become particularly effective. When one group captures sections of the state, they are taking power for themselves and denying it to competing groups. The case studies will show how Shia organizations captured important state security forces in the early and middle years of the US presence. Moqtada Al-Sadr and his organization came to control many of the local police precincts, as well as taking over local judicial functions. The US Army official war history includes a statement by the Iraqi finance minister at the time: "It was common knowledge that Baghdad's 60,000 strong police force was divided between the Mahdi Army and the Badr Organization with 12,000 former Badr Corps members absorbed into the Special Police Commandos" (US Army History, Vol. 1, p. 410). Shia organizations simultaneously ran for political office while fielding violent militias and capturing state security organs.

1.4.1.6. The United States never fully understood identity politics in Iraq.

The US failure to understand Iraq's ethnic dynamics can be addressed in more general terms. If actors are motivated by dominance-related goals, then surely these goals will determine political objectives. As noted by scholars going back to Clausewitz, to be effective, strategy must follow political objectives. When politics is perceived as a matter of domination, the stakes are very high and restraints fall. When actors engage in fights involving questions of dominance and subordination, they are not interested in vague concepts of "inclusion" and "reconciliation." The institutions of democracy will not be an end in themselves, but rather a means for exclusionary goals. With the stakes in contests involving dominance, violence is justified. Terror can be justified. Sectarian cleansing can be "normal."

A major theme of the book is that many US policymakers had little idea of the world they were entering. Following Clausewitz, the United States needed to first lay out a clear set of political objectives and then develop strategies to accomplish those objectives. Here was a central problem: US political objectives needed to consider the political objectives of their allies and opponents. US actors failed to recognize that they were playing a game where the other actors were driven by dominance concerns.

Dominance concerns can fade with time. Once a group prevails in a dominance contest, it will likely make concessions to other groups. Indeed, it is in the interest of the dominant group to do so, both to quell domestic opposition and to appear just in the international world. The losers in the competition will eventually come to accept a subordinate position and work the new situation to their own best advantage. Dominance concerns will also fade if it becomes clear to all actors that dominance simply cannot be achieved. The case studies will show how time and power shifts produced clarity in group hierarchy, which in turn produced an erosion of dominance concerns. But the contests for power and dominance unleashed and playing out in the time of US presence left a legacy that can be found imprinted in Iraqi political and institutional life; the games over dominance in the early 2000s go a long way in explaining the dysfunction of the Iraqi state in 2023.

1.4.1.7. *The United States overestimated the power of Islamic extremists.*

In the period immediately after the invasion, the United States was focused mainly on former Baathists and al-Qaeda. Indeed, Sunni extremists planted many bombs and killed many US soldiers. But the larger and longer battle was won by the Shia. They were not ready when the Jaysh al-Mahdi began sweeping through Baghdad, cleansing neighborhood after neighborhood and transforming Baghdad's very demography.

To be fair, the US invasion in Iraq was justified in terms of the Global War on Terror and aimed to pre-empt terrorist threats to the US homeland. Related to the preceding point, the political goals and understanding of the US forces did not always correspond to the balances of power and threats within Iraq.

1.4.1.8. US success often came through the agency of domestic actors rather than from US efforts.

This statement applies to both of the most famous operations of the Iraq war: the Awakening and the Surge. In the Awakening (covered in depth in Chapter 11), the strategic decisions of Sunni tribal leaders in Anbar were decisive. These tribal leaders had to develop a way to simultaneously balance against the Shia while breaking from the increasingly dysfunctional alliance with al-Qaeda in Iraq (AQI). Alliance with the United States became an optimal strategy. Tribal leaders had only a brief window of opportunity to reassert control before the Americans withdrew. They may not have liked the Americans, but siding with the United States was the only way to avoid domination by the ascendant and Iranian-allied Shia now controlling the Iraqi government. Importantly, the initiative came from the tribal elites more than from the American side. In the Surge (Chapter 13), Moqtada al-Sadr's August 2007 cease-fire was perhaps as influential as the change in US military strategy.

1.4.1.9. In battles where the United States and allies are "rolling back" an enemy rather than conducting counterinsurgency, a combination of war-fighting and decapitation can be effective.

Two chapters of the book examine battles of the United States and allies against a fairly static enemy. In the Battle of Sadr City (Chapter 12), the United States had learned by 2008 how to efficiently combine ground combat with intelligence, surveillance, and reconnaissance (ISR) capabilities to dislodge the Shia militias from control in their home base. A somewhat similar combination of strategies and tactics was used to defeat ISIS ("The Third Iraq War," Chapter 16) in the 2014–2017 war. The analysis of the conduct of the war against ISIS will be highly relevant to Section IV in its consideration of the future of US military intervention.

1.4.1.10. Weak states in modern times are likely to generate hybrid forces, especially in conflicts involving dominance contests.

Some of the fighting organizations that developed over time in Iraq blur the distinction between state and non-state. As defined by Cambanis et al. (2019, pp. 7–8), this type of organization is "the hybrid actor, a type of armed group that sometimes operates in concert with the state and sometimes competes with it. Hybrid actors depend on state sponsorship and benefit from the tools and prerogatives of state power, but at the same time the enjoy the flexibility that comes with *not* being the state and *not* being responsible for governance." The PMF of Iraq (the subject of Chapter 17) are hybrid forces par excellence. Chapter 18, on the development of Christian minority militias, and Chapters 14 and 20, addressing the role and nature of Kurdish Peshmerga, will also address the hybrid phenomenon.

1.4.2. Arguments

Another way to preview the conclusions of this book is to repackage the findings above in the form of "arguments," which also specify counter positions.

Despite all the special circumstances of the US invasion, I argue that the conflicts in Iraq resembled those in many other cases of ethnic conflict. As some readers may note from my work in Eastern Europe and other areas of the world, my general findings on group conflict support particular assumptions about human nature, specifically:

- Individuals strongly identify with groups.
- Individuals readily perceive a hierarchy of status ordering a state's groups.
- The perception of an unjust position of one's group on this hierarchy can motivate support for or participation in violence.
- Ethnic and sectarian violent conflict is most likely in a period of unstable hierarchy and especially when dominant groups perceive reversal of position. Ethnic conflict will subside once a clear and stable hierarchy re-emerges.

Certainly, not all conflicts are created by group struggle for dominance within a changing hierarchy. In his study of post-Soviet Georgia, Jesse Driscoll (2015) has analyzed a violent world driven by the strategic action of warlords, rather than groups defined by master cleavages. In her study of Afghanistan (2012), Fotini Christia sees a conflict dominated by one particular cleavage—ethnic group—while other master frames are malleable and are used only to justify alliance decisions. In his analysis of Greece during the Second World War, Stathis Kalyvas (2006) outlines how local conditions and master cleavages jointly explain levels of violence. The bottom line is that the influence of master cleavages and group hierarchy and other broad relationships is an empirical question. The saliency and power of master cleavages vary across cases and over time within cases (as addressed in Chapter 20).

For dominance-related goals to become central in a conflict, certain requirements must be met. First, individuals must identify with their group and see that group in conflict with other groups. In other words, a master cleavage must be salient. There must be a widespread perception of an "us" and a "them" in a competitive relationship. Second, there must be a means of transforming the motivations and perceptions linked to the master cleavage to actions. Usually, this ability is built on previous organization. As the case studies will illustrate, post-invasion Iraq met those conditions.

Despite its many twists and turns, the evolution of violence in Iraq has centered on the successful Shia drive for dominance in the Iraqi state. We cannot understand most of the crucial phenomena and turn of events, not to mention levels of violence and state-building, without putting Iraqi identity master cleavages at the center of our analysis. We cannot comprehend the rise of Moqtada al-Sadr and his persistence. We cannot grasp the formation of the Sadrist militias, nor the fervor driving their sectarian cleansing. We will not correctly discern the motives and strategies of the Badr organization. We will not understand the decision calculus of Sunni sheikhs at the start of the Awakening without comprehension of changes in the ethnic balance of power. Likewise, we will not understand the timing of Prime Minister Maliki's moves against fellow Shias in Basra and Sadr City without consideration of changes in sectarian power. We cannot understand how Islamic State forces swept through Mosul and Anbar Province without appreciating the lingering Sunni resentments against the Iraqi government. We cannot understand the origins and politics of the dozens of mainly Shia militias that responded to the ISIS threat. We cannot comprehend Kurdish politics, both between the Kurds and Arabs and between the KDP and PUK, without an appreciation of underlying master cleavages.

Some of the counterfactuals of the Iraq war can be considered in light of this position. Some contend that more US troops at the beginning of the occupation would have prevented civil war. Others believe that the overly widespread de-Baathification of Iraq unnecessarily pushed individuals into violent roles and sparked violent conflict. If my argument is correct, neither more US troops nor less de-Baathification would have decisively changed the overall contours of this dominance-driven conflict. These policies may have led to less death, they might have helped create somewhat better functioning state institutions, but they would not have eliminated the fundamental political and psychological foundations of the conflict.

To move the state-building question, my argument on Iraq's poor state-building record centers on the capture of many state functions by non-state armed groups. The analytical framework of the book is well-suited to evaluate state-building (see Figure 1.3 above). Most states aim to gain a monopoly over violence within its borders, or at the very least keep armed organizations out of the daily business of governance and elections. In most well-known cases of development in the West, at least, governments accomplished this goal through state control of a single military (+3) as well as control over local organs of violence such as the police (+2). With control over violence established, states often worked to bring the general population into support of the state through some version of a social contract. In terms of the spectrum of roles, the general population, even if not universally enthusiastic about the government, should cooperate with the state (+1) or at least remain neutral (0) in regard to those using violent or illegal means against the state. The state would eliminate those individuals or groups at the −2 and −3 roles through attack, arrest, or incorporation into state security institutions.

That process did not play out in Iraq. Rather, non-state armed groups not only sustained their independence, but also captured parts of the state. In Kurdistan, the two main political parties—the KDP and PUK—maintain separate lines of control through their respective Peshmerga armed forces and other less transparent security organs. In the wake of the ISIS invasion, the state partnered with Iranian-connected militias to form the PMF. The PMF is a classic "hybrid" entity. Its various militias draw salaries from the state and sometimes obey its orders, while other times pursuing their own agenda, often in conflict with the state. The Sadrists, always able to threaten violence, control selected ministries and possess state-like power in certain neighborhoods and towns.

In Iraq the distinctions between realms of religion, militia, political party, personal loyalty, and governance entities are murky. For reasons laid out in point 5 of the previous section, these actors fear elimination, or at least marginalization, by other actors. They fear that a rival might capture a strong and coherent state and are satisfied to maintain a weak one. After the invasion, the United States imposed a consociational type of system on Iraq to ensure inclusion of important groups and actors. Such systems rely on elite bargaining, grand coalitions, and a broad division of government resources. In Iraq, consociationalism evolved into a giant quota system, known as the Muhasasa system, with party/militia/religious organizations doling out jobs down to the lowest levels of governance. Despite protests against this system and its deficiencies, in 2022 incoming Iraqi Prime Minister al-Sudani did not seem prepared to challenge it.

Born in violence and chaos, the Iraqi system saw many of its early armed actors establish legitimacy, maintain power, expand their political domains, and capture government ministries and positions. As of 2023, security still ranked higher than efficiency in an Iraq lacking basic levels of trust.

What does this book argue about US involvement in Iraq? There is a straightforward story sometimes told about US strategy in Iraq. At the beginning, the US forces were not at all prepared to do counterinsurgency, so they often relied on inappropriate and counterproductive basic war-fighting tactics (firepower, use of armor, and kinetic violence, force protection in large forward-operating bases). Then, with the help of a new field manual (FM 3-24), US forces turned to a population-centric strategy often termed "clear, hold, build" (CHB). US soldiers would leave their giant forward-operating bases to take positions at small command outposts among the population. There would be a period of high violence to "clear" out insurgent forces, followed by a "hold" incorporating Iraqi forces, and then a "build" involving visible improvements in roads, schools, and services. The goal was to protect the population, convince citizens that the future lay with the Iraqi government not the insurgents, all the while building up Iraqi forces to take over. Many argue that this change in strategy produced the dramatic decrease in violence seen in the "Surge."

As the case studies of this book will illustrate, the story is not so straightforward. There were not just the two strategies just mentioned—war-fighting and CHB—but also community mobilization (alliance with local actors), decapitation (taking out the middle levels of insurgent networks), and homogenization (allowing and enforcing the separation of populations to develop defensible positions among warring sides). These five strategies were used in varying combinations at different locations and times across Iraq. The fighting was highly decentralized. Company-level commanders—captains leading 100–140 soldiers—often had great discretion, and often made deals with local opponents. In effect, there was not one war in Iraq, but many, depending on local conditions.

In this decentralized war, there were successes as well as failures, at least at tactical and operational levels. Along the lines of the two major outcomes mentioned above, the United States had two major goals in Iraq—to bring down violence and to build a functional state. In many cases, US forces did manage to bring down violence, at least in the short term. They were not so good at state-building.

What do I argue about the future of American military intervention? In Iraq, US forces did become highly proficient in "finding, fixing, and finishing" targets. By the time of the ISIS war, the United States also became better at selecting partners to aid in decapitation. In effect, the experience in Iraq provided the US military and intelligence branches with knowledge and abilities for a version of what Paul Staniland calls "violence management." Relying on selected local partners, and using precision-guided weapons, the United States could engage in what Israelis term "mowing the lawn" on a worldwide basis. While nation-building through a "clear, hold, build" counterinsurgency strategy might still be best in preventing terrorism and building up friendly nations in the long run, the Iraq experience proved the difficulty of such a strategy.

1.4.3. Variables and a Flow Chart

A third way to summarize the findings of this book is through more formal social science language. In common social science treatments, there is a test of the power of a specified cause (an independent variable) on specified outcomes (the dependent variables). Good social science theory should lay out the reasons that the causes should produce the predicted effects.

Figure 1.4 illustrates this chain as it relates to this work. The bottom left indicates the two main dependent variables of this work: violence and state-building. If violence and state-building are the outcomes at the end of the chain, what are the possible causes, or independent variables, of these observed outcomes? The upper left corner of the figures lists a few of a very long list of what are known as structural variables—stable and observable characteristics of a case. Political scientists have produced hundreds of studies assessing the explanatory power of factors related to economic wealth, geography, demography, among others, as they relate to insurgency and civil war. These structural variables are thought to strongly constrain the abilities of actors to create and sustain violence, as well as the state's capacity to build strong, legitimate institutions.

On the other hand, some political scientists concentrate on how actors can find ways or build organizations to overcome structural constraints. In this case, the focus is on the ways in which agency and strategy produce outcomes in violence and state-building.[7] In considering the Iraq conflict, the United States is the invader, occupier, and primary state-builder. Accordingly, US counterinsurgency strategy is a central focus of this work. Of course, opponents will come up with counterstrategies. It follows that the *combination* of US and opponent strategy forms the equivalent of an independent variable, a potential cause of outcomes in violence and state-building. As mentioned above, US strategy took at least five identifiable forms: war-fighting; CHB; decapitation; community mobilization; and homogenization. Although insurgent strategies were largely

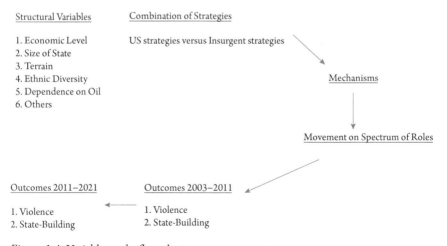

Structural Variables   Combination of Strategies

1. Economic Level   US strategies versus Insurgent strategies
2. Size of State
3. Terrain
4. Ethnic Diversity   Mechanisms
5. Dependence on Oil
6. Others

                                          Movement on Spectrum of Roles

Outcomes 2011–2021   Outcomes 2003–2011

1. Violence   1. Violence
2. State-Building   2. State-Building

Figure 1.4 Variables and a flow chart.

reactive to US strategy and cannot be as easily labeled or categorized, the case studies will identify their logic and targets. The case studies work to explicitly identify and match up US strategy and insurgent strategy.

In terms of independent versus dependent variables, readers should note that the state-building outcomes of the 2003–2011 period switch from being a dependent variable (an effect) to an independent variable (a cause) in the 2011–2020 cases. The case studies in Section III will show how specific failures in state-building during the 2003–2011 period helped lead to renewed violence (as seen in the ISIS war) and the persistence of a weak state.

The preceding paragraphs have described key independent and dependent variables. This book devotes substantial effort to trying to uncover and understand *how* the independent variables are causing the outcomes. Here, the right side of Figure 1.4 comes into play. The case studies will indicate how different strategies set off different sets of mechanisms that in turn shaped movement among the spectrum of roles. Section I lays out the concepts of mechanism and roles and specifies the links within the chain connecting strategy, mechanism, and roles. Sections II and III put these concepts and their method into practice.

The book will stress the importance of one structural variable—Iraq's demography. The fact that Iraq is a majority Shia state is fundamental to the battles over group hierarchy. Baghdad's highly mixed ethnic demography created vulnerable populations subject to ethnic cleansing. While not a major focus of the book, the importance of Iraq's dependence on oil is a major factor in perpetuating Iraq's dysfunctional political system. Yet on the whole, the book's major arguments and findings show that actors' agency, strategies, and organization have been more important than structural constraints.

In linking strategy to outcome, I will argue that US strategy was sometimes effective in quelling violence in Iraq while deficient in state building. The United States unleashed a variety of strategies and combination of strategies in Iraq. The United States became adept in decapitation, was complicit in homogenization, made tremendous but short-term success in community mobilization, and managed to clear and hold while failing to build the necessary state structures and institutions. However, none of the various strategies or their combinations produced a sustained movement into the positive sides of the spectrum of roles—loyal citizens (+1), efficient local security and police (+2), an effective army (+3).

I will argue that the US military learned important tactical and operational lessons during the Iraq war and that some of these lessons informed US efforts in defeating ISIS in 2014–2017. I will also argue that the US military and civilian policymakers (especially) will likely forget, or wrongly learn, many of these lessons going forward.

Some political scientists will no doubt be disappointed that this book does not systematically address or explicitly test arguments connected to structural variables. They will wonder why I did not engage with my fellow political scientists more directly. In fact, the very early version of this work was entitled "The Social Science Guide to the Iraq War."[8] My goal at the start was to systematically compare and contrast a very wide range of existing political science works to the Iraq war. However, it became clear to me that others could do that work better than I. As the reader will note, an in-depth analysis of political science works and their relationship to this work's framework has been moved to Appendix B. I came to believe that I could make a more significant contribution by adapting and honing a methodological framework that I had previously developed and applying that framework to guide an analysis of multiple cases in Iraq over the 20-year period after the 2003 US invasion. This approach would also allow me to readily incorporate invaluable material gleaned from fieldwork, as discussed in the following point.

1.5. Letting Actors' Voices Speak

In a recent book on modern warfare, Sean McFate laments that "PhDs who have never smelled gun smoke in battle pontificate about war" (McFate, 2019, p. 22). I am indeed one of those PhDs. I do hope that I have prevented myself from too much pontification by listening to and including the voices of not only combatants, but also policymakers and regular civilians caught up in the Iraq conflict. This book is 10 years in the making, and along the way I have tried to listen to many of those involved in the Iraq conflict.

The genesis for this project began back in 2010 when I co-organized a conference entitled "MIT Workshop on Theory and Practice in Iraq and Afghanistan," which brought together prominent academics who write on civil wars and counterinsurgency with individuals who had experience on the ground in both Afghanistan and Iraq.[9] I organized a follow-up conference the next year, entitled "Counterinsurgency and Counterterrorism, 2011," which brought together 40 academics and military personnel.[10] At the same time, I was engaged with the Naval War College Center for the Study of Irregular Warfare and Armed Groups, co-writing a case study on Iraq with Jon Lindsay (Lindsay and Petersen, 2012). I have interacted with many US military officers who served in Iraq, especially the military fellows at the Security Studies Program at MIT, since those original meetings. At several junctures in the case studies, I provide longer descriptions and vignettes from these interactions to bring abstract theory to life.

The book greatly benefits from its collaborations. Two of the key empirical chapters are co-written with US military practitioners and are based on their respective experiences and field notes from Iraq. The chapter on the Bayaa neighborhood of Baghdad during the Surge may be one of the most detailed, yet theoretically guided, ever written on that important battle. The chapter is co-written with Timothy Wright. During the Surge, Wright was serving as a captain and company commander in the Bayaa neighborhood. He used that experience as the empirical basis of his dissertation, "From Predator to Provider: The Role of Violence and Rules in Establishing Social Control," which Wright defended at MIT in 2018. The "Anbar" Chapter is co-written with Professor Jon Lindsay. Lindsay served in Anbar on active duty with the US Navy from fall 2007 to spring 2008. As the Special Operations Task Force West (SOTF-W) Nonlethal Effects Officer, he coordinated civil affairs, information operations, and tribal engagement activities in Anbar, which afforded the opportunity to visit towns throughout Anbar and interact with Anbaris involved in the Awakening and their partners in the Marine Corps. In addition to the Bayaa and Anbar collaborations, the chapter on the formation of Christian militias in Ninewa Province is co-written with Matt Cancian, a former Marine with combat experience from Afghanistan. In the course of his dissertation research, Cancian has conducted extensive recent research in the Iraqi north. Most of my knowledge on the Shia-Sunni dynamic comes from my interactions with Marsin Alshamary, who recently completed a dissertation at MIT on Shia mobilization ("Prophets and Priests: Religious Leaders and Anti-Government Protest in Iraq").[11] Alshamary's research was especially critical for Chapter 5, "Violence, State-Building, and the Sunni-Shia Cleavage."

In terms of fieldwork in the Middle East, the first empirical chapter, on the Ghazaliyah neighborhood in Baghdad, is based on a series of conversations in Amman, Jordan, with a former insurgent (along with interviews with Army officers and a translator serving in the same district at the same time). The chapter on the failure of the United States and the Iraqi state to establish local security is based on interviews with Falah Naqib, the former minister of the interior and the founder of the "Wolf Brigades." The chapter on the plight of Sunnis in the Mansour neighborhood of Baghdad is based on multiple interviews with Sunni refugees in Amman. The chapter on Christian militias is based on my interactions with Christian refugees in Madaba and Na'our in Jordan, as well as in the Ankawa neighborhood of Erbil in Iraq. For the two chapters on Iraqi Kurdistan, in 2013 I went to Erbil, Suleymaniyah, Halabja, and Kirkuk and talked with a range of officials that included Masrour Barzani (then head of the Kurdistan Security Council), Jafer Mustafa Ali (head of Peshmerga), Khasro Goran (former deputy governor of Mosul), Najmaldin Karim (then governor of the Kirkuk Governate), among others. Along the way, I held many conversations ranging from common citizens to a meeting with Iyad Allawi, the first prime minister of post-invasion Iraq.

Iraq's trajectory is often compared with Lebanon's history and evolution. To pursue this comparison in fully understanding recent Iraqi events, I traveled to Lebanon. Most specifically, I pursued the question of whether Iraq might be developing a long-term sectarian system permeated with non-state militias. In Beirut, I met with Hussein Husseini, a primary architect of the Taif Accords; among various other interactions, I also went to the Hezbollah Museum in south Lebanon to talk with members of Hezbollah to pursue questions of hybrid militias.

During the finishing stages of this book, I traveled to Baghdad to lay out my findings and major themes to receive final feedback. I was able to present many of the ideas in this book at two important speaking engagements attended by key political and military figures, including Mohammed Sudani, who would go on to become Iraqi prime minister a few months later.[12] During that trip, I also met with Ammar al-Hakim, former leader of the Islamic Supreme Council of Iraq and then head of the Hikma movement, Qasim al-Ajari, Iraq national security advisor, and Dr. Suhad al-Azzawi, director of Strategic Studies at Nahrain University, among others. I returned to Baghdad again in March 2023 to participate in events marking the 20th anniversary of the US invasion. While these forums and meetings provided some necessary corrections and additions to this book, overall they gave me confidence in its overall findings.

1.6. Concluding Comments

I started this introductory chapter by inveighing against those who overgeneralize about Iraq. There are also some who might say that Iraq has been too complicated to be understood. No one can deny that the course of the conflict in Iraq has been enormously complex. This book is dedicated to making that complexity more understandable. The first section of the book develops a method to break down insurgencies and group conflicts into their component parts and then builds back up to develop an analytical framework. Section II applies that framework to nine cases in Iraq during the period of US presence, 2003–2011. Section III applies the framework to another set of cases in the period following US withdrawal, 2011–2020, drawing out the ways the US intervention is connected to longer-term outcomes in Iraq. The fourth section of the book summarizes findings and produces summaries relevant to future US military interventions. Despite its length, the work attempts to make an extremely complex conflict more understandable. While the simultaneous pursuit of "richness and rigor" may be something of a slogan, this book makes great efforts to achieve that goal.

The Analytical Framework I

Roles and Strategy

2.1. Introduction

At the end of Chapter 1, Figure 1.4 showed a chain linking a combination of strategies to the triggering of mechanisms and, in turn, linking those mechanisms to movement on the spectrum of roles. If we understand this chain—and develop a method to systematically apply this understanding to case studies within Iraq—we will be able to understand the ebbs and flow of violence and the problems of state-building underlying Iraq's conflicts and political evolution. This chapter outlines the three core elements of the framework, concentrating on roles and strategy. The following chapter focuses on mechanisms and strategy.

2.2. Basic Elements

2.2.1. Basic Element 1: Individual Roles

In an unstable state experiencing insurgency and other forms of internal conflict, individuals move across a set of multiple roles. In much of the insurgency/rebellion literature, individuals are portrayed as deciding among just two choices, two roles—either to "rebel" or "not rebel,"—and then the analyst tries to determine the payoff structures between these two choices. Such treatment obfuscates the set of individual roles underlying most insurgencies. More realistically, individuals move along a set of roles that can be aligned along the spectrum in Figure 2.1 (a duplication of Figure 1.3, placed here for the reader's convenience).

Neutral (0): During any conflict between a government and its opponent, many individuals will choose neutrality; these actors will try to avoid both sides and to go about their daily lives with a minimum of risk. They will not

Figure 2.1. Spectrum of participation in insurgency and counterinsurgency (reprint of Figure 1.3).

willingly provide information or material support to either the government or the insurgents, nor will they participate in public demonstrations for either side.

Unarmed, unorganized insurgent supporter (−1): While avoiding any armed role, some individuals will occasionally provide information, shelter, and material support for the insurgents. While unorganized, these individuals may show up at rallies supporting the insurgents and will boycott elections and other activities that could legitimize the government.

Armed local insurgent (−2): Some individuals will adopt a role of direct and organized participation in a locally based, armed organization. In the absence of a powerful state, individuals in this role often take the form of local militia members. In the presence of a powerful state, such individuals may appear as average citizens or neutrals by day, but play the role of active fighter at night. Even the most powerful states can have trouble identifying and neutralizing actors in this role.

Mobile armed insurgent (−3): Some individuals will join mobile and armed organizations, becoming members in a guerrilla unit or rebel army. These individuals will fight outside of their own local communities.

These four roles form one side of a spectrum of participation. At the onset of an occupation or violent conflict, many individuals will begin at neutrality but then move into a role of support, and then move to even more committed and violent roles. They might also jump immediately into armed roles (−2, −3). Of course, individuals may also move among a parallel spectrum of roles in support of the government. These roles essentially mirror those above:

Unarmed, unorganized government supporter (+1): While avoiding any armed or organized role, some individuals will willingly identify insurgents and provide the government with valuable information about insurgent activity. These individuals may show up at rallies supporting the government and likely will vote in elections and participate in other activities that legitimize the government.

Armed local government supporter (+2): Some individuals will adopt a role of direct and organized participation in a locally based, armed organization that is either formally or informally connected with the government. In Iraq, organizations such as the "Sons of Anbar" provided these roles. More formally, states often develop paramilitary organizations or expanded police forces which create opportunities for armed local government support.

Mobile armed government forces (+3): Some individuals will join the mobile and armed organizations of the government, namely, the state's military.

As a measurement device, the spectrum of roles matches the analysis of many practitioners. In his estimates of the Taliban movement as of 2008, David Kilcullen estimates that there were "8,000 to 10,000 full-time fighters or 'core' Taliban, or about 25 percent of the total, typically on the order of 200 to 450 full-time Taliban per province," and that "22,000 to 32,000 fighters are local, part-time guerrillas who, as I shall show, operate on a temporary ad-hoc basis" (Kilcullen, 2009, pp. 48–49). Thus, Kilcullen separates the −3 fighters from the −2 fighters. The understanding of the −1 and −2 roles is even more critical for cases like Iraq, because the numbers participating in these roles undoubtedly outnumbered mobile fighters (−3).[1]

Several aspects of this spectrum of roles should be emphasized. First, these roles are based on behavior, not attitudes. These roles are based on what individuals actually do, not what they think. The −1 and +1 roles are mostly concerned with information provision, but also encompass voting, demonstrating, and other actions that clearly favor either the government or insurgent side.

Second, and relatedly, individuals do not always move into adjacent roles. Individuals may move off of neutrality (0) to the +1 or −1 node and then to an armed role at the 2 or 3 levels. But they need not follow that progression. Chapter 11 on Anbar Province will examine in detail a phenomenon that can be termed "flipping." Here, the state "flips" a local militia and its members from a local, armed anti-state role (−2) to a local, armed pro-state position (+2). In the case of the Awakening and the organization of the Sons of Iraq, al-Qaeda in Iraq (AQI)–associated militia members (−2 level) jumped to a corresponding pro-state position (+2). There will be other cases of individuals jumping across positions on the spectrum of roles. Individuals may move off of neutrality (0) to join either the state's army (+3) or a mobile insurgent or terrorist group (−3).

Third, it is critical to emphasize that the same individuals pass through different roles in the course of insurgency. Moving among roles is likely the norm rather than the exception. For the most part, these roles are distinct. An individual is armed or is not armed; an individual belongs to a unit that is tied to one community or fights in a unit that is mobile.

However, as examined in Section III, "hybrid" roles can emerge. In this case, actors hold two roles simultaneously. In the classic cases of counterinsurgency, this phenomenon was rare and most of the time not possible. I originally developed the spectrum of roles to study anti-Soviet resistance in Eastern Europe (Petersen, 2001). In those cases, anti-Soviet partisans did not simultaneously hold positions in the Soviet security structures.[2] There was a clear anti-state side and a clear state side, one linear line with a negative and positive side.[3] The simple form of the spectrum of roles will largely fit the Iraq case from 2003 to 2011, with some noted exceptions. However, the spectrum of roles will need significant modification to apply to Iraq from 2014 forward. As we will see in our analysis of Iraq in 2014–2021, hybrid actors become a highly significant part of Iraq's security environment. Indeed, members of Iranian-backed militias will take positions on the state's security payroll. Chapter 17 is entitled "Hybrid Actors: The Emergence and Persistence of the Popular Mobilization Forces."

Individuals clearly move across these roles during a conflict—but what forces drive them into different roles on this spectrum? This question leads to the second fundamental element of the framework.

2.2.2. Basic Element 2: Mechanisms

Keeping with a goal of breaking down insurgency into its most elemental parts, we seek to identify the small, generalizable forces that drive individuals across this spectrum of roles. In social science language, these small causal forces are often called *mechanisms*. Mechanisms are specific causal patterns that explain individual actions over a wide range of settings.[4]

Consider one particular example: "tyranny of sunk costs."[5] An old automobile that is constantly breaking down and being repaired might be retained by the owner despite the likelihood of numerous additional costly repairs due to the tyranny of sunk costs. Although the optimal choice might be to "junk" the car, the owner refuses to rationally calculate probable future costs because he or she cannot bear the thought of previous repair efforts "going down the drain." The same process might be involved in dysfunctional personal relationships or marriages. One or both partners in a relationship may find themselves continuously dissatisfied, in conflict, and on the verge of breaking up. Rather than ending the relationship, they may choose to remain together and ignore the probability that problems will recur because they cannot accept the fact that investments in the relationship have been in vain. The tyranny of sunk costs mechanism is both general in that it can be applied to a wide variety of cases (cars and spouses) and specific and causal in that it explains why an event occurs. This combination of generality and specificity is one of the benefits of a mechanism approach. Another benefit is the wide possible range of behaviors that mechanisms can encompass. Irrational psychological processes such as the "tyranny of sunk costs" or cognitive dissonance reduction are mechanisms, but so are rational adaptation and social norms. Concentration on mechanisms allows the social scientist to deal with realistic actors affected by a complex variety of forces; it forces the social scientist toward causal explanations of increasingly finer grain.

If there were hundreds of relevant mechanisms, referring to them would not help reduce complexity, but rather would be just a form of description. The approach here works from the assumption that social scientists have developed a wealth of cumulative knowledge about human behavior. Psychologists, behavioral economists, anthropologists, and others have identified individual-level causal forces that drive individuals in predicted ways. Some of these mechanisms affect individuals in much the same way across different cultures and time periods. These mechanisms fall into four general categories—rational choice, social norms, emotions, and psychological mechanisms.

Only some of these mechanisms, however, are pertinent to insurgencies or internal conflicts. To develop a relevant list, we need to rely on the extensive work and research of historians and political scientists who have covered insurgency, civil war, and internal conflict for decades. By combining insights from both the social scientists who have specified mechanisms with those who study substantive cases in depth, we can develop a manageable set of mechanisms to form a baseline for our study of Iraq. We can also use this knowledge to understand what specific mechanisms are at play at specific points on the spectrum. For example, what mechanisms move individuals from −1 (insurgent support) to neutrality (0) or government support (+1)? What mechanisms move individuals into insurgent armed roles (either at the −2 or −3 levels)? Chapter 3 discusses mechanisms in detail. Based upon an integration of social science studies and case studies of insurgency, Chapter 3 will identify a list of mechanisms that play prominent roles in insurgencies in general. Then we determine which of these mechanisms were most prominent in Iraq and how (between which nodes of the spectrum) they were likely to be operative.

The first task in "building up" is to specify how these mechanisms can operate in sequences and combinations to create movement on the spectrum. Through identifying these sequences of mechanisms, we can specify processes which might trigger and sustain insurgency. For example, mechanisms related to ethnic identity might operate to push people from neutrality to unorganized resistance (from 0 to −1), but then other mechanisms, perhaps related to considerations of safety, might be the primary force that pushes individuals into more dangerous roles of armed rebellion (−2, −3). A third set of mechanisms, possibly connected to economic factors, might sustain individuals at those risk-laden roles. There are undoubtedly different sequences of mechanisms capable of working in tandem to drive movement left or right on the spectrum of roles. Certainly, both insurgents and counterinsurgents have strategies to try to put these processes into motion, which leads into the next section.

2.2.3. Basic Element 3: Strategies

Both insurgents and governments have ideas on how to use their power and resources to move individuals up and down the spectrum of roles, how they can set these processes in motion. They hold beliefs about the means they can use to accomplish their goals. In other words, they have strategies.

We can discuss strategy in terms of the elements listed above. With scarce resources, actors will identify which elements of the population should be targeted, either negatively or positively. In Clausewitzian terms, strategies should identify a "center of gravity" or a crucial focus for winning the contest. In terms of our framework, the contenders for power (state or insurgent) will focus resources and attention to the key locations on the spectrum of roles.

Second, there is the question about how to move actors into desired roles, or move them out of undesired roles (sometimes through elimination). The "how" in the strategy refers to mechanisms. The actor's strategy will include a logic of how to push and pull individuals in the population along the spectrum of roles. In our terms, they have a theory of how to "trigger mechanisms" in a way to accomplish the strategy's goals. There may be a sequence in terms of targeted roles and triggered mechanisms.

Chapter 1 listed five distinct strategies employed in Iraq. In addition to traditional war-fighting, four counterinsurgent strategies included:

- Clear, hold, build (CHB)
- Decapitation
- Homogenization
- Community mobilization.

Each of these strategies concentrates on different nodes of the spectrum of roles. Figure 2.2 illustrates their difference in focus.[6]

2.2.3.1. Clear, Hold, Build

"Clear, hold, build" (CHB) explicitly identifies a center of gravity—the general unarmed population, or nodes -1, 0, $+1$ on our spectrum of roles. The strategy is distinguished by the way it connects movement in the general population $(-1, 0, +1)$ with warfighting goals at the $+3$ versus -3 level in a clear process. The first steps involve triggering mechanisms that move neutrals (0) and insurgent sympathizers (-1) rightward to a pro-government position $(+1)$. When occupying this role, individuals are informing the counterinsurgent forces about the presence and location of mobile insurgents (-3). CHB is built on the premise that information-collection can turn the tide of insurgency. While the population moves into the $+1$ position, the state should also be building up its army and mobile security forces $(+3)$. With the information now flowing from the $+1$ population, the $+3$ forces of the state can go after mobile insurgents (-3).

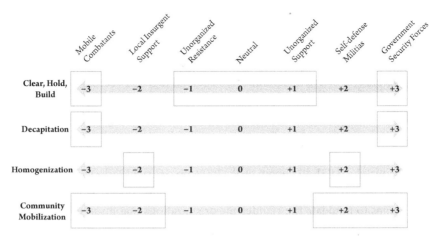

Figure 2.2. Different counterinsurgent strategies address different segments of the population.

CHB envisions moving the population through rational choice mechanisms. In terms of "winning hearts and minds," the appeal to the mind is more crucial and effective than the appeal to the heart. If the population clearly sees the state as providing better security and more economic goods, individuals will rationally calculate that their future lies with the new government and will move rightward to +1. The strategy also emphasizes the avoidance of collateral damage that might trigger emotional mechanisms capable of moving individuals leftward.

Graphically, the logic and focus of the CHB strategy is represented by the top illustration in Figure 2.2. Portraying strategies in this way is also helpful in illustrating what strategies are *not* doing. CHB does not focus on the community level of organization (the −2 and +2 levels). The strategy hopes to build a strong state that will attract individuals to its side; it does not see making deals with community leaders or allowing communities to develop their own self-defense forces as useful moves toward building a coherent state. Specifying the strategy in this way also helps us understand the conditions of when the strategy might fail. If the most important dynamics in countering an insurgency are at the −2 and +2 levels, then the CHB strategy may have troubles accomplishing its goals.

If in practice CHB does not trigger the intended mechanisms, or if it sets off intended mechanisms that counter the effects of the intended ones, the strategy is not likely to succeed. If government-aligned forces institute CHB, insurgents will surely develop a counterstrategy. Insurgents will consider how they can trigger mechanisms that push individuals in the −1, 0, +1 positions leftward. They can also focus their strategy on the vulnerable positions on the spectrum. For instance, while CHB does not focus on the −2 level, insurgents exploit that neglect by concentrating their resources on building up and sustaining local insurgent organizations.

2.2.3.2. Decapitation

A "decapitation" strategy goes after insurgent organizations (−3) directly by enhancing the acuity and coverage of surveillance and the speed and precision of strike forces (+3). When manhunts are coupled together such that intelligence from detainees and materials gathered from one raid provides leads for new raids, then decapitation efforts are often called "counter-network operations" or simply "counterterrorism." As discussed in detail in Chapter 4, US Special Operations Forces (SOF) describes this cyclic methodology as "find, fix, finish, exploit, analyze" (F3EA) (Flynn et al., 2008, pp. 56–61; Marks et al., 2005).[7]

Whereas CHB attempts to address grievance as the root cause of insurgency, F3EA aims to liquidate the clandestine organizations that insurgency requires, whatever its cause. Its goal is to kill or capture senior and mid-level insurgent commanders faster than they are able to regenerate in order to sow fear and confusion and ultimately to cause the network to collapse. Counterterrorism technology enables militaries to restore their preferred two-way relationship between +3s and −3s without having to be intimately involved with the messy population in the middle. As opposed to the logic inherent in CHB, economic development only matters insofar as it improves intelligence and assault operations, such as through the improvement of communication and transportation infrastructure.

2.2.3.3. Homogenization

"Homogenization" is another strategy, although often a passive one. Many political scientists argue that the best way to end ethnic violence is simply to physically separate the warring sides and create defensible boundaries between them.[8] Sometimes, the strategy consists of simply letting local forces (both those at −2 and those at +2) separate themselves into defensible camps. Governments do not usually choose ethnic homogenization as a strategy; it is normatively too close to ethnic cleansing. Yet, homogenization may help bring an end to violence. Governments may turn a blind eye to the process, or they may work with the result of ethnic cleansing to maintain peace.

2.2.3.4. Community Mobilization

A fourth counterinsurgency strategy can be labeled "community mobilization." Whereas homogenization, as described above, can occur without the direct involvement of counterinsurgent forces, here government security forces ally directly with +2 militias against −3 insurgents. A major part of this strategy is to "flip" or "turn" locally based insurgent organizations (−2) over to the government-counterinsurgent side—in other words, to transform individuals at −2 to +2.

Chapter 4 expands on these brief definitions. It will go into detail regarding the US military practice and logic of each of them.

2.3. Assessing Outcomes: Strategies, Violence, and State-Building

Different strategies are likely to produce higher and lower levels of violence, although all aim to lower or eliminate violence in the long run. CHB expects to produce higher levels of violence during the "clear" stage, followed by much less violence during "hold" and "build." Decapitation calls for a high level of violence against a small category of targets, while not being concerned with general violence within the population. Homogenization expects high initial violence against civilians, with a drastic lowering after boundaries have been drawn. The relationship between violence and community mobilization is ambiguous. The strategy often involves shifting alliances with local militias, which may enflame violence or create a violence-reducing balance of power. Because one strategy will be met with a counterstrategy, it is difficult to predict levels of violence from the counterinsurgent strategy alone.

Each of the four counterinsurgency strategies previously outlined contains not only a theory on reducing violence, but also a theory on state-building, even if that theory is incomplete and implicit. The state-building logic of "clear, hold, build" is the most distinct. Indeed, CHB is all about creating the conditions for state-building. A first "clear" effort pushes out the −3 forces. "Holding" involves establishing a +3 presence that convinces the population that insurgents can and will be defeated. When this stage is achieved, the population will move to the +1 node and begin providing information about the location and practices of −3 forces. A virtuous cycle ensues as more +3 forces fill territories, allowing for the establishment of state services and control. The third stage—"build"—creates and sustains these institutions, continually placing the personnel to accomplish the day-to-day bureaucratic functioning of a state.

Community mobilization offers a very different state-building alternative. Community mobilization does not so much attempt to build a new state from the bottom up, but rather to take existing organizations, even if they are local militias, and incorporate them into state structures. This strategy is statebuilding through deal-making rather than institution creation. It depends upon moving individuals and groups from −2 directly into +2 positions. The strategy, as some scholars have pointed out, has much in common with Tilly's predatory model where feudal lords were co-opted and integrated into a central state (Jackson, 2009).

Homogenization relies on natural conflict processes to help create the conditions for a new state. As many political science findings suggest, ethnic homogeneity may facilitate both the establishment of security and the efficient provision of public goods. Homogenization may limit infighting and state capture. With less divisive internal conflict, the state can develop +2 and +3 actors more readily and gain the time and space to create a functioning set of binding rules, laws, and institutions. In their application of Tilly's model to modern state formation in the developing world, Taylor and Botea find that two factors contribute to the progression of state-building: the existence of a core ethnic group, and a unifying ideology that combines nationalism and politics. Of these two factors, Taylor and Botea argue that ethnic homogeneity is a more powerful force in building a strong state (Taylor and Botea, 2008).

A decapitation strategy basically gives up on state-building. It aims only to eliminate the most openly violent and unredeemable actors of the −3 node. The implicit assumption of decapitation is that state-building is too difficult, or at least not worth the effort. The business of the United States is counter-terrorism, not state-building. The United States must let foreign peoples find their own way.

Understanding the relationship between US strategy and state-building is critical because building a new Iraqi state was perhaps the single most important goal of the US invasion. The United States and its allies did not invade Iraq in 2003 to win a war; that outcome was never in doubt. Nor was the sole reason for the elimination of weapons of mass destruction. The larger goal was the creation of a new post-Saddam state. As mentioned in Chapter 1, President Obama laid out the goals of the state-building effort: Iraq is to be "sovereign, stable, and self-reliant." These are the attributes that define a functioning state.

In conjunction with these criteria, the analytical framework provides a ready way to recognize failures in state-building. When non-state militias at the −2 level control much of the country, the state is not entirely sovereign; when mobile armed groups at the −3 level control wide swaths of territory, the state is not sovereign. If −2 militias can rapidly organize significant numbers of armed fighters, the state is not stable; if −3 forces can take territory at will, the state is not stable; if the majority of the population is willing to support anti-state armed groups with information and material goods (the −1 level), then the state is not stable. If the state cannot develop and maintain local security organs and police (+2) and allows non-state actors to control localities, the state is not entirely sovereign. If the state cannot maintain an army (+3) for external defense and internal defense, the state is not stable. If a significant percentage of the population does not cooperate with the state in terms of information provision and political support (+1), the state will not be stable. If the state depends on outside actors for external and internal defense, the state is not self-reliant.

2.4. Conclusion: Where We Are Headed

This chapter has focused on roles, the spectrum of roles, the ways different strategies can be broken down and analyzed by focusing on these elements, and the connection of these strategies to issues of violence and state-building. This method has widespread applicability beyond Iraq.

The following chapter expands the framework by fleshing out its third fundamental element—mechanisms. The primary goal of the following chapter is to draw on knowledge and findings from a variety of the social sciences to expand upon and deepen our knowledge of the mechanisms that are central to the framework.

3

The Analytical Framework II

Mechanisms and Strategy

3.1. Introduction

The previous chapter developed a spectrum of roles and showed how different strategies concentrate on specific nodes of that spectrum. While the preceding chapters defined the third fundamental element of the framework—mechanism—they did not detail types of mechanisms or specify how they are integrated with the framework. Those tasks are the goal of this chapter.

When an insurgent or counterinsurgent plays a strategy, three steps are involved: (1) the actor has scarce resources and must decide where to focus those resources, in effect specifying which positions on the spectrum of roles to focus on; (2) the actor wishes to either eliminate actors at certain nodes or push them off their present position to a different role on the spectrum; (3) the actor's strategy will have a theory about *how* to move individuals from the present node to the desired position; in effect, this theory specifies a mechanism, a reason why the action would push the individual in the desired direction. The assumption here is that these actors—insurgent leaders, government officials, military officers—believe they know how to drive this movement. Some actors believe that force and threats are the most effective tools, "sticks" over "carrots." Others might believe in buying off opponents. Then there are "shock and awe" and "winning hearts and minds."

In effect, these actors make choices about which mechanisms to try to trigger. Although they may not realize it, in their formation of strategy these actors are choosing from a broader range of potentially relevant mechanisms. This chapter will draw from social sciences and history to establish that broader range of mechanisms. It will also theorize about the power and relevance of those mechanisms at different locations on the spectrum of roles.

The framework's concentration on mechanisms will help us understand US policy shortcomings and failures. When the United States developed its strategies based on its beliefs about which mechanisms would be effective, did they consider the entire set of relevant mechanisms? Did the United States consider how opponents might trigger an alternative, and perhaps more effective, set of mechanisms? US military doctrine evolved during the Iraq conflict. The framework can help us evaluate this evolution and its possible lessons for the future. Application of the framework can also help recognize blind spots and help to understand the origins of those blind spots.

3.2. Mechanisms Further Defined

The driving idea behind a mechanisms-based approach is to reduce the level of abstraction while maintaining an ability to capture complex processes.[1] As defined here, mechanisms are fine-grained forces behind specific individual actions.[2] In terms of the framework, the mechanisms approach directs the analyst to identify *why* individuals move from one position on the spectrum to another. For instance, why does an individual move from a position of neutrality to one of informal government support (0 to +1)? Why does an individual move from informal government support to membership in a local pro-government defense organization (+1 to +2)? Mechanisms are the identifiable forces behind these concrete actions. With an understanding of how these mechanisms work in sequences comes a better understanding of broader outcomes.

One reason the mechanism approach is so appropriate for the study of insurgency is that both insurgents and counterinsurgents are often thinking in terms of mechanisms; that is, they are thinking about how to set off individual-level forces that shape behavior. Mechanisms are the basic theoretical building blocks of the contestants' actions. Of course, not all mechanisms driving behavior on the spectrum of roles are intended. As the empirical chapters will make clear, many strategies trigger unintended mechanisms. Furthermore, structural factors and a lack of resources will often prevent an actor from being able to trigger an intended mechanism. In any case, breaking down a strategy, whether it be Mao's strategy or David Petraeus's strategy, will involve a discussion of mechanisms, even if the recognition of mechanisms is more implicit than explicit.

One major objection to this method concerns the number of possible mechanisms at each step.[3] If a multitude of mechanisms is operating across this spectrum, then the method is hardly able to accomplish its goal of simplification. If an overwhelming multitude of plausible mechanisms exists, then for any given case, a user of the method might be able to pick and choose among this long list in order to fit a given argument. In that case, the method would be little different

than description. As with other social science methods, a mechanisms approach
needs to possess a measure of discipline.[4] One cannot just call anything a mechanism. My position is that the number of mechanisms highly relevant to modern
insurgency and related conflicts is relatively small. Social science and actual field
experience have gone some way in identifying common powerful mechanisms at
work in insurgencies. The next section identifies approximately 15 mechanisms
in four categories—rational choice, social norms, emotions, and psychological
mechanisms. Not all of these mechanisms were significant in Iraq. Moreover, for
any specific region and time period, a smaller set of mechanisms becomes most
crucial.

3.3. Developing a General List of Insurgency-Related Mechanisms

In developing a list of general mechanisms that have consistently operated across
modern insurgencies, it is possible to rely on four solid sources:

1. First, there are abundant histories and case studies to build upon. Since
   World War II, the world has witnessed over 190 insurgencies.[5] Scholars have
   written extensively about the Greek Civil War, Cyprus, Palestine, Vietnam,
   the Malayan Emergency, the Philippines, and many more conflicts. Through
   a thorough reading of dozens of these conflicts, one can develop knowledge
   about what types of mechanisms operate under what type of conditions.
   Iraq, while distinctive in some ways, is not sui generis. Through the use of
   comparison and intensive reading, a scholar can identify several plausible
   mechanisms operating in much the same way across insurgencies.

2. History and actual case studies provide examples of common mechanisms;
   psychology, anthropology, and behavioral economics confirm that many of
   these mechanisms are rooted in human psyche and experience. When the
   social sciences corroborate what is being observed in multiple case studies,
   it substantiates the belief in the generalizability of these mechanisms.

3. An increasingly large body of published social science articles have
   examined the power of potential mechanisms using recent data. For many
   conflicts, including Iraq, the military and other organizations collected extensive records. Numerous social scientists have analyzed these data, with
   results published in numerous scholarly journals. As described toward the
   end of this chapter, Appendix B reviews dozens of recent articles on insurgency and civil war that examine specific mechanisms.

4. Furthermore, there are also the observations from military practitioners.
   In terms of Iraq specifically, hundreds of thousands of military and State

Department personnel served in Iraq. The mechanism approach is designed to draw on this experience.

The problem with the study of insurgency, and the Iraq insurgency in particular, is not the lack of knowledge, which is sizable. Rather, it is the integration of existing knowledge. Histories, case studies, psychology, anthropology, and economics can all be tapped to identify a set of general mechanisms explaining movement on the spectrum of roles during insurgencies.

3.4. Types of Mechanisms Common to Many Insurgencies

While there are several types of mechanisms at play in insurgency, they can be grouped into four categories: rational calculation, social norms, emotions, and psychological mechanisms. This section systemically addresses each of these categories of mechanisms. For each category, I provide a basic definition, list subtypes and related mechanisms, provide examples from classic texts, mention well-known works relying on that mechanism, and describe the conditions which are most likely to trigger the mechanism. The following review relies on well-known classic texts not only because many readers will be familiar with those texts, but also because their relevance has withstood the test of time.

3.4.1. Rational Choice

The mechanism underlying most theories of insurgency is *instrumental rational choice* related to a relatively narrow set of economic and security values. Individuals are seen as coldly calculating costs on one hand and benefits on the other. In terms of the spectrum of roles, if an individual is at -1 (informal support of insurgents), that individual will calculate the costs and benefits of remaining at -1 versus the costs and benefits of moving to another role. For most individuals, the most possible and likely move is to an adjacent position. For the individual at -1, the choice set may be to either move to -2 (joining up with a local insurgent group) or to play things safe and move into a neutral role (0). Much counterinsurgency theory concentrates on "sticks and carrots" used to influence the operation of this rational calculation mechanism. Early practice in Iraq reflected reliance on this mechanism. An American military colonel serving in Iraq in 2003 stated: "With a heavy dose of fear and violence, and a lot of money for projects, I think we can convince these people that we are here to help them" (Colonel Sassaman quoted in Filkins, 2003, p. 160).

It individuals are calculating cost and benefits and choosing the optimal choice, then the questions turn to (1) the determination of costs and benefit, and (2) the information necessary to determine levels of costs and benefits. In studying insurgency, the values are economic benefits, threats, and sometimes status rewards.[6] Economically, counterinsurgents often offer jobs and payments as part of a "hearts and minds" campaign to move individuals from neutrality to informal support (0 to +1). They offer good salaries to recruit individuals into the local police and local security forces (+2) or the military (+3). Insurgents can also offer financial rewards and/or allow supporters to cash in on spoils or illegal activities.[7] Given the fracturing of the state and the breakdown in law and order, insurgents often generate income through smuggling, black market operations, and other illegal activities.

Both insurgents and counterinsurgents also try to add to the negative side of the cost/benefit balance through threats and repression. Counterinsurgents will threaten those moving leftward on the spectrum of roles; insurgents will use the stick for those moving rightward toward cooperation with the state. These threats and sanctions do not fit into a rational choice framework in an entirely straightforward way. Two related mechanisms need to be addressed—perception of a "safety in numbers" tipping point, and focal points.

As many theorists posit, support of either the insurgent or the counterinsurgent is often conditional. Insurgents and counterinsurgents threaten penalties against certain actions, but individuals will want to know the chance that these penalties will be administered. Individuals may wish to take offered rewards for cooperation with the insurgent or the counterinsurgent, but only *if* the threat of retaliation is low enough. In David Galula's foundational text on counterinsurgency, the Third Law reads: "The Third Law: Support from the Population is Conditional." As Galula states in explanation:

> The minority hostile to the insurgent will not and cannot emerge as long as the threat has not been lifted to a reasonable extent. Furthermore, even after the threat has been lifted, the emerging counterinsurgent supporters will not be able to rally the bulk of the population so long as the population is not convinced that the counterinsurgent has the will, the means, and the ability to win. When a man's life is at stake, it takes more than propaganda to budge him. (Galula, 1964, pp. 54–55)

Within the insurgency/counterinsurgency literature, individual estimation of threat is often tied to a *safety in numbers*[8] estimation. If an individual is at the neutral position (0), he or she will not wish to move to support of insurgents (−1 or −2) unless there are enough other individuals in a reference group also moving to that position to create a "safety in numbers" effect. It is dangerous to be one of a few individuals moving to a risk-laden role. The same logic applies going in the other direction, toward support of the counterinsurgent or the government.

At certain point, however, individuals come to believe that a threshold has been crossed. With the perception that local population percentages are favoring one side or the other, individuals are far more likely to seize possible benefits from active participation. When a "tipping point" has been passed, there is often dramatic movement on the spectrum of roles. Observers can see the shift in the population. Galula observed such a shift in an Algerian village after the elimination of Islamist insurgents (the OPA) and their supporters. Galula describes this case in his autobiographical work, *Pacification in Algeria, 1956–1958*:

> The change in the attitude of the population at Bou Souar after the purge was amazing, a real honeymoon. No longer did the villagers avoid talking to my soldiers. I didn't have to force the sick to visit the dispensary. Even the women came, and often unaccompanied. The villagers visited the Army post in such numbers to buy beer and soft drinks from the local canteen. . . . As the surest sign that I had hit straight at the OPA, the villagers were smoking again quite openly. (Galula, 2006, p. 122)

How does an individual gauge how many others are moving to positions across the spectrum? Is the rest of the population moving out of neutrality toward government support, or are substantial numbers moving the other way toward the insurgents? In the Galula example just mentioned, residents in the village could all see other residents talking to soldiers and drinking beer; they could see that their fellow residents had lost their fear of insurgents. Given this information, they could gauge that the chances of insurgent retaliation for these actions were low.

This discussion of "safety in numbers" leads into a consideration of a second informational mechanism—*focal points*. Focal points are events, places, or dates that help to coordinate expectations and thus actions. For governments, elections can serve as focal points. The election is held on a specific day and requires voters to go to specific locations. Every individual can see how many others are going to the polls. For the government, a massive turnout can signal its legitimacy. Through high election turnout, neutrals and those sympathetic to the insurgents must face the fact that a majority of the population favors the government. Wavering individuals may adjust their behavior accordingly by moving rightward on the spectrum. On the other side, insurgents may use specific holidays and locations to stage anti-government rallies to serve as coordinating focal points. Religion, by its regular timing of holidays and rituals, often provides focal points. In East Germany in 1989, anti-regime protestors in Leipzig knew to show up on Mondays after prayers at a local church. Protected by the knowledge that thousands of others would attend, rallies increasingly grew in size and spread to other cities in the German Democratic Republic (GDR). Although GDR leader Erich Honecker called for violence on October 9, the crowds had grown so large that his brutal security chief, Mielke, simply replied, "Erich, we can't beat up hundreds of thousands of people" (Petersen, 2001, p. 269).

While rational choice approaches would seem to be entirely straightforward, in terms of actual counterinsurgency practice there are some complexities. For example, if a counterinsurgent wishes to affect individuals' cost/benefit calculations, should it aim at current payoffs or strive to affect calculations of future payoffs? If the latter, the counterinsurgent might devote resources to high-profile public goods like dams or public schools. These projects will provide confidence in the ability of the state to prevail over insurgents, as well as to show off the government's longer-term influence. Regardless of present events and personal gains and losses, individuals will gauge that they should bandwagon with the future winner now.

On the other hand, if the counterinsurgent acts along the lines of the most famous economic theory of collective action, that of Mancur Olson as laid out in *The Logic of Collective Action* (1971), it might choose different tactics. Olson's theory holds that the promise of public goods will not drive individuals to action. By definition, individuals cannot be excluded from the benefits of public goods. Whether an individual supports the government or not, he or she will benefit from the construction of a dam or public school all the same. So why take risks in supporting the counterinsurgent and possibly becoming an individual target of the insurgents? For Olson, only "selective incentives" will drive rational individuals.[9] Selective incentives are given only to those who actually contribute. Following Olson's theory, the counterinsurgent should devote resources to establishing payrolls—only those who directly work on behalf of the state will receive the payment. Counterinsurgents could also rely on bribes or allowing selected parties control over smuggling networks. In applying Olson's theory to the insurgent side, insurgent groups need to develop a capacity for applying sticks (threats) and carrots (usually economic benefits) selectively in order for rebellion to be sustained.

There are important wrinkles to Olson's theory, though. Samuel Popkin's *The Rational Peasant: The Political Economy of Rural Society in Vietnam* is a well-known application of Olson's theory employed to explain the decisions of Vietnamese peasants to support the insurgency. Rather than simply specifying selective incentives, Popkin's work argues that insurgent political entrepreneurs can spur collective action, in Olson's theory, by turning larger "latent" groups into smaller "intermediate" groups. In the former, no single individual's contribution is significant or noticeable. In the latter, an individual's contribution becomes consequential and noticeable. Popkin wrote how successful Vietnamese rebel organizations and their local leaders broke down the larger public goods of insurgency into a series of smaller tasks in which an individual's contribution became meaningful. Rather than fighting for an insurgent victory, entrepreneurs involved peasants in local projects, such as building wells or irrigation systems. Given this action, where each individual could see the impact of his or her contribution and assess the payoff, the population was rationally drawn into the broader support network of the insurgents.

Under what conditions would we expect rational choice mechanisms to best explain movement among insurgency roles? As a choice-based explanation, rational choice would seem best suited to situations in which the cost–benefit value of one choice is clearly and consistently better than that of alternative choices. As one notable proponent of rational choice, George Tsebelis, has summarized, "actions taken in noniterative situations by individual decision makers (such as in crisis situations) are not necessarily well-suited for rational choice predictions" (Tsebelis, 1990, p. 38). When individuals are not clear about the choices that exist, or do not have enough information to calculate payoffs, other mechanisms are more likely to drive action. Insurgencies are almost always situations of upheaval, rapid change, and sudden violence. In these circumstances, individuals may not be able to calculate the value of "sticks and carrots" or selective incentives. They may put loyalty to family, clan, or nation ahead of the personal benefit of an economic "carrot." Accordingly, there is a need to specify other potentially powerful mechanisms.

3.4.2. Social Norms

Under the influence of social norms, individuals do not calculate costs and benefits, but rather follow accepted rules of behavior. Some norms are unconditional: "do X, not Y." Other social norms are conditional: "do X if others are doing X." These conditional norms often serve to coordinate actions with others. Social norms can be crucial mechanisms in insurgencies in societies with strong family, clan, or tribal elements. For example, consider an individual member of a clan who wishes to remain neutral (at the 0 level) early in the conflict. If other members of the clan move to −1 support, the social norms of the clan will also impel this individual to support the insurgents in similar fashion.[10] If the clan moves to −2 level of organized and armed support, this individual, following *social norms of reciprocity*, will likely be pulled along. Counterinsurgents may try to influence this individual's calculus through a set of individually targeted threats (prison) or benefits (payoffs, amnesty), but if the group norm is strong, these sticks and carrots will not produce their intended effect.

Unsurprisingly, norms play a powerful role in a host of well-known works explaining a range of political violence. By definition, insurgencies, as well as rebellions and revolutions, involve the breakdown of state control. As the state disintegrates, the locus of action often becomes the community. Accordingly, mechanisms associated with community critically emerge at specific junctures. In *States and Social Revolutions*, Theda Skocpol (1979) outlines a process in which changes in international competition drive states to seek to extract more domestic resources. This effort sets off internal class conflict as powerful aristocracies resist state intrusion. Although Skocpol (1979) concentrates on the state, at one point in her explanatory narrative the nature of peasant community structures emerges as a primary factor. As the domestic system unravels, differences in levels of village solidarity produce different paths to revolution across France, Russia, and China. In France and Russia, higher forms of community solidarity trigger quick violent actions; in China, political entrepreneurs must play a larger role. Although Skocpol (1979) does not use the terminology, she sketches a process in which the locus of action shifts across levels of analysis from international to state/class level to community and the norms and solidarity of those communities.

While it was not Skocpol's (1979) focus, many other social scientists have worked to specify community-level norms that generate and sustain political violence. Most famously perhaps, James Scott's *The Moral Economy of the Peasant: Rebellion and Subsistence in Southeast Asia* outlines the role of community social norms related to guarantees of subsistence and how threats to those norms ignite resistance (Scott, 1976). Roger Gould's network models illustrate the potential power of social norms of fairness (Gould, 1993).[11]

3.4.3. Emotions

Rational-choice approaches assume straightforward connections between preferences, information, and beliefs. Individuals desire things, some more than others. Thus, there is a preference order, one assumed to be stable. The individual then collects information relevant to his or her preferences and then forms reasonable beliefs from that information on how to achieve the preferred ends.

During violent conflict, the operation of this cycle is not so straightforward. Violent insurgencies involve death, destruction, and desecration—all of which can generate powerful emotions. These emotions, in turn, change preferences, shape information collection, and distort belief formation. First, and most fundamentally, emotions are mechanisms that can heighten the saliency of particular concerns. They act as a "switch" among basic desires, in effect transforming preferences. Once in place, emotions can produce a feedback effect on information collection. Furthermore, even with accurate and undistorted information, emotion can affect belief formation. These feedback effects on information collection and belief formation distinguish emotions from rational-choice mechanisms.[12] As with social norms, emotions can affect behavior in ways that can override the "sticks and carrots" policies of an occupier.

During insurgencies, the emotions of fear of anger, either arising out of the situation itself or enflamed by political entrepreneurs, can move individuals along the spectrum. *Anger* results from the belief that an actor has committed a bad action against one's self or group. Under the influence of anger, individuals no longer calculate costs and benefits in a straightforward way. Under anger, they downgrade risks and skew information processing in ways that allow for the pursuit of revenge. The emotion of anger is the primary fuel for sparking and sustaining spirals of violence, with two sides sequentially responding to the other side's attacks. In terms of the spectrum of roles, under anger, individuals will feel compelled to move out of neutrality into a more active role. Neutrals and unarmed supporters may be compelled to move to an armed role.

Under the influence of *fear*, individual perceptions of danger become heightened. Individuals may feel compelled to seek safety in ethnically homogenous areas as a form of protection. In Bosnia, Serbian militias used indiscriminate killings and burnings of villages to inculcate fear and generate flight and ethnic separation. Violence was highest in areas bordering Serbia and along the line of what would become the demarcation line between Republika Srpska and the Bosnjak/Croat-dominated Federation (Costalli and Moro, 2012; Kalyvas and Sambanis, 2005). Fear is an effective mechanism that drives ethnic separation and homogenization. Without the possibility of flight, individuals may seek safety by hiding or at least trying to stay out of the way of trouble and out of the view of combatants.

One of the most relevant emotions to invasion, occupation, and state-building is *resentment*. Perceptions of unjust group subordination create a powerful emotion of resentment. Prior to the conflict, group A might have held most of the visible positions of power and authority over groups B and C. After the invasion, the formerly subordinate groups B and C may be able to assert new dominance over A. Much recent scholarship has shown the power of group status reversals. Once a group has established itself in the dominant position in an ethnic status hierarchy, members of that group do not readily accept subordination (or even equality). In a sweeping statistical study, Lars-Erik Cederman and his collaborators have found that groups that have undergone status reversals are about five times more likely to mobilize for violence than comparable groups that did not experience status reversals (Cederman et al., 2010).[13]

Few conflict-focused political scientists address the role of emotions. As Ronald Suny summarizes: "I argue something that should be obvious, though not always for political scientists: emotions are key to human motivation. Indeed, we would not be human without them. They are a stimulus to action; they are fundamental to self-identification, to thinking about who 'we' are and who the 'other' is; they are involved in the social bonds that make groups, even whole societies, or nations, possible. And they are, therefore, powerful tools to explain why people do what they do politically" (Suny, 2004, p. 5). Political scientists who do concentrate on emotion and insurgency/civil war include Stuart Kaufman who studies the role of hatred in the Balkans and the Caucuses (Kaufman, 2001), Elisabeth Wood who studies the formation and power of pride among El Salvadorian rebels (Wood, 2003, 2008), and Donald Horowitz who studies ethnic conflict in ranked versus unranked systems in a fashion related to the discussion of the emotion of resentment above (Horowitz, 1985).

3.4.4. Psychological Mechanisms

The set of relevant psychological mechanisms can again be defined with reference to rational choice. Rational choice assumes that individuals have information and develop coherent beliefs from that information. In this vein, individuals calculate losses and gains, sticks and carrots, in a straightforward manner. Much of the field of social psychology and behavioral economics challenges these assumptions. Economists Amos Tversky and Daniel Kahneman (1991) have shown how individuals strongly prefer avoiding losses to acquiring gains. Their insights have led to a sub-field of prospect theory and the related mechanism of *loss aversion*. The related mechanism of the *tyranny of sunk costs* came up above. Social psychologists have studied the mechanism of *cognitive dissonance* for generations.[14] Cognitive dissonance occurs when an individual holds two incongruent beliefs. The psychic tension from holding these inconsistent beliefs pushes the individual toward some form of reconciliation that brings the beliefs into line. In the process, the individual may come up with a rationalization that leads to continuing a clearly suboptimal line of action. Tocqueville, Davies, and also Ted Gurr (1968) have initiated a line of logic and research on the *relative deprivation* mechanism. Then there are more commonsense psychological mechanisms, such as *wishful thinking*. Under wishful thinking, individuals desire something so strongly that information contrary to achieving that desire is ignored and unrealistic beliefs are maintained.[15] Other well-established psychological mechanisms specify how individuals process information about outsiders differently than information about insiders. The *fundamental attribution error* occurs when one explains outsider actions as a result of their internal and innate characteristics, while attributing actions of oneself or one's group to the situation.

Many political scientists, especially those studying international relations, have studied the effects of these psychological mechanisms on leadership decisions.[16] Christopher Blattman's work identifies several mechanisms which work to distort or impede a bargaining process and the ability to compromise that could prevent violence.[17] There is a significant literature addressing psychological mechanisms during postwar reconstruction. Recent applications to insurgency and violent internal struggle are fewer. This was not always the case. For example, relative deprivation was actually a dominant approach during the 1970s before quickly fading from the scene. As defined by Ted Gurr, the leading proponent of the theory, relative deprivation is an "actor's perceptions of discrepancy between their value expectations (the goods and conditions of the life in which they believe they are justifiably entitled) and their value capabilities (the amounts of those goods and conditions that they think they are able to get and keep)" (Gurr, 1968, p. 1104). Between 1968 and 1977, roughly one-third of the articles on violent conflict in the *American Political Science Review*, the field's flagship journal, employed relative deprivation theory in some form or another.

To preview the empirical findings of this work, psychological mechanisms will not play a huge role in this book, but they are well-established and should be included within the list of general mechanisms to be considered at the start of analysis. While some of the mechanisms above help explain the "triggering" of insurgency, psychological mechanisms would appear to most help explain how insurgency is sustained in the face of declining insurgent power. The tyranny of sunk costs was already mentioned above. After blood has been shed, individuals will tend to believe that it must have been shed for a worthwhile purpose; it is difficult to accept that lives may have been lost in vain. Those at the −2 and −3 levels will be compelled to fight on, even in the face of powerful government "sticks." As the wishful thinking mechanism holds, individuals might likely ignore evidence in order to maintain a belief in eventual victory, even if catastrophic defeat stares them in the face. There is also the "tyranny of small victories." In this case, the ability to inflict some pain on the government, that is, to carry out occasional successful operations against the government, will outweigh a rational evaluation of the overall course of the conflict, even when that course is downhill.

3.5. Mechanisms and the Spectrum of Roles

The three core elements of the analytical framework are strategy, mechanism, and role. Thus far, we have discussed each element separately, as well as the relationship between strategy and role (exemplified by Figure 2.2 in Chapter 2). The remaining task is to draw out the connections between mechanisms and roles.

Any given mechanism is likely to have its main effects only between certain nodes. Below, the reader will find a template that specifies when we might expect a particular mechanism to be most important in moving individuals across roles of the spectrum. This template was developed from a wide reading of historical case studies, previous fieldwork, and a multitude of social science studies of insurgency and domestic conflict, some mentioned above. In addition, this template has been derived from the reading and summary of over 60 recent articles from the social science literature on insurgency.[18] Those articles are categorized and summarized by topic and relevance to movement on the spectrum in Appendix B.[19]

The list of articles in Appendix B is not exhaustive, and tends to over-select from Middle East cases, but is large and general enough to translate much of the recent literature on insurgency into the framework's key concepts of mechanisms and a spectrum of roles. The hope is that serious students and researchers of internal conflict and insurgency will find Appendix B a useful resource.

3.5.1. Template of Anticipated Mechanisms

Movement from 0 to −1:

- Resentment versus newly empowered group
- Safety in numbers with general population as reference point
- Status rewards
- Focal points.

Movement from 0 to +1:

- Resentment versus insurgent group
- Safety in numbers with general population as reference point
- Focal points
- Rational economic decision, payouts from government, employment, etc.

Movement from +1 and −1 back to 0:

- Rational reaction to threat
- Fear (emotion).

Movement from −1 to −2:

- Social norms of reciprocity
- Norms of honor/vengeance

- Anger (vs. collateral damage, detainment, etc.)
- Safety in numbers with local population as reference point
- Material incentives.

Movement to +2:

- Social norms of reciprocity
- Anger (vs. insurgent violence)
- Safety in numbers with local population as reference point
- Material incentives/employment/bribes.

Movement to −3:

- Material incentives
- Ideological fervor
- Humiliation.

Mechanisms sustaining −2, −3:

- Psychological mechanisms—tyranny of sunk costs, wishful thinking, cognitive dissonance
- Coercion, threats against leaving
- Social norms.

Movement to +3:

- Material incentives (pay, uniforms, equipment)
- Pride (in either professionalism or patriotism).

3.5.2. Process Tracing: The Application of the Template

In the field of political science, practitioners of case studies usually claim to do "process tracing." What this means in practice is often particular to the analyst. Here, the aim is to study actors implementing strategies to set off mechanisms in order to affect the distribution of roles in the population. These are certainly complex "processes." The template helps "trace" those processes. It serves to discipline process tracing. While each case of insurgency and internal violent conflict will differ, this template reminds us what to look for in a given case. It helps us to readily identify common mechanisms at work, as well as to identify sequences of mechanisms that form processes.[20] It reminds the analyst not only to look for the mechanisms that insurgents and counterinsurgents attempt to trigger, but also those that they do not attempt, or attempt and fail, to trigger.

This template helps examine strategies. In the empirical sections of this work, several case studies will juxtapose insurgent and the counterinsurgent strategies. The case will analyze the matchup and explain how it worked to produce outcomes. How did respective strategies concentrate on certain nodes of the spectrum rather than others? How did the strategy intend to move individuals into desired role—what was the underlying "theory" of effective mechanisms?

This matching of strategies is an essential part of our analysis. As Andrew Krepinevich has written:

> (t)he essence of strategy is identifying asymmetric advantages, both our own and those of our rivals, both existing and prospective. General Rupert Smith observes that "the essence of the practice of war is to achieve asymmetric advantage over one's opponent; an advantage in any terms, not just technological." (Krepinevich, 2009, p. 15)

The method will identify how insurgents used and sometimes created asymmetries that allowed them to sustain violence and organization even in the face of Coalition technological advantages. It will also show how the US/ Coalition forces sometimes managed to counter or eliminate these asymmetries and/or use US asymmetrical advantages to greater advantage.[21]

Because the template was built from a wide range of social science studies and history, it can be used to help identify deficiencies in US intervention and counterinsurgency doctrine. If the template suggests that a mechanism is important in generating insurgency, and if US strategy ignored or downplayed that mechanism, we have identified a potential deficiency in US practice. Identifying these deficiencies helps us look toward the future of US intervention. Will future opponents of the United States hold certain inherent advantages in triggering the mechanisms most fundamental to violent processes or the blunting of state-building? What are possible US counters? If the United States is at an inherent disadvantage for one strategy, can it move to an alternative strategy?

3.5.3. General Application of the Template: Appendix A

As emphasized earlier, the analytical framework used throughout this work was created to have general applicability. It embodies a method both to guide the analysis of a particular case and to make comparisons across cases. Although this template will be used in this book to break down and match up insurgent and counterinsurgent strategies in Iraq, it should be useful in breaking down the logic and contours of many insurgencies and civil wars.

Appendix A provides an application of the framework to classic theories of insurgency and counterinsurgency. Appendix A restates Mao's theory of guerrilla warfare and David Galula's counterinsurgency theory in terms of roles, mechanisms, and strategies. The analysis then goes on to outline the matchup of these strategies in the Malayan Emergency, perhaps the most studied case in the insurgency research field.

Appendix A is recommended for those interested in classic counterinsurgency and insurgency theory, as well as anyone seeking a concise application of this book's analytical framework before moving into the Iraq study. The conclusion to Appendix A summarizes the value added of this book's analytical framework.

3.6. Mechanisms Related to Master Cleavages and Dominance

A major finding of this book is that a drive toward group dominance, as well as efforts to avoid group subordination, fueled much of the Iraq conflict and shaped its evolution. As laid out in the introductory chapter, for dominance-related goals to become central in a conflict, individuals must identify with their group and see that group in conflict with other groups. The salience of identity also needs to be translated into action. A mechanisms-based approach specifies the causal forces that heighten group identification and motivate action along group lines.

While scholars have certainly linked rational choice[22] and social norm[23] mechanisms to a heightened salience of identity, three powerful emotions best explain powerful group identification and movement across the spectrum. These three emotions are resentment and anger, both mentioned above, along with humiliation.

As outlined above, resentment forms from perceptions of unjust group subordination. By this very definition, the emotion is connected to dominance. Resentment motivates action by heightening a preference to re-establish the dominant position of one's group or to avoid being dominated; the emotion skews information collection biasing the individuals to see group dominance or subordination even in ambiguous situations. If the state is perceived as controlled or dominated by a previously subordinate group, resentment will be a force driving individuals leftward on the spectrum of roles. Resentment is a broadly felt force, likely to be experienced by many members of a group. As only some group members will take up armed positions at the −2 or −3 level, resentment's most important and clearest force is in driving members of a group toward the −1 position. From that position, resentful group members will provide information and support to those actively trying (often violently) to rectify the group's status position. In Iraq, one of the most consequential resentment-driven actions was the Sunni boycott of the 2005 elections, a nonviolent anti-state (−1) behavior.

While resentment heightens salience of a group's identity and focuses individuals' minds on the group status position, the emotion of anger is in reaction to opposing groups' actions. Anger creates a drive for revenge; violence to be met with violence. Influenced by anger, individuals are also subject to the fundamental attribution error, a psychological mechanism where blame is assigned to groups rather than individuals (Keltner et al, 1993). The angry person lowers the threshold for attributing harmful intent. Anger also tends to produce more stereotyping (Bodenhausen et al., 1994). Under the influence of anger, individuals lower their risk estimates and become more willing to engage in risky behavior (Lerner and Keltner, 2000, 2001).

The link between anger and the persistence and pervasiveness of master cleavage identity is straightforward. If identities are already salient, through history or resentment, the emotion of anger, in conjunction with its related psychological mechanisms, will drive individuals to code a violent action in group terms. "That group" committed violence against "us." Anger will drive individuals to punish the opposing group, rather than the opposing group's factions or leaders. Revenge, acted out from one side, will produce a similar action on the other side. An anger-fueled spiral ensues, heightening the salience of group identity and bolstering group stereotypes. Moreover, violence inherently creates a perception of dominance and subordination through its creation of perpetrators and victims. Violence must be met with violence not only as a matter of justice, but also to create "just" status relations among groups.

If resentment drives individuals to a general −1 position, anger has the ability to drive individuals into −2 or −3 roles. The angry individual wants revenge. But revenge is best carried out by groups, not isolated individuals. The angry individual may find an outlet in a local militia or even by joining a mobile armed group.

There is one more emotional mechanism closely connected to dominance— humiliation. While resentment is about group status and anger is about perceptions of group actions, humiliation is a combination of both. An individual experiences humiliation through a perception that a clear perpetrator has unjustly acted to reduce his or her status to a low and powerless position. In some treatments, humiliation is a combination of anger and shame (McCauley, 2017).[24] A perpetrator has acted to make a victim feel small. In the words of Evelin Linder, "Humiliation entails demeaning treatment that transgresses established expectations. The victim is forced into passivity, acted upon, and made helpless" (Linder, 2006, p. 172, qtd. in McCauley, 2017, p. 257).

Humiliation is often considered the root motivation for terrorism (Stern, 2003). The only way to confront one's humiliation and regain dignity is through violent action against the actor who produced one's position of powerlessness. Violent action itself is the clearest way to reverse the tables and establish a sense of balance, to use terror to force the perpetrator to experience powerlessness. While anger can drive an individual to seek out a vehicle for revenge, the power of humiliation can drive an individual to more extreme actions. Humiliation, it follows, can propel individuals to the −3 position. Mobile armed groups such as al-Qaeda provide the logistics and opportunities to retaliate. Such groups often possess an ideology and language directed at the humiliated individual.

While humiliation can be addressed as an individual-level mechanism driving specific movement on the spectrum of roles, the emotion also plays a more general role in Middle East conflicts and Iraq in particular. Dominique Moisi, in his book *The Geopolitics of Emotion: How Cultures of Fear, Humiliation, and Hope Are Reshaping the World*, describes humiliation in the following terms:

> If hope is confidence, humiliation is impotence, an emotion that stems above all from the feeling that you no longer in control of your life either collectively, as a people, a nation, or a religious community, or individually, as single person. Humiliation peaks when you are convinced the Other has intruded into the private realm of your own life and made you utterly dependent. Humiliation encapsulates a sense of dispossession toward the present and even more so toward the future, a future in utter contrast with an idealized, glorified past, a future in which your political, social, cultural conditions are dictated by the Other. (Moisi, 2010, pp. 56–57)

Moisi goes on to argue that the Islamic world, and especially the Arab world, can be characterized by a culture of humiliation. Of course, the Other dominating and humiliating these cultures is the West. Indeed, the West has produced searing images of domination in the Middle East. Israeli administration of the West Bank with its checkpoint systems produces daily humiliation on Arab residents; Israel's periodic wars with Gaza provide images of missiles from the sky decimating neighborhoods and spreading death among the general populace. From the experience of the United States in Iraq, perhaps no images were more humiliating than those coming out of the Abu Ghraib prison—Arab men forced onto dog piles and made to wear women's underwear.

3.7. The Way Forward

The second chapter concentrated on the concepts of roles and strategies. This chapter has focused on mechanisms. It has provided definitions, a general list of mechanisms relevant to insurgency, and a template linking specific mechanisms to the spectrum of roles, as well as addressing mechanisms central to dominance and the saliency of master cleavages. In sum, the second and third chapters have created a framework for analysis capable of breaking down and analyzing the interplay of insurgent and counterinsurgent strategies.

Chapter 4 will employ the framework to break down five counterinsurgency strategies employed by the United States in Iraq. Sections II and III will apply the framework to over a dozen cases in Iraq, covering a wide range of regions and time periods. Ultimately, these applications can produce knowledge and insights relevant to the future, as laid out in Section IV.

US Counterinsurgency Strategy and Practice

4.1. Introduction

This chapter will address all three of our core concepts—role, mechanism, strategy—through an examination of US counterinsurgency practice.[1] The chapter will survey five strategies. Each of these strategies has its own logic; each recommends different applications of force and violence; each addresses the problem of state-building in its own way. In line with our analytical framework, each strategy has an explicit or implicit theory of how to trigger mechanisms to set off processes that move individuals in desired directions on the spectrum of roles.

Accordingly, this chapter will systematically examine each of the five strategies in more depth, expanding on the brief coverage in Chapter 2. Each will be addressed in three steps—first, by laying out each strategy's logic in more detail; second, by specifying the mechanisms underlying that logic; third, by illustrating the strategy and points of contention surrounding the strategy with commentary of practitioners.[2] By the end of the chapter, the reader should have a better understanding of the strategic thinking of a primary player in Iraq, the United States, before heading into the case studies.

The case studies in Sections II and III present a largely chronological story that cannot be understood without knowledge of US strategy, the evolution of that strategy over time, and its interaction with insurgent strategies. The implementation of these strategies has had powerful effects on the building of the Iraqi state during the US occupation, as well as a lasting legacy on Iraqi society and politics up to the time of writing (2023). The reader can review Figures 1.1 and 1.2 (Chapter 1) to recall the ebbs and flows of violence across time and region in Iraq. The empirical cases will explain the reasons for these sharp increases and declines in violence. They will attempt to parse out how much of this rise and fall had to do with changes in US strategy. Just as importantly, *how* did these strategies affect such changes?

4.2. War-Fighting

Chapter 2 outlined four counterinsurgency strategies—clear, hold, build (CHB); community mobilization; decapitation; and homogenization—captured by Figure 2.2, which is reprinted here as Figure 4.1. Before going to an analysis of these four counterinsurgency strategies, we must address a fifth strategy: war-fighting. There were four planned phases to the Iraq War. As early as December 2001, General Tommy Franks outlined these phases to President George W. Bush in a briefing (Franks, 2004, pp. 340–341). Phase I established international support and capabilities to transport soldiers and materials into the theater. Phase II "shaped the battlespace." Phase III planned decisive military operations both to defeat the Iraq military and to kill or capture regime leaders. The final phase IV was "post-hostility operations." This book will focus on how the four counterinsurgency strategies illustrated by Figure 4.1 played out during Phase IV. But the fact that Phase III was an armored invasion cannot be forgotten. The first counterinsurgency strategy was primarily conducted by war-fighters with little counterinsurgency training. Unsurprisingly, these units fought insurgency through conventional war-fighting means. The counterinsurgency strategies that came later are in large part a response to the perceived deficiencies of fighting an insurgency with this strategy. In short, it is necessary to understand the strategy of war-fighting as applied to an internal conflict before we can understand what comes after.

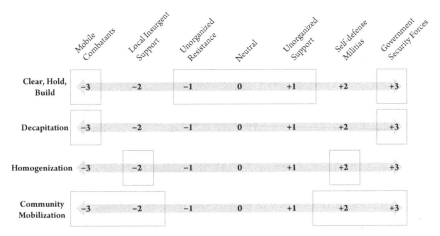

Figure 4.1. Four counterinsurgent strategies (reprint of Figure 2.2).

In terms of the spectrum of roles, war-fighting is straightforward—the military is going after the mobile soldiers of the opposing side, the −3 level. There is little concern for focusing on other nodes, especially those concentrated on moving individuals in the −1, 0, +1 non-armed positions. As the term *war-fighting* suggests, the military is fighting a war; soldiers act to "kill the enemy, not to win their hearts and minds" (Ricks, 2007, p. 234).[3] War-fighting also implies that the military is fighting the enemy, even an insurgent enemy, with conventional military means. For the United States, these conventional military means center on mobility and firepower. Primary tactics include cordon and sweep operations, harassment and interdiction artillery shelling, and showing force to create a deterrent.

Cordon and sweep, or cordon and search, operations are raids meant to encircle targets within an area. Throughout the Iraq conflict, US forces conducted these operations based on local tips. The typical operation involved setting up an outer cordon to control movement in and out of the area, then the creation of an inner cordon to seal off the area immediate to the target location, and finally an assault on the target itself. The assault team is often divided into four units: a protective unit able to produce suppressive fire if necessary; an entry team to clear the buildings of people; a search team to ferret out weapons, bomb-making materials, and contraband; and a detention and collection team to secure the human targets and material. Early in the occupation, with war-fighting the predominant mode of operation, the United States embarked on many major cordon and sweep operations. Launched on July 12, 2003, Operation Soda Mountain conducted a series of approximately 150 separate raids throughout Iraq over five days, resulting in the capture of 62 Baathist leaders. Also launched on July 12, the Fourth Infantry Division conducted Operation Ivy Serpent to sweep Diyala and Salahaddin provinces. Two months later, under Operation Longstreet, elements of the First Armored Division and the Third Armored Cavalry Regiment conducted cordon and sweep operations between Fallujah and Baghdad for two weeks. In October 2003, elements of the 82nd Airborne Division conducted sweeps in Ramadi with Operation O.K. Corral. Within the first 18 months of the occupation, General Ricardo Sanchez estimated that US forces had put 30,000 to 40,000 Iraqis into detention facilities.

Harassment and interdiction (H and I) artillery shelling involves firing into a general area in order to prevent the enemy's free movement as well as to destroy enemy morale. In Vietnam, nearly half of the ammunition used by the US Army in 1966 and 1967 was spent in these unobserved firing missions (Hawkins, 2004). Given its unclear success (and some think clear failure), General William Westmoreland reduced H and I operations during 1968, and his successor, General Creighton Abrams, nearly eliminated H and I bombing by 1970. The practice made a comeback of sorts early in the Iraq war. While

leading the 4th Infantry Division in the Sunni Triangle in 2003–2004, General
Raymond Odierno wrote, "We used our Paladins [155 millimeter self-propelled
howitzer systems] the entire time we were there.... Most nights we fired H&I
fires ... what I call 'proactive' counterfire." He concluded, "artillery plays a significant role in counterinsurgency operations" (Ricks, 2007, p. 234). In some cases,
insurgent mortars would be answered with a responding, and disproportionate,
counter artillery response. Dexter Filkins, writing of the well-known Colonel
Nathan Sassaman,[4] recalls one incident in 2003:

> By the time he ended his tour in Iraq, the insurgents had come to fear
> Sassaman more than anyone else. Whenever he left Balad, even for a
> couple of days, the insurgents would step up their attacks. When he
> returned, they would back off. Once, after Sassaman returned from a
> mission in Samarra, insurgents fired a single mortar round into his com-
> pound, as if to welcome him back. He responded by firing twenty-eight
> 155-millmeter artillery shells and forty-two mortar rounds. He called
> in two airstrikes, one with a 500 pound bomb and another with a 2,000
> pound bomb. Later on, his men found a crater deep as a swimming
> pool. (Filkins, 2008, p. 163)

Colonel Sassaman's response aimed in large part to quell insurgency through
deterrence. After the incident described above, Sassaman told Filkins, "We just
didn't get hit after that" (Filkins, 2008, p. 163).

In addition to firepower, the US and Coalition forces constantly patrolled to
maintain a visible presence. In the words of a battalion commander in Tikrit early
in the occupation, "We would not win the people of Tikrit over.... They generally hate us. We are kind and compassionate to those that work with us but most
detest us as a general rule. But they do respect power. Some have questioned our
forcefulness but we will not win them over by handing out lollipops—not in
Tikrit" (Ricks, 2007, p. 233).

As noted above, it is hardly surprising that the US military relied on war-
fighting for counterinsurgency in the period after the invasion. As no force in the
world matches the United States in either mobility or firepower, it was natural
for the US military to use these capabilities as a first choice. Moreover, the US
military has been built to use mobility and firepower to win decisive battles in
conventional wars. Ricks quotes a senior military intelligence officer on operations in 2003: "We were not very sophisticated or calibrated in our approach.
You know the old saying, 'If all you have is a hammer, everything looks like a
nail'" (Ricks, 2007, p. 195). Most importantly, the armored units that led the
invasion of Iraq were not trained for counterinsurgency. Officers such as Lt. Col.

John Nagl led a tank battalion into Iraq. He noted the wholesale lack of prepara-
tion of his unit for counterinsurgency:

> The situation wasn't helped by the fact that we were completely unpre-
> pared for the war we were about to fight. Our soldiers were tankers,
> trained and equipped to close with and destroy other enemy armored
> units. We had to learn to wage war against an insurgency rather than
> against the enemy tank units we had been designed to confront in open
> warfare. We had no training in developing an intelligence portfolio
> on individual insurgents, conducting security patrols to derive local
> intelligence, developing local governing councils, training and equip-
> ping local police forces, conducting raids to capture or kill high value
> targets . . . the list could go on for days. (Nagl, 2014, p. 69)

Perhaps most importantly, on the broadest level of strategy, an emphasis on
war-fighting usually means less attention paid to the politics of state-building.
As seen in Nagl's comment above, war-fighters are not trained for state-building.
Moreover, the tactics of war-fighting—sweeps, detentions on a large scale, artillery shelling, and shows of force—produce collateral damage and scenes of
domination which cause serious problems for state-building.

Fairly early in the war, many US soldiers came to believe that war-fighting
alone was not likely to bring about a stable Iraq.[5] Even before the dissemination of Field Manual 3-24 (FM 24), officers in the field were moving to more
nuanced counterinsurgency strategies in their localities. The four counterinsurgency strategies briefly outlined in Chapter 2 capture the differences among
these new approaches. The starting point here is the most well-known COIN
strategy—clear, hold, build (CHB). This strategy, associated with Petraeus and
others, aimed at avoiding many of the problems and consequences of the war-
fighting approach. The strategy focused on state-building and protecting the
population and winning its trust. The following section discusses CHB in depth
by breaking the strategy down into its planned sequence of mechanisms.

4.3. Clear, Hold, Build

Field Manual (FM) 3-24 is basically a handbook for CHB.[6] As Figure 4.1
illustrates, the strategy of CHB concentrates on the middle nodes (−1, 0, +
1) and the end nodes (−3, +3) of the spectrum of roles. The strategy is much
more complicated, as it envisions movement and interaction among the roles. In
effect, the strategy calls for three interlocking tasks:

A. Insurgent sympathizers (−1) and neutrals (0) must be moved into the role
    of government supporters (+1). For the strategy to be successful, these sup-
    portive individual citizens must be willing to provide information to the gov-
    ernment forces (+3) about the actions and whereabouts of insurgents (−3).
B. While building support from the population, the counterinsurgents must re-
    cruit and train indigenous military forces (+3).
C. State forces must be able to use the information flowing from the population
    to hunt down and kill or capture mobile insurgent forces (−3).

In this dynamic, the most crucial node is +1: supporters able and willing to
provide information. This feature underlies the definitional core of the mission
as "population-centric" and associates the strategy with "winning hearts and
minds." Of the three tasks, moving the population into support and informant
roles was assumed to be more important, and more daunting, than building a
state military or actually hunting down insurgents.

How does the counterinsurgent move individuals rightward to the +1 position?[7] In general, two objectives must be met—safety and legitimacy. Above
all, the counterinsurgent needs to be able to protect the population. Few
individuals will come forward if they do not feel safe to do so. If basic safety
needs are met, economic development in the way of jobs and public works can
build government legitimacy. Legitimacy can be eroded or destroyed, however,
if the counterinsurgent uses tactics that kill civilians or demonstrate dominance.
Bombing and shelling and indiscriminate force in general is to be kept to a minimum. Collateral damage should be avoided at all costs. At checkpoints, US military should work alongside local security. Patrols should be done on foot rather
than in vehicles.

Assuming the counterinsurgent is able to build up a mobile military force,
tactics must also change to gain local information and translate it into action.
Troops are to move out of large forward operating bases (FOBs) and live among
civilians in order to build networks that create trust. Increased presence and
contact allow for the creation of local censuses, which in turn allow for better
community monitoring. Over a period of time, the strategy develops a local government of state-approved officials working with the new state, replacing the un-
official and often illegitimate actors who took control of local governance during
the chaotic period after the invasion. In terms of human resources, CHB is intensive. Large force ratios are necessary but not sufficient: there must be sufficient
"boots on the ground" long enough to "clear" populated areas of insurgents,
"hold" them against relapse into violence, and "build" legitimate institutions.
Success builds on success as the "oil spot" of stability spreads.

Critically, CHB does not concentrate on local community-based forces. Proactive community resistance (−2) and militias (+2) are ignored or lumped into the other categories.[8]

4.3.1. Mechanisms

Like many Western occupation strategies, CHB greatly relies on *rational choice* mechanisms, both in terms of the effects of safety and in economics. As the strategy's essential task is to win the confidence of the population in order to gain information, consider the following example illustrating the cost–benefit involved with information provision:

> In eastern Ramadi, U.S. Army Capt. Joe Claburn visited a house beside an alley from where four guerrillas armed with automatic weapons and rocket-propelled grenades had attacked a guard tower on a U.S. base a day earlier. The man, barefoot with a carefully trimmed white beard, said he hadn't seen the attack or any gunmen. U.S. officers asked that the Associated Press not publish his name for fear of reprisals. Claburn asked the man if he was willing to signal U.S. troops when insurgents turned up. "I'm telling you sincerely, I cannot cooperate with you," the man replied, shaking his head. "We know you are trying to protect us, but the insurgents would cut off my head. . . . We are too frightened to do anything. They're everywhere. They're probably watching us right now" (Pitman, 2006).

Given this individual's weighting of costs and benefits, he should be expected to remain neutral (position 0) or even move to support the insurgents (−1). For potential supporters and informants (+1), both the probability and the cost of retaliation are very high. For the counterinsurgents under CHB, the first task is not only to actually clear the insurgents, but also to communicate to the population that the probability of retaliation has greatly diminished. Following Galula, this goal relies on the rational choice "tipping" mechanism that captures the logic of *safety in numbers*.[9] Once a certain (probably high) percentage of the population is visibly cooperating with the occupation forces, individuals will calculate that cooperation is now safe. With confidence in the strength and sustainability of security forces, individuals will bandwagon with the government side increasingly moving rightward and into the +1 position on the spectrum. *Focal points*—events, places, or dates that help to coordinate expectations and thus actions—can also serve as important informational mechanisms to move this process. Much stock is put into the "blue fingers" of voters to provide evidence of government legitimacy.

Even if security is established, that is, if the "clear" is finished, the counterinsurgents may need to provide other incentives to the population in order to hold and build. Here, the provision of private and public goods is essential to CHB.[10] In terms of private goods, discussed in terms of selective incentives in the previous chapter, many counterinsurgents see the provision of a stable job as the most powerful way to bind an individual to government support. Following the logic of opportunity costs, a gainfully employed citizen would not want to risk a paycheck through association with insurgents. While public goods are not selective but shared by all, counterinsurgents may wish to build large visible public works to establish confidence in the reconstructed state's stability and promise. In terms of public goods, electricity, sewage, and water are the most necessary and visible.[11]

To emphasize, these cost–benefit calculations and informational devices are rational-choice mechanisms. Despite the phrase "hearts and minds," the main focus of CHB is not directed toward emotions, norms, or psychological mechanisms. Consider the statement of David Kilcullen, a key participant in creating the CHB doctrine as seen in FM 3-24:

> Once you have settled into your sector, your next task is to build trusted networks. This is the true meaning of the phrase "hearts and minds," which comprises two separate components. "Hearts" means persuading people their best interests are served by your success; "minds" means convincing them that you can protect them, and that resisting you is pointless. Note that neither concept has to do with whether people like you. Calculated self-interest, not emotion, is what counts. Over time, if you successfully build networks of trust, these will grow like roots into the population, displacing the enemy's networks, bringing him out in the open to fight you, and seizing the initiative. . . . This is your true main effort: everything else is secondary. Actions that help build trusted networks serve your cause. Actions—even killing high profile targets—that undermine trust or disrupt your networks help the enemy.[12]

Note that Kilcullen equates trust with reliability. When people see occupation forces acting consistently and predictably, it is rational to expect them to do so in the near future. If occupation forces only periodically exit a giant FOB to conduct a sweep, or to occasionally give out goods or money, these actions do not project reliability. On the other hand, under CHB soldiers spend their days out in the community, working out of command outposts (COPs). Locals see consistent patterns of operation and can judge the value of cooperation accordingly. Even if they do not like the soldiers, they can still form a rational expectation about the value of cooperation and the cost of continued opposition. As Kilcullen states, "Again, emotions are secondary here—if locals like you but believe you cannot be relied on, you come to seem pathetic to them" (Kilcullen, 2010, p. 37).

However, CHB is not only built on rational-choice mechanisms; it also is based on avoiding negative emotions and preventing the triggering of violence-producing norms. These are mechanisms that drive individuals leftward on the spectrum of roles toward support of and participation in the insurgency. As outlined in the previous chapter, insurgencies often trigger emotions of resentment, anger, and fear. *Resentment* stems from perceptions of unjust political domination. An occupation, almost by definition, means that outsiders have authority over locals. CHB tries to blunt resentment through several means. As opposed to war-fighting, it downplays ostentatious displays of occupier force. At a local governance level, it aims for quick and thorough inclusion of native security elements at checkpoints and in local positions of authority. Kilcullen's view of networking requires cooperation, and thus a measure of equality, among actors.

Anger stems from perceptions of specific unjust actions committed against one's self or group. One of the major sources of this perception comes from "collateral damage" of occupier military actions. Not surprisingly, when an occupier military force kills innocents, especially women and children, anger produces a desire for retaliation. Under this emotion, neutrals will move left on the spectrum of roles, often into −2 positions, in order to gain a measure of revenge. The reduction of anger is one of the major tenets of CHB. Recall the Kilcullen quote above: "Actions—even killing high profile targets—that undermine trust or disrupt your networks help the enemy." If killing a high-profile target (possibly with significant collateral damage) provokes a high level of anger, it is not worth doing. Clearly, this view is in direct contrast with war-fighting strategies that place elimination of −3 actors above all else.

Mass detention is another cause of anger. Especially early on in the occupation, US forces rounded up tens of thousands of Iraqi men, tied their hands with flexicuffs, covered many in hoods, and dragged them off, often in pajamas. These raids often violated local codes of honor and triggered a norm of revenge. In the words of Colonel T. X. Hammes, a Marine expert advising on counterinsurgency, "Many of the arrests were done with a boot on the head, in front of his woman. . . . You've created a blood debt when you do that" (Ricks, 2007, p. 238). CHB aimed to reduce these incidents and directed practitioners to knock on doors and develop consistent and respectful practices during searches. The negative effects of the fiasco at Abu Ghraib need little explanation.

The emotion of *fear* heightens perceptions of danger and activates tendencies of withdrawal. With a focus on protection of the population, CHB prioritizes a reduction of fear. Under the strategy, soldiers should not make occasional forays and then disappear into an FOB, but should remain in the community as a constant source of protection. When fear subsides, rational calculations favoring cooperation with the occupier take over. The reduction of fear helps create the bandwagoning process leading to the surpassing of "tipping points."

4.3.2. Practitioner Experience with CHB

Many practitioners held a positive view of CHB, especially after the surge, with caveats emerging with hindsight. At the time of writing, positive treatments of the strategy are colored by the collapse of Afghanistan and the clear long-term failure of CHB there. Some hold that if CHB had been adopted earlier, a successful outcome in Iraq would have been far more likely. Even proponents, however, recognize the costs, especially in cases like Iraq. As Nagl expostulated in 2014:

> The question is not whether the classic counterinsurgency principles of clear, hold, build work; the fact that they do has been demonstrated repeatedly. The question is whether the extraordinary investment of time, blood and treasure required to make them work is worth the cost. The answer to that question depends on the value of the long-term stability in the country afflicted by the insurgency, and that answer varies by time and place. (Nagl, 2014, p. 215)

Another common view is that while the "surge," based on CHB, was an undeniable tactical success in Iraq, it did not solve larger strategic problems. Retired Lieutenant General Daniel P. Bolger, in his tome *Why We Lost*, believed that without a long-term commitment, counterinsurgency cannot succeed. He writes, "The shiny objects of counterinsurgency theory, neatly captured in FM 3-24, ended up delivering far less than expected or hoped. Counterinsurgency works if the intervening country demonstrates the will to stay forever. . . . Had America treated Afghanistan and Iraq from the beginning as the future fifty-first and fifty-second states, FM 3-24 offered a way to pacify them. Saddled with incomplete authority over Afghan and Iraqi internal affairs, inept host governments, and ticking clocks, we could not do it" (Bolger, 2014, p. 429). Bolger also cites a White House staffer who had stated, "The model had become clear, hold, hold, hold, hold and hold. Hold for years. There was no build, no transfer" (Bolger, 2014, p. 372).[13]

Others, such as Colonel Gian Gentile, assert that the decline in violence in Iraq was more related to other factors operating during the same time period than to the implementation of CHB. If Baghdad forms the central arena for evaluating

CHB, the complexity of the case prevents easy conclusions about the strategy's efficacy. As the case studies will show, as the Surge was being implemented, the demography of the city was transformed through ethnic cleansing and deals were being made with local insurgent groups.

To conclude this section, we can look back at one major element of CHB to help understand its thrust. Most proponents of the strategy seem to agree on the value of providing jobs to the population. Following the logic laid out above, employment is a way to convert angry −1s to supportive +1s. Following the view of potential insurgents as rational actors, it was better to pay the population to work on projects rather than have insurgent operations pay them to plant IEDs. In a September 2007 interview, Marine Major General Douglas Stone, Commander of US detention facilities in Iraq, made the following statement: "And I will tell you, there's not one guy in my line of work, there's not one commander that I have, there's not one guy in interrogation who won't tell you, the number one problem to drain the swap of the . . . countercoalition guys, the ones we're rolling up, is jobs" (*Washington Post*, 2007, September 18). At another point in the same interview, Stone put the logic bluntly, "If these guys don't have jobs, what in the hell else are they going to do? I mean, if somebody's going to pay them, you know, a couple of hundred bucks, they are going to go that way" (*Washington Post*, 2007, September 18).

The logic about jobs, clear in the statement immediately above, rests on a rational choice theory about opportunity costs. Individuals will forgo dangerous insurgent roles if they can gain personal benefits for moving to the +1 position of cooperation. In addition to this opportunity-cost argument, there is an alternative conception about how "hearts and minds" are won. Some practitioners focus on changing perceptions rather than payoffs.[14] For instance, counterinsurgents can create a positive perception of the government's future abilities and intentions through the creation of visible public works. When there is a general perception of a positive future, individuals move to +1 in order to prepare for that future. Lieutenant General Peter Chiarelli commanded the Multi-National Corps headquarters in Iraq under General George Casey and pushed this position. While Chiarelli agreed with Stone's assessment on the importance of jobs, he also was a strong advocate for reversing perceptions of Iraqi incompetence in providing basic services.[15]

4.4. Community Mobilization

With CHB, the counterinsurgent triggers individual-level mechanisms to move members of the general population into supporter roles (+1) and recruit soldiers into the central state security apparatus (+3). With community mobilization, the counterinsurgent interacts with groups of individuals who have been knit together through networks, family ties, or organizational history. The goal is to bring entire collectives into a supportive role. These collectives are often local, organized, and armed. Bringing them into cooperation with the state defines them as +2 on the spectrum of roles.

While CHB stresses the importance of regular engagement with local elites, the role of those local elites is limited to the provision of intelligence and recruits for +3 security forces. Community mobilization, on the other hand, calls for basically allying with local elites and bringing in their organizations intact. Although there may be plans to break up or integrate these organizations into the state, the strategy simply calls for making a deal to bring the support of the organization over to the counterinsurgent's side. CHB does not see such alliances as the way forward, especially in terms of state-building. The leaders of these groups may provide intelligence and manpower, but they usually do so only to bolster their own position. Accordingly, as outlined in FM 3-24, irregular units always pose a potential threat. As the Field Manual concludes: "If militias are outside the [host nation] government's control, they can often be obstacles to ending an insurgency."[16]

As the case studies will illustrate, today's +2 allies are often drawn from yesterday's −2 adversaries. The counterinsurgent can often "flip" a −2 group over to its own side (making them +2), but that group may later "flip" back to their non-state adversarial position (Staniland, 2012). These groups may be able to work both sides in order to manage and enhance their political influence in the community, changing back and forth, always looking for a better deal. Furthermore, even if the group does not completely "flip" into opposition, these non-state organizations will have incentives to seek their own goals rather than the state's. They can warp intelligence to send the counterinsurgent after their own rivals rather than those of the state. They can suck resources from the counterinsurgent that can be used at a later time against either the state or local enemies. They can develop leverage against the counterinsurgent by threatening to return to their oppositional position. They may be allying with the state to protect revenue streams gained from smuggling or criminal or semi-criminal practices.[17]

Whereas FM 3-24 assumes that the solution to civil war anarchy is a Weberian monopoly on violence invested in the state, the community mobilization strategy may give rise to a stable truce among an oligopoly of feudal warlords—or party bosses, mafia dons, tribal patriarchs, or whatever the polite term might be (Jackson, 2009).[18] How and whether these can be consolidated into the central state is a major research area in comparative politics, but historically the process has been both lengthy and violent (North et al., 2009; Strayer, 1973; Tilly, 1992).

Despite these potential problems, community mobilization and CHB are the most analyzed strategies in this volume. Many practitioners and academics see the reduction of violence after the surge stemming from the two strategies working in tandem, some stressing the importance of one of the pair more than the other.[19]

4.4.1. Mechanisms

There are two main mechanisms at work here. First is the self-interest and *rational choice of community leaders*. Because of their precarious situation, these leaders must think in terms of power and preservation. They make alliances, they broker deals, they bandwagon, and they balance. However, their power rests upon having a community to lead. Why do individuals within a given community follow their leaders into dangerous armed roles, even when sometimes that decision goes against a straightforward cost–benefit analysis? Here, social norm mechanisms are at work.

For many communities in Iraq, two norms are most relevant. Under *norms of reciprocity*, if most community members are doing X, the individual community member also does X. As explained in Chapter 3, under the sway of norms the individual does not perform cost–benefit calculations, but simply follows the pull of the norm. One feels compelled to reciprocate the actions of family members or friendship cliques. This mechanism helps explain how communities as a whole can turn from the −2 position to the +2 position when they are not part of a formalized structure.

A second type of social norm is often powerful in Iraq: *norms of honor*. When one actor violates a local code of behavior toward one person, family, religion, or tribe, it becomes incumbent on the offended actor to retaliate. When norms of honor are strong and occupiers violate the local code, community leaders can readily organize and generate violence. When opposing groups commit acts of violence and desecration against a group, the resulting emotion of anger serves as fuel to set the effects of this norm into motion. The combination of anger, community social norms of reciprocity, and violations of honor can propel rapid mobilization into −2 roles. Other mechanisms, such as the straightforward rational pursuit of economic goods and psychological mechanisms, may sustain the local, armed organization. The presence and power of community social norms varies across communities, and certainly varies among Iraqi communities.[20] The case studies will provide an examination of the power of these norms across region and group.

4.4.2. Practitioner Experience

As just mentioned, tribal norms and leadership were particularly strong in certain areas of Iraq, and practitioners had to adjust their policies accordingly. US

Marines developed the maps in Figure 4.2 in conjunction with their community mobilization strategy in Ramadi.[21] As marked, different tribes controlled different neighborhoods. US forces coded each tribe-neighborhood as cooperative, neutral, or uncooperative. In effect, military practitioners were coding each tribe-neighborhood according to nodes of the spectrum—cooperative as +2, neutral as 0, uncooperative as −2. Using a community mobilization strategy, the goal of the US military was to "flip" the −2 organizations to the +2 node on the spectrum, or at least move the −2 organizations to neutrality (position 0). As opposed to war-fighting, the goal was not to kill or eliminate the opposing organization. Contrary to CHB, the emphasis was on communities as a whole, not individual hearts and minds. As the notation on the left side of the bottom figure indicates, the US military created a bandwagon of community leaders, in order to change the dynamic in the city as a whole.

Practitioners did not always like this "flipping" strategy. It meant putting many of those who had killed US soldiers on US pay and support. For some, this move required intellectual and emotional reckoning. The very concept of making a deal, often with highly unsavory characters, left a bad taste for many US soldiers.

As a US Army captain leading a company in Baghdad, Tim Wright learned that making deals with former targets was an effective way to lower improvised explosive device (IED) attacks and violence in general in his command area in the Bayaa neighborhood (Chapter 10 details these experiences). In an interview in 2008, Wright referred to the most respected local leader among Shia militiamen as "Mr. X" and described him as "kind of the Tony Soprano in this area" (Dehghanpisheh, 2008). Mr. X had undoubtedly been involved in the cleansing of local Sunni population. Wright's Delta company forces had raided his home three times without success in apprehending him. Yet after arresting and releasing Mr. X's brother, Wright made contact and entered into regular communications and negotiations. Exchanges of armed fire and IED attacks plummeted. Despite this result, some of Wright's troops showed discomfort from the move:

> "It's hard," says Lt. Andrew Goehring, 24. "There are guys who condoned or supported attacks that affected our guys." (Goehring's own Humvee was blown up by an IED.) First Sgt. Darrell Snell, 38, a career soldier, tries not to think about his captain's shadowy contacts with the likes of Mr. X. Instead, he focuses on the children in the street when he goes on patrol. "I just put it in my head that the kids didn't do it," he says. "That's how I deal with it." (Dehghanpisheh, 2008)

Despite the misgivings and hard feelings that might go with this strategy, some analysts believe that making deals is the only realistic way to rebuild a state.

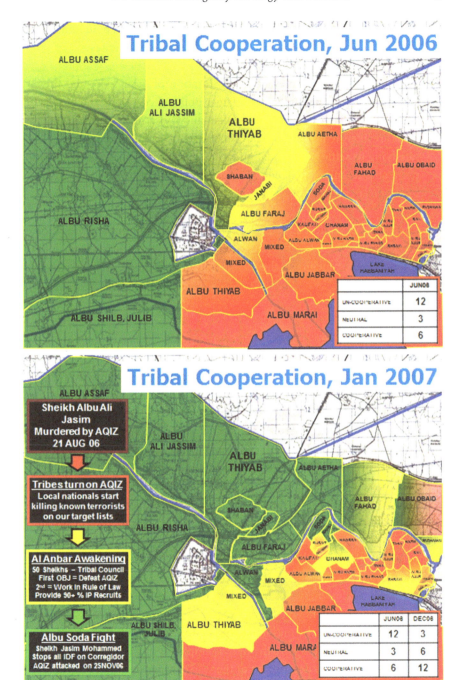

Figure 4.2. Community mobilization in Ramadi.
Source: US Department of Defense. Originally produced by 1st Battalion of the 6th Marine Regiment of the 2nd Marine Division

Colin Jackson, a professor at the Naval War College, compared rebuilding a state in Iraq to the building of states during the feudal period. He writes:

> [T]he achievable aim may be the restoration of local order and the assembly of resulting units into a larger political coalition. The bonds connecting individuals to local leaders and those leaders to national elites are likely to be personal and patronage based. While it may be less satisfying to settle for a feudal midpoint, a solid, personalistic order is preferable to an unstable equilibrium of formal institutions held aloft by legions of manpower and rivers of money (Jackson, 2014).

Community mobilization undoubtedly played a major role in the pacification of Anbar province in 2006 and the years after. The lasting question is about longer-term consequences, including the incorporation of "flipped" militias into state institutions.

4.5. Decapitation

While CHB focuses on the +1 node and community mobilization on the −2/+2 level nodes, decapitation concentrates on the +3 and −3 nodes. The counterinsurgent uses enhanced surveillance and intelligence capabilities to immediately exploit information from a raid. As mentioned in Chapter 2, decapitation efforts are often called "counter-network operations and, US Special Operations Forces (SOF) describe this cyclic methodology as "find, fix, finish, exploit, analyze" (F3EA) (Flynn et al., 2008; Marks et al., 2005) (see Figure 4.3). A decapitation strategy does not focus on population grievances. F3EA simply aims to liquidate the clandestine organizations. The goal is to prevent sustained insurgency by killing or capturing senior and mid-level insurgent commanders so quickly that there is little chance for regeneration.

In the usage in this work, the term "decapitation" is used broadly to describe targeted raids against network leadership, even if these targets are mid-level rather than senior leaders. The term "counter-network operations" is supposed to capture this focus on the middle of the organization, not just the head as implied by "decapitation," but here the term is employed as a catchall for both.

As can be seen in the description of the war-fighting strategy in the first section of this chapter, both decapitation and war-fighting advocate using military means to go after mobile insurgents. The differences between the two strategies are large, though. Decapitation is selective violence; it tries to avoid interacting with the population much at all by seeking reliable intelligence to trigger a raid and by keeping a discrete footprint. In some ways, the strategy is the polar

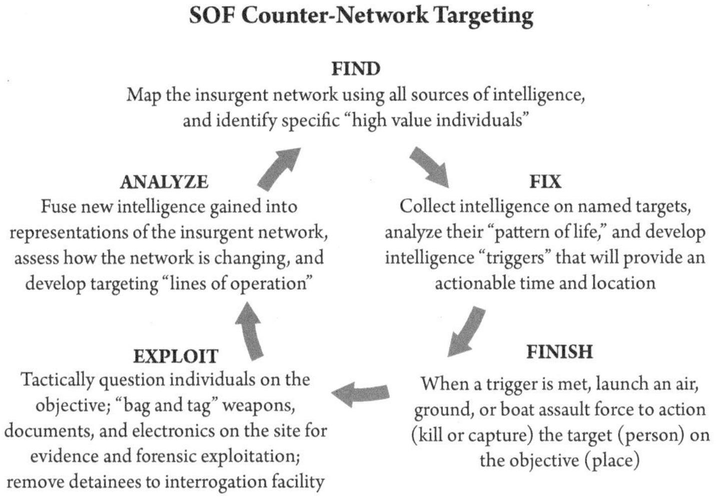

SOF Counter-Network Targeting

FIND
Map the insurgent network using all sources of intelligence,
and identify specific "high value individuals"

ANALYZE
Fuse new intelligence gained into
representations of the insurgent network,
assess how the network is changing, and
develop targeting "lines of operation"

FIX
Collect intelligence on named targets,
analyze their "pattern of life," and develop
intelligence "triggers" that will provide an
actionable time and location

EXPLOIT
Tactically question individuals on the
objective; "bag and tag" weapons,
documents, and electronics on the site for
evidence and forensic exploitation;
remove detainees to interrogation facility

FINISH
When a trigger is met, launch an air,
ground, or boat assault force to action
(kill or capture) the target (person) on
the objective (place)

Figure 4.3. Special Operation Forces counter-network targeting.

opposite of war-fighting with its highly visible and indiscriminate tactics of "cordon and search," "harassment and interdiction" bombing, and "search and destroy."

As a strategy, decapitation has had a shadowy past. Capturing and detaining targets sometimes led to torturing those targets to extract information. New technologies of intelligence collection and analysis now enable SOF to find and fix targets without resorting to such methods. Counterterrorism technology enables militaries to restore their preferred two-way relationship between +3s and −3s without having to be intimately involved with the messy population in the middle. Economic development only matters insofar as it improves intelligence and assault operations, such as through the improvement of communication and transportation infrastructure.[22]

4.5.1. Mechanisms

Decapitation is an organization-based strategy. The population's hearts and minds and its factions are not major concerns. Its goals are simple and straightforward—eliminate the insurgent leadership. The mechanisms discussed above—emotions and norms—are beyond the scope of the strategy, although some killings may create fear. The strategy does care about civilian collateral damage, with an unstated goal to not enflame the emotion of anger. With decapitation, counterinsurgents do aim, if possible, for precision strikes that are less likely to cause an angry backlash. Regarding other emotions, the population's resentments and fears are less important than success in hitting targets. The provision of goods to the population is also not part of the equation. If the strategy triggers mechanisms that might push the population leftward on the spectrum, that cost is outweighed by the benefits of cutting off the heads and crucial nodes of the insurgent organization.

4.5.2. Practitioner Experience and Points of Contention

There is little doubt that decapitation will remain a major part of US strategy, both in counterterrorism and in counterinsurgency. For many civilian policymakers, the major advantage is its cheap cost. Among possible strategies, decapitation is the cheapest in money and manpower and the least intrusive in terms of a "footprint." Operations are carried out either by unmanned drone strike or by small groups of Special Forces in precisely targeted raids. Even if one thinks the benefits of the strategy are not that high, at least the costs seem very low.

As far as military practitioners go, it is important to realize just how few soldiers are directly engaged in decapitation. The Joint Special Operations Command (JSOC) and the Central Intelligence Agency (CIA) are the central actors. JSOC was officially formed shortly after the US Embassy hostage rescue attempt disaster in Iran during the Carter administration. It draws from the military's most elite units—75th Army Rangers, Delta Force, and SEAL Team 6. The original intent was to create an elite force that would report directly to the president. As described by General Hugh Shelton, JSOC was meant to be "the ace" in the hole. "If you were a card player, that's your ace that you've got tucked away" (Scahill, 2014, p. 52). In the 1990s, JSOC pursued war criminals in the former Yugoslavia and targeted members of the emerging al-Qaeda organization. It also set up shop in the 1990s in Iraqi Kurdistan with Task Force 20. After 9/11, Secretary of Defense Rumsfeld greatly expanded JSOC's mission and, correspondingly, JSOC's capabilities. In September 2003, Stanley McChrystal became JSOC commander for the next five years. With Iraq's most wanted portrayed on a deck of cards, McChrystal and JSOC went to work. As insurgent networks proliferated, the target set expanded exponentially. As mentioned above, counterterrorism operations run on a cycle represented by F3EA. With experience under its belt, JSOC dramatically increased the speed of this cycle. Once a target was found, drones helped fix that target's location. Combat teams finished the target (capturing or killing), but now specialists accompanied the combat team and immediately exploited the information found on laptops, flash drives, and cell phones. With ever-expanding data, a rapid analysis of the new information created the abilities to immediately seek new targets. The cycle was reduced from days to hours.

There is no doubt that JSOC captured and killed a large number of important targets, and did so with increasing skill and speed in Iraq. The questions are about the overall strategic accomplishments of decapitation, as well as the trade-offs it entails in overall counterinsurgency practice. Many military service people respect JSOC, but doubt that the United States can make a dent in many counterinsurgency situations with decapitation alone, or even with decapitation combined with alliances with local groups. This opinion is certainly voiced by officers serving in the "Big Army." In 2009, counterinsurgent advocate and former tank commander Jon Nagl was asked to address Vice President Joseph Biden, a leading proponent of counterterrorism, about strategy in Afghanistan. Based on his view of Iraq, Nagl told Biden, "A counterterrorism strategy by itself was a recipe for endless war; it was necessary to resource improvements in governance, economic development, and the provision of services to the population to persuade Afghans not to support a Taliban insurgency that promised it would do all those things if it regained power" (Nagl, 2014, p. 194).

The implementation of decapitation not only is a key issue for this book and US military intervention in general, but also has implications for the organization of US military forces and the balance within the Special Forces community. JSOC represents only one side of the two sides of US Special Forces, and the smaller one at that. In the words of Tony Schwalm, a retired lieutenant colonel in the Green Berets, these two sides are "Daniel Boone" and "Superman" (Schwalm, 2012, p. 3). Green Berets are an example of Daniel Boone—someone who knows local cultures, can survive in harsh conditions, and still be able to employ violence when needed. Daniel Boone has two missions. The primary mission is unconventional warfare (UW)—training and fighting alongside indigenous groups willing and able to bring down a target government. The other mission is counterinsurgency and aims to bring SOF military anthropological skills to bear in helping CHB or community mobilization strategies. For Daniel Boone–type Special Forces, training for both missions involves learning the languages and cultures of indigenous peoples, learning how to build rapport with those peoples, and learning how not to violate local social norms or enflame counterproductive emotions. As Schwalm again relates in vivid metaphor, UW missions work to bring out a destructive force within a targeted regime: "SF brings cancer. We make the body, the host, kill itself" (Schwalm, 2012, p. 5).

The other type of Special Forces unit is "Superman." As Schwalm's "Superman" term captures, these are the elite of the elite in skills and military training. While Daniel Boone brings cancer to a festering political body, Superman amputates (Schwalm, 2012, p. 5). As Schwalm again pictures: "To illustrate, when Superman arrives, he usually says, 'I'm here to kill somebody. Where is He?' If you are that carbon-based life form and identifiable to Superman, you are probably going to die at his hands. People standing near you at the time of the hit are not going to fare well either" (Schwalm, 2012, p. 3). To complete his comparison of the two types of SOF, Schwalm states, "Superman goes, does, and leaves. Daniel Boone goes, does, and stays and stays and stays. In the end both come to the same place: killing somebody. The question becomes who pulls the trigger" (Schwalm, 2012, p. 5).[23] With decapitation, the United States will pull the trigger itself—quickly, predictably and efficiently. With unconventional warfare, the United States must take a lot of time training local allies to pull the trigger, and it must rely on them to do so when the opportunity arises.

Many Green Berets, like Schwalm, are skeptical of the ability of decapitation alone to secure victory. Schwalm noticed the shift away from UW even before 9/11. Schwalm comments on his experience with the budget process at SOCOM (Special Operations Command) during 1999:

> I watched the budget process. The commando didn't just get a lion's share; he got his before and at the expense of the guerrillas. The concept of several football players traveling toward a target in a black helicopter, doing great violence to those who needed it, and leaving before the press could get wind of it was much more appealing than Green Berets walking (possibly riding pack animals) with a group of people nobody really trusted anyway and hoping that in a few months a political objective would be achieved (Schwalm, 2012, p. 272).

Traumatic amputation, unilaterally administered and measured in hours, was much preferred by the leadership (not just at SOCOM, but at the Department of Defense writ large) over the introduction of cancer-causing agents, administered by, through, and with indigenous people, measured by months (Schwalm, 2012, p. 272).

Schwalm felt that the Afghan operation of 2003, Operation Enduring Freedom, validated the Green Beret approach, but believed that a lack of patience resulted in a reversion to overreliance on decapitation.

The controversy will undoubtedly continue. Even when effective, how much can decapitation work to achieve strategic goals on its own? How much can it combine with local forces to defeat an insurgency? Is decapitation an equal partner with CHB or just a supplement? Is the political backlash created by decapitation worth its benefits? Does wholesale adoption of a decapitation strategy mean giving up on the hard work of state-building? Section IV of this book will come back to these questions.

4.6. Homogenization

Some political scientists argue that the best way to end ethnic violence is to allow, or even encourage, physical separation of the warring sides to create defensible boundaries between them.[24] There are good examples where ethnic homogenization led to a decrease in violence. Consider the war in Bosnia (1992–1995). Ethnic cleansing during the war had drastically reduced the number of demographically mixed, contestable, and potentially violent, hot spots. At the end of the war, Serbian forces faced off against the forces of a Bosnian-Croatian alliance across demarcated lines that would become the border between Republika Srpska (RS) and the Federation. The war reduced the non-Serb population living in Republika Srpska from 46% to 3% (Pond, 2006, p. 151). Likewise, the Serbian population in the territory of the Federation had fallen from 17% to 3%.[25] It can be argued that the Dayton Accord ratified already existing spheres of control, rather than working to establish control in the first place. A NATO-led Implementation Force (IFOR) composed of 60,000 multinational troops soon took over to maintain peace.[26] Before yielding to an EU force in 2004, NATO troops served as peacekeepers in Bosnia for nine years without a single service-related fatality (Pond, 2006, p. 161). The question is whether this remarkable lack of violence is the result of a large peacekeeping force or an outcome of the ethnic separation produced by the war. The same question can be asked about Baghdad, although the path to homogenization differed.

In Bosnia, ethnic homogenization, perhaps more accurately termed "ethnic cleansing" in that case, was mainly a result of a broad Serbian strategy. However, ethnic homogenization can also occur through a multitude of local sectarian battles. In the absence of a functioning state, local power brokers, with a tribal, family, or even mafia base, may create militias or organizations (violent community organizations at the −2 level) that pursue interests ranging from survival to enrichment and honor, and they react to their neighbors doing likewise. In the process, one identity group may be forced from the community, resulting in homogenization.

As mentioned earlier, governments and occupying forces do not usually choose ethnic homogenization as a strategy; it is normatively too close to ethnic cleansing. Yet, homogenization may help bring an end to violence. Governments may turn a blind eye to the process, or they may work with the result of ethnic cleansing, as happened in Bosnia, to maintain peace.

4.6.1. Mechanisms

If members of group X are being killed in a neighborhood and the individual is a member of group X, it is a *rational choice* to get out of that neighborhood and find safety. Beyond the cost–benefit part of that choice, though, is some level of emotion.

It would be hard to believe that killing and bombings do not create the emotion of fear. *Fear* affects decision-making in predictable ways. To review from the previous chapter, under fear, individuals privilege information about danger

(Gallagher & Clore, 1985; Lerner et al., 2003; Lerner & Keltner, 2001; Mano, 1994). Individuals under the sway of fear become more risk-averse. In previous work, I have written about the instigation of the emotion of fear within the context of conflict and occupation:

> In the context of intervention, political entrepreneurs use fear to induce withdrawals of populations. They are seeking to generate fear in order to trigger the action tendency of flight. Fear is used to separate populations. Once separated, fear is used to prevent the return of refugees.
>
> Political entrepreneurs can produce flight-generating fears by instilling the belief that the threat cannot be confronted. The intent is to make the target believe that they do not possess the capacity, or have sufficient power to defeat the threat. . . .
>
> As opposed to anger, political entrepreneurs create fear through indiscriminate violence. As Richardson and others point out, it is the seeming randomness of attacks that makes them powerful. If civilians can die as easily, or even more easily than combatants, if they can die on a bus, in a restaurant, or walking down the street, then a belief of powerlessness sets in that sets off fear and flight. When a few refugee families return to an area that was previously ethnically cleansed and one of them is attacked by unknown forces during the night, fear will almost certainly dominate that community. (Petersen, 2011, pp. 39–40)

Fear accelerates flight. The emotion also helps sustain boundaries even after danger levels may recede. One effect creates demographic homogenization; the other sustains it.

4.6.2. Practitioner Experience

Consider the map in Figure 4.4. It is a map of Baghdad's sectarian cleansing created by the US military.[27] Given this is a military map, the US military was obviously aware of the homogenization of Baghdad and also aware of the "flashpoints of violence" marked on the map.

The United States also constructed concrete T-walls that reinforced the new ethnic demographic lines. In effect, although the US military could not stop the homogenization process, it did help create and sustain homogenous neighborhoods. In turn, this process helped reduce violence in Baghdad witnessed in 2007–2008. One of the major points of contention is whether this process of separation was in fact the main reason, or even a major reason, for reduction in violence in Baghdad, rather than the Surge. Because sectarian

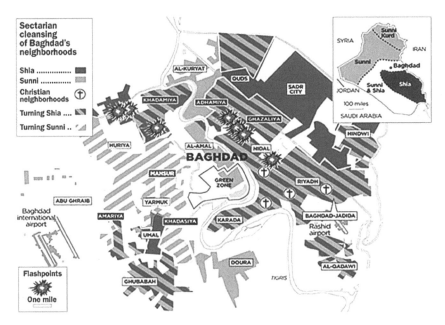

Figure 4.4. Sectarian cleansing of Baghdadgetneighborhoods. Source: Ned Parker and Ali Hamdani, "How Violence Is Forging a Brutal Divide in Baghdad," *Times of London*, December 14, 2006.

cleansing and the Surge took place at roughly the same time, it is difficult to separate out their respective effects.[28]

Academics and practitioners are aware of the potential for homogenization to affect counterinsurgency efforts. As Nagl notes in his comparison of Afghanistan and Iraq, "The success rate of rural insurgencies is far higher than those fought in urban areas because the population in an urban insurgency is already concentrated in cities and easier to separate from insurgents, using expedients like the T-walls that divided ethnic factions in Baghdad" (Nagl, 2014, p. 186). Some counterinsurgents note the costs of walling off sections of a city in order to control movement and separate warring factions. In the beginning pages of his book *Out of the Mountains: The Coming Age of the Urban Guerrilla*, David Kilcullen, one of the architects of FM 3-24 and the US counterinsurgency policy, had the following conversation with a fellow practitioner from Baghdad:

> Kilcullen: "You killed the city, mate. You know that, right?
> Eames: "What? Piss off."
> Kilcullen: "Seriously. All that barbed wire, concrete barriers, checkpoints. You shut the city down. You stopped it flowing—put it on life support. You stopped people getting around to do what they

had to do. You cut the violence, sure, but you did it by killing the city."
(Kilcullen, 2013, p. 19)

As in Bosnia and parts of Kosovo, Cyprus, and elsewhere, ethnic homogenization may separate sides and reduce the possibilities for violence. But at a cost.

4.7. Conclusions

Chapter 2 laid out a general framework for analyzing insurgencies and strategies of insurgents and counterinsurgents. Chapter 3 fleshed out the concept of mechanisms. This chapter turned its focus to the US counterinsurgents, a primary actor in our study. Along the lines of our framework, it broke down multiple strategies according to their respective concentration on roles on the spectrum and their logic of triggering mechanisms to move individuals along that spectrum in desired directions. The chapter also produced insights from practitioners on each strategy. The case studies will provide illustrations of these strategies, sometimes working in combination. One of this book's major goals is to break down US/Coalition strategy into its component parts and then examine how insurgents responded.

Section II begins with an overview of the section's chapters and goals. Chapter 5 then proceeds to outline the origins and basis of one of the book's central points—the pervasive role of identity master cleavages in affecting and shaping the evolution of the Iraq conflict.

SECTION II

THE IRAQ CONFLICT, 2003–2011

The first section of this book outlined an analytical framework able to break down the strategies, processes, and mechanisms driving the course of military intervention and insurgency. This section will apply that framework to the 2003–2011 period in Iraq, from the time of US invasion until the time of US withdrawal. Section III will cover Iraq from 2011 until 2020 (with some commentary on Iraq at the time of writing in 2023). The third section will focus on the legacy of the 2003–2011 US military involvement. Section IV summarizes the findings of previous sections and speculates on their meaning for future US military intervention.

Across its many empirical cases, this work examines variation on two highly linked outcomes: violence and state-building. The present section provides nine empirical cases which explain spikes and declines in violence and specify reasons for state-building failure at different times and various places. These cases provide a window into how strategic moves by the United States and insurgents (and their interaction) worked to set off the processes and mechanisms underlying changes in major outcomes.

The analytical framework is designed to help explain increases and decreases in violence. For violence to reach the levels seen in Baghdad during what was essentially a sectarian civil war, at least two types of movement on the spectrum of roles must occur. First, individuals must move into armed roles at the −2 and −3 nodes. These insurgent fighters will be more effective when individuals move into −1 supporting roles. Second, the state security apparatus—the police at the +2 level and the armed forces at the +3 level—needs to be relatively weak enough to be unable to prevent the killings and bombings of insurgent actors.

The question of the quality of the security apparatus leads into the other key important outcome variable—state-building. The incredible increase of violence in Baghdad and other regions in Iraq would probably not have occurred the way it did if a strong state had put effective police on the streets and mobilized a competent army or national guard to gain control of highly violent neighborhoods. As with violence, the framework points the way for an analysis of state-building. Strong states gain control over violence within their borders. Governments accomplish this goal through state control of a single military (+3), as well as control over local organs of violence (+2), especially the police. The general population, even if not universally enthusiastic about the government, should cooperate with the state and its institutions (+1) or at least remain neutral (0) and not actively support those using violent or illegal means against the state. In sum, during the process of state-building, an emerging strong state will neutralize/eliminate individuals on the left side of this spectrum and/or take actions to move those individuals to roles on the right side of the spectrum. The government will also wish to prevent leftward movement.

Successful counterinsurgency can help build a state by taking control over territory and denying control of that territory by −3/−2 organizations. Successful counterinsurgents should be able to employ physical force, if necessary, to enforce the law across that territory. In order to accomplish their mission, the +2 and +3 forces need to become professional and institutionalized. With the consolidation and professionalization of +2 and +3, and the elimination of −2 and −3, sufficient security will be established for other state bureaucracies to provide services to the population moving the population from the −1 and 0 roles to government participation and support (+1).

What makes for a weak state? In reference to the spectrum framework, a functioning state is weak when −2 and −3 groups control territory, when −2 and −3 groups prevent the implementation of centrally directed policies, when +2 and +3 groups, officially in the employ of the state (and thus with a "+" designation), carry out the agenda of non-state organizations. Also, a state is weak when the general population does not participate in or support the state's institutions either by occupying a neutral role (0) or through more active support of insurgents and non-state actors (−1).

By these criteria, the government of Iraq and its Coalition partners largely failed in their state-building project in the years following the invasion. This failure can be specified with reference to the spectrum of roles:

1. *Movement to −2*: Local armed militias formed quickly and in many cases were able to become self-sustaining.
2. *Compromise/Capture of +2 by non-state actors*: The Ministry of the Interior and local police stations were often taken over by parties and organizations for purposes against the interest of the state. As the historian Charles Tripp has summarized the situation after the 2005 elections: "Public ministries became partisan fiefdoms, farmed out to powerful factions, made more powerful by their ability to command militias that were used to terrorize political enemies and whole neighborhoods or communities seen as hostile to their sponsors" (Tripp, 2010, p. 277).
3. *The failure to build competent and professional +2 forces*: Three years after the invasion, the United States realized the shortcomings in police training and decided to make 2006 "The Year of the Police." These shortcomings were never fully overcome.
4. *The creation of −3 mobile, armed groups*: Armed and mobile groups, such as al-Qaeda in Iraq (AQI), maintained a presence in Iraq.
5. *The politicization and de-professionalization of +3*: As with +2 police units, the military was politicized and, as will be made evident with its shortcomings in facing ISIS, never fully professionalized.
6. *The failure to move the population from −1 to +1*: Non-state actors often provided the population with goods and security to a higher degree than state actors, thus winning the battle for trust and cooperation.

The empirical chapters in Section II will illustrate these specific state-building failures in Iraq. Taken in sum, these findings support one of the book's central arguments. Given the conflict's sectarian tones and strong sectarian, especially Shia, organizations, non-state actors not only denied the rebuilding state a monopoly over violence, but invaded, captured, and replaced sections of the state during 2003–2011. This fragmentation and capture of state organs would persist, and in some ways even deepen, in the post-2011 period.

Preview of Section II Chapters

Six of the chapters in Section II center on Baghdad. Baghdad is not only the largest city and capital of Iraq, but also the location of the most severe swings in violence. Recall the arc of the Baghdad line in Figure 1.1 of Chapter 1. The figure shows the number of Significant Acts of Violence recorded by US forces across Iraq from December 2004 to December 2008. Most notably, the numbers meteorically rise after the Samarra bombing in February 2006 and stunningly drop in the second half of 2007, the period of the "Surge." Figure 1.2 in Chapter 1 provides a corresponding pattern for civilian causalities across Iraq. As the capital, Baghdad is also the center of the state-building process in Iraq and the home of its ministries.

Before launching into the empirical chapters, Chapter 5, "Violence, State-Building, and the Shia-Sunni Cleavage," provides an overview of the genesis, evolution, and capabilities of Shia and Sunni organizations. It is imperative to understand the origins and power of the major actors—the Sadrists and SCIRI/Badr Organization chief among them. While these Shia actors are the most powerful in Baghdad, and will be addressed in the most detail in Chapter 5, there are many other significant actors in Iraq. Chapter 11 examines the role of tribe and family in Anbar. Chapter 14, covering the Kurdish Regional Government, addresses Kurdish groups in depth.

Chapter 6, "Ghazaliyah: Sunni Mobilization, Sectarian War, US Success and Failure," presents an excellent illustration of many of the forces connected to violence, state-building, and identity over the entire 2003–2011 period. More specifically, the chapter will identify:

- Sunni movement to −2
- Details of sectarian war between Shia and Sunni militias
- The early irrelevance of US presence and strategy in the neighborhood battle between Shia and Sunni militias
- The origins, implementation, and success of a community-mobilization strategy moving Sunni militias from −2 to +2 in the Sons of Iraq (SOI) program
- The failure of the Iraqi state to incorporate SOI participants into state institutions by failing to move them to +2 and +3 positions.

Chapter 7, "Sadr City, the Mahdi Army, and the Sectarian Cleansing of Baghdad," explains the resource base and the resiliency of the Sadrist movement. More specifically, the chapter will identify:

- Shia mobilization into −2 and −3 positions and the development of the Jaysh al-Mahdi (JAM)
- The Sadrist use of social organizations to move individuals to the −1 position

- Sadrist capture of local police (capture of +2)
- Sadrist ability to harass US and ISF forces (action vs. +3)
- JAM militia tactics used to systematically cleanse Sunnis from their homes
- The failure of US clear, hold, build (CHB) strategies.

Chapter 8, "Mansour, 2003–2007: The Failure to Mobilize Moderates," explains the lack of mobilization in a middle-class Sunni neighborhood:

- The failure to move receptive middle-class Sunnis from 0 to +1, +2 in Baghdad
- Comparison of Mansour to Ghazaliyah, explaining variation among Sunni neighborhoods.

Chapter 9, "The Failure to Establish Local Security," concentrates on the +2 node and its ramifications for violence reduction and state-building:

- Failure of US forces to build +2
- Sadrist capture of +2
- Badr Organization capture of the Ministry of the Interior, capture of Ministry responsible for +2
- The evolution of the "Wolf Brigades" and the use of +2 state security forces for political and sectarian purposes.

Chapter 10, "Captain Wright Goes to Baghdad," is co-written with Colonel Timothy Wright and is based on his experiences as a captain and company commander in the Bayaa neighborhood of Baghdad in 2007–2008. This chapter will cover:

- JAM cleansing of Sunni residents from the Bayaa neighborhood
- The operation of Sadrist social and governmental activities moving the population to −1
- The implementation of CHB and the US efforts to move the population to +1
- The Sadrist advantage in the −1/0/+1 competition stemming from their ability to take over neighborhood adjudication roles
- The development of US decapitation capabilities to identify and pursue −2/−3 leaders
- How CHB, combined with decapitation, led to successful deal-making between US forces and local opponents.

Chapter 11, "Anbar, 2003–2011: The Generation of a Community Mobilization Strategy," parallels the previous chapter on the Bayaa neighborhood. It is co-written with a practitioner—Jon Lindsay, who was serving as a Naval intelligence officer in Anbar. Both Lindsay and LTC Wright were serving at roughly the same time but in different locations. As pointed out in later chapters, the Awakening in Anbar had strategic implications for the Surge and subsequent periods. The chapter covers:

- Sunni mobilization in Anbar to the −2 position
- The failure of US CHB strategy in Anbar
- The development and implementation of a successful community mobilization strategy
- Sunni tribes "flipping" from −2 to +2.

Chapter 12, "The Battle of Sadr City, 2008: Innovations in Urban Counterinsurgency," focuses on changes in internal Iraqi political forces in the wake of Shia victory in the "Battle of Baghdad." The chapter also concentrates on the US shift from CHB to a combination of war-fighting and decapitation as US forces took on JAM in its stronghold:

- The status of ISF +3 forces
- US shift to a combination war-fighting/decapitation strategy.

Chapter 13 is entitled "The Surge: A Reconsideration." Controversy still surrounds the explanation for the dramatic drop in violence in 2007. The "synergy" argument, holding that an interaction between community mobilization and CHB produced the decline, is closest to the conventional wisdom. I argue that sectarian politics and Shia political decisions drove the outcome as much as US strategy.

Chapter 14, "Iraqi Kurdistan: Dual Cleavages and Their Impact on War and State-Building," proceeds much as the title suggests. Given relatively low violence in the Kurdistan Regional Government during 2003–2011, the focus is on state-building, or the surprising lack of it given favorable conditions. I demonstrate that the competition of two political parties (KDP and PUK), both with their own security organizations, prevented the unity and functioning of a coherent state.

5

Violence, State-Building, and the Shia-Sunni Cleavage

5.1. Introduction

One of the major arguments of this book holds that much of the variation in violence and state-building in Iraq can be explained through a full understanding of Iraqi identity master cleavages. To clarify these cleavages, this chapter describes the origins and history of the organizations that entered the contest in Iraq in the years immediately after the invasion. In the decades preceding the US invasion, several of these bodies had endured persecution and assassination of leaders. While some members of oppressed groups remained in Iraq, others fled abroad. In the wake of the 2003 invasion, various individuals and groups found a collapsed state and political and security void that offered previously unimagined opportunities for power and vengeance.

Section II will show that not all of these organizations could play the game the same way. In the struggle for dominance between Shia and Sunni, the Shia essentially win. They do so in large part because they were able to trigger an effective set of mechanisms that moved individuals into desired roles. Although they share much in common, Shia organization and demographics differed substantially from that of Sunnis. This difference helps explain Shia advantages, their relative rise in power and resilience, and corresponding changes in Shia political maneuvers. More specifically, Shia organizations mobilized early and quickly through the intensity of the resentment emotion; Shia adherents could move in sync through a norm of emulation of strong and well-known religious leaders; Shia organizations could communicate with and coordinate the actions of followers through a mosque system which created focal points and safety in numbers; Shia had a large and impermeable base in the Sadr City neighborhood; Shia organizations often benefited through their connections to Iran and its weapons and training.

This chapter will systematically examine the emergence and capabilities of Shia and Sunni organizations. The nature of these organizations can be understood through an examination of history, demographics, and institutions. To warn the reader, the next sections of this chapter are not an easy read. However, because the main arguments of this book center on the power of sectarian identification, leadership, and organization, a detailed overview is both appropriate and necessary. By the end, the reader should hopefully have some understanding of the origins and political orientations of Dawa, the Sadrists, the Badr Organization, and Iraqi political forces living abroad before the invasion. The reader should be prepared to understand the difference in capacities for mobilization between Shia and Sunni. Furthermore, the readers should understand how the Iraq's repressive history, powerful religious institutions, and sectarian differences can work to affect the mechanisms and roles at the heart of our analytical framework.

5.2. History, Part 1: The Roots of Shia Political Organization

5.2.1. The State, the Hawza, and the Dawa Party

Competition between secular and religious leaders for authority has been a source of conflict and change across many eras and cultures.[1] Iraq provides another example. The growth of the modern Iraqi state naturally produced presidents, prime ministers, and political parties all seeking power and the obedience of citizen/subjects. These actors would almost inevitably enter into a tense relationship with Iraqi religious leaders. Shia leaders in particular possessed qualities that made them formidable competitors.

Shia leaders in Iraq were capable of developing large followings for several related reasons. Above all, Shia leaders gained legitimacy and renown through their association with the Hawza, a widely revered Najaf-based Shia seminary. These well-known and respected leaders are embraced by followers in the phenomenon of "emulation." Perhaps the most important innovation in modern Shiism is the concept of *marja'iiyat al-taqlid*, or the emulation of the most learned scholars. Every member of the Shia community is obligated to select a learned *mujtahid*[2] to emulate in all sorts of religious matters.[3] In another modern "tradition," *mujtahidin* began to designate their own successors. This new tradition had the effect of crystallizing groups of adherents into a recognizable bloc as the supporters of a given cleric. Furthermore, well-known clerics within this system could develop a patronage system by gathering funds from emulators and then doling out those funds in the form of stipends to seminary students who, in turn, help collect donations from emulators in the business and other sectors. The most significant clerics, a handful at most, are thus able to create a widespread network throughout Iraq. These leading clerics not only collect money from their emulator-based network, they also could direct the votes of their followers.

Because of these capabilities, state leaders could easily conceive of Shia leaders as potential threats to state authority. Ambiguous Shia doctrines concerning the relationship between Islam and state power were also problematic. In a major difference from Sunni Islam, many Shia adherents believe that imams should hold legislative and political power. Whereas the Sunnis are limited to the Quran and the Hadith (the sayings and the teachings of the Prophet Muhammad), Shia are further guided by their 12 infallible imams. The latter believe that these imams, as direct descendants of the Prophet, are legitimate emissaries of the Prophet's message and have the authority to relay God's will to humankind. Imams have the right to issue rulings on what Islam permits, as well as to intervene in the political affairs of the Muslim community. Throughout Islamic history, there have been examples of various levels of political interference (and non-interference) on the part of the imams.

Prominent clerics in Iraq have recognized the potential explosiveness of these religious-political issues and sought paths to manage the inherent tensions between religious law and obligation on the one hand and political realities on the other. By the late 1950s, however, some Iraqi clerics believed that rising secularization threatened Islamic authority. Both the Baath Party and the Communist Party were gaining power and working hard to erode the position of Islam. Despite the chances for direct conflict with the state, some clerics were compelled to enter the political fray in the form of a political party. The result was the founding of the Dawa Party in 1958. To preview, most of the vital Shia organizations of the post-2003 period had their roots in the Islamic Dawa Party. Indeed, three of the first four post-invasion prime ministers came from the Dawa Party.[4]

Although the exact details are shrouded; most scholars agree that the key founders of the Dawa Party were Muhammed Baqir al-Sadr (Sadr I), Mahdi al-Hakim, Talib Rifa'i, and Sahib al-Dakhil. The role of the Sadr and Hakim families are crucial for our understanding of Shia organization in the post-2003 period. While Muhammed Baqir al-Sadr (Sadr I) was a founder of Dawa, his cousin Muhammed Sadiq al-Sadr (Sadr II) would go on to expand a social movement in Baghdad in the 1990s. After the Saddam regime killed Sadr II, his son, Moqtada al-Sadr, would become one of the leading figures in the empirical chapters of this book. Meanwhile, the Hakim family would produce a line of leaders (Mohammed Baqir al-Hakim, Abdul Aziz al-Hakim, Ammar al-Hakim) heading the Supreme Council for the Islamic Revolution in Iraq (SCIRI) in its various names and forms.

The founders and leaders of the party were primarily from the prominent clerical and merchant families of Najaf, thus already having societal status and power. The Dawa Party's political agenda was provocative but did not call for the overthrow of the state. According to the party's manifesto, *Al-Usus* (which was written by Sadr I), the Dawa Party was created with the goal of eventually establishing an Islamic polity through four stages. The first of these stages, the *fikriya* (the intellectual) or the *taghyiriya* (the phase of change), is meant to be a time in which the party's Islamic ideology is consolidated and disseminated to the masses. By the second stage, the *siyasiya* (the political), the party would have amassed enough public support to wage a struggle for political power. The culmination of this struggle is in the third stage, the *thawriya* (revolutionary), in which the status quo regime is removed. Finally, the *hukumiya* stage (the governmental) is the one in which the party could establish a viable political system in accordance with Islamic law and values.

The leaders of the Dawa Party knew that this ideology would put the organization on bad terms with the state, likely bringing down repressive measures. Therefore, the founders of the Dawa Party decided on a cell-style organizational structure inspired by the communist movement. The group would have a central political bureau, but it would also have geographical "cells" organized into larger groups with a vertical chain of command wherein each member only knew his immediate colleagues (the person who recruited him and the person he recruited).[5] The founders of the Dawa Party sought to establish a party that could survive intimidation tactics and whose local and regional command could not be easily identified.

While the Dawa Party itself developed means of blunting state repression, its first clerical leaders also faced backlash from the senior clerics of the Hawza.[6] One of the founding members, Sadr I, faced such pressure for his role in the Dawa Party. While Sadr I amassed his set of followers, competing clerics could rely on their own emulators to sway public opinion against Sadr I and the Dawa Party. Facing such resistance, Sadr I distanced himself from and eventually abandoned the Dawa Party in the late 1960s. Another founding member, Grand Ayatollah Mushin al-Hakim, tried to navigate a middle way by opposing the formalization of a political party, but not political action in total (Mushin al-Hakim's son, Mahdi al-Hakim, was one of Dawa's founders). Westerners often refer to "quietist" clerics, those who refrain from overt political action, versus "non-quietist" or activist clerics. Mushin al-Hakim might be counted as an early example in the adoption of "quietism." He ended up issuing a fatwa against party activism. This fatwa, in addition to the existing political and social pressures, drove many members to withdraw from the Dawa Party, leaving very few "cells" intact.

While the Dawa Party faced this set of fracturing internal issues in its early years, the coming of the Baathist regime would increase pressure from outside to new levels. In 1968, the Baathists took over Iraq and exerted immense efforts to secularize Iraqi society. These efforts were directed primarily at Shia institutions, including the Hawza and Shia figures like Ayatollah Muhsin al-Hakim. At the same time, the Dawa Party was growing, with members reaching into the hundreds in Baghdad and also expanding into the southern provinces. The Baathist security apparatus, alerted to the growth, began a series of arrests and executions that would end the Dawa Party's period of centralization in Iraq. In 1974, five leading members of the Dawa Party were executed.[7] At the same time, many of the Dawa Party's future leaders fled the country, including Mahdi al-Hakim. Despite the annihilation of many of the Dawa Party's leaders and the general crackdown on Shiism, anti-Baathist demonstrations occurred in the mid- to late 1970s. The most important of these was the 1977 Safar Intifada. In reprisal, the Baathist regime arrested and executed key leaders of the Hawza.

The Iranian Revolution in 1979 was a final breaking point for the regime. The threat from revolutionary Shia became a reality in the neighboring country. Sadr I was put under house arrest and was asked to appear on television renouncing the Dawa Party and supporting the Baathist regime. After refusing, Sadr I was arrested on April 4, 1980, and eventually executed. A few days before, on March 31, the government decreed that membership in the Dawa Party was a capital offense. This decree, added to the destruction of the Dawa Party's human and financial capital, caused the party to dwindle into virtual nonexistence. It is no surprise, then, that the Dawa Party survived the period of Saddam's rule only by functioning outside of its home country. Ayatollah al-Asifi, Nouri al-Maliki, and Ibrahim al-Jafari fled the country. These figures would become central in Iraq after 2003. For nearly a decade, the Dawa Party's leading members were centered in Iran under the leadership of Ayatollah Asifi (a staunch supporter of Ayatollah Khomeini).

5.2.2. The Emergence of the Supreme Council for the Islamic Revolution in Iraq (SCIRI) and the Badr Organization in Iran

With the demise of the Dawa Party in Iraq proper, many Shia political leaders would flee to Iran and the West, as well as neighboring Middle Eastern states. These exiles would develop a myriad of organizations. One of the most powerful and durable of these organizations took shape in Iran. The Supreme Council for the Islamic Revolution in Iraq (SCIRI) was established in November 1982 in Tehran, Iran.[8] Composed of exiled Iraqi clerics and displaced Shia organizations, the group was created to pursue an agenda of political activism leading to revolution in Iraq.[9] Unlike the Dawa Party, which strove to be a politically independent Iraqi nationalist party, SCIRI was dependent on and inspired by the Iranian revolutionary establishment. In the time period between the Sadr I execution (and the Dawa Party's effective disbandment) and the establishment of SCIRI, Iran tried and failed to unite the many splintered Shia organizations in Iraq. Of the 15 men who composed the first SCIRI council, nine of them were based in Iran, four in London, and one in Damascus. Six of them had been members of the Dawa Party. The most prominent members were Muhammad Baqir al-Hakim (the uncle of SCIRI's later head, Ammar al-Hakim) and Mahmud al-Hashimi, both students of Sadr.

SCIRI departed greatly from what the Dawa Party had been. While the Dawa Party had a four-pronged plan that happened to include revolution and the establishment of Islamic governance, SCIRI adopted the goal of the immediate, not eventual, establishment of an Islamic polity. Furthermore, SCIRI adopted Khomeini's particular brand of Shia governance, that of *Vilayet-e-Faqih* (rule of the jurisprudent). Given this Iranian influence, SCIRI's official working plan became the reproduction of the events leading up to the Iranian revolution.

SCIRI's military wing was the Badr Organization. One of the most startling developments in SCIRI was the establishment of *Faylaq Badr*, or the Badr Organization, composed of Iraqi deportees and prisoners of war. Despite being a branch of SCIRI, the Badr Organization was under the command of the Iranian government; its primary commander was an Iranian colonel, although there were several Iraqi officers in the general staff. During the Iran-Iraq War, SCIRI's Badr Organization was absorbed into the Iranian military effort. In the Iraq-Iran War, the Badr Organization's Iraqi fighters fought on the Iranian side. The Iraqi Shia community naturally had a difficult time coming to grips with Iraqis fighting Iraq. It was an uncomfortable question of nationalism versus religion. This issue would work to shape and constrain SCIRI's ventures in Iraq, especially in relationship to the Sadrists.

SCIRI and Badr would take a further reputational hit in the wake of the First Gulf War. Taking advantage of the turmoil in the wake of the war, Shia in the south of Iraq and Kurds in the north rose up against the Saddam regime. The Kurds were eventually saved by the United States and the institution of a no-fly zone. Many Iraqi Shias were expecting that the Badr Organization would use the opportunity to enter Iraq and help liberate the country from the Baathists. However, SCIRI and Badr largely stayed out of the conflict. The opposition forces were utterly destroyed by Saddam's forces. When Muhammad Baqir al-Hakim was questioned about SCIRI and the Badr Organization's absence, he responded that he had received orders from the Iranian government forbidding entrance into Iraq.

5.2.3. The Shia Exiles in the West: The INA and the INC

While one group of Iraqi exiles formed SCIRI/Badr in Iran in 1982, other exiles would develop organizations in the wake of the First Gulf War. Two distinct Iraqi organizations formed among exiles and émigrés in the West. The Iraqi National Accord (INA) started in London in 1990. Its key member was Iyad Allawi, who would go on to become Iraq's first post-invasion prime minister when he assumed the position of interim prime minister in 2004.[10] INA membership included Baathist dissidents and former Iraqi military officers. Notably, it also included some Sunnis. Unsurprisingly, given this composition, the INA theory of regime change was top-down. They wanted only to cut off Saddam and his top henchmen and leave the Iraqi state structure intact (Tripp, 2010, pp. 266–267).

The Iraqi National Congress (INC) was founded in Vienna in 1992 as an umbrella organization of mainly Shia groups. Its leader was the complicated figure Ahmed Chalabi. In October 1992, the INC held an assembly near Erbil in the KRG, then under US protection with Operation Provide Comfort. It was the first such assembly on Iraqi soil and aimed to provide the INC legitimacy. In contrast to the INA, the INC did not include Baathist dissidents. Its theory of regime change urged mass mobilization, particularly of the Shia population. INC members sought the destruction of Iraqi state structures. Predictably, Chalabi would be an influential proponent of the early de-Baathification orders of the Iraqi Provisional Government.

Given Saddam Hussein's survival after the First Gulf War, both groups found favor with Western policymakers seeking regime change. As the sanctions regime wore on, in the fall of 1998 the US Congress passed the Iraq Liberation Act, committing $100 million to support Iraqi opposition groups (Tripp, 2010, p. 267). The US government doled out $36 million to the INC alone between 2000 and 2003 (Ricks, 2007, p. 57). Political connections were as important as the dollars. Chalabi and the INC had gained favor among neo-conservatives, including some holding high ranks in the US Department of Defense, such as Deputy Defense Secretary Paul Wolfowitz and Under Secretary of Defense for Policy Douglas Feith. In a conversation between Feith and Jay Garner before the latter's entry into Iraq as the leading civilian authority, Feith is reported to have said, "You know Jay, when you get there, we could just make Chalabi president" (Ricks, 2007, p. 104). As will be noted in later chapters, the problem is that while Chalabi had great support in the US Defense Department, he had little connection to anyone in Iraq. As Bing West colorfully describes Chalabi and his influence on policy: "Compounding the problem, de-Baathification was placed in the hands of Ahmed Chalabi, a wily Shiite expatriate with chameleon political adroitness and overarching ambition whose core support lay inside the upper reaches of the Pentagon. De-Baathification became Chalabi's calling card to ingratiate himself with the Shiite community" (West, 2009, p. 7).[11]

5.2.4. The Sadrists—Those who Stayed in Iraq

The Iraqi state engaged in severe repression against Shia institutions in the period following the Iranian Revolution. In the aftermath of the First Gulf War and the Shia uprising, the Baathist regime again launched a wave of repression, this time gutting the seminary establishment. In the estimation of Juan Cole, "The repression of the Shi'ite establishment was so severe in the aftermath of the crushed uprising that Najaf became a shadow of its former self. . . . Clerics pulled back from teaching anything but the most basic classes in Shi'ite law and practice, lest their teachings be viewed by the secret police as seditious" (Cole, 2003b, pp. 549–550).

Throughout and across these periods of Baathist oppression, Sadrist leaders remained in Iraq. Muhammed Baqir al-Sadr (Sadr I) had been a brilliant, albeit junior, cleric in Najaf, and although growing in popularity, was not as widely known as some other clerics. His participation in the founding of the Dawa Party, as well as his political action and relationship with Khomeini, increased his visibility and alerted the Baathists to his dangerous popularity. He confronted the Baathist regime and was executed in 1980.

His cousin, Muhammad Sadiq Al-Sadr (Sadr II), became a major leader in the 1990s. Given the weakened position of the state under the sanctions regime, Saddam worked to co-opt Sadr II.[12] With regime leeway and some support, Sadr II established institutions for social provision and adjudication in East Baghdad (much of what would later be renamed Sadr City). Along the way, Sadr II became a major figure for emulation, both among poorer urbanites and some tribes. Sadr II's message, provision of social services, and family name helped him build a political structure. As Sargsyan and Bennett summarize:

> Sadiq al-Sadr regularly addressed people's economic problems in his sermons and helped provide social services when the Iraqi population suffered from the sanctions imposed on Iraq by the UN Security Council in the 1990's. A follower recalled: "In selecting a *marja'*, I choose the one who knows my suffering, who is close to the poor and disinherited (Sargsyan and Bennett, 2016, p. 624).

Sadr II paid a price for his fame and organizational success. After adopting an adversarial political stance to the regime in the late 1990s, along with a series of increasingly political Friday sermons, Sadr II and two of his sons were gunned down in the outskirts of Najaf in February 1999.

Sadr I and Sadr II remained in Iraq and were brutally murdered by the Baathist regime. They not only were considered dissidents, but also were recognized as great martyrs in the Shia narrative. Sadr II also left a legacy in terms of non-state governance organizations in East Baghdad. Given that the Sadr family remained and fought in Iraq, it had years to build up its popular support base—particularly from the poor, urban masses. In the post-2003 era, Muqtada al-Sadr would build on the legitimacy of his father and father-in-law's (Muqtada had married Sadr I's daughter) martyrdom as well as the Sadr II social organizations.

It must be noted that other leading Shia figures stayed in Iraq, avoided attention, and survived. Among the Hawza elite, Grand Ayatollahs Khoei and Sistani remained "quiet." In this repressive atmosphere, Sistani, with his reputation as a quietist, became a chief authority among the Shia. Also, Dawa members who had managed to avoid deportation or severe persecution formed "Dawn tandheem al-Iraq," an organization that included Mohammed Shia al-Sudani, selected as prime minister in 2022.

5.2.5. Summary

This section has explained the emergence of the major Shia actors and organizations that would play large roles in the post-2003 era. It has shown how modern Shiism developed a norm of emulation that fostered the emergence of powerful and respected religious leaders. These leaders could command resources and influence political behavior in ways that made them a threat to the state. State repression produced a splintering of the Shia opposition. SCIRI and its Badr Organization would enter Iraq after the fall of Saddam Hussein with 20 years of experience, Iranian training and weapons, and a relative lack of legitimacy due to their overly close relationship with Iran. The Sadrists, on the other hand, possessed a wealth of legitimacy through the martyrdom of Sadr I and Sadr II. Remaining in Iraq, the Sadrists also built up experience in local governance during the sanctions period. Iraqi exile groups residing in the West possessed neither arms nor legitimacy, but did have close relationships with the incoming occupation force. Some respected Shia leaders survived and bided their time through their "quietism."

5.3. History, Part 2: Shia Perceptions of Unjust Subordination

While the twists and turns of Shia religious and political organizations are relatively modern events, Shia social and political identity must be seen in a larger context. Doing so will provide an understanding of the roots of Shia resentment and motivation.

In the most general terms, Sunni Arabs had been the dominant ethnic group in Iraq since the collapse of the Ottoman Empire.[13] Under the British Mandate from 1923 to 1932, Shia Arabs totaled only 4 out of the 23 premiers, despite making up 53% of the population (as opposed to 21% Sunni Arab).[14] The British rulers of the mandate period retained Sunni Arabs for the top positions in the government and the armed forces. After independence was established in 1932, Sunni Arabs, Shia Arabs, Kurds, and various minorities possessed little in the way of common experience or identity to unify a nation.[15] Given the heritage of fragmented political rule inherited from the Ottoman system, the new military-dominated leadership of Iraq worked to centralize the education system and standardize language and culture. As Andreas Wimmer summarizes: "The fragmented, *millet*-based educational system of the Ottoman Empire was finally replaced by uniform compulsory education whereby the youth of the country was to be trained in the national virtues and assimilated into the ethnic culture of Sunni Arabs" (Wimmer, 2002, p. 178). This process of "Sunnization" accelerated under the Baath regime. Shia numbers in the Baath Party Command descended to 6% during the 1963–1970 era (Wimmer, 2002, p. 179).

With the coming and consolidation of Saddam Hussein's regime, Baathist leadership became concentrated in the hands of one clan. Members of the Begat section of the Albu Nasr tribe centered in Tikrit comprised one-third of the Revolutionary Command Council (Wimmer, 2002, p. 180). While Saddam may have built his trusted circle out of Tikritis rather than Sunnis per se, those Tikritis were Sunnis, and Saddam's tactics meant continued underrepresentation of Shia in ruling positions.

While the numbers tell a story of Sunni preponderance in positions of power, many Shia clearly perceived a subordinate status beyond those numbers. Many commentators hold that the myth-symbol complex of Shia faith and practice focuses on "chosen traumas" (Volkan, 1998). Shia are defined by their allegiance to Ali, murdered in the year 661, as well as the killing of Ali's son Hussein and 72 of his men in a massacre at Karbala. These events are commemorated in annual rituals during the first 10 days of the month of Muharram, where the events at Karbala are re-enacted in the Ashura. In his analysis of sectarian relations in Iraq, Fanar Haddad states that "Shi'a identity is intrinsically linked to feelings of victimhood and, as such, the Shi'a myth-symbol complex is replete with chosen traumas" (Haddad, 2011, p. 20). Moreover, Haddad emphasizes that the Sunnis of Iraq don't share these victim-oriented symbols.[16] The groups hold different myth-symbol complexes that separate the sects and give them different perceptions of dominance and subordination.

Even if one downplays the importance of the cultural content of the rituals themselves, the Iraqi government crackdown on the actual performance of these rituals certainly reinforced Shia perceptions of persecution. In 1977, Saddam's regime canceled the annual Shia pilgrimage of Arbaeen, a procession leading from Najaf to Karbala. As mentioned above, the cancellation led to a major uprising, put down by a bloody government reprisal and followed by a series of arrests and executions of key leaders in the Hawza.

As outlined previously in this chapter, the Iranian revolution led to further crackdowns on Shia political and religious figures. The Dawa Party was banned, with membership punishable by death. The regime executed al-Sadr (Sadr I) in 1980, and other Shia leaders were forced to flee at the time. In the wake of the First Gulf War, Saddam's regime decimated Shia rebels in a fashion that was perceived as broadly anti-Shia, rather than an attack on rebels or Shia activists (Haddad, 2011, p. 73). Haddad carries his argument forward, writing, "For the vast majority of Iraqi Shi'as, the events of 1991 can be said to have become both a chosen trauma and chosen glory: the glory of a self-sacrificing and just rebellion intertwined with the trauma of its brutal demise" (Haddad, 2011, p. 85).

In short, Shia in Iraq were historically underrepresented in Iraq, suffered regime persecution of religious practices, saw their political organizations banished, witnessed the assassination of several of their most popular leaders, and experienced massive reprisals after uprisings. At the time of the 2003 invasion, Iraqi Shia held grievances, and many of those grievances were connected to a reality and perception of second-class citizenship. As Andrew Cockburn summarized in a 2003 article, "Their common bond is a memory of discrimination, whether in the form of the mass executions common during the reign of Saddam Hussein or simply in their exclusion from power throughout Iraq's history" (Cockburn, 2003).

5.4. Shia Demography and Class Relations

On the eve of the US invasion, Shia political leadership had been persecuted, assassinated, or forced to flee to various foreign safe havens. Yet, Baghdad's demographic history had created enormous potential for Shia mobilization.

For the purposes here, the most important feature of Baghdad's demographic and political structure lies in the neighborhood of what has come to be known as Sadr City. This area of East Baghdad is beyond a normal neighborhood; in fact, 8% of Iraq's total population, and 13% of Iraq's Shia citizens, live there (Cole, 2003b, p. 546). If Sadr City was separated from Baghdad, it would be Iraq's second-largest city. As Juan Cole has summarized in the wake of the 2003 invasion, "The residents of East Baghdad live under appalling social and economic conditions, with little access to basic necessities such as sewerage, clean water, and decent housing" (Cole, 2003b, p. 546). Estimates of unemployment in the area as of 2004 ranged as high as 70% (A. Hashim, 2004).

The origins of Sadr City lie in Iraq's development. By mid-century, grinding rural poverty in Iraq's Shia-dominated south drove thousands of citizens to Baghdad. Makeshift homes, known as *sarifa*s, rapidly popped up to create a sprawling slum in East Baghdad (Krohley, 2015, p. 21). In 1958, General Abd al-Karim Qasim seized power in a coup d'état. Qasim's regime made the slums of eastern Baghdad a target for reforms (Krohley, 2015, pp. 24–28). The government demolished the *sarifa*s and replaced them with a new district built on a modern grid pattern. This new district, first named "Revolution City," would later be renamed "Saddam City" in 1982 and Sadr City in 2003. First planned to showcase the benefits of Qasim's revolutionary reforms for poor Shia, the demand for housing in Baghdad soon overwhelmed the ability of the regime to deliver. Originally planned to house 300,000 residents, by the late 1970s the project teemed with 1.5 million inhabitants (Krohley, 2015, p. 27). On the west side of Baghdad, a similar project, with similar problems, sprouted in the neighborhood of Shula. In the parlance of some US military practitioners in the post-invasion period, Shula was sometimes called "Sadr City West."[17]

Beyond the concentration of Shia poverty, two other developments worked to create a base for mobilization. First, because the Iraqi state could not fill the social and economic needs of east Baghdad's residents, non-state actors stepped in. As touched on above, Sadr II, a cousin of the martyred Sadr I, created informal Shia courts (Cole, 2003b, p. 552). His organization also sustained soup kitchens and provided other basic services. The effects of the post-1991 sanctions, evidenced in a dramatic rise in infant mortality among other measures, only served to heighten demand for these services (Tripp, 2010, p. 252).[18] These forms of non-state, local, communal organizations laid a basis for other types of local organization after 2003.

Second, to expand from above, state repression of Shia leaders and population alienated many Shia residents well before the 2003 invasion. As noted earlier, Sadr I was executed in 1980; Sadr II was gunned down along with two of his sons in his car in 1999. In the latter killing, the state would use lethal force to put down East Baghdad demonstrations, causing 54 fatalities (Cole, 2003b, p. 553). The 1999 uprising was preceded by violent demonstrations in 1977 and 1991. In sum, the state's relationship on the eve of the invasion to Saddam/Sadr City was very poor—it was both weak and repressive. The state had been too weak to provide sufficient basic services to this area. Moreover, its repression not only alienated the general population of Sadr City, but also created martyrs.

Life in Sadr City differed in many aspects from other neighborhoods in Baghdad. Before 2003, most of the city's neighborhoods were mixed in terms of Shia-Sunni numbers. Many of these neighborhoods were solidly middle class and some might be considered thriving, even in the sanctions period. In contrast to Sadr City, the Iraqi state was not weak in many of these neighborhoods, even in the 1990s. Throughout much of its period of rule, the Baathist regime could rely on huge oil revenues to wean the population off reliance on non-state communal practices to create dependence on state-based patronage. Oil revenues skyrocketed from $575 million in 1972 to $5.7 billion in 1974 and $26.5 billion in 1980 (Krohley, 2015, p. 30). Yet, as Krohley points out, "Beneath the surface of Iraq's boom in oil wealth and resulting spread of middle class prosperity to many, the Shi'a underclass had remained a distinct socio-cultural entity . . . they had remained an identifiable (and continuously expanding) bloc in Baghdad, and in the cities and towns of southern Iraq" (Krohley, 2015, p. 53). The oil revenues would collapse during the 1990s under sanctions. Most social relations deteriorated, the economy atrophied. Within the impoverished Shia neighborhoods, an entire generation of disconnected young men were primed to join with Sadr II, only to see him gunned down in February 1999.

In summary, on the eve of the 2003 invasion a massive and geographically concentrated Shia underclass possessed its own identity, an identity reinforced and hardened during the sanctions era. In Sadr II, they had a leader and a grassroots organization. With Sadr II's murder, they also had a holy martyr. After the invasion, they had the opportunity to rekindle Sadr II's previous organization. As seen in the following paragraphs, Shia had a system of mosques able to generate a common message that could coordinate action. Shia institutional structure, combined with Sadr II's legacy, "constituted an enormous force in Iraq's Shia community" (Krohley, 2015, p. 55). As we will see, after the invasion this enormous force would take a new form, with Sadr II's surviving son, Muqtada al-Sadr, assuming the leader role and thousands of young men from the Shia neighborhoods joining the follower ranks, including the ranks of the Mahdi Army.

5.5. Shia Institutions: Coordination of Action

As briefly discussed above, one of the most distinctive institutional characteristics of Shia Islam in Iraq is the norm of emulation. Lay members choose to become followers (*muqallid*) of one of a set of respected scholar-clerics. If a trained scholar (*mujtahid*) gains followers, he becomes a *maraji*, meaning a source or reference for imitation. The numbers of *marja* are not high. In 2003 in Iraq, only a handful of Grand Ayatollahs worthy of emulation existed in Iraq. These two features of Shia Islam produce potential leaders with considerable legitimacy and authority. Shia Islam possesses an institutional hierarchy that is independent of the state.[19] Although this hierarchy is informal and based in tradition, the trained clerics at the top of the hierarchy are well-known to the population. The result is that Shia practice in Iraq produces a small number of powerful clerics who are able to direct their followers in both religious and political-religious matters.

Related, the Shia mosque system in Iraq also works to coordinate action. After 2003 and the fall of the Baathist regime, Shia mosques began holding Friday prayers, including sermons. These sermons provided an opportunity for the emulated cleric to give directions and information to his followers. Some Ayatollahs were able to pass the same directions and information through a network of mosques. Local Shia imams were always connected to one of the *marja* either as followers or emulators. Through this top-down connection, many followers were hearing the same message at the Friday sermon. No Sunni cleric was able to do the same. As opposed to their Shia counterparts, Sunnis lacked a hierarchy and thus lacked leaders likely to possess a network of mosques. In Patel's words, "They lacked an organizational structure that could consistently induce preachers to deliver the same message in different localities" (Patel, 2017, p. 218).

In terms of the analytical framework of this book, Shia religious institutions are structured in a way to produce focal point mechanisms conducive to mobilization in a way that Sunni religious institutions are not. David Patel has written a long manuscript detailing the influence of focal points in post-invasion Iraq and how the presence and absence of focal points explain the difference in mobilization between Shia and Sunni in the post-invasion period (Patel, 2017). For Shia congregants, the follower not only heard the message, but could see that others heard the message. The Friday sermon coordinated the expectations and potential action of thousands of followers. Patel summarizes a process where religious authority merges into political authority:

> The ability of religious authority to expand to new domains is partly rooted in a belief by each follower that a sufficient number of other followers will obey an injunction, often making obedience a best response for the individual. As Iraqis saw other Iraqis following religious authorities' statements and rules, they formed expectations that others would also follow future statements and rules. Religious authority expanded into a sort of political authority; an authority became more authoritative. (Patel, 2017, p. 175)

Patel argues that in many neighborhoods with a Shia mosque, Friday prayers were able to coordinate action to provide local public goods such as trash collection and local security. At a broader level, Shia clerical leaders were able to direct voting in elections. Patel forcefully argues that Friday sermons, and the common knowledge they produced, could not push individuals into higher-risk actions that they did not wish to do. In terms of the framework, they could move individuals to the +1/−1 position, but not to the +2/−2 position. Sermons could not "create militias" (Patel, 2017, p. 137).

It is worth noting that Friday prayers not only served as focal points but could also provide estimates for the safety-in-numbers mechanism crucial to movement to both the 1 and 2 nodes. Other religious gatherings and protests could provide similar information. As we will see in the cases, some Shia clerics, such as Muqtada al-Sadr, could bring large numbers out in the street. Again, Sunni religious leaders could not generate these large rallies. To preview the course of events in the empirical chapters, two Shia clerics were able to harness the combination of authority, a network of mosques, and a coordinated message at Friday prayers to mobilize followers—Grand Ayatollah Sistani and Muqtada al-Sadr (who built on the authority and mosque networks of his father).

5.6. Sunnis in Comparison

The previous pages have addressed the capabilities of Shia organizations by examining historical, demographic, and institutional foundations. Sunni capabilities can be addressed through comparison. Due to historical subordination, Shia were motivated by long-term resentment and a culture of martyrdom and victimhood. Sunnis possessed no such history or culture. In fact, in the period immediately following the invasion, many Sunnis did not even strongly identify as Sunnis. Sunni symbols were unconsciously aligned with the Iraqi state where, as argued above by Wimmer, Sunni culture served as the basis for assimilation to Iraqi nationality. As often noted, due to a lack of group struggle, the identity of members of dominant groups often lacks salience. Post-invasion changes would certainly provide that saliency. An interview in the *New York Times* provides an illustration of how sectarian identity, as well as the perception of reversal, became basic features of Baghdad life:

> "We were shocked, really," she said. "We use to have friends, neighbors. In every moment, when you met a person, you didn't think: Is he Shia or Sunni? Of course you'd notice, but it didn't matter." Then at some point, she said, it switched; sect became the defining characteristic for Iraqis. Her Sunni friends told her she did not understand. Being Sunni used to count for something, they said. (Cave, 2007)[20]

The Coalition's early orders for de-Baathification and disbanding of the military were a first shock. Some saw these events as not only eliminating the influence of Saddam followers, but of Sunnis more broadly. Even those who considered themselves cosmopolitan or secular eventually could no longer avoid thinking in sectarian terms.

The result was that both Shia and Sunni would be motivated by resentment. The 2003 invasion allowed Shia an opportunity to eliminate their perceived position of unjust subordination. It could be "their turn" now. Within a few years, Sunnis were forced to deal with a blatant status reversal. There is little question that many Sunnis experienced resentment after the invasion and the constitution of a new government. There was resentment not only against the foreign armed occupation force, but against the Shia who would now occupy a dominant place on the Iraqi hierarchy. The Sunni boycott of the 2005 elections provided stark evidence.

In terms of demography, Sunnis had no huge, dense, and impoverished area similar to Sadr City. The most purely Sunni area could be found in Anbar province, where tribal and family identity often superseded sect. Sunni numbers and concentrations also would decline during the conflict. Sunnis were more likely to hold powerful positions in the Saddam regime and accordingly had both the incentive and the means to flee. The title of a book written by Deborah Amos is telling: *The Eclipse of the Sunnis* (2010). In its foreword, Amos writes that by 2009 two million Iraqis had fled the country, with only about one hundred thousand returning. Of those who left, sixty percent are estimated to be Sunnis (Amos, 2010, p. x). For a significant number of Sunnis, fleeing the country was a better strategy than remaining and mobilizing. The contrast with Shia could not be starker. In the aftermath of the US invasion, Shia exiles flowed into Iraq, while Sunnis living in Iraq exited.

Shia religious institutions were more capable of mobilizing and coordinating action than Sunni religious organizations. To pick up on the previous discussion, Sunni structure is decentralized. Without the norm of emulation, religious followers do not pledge allegiance, or provide monetary support to one of a handful of Sunni elite clerics. The mosque system is also decentralized and not geared to disseminating a common message. In Patel's description of Sunnis, "They lacked an organizational structure that could consistently induce preachers to deliver the same message in different localities" (Patel, 2017, p. 218). Without this structure, Friday sermons differed across mosques and could not serve as coordinating focal points to generate movement.[21]

Sunnis did have potential sources of people and resources less available to Shia. Sunnis were more likely to be members of what the United States termed "former regime elements," or FREs. As the empirical chapters will show, significant numbers of FREs, especially military officers, did form the core of some resistance and militia cells. However, Sunni mobilization of state personnel and resources would be hampered by the transformation and destruction of the Iraqi state. Before the invasion, many commentators talked about two different types of an Iraqi state: a public state and a private state. As historian Charles Tripp has summarized:

> There existed in Iraq a dual state. The elaborate bureaucracy of government agencies, state-run enterprises and organizations formed the public state in Iraq. They comprised the ministries, the official associations, the armed forces and the Ba'ath party. But behind this lay a "shadow state," formed by networks of associates, chains of patrons and clients, circles of exclusion and privilege emanating from the office and person of the president. This was the real nexus of power. . . . Estimated at 500,000 or so, including dependents, these were the people Saddam Hussein needed to convince both that his leadership was better for their interests than that of any imaginable alternative and that they would lose everything were he to be overthrown. (Tripp, 2010, p. 259)

In the wake of the invasion, the public state simply disappeared. Looters ransacked state offices, if the state employees had not taken everything before them. Effective and motivated FREs likely came from Saddam's "shadow state." If the members of this group were not sufficiently in the shadows, they often became targets of killing and revenge. Shia religious structures were in general a stronger and more robust base to generate resistance than the remnants of a shattered state system.

There was one powerful purely Sunni source of power: transnational Salafist forces. The most famous of these groups, at least in the early years after the 2003 invasion, was Osama bin Laden's al-Qaeda (Byman, 2015).[22] In the early stages of insurgency, the most important Salafist group was al-Tawhid wa al-Jihad (Monotheism and Holy War), led by Abu Musab al-Zarqawi. At first Zarqawi was not aligned with al-Qaeda, but after highly visible kidnappings and terrorist acts (most famously the videotaped execution of American Nicholas Berg), a merger was made in 2005.

With less ability to build organizations from the bottom up, these transnational organizations used terrorism to destabilize the new Iraq. In terms of emotions, resentment alone may not be enough to establish spiraling violence. It is the emotion of anger that can ignite and fuel a cycle of violence and revenge. To recall from Chapter 3: anger results from the belief that an actor has committed a bad action against one's self or group. Under the influence of anger, individuals no longer calculate costs and benefits in a straightforward way. Under anger, they downgrade risks and skew information in ways that allow for the pursuit of revenge. In terms of the spectrum of roles, under anger individuals will feel compelled to move out of neutrality into a more active role.

Given the sectarian identities at play in Iraq, political entrepreneurs found ways to unleash anger and move individuals into armed roles capable of exacting revenge. One of the most well-known examples is the effort by AQI leader, Zarqawi, to foment civil war between Sunnis and Shias. Here is a description of his strategy, based largely on a captured letter of Zarqawi:

> As Zarqawi described in his letter and subsequent broadcasts, his strategy in Iraq is to strike at the Shia—and therefore provoke a civil war. "A nation of heretics," the Shia "are the key element of change," he wrote. "If we manage to draw them onto the terrain of partisan war, it will be possible to tear the Sunnis away from their heedlessness, for they will feel the weight of the imminence of danger." Again, a strategy of provocation—which plays on an underlying reality: that Iraq sits on the crucial sectarian fault line of the Middle East and that a conflict there gains powerful momentum from the involvement of neighboring states, with Iran strongly supporting the Shia and with Saudi Arabia, Kuwait, Jordan, and Syria strongly sympathetic to the Sunnis. More and more, you can discern this outline in the chaos of the current war, with the Iranian-trained militias of the Shia Islamist parties that now control the Iraqi government battling Sunni Islamists, both Iraqi and foreign-born, and former Baathists. (Danner, 2005)[23]

While many types of killings and bombings depend on local incentives and constraints, the timing of elections, and other specific factors, Zarqawi's targets followed the general logic of creating anger and spiraling violence, at least in its early renditions.[24] The target set included motorcades of specific Shia political figures. Insurgents attacked the Dawa Party, car-bombed Sadr's office in the Shula district of Baghdad, and hit police stations associated with Shia dominance in Karada, Saydiyah, and other towns. One summary statement written in May 2005 read, "Political leaders fear that insurgents have intensified their campaign to drive a wedge between Sunnis and Shiites and that they are trying to ignite a civil war. Last month, Shiite leaders accused the largest Shiite militia force of complicity in the killing of Sunni clerics" (Oppel Jr. and Tavernise, 2005).

There were also Salafist organizations originating on Iraqi soil and maintaining their independence from al-Qaeda (Hashim, 2009, pp. 19–21). These native Iraqi groups turned to Salafism as the most effective and logical way to counter Western influence and Shia power. The most well-known groups in this category include Ansar al-Sunna (founded November 2003) and the original 1920 Revolution Brigades (founded July 2003). These organizations would undergo splits and new homegrown Sunni

Salafists organizations would emerge. Finally, the humiliating defeat of the Iraqi Army and foreign occupation did help create a few purely nationalist resistance groups (Hashim, 2009, p. 19). These groups were generally small, and for those groups who sought an ideology to guide the organization, Islam usually provided the justification.

5.7. Summary: An Application of the Framework for Specification and Summary

One of the major arguments of this book is that the contours of the Iraq conflict have been driven by the power of identity master cleavages and the perceptions and clarity of ethnic hierarchy. Two phenomena are necessary for identity master cleavages to become decisive in driving the origins and evolution of a conflict. The identities must be salient. As this chapter has laid out, Shia identity in Iraq was pronounced, mainly through actions of the modern Iraqi state. That state engaged in exclusion and repression; it created martyrs and movements. The Iraqi state's crackdown on essential Shia religious practices such as pilgrimages enflamed resentments. Additionally, Iraq's demography, with concentrated slums in East Baghdad and elsewhere, heightened the Shia sense of marginalization. With saliency of identity came perceptions of hierarchy, of dominance and subordination, along with related emotions.

The second necessary condition for a master-cleavage-driven conflict is organization. There must be a way to translate identity-based grievances into action. There must be a force able to sustain action based on identity. As this chapter has described in detail, the course of modern Iraqi history produced several powerful Shia actors that would emerge after the US invasion and carry out sectarian-oriented agendas. Contrary to many US expectations, Iraq was not a blank slate. On the Shia side, Dawa, SCIRI/Badr, Sadrists, the INA, and the INC all were primed to push their programs. On the Sunni side, former regime elements and transnational Salafists were ready to go. Some of these organizations were primed to capture sections of the new emerging state. Several were able to mobilize both members and weapons.

This book also makes a statement related to master-cleavage struggle: Shia essentially win. This chapter has identified several Shia advantages in mobilization that helped produce that result.

The analytical framework can be used to specify and summarize the reasons for both identity salience and Shia advantage. Below, I reprint the template developed in Section I, with the mechanisms related to the Shia-Sunni cleavage and competition in bold.

Movement from 0 to −1:

- **Resentment versus newly empowered group**
- Safety in numbers with general population as reference point
- Status rewards
- **Focal points**

Movement from 0 to +1:

- **Resentment versus formerly dominant group**
- Safety in numbers with general population as referent point
- **Focal points**
- Rational economic decision, payouts from government, employment, etc.

Movement from +1 and −1 back to 0:

- Rational reaction to threat
- Fear (emotion)

Movement from −1 to −2:

- Social norms of reciprocity
- Norms of honor/vengeance
- **Anger**
- **Safety in numbers with local population as reference point**
- Material incentives

Movement to +2:

- Social norms of reciprocity
- **Anger (vs. insurgent violence)**
- Safety in numbers with local population as reference point
- Material incentives/employment/bribes

Movement to −3:

- Material incentives
- **Ideological fervor**
- Humiliation

Mechanisms sustaining −2, −3:

- Psychological mechanisms—tyranny of sunk costs, wishful thinking, cognitive dissonance
- Coercion, threats against leaving
- Social norms

Movement to +3:

- Material incentives (pay, uniforms, equipment)
- Pride (either in professionalism or patriotism).

I proceed systematically from top to bottom, starting with a review of the mechanisms driving individuals into the −1 role. Both Shia and Sunni were motivated by *resentment*. Shia were driven by the emotion to create and consolidate a position of dominance after a history of subordination; Sunnis were driven by the emotion in reaction to an impending loss of dominant position. The US decision to disband the Iraqi Army and ban Baathists from employment enflamed the emotion for Sunnis. Resentment undoubtedly was a driving force behind the saliency of the Shia-Sunni cleavage.

Although both Shia and Sunni were motivated by a form of resentment, motivation alone may not be sufficient for mobilization without mechanisms for coordinated action. Here we come to crucial differences between Sunni and Shia in both structure and practice. In brief, Shia religious structure and practice produce *focal points* that coordinate action. While emotions can push individuals off neutrality toward a support role (at the −1 or +1 level), individuals are most likely to move when they know others are also acting the same way. Furthermore, they are more likely to be able to coordinate their support activities—voting, showing up at rallies, donating to a cause—if they are aware of others' actions. Focal points are events, places, or dates that help to coordinate expectations and thus actions. It is worth noting that Friday prayers not only served as focal points, but also could provide estimates for the *safety-in-numbers* mechanism crucial to movement to both the 1 and 2 nodes. Other religious gatherings and protests could provide similar information. As we will see in the cases, some Shia clerics, such as Muqtada al-Sadr, could bring large numbers out in the street. Again, Sunni religious leaders could not generate these large rallies.

Next, there are the mechanisms that drove individuals into roles of local armed resistance (−2). Here, as will be discussed in the empirical chapters, the Sunni transnational AQI leader Zarqawi was a master at generating *anger* by hitting religious symbols. The bombing of the Samarra Shrine is the quintessential case. Although these strategies were transparent, they were exceedingly difficult to counter. After a sequence of AQI bombings, a prominent disciple of Grand Ayatollah Sistani told worshippers, "Submitting to one's passion and confusion will bring us to domestic sedition and eventually lead us to failure. We must go forward, be patient, and carry on building the new Iraq" (Daragahi, 2005). Prime Minister Ibrahim al-Jaafari called for a "rational, political" struggle. These calls for rationality paradoxically serve to show how much emotions were driving the Shia-Sunni contest.

Zarqawi strived to ignite a sectarian civil war in Iraq. His success brought many Shia into the streets. With these increasing numbers, state security forces were incapable of arresting offenders or militia members. In effect, spiraling violence and the numbers it generated in neighborhoods created a *safety in numbers with local population as reference point.* Joining a local militia simply became a low-risk action for many young men. This point is especially true for Shia. They can move in bigger numbers to −2 local militia positions because of the safety-in-numbers mechanism generated by large Shia gatherings mentioned above.

On movement to −3 armed mobile organization, *ideological fervor* no doubt drove some individuals on both sides. The effect may seem clearer for Sunnis, at least in their Salafist form. As we will see in Section III of this volume, ISIS declaration of a caliphate created international fervor among one set of Islamists. I have not highlighted humiliation. This emotion is formed from a cognition of powerlessness, of agency taken away. While this mechanism might be driving Arabs as a whole in relation to the West, as argued by Dominique Moisi,[25] in the struggle between Sunnis and Shia within Iraq, both sides believed they had agency to change their situation.

The question remains why more Iraqi citizens, of any sect, did not join the state's security forces as a way to defend their group. Why didn't angry Iraqis feel compelled to join the Iraqi police? The self-generating nature of sectarian violence provides an answer. Sectarian violence clearly enhances the salience of sectarian identity. In turn, heightened sectarian identity and violence intensify a preference to join a sectarian group directly involved in a struggle to defend one's group, or gain revenge against the offending group, rather than an officially neutral state. With individuals joining sectarian armed groups and committing sectarian-oriented violence, the cycle turns again, deepening and expanding both sectarian identification and hostility. While many Iraqis did join the police for material benefits, their lack of training and motivation made their movement less consequential than the movement to the left side of the spectrum. Movement to −2 and −3 would soon set off a sectarian civil war.

The analysis above also suggests why the Shia prevail in their contest with Sunnis. For one, Shia religious structure is able to provide focal points and safety-in-numbers mechanisms that Sunni religious organization cannot. Second, and very simply, there are more Shia than Sunni; additionally, some of those Shia reside in large, homogenous neighborhoods with a history of resistance.

Third, and most importantly, Shia organizations gaining prominence after the US invasion are powerful and capable. The Sadrist organizations would trigger several of the mechanisms outlined in Chapter 3. They rode Shia resentments simmering from exclusion of power. Their Friday sermons and mass rallies provided both focal points and safety in numbers. Their creation of local social organization built on local networks and reinforced social norms of reciprocity. The members of Sadrist organizations were primed to feel anger and act on it in response to AQI terrorist attacks. Their rhetoric, symbolism, and martyrdom both created and drew from ideological fervor. The Sadrists would trigger these mechanisms in order to build up their organization from the bottom up rather than the top down. The SCIRI, led by the Hakim family, would provide the basis of an influential political party, even if it struggled with the popular perception of being controlled by Iran. The Badr Organization came into Iraq as a highly disciplined and well-trained force. Its commanders could focus this militia on specific goals related to state capture. As seen in the empirical chapters, the Dawa Party played a significant role in generating roles and mechanisms related to the $-1, 0, +1$ nodes. Participation and voting in state-held elections is a $+1$ behavior; cooperating with and providing information to state security organizations is a $+1$ behavior. Because the Dawa Party comes to hold significant state power, it has the ability to draw its followers into $+1$ state-supporting roles.

Notably, the power of the sectarian organizations compares favorably against the officially non-sectarian groups entering Iraq from the West in 2003. The INA and INC had influential sponsors in the United States and elsewhere. They came into Iraq in the wake of the invasion in a privileged position. Yet, they their ability to motivate, coordinate, and sustain action in Iraq was limited in comparison to the Iraqi religious organizations. In terms of our framework, these outsiders simply could not "trigger" the relevant mechanisms to move individuals to positions of support.

5.8. Conclusion and Caveats

The empirical chapters will merge a study of US and insurgent strategic moves with the breakdown of forces connected with sectarian master cleavages outlined in this chapter. The interaction of these two strands, guided and disciplined by the analytical framework developed in Section I, will produce rich but disciplined descriptions and explanations of the course of the Iraq conflict, and lessons about the future.

Some clarifications and caveats are in order. I am clearly not arguing that the Shia-Sunni cleavage in Iraq is driven by some "ancient" religious rivalry. Despite important differences in theology, religion alone would not create a Shia-Sunni cleavage. It is a combination of factors, in conjunction with the breakdown of the state, that made the role of explicitly Shia organizations powerful. Second, as will be shown in the case studies, Shia never unite. Different Shia organizations will compete against one another politically, sometimes even violently. However, this intra-Shia competition becomes intense only after Sunni power has been eclipsed. The state of the master cleavage largely determines the intensity of intra-group conflict. Furthermore, the Sadrists themselves are a highly decentralized and fragmented group, with many factions often pursuing local agendas. The main thing that coordinated this unruly organization was its opposition to Sunnis and the goal of changing Shia status in Iraq. Finally, the power of the Shia-Sunni cleavage declined in the post-ISIS era. As emphasized in Chapter 1, the salience of master cleavages varies over time. When the clarity of a state's group hierarchy is established, violent conflict is likely to decline. As discussed in Section III, Iraq's hierarchy is established, with Shia ascendant, by 2017.

The first case studies of this section examine the conflict in Baghdad. By 2006, the Iraqi capital was enflamed in a bloody sectarian civil war. Explicitly Shia and Sunni organizations created the foundation for that war and drove its violence. Some of those same organizations captured sections of the state or its functions. We begin with early Sunni mobilization and a focus on the neighborhood in Ghazaliyah.

Ghazaliyah

Sunni Mobilization, Sectarian War, US Success and Failure

6.1. Introduction

The empirical case study chapters begin with a study of the Ghazaliyah neighborhood in northwest Baghdad. This case provides illustrations of many of the most significant aspects of the Iraq conflict as it unfolded during 2003–2011. It will provide a window into the mobilization of Iraqi military personnel and veterans, one of the strongest sources of Sunni opposition. It will provide a detailed description of the Sunni-Shia civil war in one section of Baghdad. In a classic case of community mobilization and "flipping," the course of the war in Ghazaliyah shows how insurgents who vowed to kill US soldiers in the days after the invasion came to ally with them a few years later. The case shows the flexibility of US forces and their eventual use of a combination of strategies. The broader case includes the failure, and basically refusal, of the Iraqi government in integrating demobilized insurgents into its security organs. Above all, Ghazaliyah will demonstrate the motivating power of sectarian identity in shaping the origins and contours of violence and state-building failure in Iraq.

This chapter's narrative is formed from interviews with US soldiers, a former insurgent, a translator for the US forces in the area, and members of the general population in Baghdad, as well as a small number of secondary sources. After some brief background information, the case describes the evolution of the insurgency in Ghazaliyah in five stages: (1) immediate post-invasion and the organization of insurgent factions; (2) Shia-Sunni civil war; (3) the development of the Ghazaliyah Guardians; (4) US and Ghazaliyah Guardian cooperation; and (5) the failure to integrate the Ghazaliyah Guardians into the Iraqi government and the aftermath.

6.2. Background

The Ghazaliyah neighborhood is located in the northwest of Baghdad with a population in the hundreds of thousands. At the time of the invasion in 2003, the neighborhood was mixed but predominately Shia in its northern half and more Sunni in the southern half. During the US occupation, the neighborhood was in the Khadimiyah Security District (see Figure 6.1). To the north of Ghazaliyah lies Shula, a thoroughly Shia neighborhood that would become known as "Sadr City West" to many US soldiers. Ghazaliyah and Shula are separated by a drainage ditch, known to some US soldiers as "shit river." The eastern section of the neighborhood is sparsely populated and home to the enormous Um al-Quraa mosque, originally known as the "Mother of All Battles" Mosque to honor Saddam Hussein's "victory" in the 1991 Gulf War. Perhaps unsurprisingly, the mosque would become an organizing center for the early insurgency, as well as a focal point for Sunni mobilization. The Bakria farms and Abu Ghraib lie to the west. Ameriyah lies to the south, as does Baghdad International Airport. Soon after the invasion, Ameriyah became the hub of AQI's operations in Baghdad.

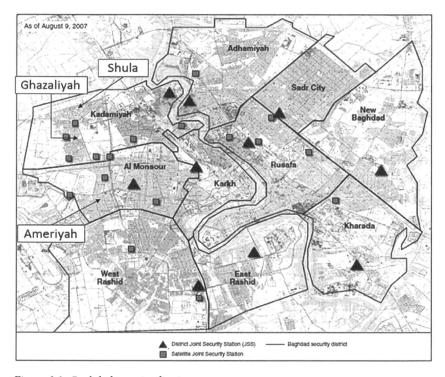

Figure 6.1. Baghdad security districts.
Source: US Department of Defense, Multinational Division Baghdad

Ghazaliyah is not an old neighborhood; much of it was built in the 1980s. Most relevant to the purposes here, seven areas (numbered *mahallas*) of Ghazaliyah were specially designated to house military and intelligence officers: areas 51, 52, 53, 681, 683, 685, and 687. Both active and retired military officers who lived in these districts had close personal ties. They lived in the same area, had similar military backgrounds, went to the same mosques. Many Baghdad residents knew of the special nature of these neighborhoods; one interviewee joked that if he knew a girl was from this area he would be hesitant to get involved with her because he would fear having to deal with a stern military father.[1]

6.3. The Immediate Post-Invasion Period and the Organization of Insurgent Factions

After the invasion and fall of Iraq, one interviewee said the area was in "tornado-like chaos." For many of the former military officers living in the concentration of Ghazaliyah neighborhoods listed above, the United States was not a liberator, but simply an invader. The country was occupied and it was natural to fight Americans. Coalition Provisional Authority Orders No. 1 (de-Baathification) and No. 2 (which disbanded the Iraqi military) cemented these perceptions in the minds of both retired and current officers.

Many US soldiers understood this motivation and sometimes labeled Iraqi ex-military insurgents as the "honorable resistance." In a 2007 interview, Col. J. B. Burton, the commander of the 2nd Brigade Combat Team, 1st Infantry Division (Dagger Battalion) made a clear distinction between ex-military and al-Qaeda in northwest Baghdad:

> you had honorable resistance members moving throughout the area. You had the 1920s Revolutionary Guard; you had the Omar Brigade; and a host of other entities that were members of the former Iraqi Army, that were now disenfranchised because they had been removed from power, had been removed from jobs and employment and were looking to oust the occupying forces from their nations. And the way to get weapons and support was through support of al Qaeda. So there was a, there was a confederation built, I believe, on the part of this honorable resistance group, to take on the fight against Coalition Forces, deny them free access to the neighborhoods, while al Qaeda went in more extreme efforts to deny any hope of progress, of growth in northwest Baghdad, while concurrently defeating the Shia expansion (Burton, 2007).

Later in the same interview, Burton reflected on his relationship with these former Iraqi soldiers after the setting up of the Sons of Iraq (SOI)/Awakening forces. He stated, "You know I meet once a week with former Iraqi Army officer leaders in, in one of our Joint Security sites. And these are men we are very comfortable with" (Burton, 2007).

The former Iraqi officers were motivated by more than nationalism and resentment of foreign occupiers. The perception of a status reversal with the Shia population was intense. These fairly wealthy Sunni military officers saw themselves as having been on top of the previous political and social world in Iraq; to be below or even equal to Shia turned this world upside down. Most veterans had fought against Iran for years during the 1980s. Now Iran was perceived to be prevailing in Iraq through Shia proxies. One must use caution when using interviews from 2015 to assess attitudes in 2003, but the contempt of Sunni officers from Ghazaliyah toward the Shia was palpable. Statements such as "they can never rule" and the Shia are "thieves/Ali Babas" were pervasive.

Based on local personalities and networks, factions began forming in the districts of Ghazaliyah filled with military personnel and veterans. One group was composed of 130 individuals, all former military officers, most who had lost their positions through Coalition Provisional Authority Order No. 2. Some officers had gone to Syria originally and then came back when they perceived it was safe to return. Five different factions with a base in Ghazaliyah soon appeared:

1. The Islamic Army
2. The Supporters of Sunni
3. The Rashideen Army
4. Tawhid and Jihad[2]
5. Hamas Iraq.

Additionally, although headquartered in nearby Abu Ghraib, the 1920 Revolution Brigade had a significant presence in Ghazaliyah. At one point, the Islamic State would also make a small presence, but did not control any territory and was described by one interviewee as "more of idea" than as a functioning insurgent group. Members of these groups used their own personal weapons, which apparently were not in short supply. Some factions buried a supply of weapons in the Bakria farms area just west of Ghazaliyah. The US military patrolled in Ghazaliyah, but did not establish any outposts.

In terms of the analytical framework, Ghazaliyah witnessed rapid movement from both active and retired military personnel into the −2 position. The emotion of resentment, both against the foreign presence and a sense of domestic status reversal with the Shia, clearly fueled this movement. Former military officers quickly formed multiple local, armed organizations through network and personal ties. Groups formed around individuals with high status in the community. Key mechanisms were resentment, social norms among local networks, and status rewards. Undoubtedly, CPA Orders No. 1 and No. 2 took away material incentives that might have worked against moving to the −2 position, but many of these military and ex-military officers were simply primed to revolt.

There was no coherent counterinsurgent strategy in Ghazaliyah in this early period. Apparently, US intelligence did not know that areas 51, 52, 53, 681, 683, 685, and 687 were filled with Iraqi military personnel. At the very least, there does not appear to be any evidence that the United States in the period after the invasion anticipated a move toward insurgency and civil war arising in this zone. US forces did patrol in Ghazaliyah, but then returned each night to the forward operating base (FOB).

6.4. Shia-Sunni War in Ghazaliyah

While former Sunni officers were organizing in central Ghazaliyah, Shia forces consolidated their power to the immediate north in Shula. Jaysh al-Mahdi (JAM) set up headquarters in Shula and began to move south. JAM's informants in these neighborhoods were locals able to distinguish Sunni from Shia residents and also able to inform on their neighbors' actions. JAM members then employed what became common tactics to intimidate Sunni residents and drive them out of the neighborhood. During their incursions, they would leave a letter with a bullet inside, or mark a Sunni-residence house with graffiti.

At first these nonviolent threats were not effective and people remained. Then JAM began killing families' sons. This escalation was effective and in one area after another people did flee. At one level, this violence could be labeled selective. However, the level of brutality increased to very high levels. One report detailed how JAM used their connections with the local police to wreak havoc on the Sunni population of Ghazaliyah:

Jaysh al Mahdi (JAM) members in Ghazaliyah were systematically killing Sunnis using police checkpoints. Operations ran 24 hours per day in four shifts of six hours each. The procedure was to use two uniformed police officers and position an officially marked police vehicle on each side of the road. The police stopped all vehicles and inspected the passengers' national identification cards to determine their sect by name and neighborhood. If they were Sunni, the police would use their radios to communicate with a JAM member on an adjacent street who was not a policeman, but wore a uniform and drove an officially marked

vehicle. The police would identify the person to JAM as Sunni. The police would inform the stopped individual that his paperwork needed
to be inspected at the police station. Another officer would enter the
vehicle and accompany the driver to a location where the JAM member
would be positioned who would either execute the Sunni, or take them
to the nearby Office of the Martyr Sadr (OMS) in al Shu'la to be killed.
The checkpoints were set up at different points on al Daghad Street. In
the Ghazaliyah police station, the entire police force was involved in
JAM activity. (Gordon and Trainor, 2012, p. 214)

Unsurprisingly, Sunnis in northern Ghazaliyah possessed no confidence in their
ability to remain in contested areas. The level of death produced a fear leading to
massive flight. One interviewee lived in Ghazaliyah as a young teen in the period
after the invasion.[3] She commented that her family could never have imagined
the level of violence that broke out, or ever conceived of such a breakdown of the
state. Her family first fled Ghazaliyah to the Baghdad neighborhood of Yarmouk,
then fled to Syria. When ISIS arose in Syria, her family came back to Baghdad.
Such was the experience of many Sunni families from Ghazaliyah.

In response to Shia/JAM incursions, Sunni faction leaders coordinated a
common defense plan. To maximize resources against JAM incursions, each faction was designated a specific area to defend. They positioned members on roofs
for surveillance and rapid response using mobile phones for communication.
Their main weapons were rocket propelled grenades (RPGs) and small arms,
but they also used IEDs to help block JAM movement. The Sunni group operations were purely defensive. In the estimation of the Sunni leaders, there was
no way to go on the offensive against JAM forces, especially given their support
by the Iraqi Army. Fighting took place at boundary lines and across fence lines.
Unlike other ethnic battles, Ghazaliyah did not see a tit-for-tat spiral model of
killing because the Sunni forces did not have the ability to make incursions into
the Shia/JAM/Army-held territory. Gains and losses were gradual in nature.

The Sunni faction organizations also made another move—all five Ghazaliyah-
based factions developed a relationship with al-Qaeda in Iraq (AQI).[4] This alliance provided logistics, information, and access to weaponry for each of the
factions. In the north, Shia groups, even if local, were tied to JAM and its leadership in Sadr City. In both Ghazaliyah and Shula, locals armed groups allied with
outside organizations with mobile fighters.

By 2006, the Sunni-Shia fighting transformed the demography of northwest
Baghdad. Hurriyah was a predominately Sunni neighborhood in 2003; it was al-
most completely Shia by 2006. Other surrounding districts saw the same effect—
Abu Ghraib and Shula in particular. Many fleeing Sunni ended up in southern
Ghazaliyah, seen as a safe Sunni pocket. There, Sunnis took over abandoned

Shia houses; Shia did the same in neighborhoods to the north. The result saw Ghazaliyah divided in half, with separate Shia (north) and Sunni (south) sides. The Shula/Ghazaliyah area of Baghdad became ethnically unmixed with a rough balance of power.

In terms of the framework and its spectrum of roles, in the northern section of the area, local Shia (−2) fighters allied with or became local fighters for JAM (−3). In the southern area, local Sunni militias (−2) allied with AQI (−3). At the population level, the emotion of fear accelerated levels of flight; it was very difficult to remain neutral. As ethnic tipping points were passed, the population fled into homogeneous zones and became a support base (−1) for factions/insurgents. The US military accepted the separation of the population in their terminology, recognizing a "Shia support zone" and "Sunni support zone."

The US military developed new tactics, but still failed to develop coherent counterinsurgency strategy, even years after the invasion. US forces still did daytime patrols. The US military gave out cell phones for the population to call in tips and report attacks. However, JAM struck quickly at night and the US forces were unable to respond from the FOB quickly enough, leaving JAM operations largely unaffected. Sunni militias had little contact with the United States at that time. In the interviewees' opinions, Coalition forces were simply not that relevant to the local battles in Ghazaliyah. Remarkably, Iraqi Sunni and Shia forces were fighting a bloody civil war while US armored units drove past, seemingly oblivious.

6.5. The Creation of the Ghazaliyah Guardians

The local Sunni militia leaders in Ghazaliyah were keenly aware of developments in the areas around them. Anbar Sunni tribal leader Sheikh Sattar Abu Risha had been in contact with at least one faction leader in an effort to recruit Sunni fighters in Baghdad to Anbar province. Sunnis in Ghazaliyah were also aware of the Sahwa, or Awakening, in Anbar. In September 2006, 30 Anbar Sunni tribes had organized and allied with the United States against AQI.

At first, many Baghdad residents did not believe that the tribal dynamics in Anbar had relevance for the capital city. Anbar was ethnically and economically more homogenous; insurgents there did not have to deal with the demographic complexities of Baghdad or an overwhelmingly powerful Shia militia. In Anbar, tribal leaders had enough clarity and sway to make firm deals.[5] It was much harder to organize in the more socially complex Baghdad.

The events in one neighborhood in Baghdad would work to change the calculations of Sunni insurgent leaders in Ghazaliyah. By far the most important signal came from events in Ameriyah, a Sunni stronghold just to the south of Ghazaliyah. The two neighborhoods possessed several common features. Ameriyah and the southern section of Ghazaliyah were havens for Sunni refugees fleeing Shia and JAM violence. Both were under extreme pressure from armed groups, although these threats differed. In Ameriyah, AQI, not JAM, had become the primary threat against local Sunni control. After a bout of excessive AQI violence, Sunni insurgents battled AQI for three days at the end of May 2007. Following up on tacit cooperation between the Sunni insurgents and US forces during that battle, a local insurgent faction leader, Abu Abed, negotiated an alliance with the United States. As a result, the "Ameriyah Knights" were born (*The US Army in the Iraq War*, Vol. 2, 2019, pp. 177–182).[6] Within a matter of months, AQI was purged from Ameriyah.

Militia leaders in Ghazaliyah took note and soon acted.[7] By late 2006, Sunni insurgent leaders in Ghazaliyah believed that JAM and the Shia had won the battle of Baghdad. Despite support from AQI, the Shia were poised to capture Ghazaliyah. In the words of one interviewee: "Let me be totally honest, we had a decision to make, do we wish to be with the US or Iran?" The United States was the better choice, the lesser of two evils. The move was driven by desperation more than anything else. Without the Americans, the Sunni fighters in Ghazaliyah believed they would have lost. While siding with the United States would make local Sunni insurgents enemies of AQI, it could be decisive against the Shia threat.

As described above, Ghazaliyah factions developed around high-status individuals. The two individuals who would become most influential in changing the course of the war in Ghazaliyah were Shuja al-Adhami and Mohammed Raad Ali. Al-Adhami served in the Iraqi Army as an artillery officer during 1975–1998. He earned six medals in the Iran-Iraq War. Originally from Adhamiyah before retiring to Ghazaliyah's military housing section, he possessed long-term ties to the area. Ali was a former Iraqi Army major who commanded Special Forces and airborne units. Neither of these men was considered particularly religious or ideological.

With Ameriyah as an example, and a sense of the changed decision calculus of Sunni faction leaders, the United States went to a group of "local councils" composed of sheikhs, notables, and elders who served as intermediaries to the armed factions. These intermediaries approached al-Adhami and Ali. The United States offered to create a local self-defense group with 450 salaries.[8] Al-Adhami was tasked to raise this force. He called the leaders of the five factions together at his house. Each of the five factions listed above would control 50 positions. Al-Adhami would pick a group of 50 to fill the quota for his own group while retaining the right to fill the remaining 200 salaries at his own discretion. The result was the formation of the Ghazaliyah Guardians. Ali created his 50-man unit around a kernel of 15 followers. They were young, and 13 of them had been ex-military. These 15 became lieutenants. Ali brought in a list to fill out the remaining 35 positions. The US military did minimal vetting. Al-Adhami filled his positions mainly through former military connections.

In summary, the equilibrium of our second period no longer held. For survival reasons, Ghazaliyah insurgent leaders broke their alliance with AQI and sided with the United States. On the spectrum of roles, −2 flipped to +2. The new organization, the Ghazaliyah Guardians (GG), followed the same patterns as in the post-invasion period: positions were divided along five militias, based on networks and local leadership.

As with the Ghazaliyah factions, rising violence drove the United States to reconsider its strategy. Three of the four strategies outlined in Figure 2.2 (Chapter 2) were instituted almost simultaneously. The flipping of the Ghazaliyah militias was a classic case of community mobilization. President Bush's January 2007 announcement of the "Surge" initiated a full-scale clear, hold, build (CHB) strategy with US forces moving out of FOBs into the neighborhoods and into command outposts and joint security stations (JSS).[9] This campaign, initiated in February 2007, was called Operation FARD AL QANOON (ENFORCING THE LAW in Arabic). US forces designated Ghazaliyah as one of the first areas for the construction of JSSs (*The US Army in the Iraq War*, Vol. 2, 2019, p. 99). By May, 65 of these small bases were operating in Baghdad.[10] In addition to community mobilization and CHB, US forces also engaged, perhaps tacitly, in the strategy of homogenization. Indeed, whole neighborhoods, with now previously cleansed and homogenized populations, were separated with concrete barriers.

6.6. US and Ghazaliyah Guardians (GG) Cooperation

The United States accepted three local leaders as colonels for the newly created GG—Shuja al Adhami, Mohammed Raad Ali, and Ayad.[11] The latter deferred to al-Adhami and Ali, who were by far the most powerful.[12] As indicated by Figure 6.2, each colonel in the Guardians commanded one of the color-coded districts. Col. Ali commanded the Guardians in the northern district (, Col. Al-Adhami the southern district, and Col. Ayad the eastern area. Each GG colonel commanded his own troops, but was in daily consultation with his US counterpart. In return for their service, members of the GG received a regular salary (completely paid out of Commander's Emergency Response Program (CERP) money) and the status rewards of uniform, radio, and wearing of the GG patch.

As the Guardians were formed during the Surge period, the map also indicates US/ISF joint security stations and checkpoints now established throughout Ghazaliyah. While the GG were formally linked to US/ISF armed

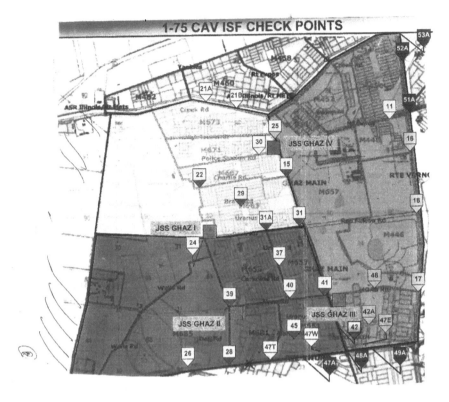

Figure 6.2. Ghazaliyah checkpoints, joint security stations, and locations of Ghazaliyah Guardian units.
Source: US Department of Defense, US Army 1st Cavalry Division

forces, they themselves could not carry weapons. The local US commanding officer had the power to hand out a weapon card (basically a permit) to an individual. This ability gave the commander important leverage. If members of the GG were especially helpful, the US commander would grant the much-desired weapons card. One US commander said he ended up granting a weapons card to about one-third of the GG members in his district. Because they had previously worked with AQI, the GG members were readily able to identify local AQI members and AQI supply lines. With the information coming from the GG, the Coalition forces arrested several AQI members and informants and uncovered arms caches.[13] The GG also worked alongside US and ISF units on patrols and checkpoints. Because these former insurgents had become expert at moving goods and weapons into Ghazaliyah, the GG were very effective at detecting smugglers and illegal materials at the checkpoints. Because the GG knew the physical geography of the area inside out, their presence on night patrols was especially helpful. The GG also formed a reserve for any emergency situation that might arise.

The US change in strategy and tactics dramatically decreased insurgent violence in Ghazaliyah. With the US move to command outposts, alliance with Sunni militias through the GG, and the building of T-walls and restriction of movement, US military deaths fell from 34 in the previous period to zero. While the Shia forces consolidated their position in Shula to the north, they ceased making incursions into central Ghazaliyah. With the lack of any local allies, and the precedent set in Ameriyah, AQI left Ghazaliyah without major fighting.

AQI continued to make targeted attacks, particularly against the GG leaders and their families. In response, Col. Ali sent his family out of the country. His own headquarters were placed next door to US headquarters. Members of the GG accompanied Col. al-Adhami's children to school, and four armed guards escorted his wife to the market. Col. al-Adhami was not lucky himself. AQI attacked and wounded him five times, the last attack producing a serious and lasting injury to his leg, chest, and right eye (with two others in the same vehicle left dead).

Using the powers gained from this merger, the former Sunni militia members could turn some of their attention to nonviolent work. In addition to security work, the GG had two other duties that increased their popularity with the population. First, they were put in charge of distributing cooking oil. Cooking oil had been distributed in a state-sponsored ration system, so the Guardians were taking over a significant and highly visible state function. Second, and perhaps most important, they were tasked with returning property and homes to their original owners. The Sunni population saw Sunni Iraqis in uniforms return Sunni homes to their previous owners. This sight, perhaps more than any other, served to enhance the standing of the government for the residents of Ghazaliyah.

In summary, the United States essentially implemented three different, although connected, strategies during this period. The US military instituted elements of CHB, if not the entire strategy. The placement of JSS seen in Figure 6.1 above is a clear manifestation. Clearly, the community-mobilization strategy yielded immediate positive effects, especially in the reduction of violence. Homogenization occurred, and at a massive level. Although dismissed by some analysts, it is almost impossible to write off homogenization as a cause of the drop in violence in Ghazaliyah. By the time the United States fully implemented its program, there were only 12 walking entry/exit points in all of Ghazaliyah. Those points were guarded by the US/ISF with GG support. Although movement from the Bakria Farms on the western edge of Ghazaliyah was difficult to prevent, movement into and out of Ghazaliyah was challenging. In terms of homogenization, Sunni and Shia had been thoroughly separated and now movement was restricted. The drainage ditch known as "shit river" formed a defensible northern boundary against Shia forces in Shula. Overall, the T-walls seemed effective on many levels. As reported in the US Army history, "In one notable case, with the support of local Sunni leaders, Burton's 2d Brigade, 1st Infantry Division, erected concrete walls around northern Ghazaliyah to stymie JAM death squads, after which the neighborhood's murder rate dropped by 50 percent the following week."[14]

The change in US strategy produced desired movements along the spectrum of roles. Ghazaliyah saw a consolidation of the new +2 units. There was also the elimination of significant −2 units (by their switch to +2) and −3 organization (AQI departure due to lack of support) from Ghazaliyah proper. Moreover, the general population itself substantially moved into +1 roles, especially spurred by the return of houses (administered by fellow Sunnis) and the increase in safety.

6.7. The Failure to Integrate the Ghazaliyah Guardians into the Iraqi Government and the Aftermath

Members of the GG were shocked when the United States turned the GG over to the Iraqi government. While the United States envisioned at least a partial transformation of SOI/Awakening units from militias into official government employment, the Sunnis of Ghazaliyah had little confidence. There would turn out to be good reasons for their skepticism.

The first government tactic for diminishing the role of the Sahwa units was to block the payment of salaries. In May 2009, GG Colonel al-Adhami complained, "I have 170 Sahwa fighters and 40 have already left their posts to drive taxis, sell groceries or do construction, and why? Because they have children to feed and can't bear the government's delay" (Rasheed and Cocks, 2009). Other measures were not so straightforward. In 2008, for example, officials from the Iraqi government told former SOI members to go the airport to apply to join the Army. While there, the former SOI members were arrested. The United States worked to get them released. Furthermore, leaders from Ghazaliyah were led to believe that they would become commanders of a police station. When the Iraqi government said no, the United States then tried to negotiate a new agreement. There were many similar single actions that amounted to a blocking of integration at the aggregate level. The Iraqi government appeared to incorporate a small number of Sahwa members into the state, but just enough to tell the international community that they had no blanket policy against former Sunni combatants.

In Iraq, Sahwa members' frustrations grew. After a spate of attacks on Awakening Council patrolmen, GG leader Shuja al-Adhami accused the Iraqi government of collaborating in the attacks. After the United States withdrew, even the pretense of incorporation disappeared. The GG were dissolved and ceased to exist. Very shortly after the last US troops pulled out, al-Adhami was arrested and charged with helping plant IEDs against Shias. He served one year in prison. When he was temporarily released in 2012, he fled the country. Raad Ali had been arrested and harassed since 2009.

The United States was complicit in these arrests. Hoping that it might serve to help integrate Sahwa members into new state positions, the United States handed over files and information on members—files containing information on previous insurgent activity as well as addresses and phone numbers. The Maliki government used the information on previous insurgent activity to charge members with crimes or to justify exclusion from state employment. Less savory elements of the regime used the addresses and phone numbers to track down former members for even more nefarious purposes. In the words of more than one US soldier, "We really fucked those guys."

6.8. Conclusion

The Ghazaliyah case demonstrates the impact of both identity and organizational factors. In terms of roles and mechanisms, these actors were almost immediately driven from neutrality (0) by strong emotional resentments. As veterans who had fought long wars for Iraq, they perceived the US occupation as illegitimate. As Sunnis, they powerfully resented their perceived subordination to Iranian-connected Shia.

They quickly formed local armed organizations (−2) through network ties and social norms. In the wake of the invasion and occupation, five significant local militias (−2) formed. These organizations were able to sustain themselves from 2003 to 2006 and form a fighting alliance to defend their community against the JAM onslaught. Their alliance choices became a matter of survival. In order to fend off JAM-aligned forces coming from Shula, the Sunni militias sided with AQI. When it became apparent that the AQI alliance could not save them from the Shia forces, they were able to coherently move in mass to partnership with the US military (+2).

For a time, these strategic moves appeared to save the Sunni insurgents from both extinction and Shia dominance. This outcome was not to be. While their strategic moves saved them from the Shia JAM forces, those moves were insufficient to prevent the Shia-dominated Maliki government from eroding and then eclipsing the Sunni move into the Iraq government. While the United States had "flipped" insurgents into roles of "Guardians," they did not have, or did not use, the power to force the Maliki government to convert these Sunni actors into integral members of the state. It would not be fair to single out Maliki for these policies. No Shia leader would have likely acted differently against these Sunni former insurgents. The history and power of the Shia-Sunni cleavage was the driving force here, not personalities.

As discussed in Section III of this book, the Maliki regime continued to conduct a political, and sometimes violent, battle against perceived Sunni enemies in the period immediately before and after the US withdrawal. In the end, many of the Ghazaliyah Guardians fled to Syria or Jordan. Later, some would go on to join the Islamic State.

Sadr City, the Mahdi Army, and the Sectarian Cleansing of Baghdad

7.1. Introduction

The resilience of Muqtada al-Sadr and his supporters is one of the fundamental puzzles of war and politics in modern Iraqi history. Consider the evolution of the Sadrists. In 2004, Muqtada instigated an uprising that resulted in the decimation of his Jaysh al-Mahdi militia (JAM, sometimes also called the Mahdi Army). Yet by 2006, using Sadr City as a base, JAM had developed into a sectarian cleansing machine, systematically purging Sunni residents from one Baghdad neighborhood after another, sweeping west and south through the capital city to transform the city's very demography.

In 2008, Nouri al-Maliki ordered Iraqi forces, in conjunction with US forces, to break JAM and the Sadrist hold over Sadr City. Again, JAM was devastated. Seemingly beaten, Muqtada al-Sadr disbanded JAM and fled to Iran. Yet a few years later, Sadrist followers were marching in mass in the form of the Promised Day Brigade, a new armed group. In the wake of Islamic State (ISIS), Sadrist militias joined the Popular Mobilization Forces (PMF) as hybrid groups. In 2014, the Peace Brigades, with thousands of black clad and armed Mahdi Army members, marched in Sadr City (*Security Situation in Baghdad: The Shia Militias*, 2015). In the 2018 elections, Muqtada al-Sadr's Sairoon took the most votes; in the 2021 elections, they took the most seats. Over 17 years, the Sadrists fought, were defeated, regenerated, conducted systematic sectarian cleansing, were decimated, regenerated, transformed, and remained a dominant political force in Iraq.

This chapter will concentrate on the first regeneration of the Sadrists. How did a group so thoroughly defeated militarily in 2004 manage to rebuild and go on to conduct massive sectarian cleansing by 2006? Why and how did US strategy fail to stop, or at least impede, this development?

This chapter provides several answers to these puzzles. On the most general level, US actors simply did not anticipate a sectarian civil war breaking out in Iraq. Following a major theme of this book, US policymakers, US military personnel, and other Coalition players did not understand the power of the Shia-Sunni master cleavage or the organizations underlying it. On a more specific level, US actors did not anticipate how the very nature of Sadr City made violent conflict probable. Sadr City is a 13-square-mile area with an estimated two million mostly impoverished Shia inhabitants packed into a grid pattern surrounded by canals and large streets. Sadr City would remain an almost impregnable base of JAM (and Special Groups) operations until 2008. Yet even the 2008 battle would not extinguish Sadrist influence in Sadr City. In retrospect, in a contest riven by a Shia-Sunni master cleavage, the existence of a densely populated, impoverished, homogenous area created vast possibilities for violence and conflict.

Yet, the question of Sadrist resiliency goes beyond the two factors just mentioned. The Sadrists have survived and prospered because they can regenerate armed actors at both local and national levels. In terms of the analytical framework, while the US forces were able to eliminate individuals occupying the −2 and −3 nodes on the spectrum of roles (in both 2004 and 2008), the Sadrist organization maintained the ability to trigger mechanisms to drive individuals to repopulate these nodes. Moreover, the Sadrist organization was also able to capture local police stations in many instances, thus controlling even the +2 nodes. The Sadrists were able to capture other state functions, including social services and adjudication. In short, unlike other organizations, the Sadrists could direct movement into multiple desired roles on the left side of the spectrum (−1, −2, −3) while capturing elements of the state. In response, the early US strategy concentrated mainly on influencing the general population, doing little to impede the Sadrists at the −2 and −3 levels.

The existence of "little Sadr Cities" in the Baghdad neighborhoods of Shula and Washash also enhanced Sadrist reach and power. These neighborhoods were relatively homogenous pockets of impoverished Shia that quickly generated fighters for JAM. The Sadrists also made inroads into some middle-class neighborhoods such as Kadhimiya.

This chapter proceeds by describing early Sadrist organization and the decimation of its militia in 2004. It then details the forces in its resurrection and its expansion into the "little Sadr cities" and Kadhimiya. Using a narrative of a US soldier based in Sadr City as an S2 (intelligence position), the chapter show how US strategy failed to match up against that of the Sadrists. The result of these developments was the creation of relatively unimpeded JAM "machine" able to ethnically cleanse many of Baghdad's Sunni residents from their homes.

7.2. The Immediate Post-Invasion Period

In the aftermath of the 2003 invasion, Muqtada Al-Sadr was able to immediately capitalize on his family's legitimacy and organizational networks. Even before the fall of the Baath Party in early April 2003, forces aligned with Muqtada al-Sadr had cleared regime forces from Sadr City (Cole, 2003a). The young cleric's followers captured ammunition depots, organized neighborhood militias, and reopened mosques. Sadr-initiated demonstrations brought crowds into the streets. Muqtada al-Sadr was the heir to a revered line of martyrs. Muhammad Baqir Al-Sadr (Sadr I) confronted the Baathist state in the 1970s. His cousin, Muhammad Sadiq Al-Sadr (Sadr II), gained a massive following in the 1990s. The cousins were brutally murdered by the Baathist regime and were subsequently recognized as great martyrs in Iraqi Shia narrative. Unlike other clerics, they had never fled Iraq. Given that the Sadr family remained and fought in Iraq, it had years to build up its popular support base, particularly from the poor, urban masses.

As Nicholas Krohley summarizes, "The 'Sadrists,' as they became known, networked through the religious institutions scattered among the district's estimated two million residents and, within a few short weeks, had revived elements of the late cleric's organization and begun the process of rekindling his mass movement" (Krohley, 2015, pp. 59–60). In supporting his communication-based theory of mobilization, Patel lays out the details of the early Sadrist organization:

> Immediately after the war, Sadr's mosques began coordinating the local provision of public goods, especially order. The Hikma Mosque, for example, quickly emerged as the principal coordinator of public goods provision and information generation in Sadr City. The local Sadr office, located in the Hikma mosque in summer of 2003, established twelve committees, each with a staff of 10–15 men. Each committee was responsible for a particular issue, such as Friday prayers, outreach, health services, media, religious edicts, Islamic law courts, electricity and telecommunications, and vice and virtue. Orders came from the central office, although only once or twice per week. These orders outline the key themes of the Friday sermons, leaving out day-to-day initiatives and activities of the mosque to local officials. (Patel, 2005, p. 26)

As previewed in Chapter 5, the re-establishment of a network of mosques created focal points for the gathering of like-minded supporters. The Sadrist mosque system provided a flow of information that served to coordinate expectations and actions. It also drew crowds that provided confidence in terms of safety in numbers. It may have also tapped into forces that go beyond communicative and rational choice mechanisms. In his coverage of the Iraqi war, the journalist Dexter Filkins repeatedly went to the Mohsin Mosque in Sadr City. As he describes in passages from his book *The Forever War*:

> The men would gather at the Mohsin Mosque, ten thousand of them even in the heat of summer. They were the downtrodden of Sadr City, the Shiite slum that took up most of eastern Baghdad. At the edge of the crowd, confident young men with guns but no uniforms searched those coming in. Among the supplicants, each carried his own prayer mat to cushion his knees from the street. The sermon was outdoors. The imam would exit the mosque and climb a ladder to a raised wooden platform and look out on the assembled men on their knees. The imam would place his hands at his side to signal the beginning of the prayer: There is no God but God and Mohammed is his prophet. Then someone in the crowd would call out, then a second man, and the rest of the men would join in. Raising their arms and shouting. In a few moments the mass of men would be throbbing and contracting like a beating heart. . . . As the months wore on I went there more and more. I'd stand at the front of the crowd, at the foot of the platform, underneath the imam, just to take it in, to feel the power. (Filkins, 2008, pp. 245–246)

Using his advantages, Moqtada al-Sadr quickly went about building the foundations of a parallel state. He ordered his followers to fill vacant government positions; he announced the formation of the Mahdi Army on July 18, 2003 (*The US Army in the Iraq War*, Vol. 1, 2019, pp. 182–183). With the control of government services and an armed force as well, "the Sadrists claimed the capital's Shi'a slums as their own" (Krohley, 2015, p. 60).

Conflict between this budding "state" and US forces came early. On August 13, 2003, a US helicopter approached a six-story transmission tower adorned at the top with the black flag of the Mahdi followers.[1] As acknowledged by US commanders, US forces tried to knock the flag from the tower. Anthony Shadid summarizes, "The incident provoked a day of anger and fervor in a Shiite neighborhood already on edge" (Shadid, 2005, p. 263). The act was seen as a religious insult, a purposeful provocation. A crowd quickly grew from one hundred to three thousand and US forces were compelled to respond. US forces were met with rocks, gunshots, and an RPG, with the US soldiers responding with force. The first armed clash between US forces and Sadr residents resulted in one Iraqi dead and four injured (Wilson 2003). After the incident, US commanders promised to reduce helicopter flights and ground patrols in the area in an attempt to reduce US military footprint and to pacify local Shia leaders calling for withdrawal (Wilson, 2003). Muqtada al-Sadr's spokesman, Qais al-Khaz'ali, had given the United States an ultimatum to stop helicopter flights and apologize, "otherwise we are not responsible for whatever reactions the US soldiers might face if they entered the city" (Wilson, 2003). Anger over US incursions undoubtedly helped drive Sadr City residents to opposition roles. In July 2003, before the August events, the number of JAM militia members in fighting units was estimated to be fewer than 1,000; by April 2004, the number had risen to 6,000 (West, 2009, p. 30).

7.3. The Early Distribution of Roles

In Sadr City, individuals populated the entire left side of the spectrum of roles, −1, −2, and −3, early on. At the −1 node, the legacy and martyrdom of Sadr I and Sadr II, along with the Sadrist organization of social services, created a potential well of volunteers who would cooperate in various non-armed ways with Sadrist non-state organizations. Friday prayers provided focal points and evidence of safety in numbers to move individuals to that position. Muqtada's sermons from the Great Mosque of Kufa were widely known.

At the −2 and −3 nodes, US actions sparked the emotion of anger to move individuals into JAM in either its local or more mobile forms. It is likely that some networks of poor young men, many with some military training, were motivated to join the militia. As the US Army history summarizes, "Now calling themselves Jaysh al-Mahdi, members of this Sadr paramilitary club sought to enlarge the organization by incorporating members of the network established by Mohammed Sadiq Sadr in the 1990s. Jaysh-al-Mahdi also absorbed some of the Shi'a soldiers of the Fedayeen Saddam who lacked employment after CPA Order 2 dissolved the Iraqi security organizations. Most of Jaysh al-Mahdi's members, however, were the uneducated Shi'a males who [*sic*] the Ba'ath repressed" (*The US Army in the Iraq War*, Vol. 1, 2019, p. 183).[2]

Amir Taha argues that JAM was built from the bottom up due to the new Iraq state's inability to demobilize former armed actors of the Saddam regime (Taha, 2019). In opposition to the more common view that JAM built upon the Sadrists networks of the 1990s, Taha sees four groups as most important: ex-combatants, student militias, criminals, and members of the 1990s troubled youth. As armed entrepreneurs, the ex-combatants were the most important for building a militia. Taha explains that they were drawn to the Sadrists because the Sadrists were forming a "state within a state" with political (Tayer al-Sadr), social (office of the Martyr Sadr), and armed wings (JAM). The ex-combatants had served a state before; they were inclined to serve a state-like organization again.

This collection was ready to commit violence and repression because that is all that they knew from their experience.

By any account, the JAM militia, formed within a few months, was nowhere close to being a disciplined fighting force. There was no formal hierarchy, no centralization, no real training.[3] Despite a lack of professionalization, Sadr increased the size of the militia, seized control of Sadr City, and also moved forces into the holy city of Najaf (*The US Army in the Iraq War*, Vol. 1, 2019, p. 182). In this early period, the United States was expecting to quickly leave Iraq. State projection of force (+2, +3) was very weak, if present at all. Neither side had a well-formulated strategy at this stage.

7.4. The 2004 April Uprising

On April 3, 2004, Coalition officials suspended al-Sadr's newspaper, *al-Hawza*, for 60 days and arrested his top lieutenant, Mustafa Yaqoubi, on an outstanding warrant in the murder of Abd al-Majid al-Khoei. US intelligence analysts predicted that Sadr would respond with three or four days of demonstrations that would quickly tail off (Ricks, 2007, p. 337).

Al-Sadr responded in a sermon delivered in the southern city of Kufa. He declared, "I and my followers of the believers have come under attack from the occupiers, imperialism, and the appointees. Be on the utmost readiness and strike them where you meet them" (Ricks, 2007, p. 337). JAM fighters hurried from Sadr City to take positions around important shrines in the south. They overran the Italian and Ukrainian forces guarding CPA offices in Nasariya and Kut. JAM forces also took on the Spanish and Bulgarian forces in Najaf and Karbala, but were repulsed with the aid of US reinforcements. In Sadr City itself, JAM forces killed 8 US soldiers and wounded another 51. With an abundance of munitions, JAM units fired mortars into US bases. They also took control of all seven police stations in the Sadr City district (along with a significant number of weapons).

Sadr's moves occurred alongside a Sunni uprising centered in Fallujah after the killing and mutilation of Blackwater contractor guards. Despite the general chaos in Iraq, the United States regrouped, with the US Army's 1st Armored Division taking most of Karbala. While full of fervor, JAM lacked organization and command control.[4] Units took heavy losses. Without centralized control, and fighting across six cities, Sadr could not coordinate attacks or maintain ceasefires. A June ceasefire was officially in place until August. Sadr called for renewed fighting on August 5, with significant casualties in Sadr City but far more in Najaf. By the last week of August, JAM was on the brink of disintegration. While suffering only a handful of deaths themselves, Coalition forces killed

1,500 JAM fighters (*The US Army in the Iraq War*, Vol. 1, 2019, p. 339). Muqtada holed up in the Imam Ali shrine. Prime Minister Allawi urged the US forces to "finish the job" (*The US Army in the Iraq War*, Vol. 1, 2019, p. 338).

In the end, Muqtada al-Sadr was forced to sue for peace. An effective cease-fire was only reached through the intervention of Grand Ayatollah Sistani, culminating in an agreement that included demands for the departure of JAM forces from the city of Najaf and its shrines, creation of a demilitarized zone in Najaf and Kufa, and the appointment of Iraqi security forces to guard shrines. Following the agreement, Sadr departed the holy city of Najaf. General Casey, the Commander of MNF-I, did not regret letting Muqtada al-Sadr escape from this dire situation. Casey stated, "I didn't see [JAM] as the chief threat. In August in Najaf there was kind of a countrywide uprising. But I would say that was more of a . . . tactical threat. By that I mean it was a lot of violence in a short period of time, but it never threatened to undermine the whole mission. The main threat was the former regime insurgency" (*The US Army in the Iraq War*, Vol. 1, 2019, p. 339). General Casey came to see the US operations in Najaf as creating a "model." The United States, along with some Iraqi security personnel for legitimacy, would do war-fighting as a "stick" against insurgents. Quick economic reconstruction (226 projects and $50 million) would then form a "carrot" to win the population over to the government side (*The US Army in the Iraq War*, Vol. 1, 2019, p. 340).

7.5. The Sadrists and JAM Regenerate, 2004–2005

By the end of August 2004, Coalition forces had devastated the loose collection of fighting groups known as JAM. Two years later, JAM would march through much of Baghdad clearing the Sunni population, spreading violence and death, and capturing key parts of the state. This regeneration was achieved through multiple means: recruitment through networks and associated social norms, heightened mobilization in reaction to Sunni terrorist attacks, the influx of Iranian weapons and technology, and the capture of Iraqi ministries and state resources after the 2005 elections.[5] These can be addressed in turn.

Coalition forces had killed 1,500 JAM fighters in 2004. How would these numbers be replenished and increased? Undoubtedly, many different mechanisms drove individuals into local Sadrist militias (−2). The template lists five mechanisms motivating movement from −1 to −2:

- Social norms of reciprocity
- Norms of honor/vengeance

- Anger
- Safety in numbers with local population as reference point
- Material incentives.

The motivating power of material incentives for young male residents of the Sadr City slum are straightforward. The effects of existing networks and their related social norms of reciprocity are more debatable. There is much debate as to how much tribal relations and norms survived the modernization process in Baghdad.[6] Some scholars highlight migration patterns from the rural Iraqi south to Sadr City, with rural-to-urban migrants bringing their tribal and family norms with them. As one researcher noted: "Shia areas like Karada with high education and employment levels are not tribal based communities; no one describes themselves by tribe, they are instead known by their families. But when Baghdad was exposed to immigration from rural areas, Sadr City was established and brought tribal traditions with them" (Carpenter, 2014, p. 109).

There are many stories about mobilization in Sadr City, no doubt reflecting the reality of the many paths into the Sadrist militias. One interviewee (R1) supplied the following narrative about the nature of JAM development in Sadr City. R1 had owned a factory in Sadr City (then called Saddam City) in Baghdad during most of the 1990s and had intensive interactions with his employees. Many of the poorer Shia in the south were moved into what became Saddam City by the Qasim regime (1958–1963). These poor newcomers were later recruited into Saddam Fedayeen. They had military training and were accustomed to indoctrination. Then they joined JAM. It was a long and logical progression for a poorer and somewhat marginalized population. Also, members of the Shia Fedayeen military stationed in the south came to Baghdad in the post-invasion period to join JAM, so more than just local men were joining. Capitalizing on these primary groups, JAM could mobilize networks rather than single individuals. Of course, criminal networks also joined and often pursued their own agenda under JAM's umbrella.

Organizational and logistical developments also drove the regeneration of the Sadrists and JAM. Realizing their extreme disadvantage versus the US in weaponry, the Sadrists reached out to Iran and Qassem Soleimani, the commander of Iran's Islamic Revolutionary Guards. JAM benefited through transfers of ammunition and weapons as well as specialized training in the use of explosives (Felter and Fishman, 2008; Worsnop, 2016, p. 352). (Iran would later switch support from JAM to Special Groups, but only in late 2006.) In the words of a British intelligence officer, "They got sophisticated IED technology that was above what our countermeasures could defeat. They came back [with] different structure, covert, cellular, insurgency, closer to terrorism in its tactics than an open insurgency" (*The US Army in the Iraq War*, Vol. 1, 2019, p. 392).

Another source was probably even more important. With the 2005 elections, the winning Shia coalition of parties negotiated the control of ministries as part of the spoils process. Sadr bargained for control of ministries of health, human services, and transportation. By capturing the resource flows from these ministries, Mutada al-Sadr was able to increase and solidify the work of neighborhood offices controlled by JAM. The JAM-affiliated Office of the Martyr Sadr (OMS) distributed food and adjudicated disputes. As discussed at many junctures of this work, JAM also infiltrated and supplied local police stations. In effect, the Sadrists and JAM were the de facto government in Sadr City, controlling service provision, local adjudication, and security. As such, the Sadrists were able to build up a patronage network, and develop a consistent stream of financial and material resources. These resources could be used to fund militias and to leverage militia members' cooperation.

In Alec Worsnop's analysis, by 2006 JAM had increased its military effectiveness through both enhanced resource control and better military training.[7] Although JAM was hardly a superior fighting force in comparison to many conventional armies, JAM was now able to both initiate violence and maintain ceasefires.

7.6. Sunni Violence, AQI, and the Focus of US Forces

As outlined in Chapter 5, Sunnis did not possess the advantages for mobilization held by their Shia rivals. They had no strong territorial base similar to Sadr City; Sunni religious practice did not produce focal points or safety-in-numbers mechanisms; former Baathist networks had been decimated. Violent resistance against the US occupation would come more from without than within.

Given their relative weakness against both the US occupation forces and the Shia, AQI and other Sunni militias engaged in what Michael Boyle has categorized as "denial" attacks (Boyle, 2009). These attacks are aimed at denying the creation of a viable state. By killing large numbers of civilians, insurgents can deny the legitimacy of the reconstructing state. In terms of the analytical framework, this strategy is not meant to recruit individuals into −2 or −3 roles, or even to create informants and sympathizers at −1. Rather, the goal of mass violence is to keep people at the 0 position, to instill a freezing fear in individuals, and perhaps to inculcate contempt for the US occupation forces and their Iraqi allies by proving their inability to provide security. Daniel Byman (2015, pp. 51–54) describes the broader al-Qaeda strategy as one of attrition. The United States lacks staying power, so relentless terrorist attacks will wear it down and drive it out of the region in the medium to long run.

In either denial and/or attrition, Sunni militia bombings and AQI suicide attacks spread heavy civilian death. The Baghdad neighborhood of Dora provides a prime example. In 2004, Sunni militants bombed two churches in Dora, driving out the neighborhood's long-standing Christian community; the following year, Sunni insurgents attacked vulnerable Shia pilgrims passing through Dora on the way to the Najaf and Karbala shrines. As summarized by journalist Sam Dagher, "The predominately Sunni Arab district has become a byword for lawlessness and mayhem" (Dagher, 2007). Sunni insurgents, including most famously Abu Musab al-Zarqawi, hit one civilian target after another—the March 2, 2004, Ashura bombing killing 140, the Najaf and Karbala shrine attacks in December 2004, the February 2005 attacks when Zarqawi operatives directed five suicide bombers to Baghdad who managed to kill 39 and wound 150 during the Ashura procession, the April 2005 car bombings, and so on.

There were two major effects of these Sunni attacks on civilian targets. First, these attacks sharpened the sectarian character of violence. Singularly, Zarqawi's relentless terrorist attacks against Shia targets, in conjunction with virulent anti-Shia rhetoric, produced motivating anger and desires for revenge. As seen in its most striking form in the bombing at Samarra discussed below, Zarqawi successfully set off Shia versus Sunni violent spirals.

Second, the often spectacular nature of Sunni attacks took attention from the reorganization of Shia insurgent forces and the Mahdi Army. US military leaders, General Casey in particular, believed that the most important insurgent threat came from members of the former regime. Moqtada al-Sadr and JAM were a secondary "tactical threat" (*The US Army in the Iraq War*, Vol. 1, 2019, p. 339).

7.7. US Strategy: The Narrative of an S2

While the Sadrists were rebuilding, developing capabilities at the −3, −2, and −1 levels and gaining control of many police stations (+2), the US strategy was an early form of clear, hold, build (CHB). The following narrative of an Army intelligence officer stationed in Sadr City in 2004–2005 helps clarify both specific aspects of the contest in Sadr City and the US strategy.

In the US Army, staff positions are designated by number and letter. S1 deals with personnel; S2 intelligence; S3 operations; S4 logistics; S5 planning. This section is based on interview material from a Brigade level S2 working in Sadr City in 2004–2005 (referred to below as "R2"). His job involved partnering with the police and national security forces, developing information to confront IEDs, and collecting intelligence relevant to US-JAM competition.

The respondent (R2) saw the US-JAM struggle in this period in terms of population-centric "hearts and minds." He stated that the US forces and JAM were in a constant struggle for the loyalty of the population. Sadr would make a move and the US forces would counter, a back and forth that repeated. "It was a competition for trustworthiness. JAM did not always win that competition despite home-field advantage." In terms of the framework, the United States worked to move individuals to +1, while JAM countered to move individuals to −1.

The game was played at other nodes as well. At the broader level, JAM wanted to keep the pressure on the US military and its Iraqi counterparts. Using Sadr City as a "free zone," militia members could venture out to mortar the Green Zone and plant IEDs (attacking, +3). In a subtle interpretation of JAM strategy, R2 believed that Sadr forces calibrated their attacks on US forces. The level of violence against the US forces was enough to keep US forces occupied and off guard, but was never done at a level that would precipitate a severe and sustained US backlash. JAM seemed to target US soldiers at the company level and below. They never tried to assassinate high-level US officers. In this period after the Sistani-brokered ceasefire, Sadr forces did not wish to provoke US actions that would precipitate the level of casualties experienced in the spring and summer of 2004. They were clearly not going to cease their insurgency either.

The biggest JAM target in this period was the local Iraqi security forces, the police (+2). As mentioned above, Sadr forces took control of all seven major police stations during the April uprising. The police had "melted away." These police stations would become the focus of the back-and-forth game described by R2 during a period of 80 days of combat. US forces countered by first physically retaking the buildings. They did so under the cover of night. Second, there were patrols out of the police station, but only by US forces. AC 130 gunships went after rocket attackers. Bradley fighting vehicles were employed to counter IEDs and to shoot down alleyways.

Such kinetic tactics would not be sufficient in the long term. US forces needed to find supportive tribal leaders to help build up local security, but it was difficult to ascertain effective allies. Intelligence officers were tasked with coding tribes as pro- or anti-Coalition. R2 assessed the loyalty of tribal leaders by their level of risk-taking. If a sheikh took risks by providing intelligence or by publicly associating with US forces, a high loyalty score would be assigned. Intelligence officers also identified higher and lower hostile areas of Sadr City. The most hostile was the industrial area in the northern corner of the district, home to IED makers. The friendliest area was on Palestine Street. Both highways on the north and south sides of Sadr City were laced with IEDs. Vietnam Street was nicknamed "where Americans go to die." These area designations were used to develop plans and rules of engagement (ROE). Unmanned aerial vehicles also helped monitor the district.

US forces established a level of control, even if they did not come close to the level implied by the term "clear" in the CHB strategy. With the improved level of security, US forces did attempt to move on to the "hold" and "build" parts of the sequence. The "hold" centered on rebuilding the police (+2) presence through joint Iraqi-US patrols instead of just US patrols. R2 said this was an uncertain move. Because the US military leadership believed that a massive purge of the Iraqi local police forces would create significant political problems, US forces were forced to bring back and retain police who had recently melted away in the medium term (the major purge would come in 2007). When police were hired, a local tribal chief would come with a list. The US forces also changed standard operating procedures (SOPs) and ROE in order to present a less visible and less annoying presence, as well as to reduce the chances of collateral damage. The US military reduced their use of armored vehicles and told soldiers to avoid crowds on Fridays.

The "build" involved projects to develop electricity, sewage, and other public works projects. The US forces divided Sadr City into roughly 30 zones. Each company-level unit was supposed to take on a "SWET" (sewage, water, electrical, trash) project to build up infrastructure. Commanders made use of CERP (Commander's Emergency Response Program) money to fund these projects in their designated zone. R2 pointed out problems with the "build." The US forces had not developed communications with local leaders or surveyed what locals believed were their own highest needs. As a result, the projects were often overly ad hoc. Moreover, Sadrists took credit for the public works projects.[8]

While rebuilding the police (establishing +2), the "hold" and "build" efforts aimed at building trust in the general population. In terms of our framework, the goal was to move significant numbers of individuals to the +1 position, supportive of the government and willing to provide information to the counterinsurgents. R2 did not believe that these efforts were successful. In fact, R2 stated the single biggest problem in Sadr City was the lack of social trust. He posited historical reasons for his view. There had never been a basis for social trust in Sadr City. Before the invasion, Saddam Hussein's regime targeted Sadr City as a focus for repression and religious persecution. For R2, JAM continued this high-level monitoring. A type of surveillance state existed both pre- and post-invasion. For R2, Sadr City's residents found it normal not to trust and not to talk. While some individuals would talk to US forces on patrol, few would risk going to the base itself. The local Iraqi police were also not trusted. Sadr City residents preferred to go to a personally reliable contact rather than to the formal local security institution. After his experience in Iraq, R2 concluded that if any conflict hinges on the formation of a useful local police, the intervening force is likely to lose that conflict and should avoid getting into it in the first place.

As mentioned above, the US forces did not go after local JAM militias and military organization (the −2 and −3 nodes). They did not do so mainly because they were not able to do so, at least not without significant costs. R2 believed that the main JAM leaders did not openly meet with the US forces. Instead, JAM sent mid-level commanders. The top leadership remained mysterious to R2, who was indeed a brigade-level intelligence officer. R2 stated bluntly that the United States was never able to fully get a grasp on JAM networks during his 2004–2005 tour. At one point, R2 came across a JAM map of Sadr City that divided the district into zones of control as well as delineating commanders.[9] He also came to realize that the Shia in Sadr City had significant connections with the south and Basra, probably based on tribal ties.

As is evident in R2's narrative, the US Army was practicing a form of CHB long before the publication of FM 3-24. In hindsight, there was never any "clear" in this process. After defeating JAM in August 2004, US forces did not consider JAM the primary threat, and perhaps not a significant threat at all. The US forces appeared to tolerate the Sadrists and JAM if they did not cross certain boundaries and were happy to allow them to perform certain welfare functions (Taha, 2019, p. 1). Without the "clear," the "build" and "hold" efforts were superficial and relatively inconsequential.

7.8. Juxtaposing US and JAM Strategies in Sadr City in 2004–2005

Based on the S2's narrative and supporting information, we can outline the rival strategies of the United States and JAM (Figure 7.1). Following tenets of CHB, the US forces attempted to move the population from −1 to +1. In R2's words, there was a competition for trust. The US forces also fought an uphill battle to rebuild the +2 position. In a point that I will emphasize below, US forces did not go after the −2 and −3 level insurgents in the Sadr City.

Sadrist/JAM strategy made moves at every position on the spectrum. This full spectrum strategy should not be surprising. Sadr City was, as its name baldly points out, the Sadrists home neighborhood.

+3: JAM forces harassed the US military with mortar and IED attacks.

+2: JAM forces first took over the police stations, then infiltrated them during the US efforts to rebuild.

−1, 0, +1: JAM built their own social service offices to compete with the US and government in the "hearts and minds" competition. Mosques controlled by Muqtada al-Sadr provided an outlet for anti-occupation resentments, as well as focal points for demonstrations and communication.

−2, −3: JAM built up militias and also its capacity for moving out from Sadr City with more mobile units. After the 2004 defeat, JAM consolidates and professionalizes, at least to a degree, its forces.

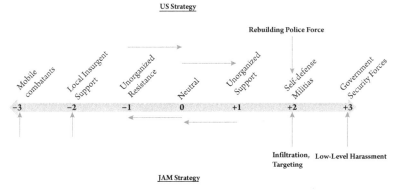

Figure 7.1. Juxtaposition of US and JAM Strategies, 2004–2006.

As Figure 7.1 illustrates, both US forces and JAM competed over the loyalty of the unarmed population, represented by the −1, 0, +1 nodes, and for control of the local police. JAM also put calibrated pressure on surrounding US forces while avoiding provocations that would have brought down severe retaliation. The major strategic asymmetry clearly can be seen in the −2 and −3 nodes. The US forces, either through a desire for a smaller footprint or a lack of intelligence, did not work to destroy or degrade the JAM militia. The force would grow both in numbers and in fighting ability. After the destruction of the Samarra shrine in February 2006, JAM would be unleashed from its Sadr City stronghold.

7.9. The Organization and Inroads of the Sadrists outside Sadr City, 2003–2005: "Little Sadr Cities"

While Sadr City was the "capital" of the Sadrists and served as a primary source for Shia power, other Baghdad neighborhoods saw a deepening of the sectarian cleavage and the development of Shia-based organization. Spikes in violence in Baghdad as a whole cannot be fully understood without a consideration of the spread and operation of JAM from Sadr City to other neighborhoods. This set of neighborhoods can be divided into two categories— "little Sadr Cities" and middle-class Shia neighborhoods.

The main "little Sadr Cities" are the neighborhoods of Shula and Washash (see Figure 7.2).[10] Chapter 6 on Ghazaliyah has already addressed Shula. Shula was a poor, largely homogenous Shia neighborhood which served as the base of attacks against the Sunni and their militias to the south in Ghazaliyah. Washash lies a short distance northeast of the Green Zone. Washash shared some struc- tural features with Sadr City. Above all, it was poor. It has been one of Baghdad's poorest areas dominated by ramshackle buildings and usually was described as a "slum" (Kukis, 2006a). The population, about 40,000 at the time of the invasion, was predominately Shia, but in a difference from Sadr City, it held significant pockets of Sunnis. At the time of the invasion, the district was a fault line between the two groups.

As in Sadr City, in the period after the invasion, US forces generally stayed out of Washash, leaving a vacuum in the wake of the invasion. US forces did not seriously contest militia power until 2007.[11] Unlike in Sadr City, where the Sadrists rapidly filled in the vacuum, Washash would witness a slower and bloodier process of Shia consolidation. While US forces did not compete for control in Washash in the 2003–2005 period, the Mahdi Army (JAM), rogue elements of JAM, the Badr Organization, and Sunni extremists including AQI did (Gaughen, 2007).

The Sadrists and JAM would come to win this competition. At first, the contest was defined by spiraling violence between Sunni and Shia forces. From 2003 to the summer of 2005, Sunni groups may have committed the bulk of these attacks, targeting polling places in the January 2005 elections in the adjacent Iskan neighborhood, marking judges for assassination, and car-bombing the local SCIRI office (Gaughen, 2007). Shia responded by attacking a Sunni mosque, killing four.

The next step for the Sadrists was to establish a wider organizational and institutional base in the neighborhood. As in other areas, the Sadrists established a social-political office, taking over many basic state functions. During the previous regime, the Baathists had converted the local Mustafa Mosque into a Party office. By 2006, the Sadrists converted the mosque/Baath office into their own command center (Rosen 2008). This office remained as a Sadrist

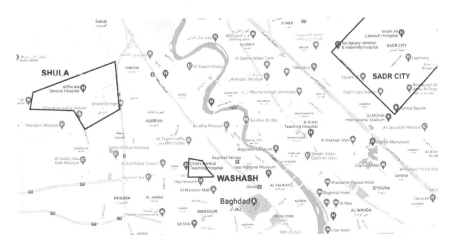

Figure 7.2. Sadr City and "Little Sadr Cities."
Source: Map of central Baghdad. Annotated Google street map.

center for distribution of much-needed humanitarian services even after the US forces raided this building in 2007 (Rosen, 2008). As in other areas, Sadrists took advantage of abandoned Sunni dwellings to dole out housing for displaced Shia coming from contested neighborhoods. As in other areas, the Sadrists and connected militias were in league with the local police. Local residents of Washash associated the local police with the Shia militias (Rosen, 2008).

These developments put the Sadrists into a superior position versus the Sunnis in Washash. In the period in question, the Sadrists and the Badr Organization were cooperating in the neighborhood, so JAM was not affected by Shia in-fighting. In short, by early 2006 the Sadrists had both a local logistical base and cooperative Shia partners to put a program of systematic ethnic cleansing into motion.

7.10. The Organization and Inroads of the Sadrists outside Sadr City, 2003–2005: Middle-Class Shia Neighborhoods

The poorest and most homogenously Shia neighborhoods served as the foundation for Sadrist organizations and militias. However, several middle-class Shia neighborhoods would become absorbed into the Sadrist orbit as well. Kadhimiyah is part of "old Baghdad," with a history and architecture dating back centuries. At the time of the invasion, it housed a middle class and mainly Shia population. It was the home of Ahmed Chalabi. Shia heritage was pronounced, symbolized by the Kadhim shrine, the assumed burial place of the seventh Shia imam (Musa al-Kadhim) and his grandson and ninth Shia imam (Muhammed al-Jawad). Immediately after the fall of Saddam, Baghdad residents surrounded the golden-domed shrine to resume previously banned Shia rituals. With the ban on Friday prayers lifted, clerics immediately came to the shrine to lead them.[12] Journalist Anthony Shadid made the following comments on the events he witnessed at the Kadhim shrine:

> This explosion of ritual was a true sign of actual liberation and unin-hibited spiritual rebirth. Here was a remembrance of things past and present, of all the losses across time conjoined into one. In chants and banners, the symbolism was unmistakable. Here, as astonished American soldiers watched, was the reclamation of a 1,300-year-old faith. "The oppression is gone, however long it took!" the crowd chanted, their voices rising as they surged toward the Kadhimiyah shrine, its four minarets newly draped in black banners, its courtyard taking on the air of carnival. "The tyrant is gone!" (Shadid, 2005, p. 165)[13]

But if there was carnival, there was also chaos. As across Baghdad, the police, and most other public service, melted away in Kadhimiyah.

7.10.1. A Narrative of the Restoration of Order in Kadhimiyah

One resident (RK) produced the following narrative about the restoration of order in Kadhimiyah:

After the invasion in 2003, the local police disappeared, leaving a vacuum in the immediate neighborhood. RK estimated that 70% of the police ran away, probably to avoid vengeance. Within the emerging anarchy, one older Shia cleric stepped in to organize locals. Using his personal connections, he recruited small committees of two or three individuals to lead in 10 different areas. In effect, the cleric managed to quickly create an informal local governance and information network. RK believed that sometimes a tribal leader or well-known businessperson could have served in the role of "first actor" in these highly localized informal structures. In RK's case, he saw the organizing cleric as a representative of Sistani, whom RK emulated. RK saw the local collective action as following Sistani's directions.

RK's local area would not remain isolated for long. RK said the informal network became incorporated into the Sadrist sphere. The Mahdi Army could use connections with local individuals to consolidate their power. RK said that locals had good reason to join up with the Sadrists because JAM could provide guns (and security) in a highly unstable and violent time. The ability to protect oneself was more important than other material incentives. The Sadrists went beyond security provision, however. RK said that the Office of the Martyr Sadr (OMS) took over control of social services in 2005. The Sadrists not only took over police functions, but also took on an adjudication function. RK said that while the former government may have existed in some official form, it had been totally discredited. The official police and the court system were "sort of a joke," not capable at all.

In the meantime, Kadhimiyah, like much of Baghdad as a whole, was becoming ethnically unmixed. Although I did not ask RK about control of housing in his local area, it is likely the OMS was involved in placing the 2,000 Shia families that fled into Kadhimiyah seeking safety (Wong and Cave, 2007). RK did provide a story of some of his relatives' experiences in finding housing. Some relatives were living in Dora, a Sunni stronghold. One night they received a "bullet letter" threatening them if they remained in the neighborhood. They moved to a new Shia area where a friend told them about an empty house. Soon after moving in, their son was taken in and interrogated by local Sadrists trying to verify the family's Shia identity. Because the son was named Omar, a traditionally Sunni moniker, the Sadrists were suspicious. While the family moved into a vacant home, they had to pay rent to the previous family, who had moved under pressure across the ethnic fault line. Unfortunately, their own house in Dora had been taken by an AQI member and was half-demolished in subsequent fighting with US forces. This story shows some of the dynamics of Baghdad's sectarian unmixing—threats of violence, flight to emptied houses, and verification of identity by militias.

In sum, RK laid out the following process for the restoration of order: (1) a local cleric, with authority deriving from Ayatollah Sistani, organized networks to produce order in a small area; (2) Sadr representatives brought this local network into their broader organization, mainly through offer of guns and security; (3) Sadr/JAM consolidated their power through the opening of social service provision offices in the form of the OMS and through their oversight and facilitation of housing during the period of ethnic separation.

The violent and sectarian nature of this process was intensified by the grisly bombing of the Kadhim Shrine on March 2, 2004, on Ashura, the holiest day on the Shia calendar. Three bombs were detonated in approximately one-minute intervals—one inside the shrine's gate, one in the courtyard, one outside the shrine in front of the Sharaf Hotel—killing and maiming several hundred pilgrims.[14] As Shadid commented, "The carnage itself sent the message of approaching anarchy, of the nearing of an abyss, as if it was understood that the Americans could say nothing to mitigate the most recent tragedies or promise anything that would end the violence" (Shadid, 2005, p. 357). Although Shia and Sunni leaders called for peace and unity at the time, such high-profile violence inevitably fueled a security dilemma, with both sides arming for protection and both sides seeing a heightened threat.

Two *New York Times* journalists, Edward Wong and Damien Cave, visited Kadhimiyah in the spring of 2007. Their report showed the lasting effects of the process described by RK in 2003–2005 (Wong and Cave, 2007). Wong and Cave stated that the Mahdi Army controlled most of Kadhimiyah. In a blurring of lines between state and militia, a Sadr loyalist led the local Iraqi Army Battalion with its 300 soldiers. The Sadrists also continued to provide food and medical aid and run underground Islamic courts. Moreover, Sadr-connected militias collected "taxes" from businesses. One southern area, however, was controlled by the Badr Organization. The Sadrists may have been the primary player in Kadhimiyah, and essentially the "government" in the most basic sense. However, the process in Kadhimiyah hardly led to a settled political and military situation. Wong and Cave describe US military interviewees as describing Kadhimiyah as a "place . . . where militia leaders, Iraqi politicians, criminals and clerics intersect and compete; a place where the Iraqi soldier protecting residents on Monday may be collecting bribes for a militia on Tuesday, praying at the mosque on Friday and firing at American troops over the weekend" (Wong and Cave, 2007).

7.11. Spiraling Violence
2006–2007: Baghdad Descends

On the morning of February 22, 2006, forces associated with AQI and Zarqawi bombed the al-Askari shrine, one of the holiest sites in Shia Islam as the location of the graves of the tenth (Ali al-Hadi) and eleventh (Hassan al-Askari) imams. Shia militias responded with attacks on Sunni targets across Iraq. In Baghdad, many of these attacks originated in Sadr City. As Bing West wrote of the Shia response,

> Urged on by Sadr, impassioned militiamen leaped into cars, vans, and minitrucks and sped out of Sadr City in East Baghdad to ransack Sunni neighborhoods and mosques. (West, 2009, p. 114)

Shia attacks produced Sunni counterattacks, leading to spiraling sectarian violence, as West's continued description of the days after the Samarra bombing.

> Unchecked by the Iraqi Army, the JAM gangs drove in packs of four to ten cars, cruising through Sunni neighborhoods to snatch the unwary, shoot randomly at houses, and speed away. Al-Qaeda struck back the next day on what was called the Brick Factory Road, a few miles south of Sadr City. Men in police uniforms stopped a dozen cars at checkpoint and machine-gunned all the occupants, killing forty-five Shiites. Two days later, JAM retaliated. A lengthy caravan of JAM toughs left Sadr City and drove south through the Shiite enclave of Jisr Diyala to the Sunni district of Salman Pak on the east bank of the Tigris. As Sunnis hid in their homes, the JAM took over the mosque, hoisted the green Shiite flag, and slapped posters of Muqtada Sadr on the stalls in the markets. (West, 2009, p. 116)

Here was a classic example of the effects of the emotion of anger. One side made it clear that they intended to hurt the other side by destroying one of its most sacred symbolic and visible sites—the Golden Dome of the al-Askari mosque. The other side, in turn, retaliated in revenge. Violence was not just a lashing out. Violence clearly targeted neighborhoods and public spaces of the offending side.

Soon, both sides were engaged in sectarian cleansing. The US Army history picked out the following passage from an interviewee for a representative example of Sunni tactics:

> The area we lived [on the western edge of Baghdad] was mostly Sunni, but there were several Shi'ite families. After the Samarra bombings, all

the Shi'ite families got threat letters from al-Qaeda in Iraq. The notes were delivered to every Shi'ite house. The letters said we were dirty collaborators working with the Americans, the Iranians, and the Jews and said we had 72 hours to leave. We didn't bother to take anything from the house, just some blankets for the children because it was cold weather then.[15]

AQI and Sunnis attacked in Ghazaliyah and Ameriyah as well as al-Jiad and Dora. The small Shia minority in Adhamiyah was completely chased out, with similar results seen in the western Baghdad suburbs of Abu Ghraib and Haswah.

Shia armed elements and supporters were more powerful sectarian cleansers than their Sunni counterparts, however. The Sadrists and JAM had already practiced their basic strategy and tactics in some neighborhoods before the 2006 conflagration. By 2006, there was effectively a model for expunging Sunnis and achieving Shia consolidation of a neighborhood. First, JAM needed to identify Sunni targets. Second, JAM would threaten these targets. Third, JAM would carry out threats against those Sunnis who refused to leave. Fourth, Sadrist offices would help displaced Shia occupy the now empty residences of the Sunni targets. JAM carried out this program with ruthless efficiency. A US raid found militia documents identifying "virtuous families" fit to stay, drafts of threatening letters to be delivered to more Sunni homes, and lists of houses where Shia families have replaced Sunni families (Kukis, 2006a). Some Sunni families received a threat in the form of a DVD that included images of houses being blown up (Kukis, 2006a). When Sunni families did not comply, they were viciously targeted. Often the male head of the household was kidnapped, tortured, and then killed. Corpses were dumped on Washash streets; one specific location came to be known as "body street" (Kukis, 2006b).

Despite its clear abilities, JAM did not perform its sectarian cleansing on its own. There was also participation by police units and support by Shia political elites. In many areas, the population saw the police as an extension of JAM, with good reason. Sometimes police participation was tacit, other times active. As reported in the US Army history: "In some instances, Iraqi security forces allied with JAM used the checkpoints to divert Sunnis to secondary checkpoints—manned by militia death squads—on side roads or behind concrete walls where Sunnis could be abducted or shot" (*The US Army in the Iraq War*, Vol. 1, 2019, p. 571). Just as importantly, Prime Minister Maliki did little to stem JAM violence. Maliki bypassed the military's chain of command to order army raids on Sunnis. The US Army history states, "The Prime Minister was essentially orchestrating raids out of Sadr City against Sunni enclaves in the capital" (*The US Army in the Iraq War*, Vol. 1, 2019, p. 627. Despite General Casey's protests,

Maliki was defiant. He believed that civil war was less of a threat than the return of the Sunni Baathist regime (*The US Army in the Iraq War*, Vol. 1, 2019, p. 585).

Once a neighborhood was transformed into a Shia dominated stronghold, it became the base for cleansing an adjacent neighborhood. Militia violence was followed by JAM and Sadrists taking over each neighborhood's social services. The JAM cleansing machine moved west and south. Across the Tigris, JAM cleansed the mixed neighborhoods of Hurriyah and Washash; east of the Tigris, JAM turned Sha'ab and Hayy al Basateen from mixed to Shia; in Shia majority 9 Nissan and Rustamiyah, Sunni minorities were chased out. It took the US military some time before it realized that the violence was conducted by mainstream JAM forces rather than rogue elements (*The US Army in the Iraq War*, Vol. 1, 2019, p. 628).

This systematic sectarian unmixing was accompanied by stunning levels and qualities of violence. In the period after the Samarra bombing, Baghdad's murder rate tripled. Soon, 30–40 corpses were delivered to the Baghdad morgue each day (*The US Army in the Iraq War*, Vol. 1, 2019, p. 541). South of Baghdad in the town of Suwayrah, in mid-2006, local police collected 339 bodies from the river, but considered that only a fraction of the total. One local fisherman told reporters, "We used to fetch them out but now there are so many we leave them. Otherwise, there would be no time for fishing."[16] The Sunnis were also doing their best on the other side of the cleavage. On November 23, 2006, Sunni forces launched six car bomb attacks within a 90-minute period, killing 181 and wounding 247 more in a Shia stronghold (*The US Army in the Iraq War*, Vol. 1, 2019, p. 629). Yet, in the post-Samarra period, eight times as many people were murdered than killed by car bombs (*The US Army in the Iraq War*, Vol. 1, 2019, p. 544).

7.12. Narrative of an MiTT Officer Working in Washash, 2006–2007: An Illustration of US Actions and Abilities in the Aftermath of Sectarian Cleansing

How did US forces operate in the environment described above? R3 deployed to Baghdad as a member of a Military Transition Team (MiTT) working with Iraqi Army trainees in the Washash neighborhood described above in 2006. As mentioned, US forces had mainly stayed out of Washash in the years immediately following the invasion. Operation Together Forward in September 2006 was one of the first major actions. The first US Command Outpost wasn't established in the neighborhood until August 2007. Thus R3 entered after Shia had taken control. At the time of his arrival, R3 believed the neighborhood had become overwhelmingly Shia in population.

The mission was to partner with an Iraqi Infantry Battalion. While the patrols of Washash were conducted solely by US units, Iraqi and US troops jointly handled checkpoints. R3 had participated in Operation Together Forward (July 9–October 26) and judged it a failure. In his view, the operation had little chance of success and worked to expose Iraqi units to retaliation. R3's unit was based on FOB Prosperity in the Green Zone. They commuted out every day to the Iraqi Battalion HQ at Muthenna Air Base. The day there began with a one-hour report on attacks, prisoners, and so on. They then made a 24-hour operational plan. Much of the training was very basic in nature.

Iraqi soldiers were not vetted, at least to R3's knowledge. They had been levied en masse, coming from the same locality, city, area. They had no incentive to fight JAM. JAM could credibly threaten any soldier who went against the Sadrists. JAM had exhibited great capacity for kidnapping in the area. Undoubtedly, JAM had infiltrated the unit. In addition, R3 said he had no interaction with the local police. He believed they were aligned with either Sadr or Badr and there was really no point in talking with them. In fact, R3 could recognize no actual police function.

R3 reported that US forces went 6–7 months without any success in finding arms caches or capturing targets in Washash. The problem was a lack of intelligence. R3 never received actionable information. He never saw a network diagram of insurgent organization or any maps outlining major Sadrist presence. R3 said his unit received no intelligence from above at all. Success came through two sources. First, the arrival of a savvy Sunni intelligence officer (S2) helped to bring down three valuable targets, including a vehicle borne improvised explosive device (VBIED) factory in quick succession. R3 believed that the unit had hit the "jackpot" with this officer and his abilities. But apparently the officer was too successful. He was quickly dismissed.

R3 believed that his biggest successes may have come from the fact that he learned some Arabic. He had one year in college and trained himself to learn basic words. He could then listen in on radio broadcasts and hear when Iraqi soldiers were talking about attacks and bombs. He could understand if they attributed the attacks to Shia or Sunni, and understand what actions they attributed to Shia insurgents. He could also read Iraqi intelligence reports, and examine the rosters.

When asked about successes and failures in policy, R3 described a lack of proper incentives for Iraqi soldiers. They had no "rotation off the line"—they could only look forward to 10 more years in Baghdad. R3 said they needed a force-generator cycle—training, cohesion-building, being deployed back home for a respite. R3 said one thing he could do was to enhance the survivability of checkpoints, a major location of death for Iraqi troops in Washash. Clearly, R3 did not have any magic bullets to solve the major problems in this district.

7.13. Results and Explanations

In the battle for Iraq's capital and central city, the Shia forces had won. In 2006–2007, Shia armed and political forces established dominance in Baghdad. The demographic changes had been stunning. Five years after the invasion, nearly 1.5 million Iraqis had become displaced persons through sectarian violence.[17] By early 2007, 5.25 million out of Baghdad's total population of 7 million lived in mono-ethnic areas (Damjuli, 2010, p. 76). With entire sections clear of Sunnis and Sunni opposition, Muqtada and the Sadrists were able to institutionalize their control. The result cemented the lines between Shia and Sunni, in demographic and territorial terms, as well as in identity and psychology.

US forces had routed the Sadrists in 2004. The analytical framework helps specify how the Sadrists rebounded after that humiliation. Their victory had come through advantages across the spectrum of roles. Either through local networks or motivated individuals, JAM managed to fill its armed ranks at the −2 and −3 levels. AQI terrorist tactics undoubtedly drove some into these ranks. After its 2004 devastation at the hands of the US military, JAM had developed at least a semblance of an organization with a minimal level of command. The Iranians had supplied weapons able to damage the superior US forces. JAM's cleansing operations were systematic and involved coordination with Sadrist social organizations such as the Office of the Martyr Sadr. By relying on local Shia residents for intelligence and replacing loyal Shia followers in the homes of fleeing Sunnis, the Sadrists developed connections with unarmed civilians. The left side of the spectrum was filled—unarmed residents at −1 working with local JAM at −2, while mobile JAM at −3 worked its way across Baghdad neighborhoods.

Perhaps more stunning were the Sadrist tactics on the positive side of the spectrum. As JAM infiltrated or took over local police stations (+2 level), citizens had nowhere to turn for security. As discussed in a following chapter, the Shia Badr Brigades took control of the Ministry of the Interior after the 2005 elections. At the +3 level, Maliki was going outside the command structure of the military to order Army units against Sunni targets. Meanwhile, the Sadrists, through their control of several social service ministries, were replacing the official Iraqi government with their own institutions.

The way Sadr City served as a safe haven and sanctuary for Shia forces cannot be overestimated. Until 2008, US forces were content to try to isolate Sadr City, leaving it to JAM control. If the Coalition considered that the costs of going into Sadr City in 2006–2007 were high, they had good reason for this belief. Consider the account of one interviewee (VB), a US special forces soldier. The following is a passage from the author's interview notes

> VB's unit was tasked to raid sites in Sadr City. In order to carry out this task, US SOF employed local Iraqis for reconnaissance, to take pictures and establish GPS points. The reconnaissance team working with VB's unit was "rolled up." Even though they were natives of Baghdad, they were apparently recognized as outsiders by the locals in Sadr City. When VB's unit entered, they found their informants dead, cruelly tortured, fingernails pulled off, and genitals mutilated. As VB recounted, "even though they were dead their faces had expressions as if they were still crying out from hell." VB recalled thinking at the moment of discovery that "human society is held together by very tenuous threads and these threads had come unloose in Iraq."

Geographically, the Sadrists spread out from Sadr City into the "little Sadr Cities" of Shula and Washash. Even in middle-class neighborhoods like Kadhimiyah, Sadrists sometimes managed to co-opt bottom-up organization. With the cleansing operations of 2006–2007, the Sadrists spread Shia control across even wider swaths of the Iraqi capital.

Meanwhile, undermanned US forces worked to move individuals to the +1 position. They practiced elements of CHB without any real "clear." US forces decided to try to contain Sadr City. The US forces did try to conduct clearing operations in the form of Together Forward (June 14, 2006) and Together Forward II, but those operations were focused on Sunni groups and AQI, not the Shia organizations. These operations were generally considered failures because of the nonexistence of competent Iraqi forces to "hold" after the original "clear." Meanwhile, the US forces did realize the critical importance of local security and the police. In fact, the year 2006 was named "the year of the police." By 2006, however, the problems with the local police, as evidenced in the narrative of the MiTT leader above, had become too severe for a rapid turnaround—certainly, too severe to impede the JAM cleansing operations.

But the course of the war would quickly change.

Mansour, 2003–2007

The Failure to Mobilize Moderates

8.1. Introduction

Many US policymakers who advocated the invasion of Iraq operated under the premise that Saddam's brutal regime had left the country as a "blank slate," a society characterized by a lack of competing and antagonistic groups, a society of atomized individuals yearning for democracy. These individuals would not be driven by agendas tied to identity master cleavages, they would not see the world through a lens of who would dominate whom. In terms of our framework, the bulk of the population would move almost immediately to the +1 position of unarmed support of the government. Free and fair elections would cement this position. Citizens would work with and some would join the ranks of the state security forces (+2 and +3). In short, the majority of the populace would become willing and active participants in the building of the new Iraqi state.

Indeed, many such individuals undoubtedly did exist in Iraq. In many localities, potential supporters of a democratic Iraq state-building project probably formed a majority. Tragically, many of these individuals never mobilized. In terms of the spectrum of roles, they remained in a position of wait-and-see neutrality (position 0). Moreover, many would flee the country, taking their values and skills out the game entirely. As seen in Chapter 6, in Ghazaliyah, those who mattered most in outcomes of violence and state-building were those who formed and joined militias, those who were motivated by identity and fear of dominance, those who already belonged to pre-invasion networks.

This chapter describes the failure of moderates to mobilize in the Baghdad neighborhood of Mansour in the years after the invasion and before the Surge. (There is a Mansour neighborhood and a Mansour Coalition security district which included not only the neighborhood of Mansour but several other neighborhoods. The focus here is mainly on the local neighborhood.) Mansour was a site of pre-invasion wealth and privilege and home to some of Baghdad's best restaurants and shops. Mansour's residents included much of the city's professional and diplomatic elite. Its demography was mixed, its religious practice muted. Following from above, many wealthy Sunnis in Mansour tried to remain neutral for as long as possible. When violence finally drove them to make decisions, many chose to leave the country altogether.

This chapter will produce a portrait of Mansour in the years just after the invasion by juxtaposing a narrative of a representative Sunni refugee who fled the neighborhood in 2006 with the narrative of a US Army captain stationed in the Mansour security district in 2004 and 2005.[1] This comparison of narratives aims at specifying the mechanisms and lack of mechanisms that resulted in a failure to move individuals into roles desired and expected by US and Coalition actors. It hopes to identify both the social characteristics of the Iraqi middle class and the shortcomings of US strategy that produced this outcome.

8.2. Early Occupation Dynamics

Mansour was an eventful location early in the conflict. The neighborhood was hit by forces from both outside and within. Being an elite neighborhood, the Baath Party unsurprisingly located its headquarters there. It was therefore natural that the US forces targeted Mansour for air strikes at the very onset of the invasion. US forces sent at least eight missiles into the headquarters of the Internal Security complex and leveled the Air Force command center as well.

Because Mansour was relatively wealthy, the neighborhood quickly became an early target for predators. In their study of household victimization in Baghdad, Hagan et al. (2012) found that the Mansour security district experienced the highest level of crime in the first months of the occupation (Hagan et al., 2012).[2] In the Mansour security district, over 20% or respondents claimed they were victims of assault, burglary, or theft. In the Thawra security district, composed mainly of Sadr City, only 1.9% of residents said they were victims of one of these three crimes, the lowest rate among Baghdad's security districts (Hagan et al., 2012, p. 488).[3] This comparison serves to point out three differences among Baghdad neighborhoods and the distinctiveness of Mansour. First, there was more to steal in Mansour. Second, some neighborhoods rapidly developed local security organs. In Sadr City, the Jaysh al-Mahdi (JAM) could enforce order and provide a check on local crime; Mansour had no such nongovernment security force. A third factor is that the Coalition presence and basic law were uneven or practically nonexistent in some Baghdad neighborhoods after the invasion. The uncontrolled and essentially lawless Washash neighborhood (described in

Chapter 7) adjoined Mansour. Notorious for ruthlessness, violent networks in Washash would have seen 2003 Mansour as easy pickings.

8.3. Narrative of a Mansour Resident

ZI graduated in the early 1970s with an engineering degree, served as an officer in the Iraqi Army, and participated in the 1980–1988 Iran-Iraq War. ZI later became a high-ranking engineer/manager in a manufacturing firm. ZI was a Sunni, but like his four brothers, he married a Shia woman. He held positive views of the early Saddam era, praising the gains made in education and literacy during that time. ZI saw the Iran-Iraq War as a great victory for Iraq, but one that ended up bankrupting the nation. He blamed the United States for "greenlighting" the Kuwait invasion. The 1990s had been disastrous, killing off Iraqi nationalism while empowering the Shia. Saddam was no longer up to the problems of the country and was incapable of fixing them.

Iraq was a good country and even a rich country in 1990, but by 2003 Iraq was lost. ZI welcomed the US invasion as a way to put Iraq back on track. In fact, ZI said the US forces coming was a "dream come true." However, the United States made mistakes right from the start. Coalition Provisional Authority leaders Jay Garner and Paul Bremer were incompetent, especially in disbanding the military and de-Baathification. The Iraqi Army could have easily been kept intact. From his own military service, ZI believed the Iraqi Army had British-style discipline that would have proven valuable. The United States should not have relied on ethnic categories that segregated the country. ZI referred to his own marriage to a Shia as an example that the sects could live together.

ZI provided a story of Mansour specifically. He described his Mansour neighborhood as high income and demographically mixed. Mansour was divided into five sectors. R lived in #625. Despite his high hopes, things were spoiled from the start of the occupation. Looting destroyed every institution. ZI claimed it was all Shia looting and that Shia clerics said that looting was OK, not a sin. The early problems stemmed from the nearby neighborhood of Washash. As ZI explained, Washash was a lower-class Shia area and it was the original source of troubles and the origin of looters in the first days.

After the early looting and theft, 2004–2005 was a quiet time. ZI did not anticipate the violence that would arise. One of the main concerns was lack of electricity. Everyone believed that the United States could have easily produced electricity, so if it did not, the US forces must be doing it on purpose. There was also a perception that the US spending on reconstruction was politically motivated and corrupt. The United States put too much money in "dirty Shia hands." There was a perception among Sunnis that the United States was buying off the Shia, and simply giving them money rather than reconstructing Iraq. Local contractors just took money in and did little with it.

The situation changed at the end of 2005. The first troubles came in the form of IED bombings. ZI believed that Baathist remnants possibly connected to the insurgency in Fallujah probably conducted the first bombings. Then there was escalation. Shia militants began bombing. ZI said that the IEDs had Iranian detonation devices so the bombing was directed in part by Iran or through Shia connections. ZI believed that the neighborhood was first attacked by the Badr Organization and then by JAM. ZI described JAM as more criminal and "low-minded," more likely to use extortion and act like gangsters.

The number of bombings in general increased to a point where he believed his family members had a significant chance of becoming a casualty. In response, ZI sent his family out of the country in early 2006. ZI felt that he would be able to stay. ZI's decision was based on his own view of the insurgents' bombing targets. ZI saw two targeting strategies in play. In early 2006, actors targeted large crowds to produce terror. This indiscriminate bombing could involve women and children and anyone gathered in markets or other public places. Given that this strategy was in play, ZI sent his family out of the country. The second strategy was the targeting of specific individuals with connection to the former regime, mainly military marks but also some members of the intelligentsia. ZI would be relatively safe because he was not a high-ranking target and he could avoid the public places.

Then targeting changed. Shia insurgent groups began targeting all Sunnis. This targeting went beyond hitting large gatherings to produce terror; it went beyond striking specific military and political targets. Now anyone with a common Sunni name, Omar or Bekr for example, could become a target. The violence was blanket sectarian violence. This turn produced too much risk for ZI. Someone connected to the Badr Organization warned him that he could be a target, so he left the country in December 2006.

ZI had decided to remain neutral throughout 2003–2006. He did not believe that the Sunnis in Mansour had a chance to create armed self-defense units. The US forces had searched their homes for weapons and had taken them. More importantly, the Shia militias were simply too strong. If Sunnis had organized, their actions would simply have given the Shia militias a better chance to quickly kill Sunnis and achieve their goal of eliminating Sunni opposition. Staying and fighting a suicide battle would allow the Shia to achieve their goal quickly.

ZI was further immobilized by the lack of state security structures. The police were not trustworthy. More importantly, the police were no match against the militias in 2006. Counterintuitively, the checkpoint system in the neighborhood worked to increase insecurity and prevent safe movement. As ZI explained, guards at the checkpoints asked questions about who you were; they checked out ID cards and examined your name and profession. People crossing the checkpoint were completely vulnerable; they could not know how the guard was processing or sending the information. ZI believed government guards often worked hand in hand with the militias. Without a trustworthy police force and unreliable checkpoints, the best thing to do was simply to stay in one's home and reduce movement.

ZI provided specifics for his account by discussing changes he witnessed on the 14th of Ramadan Street in Mansour. This street had been one of the liveliest in this rich neighborhood. ZI responded that life on the street first significantly diminished with al-Qaeda in Iraq (AQI) bombs versus patrolling US forces. Then the checkpoint system further locked down the neighborhood. Then the Sunni-Shia battles emptied out what was left.

I had met ZI in Amman. He was one of thousands of Iraqis to have fled their native land, many of them from Mansour. In his account of Iraq, Anthony Shadid interviewed one of those remaining in Mansour during the height of the violence, a psychiatrist living in a now empty two-story house. As the doctor summarized, "Everybody has run away" (Shadid, 2005, p. 93). In Mansour, many had the resources to flee to Amman or Beirut. Anyone who could deposit $75,000 in a Jordanian bank could receive legal residence there (Amos, 2010, p. 119).

8.4. Application of the Framework

Mansour is an example of a place with a lack of movement or mobilization (staying at 0 on the spectrum and then leaving Iraq altogether). People left, people hunkered down, many people hunkered down and then left. What about the groups most likely to mobilize—former regime elements (FREs) and youth? Many FREs lived in Mansour. Undoubtedly, many of these FREs had the resources to quickly leave and achieve legal residence outside Iraq. It also seems that the youth in Mansour did not mobilize. I had interviewed one younger former resident of Mansour (DB) who had worked for the US forces as a translator before leaving the country. DB stated that a majority of his cohort and schoolmates, most belonging to the more privileged class, had fled Iraq long before the 2003 invasion. The tumultuous decade of the 1990s unsurprisingly drove many of Mansour's youth out of Iraq.

ZI and his friends who fled to Jordan also had the resources to leave.[4] They did not have strong tribal, family, or veteran networks that would generate norms to pull them into a local violent organization. They were not overtly ide-ological or religious. They looked out for their families and behaved rationally to protect their interests. Along the lines of a "tipping game" and the logic of the "safety-in-numbers" mechanism, their narratives contained an implicit threshold value that would indicate when it would be time to leave. For ZI, this value for his wife and children was passed in early 2006; for himself, the threshold was passed in late 2006. In both cases, ZI considered the forces that provide protection (or at least anonymity) and compared them to the forces which could produce danger. ZI observed other groups moving out—first Sunnis with young children, then practicing Sunnis who would be easily identified as Sunnis. ZI observed the demographics of Mansour changing as Sunnis moved out and Shia from other neighborhoods moved in. Given available and abundant resources, the rational processing of this information produced neutrality and then flight.

8.5. Narrative of a US Army Captain and Company Commander in Mansour Security District, 2004–2005

What might have kept ZI in Mansour? What was the strategy of the United States and its allies in Mansour? To address these questions, we turn to the narrative of CD, a US soldier deployed in the Mansour Security District from March 2004 to March 2005. The following section will juxtapose the narratives of ZI and CD.

Before deploying to Iraq, CD's unit had been slated to be one of the first to enter Iraq during the invasion. However, the unit was pulled off that assignment and went back to training, now for stability and support operations. At Fort Hood, Vietnam vets were brought in to talk about close combat. CD's unit understood that urban pacification would be messy and a cultural challenge. At Fort Polk, the location of the Joint Readiness Training Center, they conducted simulations for the Iraq mission. They were trained in how to deal with tribal and religious elites, with natives of the Middle East brought in to do role-playing. CD believed this training addressed the complexity of the forthcoming mission. There was one more week of training in Kuwait, before entering Iraq

CD deployed as a company commander in March 2004, stationed in Central Baghdad in the Salihya and Haifa Street neighborhoods, just north of the Green Zone. His unit had very few soldiers with combat experience (maybe 4–5); only the older NCOs had combat time. The unit first occupied a set of burned-out garages. They arrived at the time of the April 2004 Sadrist uprising. In their area, they experienced sporadic fire at night, but no serious engagements.

CD's picture of the enemy was a murky one. Coming in, CD saw the enemy as "insurgents" in a very broad and undefined way. As CD's unit arrived during Sadr's April uprising, he was aware of JAM as an enemy. In CD's words, JAM had many "thugs with a cause." AQI was not high on the list. The enemy was also "criminals" and thugs. There were various actors who simply thrived on societal chaos, either to delegitimize the new government and the Coalition, or to have an uncontrolled environment conducive to criminal activities, or maybe both. Both political actors and criminals desired disorder.

In CD's view, this vague enemy's goal was to "show the world" Iraq's instability and the inability of the occupying US forces to secure even the area around the Green Zone. To accomplish this goal, the enemy mortared US bases and the Green Zone, used VBIEDs (vehicle-borne improvised explosive devices) especially at the checkpoint around the Green Zone, and even made attempts to overcome barriers and create violence and chaos within the Green Zone. The enemy assassinated US collaborators/workers, especially translators. All of the main interpreters working with CD were eventually assassinated, four while he was there. Beyond insurgent violence, or perhaps indistinguishable from it, the neighborhood experienced criminal acts including kidnapping, assault, and theft.

What was the US strategy? CD saw the basic goal as establishing "omnipresence" in the area of operation. The enemy was amorphous and multiple. With omnipresence, they would gain intelligence to both identify and go after the enemy. CD's repeated phrase was that they needed to learn "who is who in the zoo."

CD was given little intelligence going in. He also had little contact with the local police. At one point, CD went into a local police station and saw jumper cables and a battery, probably used for interrogation. The police were neither trustworthy nor professional. At this period, there were no MiTTs to help work with the Iraqi Army. There was an Iraqi National Guard, which CD described as a "clusterfuck" marked by infiltration and incompetence.

Without significant intelligence and with essentially no local security partners, and well before the publication of the FM 3-24 counterinsurgency manual, CD employed basic Army war-fighting strategy. As an officer with the 1st Cavalry Division, the employment of this strategy was natural. As described in Chapter 4, the tactics of war-fighting include cordon and sweeps, detentions on a large scale, artillery shelling, use of armor, and shows of force. These can be considered in turn.

As an officer leading an infantry unit attached to armored brigade, CD prided himself on integrating armor into stability operations. Tanks positioned themselves at the gates into the Green Zone (2 at each position). CD would use other tanks for deployment (they did not have Bradleys); they would make "thunder runs" down Haifa Street. There were also platoon level patrols (16–18 soldiers), with reinforcement in ready reserve when trouble broke out. There was always a decision on how much armor to use. If there was an attack, CD rolled out a major force. If CD had intelligence that a major attack was possible in a certain area, he would also roll out major force to that area. His philosophy was that a major presence would create a deterrent effect. CD had done his own MCOO (Modified Combined Obstacle Overlay) in order to know where armored vehicles could operate.

Army units in the area, including CD's, brought in large numbers of detainees. In the spring of 2004, US forces rounded up 263 detainees in the Haifa Street area.[5] CD explained that such a number was rare and occurred after an Army Task Force in the area was hit by 26 RPGs, eight roadside bombs, and small arms fire. In CD's recollection, that round-up was the largest during that period. Normally, CD's unit detained 3–5 at a time. Detainees were brought back to a holding area. CD recalled that their holding area was a set of cages thought to have been used by either Uday or Qusay Hussein to hold exotic animals. There was a triage-type classification of detainees (not done by CD)—criminals versus possible insurgents versus no threat. The first category was turned over to local Iraqi police, the second put in Coalition holding, and the third released. CD believed too many Iraqis were detained, partly due to the problem with "squirters." After a weapon/RPG fired, the assailant would "squirt" back into the population. There would be a tendency to make too many arrests in trying to catch the one squirter.

While major raids were planned at the battalion and not company level, CD did go on some major raids. CD did white-boarding in an effort to help plan raids. Some discussed raids were simply judgment calls— "it was difficult to know the difference between times when you knock on the door and when you blow the door off." As CD explained, before a major raid was conducted, a brief was drawn up which needed approval from higher-ups. A raid required an ability for absolute identification, requiring days of observation. Raids seldom hit a wrong target, but they did hit many "dry holes" where the target was not present. That was bad because the target now knew he was identified and would leave the area to restart the same activities someplace new. CD believed that they captured more criminals than insurgents.

As CD's unit was stationed near the Green Zone, there were many checkpoints—and many VBIED attacks at those checkpoints. CD's unit did "picking up body parts" as part of their job. There were also checkpoints at major traffic areas. When a BOLO (be on the lookout) was sent out about a VBIED, CD would set up makeshift checkpoints to try to prophylactically catch the bomber. "It was very difficult to try to find this one needle in a haystack." There were observation posts (OPs) near every mosque. Work was done to identify friendly versus hostile imams.

CD made a point about the difficulties of monitoring Haifa Street. It was basically a "canyon" of tall buildings with a street running through the heart of Baghdad. It was a main avenue for all foot traffic coming to Green Zone, as well as the main site for demonstrations. There was a huge amount of traffic moving in and out. In military terms, a unit "owns" a piece of land and is ultimately accountable for what happens on it. However, it is difficult to "own" a piece of land when people and vehicles are moving in and out of it so rapidly. There must be rapid communication among units.

CD's unit came in with little intelligence and did not receive much intelligence. The information flow consisted of a daily coordinated meeting, a weekly meeting with higher-ups and the S2 (intelligence officer). CD only received detailed intelligence from above in conjunction with major raids. For the most part, CD said intelligence coming down was scarce. The Brigade did create a "diffusion cell" that aimed to put information into a usable digestible format. CD said this goal was never accomplished during his 2004 tour. As CD summarized, "It was hard to figure out what was going on."

CD told one illustrative story that illustrated the complexity of intelligence collection in Baghdad during 2004–2005. CD identified one clear local insurgent/criminal enforcer—X.[6] A former police officer, X had 6–9 personnel going back and forth daily to Sadr City, undoubtedly in connection with JAM. CD staged an assault with two platoons—one doing cordon and one doing search. He detained the targeted group. Success seemed in hand. However, X then handed CD a card with the number of a Brigade-level S2. CD brought X into the Green Zone to Battalion HQ and was told to go to Brigade HQ. There, they know all about X—he was a confidential informant helping to develop a map of the structure of the JAM in the area. Although CD has to let X go, he did periodically raid him to limit his excesses.

Tips came into CD through civil works projects. CD provided one example. One NAC member asked the US Army to fix elevators in a high-rise building, a problem especially problematic for elderly residents. The project was good for intelligence collection. The work was indoors and not visible to outside observers. It involved constant contact with residents, some of whom became regular informants. There was a "diapers for information" relationship with one English-speaking female resident.

As outlined in Chapter 4, the US military would encourage movement away from war-fighting to CHB in the period of the Surge. This move came from clear problems with war-fighting, namely the failure to collect information, the negative reactions from collateral damage, the counterproductive use of sweeps and mass detention, and the general failure to protect the wider population.

Some of these problems were evident even during the relatively quiet 2004–early 2005 period. CD addressed one very major incident of collateral damage—the Haifa Street helicopter incident. In September 2004, insurgents used two car bombs on an attack on a Bradley armored vehicle. The vehicle was completely disabled with four injured. Army policy is to never leave a vehicle in the field so as to not have its radio and weapons going to the enemy. The commanding officer had two choices: (1) secure the area and evacuate/tow the vehicle, or (2) fire on the vehicle with a helicopter to destroy the vehicle. The officer chose the latter. Citizens were dancing around the vehicle in celebration when US forces made the destroying shots. The result was 13 dead and 60 injured civilians, with an *Al Arabiya* reporter among the dead. With media present on the scene, it was a public relations disaster.

CD described another incident involving collateral damage. CD set out to capture a local IED maker. He made a cordon around the target and then did the sweep. While CD was taking in the detainee, an Opal broke the cordon. US forces responded with heavy gunfire, as according to standard operating procedure. The Opal was carrying an innocent family, and deaths occurred. The sweep and the Opal had nothing to do with one another, an unfortunate combination of events.

8.6. Conclusion: Combining the Two Narratives

ZI and CD present the civilian and military sides of life in the Mansour Security District during 2004–2005, and in ZI's case into 2006. CD was a highly professional soldier. He led a company of soldiers who "went in hard" in an ambiguous environment. CD's war-fighting tactics—use of armor, show of force, cordon and sweep, use of detention—may have kept the lid on violence in the neighborhood during 2004–2005. But this strategy certainly did not prevent the massive burst of violence in 2006 that drove ZI and his family out of the neighborhood and the country. The deficiencies of the war-fighting strategy are clear in hindsight. These deficiencies can be highlighted with reference to the spectrum of roles:

- Failure to develop consistent tips and intelligence from the local population (lack of +1)
- No development of the local police (lack of +2)
- Incompetent Iraqi national-level security forces (lack of +3 indigenous forces).

In effect, war-fighting in the Mansour security district involved US forces trying to eliminate murky local insurgents (−2) and terrorists (−3) and did not prioritize other nodes of the spectrum of roles. The strategy failed in two distinct ways. First, war-fighting tactics produced collateral damage and detention of innocent local citizens. These tactics may have eliminated some insurgents, but they were also likely to trigger negative emotional mechanisms of fear and resentment, creating more insurgents.

Second, and more critically, a war-fighting strategy does little in terms of state-building. To create a functioning state, individuals must move into roles supporting the government, they must move rightward on the spectrum. Citizens have to move from 0 to +1, providing information and participating in normal political life. To recall the mechanisms listed in Chapter 3 related to movement between 0 and +1:

Movement from 0 to +1:

- Resentment versus insurgent group
- Safety in numbers with general population as referent point
- Focal points
- Rational economic decision, payouts from government, employment, etc.

Movement from +1 and −1 back to 0:

- Rational reaction to threat
- Fear (emotion).

ZI and many of his fellow citizens never moved out of neutrality (0). Few of the mechanisms producing movement to +1 were present. Early on, the insurgents were a murky lot and included both Sunni and Shia groups. As opposed to many other neighborhoods in Iraq, the perception of an unjust sectarian hierarchy was weak. Like other residents of the Mansour neighborhood, ZI lived a middle-class cosmopolitan life; he married across sect; he was not subject to subordination to an outside group. There was no clear target to generate resentment. Low-level violence prevented any safety-in-numbers mechanism. Mansour residents like ZI were already relatively wealthy and would not be induced by economic carrots. On the other hand, the mechanisms maintaining a neutrality status quo were present. Both rational calculation of threat and the emotion of fear deterred residents of Mansour from sticking their necks out. Even in the relatively quiet 2004–2005 period, a corrupt police, low-level violence and crime, and a suffocating checkpoint system all served to immobilize the general population.

The Failure to Establish Local Security

9.1. Introduction

The spectacular rise in violence in Baghdad in 2006 could not have taken place without the actions of Shia militias. The Jaysh al-Mahdi (JAM) and Sadrist forces held a base in Sadr City, established dominance in "little Sadr Cities," spread into middle-class Shia neighborhoods, and then moved out of these strongholds to systematically cleanse mixed neighborhoods to the south and west in Baghdad.

But the development of militias was only one side of the problem. The other side was the inability of state security organs to stop the work of militias as they moved across neighborhoods. In terms of our analytical framework, there was a problem on the negative side of the spectrum (especially −2), but there was also a problem on the positive side (at +2 and +3). This chapter focuses mainly on the +2 level. Two state institutions are most relevant to the discussion of security at +2. First, there is the local police themselves. Then there is the Ministry of Interior (MOI), which directs not only the local police but also the Federal Police, Department of Border Enforcement, Facilities Protection Service, and other smaller and more specialized security services.

There were many problems with the local police and the MOI, but the biggest problem, and the focus of this chapter, is that these state security agencies were captured by non-state actors. The Sadrist Jaysh al-Mahdi (JAM) and the Badr Corps managed to infiltrate, if not control, state security forces at several levels. As asserted by Finance Minister Ali Allawi, "It was common knowledge that Baghdad's 60,000 strong police force was divided between the Mahdi Army and the Badr Organization."[1] The state ministry in charge of Iraq's police, the MOI, was no better. As described in 2007 reports, the 11-story MOI headquarters was "'a federation of oligarchs' where various floors of the building were controlled by rival militia groups and organized criminal gangs."[2] Although not the focus of this chapter, the Iraqi Army also had its problems. As reported by US Military advisor David Kilcullen in 2007, "We did a counterintelligence assessment of an

Iraqi army battalion in central Baghdad and found that every senior commander and staff were either JAM, doing criminal activity with JAM, or intimidated by JAM" (Ricks 2009, p. 173).

This chapter is a vivid illustration of a central argument of the book. In Iraq, non-state actors captured, and often perverted, essential functions of the state. This state capture was accomplished by sectarian groups, mainly Shia, using their existing organization's abilities. The state capture of the 2003–2011 period produced a self-perpetuating dynamic lasting beyond the US presence to the present day.

The chapter will begin with the capture of local police. In building a functioning state, the creation of local security forces is critical. A strong state requires a force between the military (+3) and a supportive population (+1), an institution where citizens can go to obtain immediate safety. Without such a local presence, individuals will seek out protection on their own and may find that sanctuary in the form of anti-state local militias (−2) or even mobile insurgent groups (−3).

These local security forces should meet a set of basic standards. First, they should be professional. They should both be technically competent and follow the rule of law. Second, these forces should be accountable. Local police need to answer for their actions to the state. In turn, the state needs to know what the local police are doing. In short, there needs to be a flow of orders and information along a chain of command. Third, and perhaps most important, the local police should be loyal to the state. They should fight against the −2 and −3 levels rather than collaborate with them. In the early post-invasion years in Iraq (2003–2007), the US and its Coalition partners failed to build any of these characteristics in the Iraqi local police. They were not professional, not accountable, and not loyal.

The chapter will also describe the capture of the MOI by the Badr Organization. This case will focus on the strategic actions of Falah al-Naqib, the Minister of the Interior in 2004–2005 and the founder of police "commando" units. In the summer of 2004, Naqib attempted to create a highly professional, centralized force built from former Iraqi military personnel. These units were called "Commandos" and took on names such as the Wolf Brigade, the Hawk Brigade, Two Rivers, and Volcano. By late 2005, these forces had been captured by Badr and transformed into "hunting units," going after former regime elements. In November 2005, US forces uncovered over 150 prisoners in an underground bunker in the Jadiriyah neighborhood. As Matthew Sherman, the US senior advisor to the Iraqi MOI in 2003–2006, has described, the prisoners "weren't just held on the top floor of the bunker. It was downstairs in a more secluded area. You saw the bruises on them. You saw flesh falling off of them, and then them saying, 'Up there, on top of the tiles, is where the whips were,' where they had chains that were being used, things like that. And you were just appalled with what you saw."[3] Sections below address why Naqib felt it necessary to create police commando brigades, how they were captured by SCIRI/Badr, and how and why Badr put them to this use.

The capture of state security institutions presents challenges to the framework's concept of the spectrum of roles, blurring the distinction between positive and negative axes, between state and non-state actors. This question is addressed in the chapter's conclusion.

9.2. The Capture of the Local Police

Before the invasion, many US officials assumed that a competent +2 local police existed and could be readily maintained. While the United States was determined to disband the Iraqi Military and remove Baathist Party members from any significant position of power, the MOI and the local police were to be left largely in place. As a RAND report summarizes, "Right up until the point of ORHA's [Office for Reconstruction and Humanitarian Assistance] deployment to Baghdad in April 2003, it was thought that the predominately non-Ba'ath Party makeup of the police force meant that these personnel would be able to maintain law and order and that Coalition forces would not need to get involved in policing to any great extent" (Rathmell et al., 2005, p. 11). Martin Howard, as deputy chief of the United Kingdom's Defense Intelligence Staff, reported to the House of Commons on pre-invasion planning, "I am not aware of anything from my knowledge where we explicitly looked at how we should deal with policing in the aftermath of conflict" (Rathmell et al., 2005, p. 11, fn. 7).

This lack of attention comes partly from a lack of understanding of how Saddam Hussein controlled Iraq. In Saddam's system, many organizations, including secret police units and military units, devoted their efforts to population control. Saddam did not prioritize the local police and did not equip, train, or organize them to any great extent. They were not professional before the invasion, and the United States should not have assumed a high level of competence going in. Nor should the United States have been surprised that this weak force melted away in the first days after the invasion, many no doubt fearing retaliation for their corrupt and criminal behavior during Saddam's time.

Just as importantly, US planners did a very poor job of fulfilling the plans that did exist. The US Department of Justice recommended that 6,600 advisors be sent to Iraq to build and reform the MOI. In early 2004, there were only 60 advisors, less than 1% of the recommended number.[4] By August, there were still only 376 US and 50 non-US trainers (Radin 2020, p. 155). Moreover, these advisors did not have the security support to regularly leave the Green Zone

(*Frontline* interview, 2006). Early on, in May 2004, the military took over police training in Iraq and would be in charge until the 2011 withdrawal. CPA leader Paul Bremer objected to this move, stating, "It would convey to the Iraqis the opposite of the principle of civilian standards, rules, and accountability of the police" (Radin, 2020, p. 162). Perhaps more importantly, the US military did not see policing as a major part of its mission. The US Army's overwhelming priority was going after high value targets (HVTs). The experience of one junior officer in Baghdad in the early days of occupation is illustrative.

9.2.1. Early Training of the Iraq Civil Defense Corps: Narrative of a US Army Captain

Captain IF arrived in Baghdad in June 2003 to serve on the Regimental Staff of the 2nd ACR.[5] The AO included much of eastern Baghdad, including Sadr City. He was assigned two roles: help set up the Iraq Civil Defense Corps (ICDC) and serve as S3 (operations and training) on targeting. The ICDC was a temporary security force established to maintain local security. It operated in 2003 and 2004 before being folded into Ministry of Defense in April 2004. For the US forces, its primary role was fixed site security and route safety. As far as the ICDC job, IF had no training at all. He was given the job because he happened to be available at staff headquarters at the time.

The goal was to achieve numbers. Accordingly, vetting for the ICDC was not selective, with over 50% accepted. There was a medical exam and a form renouncing Baathist membership. Training lasted one week and centered on working in teams. The ICDC were to go on joint patrols, run checkpoints, and continue training. The first cohort was trained by September 2003. IF said the ICDC units would police their own neighborhoods. Although there might be problems with the connections among police and locals, it was thought that the advantages of having knowledge of the neighborhood would outweigh those problems. IF believed his trainees were entirely Shia. Identity issues soon came to the fore. The trainees considered the uniforms to be "Sunni uniforms" and did not wish to wear them. The US Army offered them a pay bonus to wear the uniform, but the trainees still refused. The trainees were also offended by their plastic boots.

IF saw the ICDC mission as low priority for the military. The ICDC not only served in their home areas, they were infiltrated by Shia militias. When IF was sent to train the ICDC in the south of Iraq in April to June 2004, IF reported to the Regiment head that Badr Brigades were recruiting locals to enter the ICDC. The Colonel stated, "We don't recruit Badr." IF responded, "Your squadrons do." In IF's view, the military simply wanted to put up numbers of trainees. If Badr was helping produce those numbers, so be it. The metrics of importance at the time were the number of RPGs captured and the number of HVTs killed or captured.

9.2.2. Changing Goals: Moving +1 to +2

The United States originally assumed that a significant number of individuals already existed at the +2 level at the time of invasion, a number sufficient to provide local security. When that assumption proved wrong,[6] the new goal was to professionalize the remaining local police and to move numbers of loyal citizens (+1) into the local security forces (+2). Given the breakdown of the local justice system in Iraq, in March 2004 the Bush administration decided that the Department of Defense and the US military would take over the process of MOI reform from the State Department. In June 2004, the Multi-National Security Transition Command–Iraq (MNSTC-I) began operation under the leadership of Lt. General David Petraeus. The MNSTC-I mission included reform of the Iraqi military and the Iraqi police, as well as the Ministry of Defense and the MOI.

As with IF's experience with the ICDC, the focus was on rapidly filling quotas. After the invasion, Matt Sherman, the senior advisor to the Iraqi MOI, estimated that about 40,000 Iraqi police remained serving in their previous positions. There was an immediate goal of increasing that number to 75,000 (*Frontline* interview, 2006). Target numbers expanded. Petraeus set a target to train and equip 135,000 new police. In December 2006, MNSTC-I announced it had met its target of training and equipping 187,800 police and border personnel (Perito, 2008, p. 3). Unsurprisingly, serious questions about the vetting and professionalization of these rapidly recruited and approved trainees were raised. Recruits trained at an academy in Jordan for 10 weeks. To compare, in the US mission in Kosovo, recruits had five months of classroom training before even entering the field; once in the field, they received six more months of monitoring and mentoring.[7]

While Iraqi recruits no doubt gained some measure of technical competence, their political neutrality remained a problem. Issued on April 6, 2004, CPA Order 71 decentralized authority to the provinces. Theoretically, decentralization would prevent the ability of any would-be dictator to take over the center and implement Saddam-like rule. However, decentralization also devolved the recruiting and monitoring of local police to the provincial level. States need +2 forces that are both professional and accountable. There was little accountability in this system. Matt Sherman, the senior MOI advisor, listed three issues that plagued the formation of the Iraqi police: "One, is never having a full grasp of . . . how many police came back into the ministry after the war; two, the decentralization issue; three, having so many people coming into the ministry as police officers under this 135,000 plan that you were unable to make heads or tails of who was where; and also the corruption issues, certain people taking money for their own benefit" (*Frontline* interview, 2006). While lack of professionalism and the absence of accountability pervaded the local security system, the third criterion, loyalty, was the most directly connected to the mobilization of violence.

The combination of decentralization with tens of thousands of newly armed but lightly trained police was hardly a way to prevent escalation to civil war; rather, it helped provide fuel for it. Insurgents (−2 and −3) took advantage of the US goal of quickly putting up big numbers of recruits to put their own people into the local police (+2). In many cases, the US forces provided a uniform that would confer legitimacy to anti-state actors. The incoming police force had no vested interest in the state. Short-term training and promised benefits failed to wean individuals from networks and local connections. In his March 2006 *New York Times* article entitled "Iraq's Little Armies," Matt Sherman stated that "since the Shiite-led government came to power last May, militia members have entered the Iraqi Army and police forces en masse. The danger is that many feel stronger allegiance to their militias and religious sects that to the state" (Sherman 2006).

9.3. The Capture of the Ministry of the Interior and Its Commando Units

The previous case studies of Sadr City and Washash discussed how militias associated with the Mahdi Army and the Sadrists captured the local police. US Military officers routinely wrote off the local police as either corrupt, incompetent, or both. Having connections to local Shia clerics and leaders, the Sadrists' strategy was concentrated at the community level. Their capture of the police often went hand in hand with their creation of local courts (as will be examined in more detail in the following chapter on the Bayaa case). In effect, when it came to local security and adjudication, the Sadr forces often created a quasi-state.

The political party Supreme Council for Islamic Revolution in Iraq (SCIRI), and its Badr militia, could not play the same game as the Sadrists and JAM. Having been established and based in Iran since 1982, Badr lacked legitimacy for many Shia. In the Iran-Iraq War, the Badr Army fought on the side of Iran. Its primary commander was Iranian. When Iraq soldiers in the Badr Army were killed in battle, it was the Iranian government who sent condolence messages to their families. Despite its stated revolutionary aims, Badr forces did not enter

Iraq during the 1991 uprising to aid Shia rebels. In short, Badr lacked legitimacy and popular support. Undoubtedly, SCIRI and Badr still saw the advantages of being able to project force among Baghdad's neighborhoods and communities. Given its nature as an outside actor with dubious legitimacy, if Badr was going to take advantage of the deficiencies in Iraq's local security system, they were more likely to do so not at the community level, but at the ministry level.

With decades of development, the Badr forces were well organized and disciplined. But it should also be noted that the Badr Army was composed of Iraqi deportees and prisoners of war, many with scores to settle in Iraq. Upon entering Iraq in 2003, Badr forces seemed to have two missions: first, prevent any possibility of the resurrection of a Saddam-like state that could again kill and deport SCIRI members (and threaten their Iranian patron); second, seek revenge against the Saddamist elements that had persecuted them. Both of these goals could be accomplished through systematic elimination of former regime elements. All that was needed was an efficient vehicle to go about the task. As it turned out, the evolution of the Iraq security system presented such a vehicle.[8]

To understand how this opportunity arose, we can consider the narrative of Falah al-Naqib, who rose to become MOI minister in 2004. Naqib made decisions that unintentionally led to the Badr capture of the MOI and impacted the longer evolution of the National Police. His narrative illustrates the background behind many of the central strategic decisions concerning local security in Iraq.

9.3.1. The Narrative of Falah al-Naqib: MOI Minister and Founder of the Commandos

On June 28, 2004, the Iraq Interim Government led by Iyad Allawi replaced the Coalition Provisional Authority.[9] Along with this change, Falah al-Naqib became the minister of interior.[10] In one of his first moves, Naqib sought to develop an elite force within the MOI. The force would be made up primarily of Iraqi Army officers and special Republican Guard officers who had been disbanded from the military. Unlike the police, it would be completely centralized and run out of Baghdad through the MOI. The force would be led by Naqib's uncle, General Adnan Thabit, a former prisoner under Saddam and also a tribal sheikh from Samarra.

Given the problems outlined above, Naqib believed that only an experienced and elite force with a highly centralized command system and trusted leaders outside of Iraq's corrupt political system could save Iraq. Naqib was in fact successful in developing this force, named "Commandos." The problem was that the Iraqi system soon evolved in a way that enabled the Badr forces to capture this force and use it to its own ends. This section considers two questions: Why did

Naqib come to believe that such a force, largely outside the bounds of US theory and practice, was necessary? How did Badr come to capture the force?

To answer the first question, it is useful to understand Naqib's background. Naqib was born in 1955 in Samarra to an influential Sunni family connected to the biggest tribe in the area. His father was General Hassan al-Naqib, who served as commander of Iraqi armed forces from 1967 to 1970 before running into political troubles and fleeing the country. He was an influential member in the Iraqi National Accord (INA), founded by Iyad Allawi and Salah Omar al-Ali in 1991 at the time of the first Gulf War. The Party was to be a secular alternative to Dawa and SCIRI. The INA was comprised of many ex-military and security personnel who had defected from the Saddam regime. The INA held a very different view of how to bring down Saddam than its ex-patriate rival, the Iraq National Congress (INC), connected with Chalabi. While the INC believed the best way to regime change was a broad-based revolution of Shia and Kurds, the INA called for a coup by Iraqi military and security leadership. The INA's top-down military prescription was not surprising given its membership.

Falah al-Naqib was deeply embedded within the INA community. He studied in Sweden in 1979, worked in Syria from 1980 to 1983, studied in England and earned an advanced degree in construction management engineering. After 1990, he began full-time opposition work with his father. He had known Iyad Allawi since 1993. Naqib no doubt was influenced by the INA's top-down and military-led positions. He believed that a successful military coup was possible after the 1991 war. At that time, soldiers were ripe for turning on Saddam. The sanctions regime that followed served to strengthen Saddam. Naqib stated that the sanctions destroyed Iraq more than the actual war in terms of paving the way for a society completely shot through with corruption and a state with little strength.

When the invasion came, Naqib drove from Syria to Samarra. He had not been back in Iraq since 1976, a 27-year absence. He was quickly elected to the governate's legislative body. In February 2004, Naqib was elected governor of Salah-a-Din province, a territory that included Tikrit, Saddam's hometown. He served in that position for four months. When Naqib was governor, he traveled every day from Samarra, his hometown, to Tikrit, the Governate's capital. He did not live in Tikrit, Saddam's hometown, as it was safer to live in Samarra and brave the road up to Tikrit than to live in Tikrit itself. The tribes in Samarra were at odds with those in Tikrit and there was tension among them. Naqib was a member of the largest tribe in the region and in Samarra. After Naqib's house was attacked in Samarra, a group of 300 armed fellow tribesmen came to protect it by surrounding it. Although his house was a target, tribal defense made it the safer choice in comparison with living in Tikrit.

Naqib asked for, and received, exemption for Salah-a-Din from the de-Baathification laws. He was supposed to fire 14,000–15,000 people, including 7,000–8,000 teachers. He also tried to bring back former military officers. Naqib was emphatic that only the "killers" should be kept out of government service. He stated that most of the killers had left the province to go to Baghdad, Mosul, or out of the country, so that was not a big problem for him. Tikrit, Saddam's home base, was a special problem. Naqib said that a tribal chief (Mahmoud) came to see him believing that his tribe would be targeted and persecuted because of their connections to Saddam. Naqib assured him that would not be the case, that he was not against Tikritis. The sheikh feared some of his people would take up arms if they did not have jobs. Naqib asked him what to do. The sheikh said to put them in the police. Naqib then hired 70 men into the Tikrit police force. The result, Naqib stated, was a quiet Tikrit; the payoffs and jobs were effective. Naqib stressed the inextricable linkages between tribe and police as played out in the post-invasion era. Many times, it is necessary to go to a tribal sheikh and get a list of people to fill the police. Naqib did note the downsides of this action. For example, if one member of a tribe is killed, relatives in the police might place the norm of tribal revenge above any formal rule of law. In Samarra, Naqib said he needed to form and re-form the police six or seven times because of this dynamic.

With the institution of the Iraq Interim Government and the ascension of Allawi to prime minister, Naqib took over as minister of the interior in June 2004. Given his background and record in Salah-a-Din province, he was clearly inclined to keep as much of the old state as possible, including the recruitment and hiring of former Baathists. Naqib believed that CP Order 71 decentralizing the police was a big mistake. In the early years of reconstruction, he thought that the main problem was the lack of a center able to unify the country. While decentralization might have been appropriate three or four years in the future, CP 71 was introduced way too soon.

In my conversations with Naqib, I asked him about the qualities usually associated with the creation of an effective police force mentioned above: (1) professionalization, (2) loyalty, and (3) accountability. Naqib pointed out that these criteria are the right ones for creating a force in general, but he was inheriting the police from the Saddam era. Given the unstable situation in Iraq at the time, professionalism required anti-terrorist capabilities and special training.

Given Naqib's preference for top-down and centralized organizations, as well as his desire to use experienced personnel from the Saddam era, Naqib believed that the only solution to Iraq's severe security problems was to form special units—the Commandos. These units were professional because they were formed from ex-Commandos from the Iraqi Army who were specialists in urban warfare and able to take on terrorists. As Naqib put it, these units existed, why not use them? In his opinion, it was better to use existing abilities than try to build from the bottom up, because there was no time for the bottom-up process. These units were loyal, with Naqib's uncle at the helm. Naqib claimed he did not want to put him in command right away, but things worked out that way. Also, coming from a military family and through connections from the INA, Naqib claimed he knew the officers and their background, he knew what they could do. These individuals would be outside of tribal and other networks. The units were only under the command of the MOI head, not the US or other MOI officials or administrators. Crucially, Naqib directed and approved all their missions. This limited chain of command might prevent excess leaking of information and corruption. However, no one would know what the Commandos were doing outside of Naqib and the Commandos themselves. Naqib said he approved/directed only missions that would be successful; he wanted only "victories." Any defeat would have eroded the unit's confidence, and Naqib wanted a confident, aggressive Commando unit.

From the US standpoint, Naqib's plan had several problems. The major issue was accountability. The Commandos were basically Naqib's personal force; their actions were not always even visible. A second issue was cronyism. Naqib not only appointed his uncle to lead the Commandos, but may have been filling its leadership from his INA contacts. Furthermore, it was politically problematic to fill a force with former members of Saddam's army. Yet, US officials gave the go-ahead, impressed with Naqib's self-initiative.[11]

9.3.2. The Role of Democracy in State Capture

While Naqib successfully created the Commandos, he would not control them for long. In the January 2005 elections, the United Iraqi Alliance took over 48% of the vote. For the first time in Iraqi history, the government would be dominated by Shia.[12] SCIRI/Badr was in a position to bargain for a desired ministry. Above all, they desired control of the MOI. The MOI was responsible for four civilian security services totaling nearly 500,000 members in 2008—the Iraqi Police Service (275,300), the Iraqi National Police (32,389), the Iraqi Border Enforcement Service (38,205), and the Facilities Protection Service (150,000) (Perito, 2008). The Badr forces especially wanted control of the MOI because of the Commando force developed by Naqib. With Naqib out, Bayan Jabr quickly transformed the Commandos into a tool of the Badr Organization. Badr militiamen rapidly replaced their largely Sunni predecessors. The new version of the Commandos quickly went after former regime targets. Matt Sherman describes his revelation about these operations:

You're just hearing about attacks that are happening. You're starting to see individuals get detained. You're seeing human rights issues multiply. What brought things clear in my mind was being able to find out more about the background of the individuals who were targeted. Only once I was able to understand the background of those victims did I understand why actions were being taken by some Shia members of the commandos against these individuals. What made it even more clear was it wasn't just Sunnis [being targeted]; it was also some Shias. What unified that group was that mainly these were individuals that served during the former regime, that were involved in putting down the Shia uprisings following the Gulf War. It all started to make sense as a defensive measure by SCIRI and by Badr in order to make sure this never happens again and to make sure they were able to have their own secure hold on power. (*Frontline* interview, 2006).

The torture bunkers were discovered only in November 2005. Men wearing Iraqi Police uniforms were rounding people up for detention in the bunkers. Inside the Jadriyah bunker, 166 Sunnis and 3 non-Sunnis had been tortured and ill-fed (*The US Army in the Iraq War*, Vol. 1, p. 495). Predictably, the MOI head, Bayan Jabr, played down the existence of the bunkers even after a larger system of bunkers was discovered (*The Guardian*, November 17, 2005).[13] Beyond the bunkers, Jabr purged the Special Police of 300 Sunni leaders and replaced them largely with Shia Badr Corps members; he hired 15,000 new, almost entirely Shia, recruits; he began a campaign of extrajudicial intimidation and violence in Sunni locales and neighborhoods (*The US Army in the Iraq War*, Vol. 1, p. 410).

I asked Naqib a counterfactual—knowing what he knows now, would he still have created the Commandos. He said, "that is a very good question," and sighed and sat back on his chair. He answered that he would still create the force, for basically two reasons. First, Iran and Badr were intent on killing and they would have found a way to do it even if the Commandos did not provide the vehicle for it. Second, the Commandos, in the form of the National Police, did produce effective units. By 2008, the Iraqi National Police, the successors of Naqib's Commandos, would number over 32,000 and operated across the country in cooperation with US and Iraqi military counterinsurgency forces (Perito, 2008, p. 1). In the 2015 fight against ISIS, Naqib noted, some of the most effective units were four Commando units first formed in 2004.

9.4. The US Reaction and Reform Attempts

By 2007, numerous entities came to examine sectarianism and corruption in the Iraqi MOI and Iraqi police forces. First, the US Congress formed an independent commission led by retired Marine General James Jones. Among other findings on the Iraqi Security Forces, the Jones Commission wrote of the National Police: "Sectarianism in its units undermines its ability to provide security; the force is not viable in its current form. The National Police should be disbanded and reorganized" (*The US Army in the Iraq War*, Vol. 2, p. 283). Shortly thereafter, General Petraeus sent Colonel H. R. McMaster on a two-month countrywide inspection of the MOI, again finding hopeless levels of sectarianism and corruption. The official US Army history of the Iraq war summarizes McMaster's findings: "The sectarian takeover of the ministry had taken place under the eyes of hundreds of Coalition advisers who had done little to stop it" (*The US Army in the Iraq War*, Vol. 2, p. 284). MNSTC-I leader General Dubik noted that the role of the Badr Organization in the MOI was particularly destructive due to its implementation of a clear sectarian program (*The US Army in the Iraq War*, Vol. 2, p. 284).

To be sure, the United States did push for reform both at the leadership and rank levels. All nine of the National Police brigade commanders were eventually purged, along with a majority of battalion commanders (Elliott, 2007). In November 2007, the United States finished its 3–4 week "re-bluing" program of vetting and training, essentially a purge of the ranks. Units received new names and new uniforms. In time, the National Police became a professional force. Yet, we still are left with the question of how the capture of the MOI took place "under the eyes of hundreds of Coalition advisors." Also, how did the Badr Corps manage its capture of the Commandos. After all, Iranian influence, if not outright control, of the Badr Corps was well-known. How does a non-state actor connected to a foreign power take over a security ministry?

The answer here has much to do with the political power of SCIRI. As opposed to Muqtada al-Sadr and his group, Mohammed Baqr al-Hakim's SCIRI was considered by many as a "pro-Coalition" Islamist party. SCIRI members had interjected themselves into the political process from the early post-invasion phase. Moreover, SCIRI's military wing, the Badr Corps, was professional (Worsnop, 2016, pp. 375–377). Unlike the undisciplined Sadrist militias, if the SCIRI political side called for a ceasefire, the Badr military side would stop shooting. The Badr Brigades calibrated their violence and usually avoided direct contract with American forces. In short, SCIRI/Badr were Shia the United States could "partner" with (Wright, 2018, p. 77). As the US Army History summarizes of the early occupation period: "The CPA and the CTJF-7 had bestowed much of their attention on SCIRI as one of the only pro-Coalition Islamist Shi'a political parties to have national appeal. . . . Sanchez and other CJTF-7 leaders developed close ties with Hakim's successor and Muqtada al-Sadr's principal rival, Abdul Aziz al-Hakim, to the point of having almost daily discussions with the new SCIRI leader" (*The US Army in the Iraq War*, Vol. 1,

p. 199). This relationship with SCIRI and Badr would continue for years. The Army war history goes on to state that in the struggle between SCIRI and the Sadrists, "the United States had unabashedly taken sides with the Hakims and their allies" (*The US Army in the Iraq War*, Vol. 2, pp. 71–72.).

Moreover, in the wake of the 2005 elections, US leaders actually preferred to have Jabr lead the MOI rather than Naqib. Again, the official US Army war history provides a summary quotation on US preferences:

> Lieutenant General David H. Petraeus came away from initial meetings with Jabr hoping that he would prove to be less corrupt and more focused on security than the previous interior minister Falah Haqib, whom the Coalition suspected had stacked the ministry with cronies. Naqib had also been responsible for staffing the Special Police with former officers from the Republican Guard and Special Forces, a step the Shi'a and Kurdish parties had vehemently criticized. However, Jabr quickly proved to be worse than his predecessor was. (*The US Army in the Iraq War*, Vol. 1, p. 410)

Clearly, Badr captured elements in the MOI with US help, or at least tacit acceptance. The reasons for this help are multiple. The United States may have been desperate for a Shia Islamist ally. There may have been a desire to divide and rule the Shia opposition, or to isolate the Sadrists. Alternatively, US military leaders and forces may have had some professional affinity with the professional and well-trained Badr militias, especially in comparison to the undisciplined and poorly trained JAM and other groups.

The embrace of SCIRI and the tolerance of its Badr military wing would have long-term consequences, however. The Badr organization would serve as the base of long-term non-state armed actors up to the time of writing. With its implicit deal-making with the Badr organization, the United States may have helped bring some order, and less violence, to Iraq. But it also legitimated and empowered non-state actors to the detriment of longer-term state-building. As we will see in Section III, long after the 2011 US withdrawal, the Badr Organization was still in control of sections of the MOI, directing a multitude of Popular Mobilization Force units, and dominating governance in Diyala.

9.5. Conclusions

The +2 level is critical to establish population security, especially in highly urban areas. Without this local layer of security presence, individuals will likely remain isolated and neutral (0) rather than supportive of the state (+1). The spikes in violence in Baghdad occurred mainly due to the mobilization of Shia militias in an environment of near anarchy, but there was also no brake applied by local security forces (+2). Local police stations were captured by Sadrist organizations, and the MOI and its elite units were captured by Badr. The two Shia militias appeared to have built off their respective strengths— Sadrists with their local presence and SCIRI/Badr with its political clout and internal discipline—to exploit state vulnerabilities at different levels. As Andrew Radin has summarized, "Even at the height of the Surge, based on personnel present and the understood time line of US engagement, the US-led efforts could not realistically threaten Shia control of the police throughout Iraq" (Radin, 2020, p. 168).

US personnel came in with a lack of understanding of the operative mechanisms driving individuals into and out of the +2 position. As emphasized throughout this volume, US actors constantly failed to see how identity-related mechanisms pervaded almost every cranny of Iraqi politics and state-building, including the rebuilding of local security organs. The United States was unlikely to retrain the existing Saddamist police. In seeking out newly minted replacements, the United States assumed that sufficient pay and limited training would convert "Iraqi" citizens in need of employment into loyal police. These organizations would be maintained through counterintelligence, discipline, and progress toward a perceived "inevitable victory."

These assumptions are based on rational/economic mechanisms—a basic set of carrots and sticks. Perhaps a set of carrots and sticks can move individuals into the +2 position and sustain them there in many cases of state reconstruction. However, in Iraq in the post-invasion period, many individuals who came to fill the local police and the MOI were not simply basic "Iraqi citizens" looking for a job. Many were tied to militias and networks with their own set of sticks and carrots. Moreover, many were driven by emotions that elevated revenge above following any rule of law. The Badr militia members, returning from many years in exile, had their own violent agenda against their former Saddamist persecutors. The Sadrists who filled many local police stations had their own idea of how justice between Shia and Sunni should play out.

Moreover, attempting to be an unbiased and honest police officer in Iraq was often dangerous. As we will see in Section III of this book, with the collapse of the Iraqi Army in the face of ISIS, morale—and perhaps a sense of fighting for a nation—are necessary above and beyond a good salary when an individual police officer faces threats.

9.6. Addendum: Complications with a Linear Spectrum of Roles

This chapter has illustrated how US military and civilian policymakers did not anticipate the "capture" of state security organs. Perhaps coming in with a Cold War schema in mind, capture was not the common experience of a previous era's proxy wars. During the Cold War period, one superpower usually backed a non-state insurgent while the opposing superpower supported a client state. For those conflicts, a clear linear nature of the spectrum of roles, as laid out in the beginning section, was appropriate.[14]

This chapter has shown a need to expand the concept of a spectrum of roles in certain contexts. Given a weak state, the persistence of an ineffectual and corrupt existing police force, foreign occupation, emerging power of pre-invasion organizations (some armed), and a constant and powerful presence of a neighboring state, the capture of security organs should be expected. There will then be a need to reconceptualize movement on the spectrum of roles.

Within this book, there are three different phenomena that require a modification of the spectrum. This chapter has described state capture.

1. *State capture*: As just described, in this case −2 and −3 actors and organizations infiltrate or take over +2 and +3 organizations. Infiltration and takeover can occur in different ways. Infiltration could occur by placing −2 and −3 members into +2 recruitment classes, "turning" or intimidating existing +2 and +3 members. Takeover can occur when −2 and −3 organizations capture entire units or ministries, either forcefully or through political bargains.

Some institutional settings promote capture more than others. In proportional representative systems, often no single party wins enough seats to form a government. A coalition formation process will take place in which parties will pledge support of the proposed coalition in return for control of specific ministries in the new government. Some parties may seek control of security ministries (the ministry of the interior or the ministry of defense). After taking control, those parties, especially if they have an armed wing,[15] can then fill the ranks of that ministry with their own militia members.

Chapter 6 already described a second phenomenon—"flipping"—in the case of the Ghazaliyah Guardians, an action defining the community mobilization strategy:

2. *Flipping*: As outlined in depth in the Anbar Hawija cases, "flipping" occurs when the state allies with −2 groups and incorporates those groups into state

command and pay structures. In this case, the group moves over as a collective. The new +2 groups may retain much of the form, leadership, and level of autonomy of their previous −2 existence.

Finally, Chapter 17 in Section III will analyze hybridization in depth.

3. *Hybridization*: Hybrid actors are defined as "a type of armed group that sometimes operates in concert with the state and sometimes competes with it" (Cambanis et al., 2019, p. ix). Hybrid actors receive material support and legitimacy from the state while retaining autonomy and often receiving support and direction from foreign states and organizations. Hybrid groups do not "capture" state organizations or infiltrate them. There is little that is hidden or hostile with hybrids. Rather, the state makes an accommodation, sometimes a formal one, with non-state armed groups because of weakness or affinity or common political party membership. In Section III, an entire chapter is devoted to hybrids in Iraq in the form of the Popular Mobilization Forces, a classic case of hybridization.

Captain Wright Goes to Baghdad

ROGER D. PETERSEN AND TIMOTHY WRIGHT

10.1. Introduction

This chapter examines the Baghdad neighborhood of Bayaa from March 2007 to April 2008, the period of the Surge. It is largely based on the experiences of Colonel Timothy Wright, who was serving as captain and Delta Company commander in the Bayaa neighborhood of Baghdad during that time.

Wright was a doctoral student in the MIT Political Science Program and member of the MIT Security Studies Program during 2015–2018 and completed a dissertation entitled *From Predator to Provider: The Role of Violence and Rules in Establishing Social Control*. Much of the material below is taken from that work. In his dissertation, Wright's focus was "social control," defined as "the ability of a group to shape the behavior of a population so that it consistently conforms to the group's wishes without direct supervision." Wright's goal was to identify and test what is both necessary and sufficient for a group to establish social control over a population under conditions approaching anarchy.

When Wright entered Iraq in February 2007 in command of Delta Company (First Infantry Division, 1st Battalion, 28th Infantry Regiment), he was in effect part of a group, the US Army, whose primary mission was to establish social control, ultimately on behalf of the Iraq state. In Bayaa, multiple groups could possibly gain social control over the neighborhood. In addition to the US Army, there was the local police, the National Police, Sunni networks and organizations, SCIRI, and the Sadrists. As Wright's empirical work on Bayaa describes, this competition quickly boiled down to a two-way fight between the US Army and the Sadrists. Although Wright and his soldiers managed to bring down violence, expel terrorists, and provide goods and services to the population, they did not win the contest for social control in Bayaa. The Sadrists did. Following this work's two central outcomes, this chapter explains the chain of events that led to reduced violence along with state-building deficiencies.

As the reader may note, this chapter is written in the third person. This style is partly for practical reasons. As Wright returned to active duty and was limited in terms of time and flexibility, I took the initiative to select sections of Wright's dissertation and integrate them into a narrative fitting the book's framework and adding a few things along the way. Wright then reviewed that work and suggested revisions.[1] This chapter is the longest in the book. Because I believe it is the most detailed, theoretically guided, and grounded analysis of a Baghdad neighborhood during the Surge, the length is entirely appropriate.

10.2. Wright's Mission and Resources

Before his Bayaa tour, West Point–educated Captain Wright had read Field Manuel (FM) 3-24 as well as Kilcullen's work on insurgency and Halberstam's book on Vietnam, *The Best and the Brightest*. Like many other officers, he was also familiar with the population-centric strategies and tactics employed by McMaster in Tal Afar. After witnessing the problems of a war-fighting strategy during a tour in Afghanistan ("Going after donkeys from 14,000 feet was not an effective strategy"), Wright was ready to accept and try to implement the population-centric and information-seeking strategy in the new form of clear, hold, build (CHB). In fact, Wright stated in a 2008 interview with *Newsweek*, "All the stuff in the Petraeus manual, we had kind of figured it out there (in Afghanistan). . . . It was all the stuff we had seen work on the ground" (Dehgahnpisheh, 2008).

As part of the 4th Infantry Brigade Combat Team of the 1st Infantry Division, Delta Company was responsible for implementing the new Surge strategy. Captain Wright's unit entered Bayaa in March 2007. At the time, the US military was recording two Significant Acts of Violence SIGACTS per day in his area of operation. In Wright's view, the goal or end state of the mission for his unit was not well defined. Officially, and at the broadest level, the Multi-National Division-Baghdad's mission was to "significantly reduce sectarian violence while standing up Iraqi Security Forces to allow the government of Iraq to succeed." Dropping down, the 4th Brigade's mission was to, among other things, "facilitate the local government's ability to deliver essential services to the population." Finally, the decisive point for the US Army at this time was to "win the support of the Iraqi citizens." Translated down to individual soldiers, one general idea was to "get bad guys." Another very ambiguous goal was to "be visible" as a way to show the population that insurgents could not intimidate or deter the United States. While the military would assess Wright's accomplishments with a set of five lines of evaluation—security, building host-nation forces, essential services, governance, and economics— the situation in the spring of 2007 made it clear that increased security would be required before and above other goals.

The smallest company in the battalion, Delta Company had 91 soldiers assigned, organized into a company headquarters and 4 platoons of 20 men each. Led by a lieutenant and a mix of noncommissioned officers and soldiers, the platoon was the primary maneuver unit of the company. Each platoon had four armored HMMWV (High Mobility Multipurpose Wheeled Vehicle) gun trucks with medium or heavy machine guns mounted on top, which gave each platoon full mobility to conduct mounted or dismounted patrols in the neighborhood. Soldiers in the company were armed with a mix of M4 rifles, grenade launchers, light machine guns, shotguns, and pistols. They wore full body armor, carried communications packages, and had ready access to UAVs (unmanned aerial vehicles), attack helicopters, and indirect fire. The company also had access to the full intelligence collection and analysis within the battalion and higher echelons. The company commander always had access to an assigned interpreter; every patrol had at least one interpreter able to communicate with the population. The company had access to funds to pay sources for intelligence, pay families for damaged property, and execute emergency relief projects both small and large to improve the quality of life in the neighborhood.

Going in, Wright believed that he would be confronting two enemies—AQI and JAM. It quickly became apparent that JAM was by far the more powerful and problematic of the two. To counter JAM's ascendancy, Wright attempted to implement CHB doctrine. He would then need to adjust several times. Before we get to Captain Wright's evolving tour of duty, some background is necessary.

10.3. Bayaa before Wright's Arrival

Built in the 1950s as part of a massive modernization effort, Bayaa was one of many new neighborhoods intended to pull the city into the 20th century. The streets were laid out in a perfect grid, a residential neighborhood built on previously undeveloped land. By modern standards, most streets were narrow, just over a car-width wide, but all had generous sidewalks to facilitate a pedestrian lifestyle. Along the central market street, concrete buildings stood four to five stories tall, with shops on the street level and apartments above. Homes were two to three stories tall, sharing walls with their neighbors, featuring courtyards and entry gates. Schools, administrative and government buildings, recreation areas, and public works were built on the eastern edge of the grid. Originally designated as an area for workers, Bayaa's residents were firmly middle and upper middle class with professionals from a wide variety of backgrounds. The southeastern edge was home to significant estates of very well-to-do families, and many of the traditional homes had been replaced or renovated by more modern structures.

Before the war, Bayaa was both mixed in sect and middle class.[2] By best estimates, Bayaa was approximately 70% Shia and 30% Sunni (with a small Christian population as well). If the total population of the neighborhood was estimated to be between 15,000 and 20,000, then the total Sunni population was somewhere between 4,500 and 6,000. Both Shia and Sunni mosques could be found in the neighborhood, as well as one Christian church (Coptic). The neighborhood was divided by 20th Street, a major street lined with hundreds of stores that served as a commercial hub that brought in customers from surrounding neighborhoods. Bayaa has also been home (with some periods of closure in the most violent times) to one of the region's largest automobile markets, the Al Anbar Car Fair. Bayaa's bus station served as a hub for the entire city. There were no significant sectarian differences active in the markets, schools, or parks (Gulick, 1967, p. 253).

The sanctions era failed to transform the neighborhood. Saddam's policy of reinvigorating tribes also did not seem to register in Bayaa. However, this stability did not mean that residents of the neighborhood could isolate themselves from outside events. In his book *Night Draws Near: Iraq's People in the Shadow of America's War*, Anthony Shadid recounts a visit to a gun shop in Bayaa in 2003 a few days before bombing began. The shop owner stated, "Families are buying guns like they are stockpiling food and water" (Shadid, 2005, p. 22). In his description of his visit to the Bayaa gun shop, Shadid summarized his view of the broader situation in Baghdad: "As it did for many in the city the prospect of the chaos that would follow the war colored their fear about the American attack. Faith in their fellow Iraqis was scarce for those people who were blunt, as blunt as they could be in Saddam's Baghdad, about that: they saw days of bloodletting, score-settling, and lawlessness in the near future as their brutalized society came to grips with itself" (Shadid, 2005, p. 22).

Despite these preparations, Bayaa generally remained a generally peaceful enclave within the city following the 2003 invasion. By many accounts, much of the fighting in the early years happened elsewhere. Government institutions—an Iraqi Criminal Court, a police station with a jailhouse, Ministry of Education offices, and numerous schools—all still existed in the immediate post-invasion period. All were re-established quickly, giving a sense of a return to normalcy. The car market thrived and the markets were packed with people, stalls, and businesses.

Doctors, professors, and professional politicians maintained their residence in the neighborhood and commuted to work in other places. Within the neighborhood, a variety of economic engines sustained normal life. In addition to the schools (that all required teachers, administrators, and staff), the Ministry of

Education building employed a range of office workers and bureaucrats. The university in the eastern corner of the neighborhood employed a large number of people on their relatively cloistered campus. Major infrastructure facilities, including sewer pump stations, an electricity transformer station, and a telephone tower with switchboard unit, also provided jobs and stability. During 2003–2006, the population of Bayaa shopped for food in the open-air markets that ran through the center of the car market and along the street that divided M817 and M819, with individual farmers selling vegetables and herders selling live goats that, for a few more dinars, they would slaughter and butcher on the side of the road. The *shurja* (wholesale) market on the western side of the neighborhood sold bulk goods to small shops, everything from cases of Zam Zam (an Iranian Coke/Pepsi alternative) to bushels of rice. The retail market ran from one end of 20th Street to the other, where residents and visitors from the surrounding areas bought shoes, rugs, clothes, and phones (see Figure 10.1).

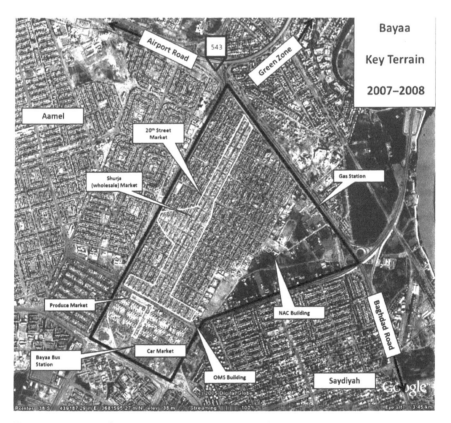

Figure 10.1. Bayaa key terrain, 2007–2008.
Source: Map of Bayaa, Baghdad. Annotated Google Earth Map.

In the immediate post-invasion years, social life in Bayaa remained vibrant and busy. Especially in the summer, the day started early, with people going to work and school by car and by foot. By midday, activity slowed in the heat, only to pick back up as the sun went down. Small restaurants and cafes were ubiquitous across the neighborhood, at which men and boys would congregate and socialize well into the evening. Sports centered around soccer, from the well-maintained sports club to the make-shift goals and fields in the car market and on the eastern edge of the *mulhallah*. There was even a small amusement park to the south of the car market. Mosques were active as well, with calls to prayer broadcast daily across the neighborhood.

In 2007, this normal life would change. Indeed, it would be shattered.

10.4. January 2007–March 2007: The Sadrists Organize in Bayaa

Even though it was not highly visible, the basis for Bayaa's transformation had been laid. Early on in the occupation, Bayaa's industrial section and car market had become a production location for Sunni insurgent car bombs; Sunni militant Tawhid and Jihad members used its gyms for meeting and recruitment (Rosen, 2006, pp. 190–191). On the Shia side, an Iraqi National Police Unit known as the Wolf Brigade (discussed in the previous chapter) was tipping off JAM about US raids in the Rashid zone (Sky, 2015, p. 213). The bombing of the Sammara mosque inaugurated Shia-Sunni clashes that would eventually transform Bayaa and all of Baghdad. The primary instrument of Shia aggression was the Sadrist movement. The Sadrist expansion reached Bayaa at the first of the year: by March, the organization's operations were in full force.

The Sadr Organization that migrated to the neighborhood was remarkably well-organized, with a clear hierarchy, chain of command, and distinct purposes for various subgroups within the organization.[3] As seen in other cases, the Sadrist organization was divided into two separate but equal parts. In effect, one part handled security functions while the other managed nonviolent services such as distribution and adjudication. Together, the Sadrists were building a parallel state.

On the one side was the Office of the Martyr Sadr (OMS). They first established an office in the neighborhood in the former criminal courthouse, declaring its arrival in Bayaa. Though the dates are fuzzy as to exactly when it became the headquarters of the OMS, by March no one in the neighborhood called it anything else.[4] The head of the OMS was the senior member of the group, and at this time, the senior authority in the neighborhood. The OMS leader was an established Shia, approximately 45–55 years old, and well respected within the organization and the neighborhood. The social services portion of the neighborhood was under his direct control.

On the other side was the Jaysh al-Mahdi (JAM). Its militia operations reflected the fragmented nature of the larger Sadrist organization at the time. There was a single JAM commander assigned to run operations in Bayaa and A'amel, the neighborhood that bordered Bayaa to the west. Like the OMS leader, the JAM commander was in his forties, and though he was originally from Bayaa, he was now much more connected to the larger JAM enterprise than to his local area.[5] JAM had three divisions based on separate missions: first, death squads focused on homogenization; second, fighters focused on denying US forces access to the neighborhood; and third, logisticians who supplied both.

The first group of JAM cells were death squads who focused on homogenizing Bayaa into a purely Shia area. As they began operations in Bayaa, external leaders recruited young men locally, creating mixed cells of external leaders and local foot soldiers to assist with the expulsion of Sunnis. They were generally armed with AK47s, pistols, and grenades, common tools in the intimidation and forced migration of families. Almost immediately, JAM developed capable, ground-level intelligence collection in Bayaa.

A second group of JAM fighters were focused on keeping US forces out of the neighborhood. Like the death squads, these cells were led by an expert who recruited local men to join, and then trained them in the technical skills they needed to attack the Coalition. These cells generally grouped around a specific skill, and in Bayaa, there was at least one cell that specialized in IEDs (more specifically, explosively formed penetrators or EFPs), one cell that specialized in indirect fire (mortars and rockets), and a third loose group that seemed to specialize in rocket-propelled grenades (RPGs) and sniper operations.

The third group was responsible for logistics, specifically, bringing in advanced weapons and ammunition necessary for the second group to conduct their operations. A specialist was brought in, apparently for coordination of weapons resupply, cache locations, and safe houses. Though rifles and pistols were ubiquitous in Iraq, mortars, RPGs, and EFPs were not readily available. The nature of these weapons indicated their Iranian origin.

The plates on an EFP were made of thick copper that was either milled from a block or cut and pressed to create the concave shape necessary to form the penetrator on detonation. This expert machining was not likely to have been done in Iraq. One American patrol was hit with an RPG-23, a modern weapon, again likely from Iran, designed to pierce tank armor from long distance. Furthermore, reports indicated that fighters from Bayaa who demonstrated enthusiasm and capability went to Iran for training, many ending up in what became known as "special group" cells.

10.5. JAM Strategy for Homogenization

As seen in other mixed Baghdad neighborhoods, JAM had a multipronged strategy for homogenization. In a first step, JAM fighters took up residence within the neighborhood and recruited locals to aid them. With fighters inserted in the neighborhood, a campaign of intimidation and sectarian cleansing could be instituted. There were at least three JAM units in Bayaa responsible for the forced migration. These groups had caches spread out across the neighborhood, in mosques and public buildings, where they kept their pistols, rifles, and grenades. They would gather at specific places (the Al Kawthar mosque, the martyr sign, at the south end of 20th street) to begin their work. They would then load into cars and patrol the streets, overtly demonstrating their freedom of movement and lack of fear of any other group.

JAM used five tactics to ethnically cleanse the Sunnis from Bayaa:

1. Identification of a Sunni household and threat: Once a family or house was identified as Sunni, they used either spray paint to mark the house with an X, or left a note wrapped around a bullet telling the family they had 48 hours to leave.
2. Kidnapping and torture: If warnings were not heeded, JAM soldiers would return to kidnap anyone living in the targeted home. At one point during Wright's tour in Bayaa, Shia insurgents kidnapped the son of a prominent local Sunni resident. The father contacted Wright's unit for help and there was a search for the son. The son did emerge but was burned and tortured. The family soon left. The effect on other Bayaa residents was powerful. In some other cases, the torture was brutal. Bodies were heavily bruised, evidence of electrical shocks and burns were common, bones were broken, and knees were drilled out with power tools. The message was clear: JAM meant what it said and had no problem following through on its threats.
3. Killings: Bodies on the street were a common sight in Bayaa, some the result of execution on a Bayaa street with a bullet in the back of the head. At other times they were executed away from the neighborhood and their bodies dumped in a prominent place. Regardless, JAM intended these killings to be a spectacle.
4. Blowing up local Sunni mosques: Sadrists cleared the neighborhood not only of Sunni people, but Sunni symbols as well. In May, two abandoned Sunni mosques were filled with explosives and imploded. On June 8, the Fatah Basha mosque was blown up, with JAM capturing the collapse of the minaret on video from a rooftop.

5. JAM did not allow empty houses to remain vacant. They were filled with Shia loyal to JAM. The OMS, the political office of the Sadrist movement, coordinated these replacements. Wright did not know who actually directed this process—whether it was JAM giving the OMS the orders, or the other way around. Either way, Sadr's forces both cleared out Sunnis and replaced them with reliable Shia in a short period of time.

To expand on this last point, the new settlers became beholden to the OMS proto-state. One of the OMS's first state-building roles was as a "housing authority" working in sync with JAM's violent program. In this violent setting, however, the OMS also took control of what was left of other state functions. This task was not difficult considering the enveloping chaos in Bayaa. Aside from schools, little was open in the neighborhood. The market was barely functional as most stores were closed. Food was available, but electricity and sewage were intermittent at best. Trash piled up on the streets. Rationed items, like cooking oil and fuel, were intermittently available. The OMS quickly set about taking control of these key resources. By March, they fully controlled the Bayaa gas station and black-market fuel sales. They repaired and fueled generators to make up for the lack of power from the Baghdad grid. They secured and guarded key infrastructure to ensure that it remained as functional as possible. They even paid people to pick up trash.

In fact, in March 2007 there was no government in Bayaa with whom US forces could partner. The court building was taken over by the OMS, and the spaces for judges at the police station were empty. Citizens could get their ration cards for gasoline and oil from the government building known as the *belladiyah*, but JAM controlled access and distribution. There were no elected officials or ministries providing governance, administration, or conflict resolution. Except for their security forces, the reach of the central government extended to the walls of the Green Zone, and not beyond, and in the case of Bayaa, those partners were weak at best.

10.6. Captain Wright and Delta Company Arrive in Bayaa in the Midst of Sadrist Cleansing and Implement a Version of CHB

In March 2007, Delta Company arrived in the middle of this chaotic scene. Wright was knowledgeable and ready to implement the new form of CHB expostulated by FM 3-24. This strategy gave form to the vague directions to "be visible," to "go after bad guys," and establish a presence and face up to intimidation. In Wright's understanding, the strategy called for the following tactics:

1. Creating and guarding checkpoints: For the first three months of its deployment, Delta Company was exclusively responsible for one critical checkpoint entering Green Zone. One platoon out of the company's four platoons was supposed to guard Checkpoint 543 at all times.
2. Dismounting and "walking around": In first weeks of the tour, Wright ordered his units to dismount and try to "meet folks." Sniper fire soon made this tactic impossible. The US forces still wanted to maintain personal contact, but would do so through randomized, 20-minute maximum visits.
3. Deliberate raids: Raids were conducted only after enough intelligence had been collected. With information coming in from the population, Wright became knowledgeable about JAM meeting points, such as the local gas station.
4. Direct fire engagements, avoiding excessive indirect fire: When insurgents fired on Delta Company, units responded, with effort to avoid civilian casualties; 50-caliber machine guns were only used in the absence of civilians.
5. CERP payments: Wright administered micro-grants but only during the last four months of the tour.[6] The US Army also put money into trash removal, sewage pumping, and other public works.

The strategy and tactics were those of CHB as laid out and discussed extensively in previous chapters. The strategy was a clear failure in the first half of 2007.

As outlined in previous chapters, CHB sees the counterinsurgency battle as a contest involving three actors: government security forces and Coalition partners (+3); "a neutral or passive majority" of the population (−1 to + 1); and irreconcilable insurgents (−3). The strategy relies on recruitment and training professional indigenous military and police forces, economic development to "win hearts and minds" and convert and/or retain the support of the population, and the use of information from the population to kill or capture insurgents. The strategy also recommends taking great pains to minimize collateral damage that might alienate the population.

Like many Western occupation strategies, CHB greatly relies on rational choice mechanisms, both in terms of the effects of safety and in economics. For the counterinsurgents under CHB, the first task is not only to actually clear the insurgents, but also to communicate to the population that the probability of retaliation has greatly diminished. This goal relies on the rational choice "tipping" mechanism capturing the logic of safety in numbers. Once a certain percentage of the population is visibly cooperating with the occupation forces, individuals will calculate that cooperation is now safe. As more and more join in a cooperation bandwagon and with knowledge of the strength and sustainability of security forces, the move rightward on the spectrum toward cooperative roles becomes a strong wave. Focal points—events, places, or dates that help to coordinate expectations and thus actions—can also serve as important informational mechanisms to move this process. CHB is also based upon avoiding negative emotions and preventing the triggering of violence-producing norms. The strategy is particularly concerned with diminishing the population's fear of the insurgent. The reduction of fear helps create the bandwagoning process, leading to the surpassing of "tipping points" which in turn can drive the population rightward on the spectrum. The rightward movement in turn leads to the conditions for effective state-building.

Certainly, US forces did not prevent the violent ethnic cleansing of Sunnis during the early months of the Surge strategy in Bayaa. There are both obvious and less obvious reasons for this failure. Clearly, there was a shortage of manpower. Delta Company needed to devote an entire platoon to controlling one broad intersection. The neighborhood contained dense urban terrain that was home to approximately 15,000–20,000 people. At any given time, Delta Company could only provide two or three platoons to cover any emergency or conduct an operation. There were also constraints on mobility. The narrow streets of the neighborhood made travel by HMMWVs difficult. EFPs were almost impossible to see before detonation, making any movement risky. Also, few of Delta Company's small number of soldiers had any combat experience.

Given resource constraints, several tactics were considered but were found untenable. In trying to counter ethnic cleansing, it would have been helpful to conduct a census to gauge demographic change and anticipate where JAM would push next. In a nearby AO (area of operations), US forces had taken a census, but it took nine months and took up a huge amount of resources. In Bayaa, the ethnic cleansing was completed in three months.

As covered in the following section, there was also no way to involve the local police. Wright had no relationship with the local police commanders. The rank and file could only be used as traffic cops or security guards. Development of the police was a low priority, even during the so-named "year of the police" in 2006. The only useful units were remnants of the National Police Wolf Brigades who had been assigned to localities. Wright did have contact with the unit leader who provided some help in the Shia areas, but serious concerns over general competence and specific loyalties made full collaboration problematic at best.

There was no way to totally isolate Bayaa through wall-building, in Wright's estimation, nor would such isolation have been desirable. For instance, separating the car market would only have produced a backlash from the merchants there. There was no way to keep people from using the bus station in Bayaa.

Because there had been little previous US presence in the AO, there was little intelligence to build on. Nor would useful information be coming down from higher levels. Intelligence collection had to be done at the company level, and there was great variation in the type and amount of intelligence across AOs.

10.7. Sadrist Strategic Adjustments: Aggressive at Every Node of the Spectrum

JAM had begun their homogenization process before Wright's forces entered Bayaa. As the US forces developed new tactics and intensified previous ones, JAM would also make adjustments. Given their resources and experience, they were able to do so.

To efficiently carry out their anti-Sunni operations, JAM needed to deny US access to the neighborhood. JAM incorporated a variety of tactics with their specialized cells. They established and maintained limited points of access into the neighborhood. When the violence broke out in 2006, most neighborhoods attempted to harden their areas by emplacing barriers and obstacles at the ends of streets leading in and out. Although the major original impetus for these barriers was toward sectarian rivals, JAM found that the barriers were also helpful in denying access to the Americans. Bayaa, being laid out on a grid, had over 70 ways a vehicle could drive in and out. In March, less than 10 remained open, JAM blocking the rest with piles of dirt, cinder blocks, concrete barriers, or wire. JAM established a network of people who would watch the entrances and alert the area when they came, either by "flipping pigeons" (releasing or scaring off birds from the rooftops), calling key leaders, or having Shia mosques play certain types of music. If they could not physically deny access, they could at least control it enough to know (most of the time) exactly where Delta Company was and what they were doing.

JAM made strategic decisions about where, when, and how it attacked Delta Company, employing specific weapons to gain maximum effect on both Delta Company and the population. Broadly speaking, JAM used precision weapons and tactics in Bayaa, but was more likely to use imprecise and explosive weapons and tactics elsewhere. Outside the neighborhood, JAM's most dangerous and casualty-producing weapons was the EFP, and they used it extensively during this phase on the routes that bordered Bayaa.[7]

JAM's use of EFPs was effective for multiple reasons. First, and in the best case, Delta Company would take serious casualties and stop coming into the neighborhood.[8] Second, they knew that detonating multiple IEDs along the same route would cause the US forces to restrict its use, giving the US fewer access points to the neighborhood and JAM greater freedom of movement. Third, by setting IEDs off near police or National Police checkpoints or positions, it would sow distrust between US forces and their nominal partners. Finally, striking an IED often caused units to wildly overreact, especially if soldiers were wounded, maimed, or killed. Untrained units (such as supply convoys) would often fire indiscriminately into the neighborhoods surrounding the detonation. Trained units might sweep through the area to try to catch the trigger man, kicking in doors and searching houses. Whether by untrained or trained units, these responses did little to encourage the population to support Delta Company.

Inside the neighborhood, JAM employed snipers. These snipers were probably well-trained given their ability to make head-shots against multiple members of Wright's Delta Company. Also, JAM insurgents used RPGs and machine gun fire within the neighborhood.

In sum, in Bayaa the JAM-OMS strategy addressed almost every node on the spectrum of roles. The primary objective of the Sadrists was to clear the neighborhood of the Sunni population and replace those residents with loyal Shia. The bifurcated organization—JAM mobilizing large-scale violence, and the OMS building a proto-state—was highly effective. To understand why, we can consider the strategy node by node, starting from the left side:

JAM brings in fighters at the −3 level: By this point, some JAM units were specialized in using IEDS, especially EFPs. Additionally, Iranian-supported "Special Groups" forces were trained and equipped to create havoc against US forces.

JAM builds up the −2 position: Sadrist fighters were relocated to Bayaa, forming a local armed base. These fighters were joined by locals recruited from the neighborhood itself.

OMS housing and services bolster −1: The most important resource provided by the OMS was housing. Though the program would not get into full force until months later, in March, Shia began migrating into the neighborhood. Enticed by nice homes and a Shia-friendly neighborhood, families from across Baghdad began coming into Bayaa. They simply had to go to the OMS to receive a house and a small amount of cash to get started. At this time, it was unclear whether the OMS was perceived as a benefactor by the new residents of Bayaa. Clearly, these selected recipients of housing would be more likely to support and pass information on to JAM/OMS than to Coalition or Government of Iraq forces.

JAM violence targets Sunnis at the 0 and +1 level: Threats, kidnappings, torture created an intolerable level of fear among the Sunni population. Most opted to leave the neighborhood.

JAM likely infiltrates the local police at the +2 level: By the time Wright got to Bayaa, it was common sense that the local police were likely infiltrated and of little use, thus Wright's lack of contact with them.

JAM and Special Groups attack US and Iraqi at the +3 level: As described above, the US forces came under constant pressure.

10.8. Explaining Early Sadrist Victory: Strategic Mismatches between Sadrist and US Strategies

Above all, it is clear that the Shia won. The following summary by a *Los Angeles Times* staff writer in August 2007 was written after visiting the adjoining neighborhoods of Amil and Bayaa and interviewing several residents and is worth quoting at length:

> The expressway skirting the Amil neighborhood in Baghdad is only a couple of miles from Mahmoud Mekki's home, but it might as well be a hundred. To reach it, Mekki must pass checkpoints guarded by Iraqi police commandos who he says are really Shiite Muslim militiamen trying to drive Sunni Muslims out of Amil. So Mekki, a Sunni, remains holed up in his home, dependent on sympathetic Shiite neighbors to pick up his groceries and run other errands.
>
> "I ask you to help us!" Mekki sobbed on the phone late one hot July night. "I don't want democracy! I just want security."
>
> Iraqi and American military officials say incidents of sectarian "cleansing" in Baghdad have decreased since a U.S. military clampdown began in February, but what is happening in Amil and neighboring Bayaa belies the claim. Since May, Iraqi police say, more than 160 bodies have been found in Amil and Bayaa—men without identification, usually shot and bearing signs of torture, hallmarks of sectarian death squads. On many days, the number of corpses found in the two neighborhoods account for half of those picked up across the capital. Before the war, Amil and Bayaa were middle-class neighborhoods where Sunnis and Shiites lived easily among one another. Now, not only are they mainly Shiite, but they have become prime territory for Shiite militias looking to expand into the surrounding Sunni-dominated areas. (Susman, 2007)

In Bayaa, most Sunni residents had abandoned the neighborhood by the end of May 2007. Sunnis had been gradually expelled through threats and violence, although their departure was not block by block, street by street, but more like "disappearing measles," with people leaving one house in one section of the neighborhood while another family was leaving in a different section.

In the period following the destruction of the Sunni mosque, US patrols noticed significantly increased numbers of Shia flags, banners, and propaganda, and cars were driving up and down the streets playing distinctly Shia songs. People seemed to be in a good mood. When asked why, they responded, "This is our neighborhood, and we are celebrating" (Schemm, 2007). As Wright recalled, there was one point at which Shia essentially declared victory in the neighborhood. Although it was a mystery to Wright and to the soldiers in Delta Company, Shia held a celebration establishing that Bayaa had become "Shiaville," in Wright's terminology. Shia insurgents took control of much of the neighborhood in three months after the arrival of Delta Company.

In order to fully understand the forces underlying Sadrist success, we can juxtapose both US and JAM strategies and tactics along the spectrum of roles. We can examine the sequence of moves and whether and how those moves triggered intended mechanisms to move individuals to new positions (Figure 10.2). As a central goal, CHB aims at moving individuals from the −1 and 0 nodes to the +1 node largely through rational choice mechanisms. Individuals essentially play a "tipping game" and move to state support when they see other individuals move to +1 without retaliation. Focal point mechanisms, such as elections, help show when that point has been reached. Individuals also move from −1 and 0 to +1 through economic "carrots," seeing better material outcomes through such a move. When the state supplies both safety and material goods, the state gains legitimacy. During the CHB process, the state is also developing security forces, mainly at the +3 level, to go after −3 individuals now identified by a state-collaborating general population. These forces provide more visible security, generating a virtuous loop between increasing safety and increasing information.

The Sadrist strategy blunted the triggering of every intended mechanism of US CHB in Bayaa. JAM violence prevented anything close to a "tipping point" being reached. JAM attacks, kidnappings, and torture created both rational reasons for Sunni citizens to leave and the emotional mechanism of fear that could produce panicked and rapid flight.

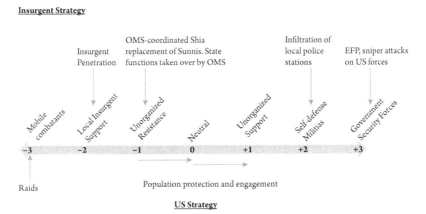

Figure 10.2. Juxtaposition of US and JAM strategies in Bayaa.

In terms of the production of material goods and adjudication, the OMS provided its Shia clients with superior offerings. The US strategy was based on an erroneous view of the state-building project in Iraq. CHB is based on the idea that there will be time to build a state and there will be a lack of serious competition in state-building. In Iraq, as discussed previously, both Iraqi expatriates and many US officials believed that post-invasion Iraq would produce a "blank slate" for building a democratic state. After a quick "clear," there would be a relatively easy road to "build." Instead, the Sadrists had the ability to take over basic state functions while the Iraqi government flailed or simply failed to show up. In Bayaa, the Sadrists moved the population to −1, rather than the state convincing individuals to move to +1.

The Sadrists and JAM also filled the −2 and +2 holes unaddressed by CHB. In Bayaa, arguably, the decisive nodes were located at the local, armed level. On the resistance side, the Sadrists recruited locals into their organization who could provide both intelligence and threats against Sunni targets. The −2 organization was composed of an effective mix of outsiders with previous experience in ethnic cleansing tactics combined with local Shia networks. On the state side (+2), the local police were co-opted. The US forces did not trust them, did not interact with them, and did not have them as local allies. Crucially, the US forces did not have a local security partner.

This point deserves some attention. Three Iraqi security services were present in Bayaa. The local police, commonly referred to as Iraqi Police or IPs, were similar in many ways to the local police throughout Baghdad. The second security service was the Facilities Protection Service (FPS). The FPS provided fixed-site security at government infrastructure locations, such as the schools, the telephone tower/switchboard, and the sewage pump station, among others. The local police station housed approximately 40 police officers, evenly split between patrol police and FPS. The third security service was the National Police, best categorized as +3 rather than +2 because of their national and mobile nature. The National Police were significantly better equipped than the local police.

In the implementation of CHB in Iraq, each of these local armed groups was problematic. The facilities protection service was heavily implicated in JAM operations. Members of the local police were seldom invested in their jobs. Even their physical facilities were sub-standard.[9] Their number one priority was survival; priority number two was making money. Stopping crime and maintaining order fell to a distant third. While showing up for work meant they got paid, incentives were low to do anything that might risk one's life. Like the FPS, the local police were Shia-dominated and had strong sectarian leanings. In Bayaa, the National Police appeared sympathetic, if not outright supportive, of JAM and the Shia expansion. It was also clear that there was little enthusiasm on the part of either National Police battalion in the area to head-on challenge any militia, whether it was Shia or Sunni.[10] Fighting of any kind, except for self-preservation, seemed to be beyond the National Police's agenda. They were outsiders, with little local knowledge, few local connections, and no hard incentives to protect Sunnis.

10.8.1. Sunni Marginalization in Bayaa

The Sunnis of Bayaa simply did not possess the organization and resources to match the Sadrists. Isolated and under pressure, the Sunnis of Bayaa attempted to fight back against their eviction, but without much success. Their strategy had three lines of operation: resist eviction, get outside help to weaken JAM by attacking it, and collaborate with US forces to gain sympathy and improve the Coalition's chances of halting the JAM expansion. The Sunnis' greatest tool to combat Shia expansion was the car bomb. On multiple occasions, Sunnis used car bombs in areas of Shia concentration in retaliation for the forced migration. However, that tactic backfired. On May 6, in an attempt to push back hard against the forced migration and killing, a car bomb was detonated at the southern entrance of the 20th Street market, a fully Shia area of the neighborhood that was busy with people shopping for food and groceries; 33 people were killed and over 70 wounded, a massive loss of life for the area. This major killing event triggered a major US sweeping exercise of the neighborhood. JAM was able to weather the US clearing operation. The Sunnis were not so lucky. As the US unit began clearing, they pinpointed the major Sunni cell's location and raided the premises. There were no more major Sunni attacks in Bayaa after that.

When US forces prepared to pacify Baghdad, they believed that Sunni resistance would be a larger problem than the Shia Sadrists. After all, AQI bombs were wreaking fear and havoc in Baghdad. As throughout most of the US time in Iraq, the military poorly understood the nature and underlying goals of the sectarian conflict. They overestimated state forces while failing to understand the ability of non-state actors to create and target violence. Most fundamentally, the US forces originally underestimated the power and capabilities of the Sadrists and JAM.

10.9. Bayaa, July–November 2007: The Game Changes

10.9.1. Sadrist Change in Strategy

As described earlier, JAM and associated Special Groups units systematically moved across Baghdad neighborhoods. They had launched their movement into Bayaa from Amel. By the summer of 2007, they were using Bayaa as a base to move into Saydiyah, the neighborhood immediately to the southwest. Correspondingly, most Special Groups attacks in Bayaa ceased.

In their place, the local JAM members who filled a supporting role over the past three months transitioned into leadership roles. As JAM in Bayaa took on a more local identity, targeted killings dropped considerably, while advanced attacks on US forces—RPGs, EFPs, and mortars—remained relatively constant. Special Groups had done their job well, training their replacements and establishing lines of communication into Bayaa that allowed local JAM to continue the fight against US forces. Finally, and most importantly, as Special Groups moved on, the OMS and its lines of operation moved to the forefront of the Sadrist Organization in Bayaa. While JAM retained its autonomy to attack US forces broadly and Delta Company specifically, the OMS in Bayaa increasingly directed JAM's overall role. Local objectives and functions moved to the forefront of Sadrist activities in this phase. In effect, JAM was used to support social services and the OMS, rather than the other way around.

With the OMS in ascension, a more structured organization emerged. The OMS leader, Mohammed, was now at the head of the organization. His office and staff were at the OMS, and he effectively managed and controlled Sadrist business in the neighborhood. There were four sub-departments: administration, logistics, money collection, and operations. Administration and logistics controlled the management of the OMS's civil service functions. Money collection and operations were local JAM members who now implemented the OMS's policies, decisions, and directives. Unlike the Special Groups, these new JAM leaders were younger, less skilled, and less experienced. Though capable, they were less organized and less professional than previous JAM leaders. Money collection was run by Fadhil "Dauria," or Fadhil "patrol," a nickname given to him as the leader of the group that patrolled the neighborhood, collected money, and enforced the OMS's rules. The Operations group was led by Mustafa, a local JAM member who had proved himself an effective fighter over the past three months under Special Groups. He was in his twenties, brash, and cocky. The group he led was composed of family members local to Bayaa and of similar age and personality. He had two other lieutenants who ran their own cells, and between the three of them, they were the primary JAM presence in Bayaa. They served two purposes. First, and along with Fadhil, they patrolled the neighborhood and acted as JAM muscle and enforcement. Second, they retained the responsibility and authority to attack Delta Company to weaken their ability to challenge the OMS for control. Based on reporting, however, it was never entirely clear if the specific orders to attack Delta Company came from Mohammed or were the operations group's desire to continue their Special Groups mission. Whether operating at the behest of Mohammed or tolerated by him as they pursued their own agenda, the effects of their operations benefited both.

The reformed Sadrist OMS/JAM organization pursued several objectives. Above all, the sectarian/demographic transformation was effectively consolidated. Remnants of Sunni culture were removed, and the migration of Shia families into the neighborhood continued at full pace. By the end of the fall of 2007, few Sunni houses were empty. Nearly all had been filled by Shia families new to the area. Enticed by nice homes and a Shia-friendly neighborhood, families from across Baghdad began coming to Bayaa, signing in with the OMS, and receiving "start-up" money.

The Sadrists, through the OMS, also provided needed services. As violence continued, most normal activity in Bayaa was shut down. As already mentioned above, the OMS stepped in as a proto-state. The OMS instituted taxation measures. They controlled contracting in the area. Any contractor who wished to do work on Coalition projects in the area had to get approval from the OMS to submit a bid. This ensured that local work fell under the OMS purview, and the OMS got a kickback. When NGOs or the Coalition independently contracted workers and sent them into the neighborhood (such as street cleaners, trash removal, or painting), these workers were compelled to give up a portion of their salary to the OMS or be kicked out. As a result, the OMS could either take credit for improvements to the neighborhood made by the Coalition, or at the very least, profit from those contracts on the side.

Importantly, the OMS established a system for rule-making and enforcement. First, by establishing their patrol and collection operations, the OMS established a monitoring mechanism on the population. Fadhil and his group were effectively the OMS's beat cops, moving throughout the neighborhood and ensuring that people were acting in accordance with the OMS's rules. Mustafa and his cells provided similar functions when not attacking Delta Company. Violators were either dealt with on the spot or were brought to the OMS for questioning. This enforcement mechanism was not just a resource and benefit for the OMS.

Furthermore, the OMS began providing a resource for people in Bayaa to resolve their disputes. By July, the OMS had established a court system within the neighborhood. If any member had a problem with another, they went to the OMS to get it solved. Starting at 4 p.m., OMS leadership would hear claims from the individuals. They made arguments and presented evidence against the perpetrator. As necessary, the operations division would bring the accused to the OMS to defend themselves. After hearing the evidence, the OMS would make a ruling for punishment and/or recompense. The operations division would ensure that each party met their requirements to satisfy the ruling. Given their well-earned reputation for application of violence, the system was remarkably effective in maintaining order. In Wright's research, as we will come back to below, the Sadrist move to gain control of adjudication functions may have been critical.

10.10. Delta Company Changes Strategy

This section addresses each of the five strategies in turn.

10.10.1. Continuing Clear, Hold, Build

The US Army and Wright's Delta Company continued to implement a form of CHB. They continued to focus on protecting the population during this phase, and as security for the population improved, they began increasing the distribution of goods and services to Bayaa. After three months of hard fighting, Delta Company adapted its tactics—its daily patrolling, deliberate operations, and targeting—to more effectively counter JAM operations in the neighborhood. Patrolling was focused on expanding the company's understanding of what went on day to day in the neighborhood. With less overall violence, Delta Company could focus operations on developing relationships with various influential people in Bayaa (religious leaders, local political figures), mapping essential information (migration patterns, electrical systems, nascent Iraqi government structures), and conducting reconnaissance of JAM-associated buildings and targets.

Intelligence collection increased during this period as well. Through a tip card program, Delta Company began to build a stable of neighborhood informants that could provide a variety of human intelligence. Usually meeting in the Green Zone or talking over the phone, Delta Company began to build a picture of how the OMS and JAM operated, their patterns of life, and the effect that operations were having. Some of it led to raids (and when successful, informants were paid well), but most filled out information about the organization and the nature of life in Bayaa beyond those doing violence.

Deliberate operations centered around disrupting the OMS/JAM operations in the neighborhood. Sometimes there were searches of buildings reported to contain caches; other times they sought to catch JAM members conducting illegal operations in the open. For example, JAM's use of the gas station to generate revenue was well known, so Delta Company started showing up at the gas station at random times and searching the workers for guns and connections to JAM.

Although Delta Company's main work was still on "clear," they increasingly engaged in "build" activities. The brigade funded a $74 million contract to support reconstruction efforts across West Rasheed, including Bayaa, to clear trash, build fences, install power generators, and fix sewage pipes (Partlow, 2007). The company also began an initiative to fix broken power transformers within the neighborhood to ensure more even distribution of power across the grid. Barriers were brought in to better control traffic on the southern end of the neighborhood where Sunni car bombs had attacked the market and on the northern end where IED cells had triggered overreactions by passing convoys.

There was also a push to find new leadership within the neighborhood who could serve the interests of the population. After months of working with the Neighborhood Advisory Council, Wright concluded that the Neighborhood Advisory Council was an isolated entity, one that could neither provide useful information about the neighborhood nor speak for its needs.[11] Therefore, the company sought to broaden its engagement to others who might have more influence over what went in in Bayaa. At various times, the company met with local politicians, business leaders, tribal sheikhs, and even the leader of the SCIRI *husseniyah*. The goal was to establish who had real power and influence in Bayaa to work with Delta Company to cooperatively reduce violence and to focus reconstruction on the areas most needed.

It should be noted that, contrary to Surge prescriptions, Delta Company never established a combat outpost in Bayaa. Tasked with maintaining security 24 hours a day, 7 days a week, on the highway interchange at Checkpoint 543, establishing and securing a combat outpost would have left little combat power available to the company to conduct operations inside the neighborhood. Though they had no place to "live" inside the neighborhood, they tried to maintain a constant presence by establishing a near-continuous patrol schedule, maintaining at least one platoon on patrol inside the neighborhood while a second secured CP 543 on the northern corner of Bayaa, able to react in an emergency inside the neighborhood as necessary.

10.10.2. Rejection of War-Fighting and Community Mobilization

Delta Company's investment in Bayaa remained high, though many had lost the cautious optimism that permeated the company in March. In Phase I, Delta Company had taken as many casualties as any other company in the brigade. This took its toll on the soldiers. Many advocated for a more muscular approach in the neighborhood, such as responding to any attack with overwhelming violence, aggressively searching houses, and increasing detentions of people with little cause. Some wanted to "send a message" to the neighborhood that if Delta Company was attacked, the company would counterattack against anyone who was near. They felt that the company ought to push the rules of engagement to their limit. Though these approaches were rejected, the possibility of Delta Company shifting to a more coercive, rather than protective, approach in Bayaa was nearer than many expected it ever to be. Over time, tactical adaptation led to fewer casualties and more effective targeting, and morale improved, but the fatigue of continuous operations remained.

During 2006–2007, US forces first allied with Sunni tribes in Anbar and then with Sunni elements in Baghdad and elsewhere through the Awakening or Sons of Iraq movement. Sunnis approached US forces to do the same in Bayaa. They claimed that they would go into Bayaa and clean up all the bad guys and solve the problem themselves. Wright saw this offer as a thinly veiled attempt at revenge. The offer was quickly rejected. US forces saw little role for armed Sunni groups in Bayaa. Eventually, in an agreement signed among Sunni and Shia leaders in March 2008, Sunnis would be allowed to re-enter the neighborhood to evaluate their homes and businesses. If their house or business was empty, they could petition to move back in immediately. If occupied, they could submit claims for rent to be paid to the council. No one would be evicted.

10.10.3. Homogenization and Decapitation

As detailed above, Bayaa had become a homogenous Shia area by mid-2007. Overall violence fell as Bayaa went from a being a contested zone between Shia and Sunni to a secure launching base to continue operations into neighboring Saydiyah. With this change, Special Groups moved out. Correspondingly, JAM/ OMS could turn their focus to social and political goals. Civilian casualties fell because there were few remaining Sunni targets. The now locally led JAM did continue attacks on Coalition forces. There was little that US forces could have done to prevent homogenization of Bayaa. Still, US forces did reap some benefits. Shia forces did greatly diminish AQI's activities in Bayaa; Shia forces were able to provide protection for their own population, now including Shia refugees fleeing remaining conflict zones.

The biggest active change for US strategy came in the increasing use of decapitation. Over the first month, information from the local population did flow in. Much of that information was not useful, as it came from residents with grudges informing on a neighbor for purposes of revenge or gain. Information also came in during the course of regular contact with members of the Neighborhood Advisory Council (NAC). However, as Delta Company's human intelligence network expanded, it was able to feed the battalion with ground-level information that drove higher-level collection across a wider spectrum of intelligence assets. Battalion-level analysts helped Delta Company refine the structure of the OMS/JAM organization, pulling in additional sources that corroborated ground-level reporting, and opening new leads for striking at the organization. These assets helped find and fix members of JAM in Bayaa, leading to an increasingly successful cycle of raids in the neighborhood. Over time, Delta Company became less reactive to JAM. Though the company was still periodically attacked, the opportunity to kill or capture the perpetrator was no longer limited to the attack itself. If Delta Company was unable to catch or kill the attacker at the point of contact, it combed its source network, monitored reporting, and eventually put together the information necessary to capture him in a raid at a later time.

To an extent, the CHB strategy was working. CHB cultivates +1 support in order to gain information for +3 security forces to go after −3 insurgents. In Bayaa, the population provided enough tips for Captain Wright to develop targeting charts capable of allowing deliberate raids. Wright started with names and descriptions on an XL spreadsheet. He managed to produce complicated diagrams and a flow chart by May 14, 2007.[12] With these connections outlined, Delta Company could conduct deliberate raids in an effort to catch JAM members and also identify and detain cooperating members of the OMS.

With the development of this detailed knowledge of networks, Delta Company had also developed a clear picture of the scope of OMS/JAM operations in the neighborhood. While the significance of the OMS becoming the provider of law-and-order functions in Bayaa was not fully understood at the time, it was a clear indicator that the organization Delta Company faced was highly capable and enjoyed significant influence in the neighborhood. If the reporting was true, however, it provided the company with an opportunity to strike the OMS and potentially take out its leadership all at once. For the last two weeks in September and the first week in October, the company devoted numerous collection assets to confirming the pattern of life described in reporting. If indeed the OMS held court proceedings and dispute resolution from 4 p.m. to 6 p.m. every day, then a raid at that time could yield not only JAM operational cells, but OMS leadership as well. Using UAVs, signal intelligence, and ground intelligence collection, Delta Company confirmed the pattern. Activity increased dramatically at the OMS at 4 p.m., with significant traffic going in and out. By 6 p.m. the office closed, and people dispersed. This confirmation was significant in two ways. First, the OMS was not only providing adjudication, but it was being used extensively by the population. To the untrained eye, it appeared like any other community building, with lots of foot traffic from all types of people. Second, it provided Delta Company the opportunity to net a significant number of targets at once, potentially taking out the OMS's leadership all at once. If successful, it would be a major victory.

On October 11 at approximately 5 p.m., Delta Company raided the OMS. Jamming cell phone signals and approaching from multiple avenues of approach, three platoons converged on the OMS at high speed. They managed to get close, but not all the way to the building, before word went out that a raid was coming. UAVs observed "squirters" (people running in multiple directions like leaks out of a water balloon) off the objective just before the company arrived. Though several detainees were taken, and the OMS's activities were confirmed, none of the senior leadership was caught—success, but far short of expectations. After approximately 90 minutes on the objective, platoons began to quietly exit the area, choosing to maneuver through Bayaa to discourage the use of RPGs or EFPs. After a strike on their headquarters, JAM hit back. They struck 2nd Platoon's trail vehicle, taking the driver's leg and destroying the vehicle. Despite many people on the streets, no one saw anything.

The raid on the OMS court was an act of decapitation; its primary goal was to capture a significant number of leadership targets. While the Joint Special Operations Command (JSOC) was dramatically expanding its pace of operations across Iraq, some lower-level Army commanders were also getting in on the game, using improved intelligence to identify crucial nodes in local networks.

Critically, understanding the organization and nature of the Sadrists opened the door for accommodation between Delta Company and the OMS.

10.11. Compromises and Deal-Making

Perhaps Captain Wright's most important innovation went outside the bounds of COIN and war-fighting strategies. Given the realities of violence and the state in Bayaa, Captain Wright and Delta Company were forced to make some adjustments in strategy (Dehgahnpisheh, 2008). In the first three months of the tour, Delta Company had lost 10 of 102 soldiers, three of those killed. Shia forces had cleansed the neighborhood of most of its Sunni residents. Given resource constraints, Delta Company was doing all it could to "clear" and "hold," with very little time or resources for "build."

The strategic problem Delta Company faced can be addressed with reference to the type of organizational flow charts Wright was able to develop. The US CHB strategy focused on the middle nodes, winning over the population (−1, 0, +1) and going after more mobile JAM and Special Groups forces (−3). The actual center of power in Bayaa, however, lay at the −2 node in the form of local armed strongmen and their networks. Developing some decapitation capabilities was one way to address this problem, although, as in the example above, there was often a lack of success.

One powerful Shia militia leader became a target of Wright and Delta Company's raids—Mohammed, the leader of the local OMS.[13] Delta Company had raided his house three times in July. Failing to catch Mohammed, Delta

Company did capture and jail his brother. At this juncture, Wright made a decision to modify straightforward CHB strategy and tactics. He would not go so far as to implement a community mobilization strategy as was being employed with Sunni insurgents in other areas of Iraq and other neighborhoods of Baghdad. But he would form a sort of truce with a major −2 element in Shia Bayaa. In October 2007, Wright used Mohammed's brother (called Abdullah here) to arrange communications with the enemy. A *Newsweek* article described Wright's move (Dehgahnpisheh, 2008):

> The scene was carefully staged. Last October, Abdullah was brought, bound and blindfolded, into a quiet corner of Forward Operating Base Falcon, not far from the tent where Wright slept. There were no harsh lights or guards, just a couple of folding chairs outside. Wright wanted the session to come across not as an interrogation but as a meeting between equals. He told Abdullah to stand and carefully cut away his plastic handcuffs with scissors and lifted the blindfold. He could tell that Abdullah recognized him as the American officer who had arrested him three months before. The moment "very easily could have gone sour," Wright recalls. But the American captain did the unexpected: he apologized. He explained that detaining Abdullah had been a mistake. He said he wanted to work with him to calm Bayaa. Abdullah smiled. Wright allowed himself a small hope.

Three days after Abdullah's release, Mohammed called Wright. More communication followed. Both men agreed that they shared the same goal—reducing violence in Bayaa. The nature of the exchanges followed certain unwritten rules—there would never be a face-to-face meeting; Wright's interpreter served as a consistent go-between. Wright insisted on three non-negotiable points. First, the company was not leaving the area. They would continue to patrol, conduct deliberate operations, and work with the National Police to improve their capabilities. Second, if Delta Company was attacked, retaliation against the guilty parties would follow, just as it had over the last year. Third, Delta Company would continue to pursue those who had been violent in the past but would consider detention on a case-by-case basis.

Mohammed had his own set of expectations. Mohammed expected Delta Company to respect the people of Bayaa, entering houses and arresting people only when necessary and with evidence. Second, Mohammed would not meet publicly with Delta Company, and if any word of his communication got out to the neighborhood, the relationship would be over. Meeting with and appearing to work with US forces would undercut his status and legitimacy within his own organization and the population, potentially putting his safety at risk. Finally, he made it clear that he had no control over Special Groups. He had communication with their cells and relationships with their leaders, but he held no sway over their actions or their decisions to target US forces.

As these terms were acceptable to both parties, the two men began conversing regularly in November. Shortly after the dialogue began, a Delta Company patrol with the company commander identified an individual "flipping pigeons" to alert the neighborhood that Delta Company was present. The patrol halted, entered his house, and brought him downstairs for questioning. Within minutes, Mohammed called the company commander, demanding to know why Delta Company had violated its agreement. The commander diffused the situation, the man was released after questioning, and the relationship survived the test. Many of the communications aimed to prevent unwanted escalations. For example, Wright called Mohammed to check on rumors of armed men roaming in a Bayaa market. If true, Wright would need to send troops in response. With his knowledge of all militia movement in Bayaa, Mohammed was able to quickly dispel that rumor, thus allowing Wright to avoid an unnecessary confrontation. In another example, Mohammed called Wright to let him know that a Shia prayer tent had been set up on a major avenue and that Wright would do well to make sure his troops did not create an unwanted provocation there.

Eventually the relationship evolved to the point where Mohammed requested that certain members of his organization not be targeted in exchange for their commitment not to conduct violence in the future. Though Delta Company was wary of such a commitment, two members of the OMS leadership joined Mohammed on the Corps-level "No Target" list, meaning that no element of the Coalition—conventional forces, Iraqi Special Forces, or US special operations units—could strike or detain these people. As promised, Bayaa OMS/ JAM members whom Mohammed vouched for did not conduct violence. This type of dialogue continued throughout the phase.

Though communication was important, Delta Company continued to conduct targeted operations to capture members of JAM in Bayaa. In the month of November, three significant targets were eliminated. First, Fadhil, the cell leader who collected payments and patrolled Bayaa, was involved in an argument with an Iraqi Army checkpoint outside the neighborhood over a traffic violation. After a member of his group slapped the Iraqi soldier, the checkpoint responded with their machine guns. Among the injured was Fadhil Dauria, who suffered a stomach wound and was in critical condition. He did not return to the area. Second, Delta Company conducted a targeted operation that netted Mustafa, the long-standing leader of the operations division within Bayaa, along with most of his cell. Five days later, a raid netted a second operations cell leader and all of his men. By the end of the month, most of JAM's long-standing operations cells were dismantled. Despite Mohammed's willingness to vouch for Mustafa, the cells remained in detention. Though others took their place, the capability of JAM was significantly reduced, and remained so throughout the phase.

With this relationship in place to moderate violence, Bayaa saw fewer IED and sniper attacks. Wright was able to spend more time on the "build," spreading around CERP money in the form of micro-grants. More and more shops opened, and trash was collected.

10.12. Violence Declines; State-Building Remains Problematic

This chapter has analyzed the implementation of the Surge in one contested neighborhood in Baghdad. From the broadest view, Bayaa was one battle in the broader Shia-Sunni civil war taking place during this period. In the sweep of Shia militia forces across swaths of Baghdad, Bayaa was one of the dominoes falling on the way to Shia dominance in the Iraq capital. When we look within the Bayaa case itself, however, the outcomes in terms of violence and state-building are complex.

Consider violence first. As in other Baghdad neighborhoods, the Surge correlates with a drop in violence and the dissolution of JAM. The CHB strategy did contribute to that success. Even though Delta Company did not set up a combat outpost within Bayaa, the tactic of constant dismounted patrols and heightened contact with the population appears to have contributed to better knowledge and intelligence. The efforts to avoid collateral damage may have paid off as the public was never enflamed in protest against the US forces.

However, it would be difficult to separate the drop in violence in Bayaa from the process of sectarian homogenization. With the cleansing complete, Special Groups moved their attention and their violent capacities to Saydiyah. While JAM took on the mission to harass US military forces, violence against civilians was obviously no longer a strategic goal. Moreover, the most visible drop in violence aligned with heightened decapitation capabilities, or at least better information, that put pressure on local Shia/OMS leaders to come to a bargaining table. It was Wright's negotiations with the local Shia leader that created the drop in attacks. It was this accommodation that allowed Delta Company to move toward the "build" leg of CHB.

The connection between Muqtada al-Sadr's broader strategic move and what was happening on the ground in Bayaa is not clear. In many respects, the local dynamic appeared disconnected to the broader struggle, especially at the end of the summer of 2007.[14] As seen in the statement of the local OMS leader, he had no ability to control what Special Groups might do. Also, local JAM did not fall into lockstep with Muqtada al-Sadr's ceasefires. On the other hand, the strategic change at the local level in Bayaa mirrored that made by the Sadrists at the national level. At both levels, there was a strategic decision to elevate the social and political mission over the military one after accomplishing Shia dominance. Following the moves of Muqtada al-Sadr, the mission and goals of the OMS took priority over those of JAM in the summer of 2007.

This strategic move seemed to pay off for the Sadrists. The primary goal of the US CHB strategy is to move the population to the +1 position. For CHB, the center of gravity is the general population. The state-building goal is to connect the public to the state and its functions. People should interact with the state to accomplish their basic goals rather than to turn to non-state actors, especially those in an antagonistic relationship to the state. That did not happen in Bayaa.

As Wright assesses, by midsummer 2007, the population of Bayaa had gone from neutral (position 0) to aligned with the OSM/JAM (−1). Two of Wright's indicators support this assessment. First, despite a significant increase in intelligence coming to Delta Company from consistent source reporting and anonymous tips, these contacts were a miniscule fraction of the population. The OMS/JAM enjoyed significantly greater intelligence support from the population. Not once did a member of the community volunteer information about the OMS/JAM unless it was non-attributional. Every time a platoon moved into the neighborhood, it was under observation, despite the lower numbers of JAM operators in the area. Though the general population's relationship with Delta Company was mostly positive—there were no demonstrations, angry mobs, or popular unrest at any point during this phase—no information of substance was given following an attack on Delta Company. As Delta Company sought out new leadership from Bayaa who had respect among the population, they found that no one would act against the OMS/JAM. Second, the population did not come to Delta Company with their problems, they went to the OMS to get their disputes resolved. During the court's hours of operation, there was a steady stream of citizens in and out of the OMS building. Delta Company never observed people coming or going under duress—the population was choosing to go there. These observations were clear indicators that the OMS, not Delta Company, was providing sufficient resources for the population to establish a reciprocal relationship with them.

By the end of Delta Company's time in Bayaa, the population's position did not change despite Delta Company's successes in protection and distribution of goods. Security was improving, shops were thriving, and threats were significantly lower than they had been in well over a year. Though life had hardly returned to normal, it was markedly better than even six months prior. Delta Company was finally providing useful benefits to the population, which they were gladly taking advantage of. Of the micro-grants distributed, only a small percentage failed or disappeared. Most were successful. While not always happy with Delta Company's operations (returning automobile vendors in the car market were unhappy with the barrier plan that blocked the public's view of their merchandise), they were willing to engage with Delta Company on issues large and small in the neighborhood.

Despite all this, the population stayed with the OMS and JAM. If protecting the population was enough, then the population should have switched its support to Delta Company as JAM was reduced, violence dropped, and the threat of Sunni/Shia conflict began to recede. If distribution mattered most, then the change in tactics in the fall of 2007 into 2008 ought to have made a difference. Rather than charging rent for protection, housing, or a place to run a business, Delta Company was literally giving money away if someone had a good idea. Given that security improved dramatically in November and remained consistently low for months, and micro-grants had been underway since January, some indicators of a shift in popular support should have appeared by March if there was a change in social control. They did not.

Earlier, as Special Groups moved IEDs and RPGs through Bayaa (as they did in February), no one reported it. When the house next door was used as a prison and torture chamber, no one reported it. When Special Groups shot RPGs at a Delta Company platoon putting barriers in place in January, none of the surrounding houses saw anything. It took participation from the OMS in the reconciliation process for the sheikhs to move past the rhetoric of the previous six months and finally act. Throughout this period, intelligence reporting to the US forces and popular usage of the OMS as a resource remained constant, and in favor of the OMS. As long as the OMS regulated behavior, punished those who violated rules, and managed interactions between people, they maintained social control and retained the support of the population.

As Wright argues in his dissertation, the logic behind the population's decision-making seems sound. No matter how much Delta Company was offering, they were not offering one essential thing that the population could not provide on their own—dispute resolution. If residents came to Delta Company with a problem, there was little that Delta Company could do other than to direct them back to the Iraqi system, one that remained glaringly absent from the neighborhood. After a year's worth of work, little had changed. The Iraqi Police forces were undoubtedly corrupt. The National Police, though improving, had no law-and-order function. The courts were still ensconced behind the walls of the Green Zone and hopelessly clogged. If residents turned on JAM, they would have lost the one body that provided protection not just from external threats, but from internal threats as well. Without it, they would have been left to their own devices once again, looking at a much more anarchic situation than the one they currently enjoyed.

During the period of sectarian civil war, the OMS became the source of housing and demographic transformation. While Coalition forces could provide public goods, OMS/JAM provided selective benefits at the individual level, such as access to housing, business rentals, and dispute resolution. They also used their coercive power to control the contracting process and the behavior of individual workers, allowing them to take credit for work contracted by the Coalition. Unfortunately for Delta Company, since they could not regulate the behavior of individuals inside the neighborhood or punish the OMS for breaking these kinds of rules, there was little Delta Company could do to stop it. The OMS invested heavily in redirecting the actions of local JAM toward regulating the behavior of the population inside Bayaa. By designating specific cells to do nothing but collect payments and monitor the population (augmented with the other operational cells), the OMS invested in the mechanisms necessary for social control. Then, by establishing their de facto court system, the OMS provided a significant resource back to the population. Delta Company had no ability to regulate behavior in this way.

10.13. Conclusion

Seen in hindsight, Wright's case study of Bayaa and his assessment of the ability of groups to establish social control shed light on the resiliency of the Sadrists. As seen in both the Sadr City and Bayaa cases, the Sadrists possessed tools that were applicable across the entire spectrum of roles. They had the ability to raise militias capable of raising levels of violence. They had the ability to infringe on state-building by capturing the local police and by administering state welfare functions.

If Wright is correct, more than any other group, the Sadrists had the ability to connect to some of the basic individual needs of local citizens, especially in terms of adjudication. In the post-invasion upheaval and the near anarchy of the civil war period, the OMS could effectively become the government. US forces, SCIRI, AQI, local police, and the National Police all lacked this ability.

Anbar, 2003–2011

The Generation of a Community Mobilization Strategy

JON LINDSAY AND ROGER D. PETERSEN

11.1. Introduction

Both scholars and practitioners have addressed the Anbar case in depth and length (Couch, 2013; Gordon and Trainor, 2012; Green and Mullen III, 2014; Hagan et al., 2013; Long, 2008; Russell, 2011; Searle, 2008; Shultz, Jr., 2013; Smith and MacFarland, 2008; West, 2009). This attention is not surprising. Anbar witnessed a dramatic drop in violence. SIGACTS (Significant Acts of Violence) numbers precipitously declined (see Figure 1.1 in Chapter 1). Anbar also saw a non-state actor, al-Qaeda, largely driven from the province, if only temporarily. As late as the summer of 2006, these outcomes were inconceivable. A classified report from August 2006 by Colonel Peter Devlin, the intelligence officer for I Marine Expeditionary Force, expressed the prevailing pessimism of the time. Thomas Ricks, in his book *The Gamble*, reprinted Devlin's conclusions:

> The social and political situation has deteriorated to a point that MNF [Multi-National Forces] and ISF [Iraqi Security Forces] are no longer capable of militarily defeating the insurgency in al Anbar. . . . Underlying this decline in stability is the near complete collapse of social order. . . . Prominent leaders have exiled themselves to neighboring Jordan and Syria, including some leading imams. Despite the success of the December elections, nearly all government institutions from the village to provincial levels have disintegrated or have been thoroughly corrupted and infiltrated by Al Qaeda in Iraq (AQI) or criminal/insurgent gangs. . . .

Although it is likely that attack levels have peaked, the steady rise in attacks from mid-2003 to 2006 indicates a clear failure to defeat the insurgency in al-Anbar Province. . . . Barring the deployment of an additional MNF division and the injection of billions of dollars of reconstruction and investment money into the Province, there is nothing MNF can do to influence the motivations of al-Anbar Sunni to wage an insurgency (Ricks, 2009, reprints Devlin report pp. 331–335).[1]

The month after Devlin's report, the violence in Anbar peaked at nearly 2,000 incidents, more than in any other province in Iraq. Remarkably, the rate plunged to just 155 incidents in January 2008, the lowest yet.[2] One of the most violent provinces had become the most peaceful.

Almost all analysts point to the strategy of community mobilization to explain this unexpected and extraordinary change. Indeed, Anbar is the paradigmatic case of community mobilization, which entails cooperation between local communities (+2) and military organizations (+3) to defeat insurgent organizations (−3) and local supporters. The changing role of the Bedouin tribes in Anbar is the critical variable in this case. The local tribes, indignant over the brutal extremism and economic usurpation of AQI, made the fateful decision to cooperate with the US military. Tribesmen provided intelligence and manpower to defeat AQI, first in al-Qaim on the Syrian border in late 2005, then in Ramadi in late 2006, and in Fallujah in early 2007. Progress moved from west to east down the Western Euphrates River Valley (WERV).

Many of these tribes were collaborating with AQI before their change in alliance. In terms of our framework, many tribes "flipped" from the −2 position to the +2 position. "Flipping" is exceptionally effective as it not only takes away fighters and resources from the insurgent side, but adds them to the state's side. Moreover, because those moving to +2 had previously been in contact with insurgent −3 forces, those "flipping" possessed detailed information and intelligence on insurgent identities, locations, and tactics. They might provide that information to +3 security forces, or they might take the initiative to act on it themselves, as vigilantes. In retrospect, it is not surprising that community mobilization in Anbar helped devastate AQI during 2007–2008.

This chapter will concentrate on one major question brought to the fore by the Anbar case: What brought the highly effective community mobilization strategy into place? Section I of this book specified five US strategies—war-fighting and four counterinsurgency strategies (clear, hold, build [CHB]; community mobilization; homogenization; and decapitation). As an assumption, the section treated the United States as a coherent actor choosing a strategy, or combination of strategies, and implementing them in at least a somewhat consistent manner. The analytical framework is not expected to perfectly describe every actual event. Rather, it provides a theoretically informed template for comparison. In terms of strategy implementation in Iraq, sometimes the US forces did execute a strategic choice in a straightforward manner. We are going to argue in this chapter, in contrast, that the move to community mobilization in Anbar was not so straightforward. In effect, the initiative started from actions of Iraqi tribes, rather than from top-down decisions from US policymakers. The US military responded to the opportunities presented by tribal openings. The interactions between the tribes and the US military then set a process in motion now looked back on as paradigmatic of community mobilization.

This chapter works to explain this process. We start by reviewing the nature of the two general actors. First, we discuss the nature of the US military bureaucracy in Anbar province—its complexity, coherence in command, and flexibility in tactics. Second, we explore the tribal actors in Anbar—their modern functions, inherent norms, and command of resources. Third, we study the interactions between these two sets of actors through a chronological case study guided by our analytical framework. We consider how community mobilization interacted with other strategies—CHB and decapitation—to produce outcomes. A final section reviews findings, draws conclusions, and addresses the role of master cleavages. As many readers will note, our findings on the Anbar case presents several challenges for the standard counterinsurgency narrative.

As the reader will note, this chapter is written in the first person, sometimes using "we," as in the paragraph above. This voice reflects the long-term interaction and frequent exchanges between the two authors going back to their 2012 co-written commissioned study for the Center for Irregular Warfare and Armed Groups (Lindsay and Petersen, 2012). As mentioned in the introduction, this chapter is partly built on Lindsay's field experience, as the Navy Special Operations Task Force West (SOTF-W) Nonlethal Effects Officer from fall 2007 to April 2008, a position demanding tribal engagement and information operations across a broad number of Anbari communities, especially those involved in the Awakening.

11.2. The Counterinsurgent in Anbar: Complexity and Coherence

The Coalition occupation in Anbar was a complex system composed of different organizations, each varying considerably in their access to resources, formal authority, and organizational culture. There is no single chain of command subordinating all relevant organizations, but rather different parts of different government agencies and functional commands. This means there are many relationships across levels, such as between the US ambassador and the military commander at Multi-National Forces–Iraq (MNFI). Civilian provincial reconstruction teams (PRTs) report to the Embassy but are embedded with military units to facilitate reconstruction. "Other Government Agency" is a euphemism for the Central Intelligence Agency, which operated with formal autonomy but in coordination with the military.

Within the military chain of command there are conventional forces that run through MNFI and Multi-National Corps–Iraq (MNCI) to the divisional element in Anbar, Multi-National Force West (MNF-W). MNF-W at the time was commanded by a two-star Marine general with a Marine Expeditionary Force (MEF). There are also separate special operations forces (SOF) chains of command for "theater" and "national," or, more colloquially, "white" SOF and "black" SOF. Theater (white) SOF include Army SF and Navy SEAL units under the Combined Joint Special Operations Task Force (CJSOTF) that provide training, collect intelligence, and conduct raids in the local area, operating alongside and supported by conventional units like the MEF, but not operationally under their command. National (black) Special Mission Units such as Army Delta Force or Naval Special Warfare Development Group ("SEAL Team Six") under Joint Special Operations Command (JSOC) conduct counterterrorism raids throughout the country, drawing on their own intelligence assets including aerial drones. JSOC's TF-16 focused on targeting AQI, with a considerable amount of autonomy from both CJSOTF and MNCI.

The term "Coalition Forces" thus does really not refer to a unitary actor on the American side, let alone when Iraqi security forces such as the Army (IA) and Police (IP) are factored in. Coalition Forces included many different types of (+3) combat organizations in Anbar, imperfectly coordinated. One unintended consequence of this degree of bureaucratic overhead is that organizations have to dedicate a lot of time to de-conflicting their activities and responding to queries and directives from headquarters in their multiple chains of command.[3]

How did this complex array of forces implement strategy in Anbar? More specifically to the purposes of the present chapter, which of the organizations were structurally or culturally suited to adopt, or at least accept, a policy that incorporated Anbar's tribes? Which of the organizations would likely impede the development of tribal mobilization?

From the start, the civilians in the Coalition Provisional Authority under Bremer saw little place for "backward" tribes in the reconstruction of the Iraqi state. As the official Army history notes, "The CPA's stance toward the tribes made outreach difficult. Throughout the summer of 2003, Bremer and one of his senior assistants, Meghan O'Sullivan, viewed Iraq's tribes as an artifact of the past and were reluctant to incorporate tribal leaders into even advisory roles" (*The US Army in the Iraq War*, Vol. 1, 2019, p. 210). Although this position would eventually change, civilians would not be a force for a move toward tribal mobilization.[4] It also goes without saying that the Shia political leaders who took power in Baghdad were initially opposed to any "flipping" of Sunni insurgent groups. The United States' Shia partners did not expect to sign on to a policy that would re-arm Sunni elites who had connections with the Saddam regime, and US civilian leadership could not dismiss these concerns.[5]

In line with civilian leadership, the top levels of the military were also reluctant to adopt policies that transferred resources and power to non-state actors. As discussed in Section I of this volume, militaries prefer offensive strategies. In the face of the friction of war, a military's natural reaction is to adopt a strategy that enhances autonomy, acquires resources, improves control, reduces uncertainty, and reinforces organizational essence. Offensive doctrines are useful for all of these goals because they require a combat unit to act with autonomy on a fluid battlefield, lay in a surplus of men and material, choose the time and place of attack, and enhance a warrior identity (Posen 1984; Snyder 1984). The bias for an offensive strategy reinforces a preference for warfighting over counterinsurgency in general (Jackson 2008; Long 2016). COIN forces play defense to protect the population in a very uncertain environment. While COIN doctrine calls for a lot of troops, they are employed in missions where casualties are likely and decisive victory is unlikely. Irregular or indirect action missions require interaction with idiosyncratic local society, which does not lend itself to stereotyped doctrine and routinized training like direct-action combat missions. The "armed social worker" who drinks "three cups of tea" with the locals is at odds with the traditional self-image of the warrior, and civil affairs specialties are typically lower status compared to combat arms like armor and infantry.

More specifically, the bias for the offensive produces resistance to a community mobilization strategy. Community mobilization embraces what the military terms "engagement missions." Engagement missions are typically where military forces have the most trouble in COIN because persuasion, communication, negotiation, and alliance building are the core activities, and these are not part of regular military training regimens (or warrior "essence"). Targeting and training have more demonstrable success metrics (how many insurgents killed, how many battle drills run, etc.), whereas engagement is an ongoing and ambiguous activity. This is reflected in the greater prestige and resourcing accorded to "black" SOF units focused on raids rather than "white" SOF units with the engagement mission. In Anbar, community mobilization meant distributing power and resources to non-state actors with opaque political agendas (as well as interests in smuggling in this case). This move would not enhance the military's autonomy, increase its control, reduce uncertainty, or bolster organizational essence.

Above all, implementing a "flipping" policy meant cooperating with and supporting groups and individuals who had previously killed US soldiers and Marines.

While the "Big Army" might not be expected to develop a community mobilization strategy, other US military organizations possessed fewer constraints and an organizational culture more open to cooperation with locals.[6] One reason that the United States created Army Special Forces (SF) was to protect and maintain specialized COIN skills within an Army more focused on major combat operations. As laid out in Section I, Army Special Forces operators, especially Green Berets, were traditionally designed to cultivate foreign forces as effective partners. Ironically, as discussed in Section I, US SOF in the post 9/11 era have embraced direct-action commando and counterterrorism missions while conventional forces have been employed in COIN in Iraq and Afghanistan. (Tucker and Lamb, 2007).[7] In sum, neither regular Army nor Special Forces were particularly ready to embrace community mobilization.

On the other hand, the US Marine Corps, with its history of "small wars," modular organization, and empowerment of junior leaders, maintained its flexibility to work with local partners (Long, 2016; Russell, 2011). Austin Long has pointed out how the Marines, in contrast to the US Army, quickly adopted and thoroughly expanded cooperation with local tribesmen in Anbar. Moreover, the Marines, again in contrast to the US Army, consolidated these gains by developing an underlying set of intelligence organs in Anbar. As Long notes:

> Realizing the importance of the local relationships and dynamics that made the Awakening possible, Marine intelligence officers wrote intelligence collection plans to gather this information. Not one but two elements were created to assess this intelligence under the MEF G2. The first was the Economic and Political Intelligence Cell (EPIC) formed in the MEF Intelligence Battalion. The second was the Security, Governance, and Economics (SG&E) section formed in the MEF Radio Battalion.
>
> In the author's experience, U.S. Army units in Iraq had no comparable organizations, much less two. Army units may have collected and analyzed similar information, but it was not readily apparent that they did so in a systematic fashion. (Long, 2016, p. 199)

In sum, the US side presented a diverse and complex set of actors that, on the whole, was not likely to initiate tribal mobilization. However, there were segments and individuals within the broad set of US military actors who were more inclined and suited to pick up on the possibilities of community mobilization, even if in a haphazard way. Indeed, James A. Russell has detailed a bottom-up process of innovation in counterinsurgency practice in Anbar during 2005–2007 (Russell, 2011). Russell makes a distinction between tactical adaptation and organizational innovation. As Russell defines, "Tactical adaptation occurs when units change organizational procedures on the battlefield in order to address perceived organizational shortfalls, which are generally revealed by their interaction with the adversary" (Russell, 2011, p. 191). Russell argues, based on a series of case studies, that tactical adaptation by individual commanders preceded organizational innovation in Anbar. We come back to this point later.

11.3. Tribes in Anbar: Communities and Mobilizers

The persistence and re-emergence of the role of tribes in a largely modern society and developed state like Iraq is a complex and fascinating phenomenon.[8] Our focus here is narrower. In terms of our framework, the empirical puzzle of Anbar concerns why individuals moved into −1 and −2 positions and how tribal leaders moved entire groups from those negative nodes to the +2 position. The strategy of "community mobilization" obviously implies, first, that there is a community that ties individuals together and coordinates their actions. The concept implies, second, that the community can indeed be mobilized, usually through community leaders. We can call them "mobilizers." This section considers the nature of the tribal community and mobilizers in turn before returning to the question of movement on our spectrum of roles.

Following the lines of Donald Horowitz's well-known theories, tribes are candidates for community mobilization because of the tribe's resemblance to family (Horowitz, 1985). Tribe is about kinship, even if fictive. As in belonging to a family, membership in a tribe involves certain obligations. Family members should help each other out. The related norm is the norm of reciprocity: if member X does something for member Y, then member Y should do the same for member X. Families also often possess an identity and a sense of honor. If someone insults a member of the family, there is an obligation to come to that family member's defense. The related norm is a norm of honor: if member X has been hurt or dishonored by an outsider, then member Y should retaliate against that outsider. These two norms can work together. If a member of the family has been attacked or dishonored, and if member X is the first to come to that member's defense, then other family members are obligated by both a norm of reciprocity and a norm of honor to join X in the defense of the family.

It is not difficult to find accounts of these norms in operation in Iraq during the post-2003 period. In one example, Anthony Shadid describes how the US military's raids and use of local informers often violated a sense of honor and triggered norms of revenge both against the US and among tribes. Describing an incident in Thuluyah, in a Sunni area 45 miles north of Baghdad, Shadid relates the story of a man named Sabah, a suspected informer working with the US forces. Seen as responsible for the deaths of three local men during a US raid, Sabah is targeted for revenge. As Shadid explains:

> But on the other end of the spectrum, that tribal code stipulated a brutal frontier justice, which had come to fill a lawless void. This code, rigorous and unforgiving, was paramount.
>
> The sense of honor, pride, and dignity was what made the role of the informer in the U.S. raid so much worse. That man's presence— like a dark family secret—lurked behind every conversation that day in Thuluyah. He had betrayed the village, he had transgressed the law of the countryside, the *rif*, and no one was willing to forget. . . . The tribal traditions were at work as I spoke to the friends, neighbors, and the relatives of the late Hashim's family over those two days. Nearly all of the boy's relatives seemed to know Sabah's identity, but they hesitated to say his name to me or even to say it out loud to one another. He had to stay nameless, even if his namelessness was a façade. Identifying him would encourage vendettas and tribal bloodletting, the chaos that would follow as tribes sought their own justice for the deaths of Hashim and the other two men. Calling him by his name would make more personal the betrayal by one of their own for an enemy who had humiliated and disgraced them. (Shadid, 2005, pp. 226–227)

Eventually, relatives of those slain in the US raid demanded that Sabah's own family execute Sabah, laying out that "either they kill Sabah, or villagers would murder the rest of his family." The story ends with Sabah's father and brother killing Sabah in their backyard orchard. The father told Shadid, "there was no other choice." In this case, tribal norms mobilized one clan for vengeance and members of an opposing family to carry out that vengeance. Broader group interactions activated norms that drove individual behavior.

There is a second view on how tribes create and sustain "community." Perhaps the dominant strain in Western political science is to assume that individuals are overwhelmingly driven by the rational pursuit of individual material interests rather than being pulled along by norms. Along these lines, tribes are like labor unions. Individuals follow because the tribal leader can provide a job or a payment. The only reason tribes and sheikhs have become mobilizers in Iraq is because history left those categories and names as a residue able to provide co-ordinating devices for patronage.

From the standpoint of the counterinsurgent, the nature of the community matters. If the community is held together by reciprocity norms connected to group membership and identity, then individuals will not be able to select in and out of the community. The community will be more stable and will sustain itself in times of both low or high levels of patronage. In terms of our spectrum of roles, reciprocity and honor norms should also facilitate individuals moving as a group along the spectrum. In contrast, "labor union" communities will more likely atrophy if the flow of patronage stops. Individuals will be able to more easily defect if a better deal comes around. In general, the counterinsurgent can shape payoffs to trigger rational economic calculations, but it is far less likely to bend deeply embedded cultural norms. It follows that the counterinsurgent will be able to shape the nature of the "labor union" community far more than one permeated by strong norms.

Then there are the "mobilizers" of the community. They can be divided into three groups. Within a period of war and chaos, there will be those who claim to be community leaders but neither lead a patronage network nor possess normative power. There are those who control patronage networks and command material resources but lack traditional or normative authority. Finally, there are mobilizers who have both material and normative power.

Again, Iraq provides good examples. When the US forces came to Anbar, they were met by an ambiguous set of "sheikhs" or tribal leaders. This group included "fake sheikhs" (sometimes referred to as "Made in Taiwan" sheikhs) who controlled little patronage and commanded no normative authority. The set also included many "labor union" sheikhs who did control patronage networks but may not have had the lineal background or historical connections necessary to generate strong social norms of reciprocity or honor. Finally, there were sheikhs who possessed both material and normative power.

There is debate about the mix of community types and nature of mobilizers in Iraq and Anbar in the post-2003 period. Iraq's tumultuous modern history produced several twists and turns in state-tribal relations. In particular, the Baathist regime, along with general forces of modernization, worked to erode tribal influences in Baghdad. Given Iraq's sizable jump in oil income after 1973, the Baathist regime had the resources to vastly increase state employment and state-based welfare benefits. Given the resources, Saddam's regime could rule directly without relying on intermediate power brokers.[9] This situation, however, would drastically change after the 1991 Gulf War. The state went into severe decline, especially with the introduction of sanctions. The need for indirect rule, and reliance on "tribe," emerged again in Baghdad. By 1996, Saddam instituted fairly dramatic measures to organize state-tribe relations. The regime called for the creation of a High Council of Tribal Chiefs, decentralized some judicial and taxation functions of the state, allowed some tribal members to carry light arms, and provided tribal sheikhs benefits in the form of diplomatic passports and exemptions from military service. Saddam praised tribal values and created relationships with key tribal leaders. As Dina Rizk Khoury summed up, "For the first time since the establishment of the Republican regime in 1958, tribalism shaped elite alliances and became part of the political language of political culture. It was a politics invented by the regime to bolster its declining power" (Khoury, 2013, p. 145). In short, Saddam hoped that the sheikhs could provide an extension of state authority into localities that the weakened state could no longer penetrate.

Nicholas Krohley emphatically argues that the tribes emerging in Baghdad in the 1990s had lost any normative power. In his view, the tribe did become a possible source of material goods and safety for desperate residents. He writes:

> Baghdadis were compelled to either resuscitate long-discarded tribal identities or fabricate them entirely. The tribes that emerged in the course of the 1990s were thus not the outgrowth of a sudden resurgence of previously suppressed or obscured kinship bonds, but rather attempts by desperate urbanites to find a measure of security and stability in an increasingly volatile urban environment . . . (t)he broader tribal phenomenon of the 1990's saw a debased caricature of the traditional conceptions of honor and vengeance come to Iraq, whereby blood feuds and honor killings became intermeshed with economically- and politically-motivated turf wars. (Krohley, 2015, p. 46)

Given the diversity of views on the meaning of tribe, the question of how tribes facilitate movement of individuals on our spectrum of roles is an empirical one. Given that there are 150 recognizable tribes composed of 2,000 clans in Iraq, we would expect variation in the nature and role of tribes across region, between urban and rural areas, between rich and poor (Hassan, 2007). No doubt some tribes and clans resembled the "labor union" model of community more than others.

With this consideration of the actors in mind, the next section presents a case study guided by the analytical framework.

11.4. The Interaction of the Counterinsurgent and Tribes in Anbar: The Generation of a Community Mobilization Strategy

11.4.1. The Immediate Post-Invasion Period: Movement to –1

In Anbar, tribes are a constituent part of the general population and clearly not separate from it. Accordingly, the mechanisms moving the general population off neutrality are those affecting most tribal members. In the immediate post-invasion period, Anbar Province witnessed low levels of violence and some support for the Coalition. In terms of our framework, few of the mechanisms able to drive individuals off the neutral position were operative in the immediate post-invasion period. Certainly, there was resentment against the occupying US forces to a degree. At this point, al-Qaeda in Iraq (AQI) and its foreign contingent were not a daily source of domination. With a low level of violence, threats and fears were not pervasive; in the uncertain situation, focal points, safety in numbers, and status rewards were not relevant. All this would soon change.

US actions soon diminished any reason for individuals to move to a position of government support (+1) and sustain that position. As in Iraq as a whole, orders for de-Baathification and the disbanding of the Iraqi Army created unemployment. These orders also created resentment among Sunnis. In a February 2004 opinion poll, 42% of the population felt that the US invasion had liberated Iraq, while 41% felt it had humiliated Iraq (Langer, 2004a). The view was quite different across ethnic and sectarian lines, however; 82% of Kurds and 43% of Shia Arabs felt liberated (11% and 37% humiliated, respectively), while 66% of Sunni Arabs felt humiliated (21% liberated) (Langer, 2004b). The sense of humiliation was even greater in Anbar, where Sunnis are relatively concentrated. Moreover, Anbar's Sunni tribal leaders, considering themselves worthy of consultation and cooperation, were dismayed at the US forces' apparent disregard for tribal engagement.

As US forces tried to establish control early on in Ramadi, demonstrators came out in the streets. The US reaction was perceived as violent, callous, and provocative. A second day of demonstrations brought the same result. In the description of Dr. Thamer Ibrahim Tahir al-Assafi, Muslim Ulema Council for al-Anbar and professor of religious studies, al-Anbar University, "The next day, they demonstrated again, and the Americans treated them in the same manner, meaning their armored vehicles went right through them. A young man, an 18-year-old youth, threw a rock at an American tank, and the soldiers shot him dead. We are a tribal people, and in our tradition, we know revenge. If someone gets killed from your family, you have to kill the killer, or at least a relative of his . . ." (Montgomery and McWilliams, 2009, p. 33).

US military daily tactics enflamed local resentments. Both US military personnel and Anbari Sheikhs agree on this point. US Marine General Kelly noted that Anbaris

> would state that after Baghdad fell and throughout the summer of 2003, the Americans overreacted to small acts of resistance or violence and fought in a way that was cowardly and without honor. Here they would talk about the senseless use of firepower and midnight raids on innocent men. They said that by our escalation, we proved true the rhetoric

of the nationalist firebrands about why we had invaded, and our actions played directly into the hands of organizations like Zarqawi's AQI and Muqtada al-Sadr's militia. (Montgomery and McWilliams, 2009, p. viii)

Even at the height of the Awakening, Sheikh Abdul Sattar abu Risha still blamed the Americans for the war: "they are to blame. The first thing the Americans did when they entered Iraq was to disband the Army. They opened up the borders and allowed people to come in. They did not work with us, the people, in the beginning. Al-Qaeda was able to come in and gain influence with the people instead" (Kukis, 2011, p. 161).

In the meantime, Salafists flocked to Fallujah and Ramadi. Taking advantage of porous borders, foreign Islamists flocked to Anbar, especially Fallujah, "the city of Mosques." Foreign fighters traveled far, taking risks along the way, to perform dangerous work. They tended to be more extreme in their ideological beliefs than the native Iraqis who affiliated with AQI. AQI quickly developed a robust insurgent organization (−3) in Anbar.[10] Proof of their bureaucratic competence came when an Awakening militia in March 2007 acquired AQI documents depicting its organizational structure. AQI was divided into governates throughout Iraq. In Anbar, the provincial emir oversaw committees for media, law (Sharia), administration, internal security, and military operations. Furthermore, the Western Euphrates River Valley (WERV) was a lucrative endowment for AQI, and the Anbar governate was a net contributor to the AQI general treasury. From June 2005 to October 2006, AQI raised US$9 million in Anbar (Felter and Fishman, 2007, p. 207). AQI was an organization with the capacity to fight the Americans, identify and punish local collaborators, sustain itself, and offer benefits and opportunities to local Anbaris.

11.4.2. Tribes Are Caught between Al-Qaeda (−3) and Coalition Forces (+3): Movement to −2

Before the second battle of Fallujah, resistance at the local, armed, organized level was diffuse. Dr. Thamer Ibrahim Tahir al-Assafi's description goes on to identify how resentments led to the first movement to the −2 position: "So these people whose youth was killed by the Americans, they formed a cell, and they started looking for revenge. They found out that placing an IED [improvised explosive device] is a simple matter, so a lot of cells began forming all over the place" (Felter and Fishman, 2007, p. 34). As one blacksmith commented on his own movement to −2: "Why does one fight? Usually for money or honor. Having the Americans in our city was painful for many people, including me. As you know, there was a huge amount of weapons left behind by the collapse of the former regime, and as a blacksmith I began helping to mount heavy machineguns on trucks for fighters. . . . Some other people I knew helped make roadside bombs. We were becoming a kind of armory for the resistance" (Kukis, 2011, p. 69).

Although details are difficult to come by, the pathways taken by various tribes are informative.[11] Some tribes would remain neutral, but several were aligning relatively early with AQI, nationalist groups such as the 1920 Revolution Brigade, or both.

The Albu Fahd tribe can trace its lineage to the Bedouin tribes and is considered to follow traditional norms. Initially, the tribe appeared to refrain from overt opposition to the occupation. However, members of the tribe soured on the US presence after numerous night raids where men were embarrassed in front of their families and fellow tribal members (Todd et al., 2006, section 4, p. 22). Relations with the Coalition then became enflamed by what would become an international incident. On May 19, 2004, Coalition forces attacked what they thought to be an insurgent safe house in the small town of Makr al-Deeb on the Syrian border. The attack killed at least 40 people. According to a later Defense Department–funded study, "Tragically, the Coalition attacked what very strong evidence indicates was a wedding party being celebrated between two families of the Albu Fahd tribe." US commanders were adamant that they had done nothing wrong. The chief spokesman for the American Forces in Iraq, Brigadier General Mark Kimmett, wrote an email to reporters stating, "Could there have been a celebration of some type going on? Certainly. Bad guys have celebrations. Could this have been a meeting among the foreign fighters and smugglers? That is a possibility. Could it have involved entertainment? Sure. However, a wedding party in a remote section of the desert along one of the rat lines, held in the early morning hours strains credulity" (Fisher, 2004). General Mattis had ordered the bombing after being shown infrared images of the gathering by an intelligence officer who had woken him up at midnight to see the images. When a reporter asked Mattis how long he had deliberated before ordering the bombing, Mattis replied, "thirty seconds" (West, 2009, p. 245). There was no apology and no compensation. As US military analysts commented, "Unfortunately, there is no indication that the incident was ever resolved to the tribe's satisfaction, which likely helped persuade members of the Albu Fahd and other tribes to join the insurgency in attacking US forces, to include cooperation with al-Zarqawi" (Todd et al., 2006, section 4, p. 22). The Albu Fahd became known in some US military intelligence circles as one of the "sinister six"—the original six tribes allying with al-Qaeda.[12]

The Abu Mahal tribe, at odds with the Saddam regime before the invasion, was initially not anti-Coalition. By the end of 2004, however, they were actively fighting the Coalition and allied with various insurgent groups (Todd et al., 2006, section 4, p. 32). The tribe's geographic concentration may have influenced their decision-making. With near total absence of a Coalition presence in the remote al-Qaim area, tribal members may have needed to cooperate with AQI to prevent predation.

The Albu Issa tribe, along with the closely connected Zoba tribe, was a first mover in developing the nationalist insurgency in Fallujah. Both tribes planned and carried out attacks against US forces. The Albu Issa provided a full range of insurgent capabilities—finances, manpower, direct attacks. With connections to tribal members across the border in Syria, the tribe engaged in arms smuggling (Todd et al., 2006, section 4, pp. 42, 43).

While tribal leaders considered their strategies, Anbari society hollowed out. Fighting between Coalition forces and insurgents became intense. As described by Marine General Tariq Yusef, "The destruction in Anbar got to the state where in some areas you'd think that a tsunami went through. That's how bad the destruction was. They would fire against the Coalition forces, and the Coalition forces would fire back, and—destruction. The areas were destroyed. Work completely stopped in the province" (Montgomery and McWilliams, 2009, p. 183). The tribal system itself decayed. Many tribal leaders fled abroad, especially to Jordan. Inside Iraq, "fake sheikhs" came to the fore amid the chaos. Caught in the maelstrom, many tribal leaders saw better odds with AQI than with the Coalition.

11.5. The Sporadic Tribal Engagement Efforts of the US Forces

As discussed above, many in the US contingent at first dismissed tribes as artifacts of the past, not worthy of consideration as bases of mobilization. US tactics focused on going after high-value targets and building up the Iraqi Army.

For the military practitioners actually working and fighting in areas like Anbar, ignoring the importance of tribes was not practical. Tribes and clan structures influenced local political and security contests, even if they did so in complex and ambiguous ways. Even though civilian leadership was not supportive of local officers' cultivation of tribal connections, US officers on the ground did engage tribal leaders within the constraints of their mission. As summarized by Colonel Michael Walker, the Commanding Officer of the 3rd Civil Affairs Group, 1st MEF from October 2003 to September 2005:

> We weren't able to get, initially, the U.S. [State Department] mission behind it, which is the number-one reason we couldn't build, because at the end of the day, you follow orders. If the mission's saying this, then that's what you are going to do. But where you have your own latitude within your own AO [area of operations], you continue to keep that pot on the oven.[13]

Colonel Walker further held that Marine efforts beginning in 2004, at the level of decentralized local actors, provided the foundation for the later Awakening. Summarizing the early efforts of Marines, Walker stated: "And if they didn't advance the torch forward, they at least kept that thing lit and held onto it until someone else could move it forward" (McWilliams and Wheeler, 2009, p. 74). Colonel Walker's use of metaphors is revealing. In the years 2003–2005, Marines were providing the basis for a future community mobilization strategy by "keeping a pot on the oven" and "keeping a torch lit." That is far from the United States having a coherent strategy toward tribes during these years.

The US approach would evolve. Building on the early efforts, US practitioners began working with tribes along the line of the "labor union" theory. Along the lines of the Saddam regime, and for that matter most colonial regimes, US forces attempted the manipulation, if not outright creation, of pliable tribal leaders. Consider the following description, which is worth quoting at length:

> As information was gathered on tribes and a more complete picture of the area developed, efforts were made to establish the settlement patterns of tribes, their primary means of revenue, and their relationships with other local leaders, the government, and where possible, al-Qaeda.
>
> Once this was done, and it often took many months it not years of determined work to accomplish, a concerted effort was then made to improve the *wasta* of the paramount sheikh, which is a rough measure of his personal prestige and standing in the community, so that he could persuade subtribal members to support the government. To this end, once a paramount sheikh had been identified and had expressed a willingness to move against al-Qaeda, the U.S. forces would bolster the sheikh's position in the tribe through lucrative civil-affairs contracts, time and attention, and his integration into military planning. These efforts by the Coalition allowed the paramount sheikh to hold out the promise to subtribal leaders that if they rallied to his personal banner and rejected al-Qaeda, he would be able to provide financial benefits to their family members, predominately though CF contracts, jobs, employment with Provincial Security Forces (PSF). (Green and Mullen III, 2014, p. 29)[14]

In this approach, the US forces treat tribes as a possible resource, as projects to be shaped. The question is whether and how these tactics mapped onto the broader story of community mobilization in Anbar. While the US forces were building up the *wasta* of some local sheikhs, other tribal leaders were acting on their own. They became subjects in the story rather than objects. For example,

Staff Major General Khadim Faris al-Fahadawi, a member of one of the most important tribes in the Ramadi area, describes a mixture of proactive tribal collaboration with Coalition forces and quiet vigilantism against a common foe: "Publicly, fighting al-Qaeda was like committing suicide, so they started secretly in small groups, cooperating with the Coalition forces, and working the same way that al-Qaeda worked. Some of these groups—which they gave names like the Anbar Revolution, and the Secret Police, or the Karama Companies— they started working in secret, and they did a beautiful job. First, because they were working secretly, al-Qaeda couldn't identify the members. The emirs started losing confidence in the people who worked with them because they couldn't fight or identify these secret groups. They attacked most of al-Qaeda's central groups where they lived. This is when al-Qaeda started to crack" (Montgomery and McWilliams, 2009b, pp. 265–266).

11.6. Tribes Take the Initiative

As is well documented, after gaining a dominant position in Anbar, AQI began to regularly engage in brutality against the population. AQI went beyond mere thuggery and intimidation to engage in beheadings and leaving bodies visible. AQI closed universities, looted banks, and gained control of resources and lucrative smuggling routes. AQI took control over daily life and the government in much of Anbar. They took over government offices, placing an AQI minder alongside official directors (Montgomery and McWilliams, 2009b, p. 205).

According to Major Alfred Connable, Senior Intelligence Analysis for the I and II MEF, the tribal system in Anbar began to stabilize by 2005. Connable summarizes, "You have a tribal organization that has started to recover. You have legitimate genuine tribal leaders coming to the fore. They are starting to have more influence over the people and their province, and this is really important for the Awakening" (McWilliams and Wheeler, 2009, p. 127). These tribal leaders began responding to events affecting both tribes and the population as a whole. In the words of Ahmed Albu Risha, who would become one of the founders of the Anbar Salvation Council:

> The reason why the movement started was because al-Qaeda was intimidating the people and interfering in their daily lives. They began killing our sheiks, killing our teachers, killing our people. Civilian life stopped. So, we decided to reach out to the various sheiks in Anbar and try to turn them against al-Qaeda. . . . Al-Qaeda claimed in the beginning they were defending Islam, and people believed them. But the true Muslims began to see that Islam was under attack not from the

occupiers but from al-Qaeda. Crimes against the country were being committed in the name of Islam by al-Qaeda. They were ruining the country in the name of Islam . . . the sheiks gradually came around to this idea. (Kukis, 2011, p. 160)

The Albu Mahal tribe in Al Qaim, was the first to organize against AQI. The Salafist group's treatment of the population was brutal, including the display and mutilation of opponents' bodies (Montgomery and McWilliams, 2009, p. 144). Their actions were a direct affront to tribal sensibilities. As Sheikh Sabah, Principal Sheikh of the Albu Mahal Tribe in the Al Qaim border region, summarized, "al-Qaeda tried to isolate and to humiliate the tribals in the areas. . . . They were foreigners who entered from Yemen, Saudi Arabia, Syria, and they called themselves emirs. They wanted to have their word and their opinion over us" (Montgomery and McWilliams, 2009, p. 140).

After the May 2, 2005, assassination and beheading of Adiya Asaf, the local chief of police and a member of the Albu Mahal tribe, the Albu Mahal rebelled. AQI unleashed a coordinated a vicious counterattack. AQI fighters from surrounding provinces and Baghdad, numbering in the thousands, circled the 300–400 Albu Mahal fighters and attacked from three sides, killing 60. The tribe's members fled from Al Qaim, finding refuge with fellow tribal members living in towns far from Al Qaim. Those who could, including some sheikhs, fled to Jordan (Knarr, 2015, p. 34).

In defeat, tribal leaders reached out to Iraqi Government officials, mainly the Sunni Minister of Defense Dulaymi, who in turn reached out to US forces. In September 2005, General Casey and Dr. Dulaymi signed the Memorandum of Understanding "Concerning Training and Equipping the 'Desert Protectors.'" It was the first time that the Coalition, as well as the Government of Iraq, officially recognized cooperation with a tribal militia. The Desert Protectors were part of the Ministry of Defense (MOD), being paid and trained by the MOD at the East Fallujah Iraqi Compound. However, the unit was thoroughly tribal. Members of the Albu Mahal tribe comprised 98% of the Desert Protectors. Recruits were told that they would only operate in their tribal area. The agreement marked the start of the Awakening movement and became a model for it.

The Awakening movement would grow, with Ramadi being the key location. Sheikh Sattar al-Rishawi of the Albu Risha tribe formally started an organized campaign against al-Qaeda in September 2006. The Rishas built support for the Awakening by approaching individual sheikhs with a list documenting the crimes of AQI and comparing them to the crimes of the Americans, arguing that the former posed the greater threat and the Americans, according to Ahmed Abu Risha, "had been trying at least at building the country since they came." Of the 30 major tribes in Anbar, "[f]ifteen agreed with the way we were thinking.

That left seven tribes who were with al-Qaeda, and about eight who were neutral or sitting on the fence as we called the conference together in September 2006. At that meeting, all the sheiks publicly declared their tribes to be at war with al-Qaeda, and that's how it all began" (Kukis, 2011, p. 160). Ahmed Abu Risha pointed out that they were not just fighting for money, however: "There were many people who were earning more money in their regular job than we could pay them as policemen, and they joined anyway. They came because of the tribal ties and because the situation had gotten so bad that they wanted to fight" (Kukis, 2011, p. 161). The end result of these actions was the formation of the Anbar Salvation Council.

Despite their negative interactions with the Coalition described above, the Albu Fahd, one of the "sinister six," also flipped. Tribal members could not tolerate AQI's killings and kidnappings. The assassination of the Albu Fahd Shaikh General Nasser Abdul Kareem al-Mukhlif in January 2006 accelerated the movement of several sections of the tribe toward anti-insurgent positions.

11.7. The Awakening: Snowballing into +2

After Ramadi, the Awakening movement spread to Fallujah and across Anbar. Clearly, a "safety in numbers" tipping mechanism set in to generate widespread participation. While the initiative began from the actions of tribal leaders, US forces worked to facilitate the snowballing dynamics through contacts and negotiation with individual sheikhs.

To understand the dynamic in Ramadi, the reader can refer back to Chapter 4 and Figure 4.2. As illustrated by Figure 4.2, different tribes were powerful in different neighborhoods of Ramadi. US forces evaluated each tribe as cooperative, neutral, or uncooperative. In effect, military practitioners were coding each tribe-neighborhood according to nodes of the spectrum: cooperative as +2, neutral as 0, uncooperative as −2. Using a community mobilization strategy, the goal of the US military was to "flip" the −2 organizations to the +2 node on the spectrum. As opposed to war-fighting, the goal was not to kill or eliminate the opposing organization. As the notation on the left side of the bottom figure indicates, the US military was creating a bandwagon of community leaders, sheikhs in this case, in order to change the dynamic in the city as a whole.

It is important to emphasize that many of the leaders coming to the +2 level were not just neutrals caught between AQI and the US forces, but were major anti-state insurgents (at the −2 level). For instance, on the US list of key insurgents, Mohammed Mahmoud Latif occupied the second or third position (McWilliams and Wheeler, 2009, p. 126). Abu Marouf, the nom de guerre of an insurgent commander from the fiercely anti-American Zobai tribe east of

Fallujah, fought with the 1920 Revolution Brigade but secretly turned against al-Qaeda in April 2005 because "[t]hey cut off people's heads and put them on sticks, as if they were sheep. They cut off my brother's head with a razor. Thirteen of my relatives and 450 members of my tribe were killed by them."[15]

Although not the same phenomenon, Anbar would serve as a model for the Sons of Iraq movement outside of Anbar. As seen in the previous description of the formation of the Ghazaliyah Guardians in Baghdad, the United States managed to "flip" hardcore Sunni opposition leaders across wide swaths of Iraq.

11.8. Community Mobilization: The Institutionalization of +2

The essence of the community mobilization strategy, at least as it played out in Anbar, was a partnership between two sides with complementary resources. The tribes had manpower and intelligence, and the US forces had firepower and organization. The most obvious change may have come in terms of manpower as tribal members flooded the police recruitment centers. Ahmad abu Risha claimed: "We rounded up 4,000 police volunteers from men in our tribes. The various tribal leaders each brought recruits by the hundred" (Kukis, 2006, p. 161). As Sean MacFarland, commander of the 1st Brigade Combat Team operating in Ramadi, summarized:

> [O]ne by one, the local tribes are beginning to flip from either hostile to neutral or neutral to friendly. And that's been probably one of the most decisive aspects of what we've done here, is bringing those tribes onto our side of the fence. That has enabled us to massively accelerate Iraqi police recruiting, from 20 to 30 a month to routinely 700 guys will show up, of whom we'll take 400. (McWilliams and Wheeler, 2009, p. 178)

Awakening groups also formed Emergency Response Units. MacFarland summarized, "now we have more friendly forces than we almost know what to do with" (McWilliams and Wheeler, 2009, p. 179). The US military had these forces on payroll at $300 a month, establishing a formal connection. Some Awakening groups, like the Anbar Revolutionaries, also murdered AQI members, but they did not openly advertise these vigilante activities, and Coalition Forces did not ask too many questions.

Although AQI conducted a campaign to instill fear in recruits, managing to bomb a recruitment line and inflict major casualties, the process soon reached a "safety in numbers" tipping point. Individuals ceased to be afraid to move to +2. "The tribal leaders started gathering courage more than before and weren't as afraid of al-Qaeda as they had been. The roads were liberated. They were not under the control of al-Qaeda anymore. . . . You could tell the area was secure because the police sirens and the police lights were roaming that area" (Montgomery and McWilliams, 2009, p. 187). With the increased number of police, the Coalition could establish a checkpoint system providing a visible security presence.

The locals also produced intelligence far beyond what Coalition forces could have generated on their own. We pick up on this point in the following section.

11.9. Why Was Community Mobilization So Effective? The Role of Decapitation and Clear, Hold, Build

Section I specified five distinct strategies (war-fighting and four counterinsurgency strategies). In Iraq, the United States appears to have employed all of them at different times and places. Furthermore, actual US conduct of war no doubt mixed elements of these strategies to differing extents. This raises the question of the overlap between community mobilization and decapitation in Anbar. While the Surge, with its saturation of troops, may have produced the drop in violence in Baghdad, the Anbar case indicates something different. Violence in Anbar dropped dramatically *before* the arrival of a US troop surge. This suggests that community mobilization, without a surge, may have produced the crucial means to turn the tide. In turn, those means may have consisted primarily of intelligence given to US forces. Clearly, "flipped" tribes provided detailed information to US forces who then targeted AQI leadership. Should we attribute much of the success of community mobilization mainly to its ability to fuel the United States' increasingly capable decapitation machine?

By 2006, JSOC had become a highly capable organization, able to find, fix, and finish targets. McChrystal moved JSOC's Iraq headquarters to Balad air base in mid-2004, where he built a state-of-the-art detention facility and a cavernous Joint Operations Center (JOC) with giant screens displaying feeds from live missions and targets in active development (Naylor, 2015, pp. 253, 256). One participant recalled, "you could just reach out with a finger, as it were, and eliminate somebody" (Urban, 2011, p. 82).

When Major General Stanley McChrystal took command of JSOC on October 6, 2003, the task force in Iraq had only 250 people and lacked an efficient process for coordinating its operations and generating intelligence from them (Urban, 2011, pp. 232–233). JSOC grew from about 800 personnel when McChrystal assumed command to over 2,300 by 2008 (Urban, 2011, p. 309). He flattened the organization, energetically promoted information sharing, and brought in representatives from other agencies, including the CIA, NSA, and FBI. By late 2005 there were nearly 100 CIA and 80 FBI personnel embedded with JSOC (Urban, 2011, p. 276). Connection to the NSA Real Time Regional Gateway enabled JSOC to rapidly query mobile phone and computer data recovered in the field, improving operator access to near real-time (Signals Intelligence) SIGINT by a factor of 10 (Harris, 2014, pp. 25–38; Naylor, 2015, p. 264). During the month of August 2004, JSOC had conducted 18 raids, but by the spring of 2006 it was conducting 30–50 a week. Delta Force meticulously planned its raids for weeks in advance prior to McChrystal, but JSOC was soon launching them with little notice for the express purpose of gathering intelligence (Gordon and Trainor, 2012, p. 205).

Michael Flynn succeeded McChrystal and expanded the number of intelligence sources JSOC had available as well as its ability to analyze the data, from a single Predator in 2003 to 40 aircraft of 15 different types, manned and unmanned, to collect cell phone and radio SIGINT and persistent full-motion video (Naylor, 2015, p. 262). Flynn sometimes put as many as three aircraft on a single target in case one malfunctioned or lost the target (Urban, 2011, p. 84). JSOC also had a Computer Network Operations squadron to surveil insurgent computers and internet cafes, a unit of Iraqi agents known as the Mohawks, clandestine intelligence operatives with Task Force Orange, and professional interrogators and forensic analysts (Naylor, 2015, pp. 257–265).

JSOC conducted counterterrorism operations in Anbar through a parallel chain of command, often with little or no advance notice to MNF-W. The role of JSOC is still poorly understood, as its operations remain cloaked in secrecy, but it is widely understood that JSOC removed thousands of AQI fighters from the battlefield, many of them killed. JSOC thus represents a major pressure on AQI and the foremost implementation of the counterterrorism strategy (+3 vs. −3) in Anbar (Lamb and Munsing, 2011).

Certainly, "flipped" tribes were feeding information into what McChrystal called "the machine." Staff Brigadier General Nuri al-Din summarized, "We provided them with information about who's a terrorist, who's an insurgent, and where they're working—locations, any location that was available. . . . We gave it to intelligence, intelligence passed it to the Americans, and the Americans started attacking them from the air and killing them" (Lamb and Munsing, 2011, p. 197).

Despite the enormous advance in targeting capabilities, there are reasons to doubt that decapitation alone produced the Anbar results. First, there is a major empirical point: the leader of AQI, al-Zarqawi, was killed in June 2006. Yet, AQI still thrived. In effect, by this point AQI was built to survive decapitation. In Weberian terms, the charismatic founder of AQI created a formal-rational organization that was able to replace him with new charismatic leaders. Charismatic and even traditional authority can be useful complements in a formal-rational organization. As we will see in later chapters of this book, Zarqawi was one leader in a line of AQI/ISIS leaders.

Second, while decapitation has obvious benefits, there are downsides to the strategy, especially in term of collateral damage and friction among military organizations. To come back to our points on US military organization, sometimes JSOC and the Marines worked together, as in Rawah and Anah where joint operations captured six AQI leaders and 30 operatives and eliminated the number one high-value target on the local unit's list (Shultz, Jr., 2013, p. 182). Other times, Marine "battlespace owners" were left to make excuses about JSOC actions to angry locals without the benefit of any advance warning or knowledge about the purpose of the raid. "Sometimes our actions were counterproductive," McChrystal admitted, "We would say, 'We need to go in and kill this guy,' but just the effects of our kinetic action did something negative and they were left to clean up the mess" (Priest and Arkin, 2011).

Third, both the US forces and local tribes went after AQI. Whose targeting was decisive? The events in Al Qaim and Ramadi showed that the tribes on their own were not a match for AQI. However, once able to take advantage of US firepower and logistics, the tribes could more effectively attack AQI. In this case, it is mobilization itself, with its sharing of capabilities, rather than US decapitation strategy, that is critical. This interpretation puts emphasis on the two-way street between tribal militias and regular Army and Marines, rather than on the targeting abilities of JSOC. As an example of this shared activity, Brigadier General Haqi summarizes the nature of information exchanges between Marines and tribes:

> I attended some meetings with Sheikh Abu Risha in his house, with Marine officers there in the meeting. They were telling us about some intelligence they got from some Iraqi people about the insurgents in their area. Sometimes we corrected them and told them it wasn't accurate. You've got to be accurate. In other cases, at other times, we offered intelligence to the Marine officers, which we thought was really accurate. But the Marine officers corrected us and told us something totally different, which made us change the mission. So in general, we were correcting each other, working together, trying to support each other for a common goal—to destroy the insurgents and al-Qaeda. (Montgomery and McWilliams, 2009, pp. 122–123)

What was the relationship between community mobilization and the CHB strategy? As shown in the case study above, community mobilization in Anbar led to vastly expanded police recruitment and an enhanced and efficient system of checkpoints. These accomplishments did make the population safer. They helped lead to a tipping point that moved individuals to the +1 level, provided an environment where individuals felt safe to provide information to the state security forces, and encouraged people to participate in local government. Partnering with local tribal leaders may have produced higher levels of legitimacy to overcome previous resentment of the US presence. All these accomplishments fall into the goals of the population-centric CHB.

However, the actual implementation across Anbar of the CHB doctrine during the period of community mobilization was uneven. On the one hand, James A. Russell's study of Anbar (and Nineveh) describes a US military operating on an internal, organically driven process of innovation, combining both community mobilization and population-centric strategies. Russell recounts MacFarland's move to reach out to tribes in Ramadi (against the wishes of the Iraqi government and some in the Marines). He also describes how US forces came to see the benefits of moderating the use of force and placing units outside of FOBs and into COPs. Russell sees the policies leading to success in Ramadi as providing a model for US forces across Iraq. As mentioned earlier, Russell saw US forces driven by tactical adaptation, rather than change in broader strategy or the knowledge of new doctrine. Likewise, Daniel Green and William Mullen describe a process in Fallujah in 2006–2007 where community mobilization and CHB appear to dovetail in many respects (Green and Mullen III, 2014).[16]

On the other hand, Marine officer Scott Huesing, in his memoir of his time as company commander in Ramadi and Rutbah in 2006–2007, was loath to give up war-fighting. Huesing writes:

> It galled me to no end when I'd have to sit and listen to officers negotiate with the local sheikhs or city official in Rutbah. It was all new to me. We never dealt with it in Ramadi, at least at my level. Our mission was clear there: kill or capture the enemy.
>
> For over a decade in Iraq, the Marines had perfected the art of blowing things up, but had scarcely learned much, if anything, about building things up. It wasn't what we trained to do. . . .
>
> It boggled my mind to think how we were ever going to get our ideas of governance and infrastructure to work. By trying to impose our western ethos on a culture that couldn't even manage to pick up its own trash, or refrain from shitting and pissing in the middle of public streets? How could they comprehend how to rebuild an entire city?

They couldn't. Not the way we envisioned it for them. (Huesing, 2018, pp. 261–262)

Needless to say, the Zen-like subtleties of FM 3-24 or the nuances of CHB were not part of Huesing's Echo Company practice. To pick up on earlier points, US counterinsurgency forces were diffuse and decentralized, so we should expect to see corresponding differences in tactics and understanding of prevailing strategy.

11.10. Summary

Anbar is the paradigmatic case of community mobilization, which entails co-operation between local communities (+2) and military organizations (+3) to defeat insurgent organizations (–3). The focus in this chapter has been on how community mobilization came into place. We can break down our findings on the evolution of the Anbar case into four periods and summarize and comment on each with reference to our analytical framework and template of mechanisms.

11.10.1. Early Movement to –1 and –2

In several ways, the evolution of the insurgency in Anbar followed the contours of the template of mechanisms. In Anbar, resentment against the occupier moved individuals to the –1 position. The rapid rate of movement may have been connected to Anbar's tribal culture. Perceived insults to the tribe could trigger a sense of violation of norms of honor and corresponding desires for vengeance or compensation.

Tribes moved to the –2 position for various reasons. Mostly residing in a remote area with little state protection, the Albu Mahal may have aligned with AQI for survival reasons. The Albu Fahd, one of the original "sinister six," appear to have been motivated by anger and insult, including a wedding massacre. The Albu Issa were fervently nationalist. Tribal leaders were able to move their membership in sync to the –2 level perhaps due to social norms of reciprocity, norms of honor/revenge, and anger at Coalition strike's collateral damage. With the US force unable to identify insurgents at local level, there was little need for safety in numbers.

11.10.2. The Movement of Tribes to +2

This move is the key focus of the chapter. As our analytical framework is based on individual mechanisms at a broader level, we need to expand our focus to the broader strategic level to address the moves of tribal leaders.

One primary goal of the chapter was to assess the US role in bringing this movement about. The US military did not develop or initiate any centralized top-down community mobilization effort. If anything, neither the top civilian or military US leadership nor the Shia leaders in Baghdad enthusiastically supported alliance making with the Sunni tribes in Anbar. Rather, two stages of actions by tribal leaders themselves were at work. First, tribal leaders decided to switch from allying with AQI to attacking it. Even before the establishment of ties with the United States, tribal leaders in Al Qaim and Ramadi were taking on AQI by themselves. After failure, there was a second move to seek an alliance with the United States. The initiative for "flipping" the tribes came from the tribes themselves. Importantly, this move came before any surge of troops into Anbar.

On the US side, many individual commanders had worked with tribes long before the later community mobilization. They had been "keeping a pot on the oven" and "keeping a torch lit." When the time came, some military leaders were ready to accept the tribes' entreaties to ally. However, for US actors to totally embrace the Awakening, they had to see US interests served by the strategy. Furthermore, a third actor, the Iraqi leadership in Baghdad, also needed to approve of the move, or at least not openly reject it. Remarkably, the interests of all three actors—tribes, the United States, and Baghdad—became aligned.[17] We can consider these interests in turn.

11.10.2.1. Tribal Interests

As described above, AQI brutality and excessive religious zeal undoubtedly drove many leaders to fight the Salafists. Beyond the abusive treatment by a largely foreign group, Sunni tribal leaders needed to assess their position in Iraq as a whole. As covered in depth in other chapters of this book, the Shia militias had largely defeated and successfully cleansed large parts of Baghdad. Many Sunnis in Anbar perceived that the ascendant Shia were closely connected with Iran. This brings back one of the major themes of the book—the overarching role of the Sunni-Shia master cleavage. Even in ethnically homogenous Anbar province, tribal leaders were acting on changes in the overall sectarian balance in Iraq.

The Casey plan and the US midterm elections made it clear the United States was leaving. The Anbaris had to work with this time constraint in mind. How could they balance against the Shia and end their subordination to AQI at the same time? The optimal strategy became alliance with the United States. Tribal leaders perceived a brief window of opportunity to reassert control in the region before the Americans left. They may not have liked the Americans, but allying with the United States was the only way to avoid domination by the ascendant and Iranian-allied Shia now controlling the Iraqi government.

Why did the United States suddenly become a viable alliance partner? The answer was that the United States had lost, or at least was perceived as losing. The United States admitted its pessimism for the future in Anbar and was, corresponding to Casey's plans, getting ready to withdraw from Iraq. Along the lines of classic balance of power politics, the two weaker sides—the tribes and the United States—allied to defeat the stronger side.

11.10.2.2. US Interests

Obviously, the United States had an interest not to lose in Anbar. Community mobilization allowed the United States an escape route from losing. To repeat a central point of this chapter, US military organization was not structured to follow this interest. There were too many actors in too many organizations—Marines, Army, Special Forces, Iraqi forces, and civilians. The key military actors were not oriented to adopt a strategy which went against a bias for the offensive. Individual commanders, on the other hand, could recognize the tremendous benefits of tribal alliance in their own areas of operation. From the US side, the US embrace of tribal mobilization came more from lower-level tactical adaptation than strategic guidance or new doctrine.[18]

Ironically, the United States had to lose before it could win. The tribal entreaties to the US forces would not have occurred if the US military had been winning. The very attractiveness of the United States as an alliance partner came from its perceived weakness. For the tribal leaders, it was more honorable to make a deal with a "loser" than concede power to a "winner," especially when that deal might be able to defeat the now primary threat of AQI.

11.10.2.3. Baghdad's Interests

Finally, the Maliki government in Baghdad stifled their opposition to a US alliance with Sunnis, even Sunnis with Baathist credentials. The Maliki government pursued multiple goals, most importantly, to consolidate Shia dominance in Baghdad and to eliminate AQI with its mass violent attacks and connections to the former regime. By 2006, the first of these goals was being accomplished. The Awakening would help accomplish the second. The empowerment of Sunni tribes was a negative turn, but one that could be swallowed in the whole scope of Iraq's political competition.

In sum, all three actor's interests led them to one thing they could agree on—the elimination of AQI. And community mobilization, despite the fact that tribal militias had killed US Marines and soldiers and despite Maliki's Sunni fears, was the most effective strategy in reaching this common goal.

11.10.3. The Consolidation of +2

While tribal leaders had strategic reasons to ally with the United States, all of the mechanisms predicting individual movement to +2 listed in the template in Chapter 3 were at work. Anger at AQI's assassinations and abuse of AQI drove desires for revenge. There was the pull of social norms of reciprocity to bring whole groups quickly to +2. With growing numbers entering the recruitment lines for local police jobs, there were visible indicators of safety in numbers. Community mobilization also created new material incentives and employment opportunities. While some tribal members may have been motivated by the normative aspects of tribal membership, once in the +2 position, the "labor union" aspect of the tribe kicked in.

11.11. Conclusion

The title of this book is *Death, Dominance, and State-Building*. All three were prominent in Anbar. Many US soldiers and Marines died in Anbar. Ramadi was probably Iraq's deadliest city. AQI killed US soldiers. When AQI began killing its own tribal allies, it helped set in motion the process leading to the community mobilization outlined above.

The entire conflict in Anbar was imbued with reactions against domination. Tribal members resented the presence of the US forces, they resented the control of AQI, they feared the ascendance of the Shia and Iranians. At every step, the proud tribal members of Anbar bristled at their unjust subordination.

The remaining issue is state-building. Many US practitioners envisioned community mobilization as a way to fold Anbar's Sunni tribesmen into the security system of the Iraqi state. While community mobilization brought the tribal members to the +2 rule and US money and supervision helped keep them in that role for the short term, Iraqi government policy would not sustain Anbaris at +2 or incorporate them in large numbers into the Army and other +3 organizations. This failure would help lead to protest and ISIS victories in the longer run. That topic is taken up in the chapters in Section III.

The Battle of Sadr City, 2008

Innovations in Urban Counterinsurgency

12.1. Introduction

By 2008, Shia forces had essentially won the Battle of Baghdad. Greatly aided by the Awakening and the creation of the Sons of Iraq forces, AQI was on the run. For the Shia-led Maliki government, the first-order goals had largely been accomplished. As in many civil wars, once a side has prevailed against an out-group opponent, a new contest for power occurs within the in-group. In 2008, intra-Shia battles occurred in both Basra and Baghdad. Although these were intra-Shia disputes, in both cases the US military was dragged into the fight. How the US forces conducted their fight is a major focus of this chapter.

The essence of the 2008 intra-Shia battles concerned the weak nature of the Iraqi state at the time. The Maliki-controlled central government held very little power over either Basra, Iraq's second largest city, or the giant Sadr City neighborhood in Baghdad. Previous chapters discussed the situation in Sadr City at length. After 2003, Sadr City became close to a state within a state, ruled primarily, but not exclusively, by Muqtada al-Sadr's organization. Prior to 2008, other major actors in Iraq had little interest in challenging that status. Maliki prioritized establishing Shia dominance in Baghdad and thus had little interest in fragmenting Shia forces before that goal was accomplished. US policymakers and military did not want to go against the wishes of their Shia allies. In fact, a previous agreement between Maliki and the Coalition prevented US direct attacks into Sadr City without Maliki's approval. The Coalition had not made a major incursion into Sadr City since 2004.

Even without the agreement, the United States had little interest in going into Sadr City for fear of igniting another Fallujah-like street-to-street battle. Strategically, it seemed wise to pursue other more pressing goals, such as the defeat of AQI and the building of Iraqi forces. For the short term, Sadr City could be left alone and essentially isolated. During the Surge, US forces emplaced a massive number of four-foot concrete walls and corresponding installation of command outposts and joint security stations around the southern one-third of Sadr City (see the black lines in Figure 12.1).

In the south, the British had been assigned to control Basra. By all accounts, they had failed to do so.[1] In the nearly homogenous Shia city, militias ruled militarily, economically, and politically. The British, with insufficient forces after a rapid post-invasion drawdown, were in no position to confront the militias. After sustaining casualties, the British forces essentially made a deal—they would return to their base and the militias would not attack them. In short, Basra was outside the control of the central Iraqi state and with little interference from Coalition forces.

Given the two major targets, Maliki would work sequentially, first taking on Basra and then Sadr City. By the end of the 2008 Battle of Sadr City, the Iraqi conflict was at least temporarily transformed. The 2008 Battle of Sadr City was the last significant spike of violence in Baghdad during the 2003–2011 US occupation. As seen in Figure 1.1 in Chapter 1, the Battle of Sadr City accounts for

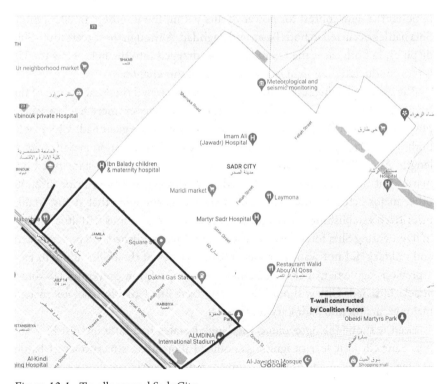

Figure 12.1. T-walls around Sadr City.
Source: "Map of Sadr City, Baghdad." Annotated Google street map.

much of the rise from roughly 700 incidents in February to over 1,200 in April. This rapid rise was followed by a rapid fall.[2] In terms of state-building, the May 10 ceasefire agreement that ended the Battle of Sadr City led to the return of government rule over a territory containing at least 1.5 million Iraqi citizens. On May 18, two Iraqi brigades occupied Sadr City without resistance. After unsustainable losses, the Jaysh al-Mahdi (JAM) militia was in no shape to challenge the Iraqi state.

This chapter begins by addressing the politics leading to the intra-Shia contest and the fighting in Basra. It then moves to a discussion focused on the transformation of US counterinsurgency strategy and tactics during the Battle of Sadr City. It concludes with comments about the resiliency of the Sadrists in the face of their seemingly decisive defeat in the 2008 fight. Observers were quick to assume the death of the Sadrists and JAM. The Sadrists' defeat was attributed not only to increased military capabilities of the US forces and the Iraqi Army, but also a decline of the Sadrists' political and social appeal. In May 2008, Max Boot summarized, "The story of the Mahdi Army's decline follows the same pattern as al Qaeda's: Not only was it routed militarily, it also made itself noxious to the very Shiite population it purported to represent and defend" (Boot, 2008). Despite this 2008 prognosis, Muqtada al-Sadr became the dominant player in the elections of 2018 and 2021. Sadrist militias would become major actors in the emerging Popular Mobilization Forces (PMF). Accounts of the death of the Sadrist movement were greatly exaggerated.

12.2. Prelude to Sadr City, 2008: Intra-Shia Competition Comes to a Head

Sensing that the time was ripe, Prime Minister Maliki made plans for Iraqi forces to move on Basra.[3] In the face of Petraeus's warnings against premature action, Maliki ordered the initiation of operation Charge of the Knights on March 23, 2008. The 10,000 members of the newly formed 14th Iraqi Army Division moved in to cordon off militia strongholds, but the operation soon stalled. Aided by the infiltration of most local Iraqi security forces, JAM's 6,000 fighters were ready with IEDs and ambush tactics. The first day of combat left 50 Iraqi soldiers dead, compared to 40 militia deaths, 120 Iraqi soldiers wounded, and dozens of vehicles lost (*The US Army in the Iraq War*, Vol. 2, 2019, p. 360). Rather than finding support from local security forces, "two-thirds of Iraqi police either deserted or discarded their uniforms to fight alongside the militiamen" (*The US Army in the Iraq War*, Vol. 2, 2019, p. 362). In the face of strong militia resistance in the Sadr-City-like enclaves of Hayaniyah and Qibla, half of the 3,000 members of the 52nd Brigade of the 14th Iraqi Army's Division deserted (*The US Army in the Iraq War*, Vol. 2, 2019, p. 362)

With fighting between government and Sadrist forces spreading across the south of Iraq (and precipitating violence in Shia areas in Baghdad), US military leaders felt the need to step in. US forces soon brought their air assets to bear, using Apache helicopters, Predator UAVs, and F-16s to attack JAM rocket teams previously identified by forward air controllers. With superior night-vision technology and constant pressure from drones, there was little let-up or opportunity for JAM forces to regroup. Iraqi reinforcements and embedded British advisors helped turn the tide and clear neighborhoods. Violence ended not only through military means, but political ones as well. Most notably, the Iranians pressured Muqtada al-Sadr to negotiate a ceasefire. In the end, JAM suffered 210 killed, 600 wounded, and 155 captured, a total estimated at about one-sixth of their Basra force. Coalition forces experienced minimal casualties (4 dead, 15 wounded) (*The US Army in the Iraq War*, Vol. 2, 2019, p. 368). The Iraqi government sent in 20,000 soldiers to keep the peace while the state re-established control over the city.

With the victory in Basra, Prime Minister Maliki saw the opportunity to finish the battle with the Sadrists by taking them on in their "capital city." In several ways, Sadr City presented a more complex situation than Basra. In addition to JAM, Special Groups (some with tight Iranian connections) and criminal networks (essentially untethered in terms of control) saturated Sadr City. Although standing JAM fighters numbered 1,000–2,000, Moqtada al-Sadr was thought able to mobilize up to 20,000 supporters if violent conflict broke out (*The US Army in the Iraq War*, Vol. 2, 2019, p. 368).

The situation in Sadr City reached a crisis point, providing Maliki an opening to attack. Concurrent with Maliki's attack on Basra, Sadrist forces launched 91 separate barrages of rockets and mortars into the Green Zone while simultaneously assaulting Iraq Security Force checkpoints around Sadr City.[4] Moqtada al-Sadr had declared an end to the ceasefire. In response, Maliki allowed Coalition forces into the south end of Sadr City; to a large degree the gloves were off. A 45-day battle began.

12.3. The Battle of Sadr City Begins: The US Forces Innovate

During the first day of the battle, JAM forces had taken over half of the Iraqi security checkpoints around Sadr City and increased rocket attacks against the Green Zone (Johnson et al., 2011, p. 4). JAM also seemed to possess an unlimited number of IEDs to use against any incursion (Spencer, 2019). These weapons, especially in the form of an EFP, destroyed six US Stryker vehicles in six days (Spencer, 2019, p. 5). JAM forces fought hard, even attempting to mass for pitched battles.

The Government of Iraq (GOI) units fighting in the Battle of Sadr City showed increasing competence from previous fights. However, social and political factors inhibited their progress. As many of the Iraqi units were from Baghdad, and east Baghdad in particular, they had reasons not to fight, partly due to legitimate fears about retaliation against their families. An estimated 700 Iraqi troops deserted in the first two days of fighting (*The US Army in the Iraq War*, Vol. 2, 2019, p. 376).

In response to JAM's solid defense and the limitations of Iraqi partners, US military forces made three moves: (1) strategically, US forces would end counterinsurgency/CHB and move to war-fighting; (2) war-fighting would be highly integrated with the surveillance and targeting practices associated with a decapitation strategy; (3) building on the existing system of walls surrounding Sadr City on the south and west, US forces would construct another and bigger wall through Sadr City to separate its lower third (with rocket bases able to hit the Green Zone) from its northern two-thirds. These moves can be considered in turn.

12.3.1. War-Fighting

After the Sadrists unleashed their rocket attacks on the Green Zone, General Petraeus informed Secretary of Defense Gates, "this week we have shifted our stance from nation-building back to warfighting" (*The US Army in the Iraq War*, Vol. 2, 2019, p. 373). War-fighting implies that the military is fighting the enemy, even an insurgent enemy, with conventional military means. For the US forces, these conventional military means center around mobility, firepower, and the use of armored vehicles. Primary tactics include cordon and sweep operations, harassment and interdiction artillery shelling, and showing force to create a deterrent.

The operation in Sadr City differed from straightforward war-fighting in some ways. Certainly, there was no indiscriminate bombing, and targeting aimed to minimize collateral damage. Cordon and sweep operations were used only in the southern third of Sadr City. Yet on the whole, as Petraeus noted, the US military did go back to war-fighting. Most striking was use of heavy armor. US forces immediately moved its fleet of M1 Abrams tanks and M2 Bradley infantry-fighting vehicles down from camp Taji to replace the high mobility multipurpose wheeled vehicles (HMMWVs) that had been the centerpiece for

CHB (Spencer, 2019, p. 4). US forces unleashed immense firepower, with the Abrams and Bradleys firing 818 main gun rounds and 12,091 25-mm rounds (Johnson et al., 2011, p. 11).

12.3.2. Decapitation

Like war-fighting, decapitation concentrates on the +3 and −3 nodes. Decapitation calls for directly going after insurgent organizations (−3) by enhancing the acuity and coverage of surveillance and the speed and precision of strike forces (+3). US forces brought a host of surveillance and precision strike weapons to the battle in Sadr City. Although Sadr City is less than five square miles in area, the US military brought two Predator drones (armed with Hellfire missiles), six Apache attack helicopters, two Army Shadow drones, fixed wing air support, guided multiple launch rocket systems (GMLRS), among other resources (Johnson et al., 2011). Continuous feeds from the Predators and Shadow drones were beamed onto multiple screens at the tactical operations center (TOC), with the visual information integrated with data received from other sensors.

There was a change in the mix of weapons and ISR (intelligence, surveillance, reconnaissance) tools. Significantly, there was also a change in the command of military arms and resources. Previously, these resources would have been under the control of the Division level or above. In the Sadr City battle, they were under the control of the Brigade Combat Team (BCT) (Spencer, 2019). Without the need to go through intervening levels of authorization, the time intervals between surveillance, evaluation, and strike diminished.

This combination of an abundance of ISR assets, along with the devolution of authority, was first brought to bear against the JAM rocket teams striking the Green Zone from the southern third of Sadr City. At the tactical operations center, intelligence personnel originally advocated strikes against identified rocket-launch teams immediately after they fired. Soon, intelligence personnel at the TOC realized they had the capabilities to follow the rocket team members back to their command location, where they would pick up additional rockets and orders (Johnson et al., 2011, p. 16). Now a strike could take out not only the rocket team but also higher-level members of the JAM network. By the end, US forces pelted JAM with 85 attacks, employing 200 hellfire missiles against Iranian-trained rocket teams (*The US Army in the Iraq War*, Vol. 2, 2019, p. 378). Raids and drone strikes, some at night, allowed no respite for JAM fighters.

JAM and Special Groups leaders had become accustomed to meeting within the Sadr City "off-limits" zone. They were unprepared when the zone was no longer off limits. Insurgent leaders expected to be safe when meeting near hospitals and mosques, estimating that the US would not strike near sensitive targets for fear of the cost of collateral damage. By 2008, however, US forces had developed a measure of precision to the point that collateral damage could largely be avoided. As the Army official history concludes, "With JAM and Special Groups leaders and fighters dying at an alarming rate, most of the remaining leaders fled to Iran to escape the coalition's increasingly lethal reach" (*The US Army in the Iraq War*, Vol. 2, 2019, p. 379). As one commentator at the Modern War Institute at West Point summarized in a 2019 study, "The small American force in the Battle of Sadr City would not have been able to accomplish its mission without the unprecedented theater-level ISR and strike capabilities pushed down to the 3rd BCT" (Spencer, 2019).

12.3.3. Building a Wall

In taking on JAM in its Sadr City stronghold, US forces effectively merged warfighting and decapitation strategies and resources. Success also came through the innovative use of T-walls. The coalition had already placed concrete barriers around the borders of the southern third of Sadr City. Then US forces built a new larger wall right through the heart of Sadr City (see Figure 12.1).[5]

In effect, US forces moved to cut off the northern two-thirds of Sadr City from the southern third by building a massive wall on Route Gold and clearing the neighborhoods of the south. The move prevented JAM rocket teams from firing on the Green Zone from their preferred launching site; it also cut them off from their control of the massive Jamila market, a primary source of funding.

The construction of the wall was a massive undertaking. Over the course of its 30 days, Operation Gold Wall installed 3,000 12-foot-high T-walls across a span of approximately three miles (Johnson et al., 2011, p. 10). As Spencer describes, "Like medieval siege engines, the units formed each night in massive convoys consisting of a tank in the lead, flatbed trucks with concrete barriers, a civilian or military crane, Bradleys, and other vehicles" (Spencer. 2019). JAM forces did all they could to impede this siege engine. They lined the route of the convoy with hundreds of IEDs, 20 IED in a single street on one day (Spencer, 2019). US armor cleared the route each day. JAM snipers aimed at crane operators; US forces responded with counter sniper fire.

The response of JAM militias to the loss of the valuable territory south of Route Irish only served to compound their deteriorating position. Waves of JAM fighters moved against Coalition positions. While JAM continued indirect fire and IED attacks in other parts of the area, it conducted complex attacks against the wall, but to no avail. Even a JAM attack under the cover of a sandstorm ended with US snipers registering 46 kills in one day (*The US Army in the*

Iraq War, Vol. 2, 2019, p. 377). In the words of one US officer, "The barrier is a magnet" (Roggio, 2008). In the words of another US officer, "JAM impaled itself on the wall" (*The US Army in the Iraq War*, Vol. 2, 2019, p. 377).

12.3.4. The End Result

Violence dramatically decreased with the building of the wall. The number of SIGACTS recorded by the 1st battalion of the 68th Armored Regiment, one of the two main units fighting the Battle of Sadr City, dropped from a high of 138 at the start of the operation to 8 toward the end (Spencer, 2019). In total, roughly 1,000 JAM fighters were killed (*The US Army in the Iraq War*, Vol. 2, 2019, p. 379). The losses compelled Muqtada al-Sadr to agree to a ceasefire requiring JAM to end its military activities and allow government forces into Sadr City. Maliki was the clear winner, JAM the clear loser. Iran lost significant ability to impose costs on the US forces. Muqtada al-Sadr attempted to distance himself from the defeat by declaring his intention to leave the political arena to pursue religious studies.

12.4. Conclusion: The Decimation of JAM and the Resiliency of the Sadrists

As outlined in previous chapters, US forces routed the Sadrists after their 2004 uprising. Yet by 2006, using Sadr City as a base, JAM was systematically taking and cleansing large tracts of Baghdad. The US forces could do little to stop them. In terms of the analytical framework, the Sadrist turnaround and their ability to beat or at least work around the American technical superiority resulted from their ability to operate across the entire spectrum of roles. From 2004 to 2007, this versatility allowed them to take the initiative in ways that took advantage of the US forces' more limited strategy. More specifically, JAM forces harassed the US military with mortar and IED attacks (vs. +3); JAM forces first took over the police stations, then infiltrated them during the US efforts to rebuild (+2). JAM built their own social service offices to compete with the US forces and Iraqi government in "hearts and minds" competition (−1, 0, +1). Also, Muqtada al-Sadr–controlled mosques provided an outlet for anti-occupation resentments as well as focal points for demonstrations and communication. Sadrist forces built up militias and also their capacity for moving out from Sadr City with more mobile units (−2 and −3).

In 2008, US forces, in conjunction with Maliki and Iraqi security forces, again devastated JAM, even ending its complete hold over Sadr City. Seemingly broken, Muqtada al-Sadr disbanded JAM and fled to Iran. The United States and its ISF allies won the Battle of Sadr City because they reduced the fight to only two nodes on the spectrum—it was a +3 versus −3 clash. The Sadrists could not use the advantages they held relating to the other positions.

US leaders explicitly moved away from CHB and its focus on moving individuals to +1. In the Battle of Sadr City, the role of the general population was not decisive. In CHB, counterinsurgents rely on information coming from a supportive population in order to find and finish enemy combatants. In the Battle of Sadr City, information came from constant surveillance by drones analyzed in a tactical operations center. Nicholas Krohley was a member of a US Army Human Terrain Team that worked in the Tisa Nissan neighborhood near Sadr City between February and December 2008. He argues explicitly that the fall of JAM was not due to neutrals or JAM supporters moving into +1 positons of Coalition support. Instead, he argues that the population was so beaten down that they withdrew or remained in a neutral position, supporting neither JAM or the Sadrists (−1), who had been the source of constant violence and turmoil, nor the Coalition forces (+1). For Krohley, the general population was not a "center of gravity at all." The Coalition military forces won not by moving an inert population, but by becoming highly adept at identifying and killing discrete insurgent networks (Krohley, 2015, p. 8). The US forces also did not rely on community mobilization or any Sons of Iraq (+2) forces or the local police (+2). While Iraqi forces (+3) played a significant role in the battle, their actions would not have been decisive on their own.

In the Battle of Sadr City, the US forces were able to force JAM to fight in a −3/+3 battle where the US military held most of the cards. Through the stunning engineering feat of Operation Gold Wall, the US forces could impose unacceptable costs on the Sadrists. JAM could not afford to lose mobility in their home base. In response to the wall, JAM was forced to abandon common insurgent methods, those relying on mobility and stealth, and fight with more direct conventional means, massing and trying to execute complex operations. In that type of fight, the Sadrists had little chance against the resources and firepower of the Americans. In Maoist terms, by walling in the enemy, the US forces created a very small sea for insurgents to swim in. Furthermore, US surveillance and firepower were exceptionally effective in that small sea.

The Coalition victory in the Battle of Sadr City was nearly total in the military sense. The United States had developed weapons, intelligence, and tactics capable of decimating Sadrist insurgent forces. Just a short time before the operation, few could have imagined that Government of Iraq forces would be marching into the Sadrist stronghold unopposed in 2008. Yet a few years later

Sadrist followers were marching en masse in the form of the Promised Day Brigade, a new armed group. In the wake of ISIS, Sadrist militias joined the PMF as hybrid groups. In 2014, the Peace Brigades marched alongside tens of thousands of black-clad and armed JAM members (Finnish Immigration Service, Country Information Service, 2015). In the 2018 elections, Muqtada al-Sadr's Sairoon took the most votes; in the 2021 election, they took the most seats.

In terms of broad contours of state-building, the rebuilding process after the Battle of Sadr City in 2008 resembled the earlier one. Although militarily defeated, the Sadrists still maintained their local social organizations. The corruption and violence of many of JAM's military units may have resulted in the loss of respect of many in the Shia population, but the Office of the Martyr Sadr (OMS) continued its functions. Sadrists controlled state ministries connected to social services and administered those ministries in ways to enhance the Sadrist organizations, rather than replace them. As described earlier, Shia organizations have the ability to send out coordinated political messages to their followers through their centralized mosque system. Above all, Sadr City still existed. There was still a 2 million contiguous Shia section of Baghdad. "Little Sadr Cities" existed in Shula and Washash. This structural reality was not going to change in the near and medium term. In effect, despite their missteps, the Sadrists still possessed the opportunities and levers to move individuals to the −1 position on the spectrum. Given the size of the Shia population, the strength of Shia identity, and the lack of opportunities in the Iraqi economy, the Sadrists could also mobilize significant numbers of youth in local militia groups (−2) whenever threats appeared. Given many years of fighting, as well as continued access from various sources of weapons, the Sadrists maintained an ability to create mobile armed militia units (−3). Moreover, the Sadrists also continued to infiltrate local police stations (+2).

The resurrections of the Sadrist organization lead to an understanding of resilience in general. Here is a hypothesis: the resiliency of an organization in a contentious and often violent conflict is determined by its ability to repopulate nodes across the spectrum of roles after defeat. If this is correct, then some of Muqtada al-Sadr's strategic decisions make more sense. Why did Muqtada al-Sadr disarm JAM and flee to Iran? Perhaps he considered that his political base of poor Shia is not going to disappear, that his system of mosques is going to survive, that he will always be able to raise militia members and always be able to threaten opponents. Then why not absorb temporary defeats and wait to fight another day?

Finally, the intra-Shia battles of 2008 reflected a larger aspect of state-building in Iraq. Maliki moved against Basra and Sadr City in order to consolidate central state control over large populations outside that control. It was also a move that could consolidate Maliki's personal power over all of Iraq. While Maliki found some short-term success, in the long run no leader would gain such power. Competing forces—Badr, Sadr, Iranian-controlled Special Groups, Kurdish parties—would retain their capabilities and use them to perpetuate a fragmented state. Those multiple groups had no interest in the creation of a system which might give rise to another Saddam-like strongman.

13

The Surge

A Reconsideration

13.1. Introduction

The dramatic decline of violence in 2007 and 2008 is one of the most important phenomena of the Iraq war. The most basic measures of Iraqi violence— US SIGACTS numbers and Iraq Body Count figures—both provide evidence for this stunning drop. Referring back to Figure 1.1 in Chapter 1, SIGACTS numbers fall from a peak of nearly 3,500 to under 1,000 in a span of a few short months. For our purposes, the numbers of civilian casualties found in the Iraq Body Count figures may be more relevant. As seen in Table 13.1, the number of civilian casualties doubles from January 2006 (1,546) to November 2006 (3,095). By the end of 2007, the count falls by two-thirds to under a thousand. By the tail end of 2008 (after a rise related to the battle of Sadr City), the number of Iraqi casualties is around one-sixth the figure two years earlier.

Explainin g variation in violence is one of the key outcomes of interest throughout the book. So is examining the interaction of strategies that created that violence. There are few more intense or lasting controversies than the debate over what caused the numbers seen in Table 13.1. Two specific arguments stand out. One holds that the "Surge alone" is responsible for the decline. That argument emphasizes the success of one of our counterinsurgency strategies— clear, hold, build (CHB)—above all others. The second much-cited position is the "synergy" explanation. In that argument, the Surge interacted with the Awakening to produce the drop in the violence. In the terms here, synergy essentially holds that two of the strategies—CHB and community mobilization— worked in conjunction to produce the drastic decrease in casualties.

This short chapter will not end the debate over the efficacy of the Surge. Rather, the goal here is to reconsider the two arguments just mentioned in light of this book's emphasis on identity, hierarchy, and Iraqi agency. The chapter will

Table 13.1 **Iraqi Civilian Casualties 2006–2008**

	Jan	Feb	Mar	Apr	May	Jun	Jul	Aug	Sep	Oct	Nov	Dec
2006	1,546	1,579	1,957	1,805	2,279	2,594	3,298	2,865	2,567	3,041	3,095	2,900
2007	3,035	2,680	2,728	2,573	2,854	2,219	2,702	2,483	1391	1,326	1,124	997
2008	861	1,093	1,669	1,317	915	755	640	704	612	594	540	586

first briefly review "Surge alone" and "synergy" and then go on to challenge and reinterpret some of these studies' major conclusions.

13.2. The Surge

President Bush officially announced the Surge on January 10, 2007.[1] The Surge had two main elements. Above all, it would put more "boots on the ground." The United States would send five additional brigades totaling more than 20,000 soldiers to Iraq, soon to be followed by 7,000 more. In March 2007, total US troop strength in Iraq was 152,000, on its way to a September 2007 peak of 168,000. Second, these troops would be implementing a new population-centric strategy. Instead of residing in large forward operating bases (FOBs), soldiers would relocate to smaller command outposts (COPs) within neighborhoods. Instead of venturing out of FOBs in armored vehicles, soldiers would conduct dismounted patrols. Moreover, the Surge concentrated troops in certain locations to produce an overmatch against insurgents. As Baghdad was the original focus of the Surge, troop numbers there nearly doubled. There was also a change in command to carry out the new strategy. General Petraeus replaced General Casey as Commander of the Multinational Force Iraq. General Petraeus was one of the creators of *Field Manual (FM) 3-24: Counterinsurgency*, which served as a guide to the new population-centric strategy.

In terms of our framework, the Surge practically defines CHB. As outlined in the first section, the strategy valued security for the general population as the single most important goal, the center of gravity in military terms. If counterinsurgents could produce a widespread perception of safety, higher numbers of neutrals, along with many who had accepted insurgents as a necessary evil, would move into a position of government support (effectively moving 0, −1 to +1). Accordingly, members of the population would increasingly come forward to identify insurgents and inform on their practices without fear of retaliation. With better information, Coalition troops and Iraqi partner forces (+3) could efficiently strike against insurgents, terrorist forces, and foreign fighters (−3).

The Surge was a clear departure from the previous strategy led by General Casey. That strategy heavily focused on standing up Iraqi troops (+3) to take over from the Coalition. Casey, and others, believed that close contact between US troops and the general population was counterproductive. The presence and actions of foreign troops would naturally create "antibodies" in a way that the human body reacts to foreign objects. Natural resentments would keep fueling the insurgency rather than quelling it. Highly concerned with Iraq's sovereignty, General Casey much preferred that Iraqi government forces would be killing insurgents in Iraq, not US forces. The Surge, taking a completely different direction, was based on US forces taking the lead and doing the killing.

The Surge was controversial at the time of its implementation. The day after Bush's announcement on January 10, Republican Senator Charles Hagel called the move "[t]he most dangerous foreign policy blunder in this country since Vietnam" (Schwin and Rupar, 2007). In February, the House of Representatives passed a resolution opposing the Surge by a 246–182 margin. Even after the implementation of the Surge and evidence of declining numbers of casualties, skeptics abounded. Famously, Hillary Clinton told General Petraeus during his September 10–11 report to the US Congress that his positive report required a "willing suspension of disbelief." While campaigning for the presidency in November 2007, Joe Biden stated, "This whole notion that the surge is working is a fantasy." [2]

Today, the debate is not about whether the Surge was a "foreign policy blunder." Given the dramatic drop in violence, the term "blunder" does not seem to fit.[3] Rather, the question is how much the Surge should be credited in the successful reduction of violence.[4] The Surge was a clear strategic change, but the entire strategic landscape in Iraq was markedly evolving at the time.

Chapter 4 outlined four different counterinsurgency strategies—CHB, community mobilization, decapitation, and homogenization. Each of these strategies, or elements of them, played out in Baghdad during late 2006–2008. Consider each in turn. As noted above, the Surge was a version of population-centric CHB. On homogenization, at the time of the implementation of the Surge, the demography of Baghdad was being transformed. The Sunni and Shia populations had largely "unmixed" by the end of 2007. Many commentators have attributed the drop in violence to these demographic changes. Sunnis and Shia stopped killing each other because of an absence of available local targets— "there was nobody left to kill." Chapter 11 covered the origins of US community mobilization strategy in Anbar. An Anbar Salvation Council formed in the fall of 2006 and soon gained Coalition support. The Awakening in Anbar inspired and provided an example for the Sons of Iraq (SOI) community mobilization efforts in Baghdad and other areas of Iraq. Chapter 6 already outlined in detail the community mobilization process as it played out in the Ghazaliyah neighborhood in Baghdad. Regarding decapitation, by the time of the Surge, JSOC had developed a high capacity to kill or capture significant numbers of high- and middle-level insurgent leaders.

In addition to the appearance of our four counterinsurgency strategies, intra-Shia divisions emerged at the same time as well. Nouri al-Maliki, a senior member of the Islamic Dawa Party who had fled a death sentence and spent 24 years in exile, became Iraq's prime minister in April 2006. Due to the power and representation of the Sadrists in the new government, Maliki's rule depended on accommodation with the Sadrists. On several occasions, Maliki blocked the Coalition from conducting operations in Sadr City in support of this alliance (*The US Army in the Iraq War*, Vol. 2, 2019, p. 69). Despite the Sadrists' power, Maliki constantly sought to gain an ability to end dependence on the Sadrists. On November 30, 2006, the Sadrist bloc walked out of Parliament. Prime Minister Maliki saw an opportunity to marginalize the problematic Sadrists. Maliki forged an agreement with Hakim and SCIRI. He also tried to fracture the Sadrists' own internal structure by making overtures to Sadr-allied leaders like Qais al-Khazali of Asaib Ahl al-Haq (AAH).

13.3. Synergy

Many explanations of the dramatic drop in violence recognize that multiple and interacting factors were probably at work. Biddle et al. (2012) argue that the combination of the Surge strategy with community mobilization (the Awakening) jointly produced the drop in violence.[5] Neither would have been sufficient to produce the drop in violence on their own. Moreover, the interaction of the strategies, rather than their simultaneous occurrence, is what caused the effect—thus the term "synergy." By itself, the number of troops involved in the Surge would have been too small to produce the drop in violence, even with its more efficient tactics. As the authors state:

> For synergy proponents, the Awakening was thus necessary for the surge to succeed. In this view, the Awakening had three central effects. First, it took most of the Sunni insurgency off the battlefield as an opponent, radically weakening the enemy. Second, it provided crucial information on remaining holdouts, especially AQI, which greatly increased coalition combat effectiveness. And third, these effects among Sunnis reshaped Shiite incentives, leading their primary militias to stand down in turn. (Biddle et al., 2012, p. 24)

The title of the Biddle et al. article is "Testing the Surge." The critical evidence for the test comes from one main military variable—the timing of the stand-up of SOI in a given area of operation (AO). If the Surge alone (numbers of troops and new tactics) was sufficient to reduce violence, then violence (as measured by SIGACTS) should be declining in a steady fashion over time in the AO. If the synergy argument is correct, the authors argue, then we should see the sharpest drop-off of violence in the period following the stand-up of the SOI in the respective AO. As the authors summarize, "the synergy thesis implies that for any given AO, the reduction in violence before the SOI standup should be too slow to pacify the AO before the surge's end" (Biddle et al., 2012, p. 27). The authors find that in 24 of the 38 AOs studied, violence trended down more after rather than before the SOI stand-up (Biddle et al., 2012, p. 28). Given this finding, the authors conclude, "It was not until the Sons of Iraq stood up that bloodshed fell fast enough; without them, our findings suggest that Iraq's violence would still have been at the mid-2006 levels when the surge ended" (Biddle et al., 2012, p. 36).

The authors argue for the crucial importance of the interaction of two counterinsurgency strategies—CHB and community mobilization. They explicitly argue against homogenization; they admit that they cannot directly test decapitation due to an absence of data.

13.4. A Reconsideration: Politics, Dominance, and Agency

I have previously stressed that the conflict in Iraq can be characterized by its changes in status hierarchies and the accompanying intense resentments. Before turning to the Iraq case specifically, we can first consider several hypotheses that can be applied to status-based conflicts in general. Consider a case where group A has dominated group B historically, but now group B has reversed this hierarchical relationship and has become clearly dominant over A. Also assume that these groups have competing internal factions. The following hypotheses result:

1. If B has clearly achieved dominance over A, B will likely stop major attacks against A. Achieving dominance does not require the physical extinction of the opposing group, only the clear ability to command a position of political authority.
2. If B has clearly achieved dominance, then B may even begin to make concessions to the now subordinated A group.
3. If B is still struggling to establish dominance over A, factions within B will refrain from infighting. If dominance is the overarching goal, internal factions of B will try to maintain coordination of efforts until that goal is achieved. These factions (despite unavoidable and even intense frictions) will not make major assaults on each other.
4. If B has clearly achieved dominance over A, then we should expect internal factions of B to begin fighting among themselves. If the primary goal is secure, then secondary goals will be pursued, including the pursuit of power within the group.

The value of examining these hypotheses in the Iraq case is shown by their relevance to the patterns of violence seen in other cases of ethnic cleansing. In his testimony to the US Senate in 2008 on Iraq, Stephen Biddle mentioned the Bosnian war of the 1990s as a useful referent (Biddle, 2008). Indeed, both cases witnessed massive levels of violence and ethnic cleansing. I have argued elsewhere that the Bosnian violence and cleansing were driven by a distinguishable political program (Petersen, 2011). Serbian forces aimed at rapidly carving out a new Serbian political entity with a clearly dominant Serbian demography and defensible borders. The variation in violence across time and across municipalities corresponds to this program. Almost half of all victims died during the first three months of the war (*Bosnian Book of the Dead*); violence was highest in ethnically polarized municipalities, that is, where two groups faced each other in roughly equal numbers, in effect, where no group was dominant (Costalli and Moro, 2010). Violence was high in areas bordering Serbia and along the line between what became Republika Srpska and the Federation (Costalli and Moro, 2010). This pattern of violence illustrates the political program behind it. Serbian actions seem clearly aimed at quickly clearing areas that were strategically crucial to constructing a viable Serbian entity. The violence was aimed at "cleansing" the most highly contested areas (those where Muslims and Croats could maintain majorities and control of local governments) and "cleansing" the crucial areas along the borders that would define the new entity.

Crucially, the strategy required rapid population change. The strategy did not so much depend on killing enemy fighters as on driving large numbers of out-groups from contested and strategically important regions. Serbs did not aspire to driving every non-Serb out of Bosnia, an impossible task in any event. Even in any given municipality, once dominance was achieved violence drastically declined (hypothesis #1 above). Furthermore, the boundaries created through indiscriminate violence, ethnic flight, and demographic homogenization became the basis of the Dayton Accords. The Dayton Accords ratified already existing spheres of control, rather than establishing control in the first place. Ethnic cleansing had homogenized much of Bosnia's territory and had reduced the number of contestable, and potentially violent, hot spots. With Serbs clearly dominant in the Republika Srspka territorial half of Bosnia and a clear and institutionalized balance between Bosniaks and Croats in the Federation half, hostilities could cease and deals could be made (hypothesis #2 above). While the war outcome was still in doubt, Milosevic was able to keep most Serbs on the same side (hypothesis #3). When it became clear that the best the Serbs could do, and indeed would do, was to establish dominance in one half of Bosnia, Milosevic ceased to support many Serbian forces and populations. Most famously, he tacitly cooperated in the ethnic cleansing of Serbs in Croatia's Krajina region, thus facilitating the Croatian state's dominance over its entire

territory (hypothesis #4) and ending all violence there. In his 2008 Senate testimony, Biddle attributed the end of violence in Bosnia to the presence of international peacekeepers. It is more likely that violence ended in Bosnia because
the main protagonist's dominance-seeking political program had achieved all
it could. Groups "unmixed"; lines between groups were solidified; new intra-
group battles could commence.

There are many other instances in civil wars, even ones not defined by ethnic
and sectarian divisions, where actors employ violence against civilians in an effort to establish political dominance. In her work on the Spanish Civil War, Laia
Balcells addresses the puzzle of why and when we see violence against civilians
behind the front lines in conventional civil wars (Balcells, 2010). There would
seem to be no military reason for killing civilians in cities far from the front.
Balcells does identify a political reason, though. In her analysis of over a thousand municipalities, she finds that direct violence against civilians increased
where pre-war electoral competition between rival political parties and factions
was near parity. In effect, in a country riven by an ideological political master
cleavage, violence did not occur in places where one side was clearly politically
dominant over the other. Rather, violence was a way to transform the political nature of a locality from ambiguous and contested to clear and dominated.
Violence follows the lines of the society's master cleavages (Balcells, 2010,
p. 296).

13.5. Bringing Politics (of Dominance) Back In

If the struggle in Iraq is viewed as a struggle about dominance, then one central
fact must immediately be recognized: by early 2007, at the time of the Surge,
Shia had become dominant in Baghdad, the capital and the central site of Sunni-
Shia competition in Iraq. Our previous case material provided rich illustrations
of this fact. In Ghazaliyah, the Sunni militia leader only made the radical move
to partner with the United States after recognizing that the Shia had essentially
won the larger battle for Baghdad. Recall the interview done in Amman, Jordan,
with the Sunni refugee who fled Mansour, never to return. He had earlier sent
his family out of the country; he left when he realized the game was over. In
the Bayaa chapter, the US Army Captain Wright, in charge of one section of the
neighborhood, recalls that one day Shia flags simply sprouted up in the locale.
The game there was somehow over; Bayaa was now a Shia territory, significantly
cleansed to the point that Sunnis were no longer contestants.

The maps in Figure 13.1 illustrate (clockwise from upper left) the unmixing
of Baghdad from the time of the invasion in 2003, the situation at the beginning of the JAM cleansing campaign in 2006, demographics in early 2007, and

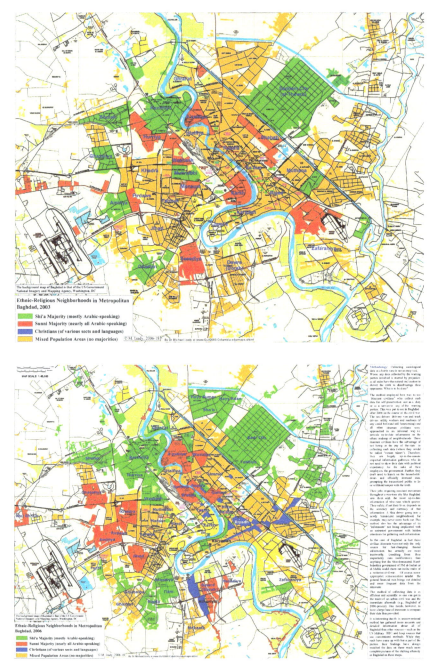

Figure 13.1. Changing demography of Baghdad.
Numbers from Iraq Body Count.
Source: Original maps created by Dr. Michael Izady via Gulf/2000

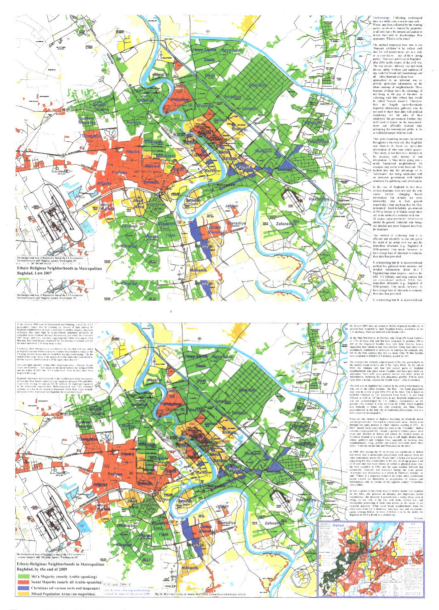

Figure 13.1. Continued

finally the situation as the United States began preparations to exit at the end of 2009. In effect, as also demonstrated by the statements above, Shia had become dominant in the majority of Baghdad's neighborhoods by 2007. As indicated by the bottom right figure, that dominant position would not change over the next three years. That position was still largely unchanged in 2023.

The demography of Baghdad changed—shifting to produce a dominant and contiguous Shia zone. Beyond that, US Surge tactics helped consolidate Shia gains. Recall the conversation in the section on homogenization in Chapter 4. In the beginning pages of his book, *Out of the Mountains: The Coming Age of the Urban Guerrilla*, David Kilcullen, one of the architects of FM 3-24 and the US counterinsurgency policy, had the following conversation with a fellow practitioner from Baghdad:

> Kilcullen: "You killed the city, mate. You know that, right?
> Eames: "What? Piss off."
> Kilcullen: "Seriously. All that barbed wire, concrete barriers, checkpoints. You shut the city down. You stopped it flowing—put it on life support. You stopped people getting around to do what they had to do. You cut the violence, sure, but you did it by killing the city.
> (Kilcullen, 2013, p. 19)

In effect, after Shia militias made their gains in 2006, the US forces helped secure those gains through the construction of massive numbers of T-walls. These barriers, along with the solidification of Sunni populations and defenses, would raise the costs of further Shia advances. But they also acted to lock in Shia dominance in Baghdad.

If we take the view that Iraq's conflict was driven by dominance issues, then we must re-evaluate our views of the strategic calculations of the key actors in light of Shia victory and consolidation. Foremost among those calculations is Muqtada al-Sadr's declaration of a unilateral ceasefire. Biddle et al. (2012) recognize that JAM militias had systematically worked out of its base in the northwest of Baghdad to clear Sunnis both from mixed areas and from majority Sunni areas. As they note, JAM drove into the heart of the Sunni area of Baghdad to destroy the Sunni dominant position. The districts of Karkh and Mansour were not only large—10–20 contiguous square miles—but heavily populated, with 1.5 million residents. By mid-2007, Shia forces had driven half of the population out and replaced it with Shia squatters (Biddle et al., 2012, p. 17).

Why did these attacks stop? Biddle et al.'s synergy argument rests almost solely on the production of higher costs to the Shia forces. Biddle et al. argue that there were more neighborhoods to be conquered and JAM would have done so if not deterred by the military power unleashed through the Surge in combination with the Awakening. Sectarian cleansing stopped, in Biddle et al.'s (2012) view, because of prohibitive military costs of continuing action. Correspondingly, Muqtada al-Sadr issued a unilateral ceasefire because he could not absorb the military punishment doled out by more numerous, more capable, and better-informed US and Iraqi forces. Following this line of thought, Biddle et al. (2012) dismiss the importance of sectarian cleansing in explaining the 2007 drop in violence.

It is clear that Muqtada al-Sadr and JAM were encountering much higher military costs because of the Surge and/or synergy and that those higher costs went into strategic calculations. But what about the benefit side for continued Shia fighting and cleansing? If the Shia had already gained dominance in Baghdad by early 2007, what was to be gained by continuing to press into remaining areas? If political dominance is the goal, it was not necessary to take over every neighborhood and cleanse the area of every out-group member (hypothesis #1). In Baghdad, it was not possible, or even desirable, for Shia organization to drive out all Sunnis. Sunnis were no longer dominant even in Karkh or Mansour; Sunnis only consolidated positions on the margins of Baghdad; they needed to side with the Americans to survive; the huge numbers of Sunni refugees and internally displaced were not likely returning to their homes, let alone return to dominant social and political positions. It is true that military costs must be considered. Why continue fighting if you are going to get bloodied? But the better question here is—why continue fighting and getting bloodied if you have already won?

Along these lines, we should further consider the specific benefits of the gains that Shia forces had already made. In the broader political viewpoint, not all neighborhoods, territories, or AOs (to consider Biddle et al.'s [2012] level of analysis) are of equal importance. If organizations on one side of a sectarian master cleavage are pursuing dominance, they will want to gain that dominant position by combining contiguous and defensible districts in the most important city (likely the capital). Biddle et al.'s (2012) treatment of Baghdad has limits on this score. Biddle et al. (2012) examine 38 AOs, finding that 24 saw a decrease after the stand-up of SOI units. However, as pointed out by Hagan et al. (2013), their sample includes only one neighborhood east of the Tigris River in Baghdad, thus basically excluding from consideration an area containing one-third of Baghdad's population (Hagan et al., 2013).[6] In the larger strategic sense, Shia control of this large territory is important for explaining the drop in violence. In effect, Shia organizations and militias had a starting large base area, they expanded that base and diminished the Sunni demographic base through incursions to the west and east, and after achieving dominance through these incursions, decided that the costs involved with further fighting were not worth the effort.

Because Biddle et al. wish to concentrate on testable hypotheses, they do not spend much time on Sadrist decision-making. Commentators have seen this as a problem. In an *International Security* forum debating the synergy argument, participants Hagan, Kaiser, and Hanson baldly state, "To be sure, there was a downward plunge in violence in Iraq, but it was likely more closely linked to al-Sadr's August 2007 cease-fire than to the stand-up of the SOI" (Hagan et al.,

2013, p. 176). Biddle et al. defend themselves against charges of ignoring or overly downplaying Iraqi internal political dynamics and al-Sadr's ceasefire. They state that the ceasefire was "important but secondary" (Hagan et al., 2013, p. 196).

Examining the Surge case with an eye on dominance politics also helps explain other political decisions that helped produce the drop in violence. As noted above, the Sadrists cost–benefit calculations included not only higher military costs, but also costs stemming from the emergence of higher levels of intra-Shia political competition. This leads to a question: What accounts for the timing of intra-Shia conflict? Why are these conflicts, which had been bubbling under the surface in previous years, only breaking out in full form in 2007? A framework highlighting dominance provides a ready answer (see hypotheses #3 and #4). When there is a main battle being fought along lines of a master cleavage, there are usually conflicts and imbalances within any side of the cleavage. Given this reality, battles are likely to be fought sequentially. Once the main battle is no longer being fought, actors turn to the secondary battle. By 2007, the civil war between Shia and Sunni in Baghdad had reached clarity with the Shia victory. Actors then predictably turned to going after in-group rivals. The behavior of Prime Minister Maliki is illustrative on this point. He sided with and protected the Sadrists during the height of the sectarian war. When the Shia victory was clear, Maliki dropped his previously fervent opposition to the inclusion of Sunni in security organs and consented to the development of the SOI (along the lines of hypothesis #2). Maliki then boldly pursued enemies within the Shia bloc after Shia had gained dominance. As we will see in later chapters, after consolidating his position in intra-Shia politics, Maliki again goes after Sunni targets.

13.6. Conclusions

The stunning drop in violence in Iraq during 2007 is one of the major questions of the entire war. The fact that many different strategies and political maneuvers took place during 2006–2007 produces a complexity that seems almost impossible to unravel. Some explanations, those based on the security dilemma or deterrence theories, stress security factors. Biddle et al.'s synergy argument likewise concentrates on military costs.

Other analysts believe these arguments are wrong, or at least incomplete. In their critique in the *International Security* forum, Jon Lindsay and Austin Long hold that

> Biddle et al. have little to say, however, about specific Iraqi strategic choices, how important they were, or indeed whether they even required extensive U.S. encouragement. Methodologically, Biddle et al.

fail to adequately measure or infer the causes and consequences of Iraqi calculations. They rely heavily on the accounts of U.S. personnel and on SIGACTS (significant acts) recorded by U.S. forces, but these sources reveal little about ethnic cleansing, factional fighting, systematic criminal violence, or third party (Iranian) intervention that may have occurred with little relation to the disposition of U.S. troops. (Hagan et al., 2013, pp. 186–187)

I also argue that war and politics cannot be so easily separated. Clausewitz's famous dictum may prove stronger for civil war than interstate war. Killing and threatening civilians in civil war usually has a political purpose. Since the beginning of this book, I have argued that violence in Iraq has often been motivated by a desire to dominate or avoid subordination. There was a goal behind the systematic neighborhood-by-neighborhood sectarian cleansing of Sunnis by JAM and the Badr Organization: the establishment of Shia dominance in the capital city. The reason for night letters and bullets in envelopes and graffiti on houses was not to make it easier to kill Sunnis, but to drive them out and replace them.

Iraqi Kurdistan

Dual Cleavages and Their Impact on War and State-Building

14.1. Introduction

As outlined since Chapter 1, Iraq has struggled since the 2003 invasion to build a functional state. I have argued that the failure to evolve toward a more coherent state stems from the way non-state violent actors have either captured or merged with the Iraqi state. The Sadrists, the Badr Organization, Iranian-backed militias, and others established legitimacy and staying power. These groups honed their abilities to meddle and monitor nonviolent aspects of the state, controlling ministries and developing entrenched patronage systems. Given the lack of trust among all major actors, there is no incentive to change. There is little desire to move toward a coherent, centralized state which could serve as a platform for a Saddam-like strongman. A system based on a bargained division of government security organs and oil resources may not be efficient or just, but it is safe and satisfactory for the current set of power holders.

The Kurdistan region and the Kurdistan Regional Government (KRG) are an essential, and typical, part of this system.[1] The political power in the region lies with two major political parties: the Kurdistan Democratic Party (KDP) and the Patriotic Union of Kurdistan (PUK). These two parties maintain separate lines of control through their respective Peshmerga armed forces and other less transparent security organs. These autonomous security institutions prevented a monopoly over the legitimate means of violence and helped sustain non-transparent control of state resources and patronage. This chapter will show how institutions of violence, a focus of this book's analytical framework, are inextricably linked to state-building. Mirroring a dynamic seen in Iraq as a whole, a mix of competition, cooperation, and outright violence between these two dominant forces has led to a weak government.

This outcome was not predicted. The failure of the KRG to live up to its long-term potential can be glaringly illustrated by comparing the promise of the entity in 2010–2013 to events only a few years later. Kurds had talked about the KRG capital of Erbil becoming a "new Dubai." When I was in Erbil in 2013, the claim seemed to have merit. The construction of new gleaming buildings indeed brought up such comparisons. But compare the promise of that time to the reality only a few years later. In 2021, in great contrast, migrants from the KRG, among other desperate peoples, crowded along the Belarus-Polish border. One commentator from Iraqi Kurdistan wrote: "(t)he mass exodus of Kurds . . . is not a simple story of migration or even about fleeing injustice, corruption, intimidation and authoritarian rule in the Kurdish region. It is the story of a broader failure. The failure of what was once touted as a regional success story is a loss for the whole Middle East" (Chomani, 2021).

This outcome is all the more puzzling because the KRG seemed to hold many state-building advantages. During Iraq's bloody civil war, the KRG saw little violence. Referring back to Figure 1.1 in Chapter 1, the north region never approached 500 SIGACTS in any month and was below 100 in most months. These numbers were vastly below those experienced in Baghdad, central Iraq, or Anbar. They were significantly lower than adjacent Nineveh but rivaled those seen in the south. Second, the KRG has been closer to a de facto state than a federal region of Iraq.[2] While the 2005 Iraqi constitution devolved significant powers to the regions, even within that decentralized system the KRG was establishing de facto state authority and impinging on the prerogatives of the central government. The KRG established a Department of Foreign Affairs in 2006.[3] In August 2007, the KRG adopted its own oil law and promptly made deals with numerous foreign firms despite Iraq's oil minister labeling those deals as illegal. As detailed below, the KRG made its own defense and security policy. The KRG constitution, although never ratified, also laid claims to territory outside the three provinces defining the KRG. Given these capabilities, the KRG could largely manage its own affairs without being bogged down with the problems in Iraq proper (at least until the coming of ISIS in 2014).

While it is true that the KRG often outperformed the rest of Iraq along common economic measures,[4] Kurds have done badly on many governance measures. KRG budget and allocation systems were never transparent. The KRG has usually been seen as a patronage system permeated by family and tribal connections. Typical NGO evaluations hold that "[l]evels of corruption in the Kurdistan Region of Iraq, while lower than in Iraq as a whole, are relatively high compared to other countries in the region. Corruption challenges are rooted in the strong role that the two established political parties have in the political system, nepotism, a weak bureaucracy and difficulties associated with managing oil revenues" (Pring, 2015).[5]

One of the central arguments of this book is that non-state armed actors came to control sections of the Iraqi state, in turn, creating a weak and fragmented state. This argument is linked to another—that the conflict in Iraq has been driven by the power of master cleavages and perceptions of dominance and subordination. On this score, I will make a particular argument about the Kurds in Iraq. Kurds are subject to two powerful cleavages: Arab/Kurd and KDP/PUK. I will argue that the KDP and PUK evolved in a way to create perceptions of difference and dominance close to those experienced in ethnic and sectarian conflicts. Following the general theory laid out earlier, the clarity of hierarchy in these master cleavages has largely determined the intensity of conflict between Kurds and Arabs and between KDP and PUK. As is the case more broadly, periods of change and ambiguity in hierarchy have witnessed conflict, while periods of either clear dominance of one group or clear balance among groups saw an absence of violence.

14.1.1. The Way Forward

The present chapter and Chapter 19 in Section III examine our two main outcomes—violence and state-building—in the Kurdish areas of Iraq from 2003 to the time of writing. To recall, Chapter 5 was entitled "Violence, State-Building, and the Shia-Sunni Cleavage." That chapter provided a summary of the historical origins of the relations between Shia and Sunni, their respective organizational bases, and possibilities for mobilization. Following that format, this chapter begins with two sections describing the formation of the two powerful cleavages dividing Kurds and Arabs and KDP and PUK. It then follows changes in the clarity/ambiguity of those cleavages through a series of wars and political challenges. The present chapter will follow the Kurdish story through 2011. Following the book's general arguments, the chapter shows the development of competing party-controlled security organs that work to distort state-building in the Kurdish region.

Chapter 19 will continue the analysis of the Kurdish region up to approximately 2020. During the 2011–2020 period that is the focus of Section III, Kurdish armed forces fought a prolonged and bloody war against the Islamic State (ISIS). After several early defeats, Kurdish Peshmerga rallied and, in conjunction with the US and Iraqi forces, drove ISIS out of Kurdish-populated territories, although taking significant numbers of casualties in the process. The Kurdish role in the anti-ISIS war is addressed in some detail in the Chapter 16, "The Third Iraq War."

In total, the two chapters on Kurds will cover these critical periods:

1. The aftermath of the First Iraq War of 1991
2. The Kurdish Civil War between the KDP and PUK during 1994–1998

3. The aftermath of the US invasion
4. The Gorran challenge to the KDP/PUK dominated political system, 2009–2011
5. The war against ISIS, 2014–2017
6. The 2017 independence referendum and its aftermath.

After describing the formation of the two master cleavages, this chapter covers the first four periods. Chapter 19 in Section III, as well as parts of Chapter 16, address the last two periods.

14.2. The Creation of the Kurdish-Arab Master Cleavage

In most cases, nationalism is a modern phenomenon. This statement applies to Iraq's Kurds. During most of its reign, the Ottoman Empire maintained social control in its Kurdish regions through a system of indirect rule relying on tribal chiefs. Only in the nineteenth century did the Ottomans move to a system of more centralized direct rule, a system largely run by Sunni administrators (Hechter and Kabiri, 2008). The move to direct rule sparked resistance by Kurdish tribal chiefs. It also helped lay the foundation for Kurdish group resentments against outside rule.

In April 1920, the League of Nations awarded Britain a mandate to govern Iraq. Continuing Ottoman practices, they relied largely on Sunnis as administrators. While the British had promised Kurds significant autonomy, the 1930 Anglo-Iraq treaty did not even mention Kurdish self-determination. Meanwhile, modernization brought increasing state penetration of political and social life. A growing number of Kurds became aware of broader ethnic and religious forces beyond tribe, as well as developing a consciousness of ethnic hierarchy and subordination. Andreas Wimmer describes the interaction among modernization, perception of Arab dominance, and the growth of Kurdish nationalism:

> The spread of these ideas was closely linked to the Arabisation of the state and army and to corresponding processes of social closure that suddenly left persons of Kurdish origin outside the doors leading to power and influence at the centre, doors through which the influential, rich or gifted had passed without hindrance in Ottoman times. (Wimmer, 2002, p. 185)[6]

In response, the first Kurdish nationalist organizations formed in 1939 (Tripp, 2010, p. 108). Given the existence of a Pan-Arab movement, Iraq's Kurds could not be sure if the opposing side of the emerging cleavage would be Arabs in general or the Arabs within Iraq proper, but after 1941, it became clear that Iraq's Pan-Arab movement would not prevail. Iraqi Kurds needed to deal with their Arab counterparts in Baghdad.

At this point, Mulla Mustafa Barzani emerged as the central Kurdish protagonist. Possessing a military-political power base in Barzan, Barzani could raise armed tribal forces to attack and pressure the Iraqi government for concessions on Kurdish autonomy. Despite some early Kurdish victories, the Iraqi Army drove the rebels into Iran in October 1945 (where the short-lived Kurdish Mahabad Republic was formed). Iranian forces then drove Barzani's followers back into Iraq, where after a short period of respite, they were again driven across borders and mountains into the Soviet Union. Granted asylum, Barzani and his followers remained in exile in the Soviet Union until the fall of the Iraqi monarchy and the entrance of the Qasim regime in 1958.

During this tumultuous period, the KDP was formed, holding its founding congress in Baghdad in 1946. Although in exile in Iran at the time, Barzani was elected president; the congress adopted a Kurdish nationalist program while recognizing the sovereignty of the Iraqi state. Here was the political institutionalization of Kurdish nationalism. It came in the form of a military/political hybrid built on tribal networks, especially those of one powerful clan.

After the military coup initiated the Qasim regime, Barzani was allowed back in Iraq. While other Kurdish organizations had formed in the meantime, the KDP maintained its preeminence. Among Kurdish groups, only the KDP could raise sufficient military force to pressure the government. When Barzani's political overtures were rejected in July 1961, full-scale war soon broke out in the northern tribal areas. In 1962, a collection of largely tribal fighting units combined to form the Peshmerga. Part-time guerilla fighters became a full-time fighting organization with a reserve contingent. Moreover, in 1968 the KDP developed its own party-controlled intelligence apparatus, the Parastin. By the end of the 1960s, the Kurdish nation had a dominant political party, an army, and an intelligence arm.

By March 1965, full-scale war raged in Iraqi Kurdistan. Government troops controlled the cities and some of the rural areas during the day, but Kurdish forces held their own. In June 1966, Iraqi policymakers offered their Kurdish opponents a deal recognizing Kurdish demands for cultural and linguistic rights as well as self-government. However, Iraqi military officers pushed back. A new cabinet filled with military officers withdrew the offer. In 1968, the Baathists took power in a military coup. Their relative weakness, however, led them to offer Kurds rights and autonomy, in the form of the 1970 Manifesto, at a level beyond any previous proposal. Yet, military action and negotiations continued simultaneously. By the early 1970s, there was a Kurdish/Arab cleavage at the center of Iraqi politics, but it was unstable both in military and political terms.

By the mid-1970s, international and regional political events led Barzani to believe this unstable balance might turn to the Kurds' advantage. Iran and Iraq came close to the brink of all-out war. Aligned with Iran at the time, the United States also looked for leverage against Iraq. Both Iran and the United States found this leverage against Iraq by aiding Kurdish fighters. This strategy indeed worked. Iraq made a peace deal with Iran. Unfortunately for the Kurds, as part of the deal the Iraq regime demanded that all Iranian aid to Kurdish rebels end. Within weeks, the Kurdish resistance collapsed. Barzani and his fellow KDP leaders, as well as 150,000 Kurdish civilians, fled the country while thousands of remaining Peshmerga accepted amnesty offers (Tripp, 2010, pp. 204–205).

To summarize, modernization and outside rule led to national consciousness. In turn, this consciousness led to organizational form, conflict with the Arab center, and ultimately violence and war. While the Barzani-led forces were able to confront the center and create an unstable balance between Kurds and Arabs (as seen in the 1970 Manifesto) in the 1960s and early 1970s, the realignments of 1975 established clear Arab dominance.

14.3. The Creation of the KDP-PUK Master Cleavage

With the KDP's devastating defeat in 1975, the state of the primary Kurd/Arab cleavage had become clear. Kurds had lost. Barzani himself would die in the United States in exile in 1979. While there was no battle to be fought on the lines of the primary Kurd/Arab cleavage, attention would turn to matters within the Kurdish cleavage. As in the emergence of a Kurdish cleavage seen above, forces of modernization would again create a new and powerful cleavage, this time within the Kurds.

Perhaps the most significant force was urbanization. Based on his own origins and experience, Barzani had formed the original KDP disproportionately from rural tribal alliances. By the 1970s, Iraq's Kurdish population had grown more urban. As across the region, and the world for that matter, socialist factions rose in the new urban and more literate society. Modernization also brought bureaucratization, which at that time combined with the Barzani tribal networks to produce a patronage system. Tribal chiefs became brokers of jobs and projects in Kurdish cities. The KDP became intertwined and identified with a kinship-based patronage system (Leezenberg, 2006). On both ideological and patronage grounds, the time was ripe for the growing divisions within the Kurdish cleavage to manifest themselves.

Accordingly, upon the disastrous military outcome in 1975 and a weakened KDP, Jalal Talabani established the Patriotic Union of Kurdistan (PUK). As often noted, the PUK differed from the KDP in its more urban base, its socialist orientation, its territorial base, and its members' differences in dialect (Badini speakers in the KDP north versus Sorani speakers in the PUK south). No doubt, Talabani and the PUK were also trying to free themselves from the disproportionate power of the Barzani family (with Barzani's sons Masoud and Idris ready to take power).

While the splitting of the KDP did not fall along ethnic or class lines, the division soon became institutionally entrenched. The PUK quickly established its own Peshmerga in 1976. Young Kurdish men were now recruited, trained, and indoctrinated into two parallel and competing fighting forces.[7] Like his KDP counterpart, Talabani took on an unquestioned leadership role with cult-like properties. In some areas of Kurdistan, shop owners put up pictures of Barzani; in others, Talabani.

While most master cleavages revolve around the day-to-day mass experiences involved with language, race, or religion, under certain circumstances political divisions can equal the pervasiveness of ethnic identity through institutionalization and symbols.[8] Perhaps most critically, the establishment of separate institutions of violence and force indicate the emergence of a cleavage. Such institutions are designed to assure the prevention of domination by the opposing side. They force comparisons of power and perpetuate perceptions of the physical threats to the in-group.

14.4. The Iran-Iraq War: Death in Abundance and the Renewed Salience of the Kurd/Arab Cleavage

With Iraq and Iran engaged in a massive conventional war beginning in 1980, the Iraqi state's capabilities were stretched too thin to keep the lid on the Kurds. To compensate for a lack of troops in the north, the regime bought off Kurdish tribal leaders and gave them police powers, their forces known derisively as "Jash" or donkey foal by opponents. The Iraqi government and its collaborators were no match, especially in the mountains, for Peshmerga forces of the KDP, PUK, and a range of smaller parties. Peshmerga forces were formidable on their own, but their power was multiplied when combined with those of Iran. In July 1983, KDP forces worked in tandem with Iranian units in a successful joint operation.

In retaliation, the regime committed an act of mass killing with long-lasting resonance. Iraqi forces detained 8,000 members of the Barzani clan. While listed as "disappeared," they were certainly killed. The act was aimed at creating a deterrent for collaboration. It also appeared to be an act of revenge against the Barzanis in particular.

The massacre failed to deter Kurdish fighters. By 1987, the Iraqi government controlled most of Iraqi Kurdistan in name only. In 1987, the war took another turn when the combined Kurdish forces, the Kurdistan Front, declared an alliance with Iran. For the Saddam regime, this was an act of treason justifying any act of retaliation. As the war with Iran began to wind down, government attention turned to the north. The regime launched the al-Anfal (meaning "spoils of war" and also the name of the eighth sura of the Quran), a series of scorched earth campaigns, peaking from February 23 to September 6, 1988. Aimed at destroying the support base of Kurdish rebels, the Anfal entailed mass summary executions of non-combatants, the use of chemical weapons, forced displacement, and wholesale destruction. In all, 60,000 Iraqi soldiers took part in eight waves of attacks that may have killed 50,000–100,000 Kurds while destroying several thousand villages (Human Rights Watch, 1993).[9] One of the most well-known attacks came at Halabja, the site of a massive chemical attack and the location of a large present-day museum and memorial. With the completion of the eighth Anfal campaign, coming immediately after a ceasefire with Iran, the Iraqi regime announced a general amnesty for all Kurds on September 6, 1988. The amnesty itself was a clear sign of Arab victory. Winning sides only grant amnesty to defeated groups who no longer pose a threat.

The nature of the operations showed a clear drive for Arab domination. In most of the Anfal operations, women and children were separated from men. Women and children were interned; men executed. However, women and children from Germian (in the 3rd and 4th Anfals) were carted off to execution along with the men (Hiltermann, 2008). The apparent goal was to change the demographics of the disputed Kirkuk region. In the words of Wafiq al-Samarra'i, who was deputy director of the Military Intelligence Directorate in 1988, "You can kill half a million Kurds in Erbil, but that won't do anything. It would still be Kurdish. But killing 50,000 Kurds in Kirkuk will finish the Kurdish cause forever" (Hiltermann, 2008). As Hiltermann (2008) summarizes, the Anfal campaign was Arabization taken to a "logical extreme." He states, "Anfal, in other words, was a campaign to (1) incapacitate the Kurdish national movement by razing rural Kurdistan and killing all its actual or potential fighters, and (2) remove that movement's main prize, Kirkuk, by exterminating that particular region's Kurdish village population."

While the Kurdish-Arab cleavage obviously intensified to extreme levels, the carnage did not force a merger of the KDP and PUK. The previously established and institutionalized cleavage persisted. In fact, Talabani and the PUK communicated with the Saddam regime (Tripp, 2010, p. 234). Both the PUK and the KDP established de facto autonomy in their respective areas of support (Tripp, 2010, p. 235). In both policy and territory, the two party's actions reinforced their separate identities and institutions. This lack of clarity in the KDP/PUK cleavage would have major repercussions in the next period.

14.5. The First Iraq War and the 1991 Uprising: The Ironic End of Arab Domination and the Birth of a Kurdish de Facto State

As the United States decimated Iraq's army as it fled Kuwait toward the end of the 1991 war, Kurds again found opportunity for revolt against a weakened central government. In effect, the war weakened Arab dominance, introducing a new period of uncertainty. In March 1991, uprisings broke out across the south of Iraq, especially in Basra, Najaf, and Karbala. Having kept the Republican Guard troops in reserve for just such a contingency, Saddam deployed these highly trained units to put down the rebellion. Kurds had also risen in rebellion, taking several towns and capturing Kirkuk on March 19. As in the south, Republican Guard units again established control. With the mass killing of the Anfal only three years in the past, massive numbers of civilians fled to the borders of Iran and Turkey seeking safety. Up to two million citizens were displaced; a humanitarian crisis loomed.

The brutal and genocidal nature of the regime's previous attacks in Iraqi Kurdistan, combined with the possibility of a new humanitarian disaster, prompted international intervention. UN Security Council Resolution 688 called for protection of Kurds and laid the groundwork for the US-led Coalition's establishment of a no-fly zone north of the 36th parallel in Iraq. Operation Provide Comfort (I and II) and the follow-on Operation Northern Watch essentially guaranteed autonomy in Kurdistan up to the 2003 invasion.[10]

These events became a watershed moment for most Iraqi Kurds. Kurds would never again need to fear being dominated within the core Kurdish region by the Arabs to the south. The Saddam regime's systematic killing, use of chemical weapons, death of non-combatants, and other atrocities of the Anfal and Halabja had made Arab domination of the Kurds illegitimate in the eyes of the international community, not to mention in the eyes of the Kurds themselves. From 1991 until 2003, the Iraqi Kurds would rule as their own de facto state, a highly problematic one, as we will see shortly, but still a de facto state. After the invasion and state reconstruction in the post-2003 period, the KRG continued its existence as a de facto state. Ironically, the depth of the losses of the late 1980s provided the basis for this political victory. In comparison, the Shia Arab rebels of the south received very little support for their suffering and aspirations.

14.6. The KDP/PUK Cleavage Comes to the Fore: Kurdish Civil War and Its Aftermath

With clarity on the Kurd/Arab cleavage, attention again turned inward. There was no clarity on the KDP/PUK dimension. In May 1992, the international community administered elections to a Kurdish Assembly. Both the KDP and PUK took approximately 45% of the vote. This balance did not prove to be stable. The entire system came under incredible pressure due to a double embargo—international sanctions against the Saddam government, and the Saddam regime's economic blockade of the Kurdish region (Tripp, 2010, p. 255). Widespread shortages and unemployment rocked Iraqi Kurdistan. In this volatile situation, both Masoud Barzani and Jalal Talabani removed themselves from direct participation in the KRG to build their own patronage networks. These parallel networks were territorially divided, the KDP in the north and the PUK in the south, but not strictly so. Moreover, tribal leaders often played both sides seeking a better deal; sometimes factions emerged within tribes, some going with the KDP, others with the PUK (Leezenberg, 2006, p. 165). In some areas, urban warlords such as Mamand Qashqai in Erbil played the PUK and KDP against one another and successfully controlled entire neighborhoods (Leezenberg, 2006, p. 167). In this situation, both sides competed over three sources of money and power—the distribution of international aid, oil revenues, and control over smuggling routes. It was not at all clear which side would prevail.

That the KDP and PUK developed ties to different foreign sponsors complicated the struggle. The regional basis of the cleavage became heightened through KDP connections with Turkey and PUK ties to Iran. Baghdad, in the meantime, was happy to see both sides suffer. As explained to the author by Mohammed Tofiq Rahim (known as Hama Tofiq), a former PUK official, all of the surrounding states—Turkey, Iran, and Iraq proper—had incentives to fund an intra-Kurd war and thus contain the Kurdish "problem."[11]

The contest turned violent beginning in December 1993. The fighting became serious in May 1994 when a dispute over land rights in Qala Diza pitted a tribal claimant against non-tribal farmers. While seemingly an unimportant incident, its nature illustrated basic issues about property rights and jurisdiction that separated the KDP and PUK. Each side expelled the other's Peshmerga units from their respective zones, and war escalated (Lawrence, 2008, pp. 68–69). In December 1994, PUK forces launched a large-scale offensive and captured Erbil, the Kurdish capital. Casualties mounted throughout 1995. In August 1996, the KDP allied with Iraq forces, 30,000 strong, and seized Erbil and Suleymaniyah. The PUK, with support from Iran, retook Suleymaniyah.

The fact that the KDP called in Saddam's regime after the atrocities of the 1980s may seem astounding at first glance. However, the action emphasizes two qualities concerning master cleavages at the time. First, the KDP could call in these Arab forces because they knew they would soon leave. Kurdish autonomy, if not independence, had been secured. Iraqi forces stayed only two months, a time sufficient for Saddam to establish his continued relevance. Second, this action illustrated that the KDP/PUK contest not only had become the primary cleavage and struggle in Kurdistan, but also had become existential in nature.

Neither side would want to go to the brink again. It was time for a brokered deal that would create a clear and stable balance.

The United States played the role of broker for that deal. The Washington Agreement was signed by Barzani and Talabani in September 1998. Most importantly, the pact demarcated territorial zones, each with its own capital. It also formalized the sharing of revenue and committed both sides to keeping out Iraqi troops and the Kurdistan Workers Party (PKK). The United States formally pledged to use force to protest the region from aggression by the Saddam regime.

The 1991–2003 period also saw the deepening of the KDP/PUK cleavage in terms of security institutions. In a discussion of Kurdish identity and state-building, Dylan O'Driscoll and Bahar Baser eloquently summarize how the separate security institutions of the KDP and PUK help propel two different Kurdish nationalisms:

> If nationalism in the KRI (Kurdistan Region of Iraq) is understood as involving multiple actors trying to gain and maintain power within the region and from Baghdad, having separate military wings—two branches of the Peshmerga linked separately to the KDP and PUK directly—can aid this process and create distinctive divides amongst the population. When these two separate militaries are paired with the geographic separation of KDP and PUK territory and the competitive discourse of Kurdishness between the two parties, it becomes evident that two different forms of Kurdish nationalism have occurred simultaneously. Moreover, due to the history of civil war between these two parties and their military divisions, their continued separation prevents a unified Kurdish nationalism and enhances the prospect of the military being used to maintain power within the KRI. It also gives rise to internal security threats, instability and weakens the government. (O'Driscoll and Baser, 2019)

The Peshmerga became both more professionalized and more numerous. With a secure zone and revenues from border crossings, Peshmerga members received regular salaries. Given the economic crisis in the region, young men had few other opportunities for employment.

The KDP would develop a Peshmerga eventually totaling 50,000 (members in Unit 80), along with a paramilitary "Zerevani" force with at least 45,000 members, in 2006.[12] The PUK military would eventually come to number 48,000 (members of Unit 70), with a paramilitary "Bargry Firakawtin" with perhaps 10,000–20,000 personnel. More than ever, the KDP and PUK became separate political-military hybrids.

This lack of separation between politics and military became most problematic in the form of the Asayish.[13] Established in 1992 to fill the security vacuum after the 1991 uprising and Iraqi government withdrawal, the Asayish (meaning "security") drew members from the Peshmerga to create an organization for internal security matters (Chapman, 2009, p. 183). Essentially, it was an FBI for the KRG. Only in the KRG, the Asayish have always been a party-controlled FBI. This has always been true, despite changing government versus party status of the organizations. In 1993, the KDP and PUK party-based Asayish were attached to the Ministry of Interior of the KRG (Bakr, 2021, p. 10). When the KRG broke into two halves in 1994, each half put the Asayish under their own Ministry of the Interior. In 2004, the KDP-dominated government transferred the Asayish to control by a party-controlled committee. The PUK followed suit in 2005 (Chapman, 2009, p. 183).

14.7. The 2003 Invasion and Aftermath: Little Change in the Kurd/Arab Cleavage and the Institutional Deepening of the KDP/PUK Cleavage

This section comes back to the central questions of violence and state-building in Iraqi Kurdistan from 2003 to 2011. As mentioned at the beginning of the chapter, the region saw relatively little violence during this period. The invasion and its aftermath only served to strengthen the Kurdish hold. In Iraqi federal politics, as noted earlier, the KRG possessed broad constitutionally supported autonomy. Furthermore, the KRG received a share of the federal budget proportionate to the KRG share of the Iraq population. In fact, the Kurds could play things two ways—act as a de facto state on the one hand, while still wielding considerable influence in Iraqi national politics. This dual role was best illustrated by the fact that while Masoud Barzani was president of the KRG, Jalal Talabani held the position of Iraqi president. In the 2005 Iraq elections, the existence of a united Kurdish list gave the Kurds (in reality, Barzani and Talabani) enormous leverage in the post-election bargaining, especially as the Transitional Administrative Law required a two-thirds majority to form a government.

At the international level, the Kurds, in reward for their valuable support during the invasion, possessed a reservoir of goodwill from the United States, along with US promises to maintain Kurdish autonomy. As noted by Gareth Stansfield in 2006, "the Kurdistan Region had achieved a degree of semipermanency in the minds of many regional capitals (possibly even in Ankara), and international actors were increasingly viewing the region in a similar way" (Stansfield, 2006, p. 264). In the period after the invasion, the KRG became sufficiently wealthy and powerful to conduct its own foreign policy. In a series of interviews conducted in the KRG and Kirkuk in 2013, I spoke with Hemin Hawrami, the head of foreign relations for the KDP. Hawrami boasted of Kurdistan's ability to make deals with Turkey and others on Kurdish terms.[14] Hawrami, echoing many others, downplayed the ability of the Iraqi central state and army to pose a significant threat to the KRG.

Despite their differences and bitter history, both the KDP and the PUK were on the same page regarding the major issues regarding Kurd/Arab relations. In an interview with the author, Hakim Qadir, a long-time leader of the PUK, stressed two things.[15] First, the PUK differed greatly from the KDP in its social democratic orientation and anti-tribalism. Second, in terms of the major issues with Arabs, the PUK and KDP were in sync on the reversal of Arabization and the settlement of the issues in the disputed territories on Kurdish terms.

With new resources and official status, the KRG institutionalized the memory of Kurdish persecution by creating a Ministry for Martyr and Anfal Affairs. As Minister Sabah Ahmed Mohammed (known as Mamosta Aram) explained to the author,[16] the ministry's mission was to establish the truth and educate the public about five major events: (1) the killing of 8,000 members of the Barzani tribe; (2) the 5,000–10,000 killed in the chemical attack at Halabja; (3) the eight genocidal campaigns of the 1988 Anfal; (4) the border deportations of the 1970s; (5) the expulsion of the Fayli Kurds (Shia Kurds some with historical ties to Iran, many involved in business; 40,000 were expelled in the 1970s as Iranian spies).[17] Taken as a whole, these five phenomena establish a history of victimhood so long, so pervasive, and so diverse that there can be no going back; Kurdish separation is necessary and non-negotiable.

The separation of the KRG from Arab Iraq was also reinforced by the declining status and use of the Arab language, now eclipsed by Kurdish, as well as by increasing numbers choosing English over Arabic as a second language. In a 2007 survey in the universities of Salah al-Din, Dohuk, and Suleymaniyah, only 2.2% answered that they felt "more Iraqi than Kurd," with 1.3% labeling themselves "Iraqi Kurd." Over 95% chose "Kurd" (17.3%), "Kurdistani" (73.1%), and "Kurdistani but not Iraqi" (5.1%)" (Yoshioka, 2020). As one Kurdish KDP member of the Iraqi Parliament told me, the de facto independence of the KRG was a "fact on the ground," recognized by the Sunni parties as well as Maliki. Although the path was uncertain, de jure recognition was only a matter of time.[18]

In sum, in the post-invasion period, there was clarity in both master cleavages. Kurds ruled the KRG proper with little interference from the Arab south (the disputed territories were another matter). The KDP/PUK cleavage was stable as both the KDP and PUK possessed unrivaled and uncontested political and economic powers in their respective regions with the KRG. Much of this power, and stability, derived from the nature of the KRG economy. Money came in through non-transparent oil revenues. The money went out to a bloated number of public servants who comprised roughly half of total employment. This situation was ideal for patronage politics. There was essentially no private sector. As Denise Natali laments, "The distinction between state and society is undeveloped. Here, you have a relationship of dependency, like one between a big daddy and child" (Healy and Abdulla, 2011). In the KRG, there were two "daddy's—the KDP and the PUK—and both could ensure their respective power through the oil money they could control.

This system was glued together by the robust and separate security organs of both the KDP and PUK. As noted, both had their own army in their respective Peshmergas. Both had paramilitaries. Both had their own party-controlled security organs in the Asayish. The party control of these non-transparent security organs provided a means to recruit loyal personnel, control patronage, and build party support. Given these powers, there was little incentive either to upset the balance versus the opposing party or to build a more efficient state. In 2006, the KDP and PUK signed the Strategic Agreement, a power-sharing deal aimed at splitting power in the KRG on a 50:50 basis (Bakr, 2021, pp. 7–8).

Both parties maintained the functions and size of non-transparent security actors such as the Asayish. The Asayish and its negative effects on state-building will be discussed at length in Chapter 19 on the KRG in Section III. Here, consider the role of the Asayish in the disputed territory of Kirkuk in the period after 2003. As an International Crisis Group report describes:

> The *asaesh* have carved out an autonomous security role in Kirkuk and elsewhere, accountable only to their political bosses. While the US has credited the *asaesh* with maintaining security in Kirkuk and the *asaesh* themselves have emphasized their professionalism, there is no doubt that much of the ethnic tension in Kirkuk has focused on what are seen as arbitrary and discriminatory practices by this irregular security force. (International Crisis Group, 2006, p. 20)

After discussing how estimates of the number of Asayish in Kirkuk Governorate varied between 4,000 and 14,000, the ICG report concludes: "Whatever the exact number, which may be difficult to verify, their impact has been enormous from the moment they arrived in 2003 to fill the vacuum left by the former regime's overthrow" (International Crisis Group, 2011, pp. 20–21).

14.8. The Gorran Challenge to the KDP/PUK
Dominated Political System, 2009–2011

In 2009, a faction of the PUK broke off and formed the Gorran ("Change") movement to confront the two entrenched parties. Following public protests in 2011, the end of the period covered in this chapter, Gorran listed demands for reform. These demands included transparency in finances and reduced party monopolies in allocation, reduced corruption, reduced party influence in the media, and independent judiciary and prosecutorial system, and a de-politicization of security services.[19]

In the summer of 2013, the author interviewed Mohammed Tofiq Rahim (popularly known as Ham Tofiq), serving then as the director of external relations for Gorran.[20] Along with Nawshiran Mustafa, Rahim had been one of the founders and major leaders of the Gorran Party. After serving in the PUK Politburo for 20 years, Rahim became Gorran's first official spokesman. Rahim defected from the PUK in 2006 after what he claimed were rigged elections within the PUK. As he explained, Gorran was a response to the Stalinist/Baathist type of structure of the KDP and PUK and their regional division of spoils.

As Rahim explained, the two major parties controlled the money flowing into the KRG in a non-transparent fashion. The KRG relied on its share of Iraqi oil money to fund the KRG de facto state; there were no income taxes or sales taxes. When the money flowed in, 48% went to the PUK and 52% to the KDP. After that, no one really knew where the money went. With these oil funds making up 97% of the KRG's budget, and with 1.4 million KRG government employees, the funds no doubt were eaten either by patronage or by corruption.

Gorran was basically calling for a strengthening of the KRG state with a corresponding diminishment of the KDP and PUK hegemony. In Rahim's view, the first step was likely an independent judiciary to force transparency, both political and financial. The transfer of security forces from political party control to state control was also necessary and could again be accomplished by changes in funding. Gorran itself was committed to never forming a militia of its own. Indeed, Gorran listed the de-politicization of the security forces as a primary goal. Their platform stated that the armed forces and intelligence should be controlled by the government, not political parties. The Peshmerga were not the only security force that needed to come under state control. The Gorran platform stated, "[Asayish] play the most fearsome role when they become a militia force to oppress the people, a hidden force for the party to restrict, a means to inflict fear, interfering in the political map and cleansing the rivalry and internal differences."[21]

In response to the growing challenge from Gorran, the KDP and PUK formed a bloc for the 2009 elections. Their alliance controlled 59 out of 111 seats, limiting Gorran to 26 seats and the Reform bloc (including socialists and Islamists) to 13.[22] The two main parties sustained their power and form of rule, although with a weakened PUK.

This outcome was hardly surprising. From 2003 to 2011 in the KRG, there was one major and balanced master cleavage. The most salient master cleavage was not that of Kurd/Arab, despite the fact that this cleavage did tower over much of the twentieth-century Kurdish experience. Rather, it was KDP/PUK. That cleavage was largely in balance, at least until the Gorran challenge. With clarity and dominance in the home region in the Kurd/Arab cleavage, and a clear balance in the KDP/PUK cleavage, Iraqi Kurdistan experienced little violence. While the state was divided and weak in most Western conceptions, both the KDP and the PUK enjoyed a period of stable control. For both parties, this equilibrium was not to be upset. Even though they had fought a bitter civil war in the previous decade, the KDP and PUK would come together to fend off the Gorran challenge.

No doubt Gorran faced a severe challenge in trying to bring down KDP/PUK hegemony. By 2009, the KDP and PUK were not just opposing political parties, they were the face of each side of a political-societal cleavage—their history of competition and sacrifice, symbols, and personal identification with leaders. The KDP and PUK had their own military units, uniforms, heroes, and martyrs. The KDP and PUK provided a system of meaning and belonging that underlies the power of a societal cleavage.

On the other hand, Gorran was a political movement. It talked in largely technical terms of transparency, good governance, and judicial independence. It refused to field its own Peshmerga. It had no real historical narrative. It consciously avoided personality cults and family connections. It had little of the passion to produce the long-term identification effects underlying a societal cleavage.

14.9. Security Institutions, Dominance, and the Prevention of Dominance

While the history and evolution of Iraqi Kurdistan produced the deep cleavage between the KDP and the PUK, the nature of the two political parties' less transparent security institutions helped maintain their dual hegemony. In order to flesh out this point, we can return to our spectrum of roles to analyze these security institutions, concentrating on the 2003–2011 era. The reader can refer to Figure 14.1. As the figure illustrates, there are not just one set of state security institutions at the +2 and +3 nodes. Rather, there are three. This complex set of +2 and +3 organs maintains balance and stability, but also guarantees state dysfunction.

After 2003, the KRG was integrated into the federal system of Iraq. The Iraqi Army (+3 on the Figure 14.1 central arrow) had the right to enter KRG territory and protect borders. Some Kurdish individuals served in the Iraqi military.[23] The KDP and PUK maintained their own Peshmerga (mobile +3 fighting units). These +3 fighting forces are the ultimate guarantee against domination by opponents. These Peshmerga forces are backed by paramilitary forces under the Ministry of the Interior. The KDP-affiliated force is the Zerevani, numbering 30,000 around 2015 and able to fight alongside the Peshmerga on front lines. The PUK-affiliated paramilitary is the smaller Task Force Black.

The Peshmerga and associated paramilitaries are not the only party-based security forces of the KDP and PUK. Both parties possess their own police and intelligence units that operate to maintain security at local levels. The nature of the Asayish was mentioned at points above. In 2004, the KDP removed its Asayish units from the Ministry of Interior's control to that of a KDP party committee, with the PUK following suit the next year (Chapman, 2009, p. 183). The Asayish conduct internal security and administer checkpoints to control local movements. As mentioned above, they are often seen as a non-state party-controlled FBI equivalent. Other party-based security organizations are even less transparent. The KDP developed an intelligence-collection unit known as the Parastin back in 1968, although it was not officially named until 1991. As usual, the PUK followed the KDP example and developed a parallel party intelligence-collection unit known as the Zanyari in 1991. Both were headed by

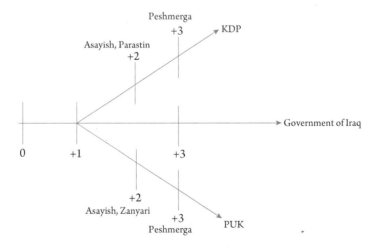

Figure 14.1. Multiple government security forces of the KRG.

either family members or close associates of the Barzanis or Talabani, respectively (Chapman, 2009, pp. 204–205).

In terms of our spectrum of roles, the Asayish, Parastin, and Zanyari operate to maintain local security at +2. Figure 14.1 emphasizes the lack of a Weberian defined state in the KRG during the 2003–2011 period. There is no legitimate monopoly on the use of violence.

The United States pushed hard for the integration of KRG security forces. As will be addressed in Section III, starting in 2010 and again at the end of the ISIS war, there was a move to attempt to merge the KDP and PUK security forces. There was also some thought of integrating, or at least better coordinating, the KRG-based Peshmerga with Government of Iraq military structures. In effect, the +3 forces seen in Figure 14.1 would be collapsed. Such a reform would move the KRG and Baghdad toward unified state control with an established chain of command and perhaps common training and professional standards. There was also discussion of the integration of the Asayish, Parastin, and Zanyari.

As Chapter 19 will describe, this integration plan did not go smoothly. Neither the KDP nor the PUK were willing to completely integrate their Peshmerga forces, despite the formation of some integrated units. These organizations are insurance for each party, a way to maintain autonomy and a way to monitor and administer patronage. The surest way to avoid dominance is to maintain a measure of control of the means of violence.

14.10. Conclusion

The evolution of Kurdish politics is largely a story of the creation and evolution of master cleavages. Kurdish nationalists arose to confront an Arab state. Then one set of Kurdish nationalists, in the KDP, came to face off another set of Kurdish nationalists in the PUK. The saliency and balance among these cleavages determined the mobilization and direction of violence. The 1991 Iraq War ended with Kurds clearly dominant in their northern region. With the Kurd/Arab cleavage far less salient, the unclear relationship between the KDP and PUK became the primary contest. The Kurdish Civil War in 1994–1998 led to a brokered and clear-cut balance between the two sides. The situation of KDP-PUK dual hegemony, combined with Kurdish dominance in the KRG proper,[24] lasted through the 2003 US invasion and survived a challenge from the Gorran movement in 2009. In sum, during the period of focus of Section I (2003–2011), the Kurds had clearly ended Arab dominance and the KDP and PUK existed in a well-defined balance. The result was a low level of violence, accompanied by inefficient, non-transparent, and patronage-based state-building.

The KDP and PUK sustained their balance and respective autonomy through the creation and development of party-controlled, non-transparent security organs. Born in war and violence, both parties maintained their power and identity through an organization that never clearly separated the military from the political. In a world of Saddamist atrocities and intra-Kurdish civil war, neither the KDP nor the PUK was ready to give away the tools of force and violence that guaranteed freedom from domination. This system has not delivered a strong, effective, and efficient state in the long run. Its state-building failure is seen in its corruption and its failure to deliver many state services. This system has resisted reforms and excluded reformers.

A question of interest for this book concerns the ability of the United States to rebuild a state after war. Could the United States have set Iraqi Kurdistan on a better path toward a coherent and functioning de facto state? Perhaps US policymakers could have more effectively used their leverage to force reforms on the KDP and PUK. Perhaps they could have more forcefully supported the reformist Gorran party. Or perhaps the impediments to stronger state-building in the KRG were based in long-term historical processes unamenable to influence. Maybe the distortions in the political-security institutions of the KRG were too embedded to be changed. Perhaps the US military was satisfied with its relationship with existing Kurdish security forces and had no desire to reform them, let alone support the non-militarized Gorran.

Chapter 19 will revisit the KRG. After discussing the persistence of the KDP/PUK balance in the years immediately after the 2011 US withdrawal, that chapter will analyze the changes in cleavage structure and their effects on violence and state-building, concentrating on two critical junctures: the war against the Islamic State during 2014–2017, and the political failure following the 2017 independence referendum. This chapter did not address the status of the disputed territories. From 2003 to 2011, that dispute remained muted. That will change.

SECTION III

IRAQ, 2011–2020

III.1. Review of Section II

Section I developed an analytical framework based on concepts of roles, mechanisms, and strategies. Section II applied that framework to several empirical case studies during the period stretching from the invasion in 2003 to US withdrawal in 2011. Before previewing Section III, this is an appropriate place to stop and reconsider some of the central arguments of the book.

The conflicts in Iraq, at their essence, have been driven by a pursuit for group dominance. The best predictor of violence and peace can be found in the nature of group-based hierarchy. As postulated in the first chapter, ethnic and sectarian violent conflict is most likely in a period of unstable hierarchy and especially when dominant groups perceive a reversal of position. Ethnic conflict will subside once a clear and stable hierarchy re-emerges.

Section II ended with the US withdrawal in 2011. At that time, the Shia-Sunni civil war had left the Shia dominant in Baghdad. There would be no more major sectarian war in the Iraqi capital. Iraq as a whole was another matter. Sunnis had been weakened by ethnic cleansing internally and the flight of the Sunni middle class across borders. On the positive side, the Sunni Awakening had produced Sunni victors in Anbar. Sunnis could reasonably hope for a balanced position vis-à-vis the Shia, while some Sunni still dreamed of a return to dominance. The previous chapter outlined the creation and evolution of dual cleavages experienced by Kurds over several decades. By 2011, Kurds were securely dominant in their central home territory. There was still uncertainty in the Arab/Kurd cleavage over the disputed territories. In 2011, the KDP/PUK cleavage remained balanced and able to fend off political challengers. Most Kurds firmly believed that independence was a realistic middle-range possibility.

A second major argument addressed failures in state-building. The analytical framework of the book is well-suited to address those shortcomings. The previous section outlined cases where the population remained neutral or more connected to non-state organizations (−1) than the Iraqi state (+1). It presented cases where non-state actors captured the Ministry of the Interior and local police stations (+2). There were cases where non-state local, armed militias (−2) quickly formed and became self-sustaining. The Iraqi Army (+3), despite billions of US dollars put into the effort, was never fully professionalized. Despite Iraq's decline in violence, Iraq was not progressing toward a fully functioning state. In Kurdistan, the KDP and PUK maintained separate lines of control, employing the power of multiple security organs.

The difficulties of state-building ran deep. The preceding empirical chapters have illustrated the origins and suggested the intractability of the problem. As stated in Chapter 1, "Born in violence and chaos, the Iraqi system saw many of its early armed actors establish legitimacy, maintain power, expand their political domains, and capture government ministries and positions." None of these actors desired to move toward a system that could produce a Saddam-like strongman or block the distribution of government spoils.

A third major argument addressed the nature of US involvement. The preceding chapters have illustrated, in detail, US employment of multiple strategies and various combinations of those strategies at various times and locations. The chapters also show a range of failure and success. The case studies have made the point—put forth in Chapter 1—"that there was not one war in Iraq, but many, depending on local conditions." A full and systematic accounting of the strategic match-ups of counterinsurgent and insurgent strategies must wait until Chapter 21. One clear lesson, though, is that the actor who can operate across the entire spectrum of roles, such as seen with the Sadrists, will likely possess an unexpected resiliency.

III.2. Preview of Section III Chapters

Section III will continue to draw on the analytical framework to examine the legacy of US strategies and the evolution of post-US Iraqi war and politics. To preview some of conclusions of the section:

After the ISIS war and the failed Kurdish referendum, the group hierarchy in Iraq became clear. Sectarian war had ended in Iraq. Kurdish independence again became a distant dream. The Shia were on top and factions of the Sunnis and Kurds had to make deals from a subordinate position. The most powerful contests emerged, as one would expect, from within the Shia block. The Iraqi state remains fragmented and weakened, in some ways, more so than in 2011. The reasons for this continued weakness remained the same. Most significant political actors preferred a weak non-threatening state despite its deficiencies. The United States would again militarily intervene, this time to help defeat ISIS. Important lessons would be learned in this successful, if long and destructive, fight.

The following is a summary of each of the Section III's six chapters:

> Chapter 15, "Hawija: Explaining Sunni Resurgence," serves as a bridge between Section II and Section III, showing how the power of Sunni resentment against the Shia-dominated state helped maintain the potential for violence and state breakdown across more than a decade. The chapter breaks down both the US military strategies during 2003–2011 and the Iraqi government strategies from 2011 to 2017 and matches those strategies with those of Sunni resistance groups, sometimes operating in conjunction with ISIS. The Hawija chapter will illustrate the persistent power of the Shia-Sunni master cleavage despite, and because of, changes in US and Iraqi state strategies.

> Chapter 16, "The Third Iraq War," begins with the collapse of the Iraqi Army (+3) and the coming of ISIS. The chapter focuses on US strategy, outlining the development of a new strategy combining decapitation and war-fighting, a model with great significance for the US military in the future.

> Chapter 17, "Hybrid Actors: The Emergence and Persistence of the Popular Mobilization Forces," will explain how the collapse of the Iraqi Army, the weakness of the Iraqi state, and the incentives of sectarian and ethnic political actors came together to form a new type of security actor—one challenging the linear nature of the spectrum of roles by combining both state (+2/+3) and non-state (−2/−3) qualities. The chapter explains how Iraq's master cleavage politics work to sustain these hybrid forces and in doing so work to sustain a weak and fragmented state. The emergence of hybrid actors suggests ways in which practitioners must reconceptualize the state in future conflicts and interventions.

Chapter 18, "How Minorities Make Their Way: The Case of Christian Militias in the Nineveh Plains," expands on the issue of how actors operate in Iraq's fragmented state and security environment. While the book concentrates on Iraq's master cleavages, like almost all states, Iraq contains significant minorities. The chapter explains how and why sections of a minority group moved from relative pacifism to the creation of militias. The chapter explains how one major minority, the Christians on the Nineveh Plain, have dealt with Iraq's weak state and the existential threat from ISIS. The chapter is co-written with Matt Cancian, who has extensive fieldwork experience in the region.

Chapter 19, "The Kurdistan Regional Government Revisited: Death, War, Machinations, and Little Change," continues the story of the Kurdish region of Iraq. The chapter is centered on the disastrous independence referendum of 2017. It will again show the persistent influence of master cleavage politics both between Kurds and Arabs and between the KDP and the PUK. The chapter will again show how a fragmented security system underlies a weak state overall.

Chapter 20, "The Decline of Dominance Politics? Emotions and Institutions in Iraq 10 Years after the 2011 US Withdrawal," examines the state of the Shia-Sunni cleavage in Iraq, arguing that clear Shia political dominance has ushered in new possibilities for progress in Iraq.

Hawija

Explaining Sunni Resurgence

15.1. Introduction

This chapter presents a case study of Hawija, a small homogenous Sunni Arab city located in the Kirkuk Governorate about 55 kilometers west of the city of Kirkuk. As indicated in Figure 15.1, the history of post-2003 Hawija can be divided into seven periods. The first runs from the beginning days of US occupation until after the April 2004 uprisings. The second begins when US forces institute a version of clear, hold, build (CHB) counterinsurgency strategy. In the third period, the US incorporates community mobilization into its overall strategy. In the fourth period, a new US commander implements a more intensive form of CHB. In 2011, US forces leave Iraq. The fifth period covers Hawija from the US departure until the ISIS takeover in August 2014. The sixth period starts with the ISIS 2014 offensive and ends with its expulsion from Hawija. Finally, the last period addresses the period from the expulsion of ISIS in Hawija in October 2017 until the time of writing.

To frame one central question of the chapter, what is the relationship between periods 2, 3, and 4—the periods of US led counterinsurgency and state-building and the events in the periods coming after the 2011 US departure in periods 5, 6, and 7? In other words, can we specify a legacy of the US presence in Hawija, and perhaps in Iraq more generally?

Hawija is a good case to begin this examination because of what happened there in periods 5 and 6. In April 2013 (period 5), forces from the Iraqi Army's 12th Division raided a protest camp in Hawija, killing dozens of civilians. The Hawija events helped add fuel to broader Sunni protests against the perceived anti-Sunni politics of Prime Minister Nouri al-Maliki. The deadly raid in Hawija would precipitate further protest and violence

Figure 15.1. Hawija timeline.

across the Sunni north and west, helping lead to the most violent month in Iraq since 2008. In August 2014, Hawija would fall into the hands of ISIS (beginning period 6). In the view of many commentators, Hawija was ripe for an ISIS takeover. The International Crisis Group's Joost Hiltermann went so far as to state that Maliki's violent repression in April 2013 was a catalyst "turning the town into a poster child for all the ills that would facilitate the Islamic State takeover one year later" (Hiltermann, 2016). Peter Schwartzstein wrote an article for *Reuters* entitled, "The Perfect Recipe for Making Jihadis Was Developed in This Small Iraq Town" (Schwartzstein, 2016). In 2015–2016, the Iraqi armed forces moved northward to displace ISIS from its captured cities. On the way north, political leaders decided that security forces should bypass Hawija and conserve their power for the bigger prize of Mosul. With already overstretched resources, the battle to take problematic Hawija, a fight that could potentially involve a disproportionate amount of resources, could wait.

Why did Hawija become a catalyst for violent conflict and a thorn in the Iraqi state's side? What was the role of US policy and strategy in producing, or at least failing to prevent, this outcome? There would seem to be multiple possibilities. US actions in periods 1–4 could have created or exacerbated the factors underlying the turmoil in period 5. Alternatively, the situation in Hawija could have been even worse without US intervention. Or perhaps US actions might not have made much difference at all in the longer run.

The problem was certainly not the lack of pacification efforts by the Coalition from 2003 to 2011. As this chapter lays out, US forces in Hawija employed flexible and well-resourced counterinsurgent strategies. Coalition strategies were effective in reducing open violence in Hawija. The problems, as the conclusions to this chapter will outline, had to do with the underlying forces impeding state-building. The chapter, informed by insights of multiple US Army personnel who served in Hawija, proceeds chronologically through the seven periods before systematically applying the book's analytical framework to draw connections among strategies and outcomes across the periods.

15.2. Structural Factors: Geography and Demography

There are two highly significant geopolitical facts about Hawija. First, in terms of geography, the city of Hawija and the Hawija District lie within the Kirkuk Governorate (see Figure 15.2). Only 55 kilometers separate Hawija from the city of Kirkuk. As discussed in Chapter 19, the status of Kirkuk is one of the single most important and thorny political issues in all of Iraq. While the Iraqi Constitution of 2005 outlined a path toward the solution of Kirkuk's status (reversal of previous Arabization policy, census, referendum), that path has never been taken. In this political state of limbo, from the time of the invasion on, Kurdish parties slowly took control of many of Kirkuk's administration and security organs. Kurdish actors not only solidified their power in Kirkuk proper, but also took control of Kurdish-majority areas north and east of the city.

Many Kurds possess an understanding of the likely future borders of an independent Kurdistan. Here is where the second structural variable comes in: Hawija's population is almost entirely Sunni Arab (roughly 98%). In any future Kurdistan, either in terms of an independent state or an expanded autonomous region, Hawija will be an Arab city located either just outside or just inside the border between Kurd and Arab. From the Kurdish perspective, Hawija's geography and demography meant that it needed to be controlled, if not ruled. What has this meant in practice for Hawija? The composition of security forces became a key issue. In the Kirkuk Governorate, many of the district police were

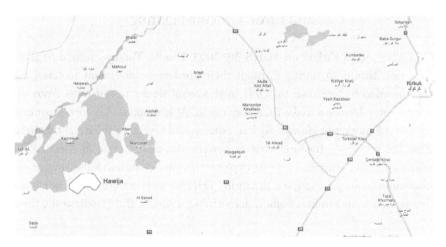

Figure 15.2. Map of Hawija.
Source: Map of Hawija and Kirkuk Province. Annotated Google Street Map.

former or current Peshmerga. In fact, the police operating in Hawija could sometimes be seen wearing Peshmerga uniforms.[1] US Special Operations Forces (SOF) would at times enter Hawija accompanied by Kurdish/Iraqi SOF for searches and raids.[2] The district police would establish the cordon and the Kurdish SOF would conduct the search. One military officer related how he saw Kurdish Peshmerga lining up Sunni Arabs on their knees for hours at a time during these cordon and search operations, as late as 2009.

Hawija's location on the Kurdish-Arab fault line and inside the Kirkuk Governorate provided one set of problems. Another major issue was Hawija's political-demographic history. As a reliable Sunni stronghold in the region, the city possessed a strong relationship with the Saddam regime. As one US military officer noted during his tour in 2006, "This area was very well taken care of by Saddam Hussein. When Saddam Hussein was removed from power, their life-style took a step back."[3] Furthermore, Hawija is the home of many retired and disbanded Iraqi military personnel. Correspondingly, influential Baath Party members lived in the city. Given Hawija's demography and Baathist history, the end of Saddam and the rise of Shia to power in Baghdad naturally produced trepidation.

In short, in the period after the invasion, geography and demography had put the Sunni residents of Hawija in an unenviable position. They were at odds with now locally powerful Kurds, at odds with the ascendant Shia in Iraq as a whole, and at odds with US occupiers hunting former regime members.

15.3. Period 1: Early Occupation, Insurgent Trial and Error, US War-Fighting

US forces seized Kirkuk on March 30, 2003. Due to Turkey's refusal to allow Coalition troops to transit through their borders, soldiers and material initially needed to be flown in. Only after several weeks would units from the 4th Infantry Division make their way north. At the outset, US forces concentrated on Kirkuk, not Hawija. Kirkuk experienced several problems at this time. Essential services—trash, electricity, sewer—did not operate in Kirkuk. The police and Iraqi army had no security presence, and sectarian killings were not uncommon.[4] Surprisingly, the situation in Hawija was very different. Here is the description from a military officer active in both Kirkuk and Hawija at the time.

> When I first I went to Hawija, I estimate early May, it was eerie. The streets were clean, the trash was being picked up, there was electricity (couple hours a day, and generators the rest of the time) there was no looting like we saw in Kirkuk. It was extremely orderly. They had a mayor,

a police chief—all the civil servants were present and functioning. That was the first odd thing. People in the street, only a few there, stopped, watched us pass and glared. It was considered unfriendly from the first patrol, though no shots were fired. It would later be deemed hostile and would remain that way until we left in Feb/Mar 04, and handed over to 1st Brigade 25th Infantry Division.

In effect, the state had collapsed in Kirkuk, but not in Hawija. The interviewee also reported that the power brokers within the city of Hawija, as opposed to outlying rural areas, were not tribal leaders. The mayor and local police chief were relatively young and seemed to operate outside the tribal norms and structures found elsewhere in Sunni territories.

The most likely explanation for the differences between Kirkuk and Hawija are demographic and political. Sunnis comprised 98% of Hawija's population, many involved in Baathist networks and retired military officer associations. Despite the upheaval produced by the invasion and early occupation, this social and political foundation continued to provide for coherent functioning of the state. Despite, or perhaps because of this existing order, Hawija's population was hostile to US forces. These two qualities—relative state coherence and hostility to outsiders—characterized Hawija's politics through periods 1–4.

US forces encountered low-level harassment and violence in Hawija almost from the start. The first FOB (forward operating base) set up in the area was Gains Mills in Yachi, on Route Denny running between Kirkuk and Hawija. In August 2003, US forces set up FOB McHenry, which lay outside of Hawija city proper and would serve as the base of US military operations until the US withdrawal. FOB Gains Mills was hit by incessant mortaring. In the fall of 2003, the base experienced 100 straight days of mortar fire, usually just after the call to prayer in the morning or the evening. As the 1-12 Infantry handed over operations to the 25th Infantry Division in March 2004, it was shelled on the way out of town.

Up to April 2004, Hawija was marked by both general public order and low-level organized violence. On April 7, 2004, however, Hawija witnessed a major escalation.[5] Across different regions, Iraq was witnessing major violence. Sunni insurgents attacked US forces in Ramadi, Fallujah, and Baquba. Mahdi Army forces attacked US troops in Baghdad's Sadr City as well as in Najaf, Karbala, and other Shia-majority cities in the south of Iraq. Either in response or in coordination, insurgents in Hawija launched a coordinated attack on the US Army's 1st Battalion, 27th Infantry, in charge of Hawija. Chanting in support for Sunni insurgents in Fallujah, demonstrators descended on the municipal building where the city council was holding a meeting (McGrath, 2012, p. 4). An initial exchange between an RPG-wielding insurgent and a US rooftop sniper broke the peace. As the crowd dispersed, and US reinforcements from FOB McHenry entered the area, dozens of insurgents engaged US forces. A running battle over a substantial area of the city ensued. Insurgents fired machine guns and RPGs against lightly armored US forces. At one point, insurgents were able to coordinate an ambush with a volley of three RPGs against advancing US troops. The US forces responded to push the insurgents out in the open in the northwest section of the city, where they could be decimated by Apache helicopter fire. However, as US forces advanced, "[t]he enemy had broken up into groups of individuals and had gone to ground within the urban landscape" (McGrath, 2012, p. 13). The Apaches, on station, were never used. Insurgents demonstrated some ability to put together a sizable attack, but they did not fare well in terms of casualties. While the US forces suffered 6 wounded, insurgent figures were 35 dead, 45 wounded, and 58 detained (McGrath, 2012, p. 14). Realizing that they were no match for the US Army in direct engagements, the insurgents employed less direct methods over the next several years.

During this period, US forces focused on the pursuit of high-value targets and conducting major sweeps. As early as July 2003, Operation Ivy Serpent cleared the transportation routes along Highway 1 and sought high-value targets in an area that included Hawija. Soon after, in December 2003, Operation Bayonet Lightning specifically targeted Hawija. Operation Wolfhound Power soon followed. This period saw the US forces employing basic war-fighting strategy with kinetic (−3) forces, going after armed insurgents (at the −2 or −3 level).

15.4. Period 2: Insurgent War of Attrition and US Clear, Hold, Build

A total of 130 IEDs exploded in the area of FOB McHenry in 2004, and 900 in 2005 (Taylor, 2006).[6] By early 2006, the infantry regiment based at FOB McHenry (two miles from the city center) was finding 3–5 roadside bombs a day (Adriaensens, 2013). During one period in 2006, US forces based at FOB McHenry suffered 18 dead, including 5 from an IED created from a modified surface-to-air missile hitting a Humvee (Adriaensens, 2013). Insurgents threw grenades at Humvees on patrol and snipers took aim at US soldiers (Murray, 2006). Mortars hit FOB McHenry at a high enough rate that soldiers developed a musical system to inform troops about the direction of incoming versus outgoing fire. Shelby Monroe, an embedded reporter, described FOB McHenry's warning system in July 2006 (Monroe, 2006):

Just as the base in Kirkuk has a warning system, so does McHenry, which was explained to me by Sergeant Major David Allard. When the base is being fired upon, country music is played over the loudspeaker system. When there is outgoing fire, rock and roll is played. Controlled blasts are introduced by classical music. I thought this was a nice way to handle the unpleasantness, and I thought Sergeant Major Allard was exceptionally friendly. I learned he was injured in an attack on a patrol just a few hours after our conversation. Thankfully, his injuries were minor, but seeing how quickly a life can be altered was unsettling. Later that night, I was almost bounced out of my cot by some unbelievably loud rock and roll, followed by a series of equally loud booms that vibrated through the floor of the tent. But at least it wasn't country.

US forces could not help but know insurgent tactics through experience, yet they did not fully comprehend insurgent identity during the 2004–2007 period. From the perspective of some US military at this time, a combination of locals and outsiders seemed to comprise the enemy.[7] In retrospect, this combination of outsiders and locals probably took organizational form in the Jaysh Rijal al-Tariqah a-Naqshabandia (JRTN). With roots going back to the 2003 invasion, JRTN announced its official presence on November 30, 2006, soon after the execution of Saddam Hussein (Adnan and Reese, 2014, pp. 12–14). Although the organization's name comes from the Naqshabandi order of Sufi Islam, its leadership largely derived from the Baathist Party, and its rhetoric and symbolism are more nationalist than religious. Its founder and leader was Izzat Ibrahim al-Douri, former vice president of Saddam Hussein's Revolutionary Council; al-Douri was the "king of clubs" in the US "most wanted" deck of cards (Knights, 2014).[8] The US State Department estimated its membership at 5,000 fighters in 2013 (US Department of State, *Country Reports on Terrorism 2017*). While the leadership of JRTN was Baathist and ex-military, its fighters often came from local tribes. Many of its battles were clearly pitched by locals. In terms of our spectrum of roles, JRTN was a hybrid of −3 leaders and −2 local associates. As the home of many military and Baathist figures, Hawija was a natural base for JRTN.[9] Confirming this connection, one of the early US raids pursuing high-value targets captured al-Douri's private secretary in Hawija.[10] Crucially, the JRTN would become the second most powerful Sunni insurgent group in Iraq during the years 2013–2016, second only to ISIS (Center for International Security and Cooperation, "Mapping Militants").

In response to this enemy and its tactics, the US military went from a warfighting and kinetic-based strategy to basic clear, hold, build (CHB):

"Clear" continued much as before. In March 2006, Operation Scorpion targeted eight villages in and around Hawija. Operation Guagamela searched for suspected AQI members in the area between Kirkuk and Hawija.

"Hold" involved presence patrols and increasing training and use of Iraqi security forces to establish long-term order. While Iraqi security forces played no role in the April 2004 Battle of Hawija, the US forces would train and stand up the 207th Iraqi Civil Defense Corps in Hawija (later becoming 1st Battalion, 2nd Brigade, 4th Iraqi Army Division, eventually assuming complete responsibility for security operations in Hawija).

"Build" incorporated high-visibility public works projects, including a prominent water-treatment plant. There were also smaller projects such as paid local teams to collect garbage. The Army established a Project Coordination Center to help plan the construction of roads and public-use buildings in the Hawija area (Monroe, 2006).

In sum, during the 2004–late 2007 period, a rough equilibrium obtained. As a *New York Times* article summarized the situation at the time of the 2005 parliamentary elections, "Hawija is a bastion of the insurgency in the so-called Sunni triangle, an area of northern Iraq that has remained loyal to Saddam Hussein. . . . Throughout the war, American forces have repeatedly raided Hawija trying to stamp out the insurgency there. But the Sunni Arabs in the town have resisted the foreign military presence and the new Iraqi government" (Wong, 2005).

Although exact numbers are impossible to specify, individuals in Hawija clearly occupied all the roles on the left side of the spectrum:

(−1): Hawija's population turned out in significant numbers to protest the execution of Saddam Hussein in 2006. The population showed little desire to turn in insurgents. Voters supported a neo-Baathist Arab Political Council formed in 2003. Although they avoided election boycotts and participated in key votes, they did so only to keep the small Kurdish minority in the district from coming to power.

(−2): Local organization of insurgency had fertile ground in Hawija. The city was home to many Iraqi former military and Baathist officials, including top officers in the Republican Guard and the Mukhabarat, as well as strong tribal organization dominated by the Obeidi and Jibouri tribes.

(−3): Leaders of JRTN apparently had connections in Hawija. Other Sunni armed groups may have also been present, although information is sparse.

15.5. Period 3: Community Mobilization

In 2007, many tribes in Hawija followed the Anbar "model" in both experiences and reactions. AQI's killing of prominent leaders of the Jibouri and Obeidi tribes, the dominant tribes in Hawija, caused a recalculation of strategy. Sheikh Abdel Rahman al-Assai, head of the Obeidi Tribe, stated bluntly, "It is a terror campaign against our leaders."[11] On November 28, 2007, a dozen sheiks met near Hawija to pledge 6,000 fighters to an alliance with the Coalition forces against AQI. The tribesmen would man 200 checkpoints (for $275/month per man) as part of an effort to identify insurgents and close off their escape routes. In May 2008, tribal leaders signed Son of Iraq contracts near Hawija.

From the US side, this alliance could provide substantial information. "(T)he Hawija area will be an obstacle to militants, rather than a pathway for them. They're another set of eyes that we needed in this critical area," stated Major Sean Wilson, with the Army's 1st Brigade, 10th Mountain Division for the *Associated Press*.[12] Other soldiers recognized the necessity of aligning with tribes in this area. As stated by LTC Drew Meyerowich, a battalion commander in Hawija (Alberts, 2006):

> The people in this province have lived thousands of years within a tribal system. So when you are trying to help provide a representative government in a society where tribal grand sheiks are the ones that historically provide for people, [our effort] will not be successful unless the tribes are part of that process.

Other military personnel justified the move toward a community-mobilization strategy in terms of democracy promotion:

> If the sheiks feel like they are being ignored by the government they will communicate that to their people. By ignoring their interests, you would be crippling any effort to build a legitimate democratic government, if you are not representing the tribal voice in the Iraqi government then the government does not truly represent the people in this district.[13]

As in other areas of Iraq, collation casualties dropped precipitously after the formation of the alliance with tribal leaders. In fact, Centcom reported an 80% decline in violence in the Hawija District in the first six month of the alliance (December 2007 to May 22, 2008).[14] The reasons for the decline were likely multiple—information provision, in-group policing, more time for US forces to go after insurgent actors, mobile insurgent groups leaving the area in the absence of local support.

This success did come with a price, however. As local non-state armed actors gained heightened status and power, they also gained leverage to make deals, usually tacit ones, with the US forces in Hawija. One interviewee commented that the previously deployed Army infantry battalion may have "lost its fire" and was prepared to accept local demands too easily.[15] In one of these deals, US forces did not patrol in one area east of Hawija proper for several years. The area was officially the Mahuz triangle, but it also came to be known as a "black hole" or "Bermuda Triangle."[16] In effect, the US forces agreed to a "no-go zone" where locals could maintain complete control.

Meanwhile, when raids were conducted in other parts of the district, the government forces were the Kurdish police, often wearing Peshmerga uniforms. Apparently with no objection by the US military, Kurdish-associated forces conducted cordon and search sweeps in Hawija, often lining up Sunnis on their knees for hours. As mentioned earlier, one US interviewee saw this practice early in 2009 and it "made him queasy in his stomach."[17]

In summary, the US strategy shifted from CHB to community mobilization in late 2007. Violence declined dramatically. The state-building story was another matter. While soldiers justified the empowerment of local tribal leaders with reference to heightened legitimate representation, tribal leaders and murky networks were controlling parts of Hawija District unimpeded. Meanwhile, Kurdish forces raided what they saw as problematic (from their own perspective) areas not only with impunity, but with US assistance.

15.6. Period 4: US Forces Implement a More Intensive Clear, Hold, Build

When the Second Brigade Combat Team, 1st Cavalry Division took over in FOB McHenry in January 2009, its leadership was intent on changing course from its predecessor.[18] Under the direction of Battalion Commander David Lesperance, US troops would institute far more aggressive policies, in effect instituting more assertive forms of clearing, holding, and even building.

The question in Hawija, perhaps more than any other area in Iraq, concerned the identity and nature of the enemy. Aggressive policies would be instituted, but against whom? In the view of one senior officer (TB),[19] the enemy at this time was local, not coming from outside of the city let alone from foreign states. He supported his statements by pointing out that IED weapons were created by standard shells, available to locals, as opposed to more complex weapons from outside. He assumed that networks of former Baathists, probably connected to

JRTN, formed the base of the insurgency. He did not see any evidence of AQI's significance. The insurgents did not appear overly or specifically religious, nor were they overtly tribal. In 2009, the United States was still paying the Sons of Iraq and was therefore a source of money to the tribes. The respondent believed that the tribes were probably "playing possum" and laying low during this period (the respondent mentioned the Jabouri specifically in this context). In sum, from the point of view of one officer serving in this period in Hawija, the enemy was "more mafiosi than a branch of a nation-wide insurgent organization." Despite the overall success of the community mobilization strategy, the US forces were occasionally attacked by opaque, violent, local networks. Despite his use of the term "mafiosi," he believed that the attacks versus the US forces were driven primarily by nationalism, not by criminals trying to gain straightforward economic gains. The attacks seemed to be calibrated to maintain pressure and to delegitimize the government.[20]

TB relayed one incident in 2009 that helps to illustrate the ambiguous nature of the insurgency in Hawija in 2009. In one common tactic, insurgents pay people a small amount to stand in a group at a corner. Then, as a convoy rounds the corner, the crowd splits and allows a bomb thrower to step out and lob an explosive device on top of the last vehicle in the convoy, not allowing the vehicles in front to fire back immediately. In one instance, the crowd (TB estimated at 20) parted and an insurgent lobbed an explosive device (made from materials from the former Yugoslavia) toward the last vehicle. The US return fire hit an eight-year-old in the bottom of the leg but the bullet traveled upward into his mid-section. He died in the hospital. Commander Lesperance refused to pay compensation, saying that if you bring an eight-year-old to an attack, the United States is not at fault if he gets killed. The specific identity of the attacker and the motivation of the crowd (money vs. nationalism) was not clear. The US response produced collateral damage, but the overall effects of that damage were also difficult to determine.

While violence was at a relatively low level at the beginning of 2009, there were still mortar attacks and IEDs. Second Brigade Combat Team, 1st Cavalry Division expanded their range of tactics both militarily and politically.

15.6.1. Changes in Kinetic Strategy

The following changes were implemented:

1. The elimination of "no-go zones": Formerly, US troops would not patrol or go into an area east of Hawija. Now an entire company was sent to saturate this area with troops. This increased presence did draw more fire.

2. The use of "baiting tactics": US forces would do route clearance of roads to clear IEDs. Oftentimes, insurgents followed the route clearance to immediately replant IEDs. US units went undercover (in blackout) to follow up and catch the IED planters.

3. The use of mine resistant ambush protected vehicles (MRAPs) to move more aggressively against IEDs: US forces in Hawija during this period took many hits but with no killed in action (KIA) events, even when a vehicle had been flipped over by the explosion.

4. The use of smaller bore ammunition in order to avoid collateral damage and to fire more often and more accurately

5. The use of more dismounted teams and ground patrols

6. Active intimidation: Units would park outside a suspected insurgent's home for 30 minutes, sometimes knocking on the door and asking whether the suspect was planning on going out that night, for example.

7. Joint patrols

8. Reduction of unilateral raids: The Government of Iraq forces increasingly took the lead. Early in the period, ISF forces did the cordon while US forces did the search; this changed over time.

9. The US forces avoided doing detentions; the "rule of law" was to be instituted by Iraqi forces.

15.6.2. Non-Kinetic Strategy

Here, many of these tactics were continued use of standard practice.

1. Renting billboards, turning out leaflets, "putting out facts"

2. Use of CERP money: The most senior officer I interviewed believed that CERP money on roads was most effective. It had two positive effects—public relations and better mobility for the US Army. He did not think schools were a good investment.

3. Micro-grants (not loans), usually $500 (Figure 15.3): One interviewee believed these micro-grants were effective because it gave the US military a reason to check up on the grantee in person.[21] While ostensibly checking on whether the grant money had been used for the stated purpose, military personnel could query the grantees for information on insurgents. The grants could provide a means of constant contact which would not definitely identify participants as informants. COIST (Company Intelligence Support Team) identified people suited for the dual purpose of the micro-grant based on HUMINT sources. A "source pool" was developed.

Figure 15.3. Micro-grant in the Hawija area: 1st Battalion, 8th Cavalry Regiment, 2nd Brigade Combat Team, 1st Cavalry Division delivers a micro-grant to Abd Ali Ramadan, an Iraqi businessman who plans to use the funds to improve his business.
Source: US Department of Defense

4. Micro-grants were withheld from the former "no-go" zone now held by Company B. The withholding of this money gave the US military leverage there.
5. Commander Lesperance made public threats versus the population, stating at a meeting: "You kill us, we kill you."[22]

US forces did not suffer a KIA in Hawija in 2009. The US closed the "no-go zones." However, not all of the tactics worked. There was little success in pursuing mortar teams. The provincial police were not cooperative. Planned ambushes seldom worked. Raids were seldom successful because the insurgents had too much warning before the assault team could reach the destination.

In period 3 of our timeline, the US military established a Sons of Iraq (SOI) force in Hawija with highly positive effects in reducing violence. In contrast, interviewees did not ascribe the same significance in this period 4. The program seemed to have become a routinized patronage system disconnected from real security or governance functions. One respondent described a tribal-based system of "managers" with subordinate "foot soldiers" numbering from 30–40 to hundreds for each manager. He estimated that 80%–90% of the foot soldier's salary went back to the sheikh/manager. He recounted witnessing a soldier being paid and then turning around to hand the money to the sheikh/manager without even bothering to leave the office.[23] The actual duties and competencies of the SOI were minimal, with the primary, and seemingly only, duty being the control of static checkpoints. The SOI were never even minimally folded into the Government of Iraq.[24] Another respondent noted that no progress was made in integrating the SOI with local police forces; in fact, he was not aware of any interaction at all.[25] The SOI and police operated in separate realms and with an absence of trust.[26] While the SOI received money for salaries, US forces passed out large sums to Police Captain Hassan.[27]

There was also a big political problem. In late 2009, at end of the Combat Team's tour, the Iraqi government was already purging unwanted individuals from the local government. The Kurdish issue was never addressed, leaving questions of group hierarchy unaddressed. In the opinion of the main interviewee in this case, everyone anticipated a future evening of the score with accounts due after the departure of the United States.[28]

In terms of the spectrum of roles, the population might best be described as occupying a neutral position. Citizens participated in elections, on the one hand, while providing little information to security forces on the other. While violence was minimal, local insurgent groups, as seen in the next section, had not gone extinct. There was little activity of mobile armed insurgents.

Things were about to drastically change. Period 5 would witness movement leftward into the −1, −2, and −3 roles.

15.7. Period 5: Protests, Violence, and Master Cleavages

In the Status of Forces agreement signed in 2008, the United States agreed to completely withdraw by December 2011. The United States met that deadline. The US withdrawal made it easier for Prime Minister Maliki to pursue a sectarian agenda. This agenda involved both acts of omission and commission. The Maliki regime failed to integrate Sunnis into Iraq's political system in Baghdad. Although the Justice and Accountability Law was supposed to ameliorate the harsh consequences of de-Baathification policy, Sunnis still railed against that policy's discriminatory effects, especially in terms of the law's effects on Sunni representation in the judiciary and security services.[29] Maliki's government failed to follow through with incorporating the Sons of Iraq groups into the state's forces. Likewise, Maliki used Iraq's counter-terrorism law (especially Article 4) as a way to target Maliki's Sunni opponents. In effect, Sunnis sensed that Shia disproportionately held positions of visible force and domination— soldiers, judges, police.

Maliki's specific actions in the period immediately after US withdrawal soon gave vivid form to these perceptions. First, in December 2011, Maliki employed Iraq's laws to go after Vice President Tariq al-Hashimi, one of Iraq's most senior Sunni political figures, on charges of supporting terrorism. On December 20, 2012, Maliki ordered the arrest of Finance Minister Rafi al-Issawi, the most senior Sunni politician in Maliki's own cabinet, again on terrorism charges.[30] The method of arrest surely aroused passions. After Iraqi special forces surrounded al-Issawi's office and residence in the Green Zone, al-Issawi managed to escape arrest by making it to the home of Parliament Speaker Osama al-Najaifi, where he announced that 150 members of his family, bodyguards, and staff had been arrested (*The US Army in the Iraq War*, Vol. 2, p. 582). Al-Issawi, also leader of the Albu Issa tribe in Anbar, became a symbol of resistance to the Maliki regime. Sunni Arab sensibilities were already enflamed by the experiences of embattled fellow Sunnis next door in Syria. After Maliki's arrest of major symbolic Sunni political figures, mass protests arose in Mosul, Fallujah, Ramadi, Tikrit, the Adamiyah neighborhood of Baghdad, Hawija—basically every Sunni population center in Iraq. These protests continued day after day with Sunni speakers, including former leaders of the SOI, pouring out outrage in televised speeches against the Maliki government.

Maliki was forced to respond. He sent security forces, composed mostly of Shia units, to surround multiple protest camps. Although mainly peaceful, soldiers killed nine protestors and wounded 60 others on January 25 in Fallujah. Sunni gunmen responded by killing two soldiers at a checkpoint (*The US Army in the Iraq War*, Vol. 2, p. 583). Violence escalated across many locations in Iraq. With tensions high following provincial elections on April 20, gunmen killed an Iraqi soldier at a checkpoint in Hawija. Iraqi commanders laid down a deadline for the gunmen to be identified and turned over. When the deadline passed without compliance, Iraqi forces carried out a well-coordinated and planned operation in the early hours of April 23. The result was bloody. The International Crisis Group listed 50 protesters killed and 110 wounded.[31]

The local response in Hawija was swift. The reaction was also noteworthy for its activation of local armed organizations (−2 groups). Saddoun al-Obaidi was a tribal leader and also one of the leaders in the Hawija protests. After the Hawija attack, he stated, "The peaceful demonstrations are over, due to what happened today. Now we are going to carry weapons. We have all the weapons we need, and we are getting support from other provinces" (Arango, April 23, 2013). As the International Crisis Group emphasized, "The impact of Hawija was profound. They empowered more extreme elements among the demonstrators, while giving a green light to former resistance groups to stage armed retaliations" (International Crisis Group, 2013, p. 32). While JRTN had lain low in the years prior to the protests, they emerged in the wake of the massacre and showed their violent potential. As the US Army History records:

> The massacre in Hawijah touched off the most intense fighting Iraq had seen since 2008, most of it in sensitive areas along the Green Line. Hours after the Hawijah incident, Sunni militants who were likely affiliated with the Naqshbandi Army (JRTN) overran government troops in towns south of Kirkuk and cut the main Kirkuk-Baghdad highway, leading to several days of battles with government troops before the insurgents withdrew. (*The US Army in the Iraq War*, Vol. 2, p. 585)

If the military's aggressive action was meant to deter Sunni protesters across Iraq from further violence, it failed.[32] On April 25, protesters turned violent in Mosul; on April 27, Fallujah followed. As in Hawija, tribal sheiks mobilized their members (Arango, 2013).[33] Osama Nujaifi, the Sunni Speaker of Parliament, concluded, "Now there are clashes taking place between Iraqi tribes and the Iraqi Army. We call on the armed forces not to obey the orders to attack the demonstrators or shoot Iraqis, and we call on the tribes to cease fire and be calm" (Arango, 2013). Despite such appeals, by the end of April, Iraq's death toll tied to political violence reached 700, the most deaths in any month since 2008. At the end of period 5 of the timeline, the events in Hawija had been critical in setting off a cascade of protests across much of Iraq. In effect, Hawija was now subsumed into broader Sunni politics. With reference to our major outcomes, violence was at the highest level since 2008. In terms of state-building, the central Iraqi government was losing control over several Sunni areas; its basic legitimacy was in question. In addition, the saliency of the Sunni-Shia cleavage was as high as ever.

In terms of our framework, the general Sunni population, as witnessed by mass protests in almost every Sunni city and neighborhood, had moved from neutrality (0) to insurgent support (−1). Local armed groups (−2)—insurgents like JRTN as well as tribes—mobilized for anti-state action. As shown by their visible roles during the 2012–2013 protests, tribal actors no longer "played possum." As noted by the International Crisis Group, "Sunni armed groups that for the most part had been relatively quiescent over the past years are slowly but steadily reappearing, finding evermore recruits among young protesters disillusioned with peaceful dissent" (International Crisis Group, 2013, p. 33). Here, we see both the re-establishment of −2 groups and the movement of −1 actors into armed local roles (−2). As we see in the next period, ISIS would fill in the role of mobile armed insurgents (−3) and capitalize on the political turmoil roiling Iraq's Sunni Arab population.

15.8. Period 6: The Coming of ISIS

In late December 2013, the Maliki government decided to raze the protest camps in Fallujah and Ramadi, partly on the grounds that they were becoming ISIS sanctuaries. Maliki's move was met by fierce resistance. In Fallujah on January 4, 2014, a collection of Sunni groups—Baathist, tribal, ISIS—pushed the ISF out and took control over the city. These anti-state forces were loosely coordinated, if at all. An ISIS-led offensive, with clear help from JRTN, captured Mosul, Iraq's second largest city, on June 10. In the same general campaign, ISIS took control of Hawija as well. Kurdish and other forces managed to successfully defend Kirkuk and Erbil. The two sides faced off across a front line.

The exact relationships and interactions among ISIS, the general population, and locally or regionally based Sunni insurgent organizations were complex. Most agree with a summary from the US Army History that stated, "The Maliki government had a larger problem than just ISIS. The rebels were a broad front that included ISIS, other longstanding insurgent groups, and some parts of the Sunni Awakening" (*The US Army in the Iraq War*, Vol. 2, p. 592). Analyst Michael Knights summed up the importance of Iraqi Sunni groups, stating, "They (ISIS) couldn't have seized a fraction of what they did without coordinated alliances with other Sunni groups" (Arango, 2014).

As described earlier, in the area around Hawija the most powerful Sunni rebel organization was almost certainly JRTN. After the fall of Mosul, JRTN's leader Izzat al-Douri gave a speech calling ISIS "heroes and knights" while calling for unity to defeat the Maliki regime. The JRTN was also considered the most influential actor in founding and guiding the General Military Council of Iraqi Revolutionaries (GMCIR), an alliance mainly of nationalist and secular insurgency groups led by Baathist army officers and drawing on Sunni tribes that surfaced after the events of late December 2013 in Anbar.[34] The GMCIR was one of three major Sunni resistance "systems" of that time. Figure 15.4 illustrates the range and territories of these systems.

Despite being on opposite ends in ideology, the JRTN/GMCIR participated with ISIS in the taking of Fallujah and Mosul.[35] Early cooperation gave both groups value—the largely foreign ISIS gained legitimacy through a relationship

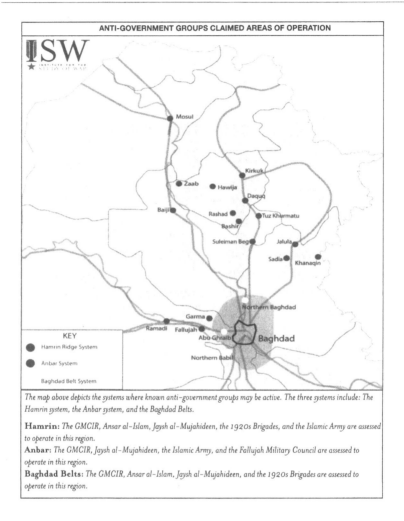

Figure 15.4. Anti-government groups claimed areas of operation.

with the locally based JRTN and its Baathist leadership. In return, the JRTN benefited from the military power and prowess of ISIS.[36] Along these lines, ISIS inserted Azhar al-Obeidi, a Baathist former Iraqi Army general, as the new governor of Mosul, and Ahmed Abdul Rashi as governor of Tikrit. As Ken Pollock noted, the Baathists "have a long history of running Iraq, so it just feels right and natural to the people that they should be in charge" (Harris, 2014).

Given the secular and nationalist nature of the JRTN and the GMCIR, any alliance with the transnational and Salafist ISIS was likely to be short-term and fragile. About the only quality the groups held in common was a mutual hatred of Maliki and Shia and a related desire to bring down the government in Baghdad. The inevitable "divorce" between the groups was foreshadowed early on, with violence again in Hawija. Days after the taking of Mosul, JRTN and ISIS members tangled, leaving 17 dead. As ISIS rule proceeded, predictably so did its brutality. In Hawija, residents described "public beheadings in the city square, people shot in the foot if caught with a cellphone, and beatings for such offenses wearing dishdasha hems too low or beards too short" (Zucchino, 2017). In August 2016, ISIS executed 85 civilians in Hawija, including women and children, while holding hundreds more hostage (Abdallah, 2016). With frictions growing, Sunni tribes confronted ISIS. In these disputes, JRTN backed the tribes.[37] When ISIS killed Christians and Yazidis, JRTN put out a statement condemning persecution of minorities. In short, the union between the Sufi/Nationalist/Baathist JRTN and Salafist ISIS lasted long enough to oust the Iraqi government and military from the region, and not much longer, although occasional cooperation in the face of specific mutual threats did occur.

15.9. Period 7: The Defeat of ISIS, Uncertain Future

The following chapter will examine how the US forces and Iraqis instituted a combination of war-fighting and decapitation against ISIS. In terms of the framework, the anti-ISIS war pitted a +3 government force against a –3 insurgent. The weary population had returned to a waiting neutrality, while local armed groups (–2)—tribes and insurgent groups like JRTN—no longer had the desire to ally with ISIS, nor the ability to put up a fight against Iraqi and US forces.

As of February 2016, Hawija remained one of ISIS's last urban strongholds in Iraq (Figure 15.5). An estimated 1,000–1,200 ISIS fighters remained in the Hawija pocket (Flood, 2017, p. 24).[38] As mentioned above, the US-Iraqi strategy was to take the prize of Mosul first before coming to take care of the less important and possibly problematic Hawija.

The Hawija offensive began on September 21, 2017. The combination of forces was notably diverse and included the Iraqi Army's 9th Armored Division, the Iraqi Special Operations Force's Golden Division, the Emergency Response Division, units of the Federal Police, and Popular Mobilization Forces (PMF) composed of mostly Shia militias allied with Iran. The United States would conduct 23 air strikes during the offensive.

Notably, Kurdish Peshmerga Forces were not involved. As discussed elsewhere in this book (Chapter 19), Kurds had conducted an independence referendum on September 25. The voting involved Kirkuk city but not Hawija. With the ISIS war winding down, Kurds turned their attention to the future status

Control areas as of February 9.

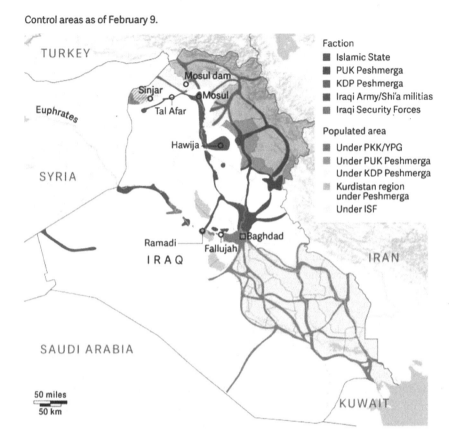

Figure 15.5. Control of areas as of February 9, 2016.

of both Iraqi Kurdistan and the disputed territories. In most Kurdish imagined futures, Kirkuk city and surrounding areas would be integrated into a greater Kurdistan, but Arab-dominated Hawija would be left out. Although Kurdish Peshmerga had intervened in security matters in Hawija during the US presence, Kurds had little reason to expend military or political resources on Hawija at this key strategic juncture. Hawija was still caught in the middle of the unsettled struggles among major cleavage groups. At this particular juncture, Shia militias were more of a problem for Hawija's Sunni actors than Kurdish Peshmerga.

Unexpectedly, ISIS did not put up much fight to defend Hawija. Iraqi forces entered Hawija city on October 4 and the city center the following day, facing little resistance. Apparently, many ISIS fighters fled to the northwest to surrender to Kurdish forces rather than face the wrath and punishment of Shia PMF forces.

JTRN maintained an online presence, but not much else. Widely considered the second most powerful Sunni insurgent group after ISIS, evidence of their continued activity became difficult to find. Their founder and leader for many years, Izzat al-Douri, died in 2020 of natural causes at the age of 78. ISIS still continues in guerrilla/terrorist form, with some activity around Hawija, but as of 2020, it was a shell of its former self (International Crisis Group, 2019). After its reign of brutality, it is hard to conceive of Hawija's population welcoming ISIS back in any way. Some analysts believed that Iraqi Sunnis as a whole would see siding with extremists as an unviable strategy and, therefore, reconciliation with Shia as the only path forward.[39]

15.10. Applying the Framework across the Seven Periods

We begin this section by reviewing changes in US and insurgent strategies. The boxes and rectangles in Figure 15.6 indicate the strategic focus of US counter-insurgency policy. The corresponding insurgent strategy is described below the spectrum figure.

15.10.1. Analysis

Comparing across this sequence, several features readily stand out. First, the sequence starts and ends with war-fighting: +3 against −3. In periods 2, 3, and 4, the US forces devoted focus, time, and money toward moving members of the general population from pro-insurgent support (−1) and neutrality (0) to participation in pro-state actions (+1).

The greatest changes in violence and the biggest shifts in the evolution of conflict occurred when one side or the other covered the full range of roles on their respective side of the spectrum. Insurgent violence declined the most in period 3, when the US and allies filled in the +2 node through community mobilization, along with the CHB efforts at +1 and +3. On the other side, the Iraqi state collapsed quickly and thoroughly when Sunni protesters, local Sunni armed groups, and ISIS covered all the negative nodes in period 6. These outcomes suggest that changing movement to or away from any single node may be insufficient to produce massive change.

That said, if any node is critical, and not well understood, it is the −2/+2 nodes. Community mobilization was correlated with a drop in violence in Hawija. Community mobilization can be effective for many reasons. It transforms an opponent into an ally; it removes an ally for opponents; it provides access to the knowledge of local armed actors who will likely possess valuable information on the identities, whereabouts, and tactics of mobile insurgent actors with whom they had previously allied or cooperated; it provides highly capable managers of checkpoints.

Period 1

US strategy: Warfighting, pursuit of high value targets (+3 forces go after –3).

Insurgent strategy: Major battle in April 2004, then local forces move to insurgent tactics.
Violence level is high.

Period 2

US strategy: Move to CHB with a population-centric focus. Attention is on moving Hawija
population to +1 position. Raids continue.

Insurgent strategy: Local forces —JRTN and tribes—appear to consolidate and standardize resistance (–2).
Constant level of mortar attacks, sniper fire, IEDs.

Violence level remains high.

Period 3

US strategy: Implementation of community mobilization. Local tribal groups incorporated into the Sons of Iraq
movement (–2 flipped to +2). In effect, US strategy filled in all of the positive nodes. However, deal making with
tribes and locals includes acceptance of a no-go zone for coalition forces, indicated by the lack of a box for –2
and –3.

Insurgent strategy: Tribes align with coalition forces, yet bargain for ways to retain autonomy.
Violence declines dramatically.

Period 4

US strategy: More intense form of CHB. Elimination of no-go zones. Ramped up economic programs.
Less focus on community mobilization, although tribes were on the payroll. Tribes clearly retained autonomy
and were not integrated into the government to any significant extent. There appeared to be little focus on the
local police.

Insurgent strategy: Little change, wait and see
Violence remains low.

Figure 15.6. Changing strategic match-ups in Hawija.

Period 5

Government of Iraq strategy. Military crackdown on anti-government protesters

Insurgent strategy: Mass protests (−1). Reappearance of JRTN and other local armed actors (−2)
Violence: Significant increase

Period 6

Government of Iraq Strategy: Iraq Security Forces defeated and then absent

Insurgents: Population (−1), local armed actors such as JRTN (−2), and ISIS (mobile armed actor), all mobilized.
The negative side of the spectrum is now filled.

Period 6B:

Coalition forces engage in war-fighting. Collection of forces—Iraqi Army's 9th Armored Division, the Iraqi Special
Operations Force's Golden Division, the Emergency Response Division, units of the Federal Police, and PMF
forces—aided by US air power decimate ISIS.

Insurgents: ISIS repressive actions de-mobilize the population (−1 now to 0). Alliance of convenience among local
Sunni armed groups and ISIS dissolves (−2 becomes non-functional). ISIS eventually decimated.

Figure 15.6. Continued

Community mobilization, however, presents risks. If "flipped" in one direction, the −2/+2 actors will likely retain the ability to "flip" back to their former position. In Hawija, tribes had reasons to temporarily side with the United States. Not long after, they had reasons to side with ISIS against the Iraqi government. Because many of these groups grew organically out of the local environment, it is difficult to ever eliminate their basis for regeneration. It is also difficult to tie them to one side of the spectrum. Tribes will respond to the best "deal." But is giving these actors a "good deal" in the short run a reliable way to build a state? Notice that community mobilization in period 3 apparently involved deal-making in the acceptance of a "no-go zone." In period 4, the main activity of tribes was to collect a salary; the money seemed to be almost entirely for pacification, rather than part of a process of incorporation into state services.

Finally, notice how little the above analysis discussed the police, a local state-based +2 organization. None of the soldiers who contributed to the narrative above had much interaction, or even much to say, about this potentially critical security organization.

To further rely on our analytical framework, we can better understand the reasons for movement seen in the sequence above by reviewing the template of mechanisms, reprinted here.

15.10.2. Template of Mechanisms and the Spectrum of Roles

Movement from 0 to −1:

- Resentment versus newly empowered group
- Safety in numbers with general population as reference point
- Status rewards
- Focal points

Movement from 0 to +1:

- Resentment versus insurgent group
- Safety in numbers with general population as referent point
- Focal points
- Rational economic decision, payouts from government, employment, etc.

Movement from +1, and −1 back to 0:

- Rational reaction to threat
- Fear (emotion)

Movement from −1 to −2:

- Social norms of reciprocity
- Norms of honor/vengeance
- Anger (vs. collateral damage, detainment, etc.)
- Safety in numbers with local population as reference point
- Material incentives

Movement to +2:

- Social norms of reciprocity
- Anger (vs. insurgent violence)
- Safety in numbers with local population as reference point
- Material incentives/employment/bribes

Movement to −3:

- Material incentives
- Ideological fervor

Mechanisms sustaining −2, −3:

- Psychological mechanisms—tyranny of sunk costs, wishful thinking, cognitive dissonance
- Coercion, threats against leaving
- Social norms

Movement to +3:

- Material incentives (pay, uniforms, equipment)
- Pride (either in professionalism or patriotism).

Consider movement in the general population along the −1, 0, +1 nodes first. In periods 1–4, Hawija provided an experiment where rational-choice mechanisms theoretically able to push individuals to the +1 node were set against an emotional mechanism theoretically pushing them to the negative side. To recall, CHB relies on rational economic decisions, payouts from government, employment, and other "carrots." Theoretically, when individuals clearly see that their economic futures lie with the state and not the insurgents, they will provide information to state security forces, vote and participate in councils, and generally cooperate with government initiatives (+1 behaviors) while eschewing those of its opponents. In periods 2, 3, and especially 4, US forces were providing funding and support for local construction and employment.

On the other side, the emotion of resentment, stemming from perception of unjust group subordination, theoretically would drive individuals toward −1 in this case. Hawija's nationalist/Baathist Sunni residents encountered US military forces daily. They witnessed Kurds and their Peshmerga conducting security operations. They saw the ways in which Americans closely cooperated with Kurdish forces in those operations. Hawija's Sunni citizens understood Shia dominance at Iraq's center. The social and political bases of resentment were no doubt present in Hawija.

At the time of the US departure, there might have been reason to believe that the rational-choice mechanisms pushing individuals to +1 had their effect. As this chapter has shown, through the application of multiple strategies and variants of strategies, US military forces managed to dramatically reduce levels of violence. By 2009, some major impediments to state-building had been removed. The conditions for the rational choice economic mechanisms to bind individuals to the state seemed to be ripe. But this was not the case. After the US departure (period 5), Maliki's policies, along with actions against key Sunni figures, produced massive anti-state protests (movement to −1). Any effects of the 0 to +1 rational-choice economic mechanisms quickly evaporated with the specter of Shia dominance. Indeed, in period 6, many Hawija residents would move to −1 in support of ISIS. In the medium run, the resentment mechanism clearly prevailed over economically based rational-choice mechanisms. It is difficult to assess whether those economic mechanisms ever had much of an effect.

Next, consider movement to the −2 and +2 nodes. Movement from the unarmed roles (−1, 0, +1) to armed roles involves higher costs and risks. Why would rational individuals accept these costs and risks? No doubt some did so for material rewards. But it is likely that many individuals who were members of tribes (and likely veterans' networks) probably were not constructing a careful balance sheet for costs and benefits when their groups organized and mobilized. Rather, when a number of fellow members moved, some individuals likely felt a "pull" to go along, to do the appropriate behavior, to reciprocate the actions of their primary social group. While such social norms of reciprocity are not always active, in periods of upheaval and uncertainty they can become primary driving forces for action. Although we should not exaggerate the role of norms of honor and vengeance in Arab society, they probably also played a role, in addition to reciprocity norms.

For counterinsurgents, social groups with this normative foundation prove problematic. Modernization surely changed the meaning of "tribe" in Iraq. Urbanization and education no doubt diminished tribal influence. But even with the vast impact of modernization, underlying group norms—of reciprocity, honor, vengeance—remain a part of the culture and identity. Even when counterinsurgents appear to destroy the open organizational forms and functioning of these groups, the ideas and norms underlying the group may still exist, lying dormant. Under quickly changing circumstances, these normative mechanisms may be able to move individuals at specific roles on the spectrum. These norms explain why entire networks move into the −2 role, and how leaders can "flip" most of the members of their group en masse to the +2 role. In the Hawija case, social norms help explain the coherence of tribal mobilization.

They might also help explain why the JRTN, which appeared marginalized in periods 3 and 4, managed to emerge as a significant force in periods 5 and 6.

Other mechanisms clearly played a role in the Hawija story. The "safety in numbers" mechanism helps explain the mass rallies of 2013–2014. Sunni resistance numbers passed a threshold—within the large crowds, the chance of physical repression for any given individual declined to an acceptable figure. The predicted emotions of anger and fear played their anticipated roles. The emotion of anger can help explain the movement to −2 in the wake of the Hawija massacres in 2013. ISIS rule very likely generated fear, as well as rational evaluations of threat, driving individuals back to neutrality (0) in period 6. Ideological fervor no doubt drove many to ISIS (−3). However, ideological fervor probably fueled the actions of foreigners more than those of Hawijians. Locals sought to borrow ISIS's military, rather than ascribe to its Salafist religious practices.

15.11. Conclusion

Our two main outcome variables are violence and state-building. As this chapter shows, violence varied considerably in Hawija. US forces and their strategies successfully reduced attacks and bloodshed, albeit far from eliminating them. US counterinsurgency strategy often prevented the movement and presence of −3 actors in Hawija. US strategy also constrained anti-state violence of local actors (−2) for a substantial period of time.

The story on state-building is another matter. US forces were indeed holding and building, but they were doing so for a territory that would soon become dominated by JRTN, tribes, and ultimately ISIS. No trust developed among the Government of Iraq and local leaders. Tribes and FREs always maintained a basis for future violent actions. In the broader scheme of things, US forces seemed to be strangers passing through town, strangers who could not see how the future would play out. Here, we come back to a basic question: Why did Hawija become a catalyst for violent conflict and a thorn in the Iraqi state's side? What is it about this city that prevents it from being incorporated into larger state structures? As one commentator summarized in 2016 as Iraqi forces bypassed Hawija on the way to Mosul:

> But Baghdad's decision to bypass Hawija on the way to Mosul has done little to address the resentment at the heart of 2013's unrest. Hawija today is a symbol of the government's inability to project its authority into key contested zones across Iraq, as overstretched forces double down in Mosul. As events three years ago in Hawija showed, poor central government responses to local grievances can precipitate national

catastrophe. Ignored by the political establishment in Baghdad, Hawija's
residents are at the mercy of groups with few incentives to respect their
wishes or autonomy. (Schweitzer, 2016)

This passage raises another question, though. Could any conceivable central government in Baghdad solve the problems created by Hawija's demographic and
geographic position? Even if there were smarter, more liberal, more inclusive
leaders in Baghdad, could they have changed the Kurd's incentives to contain
Hawija or transform the desires of Hawija's Sunnis to be free of Shia influence?
US occupation, with its troops and money, could keep the lid on these problems.
But what could actually resolve these issues?

In many ways, Hawija is a story that emphasizes the ubiquitous power of
master cleavages in shaping the course of conflict. In brief, the Sunni residents of
Hawija are short on allies. The Kurds wished to keep them under their thumb;
the US forces, besides being foreign, were too closely allied with the Kurds to
be of help; the Shia saw them as sympathizers with Sunni extremists and former
Baathists; their fellow Sunnis were geographically a step too far away. With these
master cleavages so salient and pervasive, and the state beginning from such a
weak position, resentment was likely to overpower the mechanisms the US and
Coalition forces believed would prevail.

The Third Iraq War

16.1. Introduction

The war against the Islamic State (ISIS) was the third Iraq war fought by the United States in less than three decades. The first war was brief: 42 days of intensive bombardment, followed by an armored attack into Iraq lasting 100 hours. The United States suffered only 146 killed in action, while Iraqi losses were estimated in the range of 20,000.[1] The second Iraq war was the focus of the previous section of this book. It was not brief, and it was bloody. When the last US combat troops left on August 31, 2010, there were 4,421 fatalities and nearly 32,000 wounded.[2]

After ISIS gained control over wide swaths of Iraq, the United States found itself drawn into a third Iraq war. This time, things would be different. The Obama administration was determined to avoid *any* US casualties. Drawing upon experience from the 1999 Kosovo conflict, the United States would fight its end of the war almost entirely with air strikes. Indeed, the US intervention would make 33,000 strikes against 100 sites. But there was a wide gap between the 1999 Kosovo air campaign and the third Iraq war. In the 15 years between the wars, the US military had made incredible advances in intelligence, surveillance, and reconnaissance capabilities. They also had experience of more than a decade in using these abilities in Afghanistan and Iraq. By the third Iraq war, the use of remotely piloted aircraft (RPA, better known as drones) had become a highly integrated part of warfare. While the second Iraq war had already produced what some called "the first cyber war" (Harris, 2014), the third Iraq war possibly carried the progression of modern military intervention to a new dimension.[3] General Petraeus would describe the result of this evolution of capabilities as creating a "new way of waging war":

> Over the ensuing several years, a new way of waging war evolved, largely unprecedented in its methodology and application of modern

technology. The employment of an enormous constellation of manned
and unmanned intelligence, surveillance, and reconnaissance assets together with air and ground-launched precision strike munitions—all
guided by the industrial-strength fusion of all forms of intelligence—in
order to enable host nation forces with whom coalition advisors were
located, has been a path-breaking approach. And, over time, the ability
to conduct precise airstrikes on a significant scale without forward
controllers on the ground added a hugely important component.[4]

Those tasked with carrying out this new way of waging war often came to the
same conclusion. In a jointly written book, Major General Dana J. H. Pittard, the
US task force's commanding general, and Wes J. Bryant, a joint terminal attack
controller (JTAC) whose job was to coordinate and control air strikes, described
the impact of Operation Inherent Resolve: "America's new war on ISIS changed
things. The Obama administration restricted U.S. military combat action against
ISIS almost solely to an air campaign, and in doing so inadvertently wrote a new
chapter in U.S. military operational history" (Pittard and Bryant, 2019, p. xiv).

This chapter analyzes this "new chapter," this "new way of waging war" in line
with the analytical framework and major themes of this book. As in the words
of the title, there was certainly death, and done in new ways. Less obviously, the
contours of the third Iraq war were shaped by considerations of dominance; the
war was again necessarily tied to rebuilding a badly damaged state. Moreover,
Operation Inherent Resolve and the third Iraq war produced a model of small-
footprint warfare for the future. The concluding section returns to the potential
meaning of this model for future US interventions.

16.2. Application of the Framework

The third Iraq war involved a wide set of players. As discussed below, the United
States formed a broad coalition involving NATO allies as well as Arab states. The
ground forces included not only the Iraqi Security Forces (ISF) of the Army
and National Police, and the Iraqi Counter Terrorism Service (CTS), but also
Kurdish Peshmerga units and various militias under the umbrella of the Popular
Mobilization Forces (PMF), many connected to Iran.

Despite these multiple forces, the US strategy in practice was to conduct a
war at only the −3 and +3 nodes of the spectrum. The US strategy was a combination of war-fighting and decapitation. The strategies of both decapitation
and war-fighting, while very different in many aspects, do aim to limit war to
a contest between the armed and mobile forces of state versus opponents.[5]
Decapitation calls for going after insurgent organizations (−3) directly by

enhancing the acuity and coverage of surveillance and the speed and precision of strike forces (+3). The third Iraq war was never going to be conducted only as a decapitation effort because ISIS chose not to fight an irregular war. The ISIS program was based on the creation of a caliphate, the existence of an Islamic state. Accordingly, ISIS needed to hold territory. The control of territory allowed ISIS to perform state functions such as taxation and governance. The existence of a territorially based caliphate attracted thousands of Salafists from around the world to fill ISIS's ranks.

In the war against ISIS, the center of gravity was control of territory, not control of the population or the mobilization of organized societal groups. ISIS would fight a war to control this center of gravity. Holding territory, however, involved defending front lines and fighting along the lines of conventional war. In opposition, the US strategy could not rely only on the tools of decapitation, but would also need "boots on the ground." Technical efficiency from the air alone could not dislodge a determined organization like ISIS from its territory (Byman, 2016). ISIS could defeat a precision air war through dispersal of its forces and the physical integration of their units with the general population. The United States would need a ground force not only to provide intelligence for targeting, but also to compel ISIS forces to mass and become ready and rich targets. Furthermore, the number of targets went beyond decapitation. The target set was broader than ISIS leadership or a set of networks. In effect, the US strategy required a "war-fighting" partner to complement its "decapitation" ISR and air capabilities.

The difference between the decapitation/war-fighting strategy of 2014–2017 and the strategies of the second Iraq war of 2003–2011 were stark. Unlike clear, hold, build (CHB), the strategy wishes to avoid engagement with the general population. In counterinsurgency, such engagement is necessary for collecting vital information to identify insurgents. That was not the game in Operation Inherent Resolve. The US ISR (intelligence, surveillance, reconnaissance) capabilities were sufficient, in conjunction with the ground actions of the ISF and CTS, in identifying most ISIS targets. It would be best if the population could stay out of the way and avoid becoming collateral damage. There were also different goals in terms of state-building. CHB focuses on the long-term consequences of war, while decapitation/war-fighting concentrates on the narrower purpose of degrading, possibly eliminating, a particular opponent's organizational capabilities.

Decapitation/war-fighting also avoids community mobilization with the uncertainties and political downsides of reliance upon societal groupings. At the beginning of the third Iraq war, some commentators expected a repeat of the Anbar dynamics of the second war. In February 2014, before the United States committed to intervention, there was much talk of Sunni tribes assuming the lead in the taking of Fallujah.[6] Graham Allison listed the "reawakening" of "Sunni tribal leaders who played a vital role in the success of the Surge in 2007" as a crucial element of US strategy (Allison, 2014). The logic was that there could be a repeat of Salafist overreach with ISIS overplaying its hand, and brutalizing the population, and driving them into the arms of the US Coalition.

But these dynamics would not be repeated. As David Patel pointed out at the time in an article entitled "ISIS in Iraq: What We Get Wrong and Why 2015 Is Not 2007 Redux," ISIS differed from AQI in several ways (Patel, 2015). First, ISIS leadership in 2015 was not as foreign as AQI's leadership, so resentment against outsiders was not as intense. In the leadership at least, the gulf between secular and Islamist was also not as great. According to Patel, by 2015, ISIS had incorporated many Iraqi Baathists and ex-Iraqi Saddam-era military into its organization. Many of these secular Iraqi officers found their way into ISIS after imprisonment at Bucca and other locations during the second Iraq war. Many in this generation of officers had been trained in the 1990s during Saddam's Faith Campaign and were less tied to the secular and ostensibly Pan-Arab Baathist ideology of their predecessors who had played key roles in the secular resistance of the second Iraq war. Furthermore, unlike 2007, neither US nor Iraqi government promises of patronage and political inclusion were credible by 2014. Finally, ISIS's ability to violently deter tribal defectors was highly effective. ISIS circulated photos and videos of executions of resisting tribesmen. Many tribal leaders sought refuge in Jordan rather than try to repeat an Awakening. In terms of simple calculation, the costs were too high and the potential benefits too low.

How did the United States hit upon this decapitation/war-fighting strategy? Here we come back to the three words in the title: death, dominance, and statebuilding. This time around, the Obama administration wanted no American death at all; it wanted no perception of American dominance; it did not want to become mired down in Iraqi state-building. The Obama administration was compelled, however, to drive ISIS from its territories, even if it could not be eliminated altogether.

16.3. Choosing Partners: Efficient Killing without US Dominance

The US strategy was based as much on what to avoid as what to do. This was true for both essential questions of strategy formation: Who would fight this war? How would they fight it? On both scores, efficiency and the need to avoid perceptions of dominance were fundamental.

Consider "who" first. This war could not be a "US war." It needed to be internationalized. The easiest move on this score was to involve NATO partners.

The United States quickly recruited Belgium, Canada, Denmark, France, the Netherlands, the United Kingdom, and Turkey to contribute strike aircraft. Germany, Italy, and Poland agreed to fly reconnaissance missions (Wasser et al., 2021). This multitude of "strike" partners concealed the fact that only the United States flew bombers and the US military would perform the vast number of strikes directly inflicting death.

The war could not be the West against Arabs, or Christians against Muslims. So six Arab air forces were asked to join the Coalition (Bahrain, Jordan, Morocco, Qatar, Saudi Arabia, and the United Arab Emirates). Because it was important that Sunnis actually be involved in the killing of the Sunni Salafist ISIS, all six states flew fighter missions, rather than simply participate in reconnaissance or non-lethal operations. The actual contribution of these Arab states was marginal, although politically important. It was also difficult to keep these partners on board.[7] Morocco, Qatar, the United Arab Emirates, and Bahrain ceased strikes in the first half of 2015 as a result of the Yemen intervention. Jordan and Saudi Arabia ceased operations in the fall of 2015. Only Jordan flew missions over Iraq, the other states restricting their attacks to Syria.

The war could not be a US-Shia effort. The Sunni Arab states just listed all were sensitive to being seen in league with such an effort (Williams et al., 2014). When it came to picking partner forces on the ground, it was imperative that the United States distance itself as much as possible from the Popular Mobilization Forces (PMF), many of which were connected to Iran. One interviewee who was a high-ranking defense official (GI), described Iraqi efforts to keep Sunnis on board given the problems with the PMF involvement. GI pointed out that because of the Camp Speicher massacre where the Sunni ISIS forces murdered 1,700 Shia Iraqi soldiers (see below), Sunnis were concerned about PMF revenge attacks against Sunni populations. Clearly, being associated with such retaliation against Sunni populations would be a political disaster. To assuage those concerns, GI met with representatives from the United Arab Emirates, Qatar, and Kuwait, carrying a letter promising that no such revenge massacres would occur.

The war could not be too much of a US-Kurdish enterprise. The Peshmerga would indeed be essential US partners in moving ISIS out of the Nineveh plain. US forces had developed close relations with their Kurdish counterparts since the 1991 Operation Provide Comfort provided a safe zone in the Iraqi north. These ties had only deepened during 2003–2011. As discussed below, Kurds had to follow certain rules. For instance, Kurdish forces could help encircle Mosul, but they should not enter it. Moreover, the United States could not afford to collaborate with forces of the PKK (Kurdish Workers Party) in order to keep Turkey on board. The war had to be seen as Iraqi-led. The phrase "by, with, and through" was the rhetorical essence of Operation Inherent Resolve. There could be no images of US soldiers zip-tying Iraqis or US armored vehicles cutting through Iraqi towns. The image of US aircraft determining life and death on Iraqi soil from the sky was problematic enough.[8]

The United States had to factor in politics in its choice and shaping of partners. It also had to consider who would be efficient partners, that is, who could actually fight. There were many options, including the Peshmerga, the PMF, tribal militias, the Iraqi Army, the Iraqi National Police, local police, and the Counter Terrorism Service units. Each can be considered in turn.

Following from above, the United States has had a special relationship with the Kurds. In the war against ISIS, that was not going to change. Despite the political complexities mentioned above, long-standing relationships among US and Peshmerga forces formed a basis for cooperation in the area stretching from Erbil to Bashiqa, a designated line outside of Mosul.[9]

While partnership with the Peshmerga was natural, cooperation with other militias was problematic, if not off limits. PMF units were certainly efficient in their own way. They fought bravely in early battles and played a major role in taking back Tikrit. Their agenda, however, diverged greatly from that of the United States. Many PMF units took directions from Tehran. They flew their own militia flags rather than the Iraqi flag (Weiss and Pregent, 2015). Many were bent on revenge against the proclaimed Sunni Caliphate and its genocidal inclinations against Shia (Verini, 2019, p. 240). ISIS massacred 1,700 Shia soldiers at Camp Speicher in June 2014, and they wanted payback. Clearly, the United States did not wish to rely on foreign-directed forces bent on revenge and steeped in sectarianism.

As mentioned above, tribal forces would not repeat their "Awakening" role of the previous decade. In terms of our spectrum, the United States could not mobilize local communities (+2) this time around.

The United States would find partners within the official national security forces of Iraq. The US had spent tens of billions of dollars to build these forces. Unfortunately, most of these units were not effective combat fighters. The Iraqi Army's collapse in Mosul was nothing less than astounding. When Mosul's top Iraqi Army generals boarded a helicopter to abdicate the defense of the country's second largest city, there could be no denial that something had gone badly wrong in both the official policies of the Iraqi Army and its relationship to its Sunni citizenry. As Patrick Cockburn has summarized:

> It is difficult to think of any examples in history when security forces a million strong, including fifteen divisions, have crumbled so quickly after attacks from an enemy force that has been estimated at 6,000. Key to making this possible was the fact that the Sunni population as a

whole, sensing that an end to oppression was at hand, was prepared to lend at least their tacit support. (Cockburn, 2015, p. 64)

In the anti-ISIS war, the United States would need to partner with the Iraqi Army for both logistical and political reasons ("by, with, and through"). But it could not rely on them for combat. The National Police were little better. They were often inadequately trained and provisioned. They were also largely a Sunni force with political undertones. The local police were essentially useless, having been decimated or co-opted by ISIS.

There was one reliable, capable, and efficient force: the Counter Terrorism Service (CTS). The Iraqi CTS is separate from the Iraqi Ministry of Defense (MoD) and Ministry of the Interior (MoI). The chain of command runs through the prime minister to CTS headquarters which then directs the Counter Terrorism Command (CTC), which directs three Iraqi Special Operations Forces (ISOF) Brigades. Pay, retention, and morale were all high. As a volunteer force taking only the most committed from across Iraq's population, it was not overtly sectarian. The only problem was that the CTS was created to conduct only decapitation missions, not war-fighting. For the United States, CTS political independence, competence, and professionalism trumped its lack of war-fighting training. Journalist James Verini, who had much contact with the CTS during the third Iraq war, summarizes the unexpected role of the CTS:

> It quickly became the force in which American generals had the most confidence—one of the few, in fact, in which they had any confidence at all—and in the war against the Islamic State, CTS worked in lockstep with the Americans. It was the only unit with a direct line to air support and artillery. But not even the Americans denied CTS had never been meant for a conflict like this. Its operations were supposed to last hours, maybe a few days, not months and years. The retired American general told me, "One of the things that the CTS has developed into, that we did not envision, and that I think is not healthy, is they are now the shock infantry." (Verini, 2019, pp. 28–29)

While the CTS performed the mission of the shock troops confronting ISIS fixed positions, the Iraqi 9th Armored Division did use its heavy fighting vehicles to clear alleyways. The French supplied artillery support.

In sum, the United States chose its partners for the third Iraq war. With a desire for limited footprint and limited liability, the mission would need to be multilateral, with Arab Sunni forces in the mix. It would not involve much of a +2 component. It would avoid involvement of overtly sectarian units. The war would be fought with a division of labor among +3 level forces. The US would rely heavily on the CTS, forces that the US had largely created and cultivated on its own.

The next question became—how would the war be fought?

16.4. Fighting the War: The Development of the Strike Cell

The United States had twin goals in fighting the ISIS war: efficient killing and avoidance of political baggage. The creation of the strike cell accomplished both. In previous wars, joint terminal attack controllers (JTACs) would coordinate the air and ground efforts from a position near the front lines. In the third Iraq war, strike cells would conduct these functions from remote locations such as the grounds of the Baghdad International Airport. These remote locations reduced the US footprint. Moreover, these stable remote locations allowed for steady, integrated cooperation among a host of actors.

Indeed, the processing of nominated targets became machine-like.[10] Once a request for a targeted strike came in from either Iraqi forces on the ground or from an aircraft hovering over the battlefield, the JTAC would construct a plan to hit that target. The JTAC worked in conjunction with intelligence, surveillance, and reconnaissance tactical controllers (ITCs). The ITCs, in turn, worked with sensors on aircraft to calculate target coordinates. ITCs controlled the RPAs (remotely piloted aircraft) flying over the battlefield (although control was given over to JTACs during an actual strike) and processed the reams of information coming from drones. Two collateral damage estimators (CDE) would review the plan, run a formal analysis, and possibly make suggestions for the use of alternative ordnance. CDEs went through formal training and needed to be certified before assuming this duty. Special Forces operators sat in as liaisons for any SOF operating in the battle space. Military lawyers in the room considered the legality of the strike. Finally, the US commander (originally a one-star general), in consultation with Iraqi or Kurdish partners, would give final approval.

All of these actors could coordinate their various assignments with reference to multiple big-screen televisions in the front of the room. In the strike cell at the Baghdad Airport, one main screen was surrounded by five more big-screen televisions. The strike team could see multiple video feeds from both manned fighter aircraft and RPAs. Infrared technology heightened targeting specificity. The imagery from this technology allowed for monitoring down to the movements of individuals even as they moved through underbrush. JTAC Wes Bryant describes the details of one nighttime hunt pursuing fleeing ISIS fighters:

We watched as more squads of ISIS fighters maneuvered the tight trails of thick underbrush along the river. On the infrared video feeds, we saw them as stark black figures moving through lighter shades that depicted water and vegetation around them. They weren't running anymore. They were moving tactically and regrouping into smaller units, presumably so we couldn't hit them all at once. The ISIS fighters were clearly rattled and scared; but determined to continue the fight and hold their ground

We held off, biding our time until we could attack with maximum efficiency. After ten minutes or so they played into our hands, forming a group of about a dozen fighters. I immediately began coordinating for another strike as four of the fighters branched off again. The Coalition Reaper tracked the four, we kept eyes on the other eight with our Predator.

Within minutes in another adept strike, our Super Hornets killed the entire group of eight using two more 500-pound bombs. (Pittard and Bryant, 2019, p. 208)

The strike cell could connect to the battlefield almost seamlessly. The integration of ground forces with the strike cell was fundamental to the entire US strategy. As described by General Charles Brown, the RPA feeds allowed the strike cell's commander to "accompany virtually" Iraqi partner forces on the ground (Wasser et al., 2021, p. 85). With detailed knowledge of the situation on the ground, the JTAC, in conjunction with collateral damage analysts and other strike team members, could choose among a menu of strike options, including laser-guided 300-pound Maverick missiles, F/A18 500-pound bombs, AC-130 30-mm cannon fire, Predator drone 100-pound Hellfire missiles, as well as selectable fuse options for some munitions that allow a choice between contact blast or air blast.

The corresponding ground command outposts were not as factory-like as the remote strike cells. Although the strike cell was connected to CTS-controlled sites near the battlefield with high bandwidth communication technology, the reports from the front lines to the CTS command might be made through the popular chatroom app WhatsApp.[11] James Verini describes a CTS command outpost he visited on the edge of Mosul as rather chaotic. On the ground floor, a variety of soldiers smoked and drank tea. On the second floor, two mysterious French-speaking Europeans wearing CTS uniforms monitored RPA camera feeds and discussed strike requests coming in from the front lines. Meanwhile, Iraqi generals and officers from multiple national militaries would congregate on the terrace.

Despite appearances and idiosyncrasies, Verini pictures an efficient operation even in the front line:

> When things were busy, everyone doing their job and appreciating the others doing their jobs, the strike requests coming in, being passed up the chain, being granted, the bombs coming in, rumbling the city, the terrace was a nervy, comradely spectacle, and it gave you a glimpse of the grandeur, if I can use that word of this war, of war. . . . Words were spoken, words were written, and then missiles hurled from the sky. Words into bombs. Speech into death. The jihadis may have believed they were carrying out God's will, but the men on this terrace could summon it. (Verini, 2019, pp. 96–97)

16.5. The Unfolding of the War

US strategy unfolded and established itself across the four-and-one-half-year war. The first operations were reactions to events. By the end of the war, after over 30,000 strikes, a system was more or less in place.

In the summer of 2014, ISIS launched an offensive into Iraq's Nineveh Governorate, taking the city of Sinjar and sending much of its Yazidi minority population fleeing into the nearby mountains. Further ISIS operations left the mountains surrounded, creating a humanitarian crisis for the isolated Yazidis remaining in the mountains. In response, forces from Iraqi Kurdistan, personally directed by President Masoud Barzani, launched an offensive to retake the area. From the start, the United States provided air support targeting ISIS supply areas and vehicles. Complicating the operation politically, the Kurdish Peoples Protection Units (YPG) also participated in the battle, opening a corridor from the Syrian side of the border. With its close association with the PKK, the YPG entrance into the war brought the question of US partnerships to the fore. Who was to be avoided and who to be embraced?

While the Yazidi humanitarian crisis led the United States back into an Iraqi war, a second potential humanitarian disaster deepened the commitment. ISIS seized the Mosul Dam in August 2014. The destruction of the dam could bring flood waters pouring down the Tigris River, engulfing Mosul and even threatening Baghdad (Wasser et al., 2021, p. 134). In this case, the United States took the initiative, with Vice President Biden calling Kurdistan Regional Government President Barzani to urge rapid action. To encourage and help Kurdish forces on the ground, US air strikes against ISIS tripled from August to September and then doubled again from September to October (Wasser et al., 2021, p. 134).[12]

The Mosul Dam operation was brief but meaningful in its number of strikes, use of RPAs, and cooperation with Kurdish ground forces. US strikes were aimed mostly at destroying ISIS ground forces and thus allowing for Kurdish partners to quickly advance.[13] The proven ability of the United States to strike ISIS mobile armored vehicles both provided confidence to US allies and changed the way ISIS could fight.[14] The United States also learned that it could coordinate air strikes and ground movements without having JTACs at the front line. With a strike cell based in Erbil, information coming from CTS and Peshmerga units, combined with live feeds from Predator drones, proved sufficient, even if still problematic. The operation lacked reliable intelligence and the strike cell mainly went after targets of opportunity. Notably, the United States was cooperating with its most competent partners—the CTS and the Kurdish Peshmerga—from the beginning of the war.

Despite Coalition victories at Sinjar and Mosul Dam, ISIS remained on the offensive. Again, a major international crisis sucked the United States further into war. This time, it was ISIS assault on the Kurdish region of Kobani in northwest Syria. Although the US administration had in place an "Iraq first" policy, the imagery of thousands of refugees at the Turkish border prevented a neat sequencing of battles. In the air, US B-1B bombers from the US Air Force's 9th Bomb Squadron, aircraft capable of hovering over targets for extended periods, dropped 1,700 precision-guided munitions during a six-month rotation (Wasser et al., 2021, p. 147). On the ground, the United States was primarily supporting Kurdish YPG forces (based in Syria), along with some Iraqi Peshmerga and limited numbers of vetted Syrian opposition (VSO). Cooperation with the YPG created problems for ground-air coordination, the extent of which are unknown because the actual nature of the US-YPG relationship was not public. Perhaps the YPG could readily provide crucial information through acceptable VSO intermediaries; perhaps US ISR was capable on its own (Wasser et al., 2021, p. 149).

With the battle for Kobani underway, the United States officially recognized that they were in a war with ISIS in the long run. On October 15, Centcom put out a press release announcing Operation Inherent Resolve and making the mission retroactive to August 8. The announcement mentioned both Iraq and Syria. The war against ISIS in Syria differed from the one in Iraq in crucial dimensions. As the United States had no official relationship with the Assad government, it would have to rely on Special Forces in Syria rather than on a government-based model. The Russian Air Force would become a major player in Syria, making for a crowded and dangerous air space. Yet, the operations in Kobani reinforced the utility of air power in the territorial battle against ISIS. The third Iraq war, raging in both Iraq and Syria, was producing a distinct system of fighting that could be applied to both war environments.

In the next battle, the United States was still in reactive mode. ISIS took Tikrit in June 2014. The city was not only Saddam's hometown but was located at the intersection of major Iraqi highways. Tikrit was also the home of Camp Speicher, the site of ISIS's most symbolic and stunning mass murder. It was there that ISIS separated at least 1,500 Shia soldiers, executed them one by one, and threw them into a mass grave.[15] Importantly, the PMF was the primary force in retaking Tikrit. All major Shia militias wanted in on the action. The Badr Corps provided the largest number of troops, but Moqtada al-Sadr's Peace Brigades, Kata'ib Hezbollah, and Asaib Ahl al-Haqq (AAH) also sent forces.

The Badr Corp leader, Hadi al-Ameri, essentially threw down a challenge to US leadership, along with its Iraqi government partners, stating: "Do not trust U.S. forces; they are not able to liberate one village of Iraqi territory. Today it is our sons who are able to liberate territory from ISIS with the advising of the Islamic Republic (of Iran)" (Wasser et al., 2021, pp. 152–153). The participation of the PMF in Tikrit posed a dilemma for the United States on several dimensions. The PMF forces were fighting against ISIS and doing so while taking casualties. The PMF was popular among much of the Shia population. They were Iraqis heeding the call of the most respected Shia religious leader, successfully defending Iraq. They were pursing justice, labeling the Tikrit battle "Revenge for the Martyrs of Speicher." The PMF was fighting alongside Iraqi government forces, not against them.

The PMF militias were also non-state actors taking over essential duties of the Iraqi state. The rise of the PMF meant the diminishment of Iraqi sovereignty and the increasing influence of Iran, two phenomena completely contrary to US goals and interests. Again, questions of dominance came into play. The United States would have to marginalize the PMF in the war against ISIS, but do so in a way that the US was not pitted against Iraqi Shia.

This task involved setting up certain working rules for US-PMF relations. First of all, the United States would need to show that it would not be the PMF's air force. Second, the United States would highlight cooperation and respect with the Iraq government and new Prime Minister al-Abadi. Third, the US forces would work through Iraqi state forces (usually the CTS) as much as possible. Finally, the US military might, if unavoidable, implicitly work in tandem with PMF militias in terms of allowing them to take on certain fights. The PMF could provide needed manpower and was politically legitimate. They should not be confronted; but neither should they be embraced. The United States could not directly cooperate with this non-state actor.

Accordingly, the US forces only conducted air strikes in Tikrit for one week in late March, the last week in a four-week battle. The United States only intervened after an official request by new Prime Minister al-Abadi, and after he asked the militias to temporarily withdraw. The US forces worked mainly through the CTS in an effort to sideline the militias (Wasser et al., 2021, pp. 155–156). The US and Coalition partners ceased air operations as the battle progressed toward a final assault on the city's center. At that point, PMF forces rejoined the fighting, possibly conducting extrajudicial killings at the finish. That was no longer a place for a US presence, or even its air power.

16.6. The United States Takes a Proactive Stance

While the US actions at Sinjar, Mosul Dam, and Tikrit were reactive, US forces took a proactive stance in the battle for Ramadi. Sitting only 120 miles from Baghdad, ISIS control of the Anbar capital presented an existential threat to Baghdad. Falling in May 2015, the collapse of the numerically superior Iraqi Army in Ramadi 10 months after anti-ISIS warfare had begun was especially disconcerting. In response, US strategy changed in terms of partners and tactics.

The ground assault on Ramadi did not begin until November 2015. During the five months between the city's fall and the coalition offensive, the US military led shaping operations that hit a wide variety of ISIS targets. The overall distribution of strike types in Ramadi—military forces (36%), terrain and lines of communication (28%), facilities and resources (27%), and vehicles (9%)—remained relatively constant throughout the battle (Wasser et al., 2021, p. 160). The choice of partners was limited. In Ramadi, the Iraqi Army again collapsed in the face of ISIS and needed time to rebuild. The National Police was also limited in what it could do. Attempts to create an Anbar Sunni national guard from Sunni tribal militias collapsed (*The Economist*, 2015). Some multinational partners, especially the British, took limited, but visible, roles. Without a reliable Army or National Police, the al-Abadi regime had no choice but to rely on the PMF forces. Those forces, however, could be steered away from the assault on the overwhelmingly Sunni Anbar capital and encouraged to remain in the Salahuddin Governorate.[16] The United States attempted to minimize as much as possible the PMF's role in the Ramadi battle.

The ground attack on Ramadi lasted two months. The US strike cell was headquartered in the Green Zone near the US Embassy Compound, but the more detailed targeting work was conducted by US Special Operation Forces operating out of facilities at the Baghdad International Airport (BIAP);[17] US personnel were also embedded at two locations nearer the front (Wasser et al., 2021, p. 163). During the Ramadi fight, a chain of communications was established. Iraqi units under fire first sent targeting requests to their rear base where both ISF commanders and US SOF were present. US SOF would then relay the request to the strike cell at BIAP, setting the process described above into motion. At this point, a US one-star general held target evaluation authority.

While the ratio of ISF forces to ISIS forces was between 10:1 and 20:1, the assault still moved slowly (Wasser et al., 2021, p. 165). There was an effort to integrate a broader set of ISF actors (+3) into the battle. The CTS, the National Police, and the Iraqi Army blocked off different sides of the city. The PMF was excluded.[18] The CTS maintained its special status. In a federated strike model, the CTS worked through and communicated with US SOF. The CTS was also tasked with the most intense combat assignments, losing 200 Humvees to ISIS attacks during the approach to the city in August to November 2015 (Wasser et al., 2021, p. 166).

The fight for Ramadi was a turning point in the third Iraq war. ISIS was purged from the Anbari capital. A blueprint based on the strike cell had been established which gave confidence to both Iraqi and Coalition forces.[19] Ramadi would be the first in a falling set of dominoes.

Although Mosul would not be the war's last battle, it did essentially signal the end of ISIS Caliphate project in Iraq. The battle for Mosul, the ISIS capital in Iraq, began in late 2016 and lasted 10 months. The United States had partnered with Kurdish Peshmerga to move the front line from east to west, finally arriving at the city's border where a broader set of Iraqi state forces would take over.[20] There was a long period of shaping operations.

Meanwhile, a multitude of different militias and government forces waited to get in on the Mosul battle. On the government side was the Iraq Army, National Police, and local police, as well as the CTS; on the Kurdish side were Iraqi Peshmerga and PKK guerrillas; Sunni tribal militias tried to form a collective guard known as the Hashd al-Watani; a variety of Shia militias in the PMF waited in the wings; Turkmen militias and Christian groups such as the Assyrian Dwekh Nawsha took part;[21] the Turkish army hovered outside.

With this legion of various groups all wanting to get in on the action, it was more imperative than ever for the United States to coordinate with its most reliable partners (Flood, 2016, pp. 21–26). The US continued to expand the participation of ISF forces, with the 9th Iraqi Armored Division and the 15th Iraqi Army Division playing crucial roles. However, the CTS again bore the brunt of the heaviest fighting and casualties, suffering a 40%–60% attrition rate (Wasser et al., 2021, p. 168). In total, estimates put the number of Iraqi troop fatalities at 774, with another 4,600 wounded during the first six months of the fight alone (Wasser et al., 2021, p. 169).

Deviations from the Ramadi blueprint were small, with one exception. Tactical Directive #1, issued in late 2016, devolved targeting authority. The approval of a one-star general was no longer required for many strikes. Although some JTAC units went to the front to direct artillery fire, the vast majority of air strikes were still called from the strike cell. The capability of on-the-ground partners was enhanced through the provision of Android Team Awareness

Kits (ATAK) which allowed for the relay of imagery and coordinates (Wasser et al., 2021, p. 178). The US forces provided this technology only to the CTS and the Peshmerga. The system appeared to work. According to Brigadier Mahdi Younes, the time between ground forces reporting the GPS coordinates of enemy fighters and the corresponding air strike was now reduced to only 10 minutes (Flood, 2016, p. 24). Over the course of the battle, Coalition air strikes hit roughly the same types of targets, with the exception of a seven-fold increase in VBIED engagement.[22]

After Mosul was officially taken on July 17, 2017, Operation Inherent Resolve continued and even escalated in Raqqa, Syria. Coalition forces made 5,700 strikes, killing an estimated 6,000 ISIS fighters (Wasser et al., 2021, p. 183) and fired 30,000 artillery rounds. Syrian operations did differ substantially from those in Iraq due to the lack of official relationship with the government. US SOF dominated the operation. Yet, the fundamental operation of the strike cell and the relations between the strike cell and ground forces played out in a similar fashion.[23]

The friction among the various organizations and factions fighting against ISIS should not be underestimated. The author interviewed one Iraqi Peshmerga officer (GC) involved in the effort. GC commented on US targeting restraint, believing it to be too excessive. GC was emphatic about one event in particular during the fighting for Rabia, a Sunni Arab town of 86,000 near the Syrian border. In August 2014, Kurdish forces cleared Rabia, which led to the rare situation of Kurdish control outside of the so-called disputed territories. During the fight, Peshmerga forces called for strikes against the construction site of a hospital. Although still under construction, the structure was far along enough to have produced elevated positions looking over the entire city, ideal for ISIS fighters and snipers. ISIS forces repelled repeated Peshmerga attacks on the well-fortified structure. GC stated that US lawyers would not permit a strike because of rules against targeting critical infrastructure in Iraq. As GC bitterly concluded, "The lawyers disregarded the fact the Peshmerga fighters were sustaining casualties yet they preferred to save an uncompleted building but not the lives of Peshmerga fighters that were fighting on behalf of the free world."

16.7. Conclusion: A New Way of War?

At the end of his co-written book, General Dan Pittard makes the following summary statement about his command of a strike cell in Iraq during the third Iraq war:

> What a small group of dedicated Americans accomplished in a relatively short period of time could one day become a model for how the

U.S. could support partner nations in the future without committing a large American footprint on the ground. We hope and pray that the hard-fought combat lessons from 2014, and the successes and setbacks of our fight against ISIS throughout the region since, will be heeded in the future. (Pittard and Bryant, 2019, p. 316)

In the terms of this book's framework, what were the essential components of this potential model? After this chapter's review, some possible elements become discernible.

1. Limit the war to +3 against −3.
2. Avoid boots on the ground.
3. Choose the most efficient and politically invisible partners among +3 actors to do the war-fighting.
4. Avoid reliance on +2 or flipping −2 to +2.
5. Avoid interactions with the general population (−1, 0, +1), especially avoid collateral damage deaths.
6. Avoid visible dominance.

In the designations of the analytical framework, the third Iraq war was fought as a decapitation/war-fighting hybrid. In terms of decapitation, the US and its Coalition partners took the tools of this strategy—finding, fixing, finishing—to new levels. In terms of finding, RPAs were highly integrated with ground operations; infrared technology allowed for 24-hour monitoring. In terms of fixing, the joint terminal attack controller (JTAC) became the central figure. In terms of finishing, the range of killing weapons expanded—laser guided 300-pound Maverick missiles, F/A18 500-pound bombs, AC-130 30-mm cannon fire, Predator drone 100-pound Hellfire missiles. In terms of war-fighting, Iraqi partners were tied into this machine. Led by the CTS, a variety of Iraqi and Kurdish forces did clearing and holding, but with deep cooperation with the US strike cell system.

Each of the goals on the above list can be considered in turn:

1. The war was fought almost entirely among mobile combatant groups (+3).
2. In Iraq, the number of US boots on the ground was minimal. The numbers of US casualties were practically nil.
3. A clear division of labor was established among the CTS, National Police, and Iraqi Army, with the CTS (and Peshmerga) as the preferred partner. The US basically created the Iraqi CTS with its institutional buffer protecting it from excessive control and outside interference by the MoD and MoI. The US gave the CTS advanced technology and integrated the service with US

strike cells. The CTS took a disproportionate number of casualties with limited turnover.

4. The US strategy avoided working with non-state militias to the greatest extent possible. There was little community mobilization of tribes. There was avoidance of the PMF militias.

5. The capabilities for finishing without excessive collateral damage increased with the incorporation of collateral damage evaluators, lawyers, and technical strike capacities, including the ability to select between contact blast or air blast fuse options.

6. The United States avoided the appearance of dominance or imperialism through the recruitment of a multinational coalition that included, at first, members of Sunni Arab states. US strike cells were placed in areas away from the front lines, basically secluded within the Green Zone or at the Baghdad Airport. Low-flying air frames were avoided, with reliance on RPAs.

Whether this "new way of war" will provide a blueprint for future SU military interventions will be taken up in Section IV.

Hybrid Actors

The Emergence and Persistence of the Popular Mobilization Forces

17.1. Introduction

Two of the central phenomena of this book are violence and state-building. While the Popular Mobilization Force (PMF) militias, or the Hashd Sha'abi, were violent actors, the longer effect of the PMF will likely be on state-building. The PMF emerged from a weak state. The PMF's persistence will help perpetuate a weak Iraqi state.

The United States set out to rebuild the Iraqi state in a traditional form. Following the logic of a traditional Western Weberian state construction, the state should hold a monopoly over the use of legitimate violence and possess tight control over the organizations that commit those legitimate forms of violence. In terms of our spectrum of roles, those legitimate violent actors should only be found in professional state organizations at the +2 and +3 levels. Individuals and organizations found at the −2 and −3 positions need to be either eliminated or integrated.

Previous chapters have illustrated how the ideal state-building process failed to play out in any straightforward way in Iraq. The neat linear distinction between the negative and positive side of the spectrum of roles did not occur when non-state and anti-state groups captured +2 and +3 state security organs. Chapter 9 outlined how the Badr militia took control of the Ministry of the Interior; Chapter 7 described the Sadrist capture of local police stations. The "Awakening" and its aftermath, as seen in Chapter 11, blurred the lines between state and non-state. While tribal organizations "flipped" from −2 to +2, they were never seriously integrated into the state security system. Many tribal militias moved into an anti-state position at the −1 position by 2011 and would cooperate or make their peace with the

Islamic State in 2014. As outlined in Chapter 14, in Iraqi Kurdistan the KDP and PUK maintained separate party-controlled security organs to keep their lock on power. The presence of the United States in the 2003–2011 period did little to stop this fragmentation of the Iraqi state.

While the capture of state security organs certainly weakened the Iraqi state and the "flipping" of tribal groups failed to create sustained strengthening of the state, the emergence and persistence of the PMF present an even more severe challenge. The approximately 50 militias which came to comprise the PMF can be considered "hybrid" actors. Cambanis et al. provide one of the most common definitions and descriptions of "hybrid":

> [T]he hybrid actor, a type of armed group that sometimes operates in concert with the state and sometimes competes with it. Hybrid actors depend on state sponsorship and benefit from the tools and prerogatives of state power, but at the same time they enjoy the flexibility that comes with *not* being the state and *not* being responsible for governance. Hybrid actors seek to harness and control some but not all spheres of the state's authority. Those that survive over many years tend to penetrate the state and carve out official fiefdoms within its architecture. (Cambanis et al., 2019, pp. 7–8)

In terms of our framework, these groups are able to occupy the + 2/+3 and the −2/−3 nodes simultaneously. In Iraq, on the one hand, PMF militias are an official part of the state security system. Nouri al-Maliki's regime created the Popular Mobilization Commission (PMC) in the aftermath of the Iraqi Security Force's collapse in the face of the Islamic State. Despite his misgivings, incoming Prime Minister al-Abadi not only maintained the PMC but provided the militias an official hybrid status. In February 2016, Abadi gave an executive order recognizing the PMF as both an independent military formation and a part of the Iraqi armed forces. In November 2016, the Iraqi Parliament passed a law designating the PMF as "an independent military formation as part of the Iraqi armed forces and linked to the Commander-in-Chief [the Prime Minister]" (Cambanis et al., 2019, p. 29). Under this system, the PMF has legal parity with the Ministry of Defense and the Ministry of the Interior. The PMF is not subordinate to any other Iraqi ministry, but is an equal and legitimate armed actor under the civilian National Security Council. The PMF also received significant funds from the state budget (over \$1.6 billion in 2017, or 6% of the Iraqi security budget); in 2018, the Iraqi government equalized the pay of the ISF and PMF, further legitimizing the equivalence between state and hybrid actor (Dury-Agri et al., 2017, p. 29).

Both laws and money put the PMF on the state side (+2/+3). The actual practices of the PMF have been another matter. For the most part, the PMF operates within and across parallel chains of command. On the state side, PMF falls under the command of the prime minister and the ISF. In practice, many of the powerful PMF militias follow directions of the IRGC-Quds Force. While the Iraqi prime minister may give an order, for many militias the Iranian commanders decide whether those orders should be followed, ignored, or changed (Dury-Agri et al., 2017, p. 30). In some Iraqi regions, the direction of command is hardly clear.[1] In some Iraqi provinces, the PMF Badr Organization is more likely to give an order to the ISF than the other way around (Dury-Agri et al., 2017, p. 31). Moreover, the many Iranian-directed PMF militias often work as proxies to implement broader Iranian strategy.

But the state of the Iraqi security world in the post-ISIS era is even stranger than these contradictory and simultaneous state and anti-state positions suggest. Here is a list of characteristics of the PMF system as it stood in 2020:

- The PMF is dominated by Shia militias.
- While Shia are dominant, Shia factions following three different clerical leads are often at odds over the basic meaning and direction of the PMF.
- Several PMF militias are the legacy of "special groups" which emerged nearly a decade earlier.
- While Shia militias dominate the PMF, significant numbers of Sunni and minority militias also participate within the PMF.
- Several PMF militias have expanded their range of objectives beyond the security realm to compete as parties in elections, conduct local governance, and engage in economic enterprises.
- Despite intra-Shia conflict, there is little sign in 2023 at the time of writing, nine years after the creation of the PMF, that the PMF is going away.

In short, the PMF is a Shia-dominated, highly fragmented, ideologically incoherent, Sunni inclusive, persistent, and resilient organization propping up the Iraqi state in some ways, while pursuing anti-state goals in other areas. How did this system come into place? What are its actual components? Why and how does it persist? As already mentioned, the PMF system arose from the existence of a weak state. Once in place, the PMF system has helped to perpetuate the weak state. The PMF system persists, I will argue in the concluding sections of this chapter, because a weak, fragmented state serves the interests of key actors in Iraq.

17.2. The Emergence of the Hybrid PMF

In terms of the framework, the PMF emerged after Iraq witnessed a severe breakdown at the +3 level. As ISIS advanced, the Iraqi Army collapsed and the Sunni extremist group took over one-third of the country, threatening the capital itself. ISIS was a threat to a Shia-dominated state. As would be expected, the Shia factions and the state coalesced around a common strategy. If the state security forces could not protect the country, there were non-state armed groups that could, even if many of them were closely connected to their intrusive neighbor. On the June 13, 2014, Ayatollah Sistani issued a fatwa calling for volunteers to defend Iraq by joining Iraqi state forces. On June 15, 2014, Prime Minister Maliki established a commission to create an umbrella group of non-state militias. Tens of thousands of individuals poured into militias. As is evident from the near simultaneous actions of Maliki and Sistani, the PMF was the offspring of Shia-state cooperation. The symbiotic relationship between the two sides saw the state benefiting from increased fighting strength and popular support, while Shia militias would gain legitimacy and funding.

The Shia essence of the PMF is seen both in terms of mobilization and organization. When Sistani issued his fatwa, his appeal was nationalistic and advised volunteers to join state security forces. The actual volunteers, however, shunned the state security services to join Shia militias. In the terms of our framework, what were the mechanisms driving individuals to leave the unarmed nodes of the spectrum of roles (−1, 0, +1) in order to join Shia militias? The template in Chapter 3 anticipates that movement into a +3 role comes from pride (either in professionalism or patriotism) or material incentives (pay, uniforms, equipment). In the face of ISIS, identity-related emotions were clear drivers. According to a National Democratic Institute poll conducted in the summer of 2015, 99% of Iraqi Shia respondents supported the PMF; people sometimes referred to the PMF as the "Holy Mobilization Units" (Cambanis et al., 2019, p. 32). Volunteers could be proud of making a sacrifice for their country and religion. Those emulating the Ayatollah Sistani were also fulfilling their moral duty. Sistani declared the war against ISIS as "a sacred defense," stating that "whoever of you sacrifices himself to defend his country and family and their honor will be a martyr" (Watling, 2016). If pride is the driving mechanism, it is easy to see why individuals chose the PMF over the Iraqi Army. The reputation of the Iraqi Army after the ISIS debacle was in tatters. In 2017, a poll question asked Iraqis if the militias were positive for national security. Over 90% of Shia respondents and 64.5 from Sunni areas answered in the affirmative (in 2011 the overall score was 15.5%) (Felbab-Brown, 2019, p. 3).

Of course, with the creation of the PMF, volunteers would not only be able to act on their emotional motivations, they would also receive a salary, which brings us to the organizational side of the emerging militia system.

17.3. The Nature of the Emerging Organization: The Components of the PMF

By some estimates, the PMF was at least loosely connected to 250,000 units at the height of the anti-ISIS war, although 100,000 may have "self-demobilized" at some point (Felbab-Brown, 2019, p. 3). While all numbers related to early and often informal mobilization must be taken with a grain of salt, it is possible to estimate numbers distinguishing among those volunteering for state forces, those joining existing non-state militias, and those joining newly formed non-state militias. One appraisal of a segment of recruits during 2015 cited 24,000 expected recruits, with 9,000 joining the state forces and the remainder joining the hybrid militias (Mansour, 2018). In total, perhaps one-half of PMF units were associated with preexisting militias, including Badr and AAH, among others, with the other half forming the basis of entirely new formations (Watling, 2016). If at all accurate, these numbers suggest that while some brand-new militias were created in 2013–2014, existing militias also greatly benefited by mass mobilization and the transfer of state funds.

To some extent, the size and power of Iraq's militias mirrored the divisions within the Shia community. To recall from Chapter 5, Iraq's history had produced divisions among the followers of Hakim, Sistani, and his predecessors, and the Sadrs. The Saddam regime's repressive policies further split the Shia community by creating refugee factions in both Iran and the West. After the fall of Saddam, the Shia organizations that had remained in Iraq (the Sadrists) differed from those based in Iran or rooted in London or the United States. The PMF was, in many ways, a haphazard merger of militias coming out of these various political and historical streams.

A breakdown of the PMF along the lines of its primary unit—the brigade— provides insight into the PMF's structure and internal balance of power. The PMF is composed of approximately 50 brigades geared toward about 3,000 soldiers each. The Popular Mobilization Commission pays the salaries of these fighters but is not involved in day-to-day orders. Below is a breakdown of the numbered brigades of the PMF as of late 2017, when the organization of the war against ISIS had been well established.[2]

17.3.1. Badr Organization

The Badr Organization included the following PMF Brigades: 1st, 2nd, 3rd, 4th, 5th, 9th, 10th, 16th, 21st, 22nd, 23rd, 24th, 27th, 30th, 52nd, 55th, and 110th.

As discussed extensively in Chapter 5, the Badr Brigades were formed in Iran in 1983 as the military branch of the Supreme Council for the Islamic Revolution in Iraq (SCIRI), the Shia Party led by the Hakim branch.[3] The Badr Brigades fought with the Iranian Revolutionary Guard Corps during the 1980–1988 Iran-Iraq war. The similarities that Badr shares with the Lebanese Hezbollah are noted, with the latter seen as a model. Badr is often seen as the second most important Iranian-backed militia after its Lebanese counterpart. The Badr Organization has seen continuity in command. The militia possesses artillery and armor. Badr members have had long-term de facto control over Iraq's Ministry of Interior (see Chapter 9). In several ways, this well-developed organization had already taken advantage of the state's weakness before the ISIS catastrophe.

The Badr Organization had been practicing state capture since shortly after the 2003 invasion. With the ISIS threat, and under the cover of Ayatollah Sistani's legitimating fatwa, the Badr Organization also became expert in exploiting the new rules allowing hybrid security forces. Note that Badr commanded 17 PMF brigades in 2017, nearly a third of the total number. Some of these numbers came from its enhanced recruitment in the face of the ISIS threat. In the spring of 2014, Badr created "popular committees" to recruit fighters in Iraqi cities. After Sistani's fatwa, "one Badr Organization recruiter claimed to have received 7,000 applications."[4]

During the war, Badr forces played a leading role in Tikrit, Tal Afar, and especially Diyala. Al-Amiri was given command over Army and Police in Diyala in 2015. Badr operations in Fallujah were controversial, certainly contrary to US wishes. As in other locations, the Badr organization used its controlling position over the Ministry of the Interior to enter the city and to maintain forces in the Fallujah suburbs. In Mosul, "many fighters simply changed uniforms from military camouflage to police blue to gain entrance."[5]

17.3.2. Ayatollah Sistani and the Shrine Militias

The "shrine militias" included the following:

1. Firqat al-Imam Ali al-Qitaliya (Imam Ali Fighting Division) (2nd PMF Brigade) Najaf Alawiyah Shrine
2. Firqat al-Abbas Ali al-Qitaliya (26th PMF Brigade) Karbala Abbasiyah Shrine
3. Liwa al-Tiff (20th PMF Brigade)
4. Liwaa Ali al-Akbar (11th PMF Brigade) Najaf/Husseiniyah Shrine.

This set of brigades formed a network of "shrine militias," also known as the Atabat. Unlike Badr, the Sistani-directed shrine militias were new creations, formed specifically in response to the ISIS threat. Note that each is connected to a specific shrine. These four brigades totaled 15,000 soldiers (Associated Press, 2021, March 6). These forces are considered some of the most professional of the entire PMF.

Most PMF militias are hybrids; they have two potential masters—one the secular state, and the other a religious authority. As a creation of Sistani and his religious organization, the shrine militias reflect the Ayatollah's political philosophy. It would seem ironic, but these followers of Iraq's most respected religious leader, Ayatollah Sistani, follow the commands of the secular state more than any other Islamic PMF militia. Sistani explicitly refers to *velayet-e insan*, meaning state guardianship by the people and their elected representatives. As mentioned above, his famous June 2014 fatwa actually called for volunteers to fight under the state security forces instead of non-state militias. Sistani's call was for a temporary or conditional surge, not for a long-term PMF. Most Iranian-connected PMF militias operate under Ayatollah Khamenei's principle of *velayet e-Faqih*, or the guardianship of the Islamic jurist. Accordingly, all state decisions should be subject to approval by the supreme clerical leader. Obviously, Ayatollah Sistani's political philosophy stands in stark contrast to that of Ayatollah Khamenei.

The philosophical orientation of the shrine militias manifests itself in practice. When Iran offered the shrine militias arms and training, the shrine militia leaders directed the support to first go through the Iraqi army before distribution (Watling, 2016). During the fight against ISIS, the shrine militias closely cooperated with the chief of staff of the Iraqi Army rather than the PMC (Saadoun, 2020). They did not take orders from Iran-backed PMF leaders; in fact, Sistani instructed shrine members not even to meet with any non-Iraqi military figures (Malik, 2017). Importantly, Sistani's guiding philosophy also meant that the shrine militias would not create political wings from their militias.

The relationship between the Sistani-controlled PMF brigades and the Iranian-dominated PMC was always problematic. Among other issues, the PMC used its control over PMF finances to restrict salaries for the shrine militias. The biggest point of friction, unsurprisingly, was the shrine militias' threat to PMF autonomy. As we will see below, the shrine militias eventually made a move to leave the PMF and integrate with the Iraqi state.

17.3.3. Sadrists

These include the Peace Brigades (Saraya al-Salam) 313 and 314 PMF Brigades.

Whole chapters of the second section of this book were devoted to the Sadrists, their upswings and declines, their resilience. Although the Mahdi Army was not a well-disciplined force, it had a durable foundation in Shia society and its local networks. The previous generation of Sadr clerics and martyrs provided legitimacy and essentially a brand. The movement had a geographical capital in Sadr City, as well as satellite branches in the Baghdad neighborhoods of Shula and Washash. This foundation—set upon Shia poverty, Shia exclusion, and Shia triumph—provided the ability for regeneration and rebranding. This foundation allowed Moqtada al-Sadr to recreate himself and his organizations in new forms.

The Sadrist PMF brigades were one more round, one more creation. As outlined in Chapter 7, after JAM took a beating in 2008, Moqtada al-Sadr reoriented large segments of the militia toward social services (the Mumahidoon). Sadr also retained a small group of elite fighters named the "Promised Day Brigades." In June 2014, with the ISIS threat and mass mobilization, Sadr essentially restarted the Mahdi Army with the name of the Peace Brigades.[6] The Sadrist Peace Brigades were organized in a division/brigade/battalion/company structure. These Sadrist forces were divided along seven divisions with a total of 5,200 soldiers in the PMF and 20,000 outside of it. The Peace Brigades have many untrained soldiers, but also specialized units such as a Rapid Intervention Brigade.

As with the Sistani-directed forces, the Sadrist PMF units are at odds in many ways with the Iranian-dominated PMF hierarchy. While often cooperating with Iran and its allies, Moqtada al-Sadr often appeals to an Iraqi nationalism. The differences and competition between the two groups have resulted in Sadrist splinter groups joining with the Iranian-backed militias, perhaps most notably Jaish al-Mu'amil (99th PMF Brigade).

17.3.4. PMF Militias Following Ayatollah Khamenei/ Iran: The Persistence, Evolution, and Rise of the Former "Special Groups"

These include the following:

1. Asaeb Ahl al-Haq (AAH) (League of the Righteous) (41st, 42nd, 43rd PMF Brigades)
2. Kataeb Hezbollah (KH) (45th PMF Brigade; 46th and 47th Brigade under affiliated Saraya al-Difaa al-Shaabi)
3. Haraket al-Nujaba (12th PMF Brigade) established in 2013 by KH and AAH to funnel fighters into Syria.[7]

In 2006, Qais al-Khazali led a faction, Asaeb Ahl al-Haq (AAH), out of the Mahdi Army. From the start, AAH has been funded and trained by Iran and has operated to fulfill Iranian strategy in Iraq and elsewhere. In fact, AAH fought alongside Hezbollah in the 2006 Israeli-Lebanon War. With this Iranian connection, AAH entered the category of "special groups." AAH claims responsibility for 6,000 attacks on US forces between 2006 and 2011.[8] After the withdrawal of US forces in 2011, AAH performed the role of sectarian enforcer for the Maliki regime and also supported the Assad regime in Syria.

AAH also played a key role for the PMF in taking back territory from ISIS in Iraq. After Sistani's fatwa, Shia tribesmen entered AAH. As both a part of the PMF and an Iranian proxy, AAH receives money and support from both the Iraqi government and Iran. They used their considerable resources, including Iranian T-72 tanks, in offensives against ISIS in al-Qaim and Kirkuk. As part of Iran's regional strategy, AAH also took the key transit city of Abu Kamal on the Syrian border. AAH is devoted to the Ayatollah Khamenei, once plastering 20,000 posters of his image across Iraq.[9] At one point, the organization conducted a series of assassinations against Sadrists. In short, AAH is well trained and well equipped, commits violence against a number of opponents, and operates under almost complete control by Iran.

Through the union of five smaller groups, Abu Mahdi al-Muhandis founded Kataeb Hezbollah (KH) in 2007. While AAH split from Sadr and JAM, KH split from Badr. Like AAH, KH works as a tool of broader Iranian strategy, fighting in Syria as well as Iraq and working to establish positions along border transit areas. As with AAH, KH was designated a "special group" and officially designated as a terrorist group by the United States in 2009. Like AAH, KH launched thousands of attacks against US forces during 2007–2011, gaining renown for expertise in roadside bombs.

KH became an essential part of the PMF, establishing small local brigades specifically assigned to fighting in Iraq. As part of the PMF, KH increased its numbers. KH also came to control the PMF's security directorate and missiles directorate (Malik 2020). KH and AAH were essential forces in the early fight against ISIS in Samarra and Tikrit. Despite US actions to prevent KH from entering Fallujah, KH units established a presence there. Numerous monitors have accused KH of committing atrocities against Sunni actors in Anbar. KH not only became an essential part of the PMF, but also has provided its leadership. Muhandis became the de facto head of the PMF.[10] Some commentators have labeled Badr as the body of the PMF and KH as the brain.

With the defeat of ISIS, KH returned to attacking US targets. In September 2018, KH launched rocket attacks against the US Embassy, forcing its evacuation and shutdown. In December 2019, KH targeted an air base in Kirkuk, killing an American contractor and wounding several US troops. The US military responded with air strikes, killing 24 KH fighters. KH did not stop attacking US targets, launching another strike against Camp Taji, killing a US soldier, a British Soldier, and a US contractor.[11]

The US forces assassinated KH and PMF leader Muhandis on January 3, 2020, in the strike killing Suleimani. He became an instant martyr; billboards across Baghdad display his image and urge Iraqis to never forget his sacrifice. The role of the KH as the "brain" of the PMF continued after Muhandis's death as another KH member, Abdul Aziz al-Mohammedawi (Abu Fadak), took over a primary leadership role.

The power and persistence of the KH was illustrated by events in the summer of 2020. After becoming the new Iraqi prime minister in May 2020, Mustafa al-Kadhimi tried to take a stronger stance against the Iranian-connected militias. In June, he ordered a raid on a KH base in southern Baghdad, detaining 14 KH members. Undeterred, KH forces stormed a counterterrorism office located in the Green Zone to demand release of the KH captives. The government released all but one of them. Later in the summer, KH was believed to have assassinated Hisham al-Hashimi, a prominent critic of KH. As Hamdi Malik summarized in 2020, "Kata'ib Hizbollah has shown utter disregard for the Iraqi government's authority and a tendency to go to extremes to intimidate Iraqi politicians" (Malik, 2020).

17.3.5. Sunni, Minority, and Tribal PMF Brigades

The PMF is dominated by three Shia factions, the most powerful faction closely connected to Iran. However, the PMF has room for non-Shia militias. The list of PMF brigades below indicates the location of the brigade as well as its leadership. This list is based on designations as of late 2017.

Ninawa—Disputed Territories, liberated from ISIS:

1. 90th Brigade Sunni; Ninawa leader is MP Ahmad al-Juburi.
2. 92nd PMF Brigade, Sunni, Ninawa; associated with Ninawa MP Abd al-Rahman al-Luwaizi
3. Nawada Shammar (91st PMF Brigade) Sunni, Ninawa; associated with Ninawa MP Abd al-Raheem al Shammary
4. Ninawa Guards (201st PMF Brigade, re-designated as 57th PMF Brigade; joined PMF late, links to Turkey.

Kirkuk—Key disputed region:

1. Liwa Hashd Shuhada' Kirkuk (56th Brigade), Sunni
2. Liwa Kirkuk al-Thani (Second Kirkuk Brigade), 1,500 Arabs, Kurds, and Turkmen = mixed Sunni Arab leadership
3. 88th PMF Brigade, Sunni, Salah al-Din; leader is former Awakening leader Sheik Wanas al Jabara.

Homogenous Sunni regions:

1. Liwa Salah al-Din (51st PMF Brigade), Sunni Jabour Tribe in Salah al-Din Province
2. Quwat al-Shahida Omayyat al-Jibara (88th PMF Brigade), Sunni tribal militia north of Tikrit, close Badr ally.

Other:

1. 110th Brigade: Fayli Kurdish Badr Unit, Diyala
2. Liwa al-Hussein (53rd PMF Brigade) Tal Afar, Turkmen and Yazidi unit. Leader is Mukhtar al-Musawi, affiliated with Badr.

As is apparent from the list, many of the Sunni and minority PMF brigades originated in highly volatile areas under ISIS control or continued threat, or in the disputed areas. As discussed above, the PMF thrives in a weak state environment. Ninawa, Kirkuk, and the Sunni areas liberated from ISIS provided contested areas with little state presence.

Also apparent from the list, individual leaders, some who are members of Parliament, were making deals as part of a strategy of survival. They brought their highly parochial networks into cooperation with the Shia-dominated PMF, perhaps most often choosing the Badr Organization as partner. These individually dominated PMF units are unlikely to form a bloc. They constitute no collective threat to Shia power. But neither do the Shia militias coming from outside present a threat to penetrate the highly local and personally dominated parochial militias that formed in these areas. Here is a symbiotic relationship. Locals gain access to state salaries and weapons through the PMF as well as the benefits coming with alliance with powerful Shia militias. The Iran-backed Shia militias, through their dominance in the PMF, gain entry and allies in previously blocked off areas of Iraq.

17.3.6. Political Party-Based Brigades

Finally, there are PMF brigades clearly affiliated with individual political figures or political parties. These include the 6th,[12] 17th, 19th, 25th, 31st, 33rd, 35th. The latter group includes all small brigades, created mainly by an individual to capture PMF benefits. The 31st and 33rd are connected to Sadr; the 25th and 35th to Dawa; the 17th and 19th to Iranian-linked organizations, and the 6th to the Imam Soldiers' Battalions (Jund al-Imam) (6th PMF).

17.4. Organizational Differences among the Shia PMF Militias

As just outlined, when ISIS threatened Baghdad, volunteers flooded into different militias, many in response to Ayatollah Sistani's call. The resulting PMF brigades are remarkably diverse in political affiliation, political goals, leadership, and social base. Moreover, the differences between the three major Shia factions extend to their organizational essence.

Renad Mansour has applied Paul Staniland's framework from his book *Networks of Rebellion: Explaining Insurgent Cohesion and Collapse* to differentiate among Iraqi militias (Mansour, 2021). Staniland breaks down organizations by their horizontal ties (ties among leaders in a group) and vertical ties (ties between a leader and a social base) (Staniland, 2014). Organizations that have both strong horizontal and vertical ties are "integrated." Those organizations with strong horizontal ties among elites and leaders but without a strong connection to a social base are labeled "vanguard." Those with weak horizontal ties among leaders but strong vertical ties between individual leaders and their social base are "parochial." Those organizations with neither strong horizontal ties nor strong vertical ties are "fragmented."

Mansour identifies the key Iranian-backed KH militia as a classic "vanguard" organization. KH elites have strong connections and a common background, but they are weakly connected to any social base within Iraq. On the other hand, the Sadrist PMF militias are archetypically "parochial." Leaders have deep and strong ties to the communities they lead, but those leaders do not have strong horizontal ties among themselves. In the Sadrist case, these parochial networks have origins going back to Mohammed Sadiq al-Sadr's local political mobilization efforts from the 1990s. The KH style of organization and mobilization, as well as Badr's, goes back to Mohammed Baqir Hakim's development of the Supreme Council for the Islamic Revolution of Iraq (SCIRI) in the 1980s.[13]

After the fall of Saddam, Badr moved 10,000 fighters into Iraq, many along the Iranian border. Because these forces were created and trained in Iran, the Badr forces entering Iraq after the 2003 invasion lacked local ties. It operated as vanguard organization. Badr troops were ideologically motivated, possessed strong horizontal ties, but lacked vertical ties within local Shia communities (Mansour, 2021, p. 12). Badr, and their leader Hadi al-Ameri, then looked for ways to transform this vanguard organization into an "integrated" one with both strong horizontal and vertical ties.[14]

Similar to the Badr efforts of the immediate post-2003 period, the PMF, with Muhandis in the lead, ostensibly sought to develop an integrated Shia-led organization. The horizontal ties across the Iranian-based militias could gain power through melding strong local vertical connections with local actors (Mansour, 2021, p. 16). In terms of the framework, the parochial Sadrist networks and militias were mainly based on local armed −2/+2 roles, while the vanguard units of KH and Badr operated mainly at the −3/+3 level. Given the deeply entrenched nature of these organizations, and the lack of desire for parochial local leaders to readily give away power to outsiders, this move was destined to fail. The PMF never came close to "integration" but remained a loosely connected set of militias that were not only ideologically distinct, but also organizationally distinct.

17.5. Deepening of the PMF Role in Iraqi Politics and Society: The Fragmentation of the Iraqi State

The above breakdown of PMF brigades illustrated its highly diverse and fragmented nature. Some of its major militia factions go back decades, while some are new. Some factions are Iranian proxies, others are not, and some take advantage of the Iranian connection while having their own agendas. There is no consistent ideology about the relationship between the state and religious leaders, no common conception about a chain of command. The structures of the units vary; some are parochial and others are vanguard in nature, a few are integrated, and some are simply based on a single political or military figure. Despite this inconsistent and fragmented nature, the PMF deepened its connections with the Iraqi political and economic systems.

Critically, this fragmented set of security actors infiltrated non-security sectors of the Iraqi state, usurped government functions, and developed political parties. Fragmentation begot fragmentation. The key functions of a state are security, taxation, adjudication, and economic production. PMF groups blurred the lines between state and non-state in each of these realms. Each can be considered in turn.

17.5.1. Security

As just outlined, PMF brigades fought major battles against ISIS on most of the fronts. PMF militias also took advantage of security vacuums to take control of local security functions. Given its control of the Ministry of Interior, the Badr Organization was especially effective. After the retaking of Mosul, 60%–70% of the incoming Federal Police were believed to be Badr affiliates (Mansour, 2018). In the key strategic region of Diyala, Badr took control of the full spectrum of security organizations.

17.5.2. Taxation

PMF militias used their mobility and coercive potential to set up systems of checkpoints to collect revenues. A London School of Economics study estimated that militias were garnering $300,000 a day in just one town (al-Nidawi, 2019). Toward the end of the ISIS war, the Iraqi government expected $9 billion a year in customs revenues but received only $1 billion, the rest siphoned off by networks and local alliances among business elites, politicians, and the PMF (Mansour, 2018).

17.5.3. Adjudication

PMF groups often provided more effective and just solutions than the Iraqi state.[15] As summarized in a 2021 report by Renad Mansour:

> Even those who are not part of the social base tend to go through the PMF networks for expediency and to avoid government red tape. A tribal leader, who was critical of the PMF networks for blackmailing residents in his province of Kirkuk, acknowledged that if he encountered any trouble, his first resort was to go to the PMF. He found them quicker to respond and more effective because they were from the local area, unlike the federal police, who included officers from all over the country. A resident from Baghdad, who [*sic*] the PMF had kidnapped and later released, acknowledged that in most cases working closely with PMF parties, companies' economic committees or leaders meant that "loans can be obtained" and "projects will not be obstructed or rejected." Most interviewees—whether pro- or anti-PMF agreed that its networks were key to delivering or facilitating public services. (Mansour, 2021, p. 15)

17.5.4. Economic Production

PMF forces positioned themselves to become intermediaries in the extensive, and lucrative, reconstruction in the wake of the ISIS war (International Crisis Group, 2018, pp. 10–12). This example illustrates the benefits and costs of hybridity. As with Hezbollah in Lebanon, the PMF brigades' human capital and lack of red tape often make it more efficient in reconstruction than the inefficient and corrupt Iraqi government. Furthermore, PMF groups can also use their profits and influence from these endeavors to confront the state if conflict arises.

17.5.5. Political Parties, Coalition Government, and
Control of Ministries

The blurring of the state/non-state line is perhaps most stunning in terms of Iraq's political party system. According to Article 8(3) of the 2015 Law on Political Parties, no political party can be a paramilitary organization or even work with one. The PMF groups simply change their names or declare a "political wing" to get around this law. Indeed, the pro-Khamenei militia-political factions enjoyed tremendous electoral success in the 2018 national elections. The Fateh coalition, led by Badr's al-Amiri and composed of several pro-Iranian militia groups, took 48 seats, second only to Sadr's Sairoon coalition (with Sadr's Peace Brigades also being a militia within the PMF). Among the members of Fateh, the Badr Organization garnered 22 seats, while AAH's political Sadiquon Movement totaled 15, a collection of smaller groups taking the remaining 11 seats. The group later grew into the Binaa coalition, forming one of two poles of the Iraqi system as it stood after the 2018 elections. Such electoral success translates into control of ministries, which in turn translated into control of the appointments of high-level civil servants (the 5,000 "special grades" positions), which trickles down into control of thousands of lower-level jobs and salaries. Here is a self-producing cycle: electoral and government power sustains the funding of the weapons, training, and salaries of the PMF. Despite setbacks in the October 2021 elections, there was little sign that PMF-connected parties were getting out of the electoral politics game.[16]

17.6. Why Does the PMF Persist?

Iraqi state leaders have tried to rein in the PMF. In December 2017, with the war against ISIS winding down, Prime Minister al-Abadi offered to allow PMF forces to join security agencies connected to the Ministry of Interior or the Ministry of Defense (International Crisis Group, 2018; p. 19). He proposed transforming the PMF into a part-time reserve force. Prime Minister al-Abadi also floated a plan to transform the PMF into a civilian agency concentrating on reconstruction rather than security. PMF leaders rejected all of these proposals.

The United States certainly did not plan to help create hybrid security forces. Undoubtedly, if the United States had its way, Iraq would eliminate hybrids, or at least transform them. Indeed, many commentators have proposed methods to do so.[17] In the battle between the state and hybrid groups, the state possesses potential weapons in its judicial, financial, and security tools. The state could shift PMF members, either through high pay and/or through eliminating brigades, into the Iraqi police and army. This method was proposed for integrating Awakening members into state forces. One Iraqi social scientist suggested a freeze on PMF membership, along with a training program that would develop civilian skills; many PMF members would then move to better paying civilian jobs, producing ever declining PMF numbers.[18] The state could have the Iraqi treasury directly make payments to individual PMF soldiers, thus cutting off the PMF Commission and militia leadership from a primary means of controlling and retaining their base. The state could employ its judicial capacity and enforce the law requiring political parties to be separate from armed groups; the judicial branch could prosecute, sanction, or ban parties that fail to comply. The state could try to undercut PMF ability to collect revenues and control economic functions by removing the PMF from key oil and reconstruction industries. More radically, following the example of the United States and its assassinations of Muhandis and Soliemani, the state could use arrests and decapitation against PMF leaders. A variety of theories from the demobilization, disarmament, and reintegration literature provides possible solutions.

None of these ideas has a very good chance of coming to fruition in the near future.[19] The PMF is likely to retain its hybrid nature. First, as Renad Mansour points out in an argument against targeted strikes, "The PMF networks are diversified and span political and societal nodes" (Mansour, 2021, p. 36). There is no "magic bullet" to bring down the power of this now militarily and politically diffuse institution. Second, the very nature of "hybrid' means the organization is intertwined with the state. In Iraq, those interconnections have become very tangled as PMF armed militias become political parties, in turn becoming coalition partners and in turn becoming masters of government ministries. Badr and AAH have become part of the state. The idea that the state will take on the hybrids means that the state is actually taking on part of itself.

It is true that one of the major PMF factions—the Sistani-led shrine brigades—have opted for subordination to the state. Following Sistani's own theory of governance, in the spring of 2020 the four shrine brigades listed above asked to be detached from the PMF to become affiliated with the Iraqi Defense Ministry (Saadoun, 2020; Malik, 2020, April 29). Given their close connection with the Iraqi armed forces during the anti-ISIS fight, the move was not a surprise. It is not likely that the other PMF factions will follow. To see why this is so, we can first consider more general reasons and then go through the more specific interests of the factions outlined above.

17.7. The Politics of Dominance, or More Specifically, the Politics of Avoiding Chances of Subordination

A major finding of this chapter, in line with the basic arguments of this book, is that the PMF is the result of a weak state, and in turn the PMF perpetuates that weak state. Many Iraqi actors, including those described in this chapter, probably prefer it that way.[20] Most Shia want a Shia-dominated state. They do not want a neutral state, or a state where Sunnis would have an opportunity to regain a dominant position. A neutral state might be more efficient, but that is not the most important aspect of a state. The PMF is a Shia-dominated institution, an incoherent institution, but one that guarantees Shia dominance.

Second, Shia factions do not wish to be dominated by other Shia factions. If there was a strong state, one Shia faction could capture that strong state and diminish or eliminate Shia competitors. As is stands, there is a rough balance between the pro-Iranian Khamenei brigades, the more independent Badr Organization, and the Sadrist forces, with shrine-affiliated militias on the sidelines. As components of the PMF, each of these factions receives significant funds, as well as a measure of legitimacy. Each faction can maintain themselves within this system. Despite occasional violence among the factions, none will be able to eliminate another.

Consider the interests and nature of each faction. The Badr Organization has 20 years of experience blurring the lines between state and non-state in Iraq. They have captured much of the Ministry of the Interior and controlled the Transportation Ministry. With the PMF, they not only gain access to Iraqi state funds, but control several key localities and larger strategic regions such as Diyala. The Badr Organization translated their PMF fighting credentials into seats in the Iraqi Parliament and political influence. All the while, they have maintained their connections to Iran and its resources and training.

The descendants of the "special groups" have increased their power and numbers through the PMF (at least up to 2021). They have access to state funds on the one hand, while taking the leadership reins of the PMF on the other. For KH, AAH, and assorted Iranian proxy groups, a weak state will not threaten Iran or Shia dominance within Iraq.

The Sadrists thrive in a weak state; they are able to use their flexibility to take advantage of opportunities and to absorb blows. It is true that Moqtada al-Sadr has made speeches calling for a stronger state. Certainly, he wishes to keep Iran at arm's length. The Sadrists do not welcome the political competition from the Iran-backed militias' political wings. Still, the Sadrists have incentives to maintain the status quo. The lack of ideological or structural coherence in the PMF fits the Sadrist style and history and flexible tactics. Accordingly, the Sadrists placed some militia members in the Peace Brigades within the PMF, but keep more outside of it. The Sadrists have had little incentive to put their PMF members under a professionalized and centralized state organization rather than the loose decentralized structure that currently exists.

Even the Sunni groups and minorities have incentives to support the PMF status quo. Clear dominance of one group allows for inclusion of non-threatening smaller groups. In this case, the clearly dominant Shia can afford to be generous with benefits to localized Sunni groups. Inna Rudolf sums up the logic of former PMF leader Muhandis (often known as Abu Mahdi as in the following passage):

> The diversity of the PMU is, in part, due to Abu Mahdi's strategy for PMU dominance: as the chief architect of the PMU's organizational consolidation, he had long advocated for cross-sectarian outreach. This is not to say that Abu Mahdi was a true champion of national unity. Rather, he was a shrewd strategist who understood the benefits of at least some Sunni participation in the PMU: it is both good optics and good politics, especially in areas of Iraq that are predominately Sunni. But as this report shows, Sunni participation in the PMU also has strong local foundations.[21]

Recognizing that the Shia have won, leaders of Sunni tribes and minorities have come to carve out a role within the emerging system, especially in those areas coming out of the ISIS onslaught (the development and alignment of Christian militias in this environment is covered in the following chapter). Individual leaders in these localities undoubtedly pursue their own personal interests. But, crucially, membership of their brigade in the PMF allows connections to both the most powerful Shia militias and the state.

The Kurdish angle on the PMF has not been addressed, but Kurds have little problem with the system. After all, the KDP and PUK Peshmergas are hybrid groups themselves. The PMF sets a legal precedent for their continued power outside of Iraqi state control. Also, while Kurds have little interest in a very weak Iraqi state, they have no desire to see a powerful one either.

17.8. Conclusion

Many Iraqi citizens have developed a negative view of the PMF and its power, especially in the wake of PMF attacks on peaceful protesters. Some PMF factions, however, have gone out of their way to push back and revel in their power and position. On June 26, 2021, thousands of PMF members, including Sunni,

Yazidi, and Christians, marched in Diyala Province to commemorate the seventh anniversary of the creation of the PMF (Abdul-Zahra and Kullab, 2021). Hundreds of armored vehicles, including rocket launchers and Russian tanks, formed the backbone of the parade. Iraqi Prime Minister Mustafa al-Kadhimi presided over the parade as the official state commander in chief. The marchers held posters of Abu Mahdi al-Muhandis. A fitting juxtaposition of figures—the Iraqi prime minister and a Shia religious martyr. Both played leading roles in the PMF parade in the summer of 2021—state and PMF hand in hand.

How Minorities Make Their Way

The Case of Christian Militias in the Nineveh Plains

MATT CANCIAN AND ROGER PETERSEN

18.1. Introduction

Previous chapters have focused on how Iraq's major ethnic groups fought for dominance or tried to avoid subordination. The contest over the center pitted Shia versus Sunni. In the north, Kurds strove to maintain their position against the center while fighting among themselves for dominance within the Kurdistan region. These struggles helped create a weak state with a highly fragmented security system. As outlined in the preceding chapter, a myriad of types of armed groups, each possessing different types of connections and loyalties, comprised the hybrid Popular Mobilization Forces (PMF).

With the coming of the ISIS war, Christians in the Nineveh Plains became as vulnerable there as they had been in Mosul and Baghdad. Their most pressing concern was not dominance—it was the very question of how to survive in their native territories. As a minority, how should they fit into the complex Iraqi security environment? As this chapter will show, Christians answered this question by forming militias. In fact, in the wake of ISIS, multiple Christian militias would form. Each of these militias, too weak to stand on their own, would seek out the most useful security organization partner. A fragmented Iraqi security system provided multiple paths. The choices across a range of partners were a manifestation of that fragmented system, as well as a small reinforcement of it.

The road to this eventual result was hardly smooth. For small minorities, perhaps especially those involved in business or trade, the first strategic impulse is to keep out of politics, to keep one's head down.[1] Small minorities cannot usually make a decisive contribution themselves. Organizing armed units and siding with one side or another during violent conflict can pose grave dangers. The minority can be charged with collaboration, and collaboration with a losing side can produce severe consequences. In terms of our framework, the default logic for small minorities is to stay at the 0 position on the spectrum of roles, or even to flee if the situation becomes dangerous. Indeed, many Christians in northern Iraq tried to stay neutral for as long as possible.

However, it became increasingly difficult for Christians in the Nineveh Plains to remain neutral. Shortly after the 2003 invasion, violence and the lack of a coherent state impelled Christians in Qaraqosh to form a militia. This organization was tightly connected with Kurdish structures. When the Kurds failed to provide sufficient security in 2014, the number of Christian militias expanded and adapted to the fragmented security system of Iraq.

After the presentation of some necessary background material, this chapter proceeds in three sections, essentially small case studies: (1) Christians in Mosul: a case of neutrality going bad; (2) the development and organization of the Christian militia (movement to +2) in Qaraqosh beginning in 2004; (3) the development of multiple Christian militias (+2) in the wake of ISIS.

In writing this chapter, the two authors draw from their field experience. Matt Cancian interviewed several officers in the Nineveh Plains Guards, the largest Christian self-defense force, in the summer of 2017 in Erbil (denoted as "M" sources). In the fall of 2014, Petersen conducted a series of meetings with Christian refugees who had found safety in Jordan after fleeing ISIS (denoted as "R" sources). These refugees were mainly from Qaraqosh. Petersen also met with displaced persons from Mosul while doing fieldwork in 2013 in Ankawa, a largely Christian suburb of Erbil.[2]

The field experiences of the two authors are complementary with Cancian's research being more recent and military-oriented and Petersen's work conducted earlier and more with civilians. These equal but varied contributions are reflected in the chapter's style of voice—writing of ourselves in the third person.

18.2. Christians in Iraq: Background

The organization of Christianity in northern Iraq is complex. In general, Christians in Iraq can be categorized along two dimensions—language/ethnicity and sect. For the Assyrian minority, language forms the foundation of a broader ethnic identity. The official language of the major Assyrian churches is Syriac, a dialect of Aramaic. The other key dimension, specific Christian sect, follows the historical divide between Catholic and Orthodox (with very few Protestants). The Christian population which is the focus of this chapter is sometimes referred to as "Chaldean Syriac Assyrian," with the first term specifying the Christian sect, the second the language, and the third ethnicity.[3]

In alignment with official and common usage, this work will employ "Assyrians" or just "Christians" unless a more specific issue of sect is relevant.

As in other cases in the region, modernization and violence heightened the Assyrians' sense of group consciousness. Modernization brought increased contact with the state, which in turn often resulted in violence against minorities if they did not fit in with the state's nation-building project. The Iraqi press made claims that the Assyrians "despite the small size of their community, [were] a threat to the national integrity of Iraq."[4] In August 1933, armed forces of the Kingdom of Iraq, led by Kurdish general Bakr Sidqi, killed thousands of Assyrians, many on a single day (August 7) in and around the town of Simele.[5] Assyrians commemorate this day as Martyr's Day or National Day of Mourning.[6]

Although many Assyrians tried to remain on the sidelines in the decades after Simele, the Kurdish battles against the Iraqi state made it difficult to remain there. That fight also provided occasional opportunities to design and employ strategies that might benefit from the competition between the Kurds and the central state. Benjamen (2022, p. 90) writes of the Assyrian strategic logic during the early 1960s contest between Barzani-led Kurds and the state regime:

> But the Assyrians had placed themselves in a strategic position: By aligning with Barzani, they might benefit from the support Barzani had garnered from outside sources; but in struggling alongside the Kurds, they would be able to negotiate for additional rights either from the central government, once a peace treaty had been signed, or from Kurdish leadership, in the event that the latter won greater administrative autonomy.[7]

When the Baath Party took power, the regime promised recognition and rights for Assyrians, but after Saddam Hussein consolidated his rule, Assyrian culture and language were repressed. While not completely shut out of government employment, Assyrians were still often considered "foreign." To take one example, Saddam's deputy was a Christian; however, he had to adopt the name of Tariq Aziz instead of his given Christian name, Mikhail Youhanna. In addition to cultural repression, the regime instituted an Arabization policy regime similar to the one applied to certain Kurdish areas, entailing moving in Arabs to change the local demography (Hanish, 2011, p. 162). On the whole, from the mid-1970s until the 2003 invasion, relations between Assyrians and the state found a low-level equilibrium. The Chaldean Church officially supported the regime. There was little else any church or organization could do in this period. Individual Assyrians did play important roles in the Kurdish Democratic Party (KDP) as well as the Iraqi Communist Party.

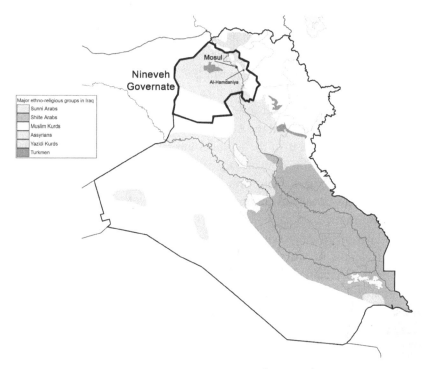

Figure 18.1. Demographics, the location of Christians (Assyrians) and other minorities.
Source: Adapted from https://en.wikipedia.org/wiki/Demogrphics_of_Iraq#/media/
File:Ethnoreligious_Iraq.svg
https://commons.wikimedia.org/wikiFile:Ethnoreligious_Iraq.svg

But this low-level equilibrium would be shattered by the 2003 invasion and its aftermath. Much of the precarious situation of the Assyrian Christians is due to geography (see Figure 18.1 and Figure 18.2). The Nineveh Plains sit between Arab and Kurdish lands. Being minorities often in conflict with the central state, the relationship between Christians and Kurds has been close. Many Christians participate in the Kurdish Democratic Party (KDP).[8] The tens of thousands of Christians populating the Erbil suburb of Ankawa provide a stable and sizable Christian presence in the KRG's largest city.[9] As an example of these positive relations, Petersen can recount a personal experience in June 2013. St. Joseph's Church in Ankawa was holding a wake for a recently deceased archbishop. A large gathering of men sat silently along the walls of the men's hall. Before taking a seat, entering mourners would greet those around them with a traditional greeting, which was returned in kind by those addressed. Many of those paying respects were Kurdish Muslims, including high officials of the Erbil government. These relations of recognition and respect were seen as ordinary. Personal relations and political ones can differ, though, as we will see below. The ISIS invasion shattered Christian confidence in the ability of the Kurds to

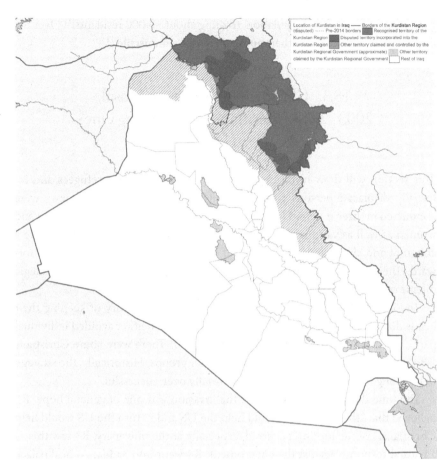

Figure 18.2. Recognized Kurdish territories and disputed territories.
Source: https://en.Wikipedia.org/wiki/Iraqi_Kurdistan#media/File:Iraqi_Kurdistan_
in_Iraq_de-facto_and_disputed_hatched).svg
https://commons.wikimedia.org/wiki/File:Iraqi_Kurdistan_in_Iraq_(de-facto_and_d
isputed_hatched).svg

provide security. The need for survival would overpower group affinity and push
the Christians into armed mobilization.

The question of minority mobilization is not just of theoretical importance. At
the time of the American invasion, an estimated 1.5 million Christians lived in
Iraq. By the time the Islamic State of Iraq and Syria (ISIS) swept through northern
Iraq in 2014, that figure may have fallen to roughly 400,000 (see Ponomarev and
Arango, 2016).[10] Without significant numbers of returns, the Iraq war and its
aftermath could lead to a near elimination of a religious minority with roots existing for nearly 2,000 years. It would not be the first time a sizable religious minority has disappeared from Iraq's mosaic of peoples. In 1900, Jews comprised

one-fourth of Baghdad's population, totaling about 50,000 residents.[11] Over the course of the next century, their numbers became miniscule.[12]

18.3. Christians in the City of Mosul, 2003–2014: The Strategy of "Keeping One's Head Down"

This section will draw from interviews with seven Christian refugees and internally displaced persons from Mosul (R sources). These interviews were conducted in three different locations during 2014–2015 and included men and women as well as various age ranges. Taken together, these interviews create a coherent and chronological narrative of Christian life in Mosul from 2003 forward. Their collective experience provides a broad illustration of the strategic dilemmas Christians faced in Mosul.

The interviewees described Christians as having a history of keeping their heads down, just wanting to be left alone. Christians neither avoided individual participation in politics, nor did they embrace it. There were some Christians who were Baathists, as with members of other groups. Historically, the strategy of blending in and remaining quiet had usually been successful.

The time during and shortly after the invasion was one of general hope. R5 believed that "the Christians would help the US and in turn the US would help Christians." While looting occurred, especially at the university, R3 saw this as a natural response against the government. R4 went into Saddam's local palace with others and observed people grabbing up the munitions and weapons strewn around the building. The first US commander in Mosul was General Petraeus. R1 was very positive about Petraeus and recalled the 28-member appointed multiethnic council as having positive effects.

In the post-2005 period, things became worse, as they did over much of Iraq. After Petraeus left, security declined, although the reasons very likely had more to do with the drastic cuts in US troop numbers than changes in leadership or overall policy. Due to the Sunni boycott of elections, Kurds became politically dominant in Mosul, exacerbating tensions with Arabs in the city. By 2006 and 2007, insecurity reached very high levels. The government was unable to offer protection. R1 stated that in one day, armed groups took over 10 police stations. Areas in Mosul became known as "dead zones." Bodies lay on the ground for 3 or 4 days. People were afraid to move them for fear of being identified and even fear of insurgents planting an IED in the corpse. The interviewees did not always know who was doing the bulk of the killing during this period. It could have been either Islamists or ex-Baathists.

The violence differed in quality, sometimes including well-publicized sensational events. In Mosul, R1 tells of an incident of a prisoner being handcuffed, led by a group of people, and then being publicly beheaded. At this point, threats against individuals were vague, although clearly in the language of the Islamic extremists. Sometimes the threat was specifically against Christians; sometimes the threats involved extortion. R3 and R4 began to stay within the confines of their neighborhood, maybe going out to the local internet cafe, but not outside the neighborhood (R3). R3 was indoors by sunset. R3 said that Christian women started to be afraid of going out without a head scarf. Christians working for the United States were assassinated.

At one point, threats changed from indiscriminate to discriminate. Threats came mainly in the forms of short-term kidnappings and extortion letters. Christian names are recognizable. As several interviewees stated, terrorists or Islamists could simply go through the phone book and find Christians to extort (R1, R2, and R8). The perpetrators sent letters to Christian homes, stating that it was necessary to cooperate with the new Islamic government. At one point, R4's family received a letter asking for $2,700 or a type of machine gun (the two were equated in the letter). The family left as a response to this letter. At 10 p.m. the family met and made a collective decision to leave. At 5 a.m. when the curfew was lifted, they fled. R4 had scoffed at his brother for leaving, but after this specific threat, he also left the next day. In 2007, two of R8's brothers were kidnapped within a span of 13 days. R8 believed the only reason they were kidnapped was because they were Christians. The kidnappers asked for $100,000. When R8's family replied that they could not pay that sum, the kidnappers told them to go to a rich businessman in Erbil to get the money. The family eventually paid $40,000.

R1's experience was more complicated, but ended with the same result. After making statements against insurgents, R1 was kidnapped for a 24-hour period and was released with warnings about his activities. Later, R1 was kidnapped a second time for extortion reasons. He was again released so he could make payment, the kidnapping having been used to establish credibility of the threat. R1 believed that he was personally targeted because of his Christian identity. As he explained, just as the Ottoman Empire taxed Christians at a higher rate than Muslims, so did Muslim insurgents see Christians as a legitimate target for money. After this direct threat in 2008, R1 decided to flee. Even after leaving Mosul for Iraqi Kurdistan, insurgents targeted him for extortion. The insurgents still had his mobile phone number. They called him and told him they would burn down his home if he does not pay. They told him he can come back, as long as he makes payment. He refused and they did in fact bomb his home.

R5 held on until the arrival of ISIS forces. R5 had left the country for several months to avoid insurgent threats. In May 2008, insurgents identifying themselves as Islamic State called R5 on his cell phone and demanded $5,000. They told him a location and time to place the money. They told him that if he went to the police, they would kill him. Moreover, they told R5 where he lived, when he was in his office, where his children went to school. The insurgents calibrated demands by the wealth of the person. While they asked R5 for $5,000, the richest in the community were given a $100,000 figure.[13] R5 avoided this pressure by leaving the country (to Malaysia) for several months before returning (R5 left in 2008 at the height of anti-Christian violence; he was encouraged by a lull in violence in 2009 and returned).

The year 2008 was perhaps the height of violence against Christians in Mosul. On February 29, 2008, the Chaldean Catholic Archbishop Paulos Faraj Monsignor Rahno disappeared and was found buried in east Mosul two weeks later. Like the rest of the Christian community in Mosul, Archbishop Rahno had been a target of extortion, paying Sunni militant groups from the church collections. The AQI-connected extorters demanded *jizya*, the traditional tax on Christians and Jews. After denouncing the protection tax on local television, Monsignor Rahno was abducted and killed.[14] Archbishop Rahno's death was a major blow to the Christians in Mosul. As R5 stated on the logic and effectiveness of the killing: "if you cut off the head of the shepherd, the sheep will scatter."

The Christians in Mosul did not develop any local self-defense organizations. Doing so might have made them an even more visible target. It is not clear how much of a difference any defense group could have made. The Christians also lacked existing building blocks to build a self-defense organization. One of the biggest differences between Christians and other groups in Iraq is that Christians do not operate along tribal lines. As Mosul descended into chaos, Christians lacked this organizational alternative for self-defense.

Neither were the United States and allied forces able to promote organization, or even to provide help. US strategy was basically clear, hold, build (CHB) throughout this period. It is obvious that "clear" was not working after 2005. Without any "clear," the "hold" tactics were of little use. The US forces did presence patrols, but the fact that US soldiers could ride through Mosul neighborhoods seemed to make little difference to the insurgents, kidnappers, and extorters. The US forces set up checkpoints but then turned them over to Iraqis, who were more connected to the insurgents than to the government. The United States was supposed to be training professional police, but none of the interviewees considered going to them for help, at least not by 2007. The US forces put money into projects to win hearts and minds, but the security issue for Christians was so overwhelming that those projects made little impact.[15]

I asked R8 if it was possible to go to the police for help. R8 said the police and the Islamic groups were the same group, or had an agreement. As mentioned above, two of R8's brothers were kidnapped. R8 said that one of the kidnappings took place near a checkpoint and the officer did not even respond to their pleas for help. R8 also said the Coalition had given out cell phones so that they could call in, but when she called, the voice on the other line told her not to call again and that they would trace the call back if R8 did call again. She said going to the Americans would get one killed. There was no anonymity, no trust in any of the government authorities. R5 backed up R8's points on the lack of trust of government authorities and the US forces. R5 believed that the police were heavily infiltrated and many were "friends of the terrorists." The US military was also not trustworthy. Bodies lay on the streets and no one did anything about it.

One of the most shocking aspects of this set of interviews was how little the interviewees even talked about Coalition forces.[16] US tactics did not address the strategic vulnerability of Christian life in Mosul. The insurgents moved from indiscriminate violence to highly discriminate violence. The insurgents could easily identify Christians and target them in personal ways in order to extort them, kill them, or drive them out. At the core of this lopsided battle was a tremendous information asymmetry between the US forces and the anti-state forces.

In terms of the framework, Christians had a preference for remaining at the 0 position. Some members did work for the US forces as translators, but some of these Christians were assassinated. Moving to +3, or even +1, could be dangerous. Christians did not form self-defense militias. R1 said this is against Christian principles—based on their reading of the Bible, their long-standing policy was always to "render under Caesar the things that are Caesar's." It may be more likely that there was simply little social basis for mobilization. Christians did not have any tribal organization, nor did they have coherent networks of ex-Baathists. Life at the 0 position became more and more constrained. Christians confined their life to the neighborhood and then the home. When threats became personal, and when those individually targeted threats came from an anonymous source, the emotion of fear helped drive many of Mosul's Christians to flee the city to the KRG.

In Mosul, Christians became aware of the power and tactics of Islamist militants. This experience would shape future considerations. Undoubtedly, Assyrians in the Nineveh Plains knew the situation of Christians in nearby Mosul and used that information to assess their options, which leads us into the next section.

18.4. Limited Moves Toward Militia Formation: The Formation of Self-Defense in Qaraqosh

Minority-group political leaders and figures have a range of choices in deciding whether and how to mobilize their populations in armed groups. First, they can simply try to stay neutral and not mobilize at all. Second, they can encourage their members to individually join an existing armed force in hopes of winning favor with that group but choose not to form an armed group based on their minority identity. Third, they can mobilize their own identity-based militia. If the third option is taken, other choices follow. Given likely political, social, and geographic differences within the minority group, how broad should the organization be? For instance, if minority X is under threat, should a leader try to form a large, but possibly less coherent, force incorporating all X's? Or is it better, or even more possible, to form a militia based on "X's in region A" or "X's of this political persuasion"? Mobilizing as a sub-group may allow the group to more coherently pursue political goals or spoils, but will also reduce the minority's leverage and increase its vulnerability. There is also the question of the militia's alliance possibilities. Given the obvious lack of numbers and power of most minority groups, there is a need to ally with a larger force for protection and resources. If there are multiple possible large alliance partners, which is the best choice?

The Christians in Mosul proper basically chose neutrality. Targeted killings and kidnappings drove them out of the city. Events played out differently in the Nineveh Plains city of Qaraqosh. The Christian city of Qaraqosh (also called al-Hamdaniyah) lay 20 miles away from Mosul and is the largest city in the Nineveh Plains.[17] A few basic demographic and political factors were central in structuring decision-making. First, Qaraqosh is monolithically Christian and has an identity as a Christian city. Many residents traveled the highway to Mosul, but in their daily lives Qaraqosh appears to have been a tight-knit self-sufficient community and not just a far suburb of Mosul. This fact seems to have created a sense of safety—why would Muslims wish to interfere in or take over a city with no Muslims? A second factor is the geographic location of Qaraqosh. Although officially in Nineveh Province, Qaraqosh lies on the border between Kurdish and Iraqi Government control (see Figure 18.2). The security forces of every group—Iraqi National Police, the Peshmerga, the Coalition forces—were operating in Qaraqosh during the 2003–2011 period.

In the summer of 2004 a Christian self-defense force was organized in Qaraqosh. According to officers in the force, the prime mover was a Catholic priest from the town, Father Louis Qassab. In response to growing violence in Mosul, he contacted Sarkis Aghajan, an Assyrian politician who was the Minister of Finance and the Economy in the KRG from 1999 to 2006. Sarkis Aghajan contacted a trusted lieutenant who had served in the Iraqi Army, Fuad Arab (a *nom de guerre*), to organize a force of Christians in Qaraqosh. Fuad Arab in turn recruited a network of Christians who were formerly members of the Iraqi Army and Intelligence Services to be the backbone of the group, and who in turn recruited younger Christians to be the junior soldiers. In effect, two powerful "first actors" were able to set off processes within two interlinked subgroups to build a self-defense (+2) organization.

From an initial force of just 245, the group (sometimes called "Church Guards") expanded to over 1,000 members who patrolled and manned checkpoints inside the city. While at first they were unarmed, they were eventually provided Kalashnikov rifles by the KRG. The decision to align with the Kurds, rather than the Iraqi state, was likely influenced by the strong ties that Sarkis Aghajan had with the Barzani family: there are reports that he grew up with Nechirvan Barzani, the prime minister and nephew of President Massoud Barzani, in Iran (Timmerman, 2008), and that he was even in the Kurdish Peshmerga (Courtois, 2009). Also, at this time the Kurds no doubt seemed more powerful, and more proximate, than the Iraqi state. From an early stage, the force, dubbed the Nineveh Plains Guards (NPG), received material aid from the KRG.

There were efforts, led by the Assyrian Democratic Movement (ADM), to establish an alternative to the KRG-sponsored NPG. There were proposals in both 2005 and 2006 to build a large US-trained and sponsored formal police force to operate across the Nineveh Plains.[18] In most accounts, the proposal was blocked by the Nineveh Governorate's Provincial Council through KRG/KDP pressure.[19] In any event, the US policy, in actual practice, was to leave Qaraqosh in the hands of the Kurds. During this time period, the Kurds were the natural government of the region.

In sum, while violence raged in nearby Mosul, Christian leaders in Qaraqosh made a decision to organize their own militia and to tie that militia to the most powerful political actor in the region—the KRG and its Peshmerga. Other leaders in smaller and less vulnerable localities chose not to mobilize an armed force. Some organizations chafed at Kurdish influence in the Nineveh Plains and called for the US forces to step in and create a Nineveh regional police force, but these efforts were in vain. Also, there were few successful local efforts to set up local police forces independent of Kurdish connections or US mentorship.[20]

Despite the creation of a local force, Qaraqosh could not stay immune from the tribulations of the region. As in Mosul, the world became smaller for the Christians in Qaraqosh. In June 2007, unidentified assailants kidnapped seven students and one teacher on their bus ride back from Mosul University. The families paid $250,000 for their return. The kidnappers were successful despite the fact buses were running in caravans between Qaraqosh and Mosul for safety purposes (Lamprecht, 2007). As one Qaraqosh priest stated, "First of all, they were kidnapped for money, and secondly, they were kidnapped because they are Christians. The minorities are vulnerable" (Lamprecht, 2007). Members of the focus group did not actually know who committed the crime. They knew about the extreme violence taking place in Mosul, and certainly knew about the number of Christian religious figures killed and kidnapped in Mosul, but they had felt safe in Qaraqosh. After the bus kidnapping, residents limited their movement and stopped going to Mosul. This event was traumatic, but nothing could prepare the population of the Nineveh Plains for what ISIS would bring.

18.5. The Coming of ISIS: The Decline of Kurdish Political Authority and the Development of Multiple Christian Militias

After taking Mosul in June 2014, ISIS paused briefly before heading east in August.[21] The ISIS invasion into the Nineveh Plains was marked by its rapidity and brutality. Residents of Qaraqosh were shocked when they were told to evacuate. They believed that the Kurds would protect them. In the account of one Qaraqosh resident:

> A ticker tape notice on the satellite news channels flashed a warning, said one resident, Wissam Isaac. Mr Isaac worked at a Qaraqosh primary school, teaching the local Syriac language, derived from Aramaic, the language of Christ. The ticker said the Kurdish army, the Peshmerga, on whom the residents had been relying for their defence, was withdrawing. "Before this time, no-one really thought we would have to leave," he said. "We trusted the Peshmerga. They said they would save us. They stayed in our houses. We can't believe this has happened." (Spencer, 2014)

The only major Christian town that wasn't overrun by ISIS was Al-Qosh in the north. The loss of confidence in the Kurds was a political earthquake for the Christians of the Nineveh Plains. While there had always been multiple political parties competing for influence in the region, before 2014 these differences did not result in the creation of competing armed groups.

The shock of Kurdish flight was accompanied by the uncertainty of not knowing which of the two competing authority structures would become the eventual liberators of the Nineveh Plains. In effect, there were now two polities competing to be the legitimate government in the Nineveh Plains: the KRG and the Government of Iraq (GOI). Neither was strong enough, or had the will, to displace the other. More importantly here, neither was strong enough to dictate terms to the Christian population or Christian organizations. Both the KRG and the GOI could produce mobile (+3) and local (+2) security forces. For Christian actors able to command an organization, the choice set broadened and contained the following realistic options:

1. Do not mobilize at all, stay neutral.
2. Mobilize and integrate with the existing Christian militia (NPG), creating one large Christian force.
3. Mobilize a new group and ally closely with the KRG.
4. Mobilize a new group and ally closely with the GOI.
5. Mobilize an independent group and occupy a position between the KRG and GOI.

As it happened, organizations covered the entire range of these options. Table 18.1 summarizes the key details about each militia. Some Christians stayed in the NPG, as the closest to the Kurds. Some split from the NPG and formed their own groups, but still maintained ties with the Kurds: these groups included Dwekh Nawsha, the Ninevah Plains Protection Units (NPU), and the Ninevah Plains Forces (NPF). Finally, one force, the Babylon Brigades, completely broke with the Kurds and threw in with the central government as members of the Popular Mobilization Forces. We cover each of these choices in turn.

Remaining closest to the KRG were the members of the NPG, now officially members of the Zeravani force under the KRG's Ministry of the Interior. As such they received salaries and training from the KRG: in the summer of 2016, Cancian visited them as they trained in Bnaslawa with members of the Western Coalition; 500 of them were receiving a two-week refresher course and morale seemed high. Abu Hakem (a *nom de guerre*), their commander, claimed that they had 2,600 members but planned to expand to 3,500. While they had hoped to return to Bartella and Qaraqosh during the then upcoming Mosul operation, these areas wound up being liberated by the central government. In the summer

Table 18.1 The Position of Multiple Christian Militias

Militia	Location of Origin	Alignment	Political Party Affiliation
Nineveh Plains Guards (NPG)	Qaraqosh	Kurdistan Regional Government (KRG): now officially members of the Zeravani forces	Chaldean Syriac Assyrian Popular Council
Dwekh Nawsha	Tel Skuf	KRG	Assyrian Patriotic Party (APP)
Nineveh Plains Protection Units (NPU)	al-Qosh	Between KRG and Government of Iraq (GOI), leaning GOI	Assyrian Democratic Movement (ADM)
Nineveh Plains Forces (NPF)		Between KRG and GOI, leaning GOI	Bet-Nahrain Democratic Party
Babylon Brigade		GOI: integrated into Popular Mobilization Units (PMF)	Unclear

of 2017 during a return visit, the NPG continued to guard refugee camps for Christians in the KRG and hoped that a change in political fortunes would allow them to return to their homes.

While the NPG was once the only Christian militia, since ISIS's attack, others have arisen. The factors behind their rise and alliances are complex, as the descriptions below certainly illustrate. They include geography, relationship to the Kurds, and their affiliations with political parties. The major point here is that with the ISIS war, combined with the fragmentation of the Iraqi security system, political actors across the region could mobilize and bargain for resources.

Dwekh Nawsha (which means "self-sacrifice" in Syriac) formed in the Tel Skuf area as the armed force of the Assyrian Patriotic Party (APP). While they are separate from the NPG, they still coordinated their operations with the Kurds, who supplied them with arms and equipment. The APP has had a tumultuous relationship with the KRG: while they were initially founded in Baghdad during the 1970s, they had to move their operations to the KRG for security reasons during Saddam's rule. Despite periodic disputes with the KRG (Assyrian International News Agency, 1999), they have mostly been safe and welcomed. The location of their base of support in Tel Askuf also helps to explain their allegiance: being closer to the Kurdish strongholds, it was more likely to be eventually liberated by the Kurds, which they eventually were.

As ISIS was rolled back by the Peshmerga, Dwekh Nawsha was able to move southward to provide rear area security. After the Tel Skuf operation, Dwekh Nawsha was put in charge of security in the town of Baqofa (CBS News, 2014). In March 2016, a US Navy Seal was killed while helping Peshmerga and Dwekh Nawsha forces defend themselves from an ISIS attack (BBC, 2016). When Batnaya was liberated during the Mosul Operation, Dwekh Nawsha was able to move there to provide security, although unfortunately it had mostly been destroyed by the fighting. On a visit to the KRG-administered border at Batnaya, Cancian noted no Dwekh Nawsha soldiers. The town was still largely destroyed, with very few residents living there. They continued to occupy some rear areas of that sector but had no frontline responsibility.

Indicating a more complete disillusionment with the Kurds than in the case of Dwekh Nawsha, two other groups not only split with the KRG-sanctioned NPG but also aligned themselves with Baghdad. The Ninevah Plains Protection Units (NPU) were formed in Al-Qosh by the Assyrian Democratic Movement (ADM). The ADM has tried to balance between Erbil and Baghdad; before the most recent elections, it had two seats in the Kurdistan Parliament and two seats in the Council of Representatives of Iraq. However, the ADM fell out with the KRG during the war against ISIS. The ADM leveraged its connections in the United States[22] to pressure to the KRG to give the NPU military facilities, while the NPU received funding from the central government (Kruczek, 2021, p. 114).

After 2014 they formed the NPU in Al Qosh, which had never fallen to ISIS and which was under the control of Peshmerga. A lack of faith in the ability of the Kurds to defend them was an explicit motivating factor. "If someone from Zakho [a town in northwest Iraqi-Kurdistan] protects the Nineveh plain, he doesn't care, because his family is somewhere else. Local people have family here, and they will not run," said Youra Moosa, an NPU political coordinator in an interview (Cetti-Roberts, 2015). After the towns of Bartella and Qaraqosh were liberated by the Iraqi Army in the Mosul Operation, despite initial attempts by the KRG to block their movement (Assyria TV, 2016), the NPU was able to move down and become the official security forces for those areas, along with another force, the Ninevah Plains Forces (NPF).

The NPF has a similar story to the NPU. It is affiliated with the Bet-Nahrain Democratic Party, which held a seat in the KRG's parliament (before the 2013 election). Similar to the NPU, it was based in the KRG's area of control and initially was supported by the Peshmerga (Hussein, 2016). During the Mosul Operation, they moved into Bartella, where they have coexisted with the NPU (France24, 2016).

Finally, the greatest break with the KRG came from the Babylon Brigade, who joined the central government's Popular Mobilization Forces (PMF). Led by Rayan al-Kildani, it is unclear what political party, if any, they are affiliated with. Even a BBC correspondent who visited their Baghdad headquarters in 2016 was "not sure how seriously to take Kildani," and implied that he believed them to have joined for the generous salaries (Bennett-Jones, 2016). It is alleged that they were sponsored by the Iranian Badr Organization (Hanna and Kruczek, 2020; Rudaw, 2021).

This proliferation of armed forces has inevitably increased hitherto latent rivalries within the Christian community. Patriarch Louis Sako, the head of the Chaldean Catholic Church in Baghdad, has spoken out against the formation of any Christian militias (West, 2016). Despite an accord in October 2016 to unify all Christian forces (Assyrian International News Agency, 2016), divisions have deepened. On July 15, 2017, clashes broke out between the NPU and the Babylon Brigade in Qaraqosh. After a brief skirmish, the Babylon Brigade members were expelled and, according to a TV station associated with the NPU's political party, the Babylon Brigade was forbidden from returning to Qaraqosh (Assyria TV, 2017). Each of the Christian forces occupied a separate area of the Nineveh Plains, with no ability to move between them.

In summary, five significant Christian militias emerged in the Nineveh Plains in the post-ISIS period. All of these organizations were armed and local (+2). As indicated in Figure 18.3, in their political alignment, these groups covered the range of options, one continuing its close relationship with the KRG, one deciding to align with the GOI and PMF, and three others positioning themselves to varying degrees between the KRG and GOI.

What accounts for this diverse range of militias? The NPG had formed earlier, had a close relationship with the KRG, and likely wanted to sustain that momentum. In the cases of Dwekh Nawsha, the NPU, and the NPF, established political parties decided to form their own militias rather than join with the NPG or try to establish a broader Christian umbrella force. With the Babylon Brigades, the promise of GOI resources appeared to be the driving force. On the whole, the story is one of a fragmented and weak state providing opportunities for political leaders to form or sustain small militias by taking up positions between the KRG and GOI. It is the nature of the system, rather than any specific group qualities, that explains the positions and distribution of groups.

18.6. Conclusions and Implications for Policy

First, after becoming direct victims of violence, no Christian groups chose neutrality. Unsurprisingly, the actual experience of violence spurs mobilization, even if the abstract threat of violence may not. Second, Christians fought in Christian militias rather than integrating into larger forces. Their militias were locally based and focused on local defense. As in much of the rest of Iraq, militia formation was mobilized along group and territorial lines. Third, in the presence of two competing potential hegemons, minority group leaders envisioned strategies that might provide both resources and autonomy. Political agendas that had lay dormant could now find life. Much as states in the Cold War period developed strategies of non-alignment between the two superpowers, minority group factions in the Nineveh Plains could mobilize organizations and

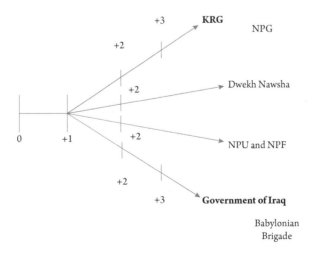

Figure 18.3. Positioning of Christian militias between KRG and Government of Iraq.

militias and position them between the GOI and the KRG. It remains to be seen whether the resulting fragmentation of the Christian minority will lead to less overall leverage and greater vulnerability in the medium and long term.

The fractured state of the Christians of Iraq does present a dilemma to US policymakers. The largest armed group, the NPG, maintains ties to the KRG, but Christian opinion on the Kurds seems to be divided. Many members of the Iraqi Christian diaspora despise the Kurds due to their complicity with massacres of Christians in the early half of the 20th century; this historic animosity, however, contrasts with the fact that since 2003 the Christians have been more secure in Kurdish areas than in the south. The diaspora's preferred solution of founding a separate Nineveh Plains region, moreover, does not seem to have the support of many Iraqi Christians who still live in the country. Many Christians are worried about encroachment by the Shabaks, a Shiite religious minority who have joined the PMF (Hanna and Kruczek, 2020, p. 10). The fundamental problem of geography, that the Nineveh Plains lie on the border of the Kurds and the Arabs, will be the primary obstacle to a solution. US policymakers who want to help the Christians will have to untangle a knot of complicated relationships and dynamics to restore Christian security. Time is not on their side. There is a very real risk that, without a satisfactory long-term solution, the Christians of Iraq will go the way of the Jews: a once vibrant community consigned to the pages of history.

The Kurdistan Regional Government Revisited

Death, War, Machinations, and Little Change

19.1. Introduction

Chapter 14 covered the Kurdistan Regional Government (KRG) up to 2011, the point of US withdrawal. This chapter takes the story forward to analyze the evolution of Kurdish politics in the period from 2011 until the time of writing. The chapter again concentrates on KRG security institutions.

To recall, Chapter 14 ended with a reworking of the spectrum concept at the center of our analytical framework (see Figure 19.1 which repeats Figure 14.1 from Chapter 14 here). This reworking was necessary because there was not a single set of +2 and +3 level forces in the KRG region, but three sets. Despite the trappings of being a de facto state, the KRG is an autonomous region within the Iraqi state. That state legally defends Iraq's border through its army and other security institutions (+3). As discussed at length below, the Iraqi government also fielded units in the disputed territories lying outside the boundaries of the KRG. Both major political parties in the KRG fielded their own +3 forces (Peshmerga) as well as paramilitaries (Zerevani), intelligence services (KDP's Parastin and PUK's Zanyari), and internal security services (Asayish). These organizations often operated in localities and are best thought of as +2 in terms of the framework.

Although by Weberian terms, all of these security forces were "legitimate" means of state violence, their overlapping missions and competing objectives were problematic both in terms of preventing violence (rather than helping foment it) and in terms of state-building (generating a system of divided political hegemony, producing streams of spoils, and preventing transparency). At multiple junctures, the United States pushed reforms to integrate the Kurdistan

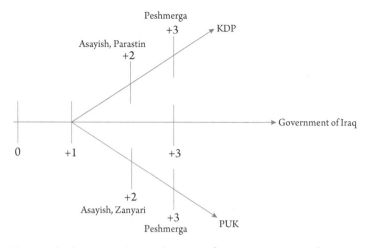

Figure 19.1. Multiple security forces of the KRG (reprint of Figure 14.1).

Democratic Party (KDP) and Patriotic Union of Kurdistan (PUK) Peshmerga forces to create a single chain of command, common standards, and overall de-politicization. The United States also hoped that the professionalized KRG Peshmerga could be better and more thoroughly coordinated with the forces of the Government of Iraq (GOI) along lines of its "One Iraq" policy. These reforms could help build a more coherent de facto KRG state and better integrate the KRG with the de jure Iraqi central state. These reforms would help manage the Kurd/Arab cleavage and work to erode the KDP/PUK cleavage.

But things did not work out that way. This chapter will outline the proposed reform attempts for the Peshmerga and other KRG security entities in both the 2011–2014 pre-ISIS war period and the period following. It will describe how KDP and PUK political organs were entangled with security institutions in ways that impeded change. The chapter will show how the flow of the ISIS war led to the 2017 independence referendum and its consequences, especially as witnessed in the disputed territories. Finally, it will come back to the general question of state-building failure in the KRG.

The conclusion to the chapter will note a remarkable phenomenon: although the KRG and its security forces experienced significant casualties in the anti-ISIS war, the overall political situation after the 2017 referendum in the KRG was still similar to that a decade earlier. The KRG retained its almost complete autonomy in the KRG proper, the status of the disputed territories was still unresolved despite the GOI's increased power in those lands, and the KDP and PUK still formed the basis of an existing master cleavage in KRG society. Despite the war and violence, reforms and referendums, change in the KRG was hard to come by.

19.2. Building the State through Professionalized and Integrated Security Forces: Attempts at Reform, 2010–2013

The KRG Parliament passed laws mandating the unification of the Peshmerga in 2007, but the process itself did not begin until 2010.[1] The United States pushed the process along by offering equipment and training to units joining integrated brigades. The goal was the creation of four new integrated brigades each year for three years (to be joined by two brigades that had been under Iraqi command until 2011). Each of these 14 brigades would have equal numbers of KDP and PUK members, as well as equal numbers of commanders. If the commander was a KDP member, the deputy commander would be from the PUK. The Ministry of the Peshmerga, not the KDP or PUK political party, would be in direct control of the brigade and would also pay salaries.

When I met with Jafer Mustafa Ali, the head of the Ministry of the Peshmerga, in June 2013, he played up these integration efforts.[2] He was pleased that 12 brigades had been integrated all the way to the platoon level at that time. He also emphasized that all Peshmerga were receiving the same training. In a nod to the building of a Weberian state, Jafer Mustafa Ali proclaimed there were now no armed forces outside the law. He also explained that the KRG and Iraqi constitutions were not in conflict in terms of ultimate authority. The Peshmerga would join Iraqi forces only in defending Iraqi borders against foreign invasion. Peshmerga would never enter intra-Arab violence. He expressed his regret that some brigades had not been united.

While the numbers of integrated units were impressive, the numbers of Peshmerga not in integrated units remained far higher. Integrated Peshmerga units would come to number 42,000.[3] In comparison, the PUK's Peshmerga, called Unit 70, would come to total at least 48,000, while the KDP's Unit 80 came to total 50,000 fighters. In addition, the KDP paramilitary force would come to number 60,000 by 2021, while the PUK's DEF grew to nearly 30,000 (Bakr, 2021, p. 10).

The KRG also made efforts to reform and integrate other KDP and PUK security and intelligence organs. The two intelligence services—the KDP's Parastin and the PUK's Zanyari—were officially merged in 2010. In 2011, the KRG Parliament established the Kurdistan Regional Security Council (KRSC) to coordinate counterterrorism and the handling of prisoners across different jurisdictions. The KRSC also was tasked with combining the Parastin and Zanyari, as well as the integration and management of the KDP and PUK Asayish.

Ironically, while in theory the KRSC's purpose was to integrate Kurdish security organs, its actual setup went on to create new parallel party-controlled institutions (Bakr, 2021, p. 11). Within the KRSC, the Kurdistan Regional Security Institution (KRSI) was set up. As the name suggests, the KRSI's duties were not unlike those of the KRSC. These dual organs, predictably, possessed their own party-based chains of command. The KRSI reported to the prime minister, who happened to be PUK, while the KRSC was under the president, who was KDP. Of course, both lines received funding from the KRG government. Here was another example of the creation of institutional hybrids. Connection to the official government provided party security institutions with legitimacy while also supporting them with financial largesse. The KRSC and KRSI budgets accounted for over 7% of the total KRG budget in 2013 (Bakr, 2021, p. 11). Most tellingly perhaps, the KRSC never had an official meeting (Bakr, 2021, p. 11). There was no need. The KDP benefited financially and politically without any actual meetings.

19.3. Why the Process of Integration and Professionalization of KDP and PUK Security Forces Was Always an Uphill Battle: Illustrative Stories from Fieldwork

Reform would always be difficult not only from political party imperatives, but also because the intelligence agencies have been historically headed by members of the Barzani or Talabani families (Gunter, 1996). It is one thing to reform an organization. It is another to reform a fusion of organization/party/family.

Nechirvan Barzani headed the Parastin in the 1990s. Masrour Barzani headed the Parastin before heading the KRSC. Masrour was the eldest son of Masoud Barzani, the president of the KRG. Masoud's second son, Mansour, is a general, as is Masoud's brother, Wajy. Masoud's nephew, Nechirvan Barzani, was the prime minister of the KRG. Another of Masoud's nephews, Sirwan, owned Korek Telecom, one of Iraq's three cell phone companies. All of these Barzanis are part of the legacy of Mullah Mustafa Barzani, the founding leader of the KDP and indisputably the leading figure in modern Iraqi Kurdish politics.[4]

The PUK also functions along family and network lines, although perhaps less overrepresented in the security services. Lahur Talabani, Jalal Talabani's nephew, headed the Zanyari, the intelligence organ of the PUK. Bafel Talabani, one of Jalal Talabani's sons, assumed the PUK presidency in 2021. Qubad Talabani, another of Jalal Talabani's sons, has served as deputy prime minister of the KRG from 2014 and up to the time of writing (2023). Latif Rashid, the president of Iraq as of 2023, was Jalal Talabani's brother-in-law. Latif Rashid and

Jalal Talabani married sisters, thus Rashid is PUK leader Bafel Talabani's uncle through marriage.

Reform is also complicated because the very roles and missions of these party-controlled and family-ruled security institutions are opaque. For instance, the functions of the Asayish are ill-defined in practice, often indistinguishable from those of the police. The Asayish are responsible for internal security in the KRG and are usually compared to the US FBI. However, the Asayish also operate checkpoints and control movement across the KRG and the disputed territories; they administer residency permits; they control border crossings; they have connections to oil production. Given their murky mission and ubiquity, it is hardly surprising that numerous human rights watchdogs criticize their actions.[5] Given this murky existence, reform is difficult because the very nature of the organization to be reformed is amorphous.

Doing fieldwork in this environment can be confusing and enlightening at the same time. To relate one experience from the summer of 2013: at 8 p.m. on one summer night, my "fixer" (combination of guide, translator, and security specialist) and one of his friends were invited to a gathering outside of Erbil and invited me to come along. After being picked up at the Chwar Chra hotel, we proceeded outside of the city, turning off on an obscure, unpaved road. The road was lined by high barbed wire fences. We passed one security checkpoint and proceeded another half mile to a gate manned by four machine-gun-wielding guards. We drove through and parked alongside a small flock of high-priced SUVs and German luxury cars. As we left the vehicle, we were greeted by our host and led to a small, perfectly leveled off grass plateau overlooking the lights of Erbil in the distance. A circle of white chairs was arranged on the lawn for guests to socialize. A large nearby table would soon be filled by impressive platters of kabobs and fish. There was also a dessert table and a second buffet table. There was no alcohol. I joined the circle of men (there were only men) sitting on the white chairs. The guests included several Syrian Kurds, three Egyptians, one mysterious Canadian seeking to do business in the KRG, one Lebanese gentleman, a Kurdish member of the Iraqi Parliament, another Kurd who worked with US defense contractors (who told me he had been to Las Vegas 14 times for conventions related to security contracting; he claimed not to drink or gamble but does like the food in Vegas), and one Kurd working with US NGOs. The food was more than plentiful and a sufficient number of servants always made certain that the pitchers of yogurt were full. It certainly would not be odd in any political system, and not in the United States, for such a group of foreigners, legislators, contractors, and NGO representatives to find themselves together for an elaborate private dinner. But who has the wealth and connections to host these events? In this case, the host was a retired high official of the Asayish; he was also closely aligned with the KDP.

A second example: one day my fixer arranged an interview with Masrour Barzani, then head of the KRSC. The interview itself went long (two and one-half hours) and smoothly, and on the whole predictably. Chancellor Barzani laid out Kurdish grievances without disclosing much about the Kurdish security apparatus itself. Soon after my meeting with Masrour Barzani, my interpreter informed me that we had another appointment for 10 p.m. in Masif Salahaddin or Pirmam, a small town outside of Erbil. There were some people there who wanted to talk with me. Pirmam/Salahaddin is home to the KDP Political Bureau and functions much like a KDP company town/headquarters. From 10 to midnight I had a conversation with two men who I assumed to be in the KRG security apparatus. I only knew them by first names. Much of the discussion was about the United States' lack of appreciation for the Kurds and their friendship.[6] Taking into consideration the whole of day, I had to ask to whom had I been talking—the KDP, the Barzanis, or the government of the KRG? Was it even possible to distinguish among them?

The fusion of family/state/party/security is admittedly rather common in many states of the developing world, especially in the Middle East. But the experiences I am describing took place in 2013—10 years after the US invasion and US efforts to professionalize and integrate security institutions. In the expectation of many in the United States, and not just the neo-conservatives, the toppling of the dictator combined with US and Western aid and tutelage, could possibly create democratic, transparent, and accountable government that could serve as an example, if not a "democratic domino," for the entire region. The place with the highest chance of success for this project would seem to be the KRG. The persistence of the impediments to state-building and reform in the KRG is testimony to the power and pervasiveness of Iraqi Kurdistan's underlying cleavage structure. The way the war against ISIS played out would provide even stronger evidence of the power of not only the PUK/KDP cleavage, but as seen in the disputed territories, the Kurdish/Arab cleavage as well.

19.4. The Third Iraq War: Potential Changes

The preceding section of this chapter identified forces able to prevent change. Despite official reform efforts, up to 2014, Kurdish security institutions still reflected the ability of Kurds to retain their autonomy versus the central state and the KDP and PUK to preserve their respective realms of control and maintain the balance between the two parties.

But if there is any great engine of change, it is war, especially an important and brutal war. The Islamic state was an existential threat to the KRG. After taking Mosul in mid-July 2014, the Islamic State marched toward Erbil, the capital of the KRG. The war itself was long, difficult, and involved significant numbers of casualties. Due to the rudimentary training and equipment of many Peshmerga units, Kurds moved to reverse ISIS gains in a deliberate manner. After taking a village or town back from ISIS, Kurdish forces would reinforce the defenses of that territory with extensive berms before moving back on the offensive. Kurdish forces took many casualties along the way—1,800 dead, 9,000 wounded, and 60 missing during the war (Palani et al., 2019).

In commonsense terms, one might have expected the ISIS war to have worked to erode the KDP/PUK cleavage. Urgent threats are known to unify groups against a common enemy. The KDP and PUK could have put aside their differences to confront and unite in order to create the most efficient force possible to confront the ISIS menace. Indeed, the Kurdish Parliament passed a decree on July 23, 2014, that all Kurdish forces should be unified within six months. The war could have possibly changed the nature of the Arab/Kurdish cleavage, especially with the collapse of the GOI Army in Mosul. Because of early Peshmerga losses and reliance on the United States for intelligence and weapons during the fight, the war might have produced leverage for the United States in its push for security organization reforms in the KRG. But there was to be little change. A review of the unfolding of the war shows why.

19.4.1. The Disputed Territories: Background and the Conduct of the ISIS War

As the bulk of the ISIS war was fought in the disputed territories, some background is necessary before the chapter returns to the just mentioned issues.[7] The disputed territories refer to those lands that are claimed by both the central Government of Iraq (GOI) and the KRG. The territories include sections of five governorates in the north of Iraq: Nineveh (sometimes spelled Ninewa or Ninawa), Erbil (Arbil or Irbil), Kirkuk, Saladin (Salah Ad-Din), and Diyala.[8] Sections of these governorates, while historically considered part of Kurdistan by Kurds, have been or continue to be under central government control.

In the wake of the 1991 uprising and the establishment of the no-fly zone by the United States, the borders of the KRG were set at the "Green Line," which excluded many areas with important Kurdish populations, most notably the city of Kirkuk (which is sometimes called "The Kurdish Jerusalem").[9] US forces took control of Kirkuk from Kurdish forces two days after the Kurds seized the city. The strains on US forces and the relatively nonviolent situation in the disputed territories, however, meant that the United States often outsourced security in many of the disputed territories to the Kurds; the Peshmerga therefore retained a presence in Kirkuk and other areas that were not governed by the KRG.

The legal status of the disputed territories was left unresolved during the American presence. Article 140 of the new Iraqi Constitution (promulgated in 2005) provided for a three-step process in resolving the legal status of the disputed territories: normalization (undoing Arabization programs), a census, and a referendum, all of which were to take place by December 31, 2007.[10] Controversies continued over whether "de-Arabization" would be a forced or a voluntary process (Senanayake, 2007). With the official "normalization" process effectively stillborn, many Kurds returned to Kirkuk outside of a legal settlement, which stoked the fears of other ethnicities (Anderson and Stansfield, 2009, p. 159). Tensions between the KRG and the GOI over the disputed territories only increased following the failure to hold the constitutionally mandated referendum. Disputes over whether the KRG was getting its proper share of the budget escalated. Figure 19.2 provides a map illustrating Kurdish presence and the location of the disputed territories.

The invasion of ISIS shattered the rough and ambiguous balance between Kurdish and Arab forces in the disputed territories. With the ISIS attack on Mosul on June 10, 2014, the Iraqi Army disintegrated. As Iraqi government forces abandoned portions of the disputed territories ahead of ISIS's advance,

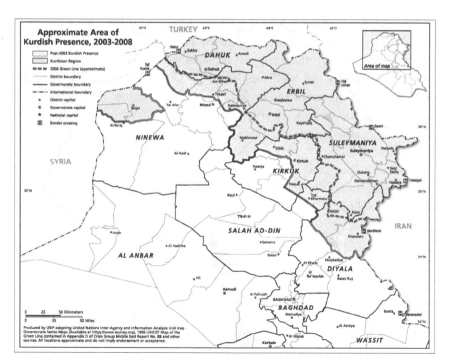

Figure 19.2. Approximate area of Kurdish presence, 2003–2008.
Source: Sean Kane, "Iraq's Disputed Territories: A View of the Political Horizon and Implications for U.S. Policy," Map 2, page 10. United States Institute of Peace, 2011.

the Peshmerga filled the void and gained control of many areas,[11] including the entire city of Kirkuk (Arango et al., 2014; Cancian, 2016). In June 2014, Barzani sent Peshmerga into Kirkuk, the Mosul Plain, Tuz Khrumatu, and other areas in the disputed territories. In a relatively short time period, Kurds had established dominance over a significant new amount of land area.

While the Kurdish Peshmerga advanced and controlled new territories during the upheaval of the ISIS war, the KDP and PUK Asayish dominated the security realm at local levels in Kirkuk and other parts of the disputed territories (International Crisis Group, June 15, 2020). Due to its better training and funding, the Asayish took over many of the roles of the local police (International Crisis Group, June 15, 2020, p. 6).

19.4.2. The Impact of the ISIS War on Master Cleavages

Despite the length and intensity of the war, the conflict did not work to integrate KDP and PUK forces. In the actual conduct of the war, KDP security forces and PUK forces fought mainly on separate fronts. The frontline was divided into eight sectors, four each belonging to KDP and PUK commanders. The PUK's Unit 70 and the KDP's Unit 80 generally served in zones corresponding to the political affiliation of the zone commander. Both Unit 70 and Unit 80 had their own "support" brigades, which manage the Peshmerga's tanks (T-55s) and artillery (Soviet D-30s); these support brigades were shuffled around to sectors of the fronts where the KRG was launching offensives. While the KDP and PUK directed their armor and artillery to desired positions, the state Ministry of Peshmerga had no tanks or artillery of its own. The two political parties and their security arms ran the war much more than the state.

The war did little to erode the Kurdish-Arab cleavage. Kurds remained unquestionably dominant in their own de facto state. For most of the war, Kurds fought along fronts far north of those involving Iraqi government forces and connected militias. Accordingly, there was little friction between the two sides.[12] Moreover, Kurdish leaders signed a Memorandum of Understanding that addressed territorial and demographic issues (Kurd Net, 2016). In sum, Kurds fought the war diligently, if not spectacularly. They also tried to avoid political conflicts with allies throughout most of the war.

While the war did not challenge Kurdish dominance in the KRG proper, it did change what had been a relatively balanced relationship between Kurds and Arabs in the disputed territories. The Kurds held the territory and had put down "facts on the ground." In 2014, Barzani provocatively claimed that Article 140 "has been implemented and completed for us" (Palani et al., 2019). The fight against ISIS had further weakened a weak central government of Iraq. The war in Syria and the continued fight against ISIS there would prevent major powers from opposing a major move.

Kurds clearly recognized Arab opposition to Kurdish moves in Kirkuk and the disputed territories. But now many Kurds believed they had the upper hand in forcing a resolution. Arabs had shown their incompetence and lack of will to defend territory in the north.[13] After Kurds displayed their loyalty and fighting prowess in the ant-ISIS war, the United States would not oppose Kurdish moves to maintain their dominant position in the disputed territories. The United States and other powers "owed" the Kurds after their sacrifice and political obedience during the ISIS fight. Such overconfidence certainly contributed to the decision to go ahead with the independence referendum.[14]

Meanwhile, in terms of the KDP/PUK cleavage, the KDP found itself in an improved position versus the PUK. Given the success and sacrifice of the war effort, the Barzanis and the KDP could feed off the nationalistic response to the war effort. KDP momentum was also helped by the decline of opposition leadership. In addition to Jalal Talabani's decline (he first fell ill in 2012 and died October 3, 2017), Gorran's leader, Nawshirwan Mustafa, also fell ill, eventually dying in May 2017.

19.5. The 2017 Independence Referendum and Its Aftermath

Changing balances of power favored the Kurds in general and the KDP specifically. In the disputed territories, Kurds were now in a favorable position versus Baghdad. The KDP was in an improved position to consolidate gains against the PUK. In 2015, Masoud Barzani was given a new lease on political life after a political deadlock in the KRG resulted in the extension of Barzani's presidency, a result many deemed illegal. As a result, Masoud Barzani had one last chance to push for the independence referendum he had long sought. While a successful referendum for Kurdish independence could not immediately provide independence, it could conserve Kurdish gains in the disputed territories and also establish the clear dominance of the KDP as the strongest representative of the Kurdish nation (O'Driscoll and Baser, 2019).

Even before the liberation of Mosul was complete, Masoud Barzani announced that the KRG would hold a referendum for independence.[15] In the run-up to the referendum, some Western observers thought Barzani was bluffing to gain concessions from the US and Baghdad. The proposed referendum was almost universally opposed by the international community. In addition to the United States, the KRG's neighbors in Turkey, Iran, and the Iraqi Arabs all

vehemently opposed the move. Only Israel was in support. Despite this opposition and other danger signals, the referendum went ahead on September
25, 2017. Importantly, the referendum was called by Barzani and not the KRG
Parliament. Also, residents in the disputed territories could vote. There was no
campaign in the KRG against independence, just a muted "No for Now" movement (led by the head of the opposition New Generation Movement party).
The referendum resulted in 93% backing independence with 72% turnout.
These numbers obscure the low turnout numbers in the PUK-dominated areas.
Turnout in Suleymaniyah was 50%, in Halabja province 54%, and only 30% in
the non-Kurdish areas of Kirkuk province. Gorran and the Kurdistan Islamic
Group (Komal) boycotted the vote, along with a section of the PUK (O'Driscoll
and Baser 2019).

Backlash against the referendum was not long in coming. For a few weeks,
tension built while Iraqi government forces gathered around Kirkuk. Politically,
the PUK was threatened by the referendum because the vote was so decisive
and it was sponsored by the Barzanis. At the same time, Jalal Talabani (who had
been debilitated following a stroke) finally died. Qassim Sulaimani went to the
funeral, and seems to have brokered an agreement between the Talabanis and
the Iraqi Popular Mobilization Forces (PMF) to hand over control of Kirkuk to
the latter.

On October 16, the PUK's special forces units withdrew from their positions
and allowed the Iraqi forces into the disputed territories. These Iraqi forces included the state-controlled forces of the Iraqi Army, the Federal Police, and the
CTS. They were accompanied by the non-state PMF and were helped at local
levels by predominately Arab local actors and police forces. In the aftermath
of the takeover, PMF forces connected with Badr, AAH, Kataib Hezbollah,
and other Shia militias patrolled areas in the south and west of the Kirkuk
Governorate. Sunni tribal PMF units operated in Hawija. In sum, a combination
of Arab forces, aided by PUK Kurdish collaboration, dislodged KDP Kurdish
forces from the disputed territories.

It would seem that Masoud Barzani did not fully understand how the referendum and actions in the disputed territories would trigger resentment, if not
humiliation, for Iraqi Arabs.[16] Between 2003 and 2014, Kurdish forces had gradually taken control of more and more territory in the disputed territories. With
the collapse of the Iraqi Army, Kurds took control over new sizable areas. The
referendum, and cooperation from the PUK, set up a counter move. The Iraqi
central state forces proceeded to roll back Kurdish control to the 2003 lines. For
some commentators, the response of the central government was entirely predictable. There was no chance that Prime Minister al-Abadi could choose to do
nothing in the face of the referendum and maintain power in Baghdad.

The actions related to the other cleavage—KDP/PUK—also seem predictable in hindsight. Christine McCaffray van den Toorn (2017) summarized the effect of the referendum on long-standing intra-Kurdish political divisions:

> The referendum has revealed and deepened the divisions among Kurdish leaders and elites and their growing rejection of—or at least compliance with—KDP unilateralism. If self-determination, the Kurds' long-held dream, cannot bring them together, then little else will. Political rivalry among the main Kurdish parties and the schisms it has created have become so deep that even the one issue that has always united the Kurds "now divides us." (van den Toorn, 2017)

While political divisions deepened, the PUK gained relative to the KDP. In the disputed territories, KDP security forces, including their Asayish, pulled out of Kirkuk and other areas. The PUK Asayish, on the other hand, remained in Kirkuk and continued to function and cooperate with federal authorities (International Crisis Group report, 2020, p. 10). In the KRG proper, the PUK did not suffer electorally for their actions. In the 2018 KRG parliamentary election, the KDP gained 7 seats (to 45 out of 111) and the PUK gained 3 (to 21). Gorran lost 12 seats, making the PUK once again the second-largest party.[17]

In overall political terms, the KDP had no choice but to recognize that the former political duopoly was back in place, at least in the short term. While the KDP could have governed alone based on its control of the 11 seats set aside for ethnic and religious minorities, they chose to continue to rule in consultation with the PUK. Institutional momentum drove the two sides together despite their bitter differences.

19.6. The Persistence and Power of Cleavage Structures I: Arabs/Kurds

In June 2013, I interviewed Najmaldin Karim, the governor of the Kirkuk Governate, in his office. He was clear that the US policy of maintaining the status quo in Kirkuk was unfortunate. He saw Kirkuk as part of Iraqi Kurdistan, although Kirkuk would need to have a special political status due to its history and demography. Four years after my visit, members of Iraqi government security forces sat in Karim's office, on October 16, 2017, in the aftermath of the referendum.[18] A picture appeared in the *BBC News* with an image of the joy of status reversal. For years, Kurds had gradually taken over parts of the disputed territories. Kurds held an independence referendum that included Kirkuk and disputed territories in a symbolic move of dominance in the region. Now Arab soldiers gloated and took selfies in the office of the Kurdish governor.

While Kurdish autonomy and de facto statehood was a fact for the KRG proper, the ethnic hierarchy in the disputed territories had been in flux, with changes favoring the Kurds. Al-Abadi's hugely popular move to send in Iraqi government forces, along with PMF militias, was as much an emotional reaction as a calculated political move. The importance of Kirkuk and the disputed territories went far beyond control of oil, despite the obvious importance of that resource. Dr. Mohammed Ihsan, who had served as minister for extra-regional affairs during 2005–2011, explained to me that previous efforts at "Arabization" of the disputed territories were not simply about Arab rights or politics. The process was about taking control of the very soil. Once the very dirt is no longer Kurdish dirt, then the territory of the Kurds becomes reduced and Kurds become increasingly marginalized. Arabization involved changing the origins of people. The process would establish that Kurds were from some other piece of dirt, from some other land, and not rightfully Iraqis.

Other Kurdish interviewees supported the emotional and symbolic importance of Kirkuk. I heard, especially from Kurdish security forces, that the Arabs (both Sunnis and Shia) will never give up Kirkuk to the Kurds and that the Kurds will never give up Kirkuk to the Arabs. For the Kurds, the Arab control of a historically Kurdish land is a symbol of unjust dominance and humiliation. For the Arabs, giving in to the Kurds in Kirkuk is also a humiliation. I asked whether the Kurds could trade oil profits for incorporation of Kirkuk. They answered that the identity politics would never allow such a trade-off, even one that on the face of it seems win-win from an outsider's perspective. They emphasized that there is no splitting of Sunni versus Shia on this issue; it is an Arab view.[19]

19.7. The Persistence and Power of Cleavage Structures II: KDP/PUK

The BBC picture of gloating Arab soldiers in Kirkuk Governor Najmaldin Karim's office mentioned just above illustrates a second theme of this chapter: the persistence of the KDP/PUK cleavage. As can be seen in the photograph, a large picture of Jalal Talabani, the leader and founder of the PUK, hangs on the wall behind Karim's desk. As mentioned earlier, Governor Karim himself was a close personal friend of Talabani. Now the PUK made deals that allowed Arabs to gloat while sitting in symbolic Kurdish offices. Apparently, for members of KDP and PUK it is sometimes better to make deals with Arabs than give in to the other Kurdish party. In 1995, the PUK leveled charges of treason against the KDP for collaboration with the Saddam regime and its temporary alliance to rebalance the KDP/PUK relationship. In 2017, in a turnabout, members of the KDP sometimes leveled charges of treason against the PUK for their "deal" with the al-Abadi administration.[20]

While the PUK and KDP are not averse to aligning with Arabs to gain the upper hand in their political struggle, both parties primarily sustained their power through their parallel sets of security forces.[21] As previously discussed in this chapter, the KDP and PUK maintain non-transparent control over the politics and control of non-transparent security organs such as the Asayish.

Toward the end of the war against ISIS, Western powers took another crack at the integration of Kurdish security forces. The United States, United Kingdom, and Germany all pushed for reform of the Peshmerga, with their efforts creating a plan entitled "Peshmerga of the Future" to be guided by a Reform Directorate within the Ministry of Peshmerga Affairs (Aziz and Cottey, 2021, pp. 235–237). This plan contained 35 detailed proposals, with the first point being the development of a common security strategy. Tellingly, even after several years of effort, there was no agreement on this fundamental issue. Apparently, the KDP and PUK could not agree on who were the Kurd's primary enemies and allies (Aziz and Cottey, 2021, p. 236). This outcome could have been predicted. The document and process could not have been expected to change the essential culture of the Peshmerga. As Aziz and Cottey (2021, p. 237) state:

> The "Peshmerga of the Future" reform plan does not really address the existing practice and culture of the Peshmerga. . . . First, most Peshmerga are members of either the KDP or the PUK and their ultimate loyalty is to their political party, not to the putative state that is the KRG. Second, the heroic-mythic status of the Peshmerga in Iraqi Kurdish society means that they are viewed as outside or above the kinds of rules and constraints which govern militaries in most modern states. Addressing these issues requires deep changes at individual, organizational and cultural levels.

Perhaps an even bigger problem was that the reform plan only addressed the Peshmerga, not the lower-level security organs. While not holding the mythic status of the Peshmerga, the intelligence agencies and the Asayish continued to perpetuate party dominance over Kurdish society through a myriad of less visible capacities. In a 2018 interview, Kurdish Parliament member Ali Hama Saleh stated, "The KDP has its own counter-terrorism forces and the same applies to the PUK. This is the case within the security [Asayish] forces; you cannot find one security officer within the security forces who does not belong to one of each ruling party" (Hama, 2019). The KDP has always controlled the Asayish in the Erbil and Dohuk Governorates in the KDP-dominated north of the KRG, while the PUK controlled the service in Suleymaniyah.

A report by Mera Jasm Bakr (2021) identifies the pervasive power and practices of these organizations. In effect, the KDP and PUK use these internal security forces to:

1. Develop revenues: The KDP and PUK use their respective Asayish units to control border access and custom revenues. Revenues from smuggling operations go to the parties.
2. Control jobs and enhance patronage: Almost 42% of the KRG's public sector funding went to the Ministry of the Interior, Ministry of Peshmerga, or the Kurdistan Regions Interior Forces. Of that figure, 57% went to the interior forces, as reported in 2020 (Bakr, 2021, p. 15).
3. Develop leadership: The KDP's Masrour Barzani and the PUK's Lahur Sheikh Jangi both held leadership positions in the interior security forces.
4. Enhance the reach of the party: The Asayish mission includes control of residency permits and the gathering of information down to local levels.

As Bakr concludes, "The MoI (Ministry of the Interior) is widely regarded as the most powerful ministry in the KRG. It is perceived as 'the real government' or 'a smaller KRG' due to its expansive power under KRI (Kurdistan Region of Iraq) law to regulate most aspects of security and administration within the KRI proper" (Bakr, 2021, p. 8).

19.8. Conclusions

This book has focused on violence and state-building. In the post-2011 period, the Kurdish regions of Iraq certainly saw violence. That violence upset the previous balance between the Kurds and the Arabs, and between the KDP and PUK. That lack of clarity led to Barzani's referendum gambit and the GOI's and the PUK's backlash.

With the end of violence, a sense of clarity returned to cleavage structures. The KRG was still a de facto state and still retained its institutional power and presence within the GOI. Rolling back Kurdish gains in the disputed territories, Baghdad gained clear dominance in the disputed territories. There was one change introducing complexity, if not affecting overall balance between Kurds and Arabs. In the disputed territories, PMF units also operated at the +2 level, taking over security duties in regions outside Kirkuk. In effect, the security field became even more crowded and complicated in Iraq's north.

The KDP was clearly the dominant political force in the KRG, but as the aftermath of the referendum showed, it still had to contend with the PUK. In the

2013–2017 period, it appeared that the KDP/PUK duopoly was on the way out. The course of events, though, returned the system to near its previous state. With Barzani's referendum move backfiring, the PUK re-established its position as the primary organized force in opposition to the KDP.

In sum, despite violence and political shifts, the nature of the cleavage system in Iraqi Kurdistan retained most of its basic qualities. There was also little change in state-building. The nature of the referendum and its outcome provided evidence that the KRG was not acting as a unified state. The borders of Iraqi Kurdistan remained undefined; the family networks and patronage systems underlying the two major parties survived; the path toward transparency, the end of corruption, and the broadening of democracy remained distant goals.

The KDP and PUK control of non-transparent security organs was a major factor in the lack of progress toward a more coherent state. The KDP and PUK retained control over their Peshmerga forces in the form of Unit 70 and Unit 80. Both parties kept control, often through family or personal networks, over their +2 Asayish, Parastin (KDP), and Zanyari (PUK) units, and used these security resources as a source of non-transparent power and patronage. As mentioned earlier, these party-controlled organs siphoned off state revenues, doled out state-funded jobs to party faithful, became a source of power for state leaders, and helped extend party control down to local levels. In sum, control of security forces, both at the +2 and +3 levels, created what is often termed a "deep state." As this chapter has shown, even the existential threat from ISIS war could not change the basic structure, division, and organization of these security forces. When the Islamic State came to the KRG's doorstep, these party-led forces largely operated along their old lines.

The integration of the KDP and PUK security forces would have been a major step in the erosion of the KDP/PUK cleavage. The success of integration might have led to a more professionalized and capable KRG security force with a single chain of command, common standards in recruitment and training, and better coordination among units and across agencies. Reform and unification would also have prevented the KDP and PUK from using their separate security forces for political purposes. In sum, integration would have strengthened the KRG in terms of state-building. This result was never close to being achieved.

It is not only the KDP and PUK who wished to block reform. The Arab-dominated government in Baghdad benefits from a divided Peshmerga. Without unity, Kurds are hindered from pushing for independence. Without unity, Kurds present a lesser challenge in the disputed territories (Aziz and Cottey, 2019). Likewise, both neighboring Turkey and Iran are more able to use divide-and-rule strategies in the current situation. In comparison, the United States never had enough "skin in the game" to force reform.

The Decline of Dominance Politics?

*Emotions and Institutions in Iraq 10 Years after
the 2011 US Withdrawal*

20.1. Introduction

As argued from the beginning pages of this book, the evolution and course of violence and state-building in Iraq have been deeply affected by the politics and perception of group dominance. At both the mass and elite levels, a desire to end unjust subordination for one's group, or to prevent the dominance of an opposing group, has shaped the evolution of the conflict in Iraq. As emphasized in Chapter 1, not every conflict is pervaded by dominance concerns. But Iraq was such a conflict. Although some argue that sectarian identity was not pervasive in pre-2003 Iraq, major Shia organizations existed both in exile (SCIRI/Badr and Dawa) and within Iraq (Sadrists) which were poised to change the status of Shia in the country. Many, perhaps even most, Sunnis may not have thought of themselves in sectarian terms before 2003. They could no longer do so in the face of elections, militia violence by both Sunni and Shia organizations, and the state capture by Shia political organizations. It was impossible to be "non-sectarian" during the civil war in Baghdad and its ethnic cleansing. In the north, Kurds did not forget previous genocidal campaigns, fought to retain their autonomy, and dreamed of independence. Kirkuk and the "disputed territories" endured as contested sites. Even beyond the US withdrawal in 2011, Sunnis protested against perceived persecution of the Maliki regime and Kurds held an independence referendum.

Yet, the saliency of dominance concerns in any given political environment will likely ebb or flow over time, or even ebb forever. In 2023, at the time of writing, there were good reasons to believe that sectarianism in Iraq was in rapid decline. Accordingly, the sectarian struggles over who is "on top" and the fears of being dominated by the "other" are waning. How should we assess the possibility of a decline in perception and saliency of sectarianism and related dominance concerns in Iraq? The analytical framework connected dominance concerns to specific mechanisms (see Chapter 3, section 3.4). A brief review of those mechanisms helps examine how recent Iraqi history may have diminished their power. To preview the conclusion, recent Iraqi history has worked to reduce the power of the emotional mechanisms connected to dominance concerns, even if Iraq's political system continues to operate along sectarian lines in terms of parties and patronage.

20.2. Mechanisms and Dominance

Concerns of group dominance/subordination can involve rational choice mechanisms. For instance, if a system is built on group-based patronage, pushing for the dominance of one's own group in the political-social system could help provide higher chances of a job and other types of personal gain.[1] Furthermore, the interaction of rational choice and social norm mechanisms can also sustain dominance concerns. It may become "common sense" that one's own group should be dominant in a hierarchy; such may be the case in a caste system. In this situation, behaving outside of the social norms (not supporting one's own group sufficiently, or reaching out and cooperating with subordinate groups, or simply pursuing equality for all individuals) could bring about a sanction from one's in-group members.

The mechanisms-based approach from the framework puts most weight on emotional mechanisms, specifically resentment, anger, and humiliation. Clearly, dominance concerns and the emotion of resentment are inextricably linked. To recall from Chapter 3, resentment forms from perceptions of unjust group subordination. The emotion has been found to be most intense after a status reversal. In that case, individuals are motivated to do whatever is necessary, often including violence, to re-establish their group's previous dominant position. Resentment skews information collection, driving the individual to see group subordination at every turn. As covered extensively in the empirical chapters, resentment motivated the majority Shia to finally establish their "rightful" place in Iraq. The emotion gave life to the latent Sunni group identity and drove key actions such as the 2005 election boycott and anti-Maliki demonstrations following the US withdrawal. Resentment may have driven active and tacit support for ISIS and other Sunni armed groups.

The emotion of anger also can work to perpetuate the saliency of group identity. While resentment is based on perceptions of group status, anger stems from perceptions of an opposing group's actions. The intensity of anger is based on the clarity of those perceptions. If an individual becomes certain that an opposing group attacked or diminished his or her group for a blameworthy reason, anger produces a desire for revenge. Anger heightens stereotyping and the tendency to assign harmful intent to the opposing group. The emotion lowers risk estimates of the costs of retaliation. Anger was the fuel for the spiraling violence after the Samarra Shrine bombing. When two sides carry out vengeance against each other over a period of time, sectarian lines are clear and the battle for dominance central.

Humiliation is a third powerful emotion connected to dominance. As stated earlier, humiliation is a combination of resentment and anger. Humiliation occurs when an individual believes that an identifiable perpetrator has purposely and unjustly acted to reduce his or her status to a low or powerless position. The humiliated individual cannot help but feel the brunt force of group subordination every day.

As laid out in the theory chapters, and as seen in the empirical chapters, these three emotions were important in moving individuals to specific nodes on the spectrum of roles. Resentment is a widespread force importantly driving individuals to sustained nonviolent support roles of insurgents (-1); anger can motivate movement and sustain action and membership in armed militias (-2); humiliation, more speculatively, drove many young men into the ranks of militant groups (-3) to fight the day-to-day sense of unjust dominance of Western occupiers.

20.3. The Decline of Resentment, Anger, and Humiliation in Iraq

As argued in the empirical chapters, in the battle over status hierarchy in Iraq, Shia prevailed. As of 2023, Baghdad is essentially a Shia-ruled city. As far as security forces are concerned, the Popular Mobilization Forces (PMF), largely Shia controlled, are as powerful as the Iraqi state security forces. Politically, Shia parties and organizations are dominant. ISIS has been defeated and there is no Sunni-led insurgent organization on the horizon.

Both Shia and Sunni had to come to grips with a transformed Iraqi society. With this adjustment, the beliefs and cognitions sustaining resentment dissipated. Shia could no longer claim subordination, neither in political terms nor in the day-to-day experiences of authority in Iraq. In the wake of ISIS, Sunni resentment had burnt out. Most Sunnis were coming to accept minority status. There would be no reversal of status. Sunni citizens had experienced devastation at the hands of the Sunni Islamic State. They were done, for the foreseeable future, with Sunni militant groups. As laid out in the previous chapter, the Kurd/Arab status hierarchy issues regained clarity. While Kurds faced no challenge in the KRG proper, the Government of Iraq had clearly come to dominate the situation in the disputed territories. Both Sunnis and Kurds realized that Shia would from now on control the political agenda. Sunnis and Kurds were now "rent-seekers" in a country "owned" by Shia.

The conditions for anger also declined. The emotion of anger depends upon a clear perception of a perpetrator and motive. During a sectarian civil war, actions are clear and usually violent. The perpetrators of those actions, as well as their motives, are also clear and obviously sectarian. By 2019, the battles in Iraq had become mainly political. Instead of combat zones there were protest sites. Many of the actors were youth who came of age well after the 2003 invasion. An International Crisis Group report written in 2016 argued that Iraq's "Generation 2000"—young Iraqis whose formative years came after 2003—did not possess the same clear ideas of group as their elders. While hardly dismissing sectarian thinking, the report argues, "The millennial generation has an amorphous identity: depending on the context and who seeks to mobilize them, ethnic sectarian, tribal, locally geographic or other sub-national identity will emerge as the avenue through which members see and challenge the establishment" (International Crisis Group, 2016).

Tracing the development of the Iraqi protests, the perception of "perpetrator" and motive became far less clear than a decade earlier. While some protests occurred as part of the Arab Spring events of 2011, the events in Basra in 2015 over electricity shortages were a turning point. Further protests in Baghdad in Tahrir Square railed against corruption. The issues were moving away from identity and more and more toward poor governance and corruption. The "perpetrator" and focus of anger became the government, sometimes specifically the prime minister.

The Tishreen protests starting in October 2019 were the largest and most sustained of the post-invasion period. With ISIS defeated, the demonstrators focused their wrath against an ineffective and corrupt government unable to produce jobs or public services such as electricity. The repressive actions of the Iraqi government now gave a new sense of "perpetrator" and "victim." At first, government action was not deadly. State forces used water hoses to disperse graduate students in September 2019 (Alshamary, December 2020). But violence escalated. Hundreds of protesters were killed or injured in October and November 2019. Many activists were assassinated. By the end of November 2019, Prime Minister al-Mahdi resigned under pressure from both the public and Grand Ayatollah Sistani. Demonstrations continued into 2020, as did violence, much of it carried out by paramilitary groups. The Sadrists first supported the protests but then some of them turned against protestors, especially in the south (Alshamary, February 2020). Grand Ayatollah Sistani acknowledged the grievances of protestors but called for mediation and reform.

If present at all, sectarianism was muted during these protests. While protestors wished to reduce or eliminate the power of PMF militias and diminish Iranian influence, they saw "perpetrators" in terms of an amorphous and unresponsive government or specific individual leaders regardless of their sect. The system itself needed major reform, not just the removal of certain actors. While Iraq's electoral rules and embedded patronage system favored the continued election of sectarian political parties, it was the broader system that was to blame. Protestors rejected Iran's interference in Iraq politics, but also railed against the United States and its assassination of Qassem Soleimani.

Anger pushes individuals to specify a perpetrator and carry out vengeance. In these protests, the perpetrators have been amorphous and multiple. The emotion behind these protests may not be anger at all, but rather rage. Similar to frustration-aggression theory, under rage multiple problems and perpetrators create an impulse to lash out more generally. There is no clear specific perpetrator to become the target of revenge. In any event, the emotions underlying the protests did not heighten saliency of sect or a specific sectarian perpetrator acting mainly on sectarian motivations. At a basic level, Iraq's political situation had become too complex to produce the clear cognitive antecedents that produce intense anger and revenge.

Finally, with the withdrawal of the West, a major source of perceived humiliation and powerlessness was no longer present. It is true that outside powers infringed on Iraq's sovereignty, with many of its major policies influenced by Iran and the United States. However, the day-to-day highly visible presence of outsiders was gone. Shia volunteers answered the call to fight ISIS, and their bravery and sacrifice in the victorious war against Daesh were sources of pride and power, even if the US-built Iraqi Army with its collapse was not.

In sum, the emotions driving movement and mobilization into roles on the negative side of the spectrum had dissipated by the late 2010s. Resentments against an opposing identity group had faded; anger against ethnically distinct others diffused or transformed into a diffuse rage; the Western symbols of outside supremacy were gone. Without these motivating emotional mechanisms in place, movement into the anti-state violent nodes would be less likely. Much of the population was frustrated with their government, likely to remain in a neutral (0) position on the spectrum either out of exhaustion or in term of "wait and see."[2]

Despite this declining power of emotional mechanisms, it was hardly the end of sectarianism in Iraq. Iraq's very institutions perpetuated group identity in ways that would be difficult to change. Sectarian dominance became a muted political force, rather than a violent one, but it persisted nonetheless.

20.4. Iraqi Institutions and Dominance

Although not explicitly stated by the US occupiers, Iraq's political system as of 2020 was quasi-consociational.[3] Consociational systems are defined by a few core features:[4] (1) ethnic parties; (2) a grand coalition that includes all major ethnic parties; (3) segmental autonomy; (4) ethnic quotas of civil service appointments; and (5) minority veto (red lines). Although not always said in plain terms, the main focus of consociationalism is the prevention of dominance and provocation. It is a system that aims to diminish the power of emotion.

Above all, it is a system designed to blunt blatant subordination. Consociationalism's principles of proportionality are designed to prevent resentment. No major ethnic group can be excluded in this system. All groups are included in political spoils and control a subscribed amount of resources. Due to the minority veto, groups can protect themselves from any dominating actions of opponents. It is also a system designed to prevent anger. As a system built on elite bargaining, consociationalism intends to avoid triggering emotions in the general population by keeping negotiations discreet; its elite bargaining and red lines prevent aggressive, public actions that might provoke anger; its segmental nature provides autonomy, self-control, and group dignity.

Iraq is not a straightforward consociational system. Its constitution does not require proportionality; after elections, the largest bloc can form a government and exclude opponents from power; in Iraq, the executive holds sweeping powers beyond what any consociational system would recommend. As pointed out by longtime Iraqi analyst Toby Dodge (2020), despite some constitutional elements, Iraq practices an informal system of consociationalism that is guided more by unwritten norms than legal constraints. Along the lines of grand coalition, all significant actors accept that the prime minister will be Shia, the president a Kurd, and the speaker of the house Sunni. Through the *muhasasa* system, an informal quota system guides distribution of jobs to parties and ethnic groups. Ethnic or sect-based organizations and parties possess significant and bargained control over certain state ministries. Through mutual agreement, if tacit, Badr predominates in the Ministry of the Interior, while Sunnis hold more positions in the Ministry of Defense. Many Shia groups hold power through corresponding PMF Shia militias. Kurds maintain autonomy while always holding the Iraqi presidency.

This system contains several elements that work to prevent dominance. There is little incentive to totally exclude any ethnic group. The distribution of security positions within this system blunts fears of violence. Multiple veto players block any rapid change. Moreover, the system is stable at its base. As a patronage system, ethnically based parties are able to distribute jobs to their members. The system activates a widespread rational choice mechanism—an individual is likely to identify with and support the ethnic organization providing a job. While the public employee payroll is completely bloated and allows incompetents to buy jobs, it also provides a social-political continuity.

Unfortunately, this system has led to poor governance in Iraq. While the system prevents dominance, it does not lead to coherent rule. As summarized in their analysis of Iraq, Ezzeddine and Noun (2020, p. 13) write:

> All parties continuously deploy all possible means to keep the others in check via control over public resources and public institutions while jealously guarding their own prerogatives and social autonomy. Paralysis is both a feature and an output of the political system, in which self-preservation is valued beyond the need for reform. Sectarian mechanisms are valued above all else because it allows established parties continuous control over political processes and enables resource appropriation. The logic of sectarian-based power sharing produces lengthy political stalemates almost by default and makes long-term decision making a Herculean task.

In interactions with policymakers, Dodge (2020, p. 148) discovered that the deal-making involved in establishing a ruling coalition involved horse-trading over 800 senior civil service jobs. Needless to say, this is not a meritocratic system geared toward preventing corruption. While John Nagle (2020) believes that consociationalism was necessary to establish order after civil war, he writes that the system became self-sustaining long after it had become dysfunctional. He writes that Iraqi consociationalism is "dead but dominant," and lives on as "zombie power-sharing."

The following chapter will discuss this phenomenon in more detail in the context of state-building failure. Suffice it to say that in the near term, and despite protests, no social revolution is on the horizon. It is difficult to assess the depth of Iraq's civil society. Analyst Marsin Alshamary holds that the protests helped build a new type of civil society—*tansiqiyyat*, defined by spontaneous groupings formed at the urban protest sites (Alshamary, December 2020). Those fitting the *tansiqiyyat* typology form a new type of activist class distinguished by pragmatism and the desire to work within the existing political system. While this new form of civil society may be able to adapt to changing conditions better than the traditional civil society organizations such as unions and cultural organizations, its vulnerability to regime repression and lack of formal organization do not threaten to change the political structure in the short or medium term. It is difficult to imagine how these non-sectarian civil society groups will ever come to displace the existing sectarian parties and their patronage power.

Furthermore, neither of the two most important external actors, Iran or the United States, has an incentive to help generate change in the Iraqi system. Iran's primary goal is to never allow Iraq to militarily threaten Iran again. Iran is content with a weak but stable Shia-controlled state on its border. For many reasons, the United States is unlikely to make any move away from the status quo. US domestic politics also puts a brake on more US involvement in Iraq, or any other extensive military intervention for that matter. Political progress in Iraq is "good enough." As previously seen in Chapter 16, Operation Inherent Resolve helped develop a relatively cheap way to deal with a major insurgent/terrorist organization.

In sum, on the one hand the Iraqi system no longer generates the types of identity-related emotional mechanisms to drive individuals toward violence-producing roles. On the other hand, the sectarian-based consensus political system produces consistent material incentives and repressive power to sustain a largely dysfunctional government. Its consociational nature provides a way to avoid the sectarian violence while failing to make necessary major reforms.

Without either strong internal or external forces pushing for change, what is the future of Iraq? One way to try to answer this question is to look at a similar type of system—post-civil-war Lebanon.

20.5. Lebanon as the Future of Iraq?

While this book is not about the Middle East more generally, let alone Lebanon, any discussion of Iraq's future almost always brings in an Iraq-Lebanon comparison. In his tome *Aftermath: Following the Bloodshed of America's Wars in the Muslim World*, Nir Rosen's first section is entitled "The Lebanonization of Iraq" (Rosen, 2010). There have been many scholarly articles assessing the comparison (Saouli, 2019). In the summer of 2018 I made a short research trip to Lebanon to try to understand the social and political dynamics that sustain Lebanon's troubled system and to assess the relevance of those dynamics for Iraq.[5] When I visited Baghdad in May of 2022, I asked policymakers and academics about the Lebanese path and whether Iraq was likely to follow it. Most had been asked this question before; for some, many times. It is a comparison that Iraqis make and are asked to make.

There are many differences between Lebanon and Iraq. Lebanon's system constitutionally enshrines ratios of Christians to Muslims in Parliament; Lebanon has no majority sect, in contrast to Iraq's Shia majority; Lebanon's Palestinian issues have no parallel in Iraq; Lebanon's economy is free market, service oriented, and based on rents from remittances and foreign investment, while Iraq's is dominated by oil revenues. Yet, there are many similarities as well.

These similarities bring up many of the key arguments of this book—changes in ethnic hierarchy, sectarian civil war, the importance of organizations, and the development of hybrid actors. After a brief review of these common characteristics, we can return to the question of whether Lebanon provides a possible, if not likely, path for Iraq's future.

20.5.1. The Ascendance of Shia Organizations

In both systems, Shia went from a subordinate group to a ruling one. In Lebanon, poor Shia were concentrated in the south of Lebanon and were badly served by the state. In 1974, a social movement arose—"Movement of the Deprived"— to address poverty. Although multi-confessional when it started, the movement naturally evolved into a Shia political force. Hussein Husseini, one of the founders of the Movement of the Deprived, said that religious/sectarian organizations needed to come and provide services simply because the state did not.[6] That movement eventually generated a militia—Amal—which became an important force in the 1975–1990 Lebanese civil war. The formation of Iranian-connected Hezbollah produced more armed Shia power.

In Iraq, Shia citizens also had an impoverished base that formed a foundation for mobilization. Shia were concentrated in northeast Baghdad, in what would become known as Sadr City. During the Saddam era, the Sadrists created social organizations based in that neighborhood to make up for the paucity of state services. After the US invasion, Shia militias grew out of the Sadrist base, the largest begin the Jaysh al-Mahdi (JAM). In both Iraq and Lebanon, a large, poor Shia population with a concentrated base first formed institutions to compensate for poor government services, and these organizations helped lead to powerful militias.

20.5.2. Weak States with Hybrid Actors

The state in Lebanon is very weak, if not practically nonexistent. Hezbollah not only became the most powerful political actor in Lebanon, its hybrid nature blurs the very lines between state and society. In 2018, I took a tour through the Hezbollah-controlled Beirut neighborhood of Dahieh which generated a powerful insight: Hezbollah is not really a non-state actor. By 2018, it *was* the state in many areas, or at least it was seamlessly interconnected with the state. I heard stories about how Hezbollah members identified criminals and drug dealers in the neighborhood and then turned them into the state for official prosecution.[7] The sectarian group and the Lebanese state had established a division of labor. Both State Police and Hezbollah checkpoints dotted the neighborhood with little observable friction. Other respondents made the point that the Lebanese state has come to rely on Hezbollah, and its Iranian subsidies, to compensate for the state's inability to provide jobs and social services.[8] Building on its Shia base, Hezbollah became not only the strongest armed force in Lebanon, but also a major provider of jobs and social services.[9]

Through its battles, and ability to fight Israel to a stalemate, Hezbollah has gained a reputation for competency and sacrifice, something the government lacks.[10] In short, the Lebanese have come to accept Shia/Hezbollah spheres of influence.[11] There is no evidence that this relationship will end anytime soon, despite the massive protests of 2020. There is no inevitable state drive to remove non-state sectarian actors from day-to-day governance. As the most powerful politico-military organization in Lebanon, Hezbollah can play divide-and-rule politics, and engage in selective assassinations, to maintain its position.[12]

In Iraq, the Shia Sadrists have also taken on usual state functions in social welfare and adjudication. The Sadrist parties have sought to control the state ministries most directly involved with social welfare. Similar to Hezbollah, the PMF gained respect through their fighting abilities. The PMF, like Hezbollah, is a major hybrid actor. While the 2021 elections may have shown the limits of PMF-connected political parties nationally, the PMF political power in some cities and regions remained undeniable as of 2023.

20.5.3. Formerly Dominant Groups Have Been Forced to Come to Grips with Status Change

While Hezbollah has become the most powerful political force in Lebanon, Christians, the former historically dominant group in Lebanon, needed to come to grips with their declining position. Most glaringly, I met few Christians who accept basic demographic estimates of their actual numbers.[13] Several of these Christians seem to exhibit wishful thinking about the future of Iran and Hezbollah. They believe that Iran is in danger of imminent collapse and will take down a totally dependent Hezbollah with it.[14] They also possess, in my view, an exaggerated sense of Western loyalty and an overestimation of the West's needs or desires to stay engaged in the region. The Christians I met were not going to integrate into some common Lebanese identity. Most already had one foot out of the country.

In Iraq, Sunnis have been forced to come to group with their reduced status position. I have argued above that they may have done so, especially after invasion and the defeat of Sunni ISIS. But in both Lebanon and Iraq, the process of status change seems irreversible.

20.5.4. The Lack of a Nation-State Identity

Almost everyone I spoke with denied that there was a common Lebanese identity or a sense of Lebanese nationalism. Two aspects produced commonalities: the

Arab language and dislike of Israel. But these are hardly the basis of any unique identity. Most Christians feel a connection with Europe more than with other Lebanese; Sunnis are tied to Syria. There is not a common history book and there are too many internal disputes. There may be some superficial sense of being Lebanese at an elite level.[15] One respondent did mention that there must be something there because after they emigrate Lebanese tend to gather in their new countries across communal lines.[16]

Whether Iraq possesses a strong national identity is an open question. While there may be a strong desire by many Iraqis to control their own affairs, there is not currently a positive common narrative about the past or the way forward. There does not seem to be a common "imagined community."

20.5.5. Coming Back to the Question

Lebanon witnessed the ascension of Shias, a decline of Christians, the take-over of state functions by sectarian actors, and the development of hybrid se-curity services—all of this occurring in a state lacking a common national identity. Lebanon experienced civil war from 1975 until 1990, finally ending with the National Reconciliation Accord, better known as the Ta'if Agreement. In the corresponding Lebanese constitution, Article 95 states, "The Chamber of Deputies . . . shall take appropriate measures to bring about the abolition of the political confessionalism according to a transitional plan." Over 30 years later, Lebanon is still controlled by a consociational and sectarian system.[17] Crises come and go, and protesters call over and over for the end of this system. Yet, the sectarian-based system has persisted.[18]

Lebanon's sect-based system has persisted for three decades despite its cor-ruption, inefficiency, and occasional disasters. It has avoided the re-emergence of long-term civil wars, at least by comparison to the 1975–1990 war (and not counting the wars involving Israel and Syria). In short, Lebanon reached a low-level equilibrium. Lebanon limped along as a sectarian-dominated, poorly governed, but somewhat stable state. Is this also the future of Iraq?

20.6. Why Iraq Will (or Won't) Follow Lebanon's Path

It would be a mistake to overdo the comparison of Lebanon and Iraq. There are many differences. Still, there is a similar overarching dynamic related to funda-mental cleavage structures. In both cases, Shia moved from a subordinate posi-tion to an equal or dominant system. In both cases, formerly dominant groups needed to come to grips with a new reality in group hierarchy. In both cases, actors have agreed on a system that mutes dominance and mitigates subordination. In both cases, hybrid security actors are powerful and tolerated. In both cases, the state is weak, as is a common national identity.

These similarities, along with the decrease in sectarian-related emotions, do provide reasons to predict that the Iraq system may continue to muddle through in a Lebanon-like way. Moving from a consensus/consociational system toward an exclusionary majoritarian system (like Britain) would involve risks. Would parties and groups excluded in one election have enough faith in the system to believe they will get a chance in another round? If not, a return to violence could not be ruled out. Also, for reasons of both security and patronage, ensconced hybrid actors have little incentive to support reform. Furthermore, but differently than Lebanon, states dependent on oil income are notorious in avoiding reform.

Some interviewees pointed out the institutional differences between the two states. In Iraq, there has been no Ta'if Accord to constitutionally enshrine a sectarian system. Others argued that the consciousness and intensity of sectarian identity has been less pronounced in Iraq.[19] Still others emphasized the differences in abilities and orientation among key actors. Many Shia interviewees foresee the decline of the Sadrists, a change that might make Iraq's political system more rational, smoother, and easier to reform. As time passes, a new generation will grow up with little connection to the period of invasion and occupation and no connection to the Sadrist Movement's founders.[20] Ammar al-Hakim stressed that Iraq will increasingly become a middle-class country, resulting in less appeal of the Sadrist's traditional message. Al-Hakim believed his Hikma Movement is primed to capture that emerging Shia middle class.

One leading politician/academic in Beirut told me he had been asked years ago whether Iraq should have its own Ta'if Accord.[21] He argued then that it was a bad idea because it would raise inflammatory issues for distribution and sustain some existing problems. However, after watching Iraq struggle for years, he might recommend it because nothing else is working. In my own view, Iraq did seem to be "muddling through" with its quasi-consociational system in March 2023. Whether that low standard will continue into the future is a difficult question.

20.7. Conclusion

The biggest difference between Lebanon and Iraq is that the United States invaded and occupied Iraq, pouring billions of dollars into state-building efforts. (In contrast, the US quickly cut its losses in Lebanon in 1983.) If the long-term consequences in these two cases bear significant similarities, what does that say about the ability of outside military intervention to design outcomes in such conflicts? Section IV of this book examines that question in detail.

SECTION IV

THE FUTURE OF AMERICAN MILITARY INTERVENTION

Chapter 21 ("Findings and Lessons") begins the final section through a review of findings gleaned from the empirical sections. It conducts this review by examining the answers to two fundamental questions pursued since the first pages of the book:

- In the contests between counterinsurgent and insurgent, what explains who wins?
- What explains the persistent weakness of the Iraqi state?

After addressing these two questions, the chapter concludes with a list of "lessons." This set of lessons is not specific to the Iraqi case. It is meant to be applied to intervention and insurgency in general. This set of general lessons forms the starting point for the remaining two chapters.

Chapter 22 considers whether US policymakers and practitioners will learn these lessons. The chapter ("Constraints on Learning") explores the organizational, political, cultural, and structural factors that could affect how those lessons might be learned, ignored, or forgotten.

Chapter 23 takes the lessons of Chapter 21, examines them in light of discussion in Chapter 22, and speculates about the future of US military intervention. It will systematically assess the possible future implementation of the five strategies (and combinations) at the heart of the book.

Given the constraints identified in Chapter 22, how will the United States envision the use of war-fighting, CHB (clear, hold, build), community mobilization, decapitation, and homogenization moving forward? The book concludes by highlighting the strengths of the analytical framework developed in Section I as a method capable of understanding fluid, violent, domestic conflicts.

Findings and Lessons

21.1. Introduction

The empirical sections have presented material supporting and illustrating the major arguments of the book. The empirical chapters also provided material for assessing our two major outcomes of interest: violence and state-building. This summary chapter will draw on the book's case studies to build toward broader theory. In doing so, we return to two general questions raised in the introductory chapter:

> In the contests between counterinsurgent and insurgent, what explains who wins?
> What explains the persistent weakness of the Iraqi state?

The chapter then proceeds to consider a list of "lessons" from the experience in Iraq. This set of lessons is meant to be general, not specific to the case of Iraq, and will serve to lead into the remaining chapters of this section.

21.2. Counterinsurgency and Violence: In the Contests between Counterinsurgent and Insurgent, What Explains Who Wins?

Any simple story of Iraq is an inaccurate one. This complexity is not surprising. Iraq is large, populous, demographically diverse, and brimming with weapons. After the invasion, Iraq experienced a brief period of relative calm, although punctuated by terrorism. There followed the emergence of insurgency, a brutal sectarian civil war, a relatively long period of gradual US withdrawal, the rekindling of Sunni resistance, the war against ISIS, and finally a problematic equilibrium. Various actors, the United States among them, had to make their way through this turbulent progression. The contest between counterinsurgent and insurgent often came down which side best made those adaptations.

21.2.1. Success by Covering the Full Range of the Spectrum of Roles (Both Counterinsurgent and Insurgent)

As a starting point, we can start with a theoretical proposition about counterinsurgent success: the more the counterinsurgent can address every node on the spectrum of roles, the more likely is success. This might be thought of as a strategy of denial. In covering the full spectrum, the counterinsurgent denies the insurgent any weak spot to attack.

As outlined by the framework, a combination of three counterinsurgency strategies can achieve this effect (see Figure 21.1). If clear, hold, build (CHB) can set off mechanisms of safety in numbers, focal points, and economic benefits, individuals might move from −1 and 0 to +1. If the counterinsurgents can institute an effective decapitation strategy, the underlying −3 networks will be destroyed. If hostile local militias (−2) can be flipped over to the government side (+2), then the state can enter antagonistic towns and neighborhoods. In effect, this combination of strategies eliminates enemies at the −1, −2, and −3 nodes while simultaneously building +1 and +2. The only remaining concern will be developing the army and other mobile state security forces.

Evidence from the cases supports this proposition. The closest the United States ever got to developing this combination of strategies was during the Surge. By 2007, the Joint Special Operations Command (JSOC) had developed sophisticated decapitation abilities and was using them across Iraq, including Baghdad. With the Awakening and the Sons of Iraq, a community mobilization strategy "flipped" thousands of former AQI allies into +2 roles. The Surge and its increase

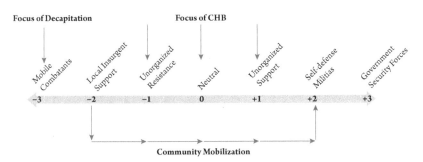

Figure 21.1. Combination of counterinsurgency strategies covering the full range of the spectrum of roles.

in troops set up local command outposts and managed not only to clear, but also to hold, many neighborhoods.

The potential for this combination is supported by Biddle et al.'s "synergy" argument. That work argued that while neither CHB nor community mobilization could produce the drastic decline in Baghdad violence seen in Figure 1.1 in Chapter 1, both could work together to leave few effective counterstrategies for insurgents.[1] While Chapter 13 presented an alternative view on the remarkable drop in violence in 2007, there is no doubt that this combination of US strategies was putting heavy pressure on insurgent forces at the time.

Other cases show US success with at least two of the three strategies working in combination. The Hawija case was divided into seven time periods (see the analysis and series of figures in Chapter 15). US forces instituted a combination of CHB and community mobilization during periods three and four. The two periods witnessed remarkably little violence (insurgent forces went underground in response, making decapitation less possible and less salient). The Ghazaliyah case during the later Surge period saw a combination of community mobilization and CHB, along with homogenization, bring violence to close to zero.

The insurgent side of the case studies also presented evidence for the power of a full-spectrum strategy—also from the insurgent side (see Figure 21.2, which repeats Figure 7.1 from Chapter 7). To recall from the case study of Sadr City, 2004–2006, the Sadrist forces managed to address the full spectrum of roles. Beyond powerful resentments driving individuals leftward on the spectrum, Shia organizations created a parallel social support system. While the United States relied on provision of material goods to drive movement to +1, Shia groups were often able to offer competing services and goods to those of the Coalition and Iraqi state. In Sadr City, long-standing social welfare organizations had been supplementing state services throughout the sanctions era. Furthermore, while

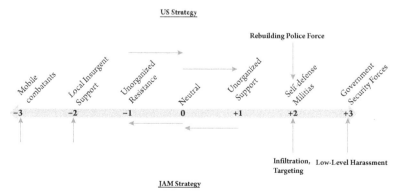

Figure 21.2. Juxtaposition of US and JAM Strategies, 2004–2006 (reprint of Figure 7.1).

the United States tried to create its own focal points through elections, Shia religious organization naturally produced effective focal points. As outlined in the Sadr City chapter, the system of Shia mosques with their coordinated Friday sermons and large gatherings efficiently produced focal points and safety in numbers. In sum, Shia and their organizations were able to trigger or take advantage of most of the mechanisms moving individuals to −1, blunting US efforts to move them rightward to +1. They were able to harness resentment, create focal points to bring out crowds, and provide goods and services on their own terms.

The Sadrists also infiltrated the local police (+2), kept up steady harassment of the US forces to keep them occupied, if not deterred from entering Sadr City, while the Jaysh al-Mahdi (JAM) developed tighter organization at −2 and −3. Their full-spectrum strategy blunted US efforts at +1 and +2 while taking advantage of the US lack of presence and action at −2 and −3. This full-spectrum strategy kept the United States at bay and allowed JAM to recover from its 2004 humiliation at the hands of the US forces. The Sadrists and JAM were the primary force in winning the Battle of Baghdad and changing the city's demography in 2005–2007.

While the full-spectrum strategy may produce success, its cost is enormous. The Sadrists could absorb those costs as they were operating from their Sadr City base and associated bases in Shula and Washash. Sustaining a surge of forces for the United States would be costly, not only in dollars, but in casualties and political capital in the homeland.

21.2.2. Insurgent Failure: Insurgent Strategies Dependent on Terrorism

Within Baghdad, for reasons outlined in Chapter 5, Sunnis did not possess a capacity for mobilization to match that of the Shia. The only strength of AQI and other similar terrorist organizations was at the −3 node. During the Shia-Sunni civil war, mobile armed fighters (−3) were coming in from outside Iraq, some willing to commit suicide bombings. The best use of this resource was in a bombing campaign against indiscriminate targets in the general population. The logic of this type of campaign was to trigger a freezing fear in the population, as well as contempt for the US occupation forces and their Iraqi allies by proving their inability to provide security (see Chapter 7). Both emotional mechanisms could work to keep the population at the 0 position. Zarqawi later sharpened the focus of the attack by hitting targets aimed at igniting violent spirals among Shia and Sunni.

While successful in setting off fear and anger, AQI's organization lacked any organic connection to local communities. It could not develop its own −2 level locally embedded cells. AQI did find local allies among Sunni −2 groups. In

Anbar, there were alliances with tribes; in Ghazaliyah, there were alliances with militias created through veterans' networks. In both of those cases, the local armed (−2) Sunni groups, unhindered by norms of reciprocity with AQI, broke off the alliance and sided with the United States. Without organic connections to local communities, there is little possibility of operating across the spectrum of roles. Emotions of anger and fear can have powerful effects, but those effects may be temporary without some type of sustaining organization and effective binding social norms.

21.2.3. Counterinsurgent Success by Neutralizing the −2 Node

Despite the AQI example, insurgents usually possess advantages against counterinsurgents at the local level. Insurgents have far better information; their threats against collaborators are often credible. In the Iraq conflict, the major −2 level actors were militias. The formation and actions of these militias took up much of this book's effort. Despite being a relatively developed and urban state, Iraq presented an environment with a high potential to trigger the mechanisms moving individuals to the −2 level. In areas with robust tribal identification, such as Anbar, social connections and norms were often able to move networks of individuals rapidly to the −2 position. In Ghazaliyah, geographically concentrated networks of veterans quickly formed multiple militias. Violent events also set off mechanisms that bolstered and sustained local armed organization. When Shia hit Sunni targets or Sunnis hit Shia, norms of honor and the emotion of anger motivated individuals to look for vehicles for retaliation, usually finding them in local armed organizations.

This discussion leads to another theoretical proposition: strategies that can neutralize the insurgent advantage at −2 are more likely to succeed. There is an additional question of the nature of "success." There are short-term successes and long-term successes; successes in reducing violence and successes in building a state.

The case studies presented cases and strategies involving neutralization efforts—the most successful case, indeed paradigmatic, being Anbar. Seen in broader context, Anbar presents a sequence of failure– success—failure. Clearly, US implementation of war-fighting and CHB was failing in 2003–2005. Then came the Awakening. With this community-mobilization strategy in place, Anbar went from a lost case to pacification. Success only lasted so long, though. With the support of local Sunni organizations, ISIS would enter a strife-filled Anbar only a few years later, igniting a conflict only ended though the region's devastation.

Having devoted an entire chapter to community mobilization in Anbar, there is no need to cover the strategy here. But it should be emphasized the US strategy involved two steps. First, the United States would broker deals with community leaders to "flip" an insurgent group from the −2 to the +2 level. After demonstrating their loyalty and competence, temporary +2 status would be transformed into permanent +2 or +3 statuses. Members of the collaborating local militia would take positions as local police officers or soldiers and officers in the Army. The second step never took place. Prime Minister Maliki did not follow through, but it is likely no Shia leader would have taken that step. They may have been right not to do so given the history and leanings of some of the members of the Awakening and Sons of Iraq. Furthermore, the United States would be gone, unable to force anyone's hand, even if it had been inclined to do so.

Anbar was not the only case of community mobilization in the book. Several case studies described instances of the first step (−2 to +2) including Ghazaliyah and Hawija. In Anbar and Ghazaliyah, community mobilization clearly led to invaluable information flows to the counterinsurgent. The strategy also removed an enemy while adding an ally. In all three cases, violence declined to low levels. In all the cases, short-term drops in violence did not prevent long-term state-building failure.

The cases also showed that community mobilization in its "flipping" form is not the only way to neutralize −2 actors. It is also possible to just make deals with local armed problematic actors. With the decentralized nature of the US military, officers down to the company level had wide latitude to deal with locals, including those armed as militias or extended networks. In the Bayaa case, company commander Wright engineered a relationship with the local "Tony Soprano" that reduced confrontations. In Hawija, US forces tolerated a "no-go zone" as a way to achieve a certain peaceful coexistence. In these cases, the costs of rooting out and taking on local armed actors outweighed the benefits. There seemed to be a tacit recognition that both sides were involved in a longer and broader game in which violent confrontation in the present had little point. Deal making, although often effective in reducing violence, is not a good way to build local government.

Another efficient way of neutralizing violence from −2 level organizations is to officially incorporate that organization into the government—the hybrid option seen in the formation of the Popular Mobilization Forces (PMF). As opposed to step 2 of the Awakening/SOI process, this alternative does not integrate individuals into existing government forces, but rather rewards existing militias with state legitimacy and resources (see Chapter 17). Organizations retain autonomy, and the ability to compete with the state. Hybridization is very problematic for state-building.

On the other side, insurgents will have success when individuals move into −2 roles. Many times, this process is outside the realm of strategic decision-making. Insurgent local militias are likely to naturally emerge from longtime vibrant local networks. The case studies showed the rapid formation of veterans-based networks in Ghazaliyah, the tribally based armed groups in Anbar, and the neighborhood-based militias rising in Sadr City.

21.2.4. Reducing Violence through Clarity in the Ethnic Hierarchy: Clarity through Demographic Homogenization

If master cleavages and concerns about group hierarchy are salient, then the conflict is unlikely to end until there is clarity in that hierarchy. Clarity can come from either distinct dominance of one group or well-defined balance among groups. Although it may be contradictory to the Western way of thinking, an outcome where one group clearly occupies the top position in a status hierarchy may be positive. When a majority group achieves dominance, resentment fades and deals can be made within the contours of the new order.

Clarity, in turn, can result from a strategy of homogenization. With this usually tacit strategy, the counterinsurgent allows the war, and its effects on demography, to play out. During the fighting, a front line may begin to develop. Seeking safety, populations "unmix," members of different groups move to where their own side is a clear majority. Focal-point mechanisms can help this process play out. Rivers form natural boundaries, but so do T-walls put up by an intervener. In the end, each side ends up dominant in their own territory.

The empirical material of this book has included cases where homogenization produced drops in violence both in Baghdad as a whole and in smaller contested areas within Baghdad. Chapter 13 presented an argument based on this logic in explaining the drop in violence in Baghdad at the time of the Surge. Shia became dominant in Baghdad after the civil war separated Shia and Sunni into homogenous zones, with the Shia masters in the majority of neighborhoods in the city. Ghazaliyah/Shula saw a drop in violence after Shia and Sunni found themselves in separate defensible zones, separated by T-walls and a canal. Bayaa saw a drop in Shia-Sunni violence after JAM had cleared out most Sunnis and gained demographic dominance.

While problematic on moral grounds, the empirical material of this book has provided support for the proposition that homogenization reduces violence.

21.2.5. Counterinsurgent Failure: War-Fighting Alone as a Counterinsurgency Strategy

In the period following the invasion, many of the US military's actions were irrelevant or alienating for much of the general population. In the invasion itself, US war-fighting success was stunning. US-led armored forces took Baghdad in a matter of weeks; major combat operations lasted only 26 days; Coalition casualties were minimal. The lesson learned from the First Iraq War was reinforced: no force in the world can match the United States in mobility or firepower. Unsurprisingly, US forces at first relied on their training and conducted a basic war-fighting strategy to quell insurgents. However, when used to conduct counterinsurgency, war-fighting left much to be desired. In contests where information is critical, armored "presence patrols" are essentially worthless. In struggles where legitimacy is important, collateral damage from indirect fire and large-scale sweeps rounding up large numbers of detainees are detrimental. Yet, the US military persisted in the use of armor, indirect artillery shelling, cordon and sweep operations, large-scale detention, and displays of force as a deterrent.

Some of the case material provided vivid illustrations of the failure of the early war-fighting strategy. In Ghazaliyah, the Sunnis and Shia fought a civil war, paying little attention to US armor parading through the neighborhood. In the Mansour neighborhood, the majority of the middle-class Sunnis slowly exited as security deteriorated despite a significant number of US troops. In Mosul, Christians hid in their homes as various militias left bodies littering the streets while US soldiers remained on their bases and in their armored vehicles.

Fairly early in the war, many US soldiers came to believe that war-fighting alone was not likely to bring about a stable Iraq. Even before the dissemination of Field Manual 3-24 (FM 3-24), officers in the field were moving to more nuanced counterinsurgency strategies in their localities. One complicating factor in strategy change, however, was the continuing utility of US armor and war-fighting capabilities in specific instances, leading into the next point.

21.2.6. War-Fighting and Decapitation: A Successful Combination for Taking Back Territory

"Insurgency" is defined in part as war without a front line of combat. If insurgents do try to take on the counterinsurgent in a head-on battle, war-fighting capabilities can be decisive for that fight. In the cases, the US military easily defeated Sadrist forces in 2004; in Hawija, US military forces thoroughly defeated insurgents in an early urban battle.

There is a second situation in which war-fighting ability is crucial. During the course of an insurgency, fighting might become confined to a certain small territory where insurgents are forced to fight a pitched battle. When that occurs, the tools of war-fighting may again become optimal, especially if combined with heightened capabilities of intelligence and surveillance. The empirical chapters identified two cases in which a combination of war-fighting and decapitation was effective. Chapter 12 described an early successful merger of the two strategies in the retaking of Sadr City in 2008. While not fought as an insurgency, this combination found another success in the war against ISIS, as illustrated in Chapter 16.

21.2.7. Counterinsurgent Failure: Clear, Hold, Build Alone as a Counterinsurgency Strategy

The framework identifies two interconnected processes at the heart of the clear, hold, build (CHB) strategy. One is moving the general unarmed population out of neutrality (0) or cooperation with the insurgents (-1) into a role of government support $(+1)$. The general population is the center of gravity in the fight. When occupying this role, individuals are informing the counterinsurgent forces about the presence and location of mobile insurgents (-3) and information-collection can turn the tide of insurgency. The second process involves building up the state's mobile security forces $(+3)$. When the process of moving the general population to $+1$ has made headway, government supporters will provide information for the newly recruited and professionally trained army and supporting forces $(+3)$ to go after the mobile insurgents (-3).

For our Iraq case, the first question to ask is whether the United States was able to trigger the intended mechanisms to move individuals to the $+1$ role. Chapter 3 ended with a construction of a template of common and established mechanisms working among different nodes of the spectrum of roles. The mechanisms most relevant to movement among the $-1, 0, +1$ unarmed roles include:

Movement from 0 to +1:

- Resentment versus insurgent group
- Safety in numbers with general population as referent point
- Focal points
- Rational economic decision, payouts from government, employment, and so on.

Movement from 0 to −1:

- Resentment versus newly empowered group
- Safety in numbers with general population as reference point

- Status rewards
- Focal points.

Movement from +1 and −1 back to 0:

- Rational reaction to threat
- Fear (emotion).

To review, CHB envisions moving the population to +1 mainly through rational-choice mechanisms. In terms of "winning hearts and minds," the appeal to the mind is more crucial and effective than the appeal to the heart. If the population clearly sees the state as providing security, ever-increasing economic benefits, and public goods such as schools, individuals will rationally calculate that their future lies with the new government and will move rightward to +1. How do individuals know when they have entered into a new secure world? Here the safety-in-numbers and focal-point mechanisms come into play. As more and more fellow citizens support the government, the less chance insurgents can single out collaborators for punishment. In terms of coordinating focal points, the United States also placed great stock in elections. When millions turn out, in spite of threats, to participate in the formation of a new government, this public signal has the potential to verify that a majority now support the government. Furthermore, by providing security to the population, CHB aims to sustain movement to +1 by preventing the emotion of fear, a mechanism capable of driving individuals back to inaction and neutrality (0).

What have the empirical chapters indicated about the success of the United States in setting off the process of moving individuals to +1 and sustaining them in that role? The evidence shows an overall lack of success. While the United States did improve security and provide economic benefits, the effect of these efforts was blunted or disrupted by a countervailing resentment mechanism driving individuals leftward toward −1. More boldly stated, material incentives were no match for group attachment, perceptions of group subordination, and the emotion of resentment.

The Hawija case study provides an illustration. The case included lengthy periods of CHB, including intensified implementation during 2009. In Hawija, US military officers poured in CERP money, awarded micro-grants, built roads, ramped up economic programs, and conducted public relations campaigns. Despite all of the effort to tie Hawija's residents to the Iraqi state, and despite low levels of violence in the latter periods of US presence, Hawija became a primary site of Sunni resistance soon after US withdrawal. Riven by reactions to Prime Minister Maliki's actions against highly visible Sunni leaders, insurgent groups reappeared and tribal forces mobilized, filling the −1 and −2 positions on the spectrum. They remained at those nodes until the coming of ISIS. Many residents would cooperate with this radical Sunni invading force against the Iraqi state. In short, most of the mechanisms driving individuals from 0 to −1 were playing out in Hawija during 2011–2014—resentment against the unabashedly Shia-dominated Maliki government, large and sustained protests generating focal-point and safety-in-numbers mechanisms. On the other hand, all of the economic investments to create a stable pro-government citizenry (at +1) had little visible lasting effect.

In broad terms, the United States made some early mistakes, or at least made some poor assumptions, that made the institution of CHB difficult. The United States pushed for relatively early elections that might serve as a focal point that would help trigger the mechanisms driving movement to +1. The hope was that seeing millions of Iraqi citizens go to the polls in defiance of threats, and holding up one's affirming blue-stained finger as evidence of government support, would serve to show the emergence of a common and legitimate new democratic state. However, the Sunni election boycott and the resulting overwhelming Shia victory in the 2005 election only served to heighten sectarian identity and Sunni resentment.

Furthermore, many of the Sunni actors who might have been most receptive to the CHB strategy had fled Iraq before it was instituted. The middle-class Mansour neighborhood was filled with professionals outside sectarian circles. They were perhaps most ready to accept democratic norms and play leadership roles in the new system. However, in the period before the Surge, the United States employed an ineffective war-fighting strategy that relied on shows of force. Few residents moved toward +1, especially in the face of emerging insurgent and criminal violence. US strategy not only failed to generate a safety-in-numbers mechanism, but also failed to prevent or reduce fear levels. As noted in the template, the mechanism of fear sustains inaction (individuals remaining at or returning to the 0 node). As violence rose in the neighborhood, many Mansour residents simply used their resources to flee Iraq, taking their essential state-building skills with them.

The Shia were a somewhat different case. Undoubtedly, many Shia were driven to end subordination to Sunni rule. Shia were not going to allow the Sunnis to regain dominance, and the best way to accomplish that goal was to become dominant in their own right. Beyond resentment, some Shia organizations could match the US strategy toward the general population by creating a parallel social system. Shia groups offered to provide competing services and goods to those of the Coalition and Iraqi state. As the Bayaa chapter illustrated, the Organization of the Martyr Sadr (OMS) provided housing—directing incoming Shia into the homes of fleeing Sunnis—as well as basic sustenance. Moreover, in Bayaa the OMS took over the role of adjudication in the neighborhood, a service outside the capacity of the Coalition. Shia religious organization naturally produced effective focal points and safety in numbers through a system of Shia mosques with coordinated Friday sermons. In sum, Shia and their organizations were able to trigger or take advantage of most of the mechanisms moving individuals to −1, blunting US efforts to move them rightward to +1. They were able to harness resentment, bring out numbers through focal points, and provide goods and services on their own terms.

Then there is the second step in CHB. In addition to moving individuals to +1, CHB requires moving motivated individuals into the +3 role. The template listed two types of mechanisms relevant to this movement:

1. Material incentives (pay, uniforms, equipment)
2. Pride (either in professionalism or patriotism).

Building a new Iraqi army was a major US goal ever since the order to disband the Iraqi Army. Very early on, a common US phrase was "when the Iraqis stand up, we will stand down." Standing up a professional Iraqi Army remained a major goal right up to US departure. Despite spending tens of billions of dollars and deploying significant numbers of military training team advisors, US and Iraqi efforts failed to produce soldiers who would stand up and fight.[2] As described in Chapter 16 on the Third Iraq War, Iraqi Army units in Mosul fled in the face of a few thousand ISIS insurgents. In retrospect, neither of the two mechanisms listed above were operative.

In terms of material incentives, Iraqi units were filled with "ghost soldiers," troops whose names appear on military rolls even while absent. Here, the soldier gives part of his salary to his officer in return for being able to return home or work a civilian job. This corrupt device provides material benefit to both soldier and officer, but is no way to build a functioning army. Following Maliki as Iraqi prime minister, an investigation commissioned by Haider al-Abadi found at least 50,000 ghost soldiers in the Iraqi Army (Morris, 2014).

In regard to patriotism and the emotion of pride, the lack of an Iraqi national identity is an obvious factor. Who would fight and possibly die for Iraq? In Iraq, Shia and Sunni, Kurds and Christians identified more with their sect than with an Iraqi nation, at least in the time period in question. While tens of thousands of Iraqi Army troops fled the Iraqi north in the face of ISIS, tens of thousands of Iraqi Shia responded to the call of Grand Ayatollah Sistani's for defense of Baghdad and Iraq. If the emotion of pride is a motivating mechanism, it clearly moved more individuals into the PMF than into the Iraqi Army. There were Iraqis who did fight with distinction, many of them to be found in the Iraqi Counter Terrorism Service. In these elite units, pay and morale were both high.

The case against CHB should be stated with some caveats. Undoubtedly, the strategy did help garner information from the population. The strategy created connections between the general population and the state. However, the Iraq case does support two general propositions. First, conflicts driven by issues of group status and hierarchy will likely see powerful emotional mechanisms outweigh economic incentives. Second, outside occupiers cannot count on controlling the informational mechanisms—focal points and safety in numbers—that affect mobilization. Local cultural and religious institutions are likely to produce the ability to trigger those mechanisms.

21.2.8. Decapitation Strategies Became Remarkably Effective over the Course of the Iraq War

During the 2003–2011 period, the US military was developing the capacity for an entirely new strategy—decapitation. Because decapitation will play a big role in the discussion of future US military intervention, it is important to understand just how quickly capacities developed over the course of the Iraq war. Consider the experience of TG, who served in Naval Special Warfare in multiple SEAL units. From 2003 until 2011, TG did six tours in Iraq (plus one shorter stay) mainly doing targeting. Examining the changes that occurred in TG's mission and capabilities over these six tours provides a good overview of the evolution of decapitation proficiencies of US forces. There were significant changes in moving from human intelligence to signal intelligence, in developing increasingly large databases, in an ever-increasing operational tempo, and in cooperating and integrating Iraqi forces.

First tour (May–September 2003): TG's unit only went after high value targets (HVT), those in the deck of cards. These targets were specified. For example, TG's unit went after the King of Clubs, Izzat Ibrahim al-Douri, described in Chapter 15 on Hawija. TG's unit also conducted raids directed by the CIA. All targeting at this point was done through human intelligence (HUMINT); there was very little in the way of signal intelligence (SIGINT). Positive identification of targets was made by a human source who would be brought along on the raid, with face covered for anonymity. Helicopter flyovers produced real-time intelligence. During this period, TG's force acted without Iraqi partners. His SEAL team worked with Army Rangers and Green Berets.

Second tour (November 2004–2005): TG was based in Baghdad. Raids were conducted from HUMINT, but in contrast to the first tour the number of sources had increased significantly. With information from multiple informants, special force operators could understand a target's patterns of behavior. This level of information was used to create a "murder board" for target selection.

Third tour (Beginning in April 2006): TG was working in conjunction with Task Force Raptor. It was during this tour that TG noted the entire decapitation process changing. Information now came primarily from SIGINT rather than HUMINT. Surveillance capacity had dramatically improved. Overhead surveillance instruments and the ability to track cell phone movement allowed detailed identification of target behavior. TG said that even though targets came to realize that their cell phones were being monitored, targets often could not restrain themselves from using their cell phones (although the most sophisticated leaders did go to a system of couriers). Also, TG's units worked not only with British SSA but also Iraqi Counter Terrorism Forces (ICTS). TG had very good relationships with the ICTS. TG described them as highly professional, some with experience from the Republican Guard. US and ICTS forces were tightly integrated. There were 150 ICTS in a company. The Task Force was the only force allowed to enter mosques and were also the first force allowed to go into Sadr City. They went after AQI targets anywhere in the theater.

Fourth tour (January 2007–April 2007): TG was based in Fallujah. By this tour, tactics developed in 2006 had been formalized into Find, Fix, Finish, Exploit, Analyze (F3EA). There was more emphasis on post-assault information collection and immediate use of that information. TG's unit collected biometrics at the target site. Among special forces units and organizations, a sophisticated division of labor began to form. Also, by this time, JSOC had developed a robust database to work from. New information at a raid site could be analyzed in conjunction with this developed database to greatly increase the tempo of operations. TG was confident that much of the rapid decline in SIGACTS was partially, if not mainly, due to the increased tempo of JSOC operations.[3] Insurgents needed time and some stability to plan new operations and they simply did not have it.

Fifth tour (April 2009–October 2009): TG was based in Basra, operating in Task Force Spartan. At this time, emphasis was placed on transition to Iraqi control before the planned US withdrawal.

Accordingly, TG's force partnered with Iraqi Tactical Support Units (TSU) and the Iraqi Army. During this tour, TG said that there were political negotiations over targets, which certainly was never happening any time before the Surge.

Sixth tour (April–November 2011): TG served in Mosul, Tikrit, and Kirkuk. On this tour, TG said his team "took the gloves off." They were not concerned with collateral damage as in earlier operations. They dealt with Iraqi Counter Terrorism, a Kurdish Partner Force trained by the CIA, and Delta. They also worked with the Iraqi Police Force, and Iraqi Army Commando Units. TG's force aimed to "take out as many bad guys as they could" in order to pave the way for a peaceful US withdrawal. While packing up and leaving, US military forces would be more vulnerable. TG believed the "gloves came off" because the Obama administration wanted to declare a peaceful end to US involvement in Iraq for electoral purposes. The targets were those who could make for a messy and deadly withdrawal. Taking them out, even with high collateral damage, was the only aim in these operations.

In sum, TG's progression of tours documented a rapid and stunning increase in technical abilities. TG's experience also showed the ways US Special Forces developed relationships with certain Iraqi units, especially the ICTS. This evolution also indicated that decapitation strategy and tactics could be calibrated to fit the changing political situation. Sometimes US Special Forces operators would choose to work closely with Iraqi forces; other times they could work separately. Sometimes US operators would be highly sensitive to possible collateral damage; other times the benefits of the target were worth the risk of civilian casualties. In many raids there would be negotiation with Iraqis over the target set; at other times "the gloves could come off."

Since the Iraq war, decapitation capabilities have only increased. There have been many more TGs serving multiple tours, learning new skills, and applying those skills in a host of new environments. It is hard to say where it all is going.

21.3. Counterinsurgency and State-Building: What Explains the Persistent Weakness of the Iraqi State?

Iraq's state-building problems have been multiple and have occurred throughout the entire 2003–2023 period (and even in the pre-invasion period). This section will discuss problems at three key junctures to summarize different types of issues. First, pre-invasion assumptions about reconstructing the post-Saddam state were far off from reality. Second, US policies during 2003–2011 were counterproductive to building a coherent state. Third, the creation of more hybrid actors and the nature of the power-sharing system post-2011 has sustained a fragmented and dysfunctional state. Accordingly, we will look at the state of state-building in the years 2003, 2011, and 2023.

21.3.1. Pre-Invasion Assumptions (or Prevarications or Wishful Thinking)

Before the invasion, many US officials believed building a post-Saddam state would be straightforward. They imagined that Iraqi society was a "blank slate." Perhaps informed by a view of the fall of communism in Eastern Europe, US and Coalition actors assumed that the former system's totalitarian legacy, with its illegitimacy and brutality, would leave behind an atomized population, a collection of individuals willing and ready to adopt a "freedom agenda."

US policymakers were not the only ones responsible for this assumption. Consider the pre-invasion recommendations of some members of the Iraqi opposition. In December 2002, the Democratic Principles Working Group of the Iraqi Opposition finished a "Final Report on the Transition to Democracy in Iraq."[4] The Working Group was composed of 32 members, mainly Iraqi exiles from a variety of opposition groups. It was supported by the US Department of State. The document was comprehensive, with many sections covering issues ranging from the "Phases of Transitional Justice" to "Reform of the Law and Order Structure" to "Vision of an Iraqi Constitutional State." In July 2003, this Working Group published a summary piece in the *Journal of Democracy*. One of the most striking passages of this report, italicized for effect by the authors, describes an expected political vacuum in the post-invasion period:

> *As a result, there are no recognized domestic political institutions, groups, or individuals that can step forward, invoke national legitimacy and assume power. A political vacuum will arise during the period of disintegration and following the downfall of the regime. Many groups and individuals will eventually emerge and compete for power, but this will only happen gradually, as the environment becomes safe for public participation.*[5]

One of the leaders of the group, the well-known Kanan Makiya,[6] published an article entitled "A Model for Post-Saddam Iraq" in the *Journal of Democracy*, with much of the material finding its way into the report.[7] Any reader of Makiya's "model" will be struck in retrospect by its wishful thinking. The article pushes three main recommendations: First, the need for federalism; second, the need for a non-Arab state identity; third, the desirability for demilitarization. Drawing from the post–World War II German example, Makiya downplays the need for security in a post-invasion state and writes off the past as a "burden" that must be cast off. As he writes, "But also like Germany and Japan both after WWII, Iraq's future lies in unshackling itself in no uncertain way from the burden of its past and in focusing all the creative energies of the country on reconstruction and cultural renewal" (Makiya, 2003).

The simple and atomized state as imagined (or purposely constructed) by some influential émigrés can be represented by Figure 21.3. Émigrés, who had been working with the United States for years, would come back to Iraq and help lead the construction of a new democratic system. After the groundwork had been laid, political parties would emerge, elections would be held, governments formed. Under the tutelage of international advisors, state institutions, free of

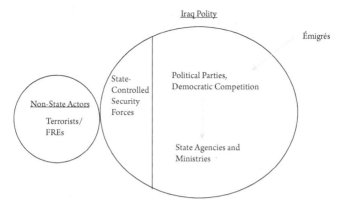

Figure 21.3. Imagined Iraqi polity.

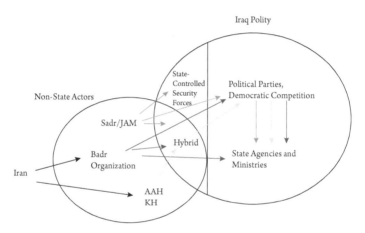

Figure 21.4. Evolution of the Iraqi polity.

their Baathist heritage and personnel, would operate under professional norms. The Baathist Party and the former Iraqi Army would have no place in this new state. The new state organs, especially security organs, must be untainted by the old system. Former regime elements (FREs) would be pushed out of the Iraqi polity world. These malefactors could be easily dealt with by the new state.

The straightforward story represented in Figure 21.3 did not play out (Figure 21.4 shows the later reality). Suffice it to say, as soon became apparent, that Iraq was far from a "blank slate." The émigré-led returning contingent tried to exclude inconvenient actors from the game. It was soon apparent that the returnees could not pick and choose among those who had stayed in Iraq. The Sadrists possessed a base in Sadr City, a legacy of charismatic leadership, and a large pool of impoverished Shia citizens willing to sacrifice, and commit violence, in order to establish their version of a just Iraqi political order. The Badr Organization brought with them many years of training and experience from their sojourn in Iran. In Anbar and localities in the south, tribes maintained both actual and latent abilities for collective action. There were also networks of veterans and former Baathists that were sometimes able to coalesce. The evolution of Iraq became complicated quickly.

21.3.2.   US Failures in the Reconstruction of the Iraqi State

A primary goal of the United States was to build a functioning Iraqi state before withdrawing in 2011. Events shortly after that withdrawal made it clear that mission had failed. The Iraqi Army collapsed in the face of ISIS, the Iraqi state temporarily lost control of a significant portion of its territory, and many Iraqi citizens did not identify with the Iraqi state. While the war against ISIS successfully liberated all of Iraqi territory, that feat was accomplished with the help of hybrid militias and the re-entry of US forces (with limited numbers but seemingly unlimited munitions). Iraq was clearly failing President Obama's three-word measure for Iraqi success—"sovereign, stable, and self-reliant."

The US legacy in Iraq contains more than a small measure of irony. While the US talked about state-building, many of its actions inadvertently created a weak state with a highly fragmented security system. The United States found itself instituting a series of different strategies, some ignoring the forces that impeded the construction of a coherent state and some actually generating those forces. A summary review of US actions at each node of the spectrum, with reference to US actions or inactions, can identify those failures.

Starting with the +3 role, the United States failed to construct a professional army with a coherent chain of command. The US training of the Iraqi Army never involved serious measures at stemming corruption. It underestimated the problem of the lack of a powerful national identity. US forces also acted in ways to promote hybrid forces. The United States was closely aligned with one hybrid force from the beginning—the Peshmerga. The US military also readily cooperated with the Badr Organization due to the latter's professionalism. From the beginning, the US military preferred interaction with already professionalized military forces to the hard work of building the Iraqi forces from scratch. US policymakers and practitioners never understood the sectarian struggle in Iraq and were never prepared to challenge the state capture of the Iraqi ministries as an essential part of that struggle. Instead of a unified state, the Badr Organization controlled the Ministry of the Interior, while the Sadrists took over administration of welfare ministries.

At the +2 node, the United States was completely unprepared to reform the Iraqi police (+2). From the beginning, a paucity of advisors plagued the first steps, and the problem was never fully addressed. For the US military, police training simply was not a priority. Police stations were easily captured or controlled by sectarian militias. Also, community mobilization requires two steps: from −2 to temporary +2 and then from temporary +2 into permanent positions in the local police (+2) or the army or national security forces (+3). In Iraq, the second step was never seriously undertaken. US pressure on the Maliki regime to do so was less than adequate. This incomplete process left many armed actors outside control of the state.

At the +1 position, after US withdrawal, the United States did little to constrain the Iraqi leadership from intensifying its sectarian politics, leading to resentment and the revolts in Hawija and Anbar.

21.3.3. The Iraqi State in 2023

These failures and missteps helped lead to a weak state. After US withdrawal, that state could not defend itself. With the coming of ISIS, and the debacle of the Iraqi Army, the Popular Mobilization Forces (PMF) emerged. Hybrid security actors became a stable part of the Iraqi system. The PMF became an umbrella group for a variety of mainly, but not only, Shia militias. These hybrid organizations soon took on political roles as well as military ones. In the Kurdish territories, the KDP and PUK controlled their own parallel, and non-transparent, sets of security institutions and used them to their own ends. As described in Chapter 18, the Iraqi security landscape was populated by so many hybrid and non-state armed actors that emerging Christian militias could shop around among various sponsors.

The Iraqi state in 2023 resembled Figure 21.4, a far cry from the simple imagined state previously diagrammed. Those coming in to build a new state in 2003 envisioned a process of the state cleansing itself from outsiders and miscreants. There would be a clear distinction about who was in and who was out of the polity. In reality, non-state groups captured or merged with parts of the state.

Figure 21.4 illustrates the status and pathways of several important groups. Asaeb Ahl al-Haq (AAH, League of the Righteous) and Kataeb Hezbollah (KH, The Battalions of the Party of God) originated as Iranian supported "special groups," renowned in part for killing US military personnel (see the descriptions in Chapter 17). Both organizations became key players in the hybrid PMF. They have used the legitimacy and resources of the PMF to branch into party and electoral politics, and then from membership in governing coalitions to positions in state ministries and agencies. Sadrists have used a variety of moves to capture and merge with the state. As cited in many of this book's cases, Sadrists have taken control of local police stations and forces, have formed PMF brigades, and have been the dominant force in elections, all the while maintaining autonomous state-like distribution and governance services. The Badr Organization produced nearly one-third of the original PMF brigades. Their capture of the Ministry of the Interior was chronicled in Chapter 9. Badr is known to be the dominant security and political force in some Iraqi Governorates.

In sum, there is fragmentation of the state in both security and governance realms. There is also an implicit agreement among this set of non-state/state actors to perpetuate this fragmentation. None of the major actors wants to see any possibility of a Saddam-like strongman emerge. To repeat from Chapter 1: If actors are worried about being dominated, and come to believe they cannot become dominant themselves, then a weak state becomes an attractive outcome. A strong state can become a vehicle for domination. If no strong state exists, there will be no such vehicle for opponents to capture. Furthermore, all of the parties have benefited from the inclusive power-sharing system that doles out the oil income–generated spoils so that each militia/party can fuel their patronage machines.

In terms of general lessons, the Iraq experience highlights several. In an intervention, the intervening forces and friends cannot choose who gets to play. Germany and Japan notwithstanding, there are few "blank slates" in the world. The intervener must be aware of the motivation and organizational power of potential actors. It should not be possible to believe that no organization would emerge from a huge slum area like Sadr City, or to believe that any intervening force could deny the leadership of such an area a role in rebuilding. It should not be possible to underestimate the potential of well-trained militias, like Badr, who have been waiting in the wings to enter the fray. Interveners should listen to émigré opposition groups with caution and question if they are just being told what they want to hear.

21.4. Lessons

This chapter closes with some lessons on intervention that should be generalizable beyond Iraq.

1. Conflicts driven by group concerns about domination/subordination and questions of group status and hierarchy are likely to be driven by powerful emotional mechanisms.

Under many conditions, it is natural for groups to struggle against subordination or compete for dominance. When there is a collapse or weakening of a state composed of a small number of salient groups with a political history imbued with group dominance/subordination, then the emotional mechanisms of resentment and anger are likely to overpower rational choice mechanisms.

2. Winning the "hearts and minds" of the population is not likely to be decisive.[8]

First, "hearts and minds" are particularly hard to control in conflicts fought along master cleavage lines. As indicated on the template of mechanisms, there are parallel sets of mechanisms, with one set moving individuals to government support and the other set driving them to insurgent support. In many cases, insurgents will be more likely to trigger the emotional, focal point, and informational mechanisms than the occupier or the state. Insurgents and non-state actors might also be able to provide some state functions as well or better than the state, especially in terms of local adjudication of disputes. Generally, the power of rational-choice economic sticks and carrots meant to induce movement to government support pales in comparison to emerging resentments driving individuals toward insurgent support.

Second, there is a question of information. The central assumption of CHB holds that winning hearts and minds can be decisive by generating high information flows from the population to the counterinsurgent. There can be valuable information coming from the general population, although that information is sometimes based in false and self-serving denunciations and is coming from unreliable sources. Truly decisive information, however, usually results from community mobilization and the "flipping" or creation of local security units. In that case, informants had actually allied and cooperated with insurgents and knew their locations and tactics.

Third, insurgency is about violence. If an insurgent develops large numbers of locally armed and mobile armed actors, and ways to sustain and regenerate those armed actors, the population will not be coming to a position of support. There will be cases where the level of violence simply overwhelms the behavior of unarmed actors.

3. Insurgents will likely hold advantages at local levels.

The key mechanism at local levels—with areas of intense interactions within communities—is the social norm. Social norms of reciprocity and norms of honor are capable of driving entire networks of individuals to local armed organization. Membership in long-standing social institutions—veterans' groups, tribes, families, local religious structures—produces and maintains these norms. Military interveners cannot replicate these entities or create norms from the air.

Because the presence of local, armed actors is so important, the counterinsurgent will need to find a way to neutralize opponents at that level (see "Counterinsurgent Success by Neutralizing the −2 Node" above). Assuming the inability or unwillingness to raze or saturate entire communities, the counterinsurgent will have three options: deal-making, community mobilization, or creation of permanent hybrid actors. All of these actions will be problematic for state-building.

4. Community mobilization is attractive but difficult to do. It will likely produce short-term gains with uncertain long-term effects.

Because the local armed level is so important but also difficult to penetrate, the community mobilization strategy is appealing. The "flipping" of these local armed groups provides valuable information, takes away an opponent, and adds an ally.

Because these groups maintain autonomy, it is very difficult to stop them from "flipping" back or perpetuating themselves in a new form. If an intervener is to institute community mobilization, there should be every effort to complete the second step of the process—to move members of the temporary group to more permanent positions in the police or army. It might also be best to try to integrate former combatants as individuals, rather than keeping groups together. On the whole, it is very difficult for any government to commit to giving security jobs, and weapons, to former enemies. This commitment problem underlies many negotiated peace settlements of civil wars. Perhaps there will be advantages in temporarily flipping local insurgent groups, but reversion should be expected.

5. The combination of a conflict characterized by dominance/subordination concerns with a weak state will likely lead to a fragmented state security structure with hybrid actors.

Following the discussion on state-building above, in violent conflicts with these characteristics, groups wish to avoid subordination to other groups above all else. A strong centralized state could provide a vehicle for domination. On the other hand, a weak state with a fragmented, if not incoherent, security system prevents the possibility of such domination. In these circumstances, a collection of actors satisfied with a division in the security realm will also be favorable to power-sharing agreement in terms of government income and distribution (especially in an oil state). If a consociational system was instituted at the beginning of the intervention, it will be very difficult to reform that system.

6. The most formidable and resilient insurgent will be the one that can play at every level of the spectrum.

Potentially formidable actors might be identified beforehand by the following characteristics: having a territorial base, possessing previous organization, representing one of the master cleavages in conflict. Organizations having only mobile fighters without a local base will be reduced to terrorism.

7. The most effective counterinsurgent will be able to create a strategy working across the spectrum of roles. This goal will require a combination of strategies.

The discussion above identified one such combination. CHB combined with community mobilization may have a good chance to succeed, at least in the short run. War-fighting and decapitation may be an effective situation in some special circumstances. One problem is that it will be difficult to determine the best combination or sequence of strategies going into a conflict. Insurgents will change their strategy, and counterinsurgents will need to change their strategy in response. It follows that flexibility should be baked into the occupier/state doctrine and field manuals. The US military has advantages in producing such flexibility. Due to the decentralized nature of its decision-making, commanders down to the company level are constantly experimenting, sometimes interacting (deal-making) with locals in innovative ways. While the military must work as a hierarchical organization, it could do better in terms of the flow of information upward and outward after successful innovations have been uncovered. Such flows of information did occur within the US military in Iraq, but those flows were often more informal than systematic.[9]

8. Staying longer may not produce better results.

One of the major findings of this study is that the United States, as an exemplar of an armed occupier, can be efficient at reducing violence, while failing as a state-builder. If there are issues involving hierarchy and dominance, there will only be so long that any outside armed force can stay without provoking resentment. Also, the problems of building the armies are not about time, but are more fundamental, involving corruption and lack of identity.

9. It is difficult to build a new army. It might be much easier to build new special forces.

Armies are large. In filling their ranks, the army will likely resemble that society from which it springs. If that society had problems and divisions, the army will likely also experience similar problems. Special forces are different. In some ways, those who strive to become members of the special forces wish to separate themselves from their society. They want to be "special." They choose a vocation that may make them feel closer to others in that vocation than they feel to their own society.

10. The US military is very good at war-fighting and finding, fixing, and finishing targets.

The invasion and elimination of the Saddamist military was stunningly swift. The US military prefers using firepower and maneuver. US special forces prefer to be the JSOC Superman over the Green Beret "Daniel Boone." The Soleimani assassination was a lethal work of art. Unsurprisingly, in the two most clearly successful operations described in this book, the 2008 Battle for Sadr City and the Third Iraq War, US forces conducted a combination of war-fighting and decapitation. But the question is—to what end?

21.5. Conclusion

This last lesson can serve as a transition. In the future, the US military will want to do what it is good at. But should it? The next two chapters lead us toward that question, among others.

Constraints on Learning

*The Influence of the Changing International System
and US Domestic Politics*

22.1. Introduction

The preceding chapter outlined and summarized the key empirical findings of this book. It ended with a series of "lessons." No one should be under the delusion that policymakers learn from such lessons and straightforwardly apply them. What might be "learned" in the policymaking world depends on many factors in the wider world. This chapter addresses six of those factors. The first three have to do with the nature of the actors most involved with intervention policy—the military, the president, and the foreign policy establishment. The other three concern trends connected with the phenomena in the title of this book—death, dominance, and state-building.

The following chapter, the last in the book, speculates about the future of US military intervention. That future will depend in part on what happened in Iraq, in part on how those events have been interpreted, and in part on how those interpretations are received. Chapter 23 will try to combine lessons gleaned from the detailed realities of Iraq's violence and politics with how that reality might be interpreted and received.[1] Admittedly, there will be much conjecture in this effort, but hopefully the consideration of the factors constraining learning found in this chapter will help make that conjecture as plausible as possible.

22.2. Military Organization

Military organizations are built on pride and action. They are not geared for introspection or self-flagellation. Unsurprisingly, the US military is primed to move on from Iraq, perhaps geared to forget. It would not be the first time the United States would try to put a troubled counterinsurgency effort out of mind. Although the Marine Corps counterinsurgency manual remained on the shelves of many officers for decades, General Petraeus would again need to reinvent COIN in Field Manual 3-24. While the Iraq experience may not match Vietnam in terms of trauma and forgetting, it is certainly bad enough.

The US military's culture enhances the ability to put counterinsurgency adventures in the rearview mirror (Nagl, 2002). Like most advanced militaries, the US military's culture favors offense over defense (Posen, 1984). It revels in firepower and maneuver. The US military prefers to study and prepare for wars with Clausewitzean "decisive battles" and a clear "center of gravity." Understandably, the US military does not like the dirty nature and opacity of internal war. In counterinsurgency, even many of the successes come through ambiguous and distasteful tactics. Furthermore, if an opportunity arises for the military to discard an unpalatable mission set they will do so, not only in practice but in peacetime training as well. Given high turnover in the military, the experience and lessons of counterinsurgencies find a hazy place in institutional memory. At the time of writing, the US war colleges were already changing their curricula to reflect these preferences.[2]

Additionally, the emergence of China as a peer competitor provides positive reasons for relegating counterinsurgency to a back burner. The ever-increasing competition with China promises a multitude of exercises where soldiers, sailors, and pilots get to shoot, sail, and fly, rather than learn how to make deals with locals in a complex foreign environment. Preparing for a possible war with China fits the organizational preferences of the US military more than remembering the complicated and sullied realities of Iraq.

At the time of writing, Ukraine and Russia were locked in a deadly attrition war. The United States was supplying massive levels of material, training, and intelligence support. This effort was likely to transform ideas of security force assistance (SFA) in the US military. The ways in which this effort might affect US military intervention more broadly were still opaque and probably dependent on how the war would turn out.

22.3. The President

Over the past several decades, the president and the executive branch have expanded control over the conduct and leadership of foreign policy, consistently eroding the power of the legislative branch. Presidential decisions and statements have the potential to change the course of US intervention policy. Certainly, the role of President George W. Bush was decisive in the decision to invade Iraq. President Bush paved the way for military intervention in Iraq by announcing a doctrine of preemption. He also changed the conduct of the war through his strong and decisive advocacy of the Surge (Petersen, 2020). In the Surge decision, President Bush was driven by his memories of Vietnam, how the defeat there created a demoralized military. The presidency's growing institutional role, along with the personal beliefs of individual presidents, can shape present intervention policy as well as constrain or promote future interventions. Certainly, President Biden has drawn lessons from past military interventions. It is worthwhile to examine at length President Biden's speech on August 31, 2021, defending his decision to withdraw from Afghanistan. He stated:

> As we turn the page on the foreign policy that's guided our nation for the last two decades, we've got to learn from our mistakes. To me there are two that are paramount. First, we must set missions with clear, achievable goals, not ones we'll never reach. And second, we must stay clearly focused on the fundamental national security interest of the United States of America.
>
> The decision about Afghanistan is not just about Afghanistan. It's about ending an era of major military operations to remake other countries. We saw a mission of counterterrorism in Afghanistan, getting the terrorists to stop the attacks, morph into counterinsurgency, nation-building, trying to create a cohesive and united Afghanistan. Something that has never been done over many centuries of Afghan's history. Moving on from that mind-set and those kind of large-scale troop deployments will make us stronger and more effective and safer at home.

Biden also stated:

> We will maintain the fight against terrorism in Afghanistan and other countries. We just don't need to fight a ground war to do it. We have what's called over-the horizon capabilities, which means we can strike terrorists and targets without American boots on the ground, very few if needed. . . . As commander in chief, I firmly believe the best path to guard our safety and security lies in a tough, unforgiving, targeted, precise strategy that goes after terror where it is today.

In terms of the present work and its underlying framework, several points are clear. First, in terms of the five strategies underlying the analysis of this work, President Biden's speech is a clear repudiation of clear, hold, build, essentially assigning it to the trash can of history. The United States can pursue its interests through counterterrorism and does not need to reconstruct a state in order to prevent terrorist attacks on the US homeland or on other vital interests. Above all, the United States should not be putting "boots on the ground" to pursue state-building. Second, President Biden's speech, at least at first glance, appears as a warm embrace of decapitation. Biden places a lot of confidence in "over-the-horizon" capabilities. If any boots on the ground are necessary, the "over-the-horizon" strategy will require very few of them. The meaning of Biden's speech for the other three strategies—war-fighting versus insurgency, community mobilization, and homogenization—is more ambiguous.

Although Biden's speech may not add up to a "doctrine," its broader outlines suggest the essential elements of an emerging grand strategy. Strategy is about matching national interests and means. In terms of defining US national interests, President Biden emphasized that the world has changed. Today, the United States must meet the following threats—"China as America's existential competitor, Russia as a disrupter, Iran and North Korea as nuclear proliferators, cyber threats as ever-evolving and terrorism as spreading far beyond Afghanistan" (Cooper et al., 2021). Military intervention in the Middle East only detracts from these threats. As stated in the Afghan withdrawal speech, "And there is nothing China and Russia would rather have, want more in this competition, than the United States to be bogged down another decade in Afghanistan." Biden has shown consistency here. As Vice President, Biden did all he could to get US forces out of Iraq, even interfering with internal Iraqi government formation to ensure the continuation of Prime Minister Maliki's continued exit-enhancing rule in 2011. Biden has been consistent: boots on the ground in the Middle East/Islamic world are not in the US national interest.

Relating to means, Biden stressed that the past litany of failures shows that military intervention should only be launched when there are "clear, achievable goals" closely tied to "fundamental national security" interests. It is difficult to imagine any form of nation-building or boots on the ground counterinsurgency efforts that could meet the criteria for "clear" goals given the ever-changing and unpredictable nature of internal war. Given often unstable nature of states emerging from violence, war, and destruction, it is also difficult to know a priori what goals are clearly "achievable." The problem is more acute if "achievability," given American's lack of patience, requires short- to medium-term success.

Biden's speech did recognize some complicating realities. He stated, "And I've been clear that human rights will be the center of our foreign policy." It is difficult to square that statement with the US capitulation to the Taliban. Early in his first term, it is not clear how President Biden would combine a foreign policy centered on human rights with an advocacy for drone strikes.

The president's statements designate Iraq as one in a collection of intervention failures. In the wake of his decision and push for complete and rapid withdrawal from Afghanistan, and his subsequent justifications, there would seem to be little room for learning from the variation seen in Iraq and described in this work.

22.4. The Foreign Policy Establishment

US presidents can shape the course of learning and forgetting about past interventions, but the US government is also run by foreign policy officials, many of whom enjoy long careers in Washington or the foreign service. In the arguments of several leading US political scientists of the "restraint school," US foreign policy has been determined in large part by an "establishment." They argue that this establishment's ideology and self-interest have perpetuated a strong, and often disastrous, interventionist policy over the past many decades.

Restraint advocates argue that in the wake of the end of the Cold War, a bipartisan consensus developed supporting an interventionist foreign policy, including the use of US military power. Intervention supporters agreed with Madeleine Albright's famous characterization of the United States as the world's "indispensable nation." Some called for the United States to act as the "world's policeman."[3] The result was a seemingly endless series of US military interventions since 1991: Operation Provide Comfort in Northern Iraq after the First Gulf War, Operation Gothic Serpent in Somalia, Operation Uphold Democracy in Haiti, Operation Deliberate Force in Bosnia, Operation Allied Force in Serbia/ Kosovo, Operation Enduring Freedom in Afghanistan, Operation Iraqi Freedom in 2003 Iraq, Operation Odyssey Dawn in Libya, and the intervention against the Islamic State in Iraq and Syria.

There are different versions of the restraint school, but all of them, in line with Biden's statement, recommend concentrating on a small set of clear national threats, avoiding all nation-building projects, and employing some form of "off-shore-balancing" to counter rising regional hegemons.[4] Accordingly, members of the restraint position saw President Biden's early statements as an indication of a clear victory for the "restraint" school over the "liberal hegemony" or "liberal interventionist" advocates embedded in the foreign policy establishment. Advocates of restraint believe that their Realist policy should have been employed throughout the post–Cold War era. Instead, the United States, following a policy of liberal interventionism, experienced one fruitless and counterproductive military intervention after the other.

The question arises of how liberal interventionists have survived and prospered given this string of interventionist failures over a 25-year period. Stephen Walt, one of the leading advocates of a restraint policy, believes the answer lies in understanding the beliefs and self-interest in the US foreign policy establishment.[5] In Walt's argument, this entrenched community came to believe that spreading liberal values is essential for US security. Often citing the findings of Democratic Liberal Peace theory (which finds that liberal democracies do not fight each other), members of the Liberal Hegemony school argue that a US-led international system could shape and sustain global liberal political and economic institutions. They also came to believe that this US-led system could confront deviant states and bring them into line at low cost and little risk. If economic sanctions didn't work, invasion was the next step in the playbook. As Walt summarizes, "Once these obstreperous tyrants were gone, the United States and the rest of the liberal international community could step in and help liberated and grateful populations create new and legitimate democracies" (Walt, 2018, p. 59).

Walt goes on to argue that for the US foreign policy establishment, these beliefs about the security benefits and low costs of military intervention are intertwined and sustained by self-interest. At an organizational level, liberal interventionists gain power and status as the implementers of intercessions. With such a consensus in play, individuals have no incentive to dissent. The consensus produces conformity. Conformity rewards compliance and punishes deviance. Furthermore, given this set of entrenched beliefs and incentives, there has been little cost of failure and a lack of accountability.

How might we see change? Walt writes that despite broad presidential powers, in terms of changing the direction, "[a] single leader cannot do it alone" (Walt, 2018, p. 19). Walt does imply that a "crushing international setback" could shake the status quo (Walt, 2018, p. 19). For Walt, only a countervailing movement within the foreign policy establishment can clearly change the liberal interventionist consensus.

Unfortunately for the restraint school, while there was a shock to the international system, it took the form of the Russian invasion of Ukraine. Many commentators and analysts saw this event as a repudiation of restraint. George Packer wrote, "This restraint is not a hard-won prudence in the face of tragic facts. It is a doctrinaire refusal, by people living in the safety and comfort of the West, to believe in liberal values that depend on American support … the war has reduced their position to rubble" (Packer, 2022). Perhaps the most consistent and known supporter of liberal interventionism is Ivo Daalder. In the wake of the Russian invasion and Ukrainian stiff response, he concluded, "The silver lining in the horror of the aggression against Ukraine is that it gives the United States and its Western allies a chance to do what they failed to accomplish after the end of the Cold War: reinvigorate international institutions and deepen cooperation on transnational threats" (Daalder and Lindsay, 2022, p. 130). The foreign policy establishment could again place the pursuit of a rules-based international order, and all it entails, at the center of the US agenda.

To come back to the core question, how will the key US policy actors come to view the adventure in Iraq in the near future (after 2023)? The discussion above suggest that the military might forget Iraq, the president might draw an overly general lesson, and the foreign policy establishment might revert back to policies supporting its own beliefs and interests. There are also broader trends at work. The future of US military intervention will be shaped by tolerance for violence, the changing international hierarchy, and the appearance of new state structures—in other words, factors related to death, dominance, and state-building.

22.5. Death

Military intervention brings death. But death has many political meanings. Some lives are much more important than others. How the United States will militarily intervene in the future depends to some extent, maybe a significant extent, on how the American public values different types of deaths.

First, there are the deaths of US civilians occurring on the US homeland. Those lives are worth more than any other. The military interventions in both Iraq and Afghanistan were justified as necessary counters to threats to the American homeland. President George W. Bush's doctrine of preemption was based on the idea that the US military must strike first before our enemies, with their terrorist connections, hit the United States. While the memories of 9/11 fade, the US public's appetite for preemptive military strikes and interventions has also declined. But what if another terrorist attack killed hundreds or thousands of US civilians in the homeland?

Second, there are the deaths of US soldiers. No doubt the US public and politicians are sensitive to these deaths. With the decline of faith in political, religious, and economic leaders, the US public sees US soldiers, sailors, and marines are one of the last sets of American "heroes," worthy of being honored at most sporting events and other gatherings. Yet, with the advent of a smaller, professional military, US military experience has become more and more disconnected from mainstream US life. While certain high-casualty events, such as the 13 military deaths at the hands of ISIS-K during the US withdrawal from Afghanistan, create a public outpouring of grief and lamentation, the casualties witnessed in Iraq were more of a daily incremental drip, largely out of sight of the US public. The wars in Iraq and Afghanistan witnessed relatively low numbers of deaths of volunteer soldiers and did not fully engage the US public. In the words of one commentator, "They allowed, so to speak, for an army at war and a nation at the mall" (Kaplan, 2021). Given the conduct and abilities of the US military to protect its force, future military interventions are likely to result in low-casualty wars. Indeed, the intervention in Kosovo was an "immaculate" war, conducted entirely from the air, with soldiers on the ground only as peacekeepers. Future public tolerance for low-casualty wars is difficult to gauge and may depend on the desires and abilities of US political leaders to make the case for sacrifice. There seems to be little tolerance for high-casualty wars.

Third, there are deaths of US contractors. These lives are worth less than any other. In World War II, the United States contracted 10% of its armed force; in Iraq, the figure was 50% (McFate, 2019, p. 128). Perhaps 15% of all contractors were members of corporate combatant organizations such as Blackwater (McFate, 2019, p. 128). No one actually knows the casualty numbers for contractors, as the US government does not keep track; however, at least one study estimated their casualty rate to be much higher than for the US military.[6] The use of contractors, if they are seen as simple mercenaries, is distasteful to many. Certainly, when Blackwater personnel killed 17 civilians in 2007 in Nisour Square in Baghdad, many in the United States were repulsed. Yet, for both financial and political reasons, the trend toward increasing use of military contractors is likely to continue. A war filled with contractors, and hidden casualties, might allow a broader range of strategies and options for military intervention.

Fourth, there are the lives of civilians in the states where the United States is intervening. In Iraq, common estimates put this figure at about 200,000.[7] Because most of these deaths were not directly caused by US military actions, the US public did not seem overly concerned. When US marines killed 26 civilians at Haditha, many shot at close range, massacre style, the squad leader was acquitted in a court-martial and the event faded in the national consciousness. Meanwhile, the shift to decapitation and drone war may actually increase tolerance for killing. Targeted killing is now supervised by lawyers. When the United States kills, it does so with official legality, with collateral damage possibilities considered and accepted. In effect, collateral damage in the forms of dead civilians is unfortunate, but legal. War may be becoming more sanitized, and perhaps increasingly tolerated.[8] The Nobel Peace Prize winner Barack Obama, perhaps unsurprisingly, greatly enhanced US drone forces and their ability to kill.

Fifth, there are the lives of civilians being killed by their own leaders in foreign states. In a 2005 World Summit, all members of states of the United Nations supported a statement addressing the international community's responsibility to intervene to prevent genocide, ethnic cleansing, war crimes, and crimes against humanity. The principle (known as "Right to Protect," or R2P) overrode state sovereignty and called for collective intervention, including military intervention, if a state failed to preserve the lives of its citizens. In 2006, Anne-Marie Slaughter, while describing R2P, stated, "From a pure international law point of view, and actually from a theory point of view, the responsibility to protect is the most important shift in the definition of sovereignty, in my view, since the Treaty of Westphalia of 1648" (Slaughter, 2006). A decade and a half later, in the wake of Iraq and especially in the aftermath of Libya, the potential of R2P to drive the United States toward military intervention seems limited. Neither the Burmese government's violence against the Rohingya nor the near collapse of the state in Haiti compelled action, or even much contemplation, of US military intervention.

Some intervention strategies are deadlier than others. Some strategies will involve higher deaths of soldiers, some will involve higher deaths of civilians, some might involve higher deaths of both. Changing perceptions of the value of life, as well as the desire to avoid taking responsibility for deaths, may affect future US military interventions. Some strategies may be taken off the table; others might be unduly favored.

22.6. Dominance

In terms of dominance, this book has focused on group hierarchies within Iraq. There are also hierarchies within the international system. These are often discussed with reference to polarity—or the number of great power peer competitors within the international arena. The Iraq conflict largely took place within an era of unipolarity. There is no question that the United States held the clear dominant position in the international system after the end of the Cold War and had no serious peer.[9] Although many argue that the United States can and will maintain that position in the foreseeable future, many others see the rise of China and other states initiating a new era that is ending American dominance.[10] In the parlance of political science, the world is currently moving from a unipolar world to either a bipolar one—with China as the overwhelmingly most important competitor—or a to a multipolar world, with Russia as well as other emerging powers such as India playing significant roles. This change in polarity will likely have broad effects on US military intervention.[11] Again, some strategies may be more or less likely to form the basis of "lessons" as the structure of world power transforms.

For many Realist theorists, unipolarity meant that the United States was unconstrained and could pursue a myriad of opportunities. With no serious rivals, the cost and risks of intervention would not significantly empower a competing rival major power because no such competitor existed. In the words of Barry Posen, the unipole lives in a "world of temptation" (Posen, 2017). Given the nature of the US foreign policy establishment described above, the temptation was to engage in state-building interventions to remove illiberal actors, using military intervention if needed, from the international system.

For many Realists, the emergence of even one peer competitor drastically changes the behavior of the former unipole. John Mearsheimer (2014) argues that because states value survival above all else, even the small chance of a major war with a competitor will force the former unipole to forgo ideologically driven temptations and instead concentrate solely on shaping the balance of power. Following this logic, the United States can no longer afford spending blood and treasure on interventions in non-vital areas. Rather, obtaining a favorable balance of power requires preventing the rival from gaining power-enhancing regional hegemony. For members of the restraint school, employing a strategy of off-shore balancing, rather than intervening with boots on the ground, will be the most efficient means for this end.[12]

Bipolarity is not determinative, however. The Cold War was a bipolar struggle that generated many interventions by both superpowers. As shown by Noel Anderson's research, one side's intervention often led to the other side's counter-invention. For instance, the Soviet invasion of Afghanistan triggered US support of anti-Soviet fighters; US intervention in Vietnam likewise produced Soviet support of the Viet Cong. With each side valuing "not losing" more than winning, each side often gave enough aid to sustain the war for many years without producing a decisive outcome. The result was many long interventions (Anderson, 2019), although with only one side at a time "putting boots on the ground" in order to avoid escalation.

Most prognosticators do not believe US bipolar competition with China will lead to this type of intervention dynamic (Christensen, 2020). Above all, Chinese leaders appear to see its comparative advantage with the United States in its growing economic power, as seen in its "Belt and Road" initiative, rather than any military intervention. As opposed to the Cold War, the ideological tenor of the competition between two market-driven powers is not the same. While the Chinese may believe that its model of a one-party state may appeal to many countries around the world, the quasi-religious nature of the Cold War, with its beliefs about contagion and dominoes falling, is absent today. Furthermore, the Chinese may have drawn lessons from US military intervention failures. Given the orientation of China as the competitor in a new bipolar system, it seems likely the constraining properties of bipolarity on military intervention would significantly outweigh those favoring intervention.

If multiple powers emerge, a situation of multipolarity, Realists predict that the competing states will seek security through the formation of alliances to create balancing coalitions. Regarding intervention, while there would be more powers with the ability to intervene, their incentives to do so would be unclear. One could imagine situations where one alliance partner was threatened by regime change or state collapse in an area vital to that state's security. Would the other members of the alliance feel compelled to militarily

intervene to maintain the capacity of their alliance partner? Would some partners in the alliance intervene believing that their participation in the alliance
would compel other alliance partners' cooperation in, or at least tolerance of,
intervention?

22.7. State-Building

There were a variety of assumptions accompanying the invasion and occupation
of Iraq. One of them held that the best way to promote peace in the long term
was through the building of a strong state, hopefully a democratic one. As in
Eastern Europe, the Saddamist totalitarian state could be swept away, leaving a
blank slate. Western interveners would build on that blank slate working toward
the Weberian standard. In this anticipated transformation, US military power
and intervention would not only sweep away the old state, but provide security
as the new state was being constructed. In Iraq, the US military, not the US State
Department, would take the forefront in developing Iraqi local political and economic institutions.

Only it didn't work out that way in Iraq. As outlined in various sections of the
book, Iraq failed every Weberian standard of a strong state. In terms of central
state sovereignty over its territory, ISIS took temporary control over large swaths
of Iraqi territory, the Kurdish Regional Government was a state within the state,
territories remained disputed, and localities have sometimes operated under
tribal and warlord influence. In terms of a monopoly over legitimate force, PMF
militias use the resources of the Iraqi state while often taking directions from
Iran. These foreign-connected militias also retain control over state ministries
and economic functions while running as political parties. In terms of legitimacy,
perhaps the most powerful political actors in Iraq were Grand Ayatollah Sistani
and Moqtada al-Sadr. The decisions and directions of both of these Shia figures
matched or superseded that of the state. It must be admitted that in terms of the
lack of a strong and well-functioning state, Iraq is more the rule than the exception, certainly in the Middle East. As outlined in Chapter 20, militias and non-
state actors have dominated Lebanon for decades. In the aftermath of Moammar
Qaddafi's removal, Libya is a divided state ruled by warlords. Syria will likely
emerge from its civil war severely fragmented.

The experience in Iraq, along with trends in the rest of the world, foretell a
different kind of world with different types of states than when the United States
invaded Iraq in 2003. There have always been weak states with hybrid actors and
a lack of a state monopoly over legitimate violence. Such states are likely to increase in the future. In a world of weak states and hybrid actors, what role should
military intervention play?

22.8. Conclusions

The findings of the previous chapter contained a level of nuance and a warning against the temptation to give into overgeneralization or to reduce the complex experience of the United States in Iraq to a set of easy slogans. Despite President Biden's clear statements about the end of an era of American military intervention, this chapter has addressed several factors which will influence US interventions in general ways. The future may be more indeterminate than many think, a point that the concluding chapter will address in more depth.

The indeterminacy regarding future military interventions is illustrated by the case of Samantha Powers. In her previous position as UN Ambassador in the Obama administration, Powers advocated US military intervention in both Libya in 2011 and Syria in 2013. President Biden nominated Powers to head the US Agency for International Development. During the 2021 nomination hearings, Senator Rand Paul asked if Powers believed her Libyan and Syrian intervention positions were mistakes. Powers made no such concession and replied, "When these situations arise, it's a question almost of lesser evils—that the choices are very challenging" (Jakes, 2021). The weight among various evils will not be clear in the future, regardless of the nature of states. Furthermore, interventions are not always straightforward cost–benefit calculations. The intervention in Afghanistan was originally driven by anger and vengeance as much as strategic logic. The war weariness and negative emotions associated with Iraq will influence interventions for the foreseeable future.

This chapter has addressed the way a changing world and changing set of US policymakers might affect future US intervention. In the world emerging at the time of writing (2023), we see an American military moving to peer-competition, grown weary of the demands and failures of counterinsurgency, but increasingly able to find, fix, and finish targets. We see a president declaring an end to an era of interventions while declaring total support for Ukraine in a war not just over territory, but for the very soul of the liberal world order. We see a foreign policy establishment shaking off a record of past intervention failures and vigorously embracing a possible second chance provided by the Russian-Ukraine war. We see an American public that will not tolerate death on its homeland, but is selective in its tolerance of death around the world. We see the end of unipolarity—maybe—and a world in which military interventions will be decided by a range of alliance considerations, rather than wars of US choice. We see a world in which rebuilding states has lost its clear meaning, as states themselves, in a world awash with guns and transnational actors, become increasingly fragmented.

So what is the future of military intervention after Iraq?

The Future of American Military Intervention

23.1. Introduction

The Iraq conflict has consumed hundreds of thousands of lives and countless billions of dollars. While the costs have been obvious, the meaning of the US adventure in Iraq for future American military interventions is unclear. This final section (IV) of the book has attempted to discern that meaning by coming back to two central questions: In the contests between counterinsurgent and insurgent, what explains who wins? What explains the persistent weakness of the Iraqi state? These two questions address the two outcomes of main concern—violence and state-building. During pursuit of those questions, Chapter 21 uncovered a series of findings and presented a list of "lessons." Chapter 22 discussed several political, cultural, and structural factors that could affect how those lessons might be learned, ignored, or forgotten by US policymakers. This chapter takes into account both the lessons and the shaping factors to project the possible future of American military intervention. It will proceed mainly by examining the five strategies outlined in the book's first section. But the final chapter must begin with a humble admission: It is very difficult to predict the future of American military intervention.

23.2. It Is Difficult to Predict the Future of US Military Intervention

A few things can be predicted with reasonable confidence. First, there is little chance that the United States will engage in a massive clear, hold, build (CHB) operation with tens of thousands of boots on the ground in the near future.

Second, the United States will continue to use decapitation as a strategy and increasingly integrate partner forces into such efforts. Beyond that, a range of possibilities will persist. While this book draws lessons from the US experience in Iraq, the next military intervention will take on its own distinct features, rather than precisely mirroring Iraq. Indeed, although occurring in roughly the same period, Iraq differed from Afghanistan, and both Iraq and Afghanistan differed from Libya.

The problem about anticipating the future of military intervention goes beyond simple statements like "no two interventions are the same." At the time of writing (2023), the majority opinion holds that the United States will avoid military intervention as much as possible. But we have seen this film before. The George W. Bush administration came into office disparaging the interventionist inclinations of its predecessor. After the 9/11 attacks, that same administration soon became the author of two of the longest and most extensive military interventions in US history. The US military interventions in Iraq and Afghanistan were the result of the 9/11 attacks and a heightened perception of terrorist attacks. Before 2001, the very idea of a generation-long global war on terror, and its accompanying interventions, was inconceivable.

While the Bush administration ridiculed interventionists before leading massive military interventions, "Right to Protect" advocates envisioned a world of legitimate military interventions arising to prevent the world's worst cases of mass killing. International support for a "Right to Protect" (R2P) reached its zenith in 2005 with its affirmation at that year's World Summit. Ideally, the United Nations would sanction interventions when states failed to provide fundamental protections to their own citizens. But if not, coalitions of the willing would step in. Indeed, the Bush administration justified the Iraq invasion partly on the principles of R2P.

Seemingly straightforward in concept, the actual practice of R2P has seen a twisted path. Ironically, the language and logic of R2P are perhaps commonly used by aggressors to justify their actions. President Putin invokes the R2P principles to invade Ukraine in order to save its Russian inhabitants from genocide (Reid, 2022). Furthermore, R2P may incentivize politically weak groups to provoke aggression to "trigger R2P" to bring in the international community on their side.[1] Because anyone with a smartphone can beam victim images across the internet, the world Wide Web is saturated with photos of suffering intended to influence international opinion. After a while, the effect is more likely desensitization than moral outrage. The bottom line is that, at least for the near future, there is no functional international norm guiding humanitarian military intervention.[2]

Neither the Bush administration anti-interventionists nor the R2P pro-interventionists could have envisioned how the future would play out. Beyond these ironic outcomes, however, the causes motivating both types of actors are not going away. Another mass terrorist attack may spark anger and fear in the United States, leading to demand for some type of military response. Human rights activists will not ignore future incidents of genocide or mass killing. The desire to save human lives is not going to disappear. Even leading restraint scholars admit a role for military intervention in some cases.[3]

While some threats seemingly come out of the blue, types and likelihood of threats might be predicted from the structure of power in the world. As discussed in Chapter 21, most analysts see the world heading toward bipolar competition between the United States and China. Bipolarity, however, is not determinative in terms of predicting military intervention. While Cold War bipolarity saw many competitive interventions, few see that dynamic as playing out in the emerging US-China bipolar contest. While one RAND study (2021) does caution US policymakers about possible Chinese interventions, most Chinese security specialists have a difficult time coming up with plausible scenarios in which the United States would be compelled to counter Chinese actions through the types of military intervention seen either in the Cold War or in the unipolar era. There is one much addressed scenario involving the collapse of North Korea. Being highly averse to a Western-allied unified Korea on its border, the Chinese might intervene to prevent regime consolidation; the United States might feel compelled to intervene in response. Another scenario involves the Chinese supporting insurgency in Myanmar with various ethnic groups as proxies and the United States being drawn in to counter. While China has interests in Central Asia and Africa, few can imagine a repeat of US-Soviet competitive intervention there. Still, no one can convincingly claim to know the exact future contours of the transition to US-Chinese future confrontations.

US-Russian rivalry also presents uncertainty. Clearly, Russia does not wish to conform to its assigned role as a lesser power. Before February 2022, much of the US policymaker world and many international relations theorists were writing off Russia as a second-rate power, a country with the GDP the same as Italy, so not to be feared. In 2014, Senator McCain dismissed Russia as "a gas station masquerading as a country" (Everett, 2014). However, after the Russian invasion of Ukraine, Sweden took the Russian threat seriously enough to end 200 years of neutrality and seek NATO protection. For the first time in decades, the possibility of nuclear war rose its head. While the United States and its NATO allies were deterred at least in part from direct military intervention by the nuclear threat, they massively supported Ukraine and built up defenses in Eastern Europe and the Baltic. While Russia will need to rebuild its forces after their troubles in Ukraine, the Russo-Ukraine war has created long-term hostility between Russia and the West with unforeseeable consequences. Russia has intervened in Syria, Georgia, and Ukraine while maintaining a military presence

in Moldova. At the time of writing, the Russian and Kremlin-aligned mercenary group Wagner was participating in armed conflicts in several African states.
Given Russia's record, it is conceivable that the United States and Russia will
find themselves engaging in competitive interventions in the Global South. But
many other scenarios are also conceivable.

Unexpected events, vacillating balances of power, and unstable international
norms produce uncertainty on the likelihood of US military intervention. There
is also the question of the nature of the intervention if it were to happen. Again,
there is a range of factors producing uncertainty. Chief among these is the emergence of new fighting technologies related to insurgency. Consider the opening
stages of the Russo-Ukrainian war. There was little anticipation that Ukrainian
forces would destroy a thousand Russian tanks in the early stages of the war.
Predictions of massive cyber war did not come to pass. The quality and intensity of the information war was a surprise. In short, the Russo-Ukrainian war
verified a well-known but often underestimated axiom. As enunciated by Ken
Pollack: "The moral of the story is that outside observers simply do not know
which countries (or nonstate actors) will prove most able to wage twenty-first
century war" (Pollack, 2022, p. 141).

Critically for the subject here, several of the emerging technologies are in-
expensive and easy to master. These technologies and weapons are likely to become increasingly available to insurgents, hybrid actors, and a range of non-state
actors. As one commentator sums up, "Lesser powers and even non-state actors can now challenge conventional militaries in ways not possible a decade
ago" (Williams, 2022). It is possible to imagine how the proliferation of these
emerging technologies might affect each of the five strategies discussed in
this book. The US advantage in war-fighting, unparalleled in the world, might
no longer be as invincible if opponents possess javelin missiles and Turkish
Bayraktar drones. There would be a cost in both US lives and materiel for any
invasion or any counterinsurgency strategy relying on armor. Likewise, CHB
presents many vulnerable targets for drones. In Iraq, the US military had to
wage an ever-changing IED war. A combination of IEDs and drones would give
insurgents deadly unmanned weapons both on land and in the sky. Also, the
United States might lose its advantage in decapitation. The enemy might also
be able to find, fix, and finish, especially in a world with Google Earth and easy
communications via WhatsApp.

On the other hand, the expansion of these weapons might present a positive side for counterinsurgents. If the United States engaged local partners in
community mobilization efforts, the low financial cost and low training costs
involved with the new technologies may multiply the value of collaboration. For
example, the United States could provide state allies and even non-state partners
with inter-operable drones (Williams, 2022). Will the changes in technology

deter or enable future US military intervention? While it is easy to imagine these costs and benefits, along the lines of the statement above it is difficult to know how things would play out.

23.3. The Future of Five Strategies

While it is difficult to predict the future of US military intervention, it is certainly not impossible. As the hundreds of pages of empirical material in this book illustrate, the Iraq war provided a trove of material on what strategies worked in that environment. An assessment of that material, along with a basic understanding of US political constraints, should produce important insights.

The following pages summarize many of those insights through the analysis of the future of the five strategies that have been at the center of this book.[4]

23.3.1. War-Fighting in Intervention

As the term *war-fighting* suggests, this strategy is about fighting a war—soldiers acting to "kill the enemy, not to win their hearts and minds."[5] The primary methods are firepower and mobility. Obviously, an invasion uses these war-fighting tools. Many US practitioners continued to engage in war-fighting as a counterinsurgency strategy long after the invasion of Iraq. They persisted in the use of armor, indirect artillery shelling, cordon and sweep operations, large-scale detention, and displays of force as a deterrent.

The deficiencies of war-fighting for counterinsurgency have been previously covered in this book. If US forces found themselves fighting an insurgency in the near- to medium-term future, they would not repeat those mistakes. Furthermore, if the United States were to invade and conduct war-fighting, opponents know enough to avoid taking the US military head-on; they would shun the disastrous attempts to try to match the United States in a war-fighting contest. Note the early learning of insurgents in Iraq. The Sadrists learned that lesson in 2004; Sunni insurgents in Hawija also learned that lesson in 2004. Opponents also know that while the United States has unchallenged military power, it also operates under heavy political constraints. Given these conditions, actors will engage in what David Kilcullen has termed "liminal maneuver"—"taking sufficiently few and ambiguous actions to achieve core political objectives, but not enough to trigger a military reaction" (Kilcullen, 2020, p. 150).

Might war-fighting be used as one step in a longer process? The United States could use its war-fighting abilities to "break" an enemy regime, then leave and allow indigenous allies to take over from there. For the near future, the United States will certainly be able to use its military superiority to "break things." The

United States can invade and overthrow governments if it wishes. This brings us to the famous "Pottery Barn" axiom of Colin Powell. In the discussion of the consequences of the US invasion of Iraq, Powell argued that the United States would inevitably become responsible for the consequences of that invasion, as in the policy of the Pottery Barn store—"you break it, you own it." But what if that is not true? Looking back at the Iraq case, what if the United States "broke it," removed Saddam Hussein, and just left? The larger question is whether the United States can go around "breaking" its enemies through relatively cheap means and then leave. The bottom line is that unless international norms (and public opinion) change, the United States is unlikely to engage in breaking things anytime in the near future. If the US military does intervene, it will likely be careful about breaking things while there, and forgoing, limiting, or altering the use of a war-fighting strategy during a longer intervention.

23.3.2. Clear, Hold, Build

While war-fighting is about breaking things, the counterinsurgency strategy of clear, hold, build (CHB) focuses on building things. Iraq showed that it is much easier to break things than to build them. Of all the lessons accumulated at the end of Chapter 21, the greatest number applied to CHB. Above all, winning the "hearts and minds" of the population will likely be insufficient. Local armed actors hold advantages in their area of operations. In contests riven by master cleavage and a pursuit of dominance, stability requires clarity in ethnic hierarchy, a task not always amenable to the Western use of sticks and carrots. Some opponents may have more tools than the occupier in moving the population to desired roles across the spectrum. Staying longer still might not produce the desired results when domestic actors capture sections of the state, hybrid actors form, and the population comes to resent a "forever" presence.

If US policymakers were to take these lessons seriously and try to learn from them, they would still think twice about ever initiating a long-term CHB project due to reasons laid out in the previous chapter. The US military wishes to move on to peer competition against China (and Russia) in the newly emerging bipolar/multipolar world. In the near future, presidents will not want to be seen repeating Iraq and Afghanistan. They will avoid being put into a position where they need to justify the US military deaths that would inevitably occur during CHB.

The problem in Iraq was not just that the United States could not achieve the lofty goals of democracy; rather, the United States, despite tens of billions of dollars spent and the work of thousands of trainers, could not build a functioning Iraqi Army, an essential part of the CHB strategy. Robert Gates famously told an assembly of Army cadets back in 2011, "In my opinion, any future defense secretary who advises the president to again send a big American land army into Asia or into the Middle East or Africa should have his head examined" (Shanker, 2011). Even the most vocal advocates of using military intervention for statebuilding, such as Samantha Powers, have changed their tune, at least in intensity.

Perhaps the biggest reason we will not see the Iraqi Surge model of CHB again is that Americans saw it not just once, but twice. In February 2009, President Obama ordered a surge in Afghanistan, sending 17,000 more troops, added to the 32,000 US forces and 38,000 NATO personnel already there. As with the Iraqi Surge, the change involved not only more troops but also a move to a population-centric strategy seen in Iraq's CHB. The consensus view is that the move failed to reach its objectives in Afghanistan as well.

A broader problem for Western state-building projects is that many of the world states are no longer states in the Weberian sense. States increasingly lack control of the legitimate means of violence and the means to project centralized power. This phenomenon will be even more pronounced in states like Iraq. Western interveners may not wish to launch state-building strategies in an environment that they cannot predict, shape, or fully understand. However, not every environment presents the same challenges as Iraq. Policymakers (and academics) could draw on the extensive experience of CHB and state-building in Iraq to more fully understand the process of state development in these countries.

23.3.3. Decapitation

For those who would give up on state-building interventions, decapitation offers an alluring alternative. There is little doubt that decapitation will remain a major part of US strategy, both in counterterrorism and in counterinsurgency. Among possible strategies, decapitation is the cheapest in cost and manpower and the least intrusive in terms of a "footprint." Even if one thinks the benefits of the strategy are not that high, at least the costs appear very low.

Recall that the term *decapitation* is used here to describe targeted raids against both broader mid-level network leadership (often described as counter-network operations) and smaller numbers of killings of senior leaders (usually termed *decapitation* and sometimes *assassination*). While the present work has been generally positive about US capabilities for decapitation, political science studies are decidedly mixed and with seemingly contradictory findings, especially in studies of top leadership decapitation. In a study of nearly 300 leadership strikes occurring during 1945–2004, Jenna Jordan found that decapitation failed to significantly degrade organizations and may have prolonged them (Jordan, 2009).

On the other hand, Patrick Johnston examined over one hundred assassination attempts carried out within 90 campaigns during 1975–2003 and found significant success in lowering violence and defeating insurgents (Johnston, 2012).[6] Other analysts have remarked on the strategy's capacity for inciting escalation or perpetuating grievances (Tecott 2016).

The broader US experience in Iraq does illuminate some decapitation shortcomings. The early experience in Iraq of decapitation in Iraq failed to meet expectations. US forces killed the leader of al-Qaeda in Iraq, al-Zarqawi, in June 2006, yet AQI still thrived. By this point, AQI was built to survive decapitation. In Weberian terms, the charismatic founder of AQI created a formal-rational organization that was able to replace him with new charismatic leaders. A year later, the US assassination of the Iranian leader and his PMF counterpart outside the Baghdad airport was a boost to the PMF legitimacy, at least in the short run. Anyone driving around Baghdad in 2022–2023 will be struck by the number of Soleimani/Muhandis billboards promising that the "the blood of our martyrs will not be forgotten."[7]

Furthermore, the early practice of President Biden's moves toward decapitation have shown that implementation of the strategy will likely involve more than "very few" boots on the ground. As previously discussed, after pulling out of Afghanistan, President Biden made a speech in August 2021 about ending "forever wars" and never putting a significant number of American boots on the ground again. Less than a year later, President Biden was authorizing the deployment of around 400–500 special forces troop to Somalia to take on Al Shabab (Savage and Schmitt, 2022). President Trump had removed a US force of 700; President Biden quickly put them back in. Under both the Trump and Biden administrations, US forces have been conducting network decapitation. President Biden's move came despite the admonishment of International Crisis Group analysts who stated, "Sending in more U.S. troops and honing in on a small number of senior Al Shabab leadership is narrow in its aims and by definition cannot end the broader military fight absent more concerted and effective diplomatic and political efforts by the United States and others" (Savage and Schmitt 2022).

These examples and findings are unlikely to make any difference for the near future of decapitation. The politics and popularity of decapitation will probably overwhelm any nuanced calculations. US presidents like decapitation (Obama, Trump, and Biden). The military likes what it is good at. The Joint Special Operations Command (JSOC) has taken on a life of its own. Indeed, it is very possible that decapitation could become the most common strategy of US military intervention moving forward. The Israelis have a phrase for the constant killing of militant opponents—"mowing the lawn." Due to the nature of the region, Israelis see militants and terrorists as inevitable as grass growing in the yard. All a state can do is develop machinery to cut the grass, a lawn mower so to speak. In a similar fashion, the United States could forgo state-building, develop relationships with special forces communities in allied states around the world, and engage in "lawn-mowing" on a global scale. The Iraq wars showed that the United States has a machine to do so. For some, the business of the United States, given what has been learned from the Iraq and Afghanistan examples, is counterterrorism, not state-building. Putting the results of Iraq in context, all the United States should hope for is short-term successes, and decapitation seems a low cost-efficient and politically desirable way to achieve those short-term goals.

As seen in the Somalia example above, even a decapitation strategy, if it is aimed against an organizational network rather than simply assassinations of very top leaders, requires a significant number of boots on the ground. Its success will also likely hinge upon local allies that are able to gather intelligence and perhaps help in raids. For this strategy to be effective, it may be easier for the United States to create its most reliable partners through training of special forces. Accordingly, the United States could downplay military-military relationships with partners around the world and instead build close relationships between US special forces and partner state special forces who could act as the eyes and ears for US decapitation.

Perhaps the biggest stumbling blocks for the development of such a strategy are legal and moral. In the consideration of death, decapitation reduces the number of US military deaths to very low levels. However, the level of foreign deaths through "collateral damage" is not insignificant. In December 2021, the *New York Times* published a Pulitzer Prize–winning investigation into civilian deaths of US air wars. The work revealed imprecision in drone targeting and the concealment of casualties. It cast doubt on the claim that the precision of current weapons, combined with oversight by legal teams, has solved the collateral damage problem.

There is also the gut emotional reaction to making decapitation central to US military intervention. One Joint Terminal Attack Controller operating in the third Iraq war described his reaction after a strike:

> The smoke slowly cleared in light winds. Soon we distinguished bodies strewn all over the west side of the berm—some with limbs separated and others in contorted positions. Those were always solemn moments, but ones we were conditioned to appreciate as warfighters battling a bloodthirsty enemy. As strange as it may seem to some, for guys like us it was a scene of somber beauty to see our enemy cut down and lying in pieces on the ground in front of us (Pittard and Bryant, 2019, p. 206).

Whether the world can become "conditioned" to appreciate this style of military intervention is an open question.[8]

23.3.4. Community Mobilization

Like decapitation, community mobilization is likely to remain in the US strategic toolbox in the foreseeable future. In Iraq, the Awakening and the Sons of Iraq movements certainly played a significant role in producing dramatic drops in violence. In September 2006, violence in Anbar peaked at nearly 2,000 SIGACT incidents a month, more than in any other province in Iraq. Remarkably, the rate plunged to just 155 incidents in January 2008.[9] One of the most violent provinces had become the most peaceful. The success of community mobilization should not be surprising given its three clear effects.

"Flipping" communities from the opponent's sphere into one's own sphere provides critical information, takes armed forces away from the insurgent, and increases manpower for the state's forces. Community mobilization is a highly effective strategy—at least in the short run.[10]

Beyond its short-term effectiveness, the strategy is attractive for reasons laid out in the previous chapter. Unlike CHB with its "surges" of boots on the ground, the strategy substitutes locals for US soldiers. The strategy usually stays out of the public eye and avoids scrutiny. The complexity of community mobilization is often difficult for even the military to fully understand. Unlike decapitation, with its sometimes wayward drone strikes killing bystanders or hitting mistaken targets, US military and political culpability for anything that goes wrong is often less clear.

Community mobilization is also likely to remain a problematic strategy. Community mobilization basically admits that the counterinsurgent will find shaping local power difficult. The logic is that it is better to co-opt local organizations and networks rather than try to fight them or shape them. The deals made between counterinsurgent and community leaders are not likely to reduce the latter's local base, agency, or autonomy.[11] That autonomy means that "flipped" groups can "flip" back to oppose the state (Staniland, 2012). These groups can work both sides, changing back and forth and always looking for a better deal. Furthermore, even if the group does not completely "flip" into opposition, these non-state organizations will have incentives to seek their own goals rather than the state's. They may be allying with the state to protect revenue streams gained from smuggling or criminal or semi-criminal practices. Some may transform into a type of hybrid actor now seen in Iraq. In a situation where the strategy is implemented across a wide number of groups, the overall situation can result in a subtle and almost feudal game involving dozens of tribes, warlords, or regional ethnic and religious groups.[12] There was a reason why CHB advocates did not see community mobilization as the way forward, especially in terms of state-building.

Different forms of community mobilization exist. In this book, the focus has been on how the United States mobilized Iraqi communities as complementary forces (to run checkpoints, go on joint patrols). The case was a partnership of an on-the-ground, in-country intervener with an internal community. Proxy warfare is a related, but different, type of relationship.[13] In proxy warfare, there is no in-country intervener. An outside power makes a deal with an inside organization, which could be a tribe or other form of community, or simply an ideological, political, or criminal organization. In the immediate post-Iraq era, the United States continued to play forms of the community mobilization strategy in Syria, even if they did not openly admit doing so. The US-backed Syrian Democratic Forces were less "democratic" than a collection of community/ ethnic groups dominated by the Kurdish Peoples Protection Group (YPG). As could be expected, the agendas of these community-based proxy groups differed from that of their US sponsor.

The United States is likely to continue practicing forms of community mobilization in the near future, but the nature of this game is usually opportunistic and ad hoc. In practice, community mobilization often has idiosyncratic origins and unpredictable trajectories. In Iraq, it was the tribes that approached the United States to make a deal after interests changed and aligned. In Syria, the United States was looking for on-the-ground short-term partners to help eliminate ISIS. Community mobilization is unlikely to be the basis of consistent US policy, even if it is very likely to be used. Unlike Biden's "over-the-horizon"/decapitation speech, or Bush's Surge/CHB move, the strategy will not be the centerpiece of a presidential speech.

23.3.5. Homogenization

In the debate about the causes of the dramatic decline in violence in Baghdad in 2007–2008, the role of homogenization is highly contested. This issue was a central focus of Chapter 13. Two lessons were extrapolated in part from that empirical case: (1) if master cleavages and concerns about group hierarchy are salient, then the conflict is unlikely to end until there is clarity in that hierarchy; (2) homogenization strategy can produce clarity. It follows that homogenization could produce a positive result. With separation and unmixing, all territories are left with a clearly local dominant majority group. Along with the construction of defensible boundaries, that dominance may lead to an end of violence, not only through eliminating security dilemmas, but by producing a more stable political order.

It is important to recall how the homogenization strategy is defined for the purposes of this book.[14] Here, homogenization is tacit acceptance of the ethnic cleansing and separation processes occurring during an intervention. The intervener is not actively engaged in population transfer. The intervener does not draw up formal legal partition boundaries, unless those become desired by the warring parties at some point. If the intervener is committing a sin with this form of homogenization, it is a sin of omission, not commission.

Governments and occupying forces do not usually openly admit to allowing homogenization to play out. Governments may turn a blind eye to the process, or they may work with the result of ethnic cleansing to maintain peace. While the intervener may not actively create defensible boundaries, it may act to enforce defensible boundaries that emerge during the struggle. Consciously or not, in Baghdad US forces constructed concrete T-walls that reinforced the new ethnic demographic lines. In effect, although the US military did not initiate the homogenization process, it did facilitate the creation and continuation of homogenous neighborhoods.

In considering a broader set of cases, homogenization strategy could be expanded and applied not only to actual interveners but also to potential interveners. Consider two different types of cases. In one set, similar to the dynamic in Iraq, interveners are present and may tacitly allow homogenization to take place. In a second type, no intervener is present when homogenization is taking place during a violent conflict. In this second set of cases, potential interveners would have at least three choices:

> First, the intervener could allow the homogenization process to continue until compact and defensible boundaries have been formed and only then send in military forces to reinforce those boundaries (probably after a ceasefire). In these cases, the intervener might be predicting, or at least hoping, that such a boundary would eventually be established. If such a boundary were never established, if one side is too small or weak to form a defensible position, ethnic homogenization might turn into genocide.

> Second, an intervener could choose to intercede earlier in an attempt to head off a bloody homogenization process. In this case, military intervention would amount to peacemaking rather than peacekeeping. This choice would also cut off the possibility of mass killing.

> The third choice would be to do nothing, to forgo intervention entirely. In these cases, homogenization might lead to a de facto partition of a state. Or it might lead to mass killings of various types. Many in the Middle East believe that the United States allowed and desired homogenization of warring communities in Syria.[15]

Given the overall reticence to engage in large-scale military intervention after the Iraq and Afghanistan wars, the United States (and Western powers as a whole) seems likely to allow more and more future conflicts to burn on, in effect the third choice above. The Iraq and Afghanistan wars have sapped Americans' compassion. Best to look away. In the absence of US will to militarily intervene, accepting homogenization (maybe even hoping for it) may become unstated policy for many of the world's most violent ethnic conflicts.[16]

23.3.6. War-Fighting and Decapitation: A Combination for Taking Back Territory

The empirical chapters identified two possibly effective combinations of strategies. Chapter 12 described an early successful merger of decapitation capabilities with war-fighting in the retaking of Sadr City in 2008. The evolution of this combination found another success in the war against ISIS, as illustrated in Chapter 16. In both cases, the combination was able to help US and Iraqi forces retake territory held by insurgents. In Chapter 21, these cases were the foundation of the conclusion that "the US military is very good at war-fighting and finding, fixing, and finishing targets."

The ISIS war also provided the evidence that it may be easier to build new special forces than new armies in overseas partners. In the ISIS war, the Iraqi Counter-Terrorism Service (CTS), as well as some Peshmerga units, did the bulk of the necessary frontal attack. CTS forces endured stunningly high casualty rates. Despite massive US training and investment, the Iraqi regular army exhibited neither professionalism nor patriotism when confronted by ISIS. It was a combination of dedicated Iraqi special forces units with US strike cells and weaponry that systematically drove ISIS out of Iraq.

This combination could form the basis of a template of a new form of war, one where the advance of specially trained units forces the enemy to concentrate their forces in response, thus creating lucrative targets for US drones and aircraft. Before getting too enthusiastic, however, it should be recalled that the ISIS war was a slow and deadly grind, taking the course of three years. Furthermore, the cities of Mosul and Raqqa in Syria were reduced to rubble in a way that resembled Warsaw after the Second World War.

23.3.7. Community Mobilization and Decapitation: A Combination for the Management of Violence

Of the five strategies, community mobilization had positive short-term results, and decapitation was impressive in its technical implementation and avoidance of American casualties. The combination of these two strategies might form the basis of what Paul Staniland has termed "violence management."[17] In this strategy, the intervener forgoes state-building but does not forgo local partnerships. The goal is to develop capabilities to disrupt challengers to the government, even if not eliminating them.

Violence management is related to "mowing the lawn," but with a larger set of tools and an in-country presence. As Staniland describes the strategy: "It has three core elements: a light U.S. ground force commitment favoring special forces, heavy reliance on airpower and partnerships of convenience with local militias, insurgents, and governments" (Staniland 2018). Many of the problems of community mobilization—uncontrolled local partners with their own agendas, the state abdicating governance in some areas—would remain. But the political costs in the United States would be greatly reduced in comparison to larger and more ambitious intervention projects.

23.3.8. Summary: The General Contours of Future US Military Intervention

The US intervention and war in Iraq have been the most important conflict of the twenty-first century so far, but it will certainly not be the last US military intervention. Members of the US military may want to get out of the postwar reconstruction business and emphasize kinetic war-fighting and deterrence, but they are unlikely to be able to extract themselves from the increasingly complicated nature of violent conflicts in today's world.

The Iraq conflict has produced knowledge and "lessons." The US security world has its own way of learning those lessons. This chapter has examined the future of the five strategies central to this book's analysis in light of those lessons and ways of learning and has extrapolated their future prospects. It has concluded that the US military will turn away from war-fighting for small wars. The United States will not wish to break something that they do not wish to own. The central mission of war-fighting will remain the main focus of the US military, but that focus, above all else, will be to develop war-fighting capacity to deter China and, to a lesser degree, Russia. Second, to echo Robert Gates, troop-intensive state-building military interventions will be unlikely. As the analysis here as made clear, those strategies failed for many reasons. After Iraq and Afghanistan, there is no political will for them. Third, there will almost certainly be a role for decapitation. The technology, as seen at work in Iraq, is too seductive. The United States, perhaps relying on transnational relationships among special forces, will likely use decapitation to erode insurgent organizations (counter-network operations) in the Middle East and Africa. Fourth, there is no end in sight for opportunistic community mobilization. If the United States is involved in a conflict, there is little reason not to take advantage of able and armed communities ready to provide manpower and intelligence to complement US firepower an organization. The Iraq experience has shown, however, that these short-term military synergies are not always compatible with longer-term political goals. Finally, the United States will increasingly accept homogenization both in its own interventions and in other cases around the world.

Two combinations of strategies perhaps seem most promising. If a fight requires taking back territory, the combination of war-fighting (with selective partners) with decapitation technologies can be used to systematically roll back insurgents. If the situation calls for violence management, the combination of community mobilization with decapitation may do the job.

23.4. Final Comments: Dealing with the Uncertainty of Military Intervention

US policymakers and military personnel will find themselves in unexpected interventions, just as they did in Iraq. How should policymakers and analysts understand the situation they find themselves in? While there are many approaches that will yield insight, I wish to conclude by highlighting the nature and benefits of the method laid out in the first chapters of the book.

Although not explicitly stated, the analytical framework is built on the assumption that there are no general laws underlying intervention or insurgency. It is a mistake to search for them. While large-n statistical studies may yield knowledge about some general tendencies, they will not be very useful in actual practice. Many of these cross-national statistical studies are based on a logic of structural constraint. They often assume a certain preference function for potential insurgents and then analyze variables that constrain those actors from achieving or pursuing those assumed goals. For example, the most commonly cited cross-national studies on civil war find that the absence of mountains to hide in constrains insurgents. A major finding is that the presence of a strong state constrains rebels. These findings are vague and often will have little relevance to any actual decision-making. In Iraq, US military personnel knew the state was weak; the mission was to find ways to strengthen it.

The case studies have emphatically shown that the analytical emphasis must be placed on actors' agency rather than laws or structural variables acting as constraints. The insurgents and counterinsurgents, as well as members of the general population, spent years adapting to a fluid and often violent situation; these actors spent years adapting to the adaptations of the other actors. This fluidity will not be captured by static variables. It is also poorly captured by methods that assume a stable preference ordering, usually an ordering that projects Western values onto the target population. In corresponding to this reality, the analytical framework developed in the early chapters of this book strived to develop an approach able to understand this constant process of adaptation. This aim was behind the all three of the central concepts of the framework: roles, mechanisms, and strategies.

Consider roles first. Individuals adapt by moving across the spectrum of roles. They often come and go from neutral positions; they can pick up a gun and they can put it down—and they can take it up again. They can choose to cooperate with the insurgent but then switch support to the government. The spectrum of roles is a central device to capture this fluidity, these constant small moves that add up to larger outcomes in a myriad of ways.

Social science has developed knowledge about the ways individuals adapt. The focus on mechanisms captures that knowledge and brings it specifically to bear on the movement among specific roles. The focus on multiple mechanisms provides a realistic approach to the complexity of human nature. Certainly, individuals calculate cost and benefits. They collect information and form beliefs about how to proceed. But individuals can actually change the way they value things during a long conflict. Emotions offer a way to understand that change. Under the intense conditions of war and occupation, individuals process information in different, but understandable ways, as established by extensive research on psychological mechanisms. Most individuals are embedded in communities and networks. We know that these ties breed powerful social norms. We have knowledge of rational choice, emotions, psychological phenomena, and norms—we have sufficient knowledge to anticipate how these mechanisms might affect movement on a spectrum of roles. Concentrating on these mechanisms allows us to develop a supple and flexible template to realistically address the fluid and complex nature of conflict under military intervention.

Strategies embody the ways actors believe they can trigger mechanisms to affect desired movements among roles. Strategies are theories about adaptation, and further, theories about how to adapt to others' adaptations. As seen in the empirical chapters, actors competing during a military intervention will change strategies over time and place. By tying the study of strategy to mechanism and role, and then matching up opposing strategies in case studies, we gain a more specific understanding of why and how one side's adaptation succeeds while another fails.

The analytical framework is geared to address uncertainty and fluidity because it is designed to be changed itself in the course of practice. Not all the hypothesized mechanisms will be observed or have explanatory worth. Other types of movement will propel a search for additional mechanisms. The spectrum of roles can be modified. As seen with the development of hybrid actors, the linear nature of this spectrum between negative and positive sides required adjustment. The method identifies important interactions and combinations. The study of Iraq started with five strategies and ended by specifying the utility of combinations of those five when the empirical analysis revealed their interactions.

A final comment—the Iraq war was traumatic. Few want to think about it. Most wish to dismiss the conflict with general statements. But the Iraq case presents us with incredible fields of variation in violence, state-building, US strategies, and opponent counterstrategies. In this book, I outlined and applied an analytical framework to understand that variation. That method is not standard; it cannot be done with off-the-shelf variables. It requires talking with many of those involved in the actual conflict. It is necessary to listen to those who fought and were caught in the fight. As a professor at MIT, I marvel at the advances in artificial intelligence and how the study of artificial intelligence is sweeping this campus and the defense institutions associated with MIT. But these machines are still a long way off from understanding the emotions, identities, and strategies that shaped the intervention and its aftermath in Iraq. I hope my effort and methods have done justice to that conflict and especially to those who suffered during it.

APPLICATION OF THE FRAMEWORK
TO CLASSIC THEORIES AND CASES
OF INSURGENCY AND
COUNTERINSURGENCY

A.1. Introduction

The first three chapters built an analytical framework based on concepts of role, mechanism, and strategy. Core insights from this framework are incorporated in the template found at the end of the third chapter. This template identifies which mechanisms are likely to be operative at and between nodes on the spectrum of roles. It serves as a guide—a set of implicit hypotheses that can be applied to any case of insurgency, not just Iraq. In political science concepts, it serves as a tool to discipline process tracing.

This template is designed to help break down the logic of insurgent and counterinsurgent strategies. This appendix provides an illustration of the framework's applicability and value through an application to two of the most famous strategists and one of the most famous cases of insurgency. First, this appendix will apply the framework to one of the most famous insurgent texts—Mao's treatise *On Guerrilla Warfare*. Second, the framework will be used to break down the thinking of perhaps the most cited counterinsurgent—David Galula. Third, the framework will be applied to both insurgent and counterinsurgent strategies and practice in one of the most studied cases of insurgency—the Malayan Emergency. This last exercise will provide an example of how the framework can match insurgent strategies versus counterinsurgent strategies and specify why one strategy prevails over the other.

A.2. Mao on Guerrilla Warfare

Chapter 5 of *On Guerrilla Warfare*, originally published in 1937, is entitled "Organization for Guerrilla Warfare." The work is not only prescriptive—detailing how guerrilla war should be fought—but also descriptive; many of the lessons learned derive from what actually transpired in the war against Japanese occupation. As Mao describes, there are different types of guerrilla units. The first is formed from the people without detailed direction from any organized body. As Mao summarizes, "Without question, the fountainhead of guerrilla warfare is in the masses of people, who organize guerrilla units directly from themselves" (Mao, 1961, p. 73). Mao provides a more vivid description of this process:

> Upon the arrival of the enemy army to oppress and slaughter the people, their leaders call upon them to resist. They assemble the most valorous elements, arm them with old rifles or bird guns, and thus a guerrilla unit begins. . . . In circumstances of this kind, the duties of leadership usually fall upon the shoulders of young students, teachers, professors, other educators, local soldiery, professional men, artisans, and those without a fixed profession, who are willing to exert themselves to the last drop of blood. Recently in Shansi, Hopeh, Chahar, Suiyan, Shantung, Chekiang, Anhwei, Kiangsu, and other provinces, extensive guerrilla hostilities have broken out. All these are led by patriots. The amount of such activity is the best proof of the foregoing statement. The more such bands there are, the better will the situation be. (Mao, 1961, pp. 72–73)

Thus Mao sees the first step in the process as a local and largely spontaneous reaction to outside rule. Then local "first actors" begin local organizations.

In Mao's treatise, these local organizations of armed resistance (the −2 level) are critical to successful insurgency. Mao spends several pages delineating the different ways that such units can be formed and maintained. He extensively discusses the ways units of the regular rebel army (−3) can support these local organizations. Specifically, a regular mobile large army unit can be dispersed and embed units locally (−3 units become −2 units); there can be a "merger of small regular detachments and local guerrilla units. The regular forces may dispatch a squad, a platoon, or a company, which is placed at the disposal of the local guerrilla commander" (Mao, 1961, p. 75) (−3 units under −2 command); local government police and home guards can be converted into local guerrilla units (+ 2 switch sides to become −2); deserting enemy soldiers can be placed into local guerrilla units (+3 become −2); "bands of bandits and brigands" can form local units (Mao, 1961, pp. 74–76).

Throughout their existence, these local units continue to develop capabilities and discipline. While they are being strengthened, the regular rebel army is formalizing their organization into a traditional squad, platoon, company, battalion, regiment hierarchical structure. At the appropriate moment, the dispersed, now better trained, local units join up with the regular army to fight a conventional and decisive battle against the weakened regime military.

In sum, Mao's theory can be broken down into stages which can be described in terms of roles and mechanisms:

1. There is immediate emotional reaction against outside rule—*anger* and *resentment* drive individuals (of many political persuasions) from neutrality (position 0) toward the left side of the spectrum of roles.
2. Local leaders, some driven by *status rewards*, form local armed guerrilla units (−2).
3. These units are continually strengthened over time. They are incorporated into a formal organization imbued with the *normative and rational mechanisms common to formal military organization.*
4. At a later stage, these dispersed, but now well-trained, local units will join up with regular army units to fight a decisive battle against the regime's forces (−2 forces transformed into −3 units).

As the reader will note, this brief outline shows the important role of strategy and organization. Mao's theory holds that the initial steps depend upon an emotional reaction against the occupier, which generates massive local mobilization. As Mao famously declares, there needs to be a "sea" in which the "fish" can swim. At a larger level, however, Mao's treatise specifies sequencing of moves concentrating on different nodes of the spectrum of roles. In the early stages when the balance of power is not favorable, the rebel forces need to build upon the features of that "sea," specifically through the creation and strengthening of local guerrilla units (−2).

A.3. David Galula's *Counterinsurgency Warfare: Theory and Practice*

David Galula's *Counterinsurgency Warfare: Theory and Practice*, written in 1964, can be seen as a Cold War contemporary counterinsurgent response to the insurgent theories of Mao and Che Guevara.[1] Chapter 7 of Galula's work

("Operations") enumerates eight steps relating to the conduct and ordering of moves in an ideal counterinsurgent strategy (Galula, 1964, pp. 75–94):

Step One: Destruction or expulsion of the insurgent forces
Step Two: Deployment of the static unit
Step Three: Contact with and control of the population
Step Four: Destruction of the insurgent political organization
Step Five: Local elections
Step Six: Testing the local leaders
Step Seven: Organizing a party
Step Eight: Winning over or suppressing the last guerrillas.

The framework serves to break down this process into mechanisms and roles. Step one targets mobile guerrillas (−3) through big initial sweeps. At this stage, Galula believes there is not enough information to go after locally embedded rebels (−2). Galula holds that uninformed action at the local level is likely to create collateral damage and do more harm than good.

The next steps concentrate on the neutral position (0). Step two establishes a grid of forces able to create a presence over a wide territory. Step three, contact with and control of the population, aims at moving local populations from neutrality to general support of the state (0 to +1). Counterinsurgents must establish themselves as the only legitimate authority in the community; insurgents must be isolated. As Galula explains (italics are Galula's):

> *In any situation, whatever the cause, there will be an active minority for the cause, a neutral majority, and an active minority against the cause.* The technique of power consists in relying on the favorable minority in the order to rally the neutral majority and to neutralize or eliminate the hostile minority. (Galula, 1964, p. 53)

Galula's specific tactics focus on one mechanism in particular—the "tipping" mechanism. Most residents will wish to remain neutral, out of the way of both rebels and soldiers. Galula believes, however, that many of these neutrals will move into a +1 position of support if they see high enough numbers of others moving to that position, that is, if a threshold is surpassed. Galula wishes to trigger this mechanism by moving numbers of residents into visible +1 positions, even by coercion if necessary. He writes:

> The battle happens because the population, which was until recently under the insurgent's open control and probably still is under his hidden control through existing political cells, cannot cooperate spontaneously

even if there is every reason to believe that a majority is sympathetic to the counterinsurgent. The inhabitants will usually avoid any contact with him. There is a barrier between them and the counterinsurgent that has to be broken and can be broken only with force. Whatever the counterinsurgent wants the population to do will have to be imposed. Yet the population must not be treated as an enemy.

The solution is first to request, and next to order, the population to perform a certain number of collective and individual tasks that will be paid for. By giving orders, the counterinsurgent provides the alibi that the population needs vis-à-vis the insurgent. (Galula, 1964, p. 81)

The ability to carry out this step requires a census, curfew, and enough military presence to produce protection.

Step four, the destruction of insurgent political organization, goes after the local rebel infrastructure, the foundation of the −2 organization. This task is only possible if step three has been accomplished and enough individuals are providing information to the counterinsurgents.

Step five, local elections, consolidates the belief that the population has moved to +1 and can go about pro-government activities such as voting without undue concern of retaliation. Elections are a classic way of producing a focal point, a visible means for individuals to gauge who is in control and how firm that control is. The elected leaders, in turn, provide the foundation for pro-government local organization, including local self-defense (+2). Step six involves testing these leaders.

Step seven aims to build local organizational success, the focus of the counterinsurgent effort to this point, into wider, perhaps national levels. The eighth step is to go after any remaining mobile guerrillas (−3).

Galula summarizes the approach in the concluding remarks to the work: "Whether in the cold or in the hot revolutionary war, its essence can be summed up in a single sentence: Build (or rebuild) a political machine from the population upward" (Galula, 1964, p. 95). In terms of the spectrum of roles, Galula's process is composed of:

1. Going after mobile guerrillas (−3) to allow a focus on the local community
2. Moving neutrals to +1 through *tipping dynamics*, using *rational choice* coercion and payoffs
3. Eliminating −2 through increased information from the +1 actors
4. Moving +1 into +2 roles for the community to rule itself, using elections as *focal points*
5. Eliminating weakened remaining −3 elements.

A.4. Comparing and Matching Insurgent and Counterinsurgent Strategies

The major benefit of translating different strategies into the concepts of the analytical framework is the ability to match up strategies of competing actors during insurgency. The framework provides a device to allow for systematic analysis of competing and evolving strategies over the course of a conflict. As mentioned before, Mao and Galula were Cold War contemporaries. Their theories present both sides of an insurgency—insurgent and counterinsurgent. By breaking down these strategies into mechanisms and roles, we can better identify how they might match up in actual practice.

A comparison of Mao and Galula produces some clear insights. Above all, Galula focused on moving neutrals into informal support of the counterinsurgent (+1). The mechanisms employed to create this movement are rational-choice sticks and carrots, combined with both of the informational mechanisms—tipping points and focal points. Galula wanted to make clear to the population that the optimal choice is support of the counterinsurgent, and he wished to produce clear visible signals to induce that choice. Galula's strategy does not see norms or emotions as central forces.

Mao's theory assumes that emotions and community-level status considerations will likely, and quickly, drive the population leftward on the spectrum. In contrast, Galula assumes that the majority of the population will sit on the fence and that minorities will be ready on two sides for *any* cause. Mao's theory allows for the force of the emotion of resentment to play a critical role. In the case of the Japanese occupation of China, Chinese resentment of Japanese rule played a major role across political groups. In his experience in Algeria, Galula believed that Algerian resentment against French rule could be overcome through the application of policies capable of incentivizing neutrals to move toward cooperation. Mao's theory holds that a key element for sustained insurgency is building local organization (−2). Galula believed that −2 level insurgents would be readily cleansed once the majority of the population became willing informers (+1). In comparison, Mao and Galula produce theories that emphasize different mechanisms. From these theories, they develop different strategies and also different beliefs about how to create and manage organizations to carry out those strategies.

A.5. The Malayan Emergency: The Interaction of Insurgent and Counterinsurgent Strategies

The practice and benefits of systematically matching counterinsurgent and insurgent strategies can be given vivid illustration through re-examination of an iconic case: the Malayan Emergency of 1948–1960.[2] The case is often held up in the counterinsurgency literature as the classic "success" case, and is often juxtaposed with Vietnam. In fact, one of the most widely read texts on counterinsurgency, John Nagl's *Learning to Eat Soup with a Knife: Counterinsurgency Lessons from Malaya and Vietnam*, is based on this comparison. As the authors of the text *Understanding Modern Warfare* summarize the influence of this case, "the iconic success story of this era, the British campaign in Malaya from 1948–1960, was mined for lessons of victory in counter-insurgency that are applicable today" (Jordan et al., 2008, p. 264). The case has lost some of its luster as an exemplar, for reasons discussed below. Here, the purpose is to show how an examination of basic mechanisms can distill a case into a form that can generate insights and comparisons.

The Malayan Communist Party (MCP) formed the Malayan People's Anti-British Army (MPABA, later the MPLA). In June 1948, the organization murdered three European planters, among others. The British response was a Declaration of Emergency which instituted a form of rule just short of martial law allowing for wide powers of detention, search, occupation of property, as well as a death penalty for unlawful possession of weapons. The Malayan Emergency would officially last until 1960.

The insurgents, in effect, played first. As in many situations, the insurgents held a weak hand. Although the British had lost their pre-war aura, they still were the sovereign rulers of a relatively wealthy colony. Several factors operated in the British favor. First, the British began with a majority of the population on their side in the contest with the Communists. Politically, the Communists were at a severe disadvantage because of their ethnic base. Chinese dominated the MCP, although they comprised only 38% of the population, in comparison to 49% Malay and 11% Indian (Nagl, 2002, p. 60). Ethnic Malay hostility to the Chinese had been recently heightened by British policy. The British gave the Chinese and Indians equal voting and other rights under the 1946 Malayan Union. In response to the Malayan Union's restructuring, Malays violently protested and all significant Malay government officers boycotted the new constitution's inauguration ceremony (Nagl, 2002, p. 62).

Second, in terms of weapons and killing power, the MCP was weak. They relied on Japanese weapons left over or captured during the Second World War (Porch, 2013, p. 253). They could mount assassinations and raids, but little more than that; they were never able to amass more than 300 fighters, with an average force of 56 men (Cable, 1986, p. 92). The lethality of the Emergency was low by comparative standards; over the course of the 12-year conflict, British and Commonwealth troops suffered only 519 killed, while the guerrillas experienced 6,710 fatalities (Cable, 1986, p. 81). Relatedly, the MPLA was further hobbled by logistical challenges. They did not possess consistent supplies of food and other necessities.

The Communist insurgents did possess one good "card," though. Much of the Chinese population lived as squatters without title to the land they lived upon. They already existed as a society apart, leery of all government representatives, and were aware of majority Malay contempt. They had moved into lands on the edge of the jungle in forest preserves or abandoned rubber groves. They were an ideal potential base for logistics and intelligence (Cable, 1986, pp. 74–75). With only this one good card, the MPLA was going to play it.

Given this source of support, the MPLA developed a series of support networks from 1949, called Min Yuen. In terms of the spectrum of roles, the Min Yuen cells were at the −2 level: organized and armed, sometimes providing part-time fighters, and always available for intelligence and food and other support. Government officials estimated the number of active guerrillas (−3) in 1949 at between 3,750 and 4,500; estimates of the total number involved as Min Yuen were at about 10 times that number (Cable, 1986, p. 78). An early British commander, Sir Henry Gurney, coming from the occupation of Palestine, stated that the Chinese squatters were "providing bases from which the bandits operate and . . . helping them, in some cases under duress and in many others willingly with food, arms, money, and other means of resistance . . . [were] a positive and formidable menace to security" (quoted in Nagl, 2002, p. 66).

With poor weapons and low numbers, but with this considerable local support base, the MPLA adopted a strategy of hit-and-run tactics against government and business targets. Given their Maoist background, the MCP planned to first cripple the economy and recruit more members. The government forces would be goaded into pursuit into the jungle, where the guerrillas would hold the upper hand. After successful attacks, the rebels would establish and expand liberated areas until the time was ripe for a climactic battle that would drive the British out (Cable, 1986, p. 73; Nagl, 2002, p. 64). In reality, the insurgents never got beyond harassing the government and business entities.

On the other side, the original British strategy failed to seriously threaten the existence of the MPLA. The first British counterinsurgency effort was essentially war-fighting. The British strategy was to use their better-trained and armed regular forces (+3) to go after MPLA guerillas (−3). The British did make some initial changes in order to pursue that strategy. In order to free up its mobile troops to hunt guerrillas, the British administration enrolled 24,000 Malays into a special force to guard tin mines, rubber plantations, and other static high-value locales (+2) (Cable, 1986, p. 75; Nagl, 2002, p. 65). Cable calls this force a "motley array of seconded civilian bureaucrats, police reserves, and ultimately, redundant NCOs of the Palestine Police" (Cable, 1986, p. 75). The British main effort was to go after the guerrillas with firepower and maneuver. Tactics included big battalion-level operations, cordon and sweep, harassment and interdiction bombing, and use of RAF bombing. In his case study, Nagl quotes General Boucher's description of the British guerrilla-centric highly kinetic strategy:

> My object is to break the counterinsurgent concentrations, to bring them to battle before they are ready, to drive them underground or into the jungle, and then to follow them there, by troops in the jungle, and by police backed by troops and the RAF outside of them. I intend to keep them constantly moving and deprive them of food and recruits, because if they are constantly moving they cannot terrorize an area properly so they can get their commodities from it; and then ferret them out of their holes, wherever those holes may be. (Nagl, 2002, p. 67)

A.5.1. Strategies and Mechanisms: Round 1

Given their constraints, the MPLA developed a strategy based upon the −2 level. The Min Yuen were absolutely critical in maintaining the relatively small and poorly equipped guerrilla force (−3). With this local support system in place, the MPLA launched small raids against the British colonial state. In response, the initial British strategy created +2 static guards, mainly using mobile military forces (+3) to chase mobile guerrilla forces (−3). In short, the British relied on basic war-fighting.

It is important to note what the British war-fighting strategy did not consider. The British strategy did not focus on the −2 level. It did not consider trying to trigger any mechanisms—rational choice, norms, or emotions—in the −1, 0, or +1 nodes. It also did not go after the source of insurgent strength, the −2 Min Yuen networks. In sum, the British strategy did not match up with the MCP strategy at all. Each strategy concentrated on different nodes on the spectrum. The MPLA strategy built on the emotions and norms of a separate squatter community. The British strategy concentrated on freeing up its mobile forces (+3) to chase, bomb, and eventually physically eradicate guerrillas (−3).

The result of this match-up of strategies was predictable. All commentators agree that the British attacks failed to accomplish its goal of eliminating the rebels. Given the information and logistical support of the Min Yuen, the guerrillas avoided the easily detectable battalion size cordon and sweep efforts of the British, with guerrillas fading into the jungle or the population. The Min Yuen also stood as a ready reserve to repopulate guerrilla losses. Bombing and periodic sweeps and maneuver warfare also failed to affect insurgent supply lines. The use of indiscriminate force only helped to push the Chinese squatter population further from the political and economic institutions of the state.

A.5.2. Strategies and Mechanisms Round 2: The British under Briggs and Templar

Lieutenant General Sir Harold Briggs became director of Operations in April 1950. In a telling passage from one of Brigg's reports, he states:

> The problem of clearing Communist banditry from Malaya was similar to that of eradicating malaria from a country. Flit guns and mosquito nets, in the form of military and police, though giving some very local security if continuously maintained, effected no permanent cure. Such a permanent cure entails the closing of all breeding areas. In this case the breeding areas of the Communists were the isolated squatter areas. . . . Once these were concentrated there might be some chance of controlling the Communist cells therein. (quoted in Nagl, 2002, pp. 74–75)

In other words, the British were now going to go after the −2 cells, the strength and center of gravity of the insurgents. And they went after this node with full force. Through a system of "New Villages," the British relocated 423,000 individuals (85% Chinese squatters) in 410 New Villages by the end of 1952 (Cable, 1986, p. 79). When Sir Gerald Templer took control of the effort, the relocation policy took on severe qualities. Templer imposed 22-hour curfews, reduced rations by 50%, and closed schools (Nagl, 2002, p. 98). There are different views of the quality of these relocation centers. Douglas Porch writes, "The goal was to move half a million Chinese into 'new villages' which turned out to be crime-infested 'rural ghettos' guarded by barbed wire enclosures and search lights that combined all the comforts of Kitchener's concentration camps minus the 'Ladies Committee'" (Porch, 2013, p. 255).

Accompanying this massive relocation effort was a change in military operations. Harassment and interdiction bombing almost ceased, airpower was limited to tactical support and making strikes only with positive visual engagement with an enemy, and armored vehicles were employed only in support of convoys. The military operated according to a principle of minimum force. There was no more massing of troops; instead the focus was on small units and flexibility. In the meantime, the British built up native +3 units, forming a Malay regiment that appealed to Malay ethnic pride and independence as well as striving to build up a Home Guard (+2).

What was the MPLA response to this change in British strategy? They simply did not have the resources to change their strategy. As the British clamped down on food control, searching every man, woman, and child as they left their village or left work at the rubber plant, the rebels went into survival mode and declined. The numbers of guerrillas killed or surrendering increased dramatically (Cable, 1986, p. 88). Also, the number of suspected subversives within the confines of the new villages dropped from 5,492 to 2,225—through relocation, monitoring, control of rations, and other means, the British effectively neutralized resistance networks (in terms of the spectrum, they moved −2 individuals to position 0).

A.5.3. Insights from the Malayan Case

One of the most commonly cited lessons from the Malayan Emergency is that counterinsurgents can learn. Nagl concentrated on the Malayan case in *Learning to Eat Soup with a Knife* for exactly this reason.[3] The British adjusted their strategy to attack the fundamental source of insurgent strength—the Chinese squatter communities. They completely changed their focus on firepower, maneuver, and mass. The British also paid attention to realistic political goals and appealed to the concerns of the Malay majority. The British changed from war-fighting mode to a more population-oriented policy, although one with draconian overtones. The British strategy changed to destroy the advantages the Communist held in the Chinese rural communities. Not all actors are able to change their strategy. The MPLA simply did not have the resources that would have allowed the flexibility to change.

A.6. Conclusion

The empirical sections of this work lay out the insurgent strategy and the counterinsurgent strategy for a range of localities in Iraq, as well as for four regions. As with the classic theories just described, the implementation of the framework will specify how these strategies placed different emphasis on different mechanisms and different nodes of the spectrum of roles. It will produce systematic matching of strategies. This matching of strategies is an essential part of our analysis. As Andrew Krepinevich has written:

> The essence of strategy is identifying asymmetric advantages, both our own and those of our rivals, both existing and prospective. General Rupert Smith observes that "the essence of the practice of war is to achieve asymmetric advantage over one's opponent; an advantage in any terms, not just technological." (Krepinevich, 2009, p. 15)

By matching up strategies disaggregated by role and mechanism, one aim is to specify and illustrate the nature of asymmetries that led to regional and local outcomes during the Iraq conflict. We will identify how insurgents used and sometimes created asymmetries that allowed them to sustain violence and organization even in the face of coalition material and technological advantages. We will also show how the US/Coalition forces sometimes managed to counter or eliminate these asymmetries and/or use US asymmetrical advantages to greater advantage.[4]

Appendix B

AN APPLICATION OF THE FRAMEWORK
TO REVIEW RECENT SOCIAL
SCIENCE LITERATURE

ZACHARY BURDETTE WITH ALEC WORSNOP AND ROGER D. PETERSEN

In an effort to build on existing knowledge from the social sciences, this appendix reviews over 80 relevant articles from major journals. Although they do not use the terminology, most of these articles attempt to test the power of a specific mechanism as it works to move individuals along identifiable nodes on the spectrum. Taken as a whole, Appendix B will provide us with some idea of the collective social science knowledge on roles, mechanisms, and strategies operating in insurgency in general and with potential relevance for Iraq.

There are eight sections. The appendix proceeds by role and mechanism, first examining works concentrating on the general population $(-1, 0, +1)$, then shifting to articles related to local militias $(-2, +2)$, and finally armed mobile actors $(-3, +3)$.

B.1. Movement among $-1, 0, +1$
Roles: Mechanisms Related to Economics/
Poverty/Employment

—Eli Berman, Jacob N. Shapiro, and Joseph H. Felter, "Can Hearts and Minds Be Bought? The Economics of Counterinsurgency in Iraq," *Journal of Political Economy* 119, no. 4 (2011): 766–819.

As the title suggests, this study directly examines the economic logic behind hearts and minds. The main independent variable of the study is the level of spending on reconstruction projects; the main dependent variable is attacks per capita against Coalition and Iraqi government forces. While the study is complex, the main hypothesis is straightforward: higher Coalition spending should produce fewer attacks. The theory underlying this hypothesis is founded on a rational choice mechanism; the authors explicitly assume a utility-maximizing community deciding between options of insurgent support versus Coalition support (Berman et al., 2011, p. 776). At the individual level, the authors clearly assume a rational actor. As they state, "This is a 'rational peasant' model, in the tradition of Popkin's (1979) description of Vietnamese peasants: noncombatants decide on the basis of a rational calculation of self-interest rather than an overwhelming ideological commitment to one side or the other." The study then lays out a three-sided "game" played among insurgent, government, and population. The value of the offers of insurgents and Coalition depends upon their signaling ability. As the authors put forth, "Signaling both capacity and commitment to providing security is critical to increasing support, cooperation, and information flow from the population. Economic aid and service provision by government could then contribute to the popular perception that the state is capable of maintaining order and enforcing security" (Berman et al., 2011, p. 772). The chain of reasoning holds that US and Coalition forces can provide signals through higher levels and specific types of economic support, which in turn allow rationally calculating individuals to see that their best interests lie with the Coalition and the new government. Accordingly, those individuals decide to forgo roles of insurgent support and move to provide support and information about the identity and location of the insurgents to the Coalition (+1), resulting in fewer attacks against the Coalition.[1]

US forces spent a lot of money in Iraq. The Commander's Emergency Response Program (CERP) alone disbursed US$3 billion across 29,975 individual projects and is used as the primary measure in the study. For their independent variable, the authors used records of daily total spending at the district level (there are 104 districts in Iraq). The study also examines what type of aid is most effective in gaining the population's support—small projects or large projects. In addition to the CERP projects, Berman et al. also examine the effect of 2,469 "large projects."

Did this massive amount of money produce the intended support? First of all, although the study is aimed at addressing economic variables, the best predictor of violence during the period under study was Sunni vote share, an identity factor. As far as isolating the effects of spending, Berman et al. found considerable variation depending on the nature and timing of the spending. When the Coalition doled out money in the form of local CERP projects after 2007, that money did correlate with a reduction in attacks. As the authors conclude, "CERP spending became more effective in reducing violence in the latter period, implying that conditions under which development aid is delivered are critical to its effectiveness" (Berman et al., 2011, p. 801). When the Coalition doled out money before

2007, or at any time in the form of large projects, there was no effect. In fact, the non-CERP spending, 90% of total aid, was found to have no effect.

—Andrew Beath, Fotini Christia, and Ruben Enikolopov, "Winning Hearts and Minds through Development Aid: Evidence from a Field Experiment in Afghanistan." Policy Research Working Paper; No. 6129 World Bank, Washington, DC. http://hdl.handle.net/10986/11950 (2012).

This study again focuses on the effect of economic aid to change attitudes and behavior in the general population. Beath et al. (2012) built their study upon the National Solidarity Program in Afghanistan. This aid program funded local projects, through both a Community Development Council and disbursement of block grants, across over 30,000 villages in Afghanistan, hundreds of them within the same small region. The program was administered over a period of years, with some villages in the same area receiving aid and others scheduled to receive aid in the future. Given these characteristics, Beath et al. (2013) could randomly select a treatment group of 500 villages (those villages that received aid) and match those villages to a control group of 500 villages (similar villages that had not yet received aid) in 10 rural districts. They then administered surveys that measured attitudes toward the government and beliefs about security and economic development.

In relation to counterinsurgency, the logic is similar to Berman et al. (2011) above. With a more positive attitude toward the government, the general population is more likely to consistently provide valuable information to the Coalition forces, which in turn will bring down levels of violence. Also, this positive attitude will likely impede individuals from moving to support roles for the insurgents. Thus, although the study measures attitudes rather than behavior, it does contain a logic explaining how these attitudes will lead to movement to +1 and away from −1 roles.

Beath et al. (2013) found that residents in villages receiving aid did possess moderately higher positive attitudes toward their economic situation and also held more positive attitudes toward the government. The authors did not find evidence of short-term improvement for security. Also, the positive effects were only found in the nonviolent villages, not in the areas of active violent insurgency in the two eastern districts in the study. This finding meshes with Berman et al. (2011) in supporting the idea that the effect of economic aid is context dependent. If there is little violence, or if violence has been reduced, then aid may persuade people to move toward +1. However, if the population is living in the midst of violence, aid does not seem influential. We also need to keep in mind that this study was conducted in Afghanistan and its findings may not easily translate to Iraq. Furthermore, for obvious reasons, the Beath et al. (2013) study was carried out in less violent areas where only 3% of respondents reported an attack in or near their village in the past year.[2]

—Benjamin Crost, Joseph Felter, and Patrick Johnston, "Aid under Fire: Development Projects and Civil Conflict," *American Economic Review* 104, no. 6 (2014): 1833–1856.

Like both Berman et al. (2011) and Beath et al. (2013), the study analyzes the relationship between aid and insurgent violence. In their case, they analyze KALAHI-CIDSS, the flagship Philippine development program which distributed aid to 4,000 villages in 42 provinces. Crost et al. (2014) examine aid distributions in 22 of these provinces through a regression discontinuity design. This design takes advantage of the fact that aid was given only to communities ranked in the poorest 25%. Their regression discontinuity design essentially looks at communities slightly below and slightly above that 25% level. In effect, we should not expect big differences between one community at 24% and one at 26%—the only major difference is that the community at 26% did not qualify for the development program and the one at 24% did. Thus they can isolate the aid variable.

Strikingly, Crost et al. (2014) find that the communities given aid experienced significantly higher levels of violence than the very similar set of communities that did not. Furthermore, they establish that political insurgent groups rather than criminal groups commit this violence. What explains this difference?

Crost et al. (2014) argue that insurgents implicitly accept the finding of Beath et al. (2013): government development aid will create positive impressions of that government and will help push members of the general population toward roles of support (+1). If the insurgents wish to block a pool of recruits from moving rightward on the spectrum, the insurgents need to impede successful development in poor communities. One obvious solution is to attack the receiving communities and diminish the success and attractiveness of that aid. In effect, the political groups committing this violence act strategically. They point out that their findings stand in contrast to Berman et al. (2011), who found that small CERP projects reduced violence after 2007. Using their view of the strategic nature of violence, they try to explain this difference: "A possible explanation is that the projects found to be violence-reducing by Berman et al. (2011) were relatively small and implemented in the vicinity of a substantial presence of US combat forces, as a complement to small unit military operations, which would explain why they did not cause an increase in violence. The KALAHI-CIDSS program, in contrast, was larger in scale, implemented by a civilian agency, and had a six-month lag between announcement and implementation. Insurgents therefore most likely had greater opportunities to act on their politically motivated incentives and sabotage the program, which would explain its conflict-increasing effect" (Crost et al., 2014, pp. 1853–1854).

—Eli Berman, Michael Callen, Joseph H. Felter, and Jacob Shapiro, "Do Working Men Rebel? Insurgency and Unemployment in Afghanistan, Iraq, and the Philippines," *Journal of Conflict Resolution* 55 (2011): 496–528.

In their study of the three states mentioned in the title, the authors find no significant relationship between unemployment and insurgent attacks that kill civilians. If there is a relationship, more unemployment drives violence down. Thus, it seems unlikely that unemployment, and the connected logic of opportunity costs, is driving individuals toward insurgent support. Perhaps many individuals do operate along the lines of opportunity cost thinking, but other forces outweigh that force.

Berman et al. (2011) can only speculate about what drives this surprising outcome. As with Berman et al. (2011), the authors develop an argument centering on the role of information in insurgency. Counterinsurgents pay for information on insurgents. When a population is in poverty, they are more likely to sell that information, and do so more cheaply. As a result, information-rich counterinsurgents have an easier time finding and eliminating insurgents. The study recognizes the difficulty of separating their argument from others. There are other variables that may be affecting both economic activity/employment and a decline in insurgent attacks. For example, the most effective counterinsurgent techniques—building walls and checkpoints—limit both commerce and insurgent attacks, and the economic variable may be spurious.

—Renard Sexton, "Aid as a Tool against Insurgency: Evidence from Contested and Controlled Territory in Afghanistan," *American Political Science Review* 110, no. 4 (2016): 731–749.

This study examines the link between government-provided aid and insurgent violence.[3] Its motivating premise is that insurgents should violently resist government aid programs because they anticipate that aid might move civilians toward pro-government support roles (+1). The main hypothesis is that insurgents' strategic response to aid projects depends on local conditions—specifically, whether the project is in a government-controlled or a contested district. While aid should have a violence-reducing effect when the government already dominates an area, it should provoke violent insurgent reactions in contested zones. Insurgents focus attacks in contested zones because they have greater capacity to operate at lower costs in those areas. This suggests that insurgents anticipate that government clear, hold, build (CHB) efforts will influence civilian hearts and minds, and their counterstrategy uses violence to prevent the government from signaling competence or buying loyalty that might otherwise move individuals away from neutral (0) or pro-insurgent (−1) positions.

A secondary hypothesis is that the type of aid matters. Insurgents should respond more assertively to projects that improve security infrastructure compared to projects with more narrowly humanitarian aims. Sexton does not fully explain the logic of this claim but notes that stopping the flow of humanitarian goods such as food and water could result in popular backlash and that attacking large infrastructure projects is logistically easier and has greater visibility.

Sexton tests these claims with data from Afghanistan in 2008–2010. The main independent variable is the amount and type of spending in CERP. To account for the interaction with territorial control, Sexton uses the location of US bases as a proxy for government-controlled areas. Data come from the Institute for the Study of War. The main dependent variable is insurgent violence, which comes from reports by the Afghanistan NGO Safety Organization. Sexton claims that top-down pressures to spend CERP funding and unwieldy bureaucratic ap-proval processes made the allocation of aid appear as if random, which can help identify the effect of spending on violence.

The results confirm that aid had violence-reducing effects in government-controlled areas but violence-enhancing effects in contested areas. There is some evidence that these effects are conditional on the type of aid, with "protective measures" in CERP spending, like watchtowers, generating the strongest pushback, whereas "humanitarian" efforts, such as food and fuel, had no statistically significant impact. Sexton evaluates potential mechanisms by testing the correlation between spending and government raids, airstrikes, and IED clearings. There is no association, which he interprets as a failure to cor-roborate the conventional wisdom that the aid reduces violence by generating more tips to selective counterinsurgent violence. Contrary to past research on the war in Iraq, Sexton also finds that spikes in insurgent violence are more strongly correlated with small projects than big ones, which might be because they are easier targets.

—Neil Narang and Jessica Stanton, "A Strategic Logic of Attacking Aid Workers: Evidence from Violence in Afghanistan," *International Studies Quarterly* 61, no. 1 (2017): 38–51.

This study examines insurgent violence in response to humanitarian aid rather than military development projects.[4] The main argument is that the Taliban attacks aid workers because they provide services that enhance the government's legitimacy and capacity. Whereas Sexton focuses on US military aid programs, Narang and Stanton extend this logic to international NGOs, such as Doctors Without Borders, that provide aid in an ostensibly neutral manner. These efforts nevertheless threaten insurgents because the government often claims credit for capturing these benefits from the international community and because it compensates for poor service provision that might otherwise fuel grievances. The main hypothesis is that variation in territorial control explains where insurgents focus attacks against aid workers. They argue that insurgents are more likely to attack in areas where support for the government is high (civilians generally occupy +1 roles) to convert government-controlled territory into contested zones. They are less likely to attack aid workers in insurgent-controlled territory because they want to avoid provoking civilian backlash where they already exercise dominance.

Narang and Stanton test these claims with data from Afghanistan in 2008–2011. They introduce a dataset of 691 Taliban attacks against aid workers drawn from Afghanistan NGO Safety Organization reports.[5] Data on the independent variable—public support for the Afghan government—comes from a mix of sources, such as Karzai's vote share in past elections. The findings confirm the main hypothesis, but suggest that the relationship is actually curvilinear. The Taliban concentrated attacks in "swing" zones where government support was neither at its highest or lowest point. They also find that attacks were concentrated against international aid workers but not Afghan organizations, which they interpret as suggesting that the Taliban knows it can exclude casualty-sensitive international organizations from operating in certain areas but calculates that Afghan aid workers are more likely to stay.

—Benjamin Crost, Joseph Felter, and Patrick Johnston, "Conditional Cash Transfers, Civil Conflict and Insurgent Influence: Experimental Evidence from the Philippines," *Journal of Development Economics* 118 (2016): 171–182.

This study examines how conditional cash transfer programs impact insurgent violence.[6] It is an empirical program evaluation of the *Pantawid Pamilyang Pilipino Program* in the Philippines. Unlike CERP, the *Pantawid* program focused on poverty reduction without considering the strategic implications of investments. For example, the attached conditions for cash transfers concerned vaccinations. Government security forces and aid administrators reportedly did not coordinate their efforts to maximize the program's effects for counterinsurgency.

The research design leverages the World Bank's decision to stagger treatment over time and randomly assign which villages received aid first. It assigned half of 130 eligible villages to start the program in 2009 and the other half to wait until 2011. The dependent variables include measures of insurgent attacks and influence according to records from the Philippine military. The findings confirm that treated villages experienced fewer attacks and decreased influence during the first year but no effect in year two.[7] This encouraging result contrasts with a previous study by the same authors that a community-driven development program also in the Philippines had led to increased violence.[8] The study attributes the difference to the difficulty of stopping cash transfers compared to infrastructure projects. These findings emphasize the importance of context. Even within the same country, regions, and general timeframe, two slightly different aid programs produced contrasting results.

The study briefly addresses potential mechanisms. Civilians in treated villages expressed higher approval of local politicians, which may suggest that the effect stems from an information mechanism of intelligence provisions (movement to +1) rather than an opportunity-cost mechanism to reduce insurgent labor supply movement away from −2/−1). Because of the proximity of treatment and control villages, higher employment in one should have spilled over to the other, so the notable difference between groups suggests that other mechanisms are more likely at play. Finally, Crost et al. acknowledge that the decline in violence may have nothing to do with shifting civilian loyalties. One common reason for insurgent attacks on civilians is the failure to pay "revolutionary taxes," so the rebels may simply have appropriated the cash transfers and had fewer reasons to harm civilians since they could pay the tax.

—Aditya Dasgupta, Kishore Gawande, and Devesh Kapur, "(When) Do Antipoverty Programs Reduce Violence? India's Rural Employment Guarantee and Maoist Conflict," *International Organization* 71, no. 3 (2017): 605–632.

This study examines the impact of jobs guarantee programs on insurgent violence.[9] The main hypothesis is that development projects will reduce insurgent activity only if local governments have the capacity to implement aid programs effectively. The treatment was a massive jobs program in rural India—the National Rural Employment Guarantee Scheme (NREGS)—and the dependent variable was a district-level dataset on Maoist violence drawn from local news sources. The study covers 144 Indian districts from 2006 to 2008. The research design leverages the program's staggered implementation across three phases. While assignment to cohorts was non-random, the authors had access to the selection criteria the government used to prioritize which districts would receive treatment first and incorporated this into the model.

The findings confirm that NREGS had a large, negative, and conditional effect on Maoist violence based on local government capacity. Whereas Sexton's measure of local capacity is based on military control, Dasgupta et al. argue that the capacity for public goods provision other than security matters (their measure is an index of service provision and evaluations of NREGS implementation). An additional test finds that the effect was greatest in villages that experienced rainfall shocks and therefore relied most heavily on income from NREGS. The authors suggest that this is consistent with the opportunity-cost mechanism and an income channel, although they acknowledge that their research design does not allow them to rule out competing explanations. The conclusion that aid's effectiveness is conditional on local governance capacity confirms the broader finding in the literature that local context matters heavily in how development shapes insurgent behavior and whether government development programs are useful tools of counterinsurgency.

—Jason Lyall, Yang-Yang Zhou, and Kosuke Imai, "Can Economic Assistance Shape Combatant Support in Wartime? Experimental Evidence from Afghanistan," *American Political Science Review* 114, no. 1 (2020): 126–143.

This study examines the relationship between economic aid and civilian attitudes about combatants.[10] It is an empirical program evaluation of a Mercy Corps intervention that randomized assignment to participate in a program involving job training and unconditional cash transfers for young, unemployed, internally displaced, Pashtun males in Kandahar. The study's chief contribution is that it has individual rather than aggregate-level data on the attitudes of aid recipients in a randomized experiment: "ironically, existing hearts and minds theories often have no measures of hearts and minds; civilian attitudes are imputed from observed changes in insurgent violence rather than from measures of aid beneficiaries' attitudes toward the combatants."[11] The dependent variables are answers to self-reported survey questions about respondents' attitudes. The study uses endorsement and list experiments to deal with preference falsification.

The findings are grim for the effectiveness of economic interventions. Vocational training had no meaningful effect on economic livelihoods or attitudes. Cash transfers produced a "boom-and-bust dynamic" with short-term spikes in support for the government but long-term resentment when economic conditions never improved. Lyall et al. identify two potential mechanisms: a "direct income channel" where improved livelihoods lead to greater government support, and an "information channel" where the aid itself signals government competence and increases support even if livelihoods do not improve. They interpret the short-term attitudinal boost from cash transfers as suggestive that the rationalist information mechanism was at work, given that there was an attitudinal change despite the lack of an impact on livelihoods.

—Jason Lyall, "Civilian Casualties, Humanitarian Aid, and Insurgent Violence in Civil Wars," *International Organization* 73, no. 4 (2019): 901–926.

This study examines how post-harm compensation influences insurgent violence.[12] The motivation is that the governments anticipate the negative strategic consequences of collateral damage and use financial compensation in response. Does that work? Lyall evaluates the effectiveness of the USAID's Afghan Civilian Assistance Program (ACAP II) during 2011–2013. The $64 million program investigated 1,061 incidents of civilian casualties and provided an average of $195 worth of compensation. Lyall leverages bureaucratic hurdles in ACAP II that caused only half of 1,061 otherwise similar investigations to result in a payment. The independent variable is receiving compensation, and the dependent variables are measures of Taliban attacks on International Security Assistance Force (ISAF) forces, Afghan forces, and local civilians. The data come from iMMAP and the ISAF's Combined Information Data Network Exchange.

The findings are conditionally optimistic about the effects of post-harm compensation. First, it reduced local attacks against ISAF forces by 23% within a two-year timeframe, but it did not reduce attacks against Afghan forces or civilians. Second, the aid was less effective when ISAF was responsible for the initial violence. Lyall interprets this as civilians demonstrating in-group psychological biases. Finally, consistent with Sexton's finding, local territorial control mattered. Payments had the largest impact when they were distributed close to ISAF bases.

This has several implications for CHB strategies. First, it provides evidence that experiencing harm does not necessarily push civilians to −1 or −2 nodes and that governments have tools to keep them from moving toward those roles. Second, psychological mechanisms can still undercut the assumption that individuals rationally update their beliefs. When ISAF forces were responsible for civilian harm, it had a much more severe impact than Taliban responsibility. In foreign occupations, this suggests that in-group biases can partially offset material deficiencies that insurgencies have relative to foreign powers.

—Daniel Silverman, "Too Late to Apologize? Collateral Damage, Post-Harm Compensation, and Insurgent Violence in Iraq," *International Organization* 74, no. 4 (2020): 853–871.

This study also assesses the effectiveness of post-harm compensation.[13] Silverman has essentially the same research question and theoretical motivation as Lyall, but the empirical analysis uses data from Iraq in 2004–2008. The independent variable is receiving a condolence payment. The data include 4,046 payments drawn from the US Army's Iraq Reconstruction Management System records, which cover a variety of programs, including CERP and USAID spending. The dependent variable is insurgent activity as recorded in SIGACTS. Data on civilian casualties come from the Iraq Body Count. The identification strategy also relies on the argument that assignment of condolence payments was as if random because of local fiscal constraints that prevented forces from making some payments but not others, idiosyncratic bureaucratic review processes, and geographic constraints based on the incident's proximity to a Coalition Civil Military Operation Center.

Consistent with Lyall's findings, post-harm compensation was associated with fewer subsequent attacks. Silverman attributes the success of condolence payments to a rationalist model of information updating about the government's intentions—the "rational peasants" model—and dismisses the notion that "ethnic partisans" have deep-seated in-group preferences. Lyall's study demonstrates that these two models are not actually mutually exclusive because post-harm compensation can lead civilians to update information about out-group actors, even if they do so in ways that exhibit some degree of in-group bias. In other words, bounded rationality is a plausible alternative explanation.

—Oeindrila Dube and Juan Vargas, "Commodity Price Shocks and Civil Conflict: Evidence from Colombia," *The Review of Economic Studies* 80, no. 4 (2013): 1384–1421.

This study examines how economic conditions—not just aid programs—influence insurgent behavior.[14] The analytical framework distinguishes between (1) an "opportunity-cost effect" in which higher wages reduce the labor supply of civilians willing to join an insurgency and (2) a "rapacity effect" in which growing wealth tempts individuals to use violence for appropriation as it becomes more profitable. The main hypothesis is that the effect of income shocks depends on whether goods are labor-intensive. When there are positive income shocks in labor-intensive industries, such as agriculture, the opportunity-cost mechanism will exert a pull away from rebellion. When there are positive shocks in industries with lower labor requirements, such as natural resources, a rapacious push toward insurgent violence is more likely.

Dube and Vargas test these claims with data on commodity prices in Colombia and local insurgent violence in 950 municipalities during 1988–2005. Colombia's top exports, coffee and oil, are the study's key commodities. The research design leverages exogenous shocks in global demand to avoid potential risks that local prices are endogenous to conflict dynamics. They find that higher oil prices were correlated with greater violence in oil-producing regions, while lower coffee prices were associated with decreased violence in coffee-producing regions. The results hold for six other Colombian export commodities.

—Andrew B. Hall, Connor Huff, and Shiro Kuriwaki, "Wealth, Slaveownership, and Fighting for the Confederacy: An Empirical Study of the American Civil War," *American Political Science Review* 113, no. 3 (2019): 658–673.

This study examines the relationship between the source of individual wealth and Civil War participation.[15] The motivating context is slave ownership and fighting for the confederacy in the American Civil War. Participation presented a collective action problem where rich Southerners had incentives to free-ride on the efforts of poor Southerners. The main argument is that the Southerners who owed their wealth to slave ownership had stronger select incentives to fight given the stakes of the war's outcome to their livelihoods. Hall et al. test these claims with a dataset of demographic information on 3.9 million Confederate citizens and an 1832 land lottery in Georgia that randomly increased the chance that some would own slaves. The findings corroborate the claim that slave ownership provided stronger incentives to fight, but they also provide some evidence that there were strong social norms rooted in martial and honor elements of Southern culture that pressured slave owners to join as well.

This corroborates research from other contexts (e.g., Dube and Vargas) that the specific source of wealth and local context matter strongly in shaping individual decisions to participate in fighting. Most studies assume that wealth creates large opportunity costs that deter participation, but that is not always the case. Second, it suggests that a mix of rational and social mechanisms can mutually reinforce pressures for civilians to move from one node to another. Both the "rational peasant" and the "rational plantation owner" models can acknowledge rational, material incentives to fight, as well as compounding pressure from social norms or psychological biases.

—Christopher Blattman and Jeannie Annan, "Can Employment Reduce Lawlessness and Rebellion? A Field Experiment with High-Risk Men in a Fragile State," *American Political Science Review* 110, no. 1 (2016): 1–17.

This study examines postwar economic interventions and ex-fighter criminal activity.[16] Although it focuses on postwar Libera rather than an active conflict zone, it does provide insights into how individuals respond to economic incentives. The NGO Action on Armed Violence randomly assigned around half of 1,1123 at-risk men to a rehabilitation program with agricultural training and cash. The dependent variable relied on self-reported survey answers, which does raise some concerns about preference falsification. Nevertheless, the study's conclusions are worth highlighting, even if tentative. First, the treatment group engaged in less illicit economic activity and expressed less interest in mercenary activities. This provides some evidence that, at least in some contexts, there is a direct income channel through which higher wages can discourage riskier behavior. Second, the effect was strongest for those in the treatment group that expected additional benefits payoffs from the program in the future. Unless recipients are lying at higher rates until they receive the entire treatment, this suggests the limits of one-off or short-lived interventions to influence opportunity costs. It also corroborates similar findings about attitudes and information sharing from Lyall et al. (2020) on the boom-and-bust cycle of single cash transfers for government support.

—Austin Wright, "Economic Shocks and Rebel Tactics," Pearson Institute Discussion Paper, 2016.

This study examines how income shocks influence rebel tactics.[17] This differs from Dube and Vargas because it analyzes the types of insurgent attacks rather than the frequency. Wright introduces a theorical framework that explains insurgent tactical choices as a function of state capacity, rebel capacity, and civilian economic opportunity costs. The main hypothesis is that income shocks can influence each of these mechanisms differently. When rebels control an economic sector that benefits, their higher resource endowments enable them to engage in more conventional tactics. When the government controls revenue from that sector, rebels are more likely to resort to guerrilla tactics. When civilians have higher opportunity costs because of wage booms in labor-intensive sectors, rebel labor supply falls and tactics become less conventional.

Wright tests these claims in Colombia during 1988–2005. The approach follows Dube and Vargas in using global oil prices as an instrument for local oil price shocks, but leverages atmospheric conditions as new instruments for coffee and coca prices. The dependent variable on the occurrence and type of insurgent attacks comes from the Conflict Analysis Resource Center. The findings are consistent with the hypothesis. Lower coffee prices reduced opportunity costs of insurgency, increasing rebel labor supply and enabling them to engage in more conventional attacks. Lower coca prices, on the other hand, undermined rebel capacity because of reliance on drug trafficking, which led to fewer direct engagements with government forces. Finally, oil price spikes benefited the government because of its control over oil production, and rebels responded to greater counterinsurgent capacity by turning to hit-and-run guerrilla tactics. These findings corroborate the rationalist mechanism that development can undermine support for insurgencies—but only if the insurgents do not control the source of wealth.

—Konstantin Sonin, Jarnickae Wilson, and Austin Wright, "Rebel Capacity and Combat Tactics," Working Paper, Becker Friedman Institute, 2019.

This study examines how economic conditions shape rebel tactics in a different context.[18] The central claim is that gathering intelligence on government forces is costly, so rebels do it less when they have fewer resources. Better rebel intelligence leads to more selective and concentrated insurgent attacks, and vice versa. Sonin et al. test this claim in Afghanistan during 2006–2014. The dependent variable is the level of randomness in insurgent attacks as measured by temporal clustering in time-stamped SIGACTS data. They also leverage US government data on Taliban surveillance operations in 2006, such as attempts to breach a base's outer perimeter to surveil targets, to test the hypothesized mechanism. The independent variable is Taliban income from opium, which is estimated from satellite imagery, UN reports, and growing season cycles. The findings confirm that the level of randomness in Taliban attacks and its ability to collect intelligence are correlated with opium revenue. When income shocks enable rebels to provide higher wages, that gives them an additional strategic tool to encourage civilians to move from neutral nodes to pro-insurgent roles, even if only intermittently scouting and collecting intelligence (+1).

—Mara Revkin, "What Explains Taxation by Resource-Rich Rebels? Evidence from the Islamic State in Syria," *The Journal of Politics* 82, no. 2 (2020): 757–764.

This study examines rebel taxation policies.[19] The motivating premise is that developing rebel governance institutions to tax and provide services seems unnecessarily costly when insurgents have access to lucrative natural resources, but some do it anyway. Revkin deductively explains this with the interaction of ideology and the costs of warfare by drawing from evidence about the Islamic State.

First, the Islamic State's Salafi-jihadist ideology called for rebuilding a traditional Islamic governance system, and some of its tax provisions came directly from the Qur'an. Second, groups are more likely to establish elaborate tax systems when the costs of fighting exceed the revenue they can acquire from natural resources. The costs of warfare were high for the Islamic State because of its expansive goals and sophisticated adversaries.

One implication from Revkin's empirical description of the Islamic State's tax policies is that insurgent groups can use economic tools as well as military threats to control the population. Some of this control can be for purely ideological ends, such as policies to tax noncompliance with behavioral mandates related to traditional dress codes and facial hair. Other aspects have more direct strategic consequences, such as using border taxes to raise the costs of civilians fleeing, which helped the Islamic State contain the population so it could use it as a resource. The Islamic State also fined the families of children who deserted after forcible conscription as a deterrent, and it allowed wealthy citizens to "pay a 'tax in lieu of jihad' to generate revenue."[20] This illustrates some ways in which insurgents can use economic tools to influence civilian choices during conflicts.

B.2. Movement among −1, 0, +1 Roles: The Effects of Indiscriminate Violence

—Jason Lyall, "Does Indiscriminate Violence Incite Insurgent Attacks? Evidence from Chechnya," *Journal of Conflict Resolution* 53, no. 3 (2009): 331–362.

During the Second Chechen War, Russian troops conducted H and I artillery shelling on settlements from 2000 to 2005. Lyall (2009) argues that this shelling was largely random, with drunken Russians firing as a simple matter of undifferentiated policy; the firing, in Lyall's (2009) view, qualifies as indiscriminate. Clearly, this tactic goes against the recommendations of FM 3-24. Lyall's (2009) method is "matching"—he matches villages with similar demographic and physical characteristics and then compares the villages that were shelled against the ones that were not shelled. His dependent variable is the mean number of insurgent attacks against Russian and Russian-allied forces during pre- and post-shelling periods.

We can discuss Lyall's (2009) findings in terms of shelled versus non-shelled settlements. The study finds that attacks in non-shelled villages averaged about 2 attacks while those in the shelled villages averaged 1.5. Thus, shelled villages had about one-fourth less insurgent attacks after being shelled. Lyall (2009) estimates that shelling helped prevent the loss of 71 soldiers' lives. As one can imagine, this article gained much attention and initiated a complex discussion about its methods. For our purposes here, it is a study that casts some doubt as to whether indiscriminate violence always leads to movement from neutrality to −1 or −2 positions.

—Matthew Adam Kocher, Thomas B. Pepinsky, and Stathis N. Kalyvas, "Aerial Bombing and Counterinsurgency in the Vietnam War," *American Journal of Political Science* 55, no. 2 (2011): 201–218.

Two years after Lyall published his study, Kocher et al. (2011) published a study of indiscriminate aerial bombing in Vietnam that reached conclusions very much at odds with those of Lyall (2009). They found that US bombing clearly moved settlements toward insurgent support. Using remarkably precise data on over 10,000 hamlets, the Kocher et al. study tests the relationship between air strikes called in on a particular locale and the level of government (versus insurgent) control in that hamlet. In his Chechen study, Lyall (2009) sought to find out if indiscriminate shelling of a village increased or decreased insurgent attacks. Kocher et al. sought to find out if aerial bombing of a village increased or decreased government control.

The use of this particular dependent variable was made possible by the Hamlet Evaluation System. The administrators of this program rated the level of presence and activity of the Viet Cong in the area of each hamlet on a 5-point scale: (1) fully government controlled; (2) moderately government controlled; (3) contested; (4) moderately insurgent controlled; (5) fully insurgent controlled. Kocher et al. collected data on their independent variable, bombing sorties, from the Combat Air Activities File which recorded all bombing runs from 1965 to 1970. With this local data, Kocher et al. could compare the relationship between bombing sorties and changes in government control levels across a multitude of hamlets. In their study, the authors compare changes in control probabilities during the period from July to December 1969. Given the five levels of control designated by the Hamlet Evaluation System, the study allows questions about the effect of bombing in this time period across villages with different levels of control. What happens when the United States bombed a hamlet in "full government control?" Does it move to embrace the insurgents? What happens when bombs strike villages moderately or fully controlled by insurgents? Do they become closer to the government?

The Kocher et al. findings are consistent across all combinations of this question—for the counterinsurgent, bombing was counterproductive. If the hamlet was in full insurgent control (category 5) in July 1969, bombing increased the chance of that village remaining in full insurgent control by about 13%. If a hamlet was in full government control (category 1) in July 1969 and was hit by bombs, it was 7.6% more likely to move out of full government control. At all five levels of control, bombing hurt the counterinsurgent and helped the insurgent.[21]

Why are the Kocher et al. (2011) findings so different from Lyall's (2009) findings? Coming second in this debate, Kocher et al. try to answer that question. They speculate that the balance of power relationship between the insurgents and the population may determine the difference. If a community solves its collective action problems and unites in the belief that insurgent actions are bringing shells down upon them, they may be able to pressure them to either leave or reduce their attacks. This phenomenon may have occurred in Chechnya. In Vietnam, by contrast, the insurgents, the highly organized and well-equipped Viet Cong, were simply too powerful to permit local residents to unite and present pressure (Kocher et al., 2011, p. 204).

We must keep in mind that neither of these studies examined Iraq. Kocher et al. (2011) studied Vietnam, a case with a massive number of US strikes. Furthermore, the Vietnamese case occurred decades before the Revolution in Military Affairs and the use of precision munitions. Lyall (2009) examined the Russians in Chechnya. He assumes that the firing was indiscriminate because of the lack of professionalization (and drunkenness) of the Russian military. Does either of these studies apply to our Iraq case? Was the violence in Iraq as indiscriminate as in these two cases? Given the differing political contexts, what can we apply? Other studies try to address the question of collateral damage in contexts perhaps more similar to Iraq.

—Jason Lyall, "Dynamic Coercion in Civil War: Evidence from Air Operations in Afghanistan." Unpublished paper, (2013).

Lyall followed up his study of Russian shelling in Chechnya with a study of US airstrikes in Afghanistan. Lyall examined 23,000 declassified air strikes and shows of force. With shows of force, planes fly over a target but do not release any weapon. In both cases of actual strikes and shows of force, the Coalition wishes to signal its ability to strike insurgents where they live. In some thinking, these actions should deter the insurgents from further violence (as well as killing them in the cases of actual strikes). Did these Coalition actions deter insurgents and reduce violent actions?

For both air strikes and shows of force, the answer is no. In fact, insurgents stepped up local violence and did so over an extended period. Lyall's interpretation of these results is that insurgent leaders need to maintain their local reputations. They need to show their audience that they cannot be intimidated by outsiders. Thus, they need to push back, even against Coalition shows of force. The data indicate that this response is not directly related to civilian casualties. With shows of force, no casualties occur; yet local insurgent leaders still respond.

Lyall's two studies appear to be in conflict. In the Chechen study discussed above, shelling reduced insurgent attacks; in the Afghan case, strikes and shows of force increase attacks. Perhaps the most important takeaway for our purposes is how these studies illustrate and emphasize the importance of local dynamics. If a locality's population plays a supporting role for an insurgent organization (−1 on our spectrum), then the leader of that local organization will use violence to preserve his reputation and prevent movement to neutrality or government support (0 or +1). This appears to be the Afghan story. On the other hand, if the community stands together and is neutral, they may be able to change the actions of insurgents. This appears to be Lyall's Chechen story.

—Luke N. Condra and Jacob N. Shapiro, "Who Takes the Blame? The Strategic Effects of Collateral Damage," *American Journal of Political Science* 56, no. 1 (2012): 167–187.

Based on a study in Iraq, Condra and Shapiro (2012) examine cases of both Coalition and insurgent acts of violence which involve collateral damage. What happens when the Coalition forces kill civilians—do attacks on the Coalition rise? What happens when insurgents kill civilians—do attacks on the Coalition fall? The authors build hypotheses about these questions based on an information theory of violence. The population is not passive; they hold a resource in terms of information. If they wish to punish the Coalition for their actions, they can withhold information from the Coalition and give it to the insurgents. Correspondingly, if they wish to punish the insurgents, they can give information to the Coalition, in turn reducing the ability of the insurgents to act.

Condra and Shapiro's (2012) independent variable is civilian casualties measured by Iraq Body Count numbers. Their dependent variable is attacks on Coalition forces measured by SIGACTS. They examined the relationship between these two sets of data from 2004 to 2009. They found that after experiencing collateral damage, civilians indeed punished, and they punished both counterinsurgent and insurgent. When the Coalition committed an act with collateral damage, insurgent attacks on Coalition force rose over the next week by 0.9 on average. When the insurgents committed a similar attack, attacks fell but at a lower rate. Also, the effects were conditioned by the political and demographic context. There was no anti-insurgent effect in Sunni areas. On the other hand, there was a stronger anti-Coalition effect in Sunni regions. The effect was strongest in mixed contested areas and in urban areas. Overall, the study supports Kocher et al.—killing civilians is a negative act for counterinsurgents. However, the study suggests that mechanisms related to backlash are conditioned on ethnic identity. The desire to punish outsiders who commit collateral damage is higher than the desire to punish co-ethnics.

—Grame Blair, C. Christine Fair, Neil Malhotra, and Jacob N. Shapiro, "Poverty and Support for Militant Politics: Evidence from Pakistan," *American Journal of Political Science* 57 (January 2013): 30–48.

Blair et al. (2013) set out to study the relationship between poverty and level of support for militants. Their test case was Pakistan, where they ran surveys that compared poor rural, poor urban, and middle-class Pakistanis and their levels of dislike for Pakistani militant groups. Their findings hold that urban poor living in areas that have witnessed violence have levels of dislike three times that of rural poor living in peaceful areas. Their interpretation bears on the issue of collateral damage. Blair et al. (2013) interpret this finding as a result of the "externalities" of militant group operations. Militant groups conduct more indiscriminate violence in poor and urban areas. Because they experience the fallout of these operations, they come to dislike militants more than either their rural or middle-class counterparts. The study supports the commonsense point that people who suffer from collateral damage blame and dislike those who committed it. Of course, this Pakistan case is not a case of foreign occupation; the study is not suited to consider the insider/outsider differences in perpetrator identity.

—Luke Condra and Austin Wright, "Civilians, Control, and Collaboration during Civil Conflict," *International Studies Quarterly* 63, no. 4 (2019): 897–907.

This study examines how civilian perceptions mediate the consequences of indiscriminate violence.[22] The main hypothesis is that civilian responses depend on how they perceive actors' intentions and efforts to keep the use of force discriminate. A secondary hypothesis is that perceptions depend partly on local territorial control. Civilians are most likely to provide information to government forces when they perceive it as exercising local control and believe the insurgents are using force recklessly (and vice versa).

Condra and Wright test these claims in Afghanistan during 2013–2015. The Afghanistan Nationwide Quarterly Research (ANQAR) survey provides quarterly data on civilian perceptions of who exercises local territorial control, whether each side is doing enough to limit civilian casualties, and willingness to inform government forces about IEDs. There is a 10% decrease in the probability of respondents expressing willingness to collaborate with government forces when they perceive the government is not taking enough steps to limit collateral damage. Similarly, respondents are 11.5% more likely to collaborate when they believe the rebel efforts are insufficient. The effect is larger when the respondent believes an actor is not doing enough to protect civilians *and* its rival controls the territory. The authors interpret this as suggesting that civilians rationally update beliefs about the combatants and the risk of informing, and the risks of collaboration are greater when aiding an actor that does not exercise territorial control. More broadly, the findings suggest the importance of perceptions rather than "objective" conditions. Taking steps to make violence more discriminate does not necessarily have a large benefit if local civilians do not perceive such efforts as serious or effective.

—Anna Pechenkina, Andrew Bausch, and Kiron Skinner, "How Do Civilians Attribute Blame for State Indiscriminate Violence?" *Journal of Peace Research* 56, no. 4 (2019): 545–558.

This study examines why civilians blame certain actors for indiscriminate violence.[23] Whereas past research emphasized the role of ethnic in-group biases in blame attribution, Pechenkina et al. highlight the role of personal experience. The main hypothesis is that blame attribution is conditional on rebel and state behavior. For example, people consider whether rebels used human shields and provoked the government to use force, even if that eventually led to civilian casualties. To test this claim, they fielded two face-to-face surveys of 2,022 Ukrainians to ask about the war in the Donbas. They found that respondents generally evaluated rebel behavior when attributing blame to the government. The exception was when individuals had personal exposure to violence during the war. Respondents with personal experience attributed blame to the government regardless of insurgent provocations. This suggests that "observers" and "recipients" of government violence attribute blame differentially. The experience could produce an emotional trigger, although the survey does not provide leverage to evaluate potential mechanisms. Another difficulty in making comparisons to other studies is that it does not provide evidence about whether such attribution was enough to change behavioral outcomes, like informing.

—Daniel Silverman, "What Shapes Civilian Beliefs about Violent Events? Experimental Evidence from Pakistan," *Journal of Conflict Resolution* 63, no. 6 (2019): 1460–1487.

This study examines how preexisting beliefs influence blame attribution.[24] The main hypothesis is that there is a strong psychological mechanism that shapes how individuals interpret basic facts about a conflict. Motivated reasoning causes individuals to interpret new information through the lens of preexisting beliefs. They are more likely to perceive a combatant's actions as selective if they have positive preexisting attitudes about it (and vice versa). Silverman tests these arguments with a survey experiment in Pakistan that varies aspects of a vignette about an air strike against insurgents, such as whether Pakistan or the United States conducted the attack. Preexisting attitudes had strong effects on how respondents interpreted the selective or indiscriminate character of an attack, even holding the reported number of casualties constant. This suggests that psychological biases may impede rational updating about a combatant's actions and intentions. For actors attempting a CHB strategy, simply placing limits on the use of force may be insufficient to persuade already skeptical civilians that such efforts are serious. One implication is that counterinsurgents might benefit from information operations to shape civilian beliefs, rather than simply letting the facts speak for themselves.

—Konstantin Sonin and Austin Wright, "Information Operations Increase Civilian Security Cooperation," Working Paper, Becker Friedman Institute, 2019.

This study evaluates the effectiveness of US information operations in Afghanistan.[25] During a mission in 2010 to clear Afghanistan's Garmer district, the US Marines implemented a Radio-In-A-Box (RIAB) program to warn civilians about the dangers of IEDs and encourage them to provide information to ISAF. The study leverages the radio signal's limited range and the period before and after the program started for a difference-in-differences design. It found that civilians within the signal's range were more likely to cooperate on IEDs than they had been before the program and compared to those out of range. While Garmer is a single case, it is also a hard case for informing because the government lacked strong territorial control.

—Sebastian Schutte, "Violence and Civilian Loyalties: Evidence from Afghanistan," *Journal of Conflict Resolution* 61, no. 8 (2017): 1595–1625.

This study examines how indiscriminate violence influences civilian attitudes.[26] The main contribution is applying a new statistical method that evaluates the impact of indiscriminate violence on downstream attacks across different levels of spatial and temporal aggregation; that is, the consequences of civilian harm may depend on where and when you look for it. In the short term, it may not lead to a large and immediate impact on civilian loyalties. Over time, there is a greater chance that it pushes civilians toward greater collaboration with the adversary.

Schutte tests this argument in Afghanistan during 2004–2010. Using SIGACTS data, Schutte (controversially) codes ISAF use of indirect fire and close air support as indiscriminate, the Taliban's use of land mines as indiscriminate, and both Taliban and ISAF direct fire attacks as selective. The dependent variable is the rate at which civilians turn in unexploded ordinance, which insurgents could otherwise use for IEDs. The model finds that indiscriminate violence produces a stronger backlash "at greater spatiotemporal distances." Schutte interprets this as civilians rationally biding their time until opportunities to collaborate at lower risk arise.

—Jake Shapiro and Nils Weidmann, "Is the Phone Mightier than the Sword? Cell Phones and Insurgent Violence in Iraq," *International Organization* 69, no. 2 (2015): 247–274.

This study examines how the risks of informing change civilian propensity to collaborate with government forces.[27] Drawing on the information-model of counterinsurgency, the main argument is that cell towers should reduce violence because they enable civilians to pass tips to government forces at far less risk than walking into police stations or bases. It uses data from 2004–2009 on the expansion of the Iraqi cell network, which was driven by an economic rather than strategic logic, and SIGACTS data on insurgent attacks. It found that expanded cell coverage reduced attacks and IEDs, and that the effect was strongest when expanding coverage into new areas rather than improving the quality of signals in existing areas.

—Andrew Shaver and Jacob Shapiro, "The Effect of Civilian Casualties on Wartime Informing: Evidence from the Iraq War," *Journal of Conflict Resolution* 65, no. 7–8 (2021): 1337–1377.

This study provides a new empirical test on the old theoretical claim that civilians retaliate by providing intelligence when a combatant kills civilians.[28] Shaver and Shapiro test this claim in Iraq during 2007–2008. The independent variable is a measure of civilian casualties according to Iraq Body Count records. The dependent variable is province-level data on tips to Coalition forces from the US government, which was recently declassified. Past studies on Iraq had to rely on indirect measures of collaboration, such as IED clearing rates, rather than direct data on intelligence. Consistent with informational theories, Shaver and Shapiro find that tips increased after insurgents killed civilians and decreased after government operations led to civilian deaths. The chief contribution is demonstrating empirically that there was a direct link between civilian casualties and downstream civilian collaboration in the form of intelligence.

—Austin Wright, Luke N. Condra, Jacob N. Shapiro, and Andrew C. Shaver, "Civilian Abuse and Wartime Informing," Pearson Institute Working Paper, 2017.

This is a similar empirical test on the link between civilian casualties and intelligence collection in Afghanistan during 2003–2014.[29] The study uses SIGACTS data on insurgent attacks and nighttime luminosity as an instrument for insurgent indiscriminate violence. The justification for the instrument's relevance is that more moonlight made it harder for the Taliban to evade security forces, so they had to rely on more indiscriminate tactics during those times. The dependent variable is the number of intelligence tips to ISAF forces. Rebel attacks that placed civilians at greater risk were associated with higher downstream levels of civilian collaboration. The contribution is empirically showing the information-sharing mechanism in another context.

—Livia Isabella Schubiger, "State Violence and Wartime Civilian Agency: Evidence from Peru," *The Journal of Politics* 83, no. 4 (2021): 1383–1398.

This study examines why civilians sometimes respond to state-imposed harm by engaging in armed mobilization against insurgents.[30] This develops Lyall's argument that indiscriminate violence by the state can actually provoke civilians to turn against insurgents.[31] The main argument is that counterinsurgent mobilization is a way for at-risk civilians to signal their loyalties and seek security. A scope condition is that government forces are harming civilians in a way that allows for some level of selectivity so that counterinsurgents will receive and respond to that signal. This is a rationalist explanation for how citizens respond to violence. The mechanism is not that the experience triggers an emotional reach and a need to fight. It is a more calculated cost–benefit calculation about how to maximize safety. It suggests that, under certain conditions, violence can move individuals into +1 and +2 roles rather than pushing them to support the insurgency. Moreover, it highlights the need to distinguish between attitudes and behaviors. The civilians in this theoretical model may dislike the government, but their behavior nevertheless still benefits it.

Schubiger tests these claims with evidence from Peru in the mid-1980s. The study leverages both an instrumental variable and difference-in-differences design that exploits geographic limitations on state violence to specific "government-imposed emergency zones." The independent variable is exposure to a violent counterinsurgent campaign during 1983–1985, and the dependent variable is mobilization in the form of civilian defense groups during 1986–1988. The findings corroborate the hypothesis that state violence can lead to autonomous civilian mobilization against insurgents.

—Evgeny Finkel, "The Phoenix Effect of State Repression: Jewish Resistance during the Holocaust," *American Political Science Review* 109, no. 2 (2015): 339–353.

This study examines how indiscriminate violence influences the latent skills a civilian population has to mobilize for resistance.[32] The main argument is that selective repression causes specific individuals to go underground to resist repression. Over time, those individuals build up skill sets, such as building clandestine ways to communicate and move, and those skills position them well to resist government security forces down the road. Selective repression solves a collective action problem to incentivize individuals to acquire costly skills, whereas indiscriminate repression does not. Selective repression at time $t-1$, then, leaves a group with skilled members capable of resistance at time t, whereas it is too late for groups to develop such skills without lead time. Finkel tests these arguments by looking at the history of repression in three ghettos in Eastern Europe before the Holocaust and subsequent anti-Nazi resistance. The main implication here is that the level of violence shapes the distribution of capabilities, not just preferences, in the population. Over time, that can influence the human capital pool for resistance groups.

—Luke N. Condra, James D. Long, Andrew C. Shaver, and Austin L. Wright "The Logic of Insurgent Electoral Violence," *American Economic Review* 108, no. 11 (2018): 3199–3231.

This study examines insurgent attacks designed to undermine elections.[33] The main argument is that insurgents use calibrated violence to raise the risk of voting and thereby suppress turnout. This decreases the government's legitimacy and support. Condra et al. use granular data and elaborate methods to demonstrate that the Taliban is highly selective in how it applies this violence, rather than engaging in indiscriminate mass attacks on elections infrastructure. This includes multiple instruments—wind conditions and nighttime cloud cover—for insurgent attacks. They find that attacks had large suppressive effects on district-level turnout in the 2014 elections. As with violent responses to aid programs, calibrated violence is a counterstrategy that insurgents use to undermine the legitimacy of a hearts-and-minds approach that seeks to provide responsive political institutions and public goods.

B.3. Movement among –1, 0, +1 Roles: The Effects of Identity

Recently, many scholars have conducted large, cross-natural studies of civil war. Most of these studies downplayed the effects of ethnicity, especially those that examined the onset of civil war. The most well-known of these were Fearon and Laitin (2003) and Collier et al. (2003). Both measured ethnicity in terms of diversity or heterogeneity of groups within a state. Fearon and Laitin (2003) found that civil war breaks out in states where conditions for the technology of insurgency are favorable. These conditions include a weak state (proxied by GDP), rough terrain, and a large population to hide among. Collier et al. argued that civil war breaks out when a state's economic system cannot provide opportunities for satisfying a legitimate economic life. The argument is based on the logic of opportunity costs, and again the key measure for the presence or absence of opportunity is GDP level.

Another group of scholars has arisen to challenge these findings. In *Inequality, Grievances, and Civil War*, Cederman et al. (2013) criticize the studies measured above for using an inappropriate measure for ethnicity. They argue that the number and distribution of ethnic groups is not as important as the political relationship among groups in a state. Instead, what matters most is their representation in the state, whether groups are included or excluded from power. As opposed to preceding studies, Cederman et al. (2013) explicitly discuss power, nationalism, and the politically relevant emotions related to power inequalities. Based on a study of politically relevant ethnic groups and their access to power in independent states from 1946 to 2009 (29,740 group years), Cederman et al. (2013) find strong support for the role of ethnicity. When a group is excluded from power, it is more likely to fight. When a group that was in power has experienced a status reversal, the effect is even stronger (Petersen, 2002).

The Cederman et al. (2013) study has high relevance in regards to status reversals and the emotion of resentment. We expect to see this mechanism help drive members of ethnic groups experiencing a status reversal from neutrality toward support of the insurgents (from 0 to −1). The relevance to Iraq is obvious. Perceiving a status reversal in the early post-invasion period (especially given the dismissal of the army and the Baathist government officials), Sunnis boycotted elections and joined insurgencies.

There are also studies that examine the role of identity specifically within the contours of counterinsurgency practice. Again, some of the most relevant work here comes from Lyall's (2009; 2013) research in Chechnya and Afghanistan.

—Jason Lyall, "Are Co-Ethnics More Effective Counter-Insurgents? Evidence from the Second Chechen War," *American Political Science Review* 104, no. 1 (February 2010): 1–20.
—Jason Lyall, Graeme Blair, and Kosuke Imai, "Explaining Support for Combatants during Wartime: A Survey Experiment in Afghanistan," *American Political Science Review* 107, no. 4 (November 2013): 679–705.

Counterinsurgency strategies, some more than others, involve raids, sweeps and operations that impact the well-being and dignity of the general population. As several studies in this review have already pointed out, these actions can drive individuals into new roles on the spectrum. Indiscriminate violence by a foreign occupier can convert +1 actors into −1 actors, for example. But will the same type of violence by the insurgents who share a common identity with the population move individuals from −1 to +1?

Established psychological mechanisms predict that these responses will be asymmetrical. Recall the fundamental attribution error mentioned in Chapter 2. This mechanism predicts that individuals will attribute an outsider's action to their innate character while attributing the actions of members of one's own group to situational factors. In the context here, when the outsider commits violence against one's community, it is because that outsider is naturally violent or uncaring; if an insider commits violence against the community, it is not because of the perpetrator's character, but because the situation may have forced the perpetrator into the action.

Lyall et al.'s (2013) survey experiment in Afghanistan provides support for this mechanism. In their survey conducted in Pashtun majority areas, respondents reported being exposed to violence at very high rates: 37% of respondents stated that they had experienced victimization by ISAF; 33% claimed victimization by the Taliban; 19% claimed victimization by both.[34] Despite apparent roughly equal numbers claiming ISAF and Taliban victimization, the effect of this violence on attitudes toward the perpetrators differed significantly. When ISAF created the harm, Lyall et al.'s (2013) survey measures indicated a drop in support for ISAF and an increase in support for the Taliban. However, when the Taliban was the perpetrator, respondents indicated only a slight drop in support for the Taliban and there was no increase in support for ISAF. Lyall et al. (2013) find what they term a "home team discount"—in that in-group victimization does not lead to support for the out-group. In effect, individuals see what they want to see. They fall under the sway of both confirmation bias (processing information to confirm what they already believe) and the fundamental attribution error. As Lyall et al. (2013) explicitly summarize in their tribal analysis, "In each case, victimization is likely to confirm the intergroup bias that negative in-group actions are situational while those of the out-group and its members are dispositional" (p. 14). In effect, the findings of the survey suggest that outsiders (ISAF) killing community members and civilians generates higher levels of violence and shifts people toward supporting the insurgency (moving them from 0 to −1), while insiders (Taliban) killing more people does not shift support toward the government (insurgent violence does not move individuals from 0 to +1). As we will come back to in the conclusion of this appendix, these findings are not in conflict with the Blair et al. (2013) study of the previous section.

In the Chechen study, Lyall (2009) asks whether co-ethnics are better at conducting counterinsurgency. During the Second Chechen War, sometimes Russian forces conducted sweeps, and other times Chechen forces who were allied with the Russians conducted sweeps. Lyall's (2009) study examines how many insurgent attacks occurred after each of these types of sweeps. He finds that insurgent attacks were 40% less after the Russian-allied Chechen sweeps than after Russian sweeps. He argues that the Chechen soldiers are better at garnering information about insurgents because they are enmeshed with the population through networks. It may also be the case that the Russian-allied Chechens were former insurgents, so they know how to operate and whom to go after based on former experience.

—Monica Duffy Toft and Yuri M. Zhukov, "Islamists and Nationalists: Rebel Motivation and Counterinsurgency in Russia's North Caucasus," *American Political Science Review* 109, no. 2 (2015): 222–238.

Toft and Zhukov (2015) address differences between ethnic/nationalist insurgent groups and ideological insurgent groups. Specifically, they test one particular element of counterinsurgency strategy—the state's type of violence. The state can either use indiscriminate violence in the form of artillery shelling and air strikes, or selective violence in the form of targeted killings and arrests. Toft and Zhukov (2015) build a dataset on North Caucasus violence collecting information related to 9,405 rebel attacks from 2000 to 2012. Toft and Zhukov (2015) use a form of a before–after analysis. For both Islamist and nationalist groups, they compare the intensity of rebel violence before and after each type of attack in similar types of districts. In the nationalist cases, when security forces used selective tactics, violence went down 5% during the following three-month period. In the Islamist cases, violence continued at the same level despite the nature of the counterinsurgent tactics, or whether the force conducting those tactics was Russian or Chechen. Toft and Zhukov (2015) reason that this outcome is explained by the organizational nature of Islamist groups. With their funding and recruits coming from outside the locales where they are fighting, Islamists are not reliant on the population in the same way as nationalists. Nationalist groups are tied to localities. Nationalist insurgents come from the local population and rely on that population for support. When the government selectively targets communities that support nationalist rebels, Toft and Zhukov (2015) reason that some of those communities respond by restraining those nationalist insurgents, leading to decreased intensity of insurgent attacks.

—Jason Lyall, Yuki Shiraito, and Kosuke Imai, "Coethnic Bias and Wartime Informing," *The Journal of Politics* 77, no. 3 (2015): 833–848.

This study examines the impact of ethnicity on collaboration and intelligence sharing.[35] The main argument is that in-group biases lead civilians to prefer cooperating with co-ethnics because civilians use ethnicity as a heuristic for trustworthiness and predictable behavior. Lyall et al. (2015) test this claim using a survey experiment of 2,700 Pashtuns and Tajiks across 100 Afghan villages in 2011. The treatment randomized the ethnic identity of the spokesperson for the Guardians of Peace program, which encouraged civilians to provide tips to security forces. The dependent variable included questions related to willingness to call the hotline or stop by military bases, as well as gauging concerns about anonymity and reprisals. The findings corroborate the prevalence of strong co-ethnic biases. Respondents were more willing to inform and less concerned about retaliation given a co-ethnic prime. Consistent with past research, respondents were also less likely to inform if they had been exposed to harm by ISAF forces in the past. Contrary to previous findings, territorial control and local development projects had no impact on willingness to inform. For the CHB strategy, this suggests that psychological mechanisms can exercise a strong influence on the flow of information in ethnic conflicts.

—Nils Hägerdal, "Ethnic Cleansing and the Politics of Restraint: Violence and Coexistence in the Lebanese Civil War," *Journal of Conflict Resolution* 63, no. 1 (2019): 59–84.

This study examines variation in the use of ethnic cleansing by armed groups.[36] The motivating premise is that insurgents often prefer to engage in selective violence but lack reliable intelligence to differentiate between neutral civilians and those supporting the adversary. Gathering intelligence is costly, and relying on ethnic identity as a proxy for support is easy. The main hypothesis is that the presence of local civilian co-ethnics makes intelligence collection easier because they can provide information on their neighbors' loyalties. Homogenous areas with few co-ethnics are at the greatest risk of ethnic cleansing. Hagerdal demonstrates this pattern with original data on violence, demographics, and migration patterns in Lebanon during 1975–1990. This suggests that an insurgent group's ability to mobilize co-ethnic civilians into +1 support roles influences their intelligence capabilities and therefore tactics.

—Janet Lewis, "How Does Ethnic Rebellion Start?" *Comparative Political Studies* 50, no. 10 (2017): 1420–1450.

This study examines how ethnicity influences the start of conflicts.[37] The fundamental argument is that previous research overstates the role of ethnicity in civil wars. Analysts often observe ethnic mobilization during a conflict and then incorrectly infer that those ethnic grievances started the war. Ethnicity sometimes becomes important in mobilizing support only after the insurgent group has already been established. Drawing on fieldwork in Uganda, Lewis creates an original dataset of all insurgent groups formed in the country since 1986 and shows that ethnicity generally impacted group survival but not creation. This suggests that ethnicity can have heterogenous effects on different roles and across different timeframes. For example, the core insurgent fighters may mobilize for non-ethnic reasons, but rely on ethnic appeals to gain unorganized support among the local population to protect them from government forces.

—Jennifer Larson and Janet Lewis, "Rumors, Kinship Networks, and Rebel Group Formation," *International Organization* 72, no. 4 (2018): 871–903.

This study builds on Lewis's research on rebel group formation in Uganda.[38] The main argument is that the ethnic composition of an area influences whether nascent rebel groups survive. Homogenous areas are more conducive to group survival in the early stages of insurgency because it is easier to keep information a secret from the government when rumors flow through kinship networks. When rumors flow through communication networks of a heterogenous population, it is more likely that some actors will leak information to government forces, which have an especially strong advantage when rebel groups are still nascent. This is consistent with Lyall's framework that in-group biases influence co-ethnic informing, but the mechanism here relies on the level of fragmentation and the length of paths in communication networks, which differ depending on ethnic composition, rather than on psychological biases. Larson and Lewis demonstrate these dynamics with formal theory and a paired comparison of early-stage rebel groups in Uganda.

—Kanchan Chandra and Omar García-Ponce, "Why Ethnic Subaltern-Led Parties Crowd Out Armed Organizations: Explaining Maoist Violence in India," *World Politics* 71, no. 2 (2019): 367–416.

This study examines how nonviolent access to political power influences support for insurgencies.[39] Chandra and Garcia-Ponce explain variation in the levels of Maoist violence in India as partly a function of marginalized groups' access to political power. Insurgents found mobilization difficult in districts where subaltern-led political parties had a strong presence, which enabled them to ensure access to services and to provide a sense of dignity and status to otherwise disaffected individuals. The mechanism therefore relies on both rational and emotional logics. Chandra and Garcia-Ponce support these claims by analyzing data on the historical vote shares of subaltern parties and district-level Maoist violence from 1967 to 2008. For CHB strategies, this suggests that political institutions provide a mechanism to crowd out violent mobilization, but Chandra and Garcia-Ponce note the caveat that timing mattered: the effect only held when the subaltern party had a strong presence before the spread of the insurgency. Otherwise, insurgents co-opted and intimidated their nonviolent competitors.

—Daniel Corstange and Erin York, "Sectarian Framing in the Syrian Civil War," *American Journal of Political Science* 62, no. 2 (2018): 441–455.

This study examines the impact of sectarian discursive frames on civilian support during civil wars.[40] Corstange and York field a survey experiment with 2,000 Syrian refugees living in Lebanon. Building on the intuition that making ethnic identities salient should help mobilize a collective response, their treatment varies whether a prompt frames the Syrian civil war as ethnic, offers no frame, or offers a number of competing frames (sectarianism, democracy, secularism, and foreign intervention). The dependent variable was a question that asked respondents to rank the importance of reasons to continue the fight in Syria. They found that sectarian frames led government supporters to place a higher value on the conflict, but this was only true when presented with the sectarian frame in isolation. The introduction of counter-narratives eliminated the effect. This suggests that ethnicity can help mobilize civilians to adopt supporting roles, but civilians are susceptible to competing narratives in the marketplace of ideas for how they should view the conflict.

Güneş Murat Tezcür, "Ordinary People, Extraordinary Risks: Participation in an Ethnic Rebellion," *American Political Science Review* 110, no. 2 (2016): 247–264.

This study revisits theories of participation in civil wars, especially ethnic conflicts.[41] Drawing from existing frameworks, it outlines a series of hypotheses about material, social, and psychological reasons that individuals join insurgencies. These include rational calculations about economic opportunity costs, security-seeking, and fear of communal sanctions for non-participation; social influences such as preexisting ethnic cleavages and kinship ties to other participants; and a psychological mechanism based in prospect theory, by which individuals with self-efficacy beliefs are convinced that their community faces an existential threat and that their participation can help prevent catastrophic losses.

Tezcür tests these hypotheses with data on participation in Kurdish militant groups. Tezcür draws from PKK obituaries for data on 8,266 combatants and from 68 interviews with participants' family members. The findings provide some support for most hypotheses except for the importance of preexisting ethnic cleavages. This suggests that there are diverse reasons that individuals join insurgencies, which highlights the importance of agency and local context.

B.4. Movement among –1, 0, +1: Mechanization

—Jason Lyall and Isaiah Wilson III, "Rage against the Machines: Explaining Outcomes in Counterinsurgency Wars," *International Organization* 63 (Winter 2009): 67–106.

Lyall and Wilson begin their study by taking the long view and examining the outcomes of counterinsurgency wars across the past 200+ years. What they find is a striking pattern where counterinsurgent victories decline from a high point of over 90% in 1851–1877 to a low point in the most recent 1976–2005 period of less than 25%.

What can account for this drastic decline in counterinsurgent success? Lyall and Wilson (2009) note that one of the biggest changes has been the mechanization of the military. In the mid-nineteenth century, armies needed to forage to sustain themselves. This necessity produced more frequent and intense interactions with the population. Even if the relationships were not positive, heightened contact and monitoring produced detailed information, the single most important factor in successful counterinsurgency. In terms of the spectrum of roles, soldiers interacting with the population were better positioned to know how to apply sticks and carrots most efficiently to move individuals away from the –1 role, if not always move them toward active collaboration (+1).

As modern militaries moved toward a goal of being able to amass forces for decisive victories, they moved away from the foraging model toward mechanization and standardization. Tanks and battleships, and later planes and helicopters, became the gold standard for what defined a good military organization. As levels of mechanization grew, the distance between soldiers and the population also grew, along with a diminished capacity to garner information from the population. While tanks might be able to intimidate intimidation was not likely to move individuals into the +1 roles crucial for producing efficient counterinsurgency.

Lyall and Wilson (2009) test their argument in two ways. First, they statistically analyze the effect of mechanization against competing variables (state capacity, terrain, proximity of conflict to counterinsurgent homeland, ethnic diversity, and specific Cold War qualities) with a dataset of 287 cases from 1800 to 2005. They find support for the negative effects of mechanization. As they summarize: "In substantive terms, shifting from the least mechanized military (1) to the most mechanized (4) is associated with a −50 percent change in expected probability of an incumbent victory in the 1918–2005 era" (Lyall and Wilson, 2009, p. 89). Although not the primary focus of the study, the article also reinforces points made above on the importance of identity. Based on a dichotomous variable, foreign occupiers are 59% less likely to prevail in a counterinsurgency than domestic regimes.

Second, Lyall and Wilson (2009) explore their argument in depth by comparing the counterinsurgency efforts of two US divisions in Iraq during 2003–2004. By the study's measures, the 4th Infantry Division was the most heavily mechanized unit in the US Army; the 101st Airborne, on the other hand, was one of the least mechanized. While the less mechanized 101st Airborne walked beats with Iraqi forces, the 4th Infantry patrolled less and did so mainly while remaining in their armored vehicles. With the 101st Airborne, Major General David Petraeus carried out a "Tribal Engagement Plan" and developed metrics based on collection of information; the 4th Infantry used metrics suited to their operations, such as number of firefights and enemy casualties. Based on better intelligence, the 101st Airborne conducted targeted raids with fewer arrests; the 4th Infantry conducted raids and arrested three times more Iraqis per day than the 101st (33 to 11). In fact, the 4th Infantry's nearly 10,000 arrests were the highest total of any division in Iraq. Lyall and Wilson (2009) quote the Army Inspector General in stating that the 4th Infantry was "grabbing whole villages because combat soldiers were unable to figure out who was of value and who was not" (p. 100). Following the expectations from the statistical study, the 4th Infantry incurred the highest number of insurgent attacks during this period (with attacks accelerating over time) while the 101st Airborne saw a rate of only 5 per day (the Iraqi average per division for this time period was 25).

Critics of this argument point out that Lyall and Wilson (2009) leave out some important variables in their study.[42] First, the work does not address possible effects of diffusion of technology and organization (as well as learning) on the insurgent side. For example, the Viet Minh themselves were both mechanized and possessed tactics to confront mechanized forces. Second, earlier counterinsurgent victories were at least partly the result of the abilities of counterinsurgents to employ unrestrained and, by today's standards, inhumane methods. Among the cases from 1832 to 1877, 12 are US victories against Native American Tribes. These cases involved the targeting of food supplies and the impact of disease. Likewise, the British tactics of the Second Boer War would not be used by the British in the post–World War II period. Both increased learning and changing international norms, neither accounted for in Lyall and Wilson's (2009) study, may play significant roles in the variation of the study's dependent variable. Others question the study's case comparison, especially in light of results for other divisions in Iraq and Afghanistan.[43]

—Melissa Dell and Pablo Querubin, "Nation Building through Foreign Intervention: Evidence from Discontinuities in Military Strategies," *The Quarterly Journal of Economics* 133, no. 2 (2018): 701–764.

This study examines how different counterinsurgency strategies worked in Vietnam.[44] To evaluate the impact of air strikes, Dell and Querubin leverage an arbitrary rounding policy in the algorithm that the US military used to determine how to allocate bombers that led to bombing only some of otherwise similar villages based on whether they were above or below the rounding threshold. The dependent variables include measures of local security and governance conditions as recorded by US military and government agents at the time. The findings suggest that reliance on air strikes fueled insurgent activity and undermined local state capacity. Dell and Querubin also leverage a spatial discontinuity between Army and Marine Corps jurisdiction to compare the impact of contrasting doctrines on otherwise similar hamlets on either side of the boundary. Army doctrine emphasized firepower and search-and-destroy operations, whereas the Marines used small teams embedded with the local population for a hearts-and-minds approach. Because the Marine approach also involved providing development aid, it is difficult to completely isolate the effect of reliance on mechanization and firepower relative to broader differences in strategy. Hamlets within the Marine area of responsibility experienced better governance, less violence, and stronger pro-government opinion compared to nearby hamlets under Army jurisdiction.

B.5. Movement to +2 (Police) +3 (Military)

—Matthew Nanes, "Police Integration and Support for Anti-Government Violence in Divided Societies: Evidence from Iraq," *Journal of Peace Research* 57, no. 2 (2020): 329–343.

This study examines how the ethnic composition of police forces influences conflict.[45] The central argument is that integrating police forces can provide a costly and credible signal to civilians that the government will not repress them, which reduces support for insurgent violence. The commitment is credible when police units are fully integrated, rather than simply containing minority-only components, because this makes unwinding integration more difficult. The mechanism is a rational approach to updating information about a combatant's intentions.

Nanes tests this argument with a survey experiment of 800 Iraqi civilians in Baghdad in 2016. The survey varied a prime about the levels of ethnic integration in the police forces and used a list experiment to gauge endorsement of anti-government violence and concerns about repression. The findings support the hypothesis that integration rather than segregated inclusion is the best method to overcome the commitment problem and that it can reduce civilian support for insurgents.

—Mara Karlin, *Building Militaries in Fragile States: Challenges for the United States* (Philadelphia: University of Pennsylvania Press, 2018).

This study examines US efforts to build militaries in weak states.[46] The main argument is that successful security sector reform is only likely when (1) the United States has "deep involvement" in the client's military affairs, and (2) there is minimal intervention from "antagonistic external actors" seeking to subvert these efforts. Deep involvement here entails "selecting the personnel who constitute the institution's senior leadership, organizing the military around countering an internal threat, and avoiding becoming a combatant."[47] Both deep US involvement and minimal foreign involvement from adversarial actors are necessary conditions for success, which is measured in terms of the client state's monopoly on the use of force.

Karlin tests these claims with four case studies of US attempts to strengthen foreign state militaries. The cases include the Greek military after World War II, South Vietnam in the 1950s, and then Lebanon, first in the 1980s and again in the early twenty-first century. Interestingly, the scope excludes cases where the United States engaged in local combat operations, including post-2003 Iraq, and Vietnam after 1961. Karlin suggests this is because of the difficulty of isolating whether these two variables explained outcomes, so the theoretical logic of the argument could extend to these cases, although the coding of "deep involvement" precludes direct military intervention.

—Oeindrila Dube and Suresh Naidu, "Bases, Bullets, and Ballots: The Effect of US Military Aid on Political Conflict in Colombia," *The Journal of Politics* 77, no. 1 (2015): 249–267.

This study examines the impact of US military aid on conflict dynamics in Colombia.[48] The independent variable is an instrument for overall shifts in the global amount of US spending on military aid, and the dependent variable is violence in the Colombian civil war. Greater aid was correlated with more attacks by pro-government paramilitary forces in areas closer to Colombian military bases. The authors interpret this as suggestive evidence that the Colombian military funneled aid windfalls to right-wing paramilitary groups, which then used those resources for attacks. But these attacks also were particularly impactful during election years to undermine local domestic politics. This suggests that actors—whether client states or their agents—can use US military aid to advance their own local agendas in ways that may conflict with other US interests or exacerbate the conflict.

—Luke Abbs, Govinda Clayton, and Andrew Thomson, "The Ties That Bind: Ethnicity, Pro-Government Militia, and the Dynamics of Violence in Civil War," *Journal of Conflict Resolution* 64, no. 5 (2020): 903–932.

This study examines how ethnicity influences the use of pro-government militias.[49] The main argument is that states rely on co-ethnic militias because ethnicity serves as a proxy for reliability that helps address principal-agent problems, but their use ultimately makes conflicts worse by aggravating ethnic tensions. Abbs et al. support this claim about the relationship between co-ethnic militias and conflict severity and duration by analyzing data from a cross-national sample of militias from 1989 to 2007. This argument suggests that governments prefer to mobilize specific kinds of individuals—co-ethnics—into security-sector roles because it makes it easier to control agents and prevent interest divergence. But Abbs et al. note that some ethnic militias are "defector" militias composed of members of the insurgency's ethnic group, such as the Kurdish Village Guard militia in Turkey. This highlights that master ethnic cleavages are not deterministic of local behavior.

—Jason Lyall, *Divided Armies: Inequality and Battlefield Performance in Modern War* (Princeton, NJ: Princeton University Press, 2020).

This study examines how ethnic exclusion influences military effectiveness.[50] The main argument is that ethnic inequalities reduce conventional military performance. The three mechanisms are grievances against the regime that diminish minority forces' combat motivation, the difficulty of inter-ethnic cooperation due to mistrust, and the greater potential of ethnic minorities to evade military service because they have access to stronger intra-ethnic networks. Lyall applies this framework to conventional wars, but one implication is that governments may often struggle simultaneously to tolerate (or encourage) ethnic inequality in their political system and to leverage ethnic minorities for counterinsurgency operations. Lyall and others have suggested that co-ethnic counterinsurgent forces provide informational advantages against insurgent groups, but there are also obstacles to integrating such co-ethnic units into traditional police and military units.

—Paul Staniland, "Militias, Ideology, and the State," *Journal of Conflict Resolution* 59, no. 5 (2015): 770–793.

This study explains variation in state strategies toward militias.[51] Staniland introduces a typology of suppression, containment, collusion, and incorporation strategies. These involve intensive lethal targeting, limited efforts to prevent a militia from growing too powerful, active cooperation, and attempts to demobilize and integrate militias into formal security structures. Staniland explanations the choice of strategy as depending on (1) ideological similarity between the state and militia, and (2) the militia's value in responding to an external threat. States are most likely to incorporate militias into their formal security forces (+3) when there is a strong ideological overlap, but the militia offers little operational value in operating independently, which makes it a "superfluous supporter." The key implication here is that states may sometimes face ideological or strategic obstacles to moving forces from +2 to +3 roles.

—Brandon Bolte, "The Puzzle of Militia Containment in Civil War," *International Studies Quarterly* 65, no. 1 (2021): 250–261.

This study examines why governments make concerted efforts to limit the strength of pro-government paramilitary forces during civil wars.[52] Bolte argues that short-term containment efforts are driven by long-term concerns about bargaining power and credible commitments; that is, strengthening the paramilitary group too much now may make it difficult to control down the road. Bolte argues that containment depends on the extent of the threat from rebels and the level of state capacity, which the study tests with a cross-national dataset from 1989–2010. The argument differs from Staniland because states can have incentives to contain militias even if they offer short-term operational advantages in dealing with external threats. One implication for community mobilization strategies is that empowering other actors in the short term can have negative long-term consequences if there are conflicts of interest in the future and the state's relative capacity is diminished.

—Tobias Böhmelt and Govinda Clayton, "Auxiliary Force Structure: Paramilitary Forces and Progovernment Militias," *Comparative Political Studies* 51, no. 2 (2018): 197–237.

This study examines how states build up auxiliary units that are not part of its traditional military forces.[53] The central analytic distinction is between paramilitary forces, which are integrated into official state command structures, and pro-government militias, which are not. Bohmelt and Clayton argue that pro-government militias offer advantages because they are cheaper and offer plausible deniability for unpopular violence. Drawing from a cross-national dataset of auxiliary forces from 1981–2007, they find that low state capacity and threats from insurgents are associated with greater reliance on militias. One implication here is that community mobilization strategies tend to partly reflect weak state capacity, not its ideal scenario.

—Govinda Clayton and Andrew Thomson, "Civilianizing Civil Conflict: Civilian Defense Militias and the Logic of Violence in Intrastate Conflict," *International Studies Quarterly* 60, no. 3 (2016): 499–510.

This study examines the impact of civilian defense militias on violence.[54] Clayton and Thomas define these militias as "sedentary and defensive" pro-government militias that "undertake intelligence and limited combat roles" without joining the state's core security forces. The main argument is that these militias provide the government with valuable intelligence that enables selective violence, but it encourages more indiscriminate insurgent violence by denying them access to local support. They confirm this trend with a cross-national dataset from 1981–2005 and a qualitative case study of Iraq during 2005–2009. This suggests that one important role for paramilitary groups is to collect intelligence because they are closer to the local population.

—Corinna Jentzsch, Stathis Kalyvas, and Livia Schubiger, "Militias in Civil Wars," *Journal of Conflict Resolution* 59, no. 5 (2015): 755–769.

This article introduces a special issue on militias in civil wars rather than introducing new scholarship, but it does briefly discuss how we might extrapolate existing theories to think about potential "triggers of militia mobilization."[55] The authors highlight bottom-up, local mobilization as a response to indiscriminate violence at the hands of either insurgents or state forces. This might be rooted in a rational mechanism of security-seeking behavior or an emotional trigger from exposure to harm.

—Matthew Kocher, Adria Lawrence, and Nuno Monteiro, "Nationalism, Collaboration, and Resistance: France under Nazi Occupation," *International Security* 43, no. 2 (2018): 117–150.

This study examines why nationalist groups still collaborate with occupying powers.[56] The main argument is that nationalist goals are indeterminate in predicting what means actors use to pursue them. Knowledge of the local political context is key to understand nationalist strategies. Kocher et al. use Vichy collaboration in Nazi-occupied France to demonstrate that right-wing groups worked with Nazi forces because it restored their access to political power that they had started to lose to left-wing parties before the war. Even left-wing groups were unwilling to mount a strong insurgent challenge to the Nazi occupation until it became apparent that Allied forces would likely defeat Germany. For CHB and community mobilization strategies, this suggests that understanding local context and the political winners and losers from pursuing different approaches is critical.

B.6. Movement from 0, −1, to −2

—Stefano Costalli and Andrea Ruggeri, "Indignation, Ideologies, and Armed Mobilization: Civil War in Italy, 1943–45," *International Security* 40, no. 2 (2015): 119–157.

This study examines the role of emotions and ideologies in civil war mobilization.[57] The main argument is that emotions, especially indignation, "push" individuals away from neutral nodes toward supporting armed mobilization. Indignation, which the study defines as an actor's response to harm done to a third party, has a strong communal effect because of its shared sense of right and wrong. Ideologies, especially radical ones, "pull" individuals toward mobilization because it connects their private grievances to collective responses. This is particularly true for radical ideologies because of their doctrinal content.

Costalli and Ruggeri test these dynamics with data from the Italian resistance movement during 1943–1945. The dependent variable is the number of partisan bands in 1944. The vote share of the Italian Community Party and the Italian Socialist Party in Italy's 1921 elections proxies for the presence of ideological networks with radical doctrines. The number of Italian soldiers from a province that died fighting abroad proxies for local indignation. The findings suggest a strong correlation across provinces between ideological networks, local indignation, and the number of partisan bands. There is also a strong correlation between bands and automobiles per person, which might represent infrastructure or wealth. Two additional tests include within-province analysis in Cuneo and Savona with a direct measure of participation as the dependent variable, as well as interviews with partisans.

—Emily Gade, "Social Isolation and Repertoires of Resistance," *American Political Science Review* 114, no. 2 (2020): 309–325.

This study examines the impact of the "built environment of conflict"— checkpoints, guard towers, and so forth, on mobilization and individuals' tactics of violent resistance.[58] The central argument is that infrastructure, in this case checkpoints, can impact social structures and individual feelings of social connection or isolation. Isolating individuals leads to feelings of hopelessness that reduce the capacity and preference for collective mobilization and lead to "unstructured, individual violence." Checkpoints that isolate entire communities but do not sever ties with those groups can generate more collective, rather than individual, resistance. The study highlights four mechanisms by which social connections support collective resistance: helping individuals cope with stress rather than being too overwhelmed to organize a response; building trust that others will follow through on promises to engage in risky activities; facilitating organization and recruitment through social networks; and building a sense of optimism about the feasibility of change. This theory is a deductive product of 71 interviews of individuals from the West Bank during the 2015 Intifada. The study contributes to understanding why some violent resistance remains unorganized (–1), whereas some develops into local collective resistance (–2).

—Anastasia Shesterinina, "Collective Threat Framing and Mobilization in Civil War," *American Political Science Review* 110, no. 3 (2016): 411–427.

This study examines the impact of threat perceptions on mobilization.[59] The main argument is that social structures mediate how individuals receive information about threats, which influences how they mobilize in response to them. The motivating premise is that patterns of mobilization in a specific war—the Georgian-Abkhaz war of 1992–1993—were puzzling because 13% of the Abkhaz population mobilized despite facing nearly impossible odds against Georgian forces. Shesterinina argues that the content of social ties determined whether individuals took self- or other-regarding responses to the threat by determining how individuals related their own behavior to a collective identity. This provides additional support that social mechanisms influence how individuals receive and process information about threats and weigh cost–benefit calculations about their obligations and optimal responses.

—Reed Wood and Jakana Thomas, "Women on the Frontline: Rebel Group Ideology and Women's Participation in Violent Rebellion," *Journal of Peace Research* 54, no. 1 (2017): 31–46.

This study examines the impact of group ideology on how insurgents mobilize women to into different roles in insurgencies.[60] The main argument is that ideologies shape how organizations address women's participation because they carry content about appropriate gender hierarchies and divisions of labor. Wood and Thomas test this claim with a cross-national dataset of rebel groups from 1979 to 2009. The findings confirm that left-wing groups are more likely to have female fighters, while Islamist groups are less likely.

—Sarah Elizabeth Parkinson, "Organizing Rebellion: Rethinking High-Risk Mobilization and Social Networks in War," *American Political Science Review* 107, no. 3 (August 2013): 418–432.

This study examines how individuals mobilize into logistics roles for insurgencies.[61] The main argument is that the formal hierarchies of militant organizations overlap with social networks (friends, family, etc.) to create pathways for mobilization. Individuals with social positions that bridge different networks are particularly useful for passing along information or money to disparate parts of an organization. The social structures that create such bridging positions create pathways to mobilize individuals into clandestine logistics networks in ways that are different from traditional mobilization into combat roles. Parkinson demonstrates this with an in-depth case study of the Palestine Liberation Organization (PLO) during the 1980s. Social networks helped build resiliency into the group when faced with external security threats, and female family members often occupied key bridge positions that made them ideal for mobilization into logistics support roles necessary to sustain the group.

—Laia Balcells, *Rivalry and Revenge: The Politics of Violence during Civil War* (New York: Cambridge University Press, 2017).

This study examines the determinants of violence in civil wars.[62] The main argument is that local rivalries and emotional triggers to seek revenge drive violence. Actors use violence against political rivals, and there is then an endogenous dynamic in which people seek revenge for past harm through violent means. Balcells tests these dynamics in the Spanish Civil War.

—Megan Stewart, "Civil War as State-Making: Strategic Governance in Civil War," *International Organization* 72, no. 1 (2018): 205–226.

This study asks why insurgent groups provide costly public goods even though civilians can free-ride on the benefits without mobilizing in support of the insurgency.[63] The main argument is that inclusive provision of public goods is not a tool of recruitment, but instead a tool of legitimacy for secessionist groups looking for recognition of their territorial control. Stewart tests this with a cross-national dataset of rebel groups and service provision from 1945 to 2003.

—Adam Lichtenheld, "Explaining Population Displacement Strategies in Civil Wars: A Cross-National Analysis," *International Organization* 74, no. 2 (2020): 253–294.

This study examines the strategic logic of population displacement in civil wars.[64] The main argument is that combatants use population displacement for different reasons, depending on the war's context and their own strategic needs. Lichtenheld distinguishes between cleansing, depopulation, and forced relocation. Cleansing involves efforts to permanently expel a particular group from a state's territory based on its collective identity; depopulation temporarily removes all civilians from an area; and forced relocation brings certain groups into government-controlled territory, such as strategic hamlets in Vietnam. Lichtenheld introduces a new "assortative" theory to explain displacement as helping states solve intelligence problems by observing whether and where civilians flee as a costly signal about their political loyalties. The hypotheses include the prevalence of cleansing in conventional wars because of the importance of territory, the greater occurrence of forced relocation in irregular wars because of the centrality of intelligence, and that weak states are most likely to used forced relocation against rural insurgencies because it has poor access to information about the population. The study tests these claims with a new dataset on displacement strategies in 160 wars from 1945 to 2008 and a case study in Uganda. Lichtenheld's study has implications for understanding the conditions under which governments might use displacement as part of a homogenization strategy.

B.7. Movement from −2 to +2 and −3 to + 3: "Flipping"

—Marc Lynch, "Explaining the Awakening: Engagement, Publicity, and the Transformation of Iraqi Sunni Political Attitudes," *Security Studies* 20, no. 1 (2011): 36–72.

Lynch (2011) describes multiple mechanisms at work. The first is attitude change through contact. Lynch points out that after 2005 the nature of contact between Americans and Iraqis changed. Contact increased became more direct; there were "endless cups of tea." Lynch (2011) describes the cumulative effect of the changed nature of the dialogue as "profound" (Lynch, 2011, p. 51). The media also became more objective. As Lynch (2011) summarizes, "Together, these led to a dramatic shift in the distribution of information available to Iraqi Sunnis, and to a reformulation of the conception of collective identity and interests underlying their strategic decisions" (p. 39).

A second mechanism was a focal point mechanism. While the private dialogue between Americans and Sunnis built trust, there still needed to be public cues that allowed actors to know what other actors were thinking and doing. Awakening leaders appeared on TV to denounce al-Qaeda. With local actors primed to shift through increased contact and information, and with higher-level leaders realizing the strategic logic of alliance change, Anbar was set to see a cascade of "flipping" toward the government side, especially during the "surge."

One of the most cited articles that address the surge is Biddle et al. (2012).

—Stephen Biddle, Jeffrey A. Friedman, and Jacob Shapiro, "Testing the Surge: Why Did Violence Decline in Iraq in 2007?," *International Security* 37, no. 1 (2012): 7–40.

This study explains the drastic drop in violence in the 2007 period to "synergy" or a combination of (1) the awakening and the "flipping" of tribes, and (2) new US strategy and tactics which provided higher numbers of troops and more frequent interactions with the population. Neither factor was sufficient. Success came through the synergies created by their combination. In this story, the only necessary mechanisms are rational-choice considerations. Sunni tribes had good strategic reasons to "flip" and the Surge gave them protection and confidence to do so. We discuss this article in detail in Chapter 11 on Anbar.

—Paul Staniland, "Between a Rock and a Hard Place: Insurgent Fratricide, Ethnic Defection, and the Rise of Pro-State Militia," *Journal of Conflict Resolution* 56, no. 1 (2012): 16–40.

Staniland has produced a series of articles on insurgent organization in South Asia, one with implications for "flipping." Studying Sunni tribal groups in Iraq, as well as groups in Kashmir and Sri Lanka, he argues that fratricide within groups is a common reason for defection to pro-state militias, while governmental policy is less important and ideological disagreements are basically unimportant. Groups switch to the government side (+2, +3) mainly because they need to survive threats to their very survival from factions within their own organization.

—Ben Oppenheim, Abbey Steele, Juan F. Vargas, and Michael Weintraub, "True Believers, Deserters, and Traitors: Who Leaves Insurgent Groups and Why," *Journal of Conflict* Resolution 59, no. 5 (2015): 794–823.

This study examines why individuals defect from insurgent groups.[65] The main argument is that the reasons people initially joined will influence their patterns of switching sides downstream. The framework distinguishes between ideological and economic joiners. The theory predicts that ideological fighters are the least likely to defect and that ideological indoctrination can also make economic joiners more committed. Conversely, economic joiners are more likely to defect given better alternative opportunities for looting or organizational attempts to limit predation on civilians. Oppenheim et al. test these claims with survey data of 1,485 former Colombian combatants collected by an NGO. The findings suggest that initial motivations for joining impacted individual decisions to defect in the future. The chief contribution of this study is that it has micro-level data on combatants rather than studying defection or flipping at the group level.

—Sabine Otto, "The Grass Is Always Greener? Armed Group Side Switching in Civil Wars," *Journal of Conflict Resolution* 62, no. 7 (2018): 1459–1488.

This study examines why armed groups, rather than individuals, flip during civil wars.[66] The theory extends to rebel groups and pro-government militias. The main argument is that a combination of organizational incentives and capacity explains these choices. First, there are stronger incentives to switch when facing greater competition in terms of the number of armed groups and when the state is weak. Switching can make a group more relevant or increase its access to resources. Second, there is greater capacity to switch when groups have internal consensus. If the group is itself already a splinter from a larger organization, internal consensus is more achievable because it is more homogenous by self-selection. Otto tests this with the History of Armed Actors Dataset with cross-national information on insurgent flipping from 1989 to 2007. The findings support the hypotheses about state capacity and splinter organizations but not the number of rival groups.

—Lee Seymour, "Why Factions Switch Sides in Civil Wars: Rivalry, Patronage, and Realignment in Sudan," *International Security* 39, no. 2 (2014): 92–131.

This study similarly examines why insurgent organizations switch sides.[67] The main argument is that groups do so opportunistically to gain an advantage over local rivals. This stands in contrast to conventional explanations of ethnic identity, ideological affinity, and territorial control. Seymour's theory focuses on local rivalry and external patronage. First, groups look for opportunities to switch sides in ways that would damage their local political rivals. Second, groups switch sides in response to foreign inducements, such as cash or military support, to do so. Seymour tests these arguments with nested analysis of insurgent flipping in the civil wars in Sudan and Darfur. The dependent variable is realignment, and the independent variables include a preexisting rivalry with another local group and patronage as quid pro quos of material rewards for flipping. Seymour complements this analysis with qualitative paired comparisons.

—Enzo Nussio and Juan Ugarriza, "Why Rebels Stop Fighting: Organizational Decline and Desertion in Colombia's Insurgency," *International Security* 45, no. 4 (2021): 167–203.

This study examines why individuals defect from insurgencies.[68] The main argument is that organizations need incentives to resolve collective-action problems inherent in mobilization. These include financial incentives, ideological appeals, and coercion. When insurgent groups suffer organizational decline from military defeats or financial losses, their ability to exercise these tools declines, so group members have fewer incentives to participate in the insurgency. For example, decreased revenue makes it more difficult for groups to retain fighters with economic motivations. Nussio and Ugarriza test this argument with data on former Colombian fighters during 2002–2017. Consistent with the hypotheses, organizational decline from decapitation and coca revenue loss correlated with increased desertion rates.

B.8. Decapitation: Versus –3

The academic position on decapitation is perhaps epitomized by two studies published in 2009–2010:

—Jenna Jordan, "When Heads Roll: Assessing the Effectiveness of Leadership Decapitation," *Security Studies* 18 (2009): 719–755.

—Alex Wilner, "Targeted Killing in Afghanistan: Measuring Coercion and Deterrence in Counterterrorism and Counterinsurgency," *Studies in Conflict and Terrorism* 33, no. 4 (2010): 307–329.

Wilner's (2010) uses the comparative case method to analyze the effects of four targeted killings of Taliban leaders in Afghanistan conducted in 2007–2008. He examines the amount and type of violence conducted by the targeted leader's organization in the period before the killing and compares it to the period immediately after. Using this before–after approach, Wilner (2010) finds that decapitation did not diminish the number of attacks. On the contrary, the overall number of attacks increased. Wilner (2010), though, states that "[o]verall levels of violence, however, are only a minor part of the analysis" (p. 319). The more important metric is type of attack. Wilner (2010) argues that the Taliban preferred attacks in the following order: suicide bombings, IEDs, and small arms and rocket fire. In his analysis, Wilner (2010) finds that the most preferred type of violence, the suicide attack, declined after decapitation. He argues that the suicide attack requires a high level of organization and planning and therefore decapitation eliminates the very ability to conduct this highly effective operation. With diminished capacity, organizations may increase the number of small arms and rocket fire attacks, but these do little damage in comparison to more complex operations. Wilner (2010) argues, in sum, that decapitation successfully "de-professionalizes" an insurgent organization.

Jordan's study differs from Wilner's (2010) in both in method and findings. Jordan (2009) does a large-n statistical analysis of 298 decapitation incidents during 1945–2004. The article concentrates on the effects of three independent variables—organizational age, size, and type (ideological, religious, or separatist). There are also three dependent variables: organizational decline, collapse, and number and lethality of attacks post-decapitation. Instead of Wilner's (2010) before–after approach, Jordan (2009) establishes a baseline rate of organizational collapse over time and then compares groups that experienced decapitation against those that did not. Jordan's approach thus captures some longer-term effects not considered in Wilner's (2010) short-term frame. Jordan's findings also differ. She finds that while decapitation may be effective against smaller, young, and ideologically motivated groups, targeting larger, older, and religious and separatist organizations is counterproductive. In these latter types of organizations, Jordan (2009) summarizes "decapitation not only has a much lower rate of success, the marginal value is, in fact, negative" (p. 754). With growth and age, Jordan reasons, an insurgent organization is likely to have developed support systems and recruitment networks as well as a deeper bureaucratization and specialization. If one leader is killed, these qualities allow another leader to quickly and efficiently step in.

Coming later in the progression of academic articles on decapitation, Austin Long's study builds from an observation about Jordan's research.

—Austin Long, "Whack-a-Mole or Coup de Grace? Institutionalization and Leadership Targeting in Iraq and Afghanistan," *Security Studies* 23, no. 3 (2014): 471–512.

After summarizing Jordan's (2009) findings on age and size and their possible effects in creating organizations resistant to decapitation, Long (2014) notes that Jordan's (2009) independent variables basically amount to proxy variables for organizational characteristics. Long (2014) asks, instead of using age and size as proxy measures for organizational qualities of specialization and bureaucratization, why not just use direct measures of specialization and bureaucratization? Long writes:

> It would therefore be ideal to isolate the actual variable of interest, in this case the level of complex structures and stable relationships, rather than probabilistic proxies. Some young, small organizations may nonetheless have complex organizations and stable relationships, while some large, old organizations may not. The ability to identify the vulnerability of organizations to leadership targeting therefore is critically dependent on identifying the level of complex structure and stable relationships rather than merely relying on the proxies of age and size. (Long, 2014, p. 475).

Using this more direct approach, Long (2014) finds that decapitation strategies will only work against organizations which do not have institutionalized command structures. Groups with institutionalized command structures can refill their ranks or transfer responsibility with little damage to the organization's efficiency.

—Patrick Johnston, "Does Decapitation Work? Assessing the Effectiveness of Leadership Targeting in Counterinsurgency Campaigns," *International Security* 36, no. 4 (2012): 47–79.

Johnston evaluates whether leadership decapitation reduces insurgent capacity.[69] The main argument is that decapitation works. Drawing on a cross-national dataset of insurgent leaders from START Terrorist Organization Profiles and a new dataset of 188 decapitation effects, 46 of which were successful, Johnston finds that decapitation is correlated with subsequent government victory and fewer and less lethal insurgent attacks. He finds no distinction in effectiveness against specific kinds of insurgencies, such as ideological or center-seeking movements. Given the extremely small sample size and numerous threats to inference, it is difficult to extrapolate much from these findings.

—Joshua Eastin and Emily Gade, "Beheading the Hydra: Counterinsurgent Violence and Insurgent Attacks in Iraq," *Terrorism and Political Violence* 30, no. 3 (2018): 384–407.

This study examines the impact of counterinsurgent violence on insurgent organizations.[70] The main argument is that low levels of violence against insurgencies can help bolster these groups by signaling their resolve and resilience, but higher levels begin to undercut their ability to mobilize support because civilians began to worry about their safety if they support insurgent operations. Eastin and Gade test this with evidence from Iraq in 2004–2009. They combine WikiLeaks and SIGACTS data on fatalities in Iraq. The dependent variable is a count of insurgent attacks. The independent variables are insurgent and civilian fatalities as measures of the rate of attrition. The findings suggest that high levels of attrition result in decreased insurgent capacity for attacks, although it does not differentiate between certain kinds of attrition, such as leadership decapitation or targeting middle-management such as bomb makers or forgers.

—Jacqueline Hazelton, "The 'Hearts and Minds' Fallacy: Violence, Coercion, and Success in Counterinsurgency Warfare," *International Security* 42, no. 1 (2017): 80–113.

This study offers a strategy-based "coercion theory" as an alternative to the logic of "hearts and minds."[71] Coercion theory rests on the heavy use of violence to undermine insurgent capacity while engaging in deal-making with local elites to collect intelligence, rather than attempting to please the broader population. Success, according to this model, does not emphasize good governance or development. Hazelton compares the track record of coercion and "hearts and minds" in canonical cases such as the Malayan Emergency and finds that coercion theory better describes government strategy in key cases attributed to "hearts and minds."

—Asfandyar Mir, "What Explains Counterterrorism Effectiveness? Evidence from the U.S. Drone War in Pakistan," *International Security* 43, no. 2 (2018): 45–83.

This study examines the determinates of counterterrorism effectiveness, which is slightly different from the context of civil wars but shares some similar insights.[72] The main argument is that a combination of legibility and speed determine whether decapitation works. Governments need to have an effective intelligence network to understand organizations and locate key actors, and they need the ability to prosecute targeting solutions quickly. The main contribution is that Mir points out that the United States has developed an elaborate intelligence, surveillance, reconnaissance (ISR) network that enables it to collect intelligence on militant activity without needing local informants, to some extent. This suggests an alternative way to engage in selective violence without relying on local support, which might be subject to the vagaries of psychological biases favoring co-ethnics, rational concerns about the risks of collaboration, or emotional opposition stemming from exposure to state-imposed violence.

—Christopher Blair, Michael Horowitz, and Philip Potter, "Leadership Targeting and Militant Alliance Breakdown," *The Journal of Politics* 84, no. 2 (2022): 923–943.

This study examines how decapitation influences the ability of insurgent groups to maintain alliance coalitions with other militants.[73] The main argument is that decapitation makes it more difficult for militant groups to sustain preexisting alliances. The potential mechanisms include decreased value of cooperation as one group collapses, the removal of interpersonal ties between leaders, preference divergence between groups as they adapt to new conditions and leadership, and concerns about operational security that raise the costs of alliance coordination. Blair et al. (2022) use the Militant Group Alliances and Relationships dataset for information on militant alliances from 1950 to 2016 with 2,613 groups. They analyze a subset of 207 terrorist groups from 1970 to 2008, and supplement this with qualitative case studies.

NOTES

Chapter 1

1. SIGACT data derived from Multi-National Forces Iraq SIGACT-III database as reported by Berman et al. (2008); troop data from O'Hanlon and Livingston, "Iraq Index." SIGACTS count a great number of different events, ranging from direct and indirect fire attacks on US troops to IED finds, whether or not there are any casualties.
2. See https://www.iraqbodycount.org/ for a description of methods.
3. This is the list distilled from an in-depth review of 40 studies and 100 documents on state-building commissioned by the Ministry of Foreign Affairs of Denmark (Jörn Grävingholt et al., 2012).
4. Margaret Coker, *New York Times*, February 14, 2018. https://www.nytimes.com/2018/02/14/world/middleeast/iraq-kuwait-donor-conference.html
5. Some readers will recognize this framework from my earlier work (Petersen, 2001).
6. In the treatment of Iraq, I will use the terms "ethnic" and "sectarian" interchangeably.
7. There are other types of independent variables—cultural, historical—that are relevant to Iraq and will be considered at various points in the book. For the purposes of this section, I have set off the major focus of the book, strategy, against the commonly accepted political science treatments with their focus on structural variables.
8. Early talks under the title "A Social Science Guide to the Iraq War" were given at Security Studies Program, MIT, September 16, 2015; MacMillan Comparative Politics Workshop, Yale University, October 13, 2015; University of Montreal, November 12, 2015; The Conference of Montreal, November 14, 2015; the Pentagon, Washington, DC, March 31, 2016.
9. "MIT Workshop on Theory and Practice in Iraq and Afghanistan," MIT, April 9–10, 2010. I was co-organizer of workshop (with Fotini Christia).
10. "Counterinsurgency and Counterterrorism, 2011," held at MIT on November 18–19, 2011. The conference was co-sponsored by the Peace Research Institute of Oslo and the Security Studies Program at MIT.
11. I served as dissertation chair for Tim Wright, Matt Cancian, and Marsin Alshamary.
12. The first talk focused on Iraqi identity issues: "State-Building in Iraq: Learning from Other Cases," Iraqi Institute for Dialogue, Baghdad, Iraq, May 6, 2022. The second talk covered strategies of counterinsurgency: "Combating Terrorism: From Conflict to Prevention," Political Science Department, Nahrain University, Baghdad, Iraq, May 16, 2022.a

Chapter 2

1. For estimates of actual fighters versus supporters, see Serena (2014, pp. 1–2).
2. Except as spies or double agents.

3. Some readers will note that in Petersen (2001), the resistance side was positive and the Soviet side negative. In this book, the resistance side is negative and the state side positive. This undoubtedly reflects some of my own orientations, but also matches the intuitions of the likely readers of the book.

4. The mechanism approach can be clearly contrasted with common alternatives. Variable-based treatments usually aim to estimate causal influence through statistical association. In this method, prediction becomes the primary goal. In opposition, a mechanism approach aims for explanation over prediction. For a discussion of the use of a mechanisms approach, see Hedstrom and Swedberg (1998). Also, see Elster (1999), especially the first chapter, "A Plea for Mechanisms." Also see Petersen (1999).

5. This paragraph is lifted from verbatim from Petersen (1999) and (2001). I include it again because it has served as a clear and concise example for various audiences of a commonly experienced mechanism.

6. This figure, as well as some of the descriptions of the figure in this section, was developed by Jon Lindsay and is addressed in more detail in Lindsay and Petersen (2012).

7. As explained in more depth in Chapter 4, we use the term "decapitation" as a general term to describe targeted raids against network leadership, even if these targets are mid-level rather than senior leaders.

8. The most well-known proponent of this position is Chaim Kaufmann. See Kaufmann (1996).

Chapter 3

1. For a general discussion on a mechanisms approach, see, among other works, Elster (1998). Also, Petersen (1999).

2. Following Elster, I have adopted an approach based on methodological individualism. Other scholars who use mechanism-based methods do not, notably Tilly, Tarrow, and McAdams (2001).

3. See King et al. (1994, p. 86) for a discussion of the issue of "infinite regress." Also see Petersen (1999) for a response.

4. As some readers might note, while the method here can be accurately described as "process tracing," it differs significantly from other practitioners of process tracing. For a well-known alternative application, see Gerring (2006, pp. 172–185).

5. The most recent PRIO data records 192 conflicts with over 25 battle deaths, 88 with less than 1,000 dead and 104 with more than 1,000 dead.

6. While economic values are most common in rational-choice treatments, some practitioners of this approach expand the nature of benefits. In some societies, choosing to become a "first-actor" in a rebellion can bring status rewards. See the example in the discussion of Mao's theory in Appendix A.

7. See Weinstein (2007) for a discussion of the relationship between insurgent groups' original endowments and motivation and discipline.

8. I italicize each specific mechanism to later use as shorthand.

9. This is so for larger populations. See the following paragraph for a discussion of Olson's theory as it applies to smaller groups.

10. On the ways such norms generate trust among group members, see Cook and Hardin (2001).

11. Related, see Staniland (2012).

12. This paragraph is largely from Petersen (2011). In his book, *Why We Fight* (2022), Christopher Blattman emphasizes the ability of affect and emotions to shape decision-making. He writes, "what's important to know is that there is no such thing as a purely reasoned decision. Emotions infuse our most clinical calculations, even the ones we think are purely rational" (p. 136). Blattman also underscores the connection between emotions and misperception.

13. Their extensive new database contains nearly 30,000 observations. Strong support for the effect of resentment status reversals is also found in Horowitz (1985).

14. Festinger's 1957 seminal work on cognitive dissonance has been cited over 55,000 times.

15. A contrast can be drawn between wishful thinking and cognitive dissonance. In the latter, contrary information is accepted. The individual manages to change beliefs in a way that reconciles the discordant information.

16. For an early examination, see *Special Issue: Prospect Theory and Political Psychology* (1992).

17. Blattman (2022) specifically discusses the availability bias, confirmation bias, and motivated biases, as well as a number of what he terms "misprojection" mechanisms, including hindsight bias, false consensus, and the lens problem. See chapter 6 of Blattman (2022) in particular. Blattman's concentration on elite-level bargaining differs from the focus here. While these mechanisms no doubt play a role in insurgency, I do not see them as central to those mechanisms driving widespread movement of the general population along the spectrum of roles.

18. Two graduate research assistants, Zachary Burdette and Alec Worsnop, did almost all of the work compiling Appendix B.

19. Appendix B categorizes these articles by topic and relevance to movement on the spectrum. After providing a bibliographical citation, each entry specifies the study's mechanism(s), how that mechanism helps explain a link between cause and effect, independent variable and dependent variable. Appendix B produces the following eight categories:

    1. Movement among −1, 0, +1 Roles: Mechanisms Related to Economics/Poverty/ Employment
    2. Movement among −1, 0, +1 Roles: The Effects of Indiscriminate Violence
    3. Movement among −1, 0, +1 Roles: The Effects of Identity
    4. Movement among −1, 0, +1: Mechanization
    5. Movement to +2 (Police) +3 (Military)
    6. Movement from 0, −1, to −2
    7. Movement from −2 to +2 and −3 to +3: "Flipping"
    8. Decapitation: Versus −3.

20. Not all of the mechanisms listed earlier in the chapter, especially some of the psychological mechanisms, are on this list. These mechanisms were deemed not as clearly significant as others.

21. As Krepinevich (2009, p. 290) goes on to write, "A sound strategy is one that leverages our asymmetric advantages to impose disproportionate costs upon the competition, making it unfeasible for our rivals to compete effectively."

22. In his book *One for All: The Logic of Group Conflict*, Russell Hardin argues that individuals identify with groups to gain economic and political advantages against other members of other groups (Hardin, 1997). Once group identity is in place, individuals then further conform to the identity to avoid being sanctioned by other group members.

23. Social norms are a basic building block of any culture. Individuals simply become habituated to certain forms of interaction with in-group members and other sets of interactions with out-group members. Social norms help create the boundaries that sustain and differentiate one group from another.

24. Also see Halperin (2015) for a relevant discussion of humiliation.

Chapter 4

1. Much of this chapter derives from Lindsay and Petersen (2012).

2. This third step relies on texts and commentary by well-known practitioners/authors/ analysts—Daniel P. Bolger, David Kilcullen, John Nagl, Gian Gentile—among others.

3. Ricks is quoting Major Christopher Varhola and Army Reserve civil affairs specialist, summarizing the position of a commanding officer early in the occupation.

4. Daniel Bolger also writes of Sassaman. See Bolger (2014, p. 149).

5. There are defenders of war-fighting as a counterinsurgency strategy. Perhaps most famously, Harry Summers argued that war-fighting was effective in Vietnam and failure came with the abandonment of that strategy. See Summers (1995).

6. For a review of this strategy, see Kalyvas (2008).

7. In some interpretations, FM 3-24 sees the population as passive. The assumption of passiveness on the part of the population is implicit in military jargon such as "human terrain"; terrain confers advantages and it can be lost, dominated, or shaped, but it is not a willful and reactive entity (thanks to Colin Jackson for this point). The treatment in this book, on the other hand, concentrates on the decisions of individuals in the population and emphasizes their agency.

8. To remind the reader, this section describes CHB as ideally presented in FM 3-24. In practice, US forces absolutely did deal with local armed actors (−2), especially with the tribes in Anbar, in the period before the Surge. In these cases, however, the communities were usually approaching the US forces, rather than the other way around. These interactions occurred in spite of the budding theory of CHB, rather than because of it.

9. See Appendix A for extended treatment of Galula's theory, including discussion of the tipping point mechanism.

10. Recall the theoretical discussion of public versus private goods in the previous chapter's section on rational-choice mechanisms.

11. The Army acronym for this "build" mission is SWEAT-MSO standing for sewer, water, electricity, academics, trash, medical, safety, and other.

12. See Kilcullen (2010, p. 37). Most of this passage is found in FM 3-24 paragraph A-26. It is also cited in Crispin Burke in *War on the Rocks* in his review of Gian Gentile.

13. Mara Karlin, in wide-ranging interviews conducted for her book *The Inheritance* (2022), encountered similar ambivalence about counterinsurgency in general. One former senior civilian official summarized, "Some think you can do COIN now; others think it's too messy." Karlin used that phrase as the heading to the section on legacy of post-9/11 war counterinsurgency practice.

14. In its review of the social science literature, Appendix B examines works related to both the opportunity cost and the positive perceptions arguments.

15. See DOD News Briefing with Lt. General Chiarelli from Iraq, September 15, 2006, https://www.globalsecurity.org/military/library/news/2006/09/mil-060915-dod01.htm.

16. See FM 3-24 MCWP 3-33.5, 5-47, 5-48.

17. This activity can be described as corruption, but it is a normal part of survival in the absence of the impersonal rule of law. COIN forces reinforce this personalized system through the use of no-bid contracts to reward local elites for cooperation—bribes, in essence, although "patronage" might be a politer term—because they provide selective incentives for keeping +2s from becoming −2s.

18. Jackson's (2008) dissertation addresses how counterinsurgents learn. Jackson argues that while militaries have an inherently hard time transitioning from a professional "operational code" for conventional warfare to triangular COIN along the lines of FM 3-24, they hardly ever engage doctrinally with the feudal state-building dynamics of civil war.

19. Chapter 13 examines these interactions, and different views of them, in detail.

20. Norms of honor can also take the form of influential religious norms. Shia religious norms may motivate people to follow the religious hierarchy. See Gates and Nordas (2013).

21. These maps are from Knarr et al. (2016).

22. Shapiro and Weidmann (2011) report a reduction of violence in the areas where new cellular phone towers are installed; this might result either from improved signals intelligence collection or more phone-in tips. Individual economic development projects can provide covers for intelligence gathering, as in an innovative British SAS scheme in Northern Ireland to operate a laundry and test all the clothes for explosive residue, as described in Moloney (2010, pp. 119–121).

23. In personal communication, I have heard that many SOF operators would prefer a different superhero analogy. As relayed to me, there is a consensus that Batman is a more useful DC comics archetype than Superman. In my friend's description, "Batman's superpowers come from (a) super-intelligent planning (b) surveillance (c) special technology (d) being a second-or-two ahead of enemies and (e) from ruthlessly disciplining the body (contra being born a mutant alien who cannot be killed). It also matters that—especially with the Christopher Nolan reboot, all about the GWOT—there is an edgy, unapologetic 'Dark Knight' piece of the Batman aesthetic that is absent in Superman, who gets by on a winning smile that sees the best in people."

24. The most well-known proponent of this position is Chaim Kaufmann. See Kaufmann (1996b).

25. On demographic homogenization and the reduction of chances for war, see Kaufmann (1996a).

26. With a population of 4.5 million, that comes down to one peacekeeper for every 75 citizens.

27. Figure 4.4 is taken from Ned Parker and Ali Hamdani, "How Violence Is Forging a Brutal Divide in Baghdad," *Times of London*, December 14, 2006.

28. This question is a major focus of Chapter 13.

Chapter 5

1. Much of this section comes from reports written by Marsin Alshamary as a research assistant at MIT. Alshamary completed her dissertation, entitled "Prophets and Priests: Religious Leaders and Protest in Iraq," in 2020.

2. A *mujtahid* is a scholar accepted as an original authority in Islamic law.

3. The practice of emulation came about in the mid-1800s under the leadership of the leading *mujtahid* of Najaf at the time, Murtadha Ansari. Ansari and his predecessor, Mohammad Hasan Najafi, transformed the Hawza in many ways. Prior to Najafi, each city in the Shia world had its own *mujtahid*, but due to a dearth of available scholars during his time, he was able to extend his authority outside of geographical constraints throughout Iraq and Iran.

4. Iyad Allawi was the first post-invasion prime minister, but was appointed by the United States, not elected. Thus the first three elected post-invasion prime ministers were from Dawa.

5. This information comes from an interview of Marsin Alshamary with a Dawa Party member from Al-Diywaniya who joined the Dawa Party in the 1970s, corroborated by other sources.

6. Much of the discussion in this section is discussed and described in Faleh Jaber (2003).

7. Arif Basri, Sahib al-Dakhil, Hussein Jalakhan, Izil Din Qabanji, Imad Tabrizi, and Nuri Tu'ma

8. SCIRI later changed its name to the Supreme Islamic Iraqi Council (SIIC) in May 2007, dropping the provocative "revolution" word. SIIC later becomes the Islamic Supreme Council in Iraq (ISCI).

9. As noted earlier, SCIRI is associated with the Hakim family. Following the murders of many of its members, surviving members of the Hakim wing of Shia clerics found refuge in Iran, chief among them being Ayatollah Mushin al-Hakim, along with his sons Mohammed Baqir al-Hakim and Abdul al-Hakim and his grandson Ammar al-Hakim (son of Abdul al-Hakim). Mohammed Baqir al-Hakim founded SCIRI (in Tehran, Iran), in 1982. After his assassination, his brother Abdul took SCIRI's leadership reins. Ammar al-Hakim then succeeded his father. Ammar al-Hakim would break off to form the Hikma movement in 2017.

10. The author met with Allawi and other key INA members in Amman, Jordan, in 2013.

11. Another Western-based Shia organization deserves mention, especially due to its connections with one of the most influential ayatollahs. The Khoei Foundation was formed in 1989 by Grand Ayatollah Abu al-Qassim Al-Khoei and is headquartered in London and Najaf. According to its website, it is one of four Muslim organizations (and the only Shia organization) to hold general consultative status in the UN. It is primarily a charitable and educational organizational with little political goals.

12. The relationship between Saddam Hussein and Sadr II is a huge controversy. Many commentators see Sadr II as essentially a useful tool of the Saddam regime, a pawn helpful in dividing Shia and reducing the influence of the Shia establishment. Our concern here is the relationship between Sadr II and the Shia in Baghdad, especially in Sadr City and other impoverished Shia neighborhoods.

13. Much of this paragraph is based on Wimmer (2002, pp. 172–183).

14. Figures are from 1932 and are cited by Wimmer (2002, pp. 173–174).

15. This point is contentious and there are opposing viewpoints.

16. In my own fieldwork experience, one Sunni interviewee took out his cell phone, showed me pictures of then Prime Minister Maliki whipping himself during Ashura, and asked how Sunnis could cooperate with people engaged in such behavior.

17. Personal experience of the author. In Chapter 6 on Ghazaliyah, Shula plays an important role as a base for the Mahdi Army.

18. Krohley (2015, p. 55) cites figures of an increase in deaths of children under five from 106,000 to 227,000.

19. Some Sunni clerics actively tried to create a Sunni establishment similar to the Hawza in the form of the Association of Muslim Scholars. For more on this, see: https://www.hudson.org/research/14304-the-sunni-religious-leadership-in-iraq.

20. For an extended treatment of the intersection of Islam with the Saddam regime and post-invasion insurgency, see Helfont (2018).
21. Also see Patel (2005).
22. See Byman (2015, pp. 115–119) specifically on Iraq and Zarqawi.
23. David Patel (2017) also discusses Zarqawi's targeting strategy on p. 198.
24. I am basing this judgment on data collected from my research assistant Jessica Karnis, who compiled a list of bombings based on information and descriptions from *Iraq Body Count*, the *New York Times*, and other sources.
25. See description of Moisi's book *The Geopolitics of Emotion: How Cultures of Fear, Humiliation, and Hope Are Reshaping the World* in Chapter 3, Section VI.

Chapter 6

1. Interview with DB.
2. Jamiat al-Tahwid wal-Jihad (JTJ) was Zarqawi's organization that evolved into AQI.
3. Interview with R.
4. As mentioned in footnote above, one of the factions was Tawhid and Jihad, Zarqawi's organization.
5. At least it was perceived as far simpler by many urban Sunnis. See Chapter 11 on the dynamic in Anbar.
6. In *The US Army in the Iraq War*, Vol. 2, 2019, pp. 177–182, from a section entitled "The Awakening Inside the Capital City," which discusses both Ameriyah and Ghazaliyah.
7. In fact, Ali came forward a week after the Ameriyah events. It would take 2½ months before negotiations became serious.
8. I use the term "salaries" here because some interviewees believed faction leaders kept some salaries for themselves rather than actually paying a member.
9. Although many of the CHB tactics had already been instituted by individual US officers in some localities.
10. Joint Press Conference, Major General William Caldwell, MNF-I spokesman, and Dr. Ali al-Dabbagh, government of Iraq spokesman, May 23, 2007. There would be a total of 76 JSS set up in Baghdad during the surge (*The US Army in the Iraq War*, Vol. 2, 2019, p. 99).
11. I am missing the full name.
12. There was some speculation that Col. Ayad was basically controlled by Ali.
13. As one Sahwa leader in Adhamiya claimed in 2009, "Without us, things would return to what they were in 2005. What Awakening guards can do in two hours, U.S. and Iraqi troops weren't able to do in four years" (Rasheed and Cocks, 2009).
14. Interview with Burton from November 14, 2007, cited in *The US Army in the Iraq War*, Vol. 2, 2019, p. 110.

Chapter 7

1. See Anthony Shadid (2005, pp. 263–265) for a description of the event and its aftermath. Also see *The US Army in the Iraq War*, Vol. 1, 2019, p. 198.
2. Also see Serena (2014, p. 65), who holds that the "networks were premised on preexisting social structures rather than on psychological factors."
3. The US Army Manual describes JAM as an "amateur organization with no formal hierarchy," p. 183. Chad Serena (2014) argues that the insurgency as a whole was always loose and shifting. Serena summarizes, "What made the Iraqi insurgency truly unique was its immensely diverse, decentralized hybrid-networked character" (Serena, 2014, p. 42).
4. For a detailed analysis of JAM's fighting ability at this time, see Alec Worsnop, "Organization *or* Community? The Determinants of Insurgent Military Effectiveness," PhD dissertation, MIT, 2016, pp. 355–357. Worsnop's dissertation research analyzes both Sunni and Shia insurgent military effectiveness throughout the war.
5. Much of this section follows the analysis from Worsnop (2016, pp. 350–354).
6. Krohley (2015) and Patel (2017) do not see much continuity, for example. The issue of tribe is reviewed in later chapters.

7. See Worsnop, "Organization *or* Community?," especially the table on p. 348.

8. A common phenomenon. See similar observations in the Bayaa chapter.

9. R2 commented that US soldiers often denigrated Iraqis as lazy and incompetent. However, when they were fighting on their own in the JAM organization, they became competent at carrying out complex operations. R2 posed the question: "what does that mean?"

10. US troops came to call Washash "Little Sadr City" (Kukis, 2006a). In my conversations, some US soldiers referred to Shula as "Sadr City West."

11. As Patrick Gaughen, researcher for the Institute for the Study of War, wrote in his September 2007 report on the Washash and Iskan districts for the Baghdad Neighborhood Project, "Until recently, this area had no persistent US force presence and the Iraqi forces in the area were ineffective."

12. David Patel (2017, p. 103). Patel states that Shaykh Mohammed al-Yacoubi, a student of Mohammed Mohammed Sadiq al-Sadr, led prayers at the Kadhimiyah Shrine on April 11; he claimed to be speaking on behalf of the Hawza.

13. After I visited the Kadhimiyah and the Shrine in 2022, I wrote the following passage in my personal journal: The visit to the Khadhimiyah Shrine reinforced my view of Shiism as its own culture. Visiting these shrines, making pilgrimages, is a core part of life for Shia. These visits are social, cultural, commercial, spiritual, ritualistic all wrapped together. They are repetitive, reinforcing, rhythmic. The Shrine links the past to the present in a highly interactive way. Every sense is involved. A powerful combination of visual and internal, sacred but also mundane in its consistency and constant practice.

14. The *New York Times* put the numbers at 178 dead and at least 500 injured. See Burns and Gettleman (2004, March 2); see Nir Rosen (2006, pp. 116–119) for a description of the bombings.

15. *The US Army in the Iraq War*, Vol. 1, 2019, p. 536. The authors are citing an interview of Ali Kadhem from Kukis (2011, p. 81).

16. *The US Army in the Iraq War*, Vol. 1, 2019, p. 571, citing Hisham Alwan and Salam Jihad, "Iraq's Tigris River Yields Hundreds of Corpses," *ABC News*, October 7, 2006.

17. Damluji (2011).

Chapter 8

1. I interviewed several Sunni refugees from Baghdad in Amman, Jordan, in 2014.

2. This study combines data from both a 2003 Gallup Poll of Baghdad and the 2003–2008 Iraq History Project Current Violation Initiative. The data cover the time period up to September 2003. As mentioned in the text, there were nine Baghdad security districts, so the Mansour district included not only the neighborhood of Mansour but several other neighborhoods. The study's authors believe that the district's level of wealth and also the Sunni composition made the area a target. See Hagan et al. (2012, p. 489). Also see the interviews included in this section.

3. See table 2 of Hagen et al. (2012).

4. I also met some of ZI's friends and fellow refugees in Amman who presented similar overall narratives.

5. See *Time* magazine, August 22, 2004, for a description of events.

6. The name is left out for confidentiality reasons.

Chapter 9

1. *The US Army in the Iraq War*, Vol. 1, p. 410. The Army history, in turn, is citing Ali Allawi's book *The Occupation of Iraq*, p. 423.

2. United States Institute of Peace report, citing a July 2007 article in the *Los Angeles Times*, p. 1. See Robert M. Perito, "Iraq's Interior Ministry: Frustrating Reform," United States Institute of Peace, May 2008. See also Ned Parker, "The Conflict in Iraq: A Ministry of Fiefdoms," *Los Angeles Times*, July 30, 2007, p. 1.

3. From an edited transcript of a *Frontline* interview with Matthew Sherman conducted on October 4, 2006, https://www.pbs.org/wgbh/pages/frontline/gangsofiraq/interviews/sherman.html.

4. As the impossibility of recruiting a high number of advisors became evident, the target numbers were lowered, from 6,500 to 1,500 to less than 350 in early 2004. See Perito (2008).

5. This section is based on conversations with IF.

6. An early report of the CPA in May 2003 concluded that the Iraqi police were incapable of providing security. See CPA, *Iraqi Police: An Assessment of the Present and Recommendations for the Future*, May 30, 2003.

7. In their 2008 summary report, one of the USIP's major recommendations was to "[t]rade the fixation on numbers for an evaluation of results." See Perito (2008).

8. Radin (2020) summarizes Shia goals more broadly: "there were two dominant Shia nationalist goals relevant to the police: to establish a prevailing role for Shia with the MoI and police organizations and to prevent the resurgence of Ba'athism" (p. 157). Radin's book (2020) recognizes that Shia groups would be decisive in the development of Iraqi security forces. Radin's overall research (also see Radin, 2012) emphasizes the primacy of local politics.

9. Based on the author's conversations with Falah al-Naqib on July 20 and July 30, 2015.

10. Radin (2020) discusses Naqib on p. 164.

11. Author's conversation with Matt Sherman, July 10, 2015.

12. The Ja'afari government was comprised of 32 ministries. Of the ministry heads, 16 were Shia, 8 Kurds, 6 Sunni, 1 Christian, and 1 Turkoman. Ja'afari was a member of the Dawa Party.

13. See https://www.theguardian.com/world/2005/nov/17/iraq.usa1.

14. As mentioned earlier, the analytical framework and the spectrum of roles were first developed from World War II and Cold War cases where Nazi and Soviet organizations were clearly distinct from resistance and insurgent organization. See Petersen (2001).

15. In some democratic states with conflicts, organizations have both a political wing, which competes in elections, and an armed wing. The political party Sinn Fein, with its close association with the Irish Republican Army, may provide the best-known example.

Chapter 10

1. Matt Cancian, working as a research assistant and having served in Afghanistan as a Marine, made valuable suggestions on this chapter.

2. For a description of Bayaa, see Carpenter (2014, p. 17). Carpenter's study examines 10 Baghdad neighborhoods, including Bayaa, and compares these neighborhoods along lines of population mixing, income, and education. Bayaa rates as "mixed" in demography, "moderate to good" in income, and "moderate" in education. See Carpenter (2014, tables on pp. 11, 111).

3. Wright did not know about this organization in this detail at the beginning of his tour. Reports of this level of organization came in March and April, but confirmation of their accuracy did not happen until much later.

4. The expression OMS described both the Organization and the Office of the Martyr Sadr. The acronym OMS was used to describe both.

5. This JAM leader had been captured by US forces approximately a year or two earlier, but subsequently released. Though it is unclear if he was a militant before he was captured, he definitely was when he was released—a possible case of radicalization while in the penal system.

6. Wright was positive about micro-grants— "just doing shit" could have a significant impact. Shops began to reopen at the end of the tour.

7. In Bayaa, JAM used explosively formed penetrators (EFPs), almost certainly from Iran, against Coalition vehicles. Only once during his tour in Bayaa did Wright's forces encounter a pressure plate IED. This ratio indicates the support of Iran for these JAM forces.

8. Wright noted that although it seems unlikely that a US unit would just quit, a company commander in another battalion was relieved of command after he stopped patrolling his neighborhood after a series of especially brutal attacks. For weeks, he had his platoons pull off to the side of the road and falsely call in checkpoints inside their area of responsibility.

9. In Bayaa, there had been two police stations, but repeated attacks reduced it to one, situated at the north end of the market street. Located in a three-story building on a corner of the widest street in the neighborhood, the station had a bunker-like feel. Access to the station was blocked by a mix of chains, barricades, and concrete walls guarding against bombs, RPGs, and small arms attacks. Inside there were offices, an arms room, and a detention facility, little more

than a large concrete room with a barred door where people were held indefinitely. One Delta Company soldier described it as "hellish."

10. For the National Police to conduct mounted or dismounted patrols in Bayaa, they required US presence, partly to keep them on task and partly to prevent sectarian behavior. The assessment of the National Police Training Team assigned to them was that out of any group of 100, they had 25–30 quality soldiers. While their organizational capacity was higher than the local police, they were, at best, a year behind the Iraqi Army in their development.

11. When it first took over, Delta Company was introduced to the Bayaa Neighborhood Advisory Council. This eight-person body had a chairman, assistant chairman, and committees for education, youth services, widows and orphans, women's issues, and economics. One of the members was a sheikh, another was a professor of political science, and all were residents of the neighborhood. Delta Company initially understood this council to be the elected leadership of Bayaa and part of the government of Iraq. After the first few meetings, it became clear that this was not true.

12. For reasons of confidentiality, these charts cannot be included here.

13. Not his actual name. In other writings, Wright referred to this individual as a "Tony Soprano" of the neighborhood and also "Mr. X."

14. On August 29, Sadr decreed a ceasefire in Baghdad and Iraq to last for six months, yet there was little change in West Rasheed. The expansion into Saydiyah continued, as did fighting between JAM and Delta Company in Bayaa. There were 14 small arms attacks in September and 13 IED attacks in October, numbers which exceeded levels of both types reported in April and May. Indirect fire attacks into Saydiyah started in earnest at the beginning of September, and the push for JAM dominance did not halt with Sadr's call for peace. Total attacks in Bayaa actually increased from 31 in August to 37 in September.

Chapter 11

1. Emphasis in original. Made public by the *Washington Post* in November 2006, http://www.washingtonpost.com/wp-dyn/content/article/2007/02/02/AR2007020201197.html.

2. To review, Significant Acts of Violence (SIGACTS) include direct fire attacks, indirect fire, improvised explosive device (IED) detonations, and IED discoveries reported to or observed by US forces. Figures from US Multinational Force West (MNF-W) figures, in Anthony H. Cordesman, "Violence in Iraq: Reaching an 'Irreducible Minimum,'" Center for Strategic and International Studies (February 25, 2008).

3. Robert Komer (1972) ridiculed the insulating effect of this system in his study of the US COIN effort in Vietnam.

4. Among civilian organizations, the CIA appeared to hold a different position, although the documents needed to pursue this point are classified.

5. In a more general point, by 2005 there were serious splits among the civilian leadership. Secretary of Defense Rumsfeld and Secretary of State Colin Powell were at odds and NSC head Condoleeza Rice was ineffective. Although beyond our scope in this chapter, these divisions clearly hindered rapid changes of strategy.

6. It should be noted that the Army also operated from more severe logistical constraints than the Marines. The Army's primary mission, to fight a large ground war, entailed heavier equipment and logistical constraints.

7. Rothstein describes SOF, therefore, as more "hyperconventional" than unconventional. See Rothstein (2006).

8. See Faleh and Dawod (2003) for a thorough treatment of the subject. For a concise overview of Iraqi tribal structure, see Khan (2007) and Dawod (2003).

9. For a historical overview of direct versus indirect rule in Iraq, see Hechter and Kabiri (2008).

10. At the time, AQI depended heavily on foreign fighters, which necessitated an elaborate support network to recruit, train, and deliver them. A Coalition raid in October 2007 near Sinjar, a town on the Syrian border, recovered nearly 700 records of foreign personnel entering Iraq throughout the previous year; they were predominantly male students in their early twenties from Saudi Arabia, but also from Libya, Yemen, Syria, Algeria, and other countries. See Felter and Fishman (2007) for a detailed look at AQI's bureaucracy.

11. The descriptions in this section are largely taken from Todd et al. (2006).
12. Bill Roggio, "The Sunni Awakening," May 3, 2007, admin@longwarjournal.org | @billroggio. The "sinister six" is a reference to a set of comic book villains.
13. See McWilliams and Wheeler (2009, p. 72) interview with Colonel Michael Walker, the Commanding Officer of the 3rd Civil Affairs Group, 1st MEF.
14. To see a very similar practice in colonial practice, see David Laitin's account of the British in Nigeria in *Hegemony and Culture: Politics and Religious Change among the Yoruba* (1986).
15. Patrick Cockburn, " 'If There Is No Change in Three Months, There Will Be War Again,' " *The Independent*, January 28, 2008.
16. See chapter 3 in Green and Mullin (2014) in particular.
17. See Lynch (2011) for an explanation that places emphasis on trust-building processes that reshaped attitudes and enabled Anbari-American cooperation, as opposed to an explanation based on a harmony of interests, which we emphasize here.
18. This point supports Russell (2011).

Chapter 12

1. Jack Straw, British foreign secretary during 2001–2006, explained British failure in Basra as a result of the overall number of soldiers Britain had at its disposal. In his view, the rapid drawdown in 2003 and the subsequent inability to prevent militia control of Basra could not have been prevented because the British forces were simply stretched beyond their limits (meeting of Jack Straw with MIT Security Studies members, April 6, 2017).
2. The numbers are Significant Acts of Violence (SIGACTS). Sadr City was not the only location of combat against Sadrist forces at the time. Coalition forces were fighting against JAM and Special Groups opponents in other Baghdad neighborhoods at the time.
3. As the official US Army history states, "As the US-led insurgency had begun to quell the Sunni insurgency in late 2007, Maliki could afford to start looking at other areas that posed a threat to his government, and Basra clearly stood out" (*The US Army in the Iraq War*, Vol. 2, 2019, p. 358).
4. *The US Army in the Iraq War*, Vol. 2, p. 372. It is not clear if Sadr had previously planned this attack or whether it happened because of Maliki's move on Basra. The official Army history supports the former. In any event, the attacks were either started or sustained as a political response to Maliki's Basra move.
5. This map is taken from Roggio (2008), which in turn was originally created in the *Washington Post* on April 24, 2008.

Chapter 13

1. For an intensive examination of President Bush's decision to initiate the Surge and gain political buy-in, see Sayle et al. (2019). For my own review of this book, see Petersen (2019).
2. Biden's overall views on Iraq at the time stressed political decentralization as key to a lasting peace. Biden did not believe the Surge was accomplishing anything significant in terms political reconciliation.
3. Although see Sjursen (2017) for a retrospective view of the Surge as a disaster.
4. There is also the question of whether the Surge accomplished any significant political goals, an issue addressed in Sections III and IV of this book.
5. This article was the subject of a subsequent debate that can be found in Hagan et al. (2013). This symposium included one contribution by John Hagan, Joshua Kaiser, and Anna Hanson, and another by Jon R. Lindsay and Austin G. Long, as well as a response by Biddle, Friedman, and Shapiro.
6. Hagen et al. also criticize Biddle et al. (2012) on grounds that only two Baghdad neighborhoods in their sample—Dora and Sayidiyya—fit their synergy model (Hagan et al., 2013, p. 174).

Chapter 14

1. This chapter benefited by reports from Sara Plana and Matt Cancian, working as research assistants.
2. Section IV states that the Iraqi Federal Government is supreme in power to the regional governorate only in international relations, national security policy and border protection, and formulation of fiscal and customs policy. Article 114 designates another set of powers that are to be shared between center and region. These powers include regulating electricity, environmental policy, planning, public health policy, and education. Article 115 grants all remaining powers to the governorate.
3. KRG officials cited Article 121 of the Iraqi Constitution justifying this move. Article 121 gives regions "the right to exercise executive, legislative, and judicial powers."
4. As reported in a 2010 book, per capita income in the KRG was about 25% higher than in the rest of Iraq at that time (Tripp, 2010, p. 309).
5. Pring's piece was written in 2015 as a summary of corruption in Iraqi Kurdistan over the previous 10 years.
6. See Wimmer (2002, pp. 166–195) for a broad discussion of the rise of Kurdish nationalism.
7. For an extended discussion of the broader history and mythical meaning of Peshmerga forces, see Aziz and Cottey (2021), especially pp. 233–235.
8. In my own personal experience, most members of the KDP can readily tell stories of Barzani family sacrifice and heroism. These narratives resemble those of many nation-founding myths.
9. *Iraq's Crime of Genocide: The Anfal Campaign against the Kurds* (Human Rights Watch, 1993).
10. See Weiss (1999, pp. 43–68); Freedman and Boren (1993).
11. Interview with Mohammed Tofiq Rahim (known as Hama Tofiq) on June 19, 2013, in Suleymaniyah. Rahim was emphatic in stating that, despite this outside interference, the KDP had no right to bring in Saddamist forces during the civil war.
12. These figures are from Bakr (2021, pp. 8, 10).
13. The KDP Asayish's name is Hezakani Asaishi Parti, while the PUK's is Hezakani Asaishi Yaketi.
14. Author's interview with Hemin Hawrami at KDP Foreign Relations Headquarters in Salah-a-Din, KRG, Iraq, on June 12, 2013.
15. Author's interview on June 18, 2013, with Hakim Qadir, member of the PUK Political Council and Leadership Council of the PUK, former member of Jalal Talabani's personal security detail in 1991, head of PUK security department for PUK in 1996, mayor of Suleymaniyah 1997–2000.
16. Author's interview with Minister Sabah Ahmed Mohammed (Mamosta Aram) on June 9, 2013, at the Ministry for Martyr and Anfal Affairs, Erbil, KRG, Iraq.
17. On the Fayli Kurds, see Eskander (2006).
18. Interview with QL, June 4, 2013.
19. From the Gorran website (https://gorran.net/?En?Detail.aspx?id=25&LinkID=132) accessed by Sara Plana for 2017 report. Gorran began writing down their platform for various pressing reforms after the 2011 protests.
20. Author's interview in Suleymaniyah, June 19, 2013.
21. Gorran Security Platform from 2011.
22. Eleven seats were set aside for Christian and Turkoman minorities. Nine of those members allied with the KDP-PUK Kurdistani list.
23. In my own interviews, Kurdish experience in the Iraqi Military was not positive. NN reported being ignored by Arab troops and basically doing nothing while stationed in Baghdad. GC went for training in Baghdad in 2008, shuttling back and forth from the Sunni base in Rusafa and the Shia base in another neighborhood, hoping not to be caught by Shia militias and killed.
24. I am using the term "KRG proper" to refer to the three governorates officially designated as a region and not including the disputed territories.

Chapter 15

1. Interview with TB.
2. This paragraph is based on interviews with TB and XR. Serving in 2009–2010 in Hawija, XR saw the visible presence of Kurdish forces in the counterterrorism units as a major problem, believing these Kurdish forces were pursuing their own agenda rather than the state's.
3. Major Brian Payne, operations officer for the 2-27th, cited in Murray (2006).
4. The information on early conditions in Kirkuk and Hawija comes from interview with JQ.
5. Much of the description of these April 7, 2004, events come from McGrath (2012, pp. 1–18). The Battle of Hawija is also the subject of an episode of *Combat Zone* (Season 1, Episode 10).
6. Taylor (2006). Taylor is citing numbers provided by Sergeant First Class Kevin Kincheloe, platoon leader.
7. Major Ben Payne, operations officer for the 2-27th in 2006, voiced this opinion in Murray (2006).
8. Al-Douri had been ordained as a Naqshabandi sheikh (Knights, 2014).
9. As an example of common thinking, Tim Arango labels Hawija a "Naqshabandia stronghold." See Arango (2014).
10. The operation was part of "Red Dawn," a month-long effort to capture Saddam Hussein (*The US Army in the Iraq War*, Vol. 1, p. 273). Despite a $10 million reward for information leading to his capture, al-Douri remained at large, eluding manhunts for 17 years until finally dying in 2020 at the age of 78. See Abdi Latif Dahir and Hassan (2020). https://www.nytimes.com/ 2020/10/29/world/middleeast/izzat-al-douri-saddam-hussein-iraq.html
11. "Iraq's Hawija Sunni Tribes Declare War on Zarqawi," *Middle East Online*, June 3, 2006.
12. "6,000 Sunnis Join Pact with US in Iraq," *Associated Press*, November 28, 2007.
13. Captain Jeff Fuller, Fire Support Officer 2-27, quoted in Alberts (2006).
14. Centcom report, MND-N PAO, May 21, 2008.
15. Interview with TB.
16. Informant FG employed these terms after entering the Hawija district with the rotation of forces in January 2009.
17. Interview with TB.
18. Much of this section relies on information from conversations with XR, FG, and two separate interviews with TB.
19. Interviewee TB.
20. The other two respondents, interviewed separately, had slightly different takes on the nature of the enemy. While they agreed that AQI was not a major factor at the time, they possessed different ideas about the centrality of JRTN.
21. XR disagreed, at least in terms of the micro-grants boosting the local economy.
22. Interview with TB.
23. Interview with XR.
24. XR's skepticism increased when the Hawija SOI was implicated in placing IEDs.
25. One of the SOI commanders had been a former brigadier general in the Iraqi Army. The relationship between such high-ranking former military officers with local police was unclear.
26. Interview with FG.
27. Interview with FG.
28. TB, the primary source for this chapter, described himself as "not so big on hearts and minds." He believed, even in 2009, that the threat of force was absolutely necessary to influence the population in a positive direction.
29. Four parties openly declared their opposition to the law, including the Iraqi National List (led by Iyad Allawi), the National Dialogue Front (led by Salih al-Mutlak), and two small factions within the Iraqi Accord Front, the main Sunni parliamentary bloc.
30. International Crisis Group, "Make or Break: Iraq's Sunnis and the State," *Crisis Group Middle East Report*, No. 144, August 14, 2013, pp. 1–2. The report leads off with details on the security forces' move on Issawi's residence.
31. Figures differ. The Iraqi Parliament report lists 40 civilian and 3 military deaths. The Iraqi Ministry of Defense lists 23 "militants" and 3 soldiers killed (*The US Army in the Iraq War*, Vol. 2, pp. 584–585).

32. This interpretation can be found in International Crisis Group, "Iraq after Hawija: Recovery or Relapse?" April 26, 2013. Also, see International Crisis Group, "Make or Break: Iraq's Sunnis and the State," p. 32, for discussion of the military organization of tribes immediately after the Hawija events.

33. Arango (2013) describes almost immediate mobilization in Ramadi.

34. Although considered its driving force, technically the JRTN was not a member group of the GMCIR. The 1920s Revolutionary Brigades also belonged to the alliance. For a detailed description of the factions within the GMCIR, see Adnan and Reese (2014, pp. 12–16).

35. See Abdulrazaq and Stansfield (2016), p. 539. The authors describe the GMCIR as a decisive force in Anbar during December 2013–January 2014.

36. Letta Tayler, a senior researcher with Human Rights Watch, articulates this view in Shane Harris, "The Re-Baathification of Iraq," *Foreign Policy*, August 21, 2014. https://foreignpolicy.com/2014/08/21/the-re-baathification-of-iraq/.

37. Adnan and Reese, p. 16.

38. Estimates of the number of ISIS fighters vary.

39. International Crisis Group (2019) includes a passage: "Even the idea of Shiite or Iranian influence is totally accepted. It's better than ISIS. They're both bad, but ISIS is worse" (p. 11).

Chapter 16

1. The numbers are from Keaney (1993). This US Air Force commissioned report estimated 10,000–12,000 Iraqi combat deaths in the air campaign, and up to 10,000 casualties in the ground war.

2. This number is from the BBC, "Iraq War in Figures," December 14, 2011. https://www.bbc.com/news/world-middle-east-11107739.

3. See especially Chapter 1, "The First Cyber War," pp. 3–24.

4. From David Petraeus's "Foreword" in Pittard and Bryant (2019, p. xi).

5. See the discussion in Chapter 4 distinguishing the two strategies. As laid out in that chapter, the differences between the two strategies are large. In some ways, decapitation is the opposite of war-fighting, the latter with its highly visible and indiscriminate tactics of "cordon and search," "harassment and interdiction" bombing, and "search and destroy." Furthermore, decapitation is driven by a desire to minimize casualties; war-fighting requires "boots on the ground" and casualties are unavoidable.

6. See Gordon and Adnan (2014). The article sites Brett McGurk, the State Department top official on Iraq, as stating, "The plan is to have the tribes out front, but with the army in support."

7. See Wasser et al. (2021, Figure 2.3, p. 36).

8. According to one account, on the eve of the battle for Ramadi, the US offered AH-64 Apache attack helicopters with their Hellfire missiles to the Iraqis. President al-Abadi turned it down, "presumably because low-flying helicopters were more visible than fixed-wing aircraft and smaller RPAs and brought back memories of the 2003–11 U.S. intervention, which was still a sensitive topic" (Wasser et al., 2021, p. 36).

9. GI, a high ranking Iraqi defense official, stated in an interview that the Peshmerga forces were overrated and not needed to retake Mosul. It was good that they agreed to remain at a designated line for seven months. GI also said that although weapons transfers to the Kurds must go through the Iraqi government, the Kurds received all that they asked for.

10. In this paragraph, I am summarizing from Chapter 27 of Pittard and Bryant (2019) and from Wasser et al. (2021, pp. 25–26).

11. See Verini (2019, p. 97). This paragraph summarizes Verini's time at that particular CTS outpost.

12. There was also a political element for this increase. Under pressure, including from the United States, Prime Minister Maliki stepped down at this time. Increased US support undoubtedly was meant as a signal of support to the new, and hopefully more inclusive, Iraqi leadership.

13. In the Mosul Dam operation, 78% of the targets were ISIS military forces, in comparison to 25%–35% in other battles of Operation Inherent Resolve. See Wasser et al. (2021, p. 138).

14. The author had an opportunity to speak at length with a Kurdish officer deeply familiar with the Mosul Dam operation (interviewee GC). GC related that the Peshmerga had officers

specially trained to call in strike coordinates. Despite training, most information was sent by regular phone using WhatsApp. Most target requests were for close air support against visible ISIS fighters and their positions, along with ISIS Humvees.

15. See Verini (2019, pp. 121–122) for a description and discussion of the political fallout from this massacre, including its impact for driving Iran into the war.

16. *The Economist* analysis of October 31, 2015, describes a "deliberate division of labour between the Hashid al-Shabi militias and the government-controlled Iraqi Security Forces.

17. Dana J. H. Pittard and Wes J. Bryant's book *Hunting the Caliphate* (2019) is largely based on the operations conducted at BIAP.

18. In *Hunting the Caliphate*, Wes Bryant discusses the exclusion of PMF. He agrees that the exclusion of AAH and KH were necessary but believes that common cause could have been made with the Badr Corps (2019, p. 79). The defense officials I talked to in Baghdad, including Qasim al-Ajari, the National Security Advisor, had a generally positive view of the PMF.

19. Pittard and Bryant (2019) list the number of killed ISIS fighters at 300 a week at one point (p. 188).

20. The Kurds, the Iraqi government, and the Coalition all agreed that the Peshmerga should halt their advance at Bashiqa (Verini, 2019, p. 191). The Kurdish involvement in post-2003 Mosul politics was complicated. Many Sunni residents in Mosul undoubtedly resented the Kurdish presence.

21. See Chapter 18 in this volume for more on the Dwekh Nawsha.

22. See Wasser et al. (2021, p. 171). Recall that the passage from Verini earlier in this chapter described a forward command post in the Mosul battle. Verini discusses the capabilities of the CTS and the National Police on pp. 240–241. After explaining the connections of the National Police with Shia militias, he writes, "Unsurprisingly, the federal police in Mosul fought sloppily. This was partly because many of them didn't much care what happened to Moslawis, partly because they were barely trained—three weeks of basic training for new recruits, then into the field—and partly because they were, despite the foreign help, badly provisioned."

23. Although space does not allow for a more extensive discussion of the issue here, there was a change over time in the nature of targeting from "dynamic" to "deliberate." The former designating strikes taking place in active battle, often in conjunction with close air support (CAS); the latter focused on targets beyond the Army's fire support coordination line (FSCL). Deliberate targeting is more strategic in the sense of destroying the enemy's logistics and command centers through deep interdiction. For a discussion of these issues, as well as a critique of President Obama's lack of support for deliberative targeting, see Lambeth (2021).

Chapter 17

1. For a discussion of the ambiguous nature of the PMF and proxy war in general, see Ollivant and Gaston (2019, May 31). For a longer, extended treatment, see Olivant and Gaston (2020).

2. I have created these lists from Dury-Agri et al. (2017). Also see al-Tamimi (2017) for a corroborating review.

3. Name changes can be challenging for many groups. The Badr Brigades became the Badr Organization for Reconstruction and Development in 2003. SCIRI (Supreme Council for the Islamic Revolution in Iraq) became ISCI (Islamic Supreme Council in Iraq) in 2007. In 2012, ISCI distanced itself from Iran, and the Badr Organization then broke with ISCI to maintain its Iran connection. Al-Amiri became both the political and military leader of the Badr Organization after the split.

4. See https://www.counterextremism.com/threat/badr-organization.

5. See https://cisac.fsi.stanford.edu/mappingmilitants/profiles/badr-organization-reconstruct ion-and-development#text_block_19346. Also see Toumaj (2017).

6. A more accurate translation is "Peace Companies," but "Peace Brigades" is the common English moniker.

7. Other Iranian-controlled PMF brigades include: Kataeb Sayed al-Shuhada (2013) (14th PMF Brigade); Saraya al-Khorasani (2013) (18th PMF Brigade)—formed quickly after June

2014 with direct assistance from Iran' Kataeb Ansar al-Hojja (29th PMF Brigade); Kataeb al-Imam Ali (40th PMF Brigade).

8. See Stanford's Mapping Militants project. https://cisac.fsi.stanford.edu/mappingmilitants/profiles/asaib-ahl-al-haq#text_block_19296.

9. See https://cisac.fsi.stanford.edu/mappingmilitants/profiles/asaib-ahl-al-haq#text_block_19296.

10. Officially, Muhandis was deputy chairman of the PMF commission (PMC).

11. See https://cisac.fsi.stanford.edu/mappingmilitants/profiles/kataib-hezbollah.

12. ISCI controls the 7th, 8th, and 28th.

13. Recall Chapter 5.

14. When Muhandis split from Badr to from KH, he maintained the vanguard structure.

15. See Chapter 10 on the Bayaa neighborhood in Baghdad and the key role of adjudication in establishing group influence.

16. While Fateh took only 17 seats, the party still took 467,000 votes, nearly as many as Maliki's State of Law Party. The different result between 2018 and 2021 reflected not only party popularity, but changes in Iraq's electoral system.

17. See, for example, Felbab-Brown (2019).

18. Interview with ZUZ. This plan was a good example of a gradualist, non-confrontational approach. Most of my conversations on the PMF during the 2022 visit accepted that more direct methods were not possible.

19. During one conversation in May 2022, one Iraqi official (GI) emphatically told me, "The PMF is here to stay!" He cited its legal entrenchment, its sacrifice and legitimacy, and its ability to provide employment. As a sign of the integration of the PMF, for a number of years the administrative centers of the Iraq Army, Iraqi National Police, and PMF were clustered together in the middle of Baghdad along the Tigris river.

20. See Ollivant and Gaston (2019) for a persuasive argument that local interests of militia actors prevail over foreign interests.

21. Inna Rudolf, "The Sunnis of Iraq's Shia Paramilitary Powerhouse," *The Century Foundation*, February 13, 2020. https://tcf.org/content/report/sunnis-iraqs-shia-paramilitary-powerhouse/.

Chapter 18

1. Some scholars refer to Iraqi Christians as being in the class of "second-order minority," defined by Barter (2015, p. 128) as "a community which forms a self-identified ethnic or religious minority dominated by an ethnic group which represents a national, or first-order minority." In the present case, Kurds are a first-order minority while Christians are a second-order minority.

2. The authors have published a shorter version of this paper focusing on the post-2014 period. See Petersen and Cancian (2018).

3. The 2005 Iraqi Constitution officially uses the moniker "Assyrian" to refer to this group. In addition to Chaldeans, the Nineveh Plains also hold small groups of Syriac Orthodox, Syriac Catholic, Armenian Orthodox, and Armenian Catholic in the region. In her 2022 book, Alda Benjamen uses the term "Assyrian" broadly (p. 2). The use of the term "Christian" is apt for the many cases in which violent Islamist groups, who did not care about specific sect, were the main actors.

4. Quoted in Benjamen (2022, p. 17).

5. August 7, known as the Simele Massacre. See Eliza Griswold (2015), who mentions a figure of 3,000. Benjamen (2022) lists figures of 300 killed in the village of Simele itself, with a possible 6,000 dead in the 100 surrounding villages (p. 17).

6. The Simele massacre is still not recognized by the Iraqi state (Benjamen 2022, p. 17).

7. Kurdish forces incorporated Assyrians in the mid-1970s.

8. Petersen interview with KDP Christian officials in Ankawa. Interview ZP.

9. Field notes (R), June 13, 2013.

10. See Ponomarev and Arango (2016). The last census in Iraq that included Iraqi Kurdistan was taken in 1987 and counted 1.4 million Christians. That census was problematic as the ongoing Iraq-Iran war might have affected the count.

11. Museum of the Jewish People website, http://www.bh.org.il/jewish-community-baghdad-iraq/.
12. See David Wright, "Vanishing History: Baghdad's Last 21 Jews," *ABC News Nightline*, January 30, 2004. As mentioned in the title, this report puts the number at 21.
13. One of the members of the Qaraqosh focus group discussed below had a father living in Mosul, where he was kidnapped and tortured. The kidnappers called on the phone and asked for $50,000. They identified themselves as Islamic/AQI (R4 of focus group).
14. This description of Archbishop Rahno's demise can be found in Deborah Amos, *Eclipse of the Sunnis: Power, Exile, and Upheaval in the Middle East* (New York: Public Affairs, 2010), pp. 23–29.
15. R7 was emphatic in stating that state services such as electricity and water did not improve even during the lulls in violence.
16. Recall a similar impression of US forces in the post-invasion period in Ghazaliyah (Chapter 6).
17. This section is based mainly on a focus group session conducted with a group of 15–20 Christian refugees from Qaraqosh in 2014 (R sources). They found safety in Jordan after fleeing ISIS.
18. See Youash (2007), Iraq Sustainable Democracy Project policy briefing, "Creating a Nineveh Plain Local Police Force: Overcoming Ethno-Religious Minority Insecurity," September 2007, for an example of forceful support of this project.
19. Benjamen (2022) mentions the two attempts to create local police forces in the Nineveh Plains, stating they were blocked by the KRG (pp. 228, 230), citing Youash (2007).
20. Ironically, US political presence may have been stronger in the area after US military withdrawal from Iraq in 2011. The United States Institute of Peace (USIP), along with the Institute for International Law and Human Rights, worked to set up the Alliance of Iraqi Minorities in 2010, bringing together the Christian, Yazidi, Sabean-Mandeans, and Shebaks into one civil-society organization (Omestad, 2012). This organization lobbied for changes in minority representation in textbooks and better infrastructure in minority areas. Jason Gluck, a senior program officer in USIP's Rule of Law Center, stated in late 2012, "By bringing minorities together and supporting them to cooperate on common and universal goals, USIP has empowered these communities to help themselves. It has helped create institutions that are self-sustaining and truly Iraqi-owned" (Omestad, 2012). Unfortunately, any such hopes were shattered for Qaraqosh and other minority communities in the Nineveh Plains with the invasion of ISIS in June 2014.
21. Much of this section is taken from Petersen and Cancian (2018).
22. See statements by Anna Eshoo, an Assyrian-American Congresswoman (Eshoo, 2005) and the active Facebook Page of the ADM in Illinois (Facebook, 2022).

Chapter 19

1. As much of this chapter is devoted toward understanding the role of the KDP and PUK security institutions, many of the chapter's insights come from interviews in 2013 with both high-level and lower-level KRG security leaders. Interviewees include Masrour Barzani, then councilor/head of the Kurdistan Security Council; Jafer Mustafa Ali, minister for Peshmerga affairs; and various lower-level security and Asayish members. The chapter will also address the disputed territories, relying on interviews with Dr. Mohammed Ihsan, minister, General Board for Kurdistani Areas Outside the Region; Najmaldin Karim, governor of the Kirkuk Governate; Khasro Goran, former deputy governor of Mosul.
2. Interview with Jafer Mustafa Ali at Peshmerga Headquarters in Erbil, KRG, Iraq, on June 11, 2013. He is a legendary figure in the PUK Peshmerga.
3. The figures in this paragraph come from Bakr (2021, p. 8), and represent numbers in 2021.
4. As of 2023, Nechirvan Barzani had become president and Masrour Barzani became prime minister. Masoud Barzani stepped down from the KRG presidency in the aftermath of the 2017 independence referendum.
5. See, for example, Human Rights Watch and Amnesty International reports, including: https://www.hrw.org/reports/2007/kurdistan0707/5.htm and https://www.amnesty.org/download/Documents/48000/mde140062009en.pdf.

6. Perhaps the most interesting part of the conversation was when I brought up the dictum often attributed to Henry Kissinger that "America has no friends, only interests." This comment provoked a long and angry diatribe against Kissinger and his betrayal of the Kurds, as well as attacks on my apparent belief that interests and friendship can be separated.

7. This section is based on Matt Cancian's research assistant report.

8. Some definitions include parts of Wasit province.

9. See "The Other Jerusalem," *The Economist*, April 4, 2007, http://www.economist.com/node/8976641.

10. See The Government of Iraq, Ministry of the Interior, "Constitution of Iraq."

11. Space does not permit a discussion of the complex battles fought at Sinjar and Mosul Dam.

12. Interview with Peshmerga officer.

13. Interview with Mohammed Ihsan.

14. In my 2013 interview with Jafer Mustafa Ali at Peshmerga headquarters, he ended by stating that the Peshmerga have the spirit to defend the country; they have no choice given the threats. They can deal militarily with the Arabs. He asked my opinion of what will happen. I mentioned that little can be negotiated until a "normalization" of the situation occurs, as is the official language on the process for resolution on Kirkuk. Jafer's final statement was that "maybe we will have to normalize them through force."

15. This was not the first Kurdish independence referendum in the post-2003 period. There was also a referendum in 2005.

16. There was much debate on Barzani's calculations. Masoud Barzani himself stated: "I am very proud of the result. I am very proud that we have given the opportunity for the Kurdish people to express their vote—and I do not regret it" (Arraf, 2017). Barzani further stated, "We were expecting some kind of reaction, but we had not calculated on military attack" (Arraf, 2017).

17. The anti-establishment movement first formed by Gorran fragmented by 2018, finding form in the New Generation Movement and the Coalition for Democracy and Justice (CDJ). The CDJ was founded by Barham Salih, who left the PUK but has since returned. The New Generation Movement was founded by businessman Shaswar Abdulwahid Qadir. The division of the opposition parties meant that they were less likely than ever to wrest control from the governing duopoly.

18. The picture I am describing originally comes from Rudaw (English) Twitter site, October 16, 2017. #BREAKING: Iraqi forces are inside the office of Najmaldin Karim, governor of #Kirkuk city. #KurdistanBlockade.

19. These views were expressed by a range of contacts, but most specifically by NN (Asayish) and VI (former Peshmerga).

20. Masoud Barzani himself makes this charge. See Arraf (2017).

21. The KDP and PUK use of security forces for political reasons is detailed in Hama (2019).

Chapter 20

1. I am aware of the collective action problem here, but also aware that in actual behavior many individuals simply don't behave that way.

2. There were, however, tens of thousands in the hybrid PMF.

3. Much of this section is informed by Ezzeddine and Noun (2020).

4. The foundational work on consociationalism is Lijphart (1969).

5. During the trip, I interviewed Hussein Husseini, considered the father of the Ta'if Accord, visited the Hezbollah Museum in Mleeta and talked with Hezbollah representatives, took a quick tour of the Hezbollah-controlled Dahieh neighborhood in Beirut as well as Sabra and Shatilla camps, interviewed numerous leaders of Christian political parties, and talked with a variety of academics.

6. Author's interview with Hussein Husseini.

7. Interview with LZD.

8. Interview with LHT.

9. For example, my driver/translator in Lebanon needed $10,000 for his daughter's heart surgery. Hezbollah provided the funds, not the state.

10. Interview with LSN.

11. Interview with LAT. Also, as Hezbollah members are citizens of Lebanon they have a right to control their own affairs in conjunction with the state; not so for non-citizen Palestinians (LZD).
12. Interviews with LAT, LHT.
13. Interviews with LQF, LBF.
14. Interviews with LAT, LQF.
15. LHT.
16. LAT.
17. Lebanon was often cited as a successful consociational system before the 1975–1990 civil war.
18. At the time of writing (2021) the Lebanese system was facing one of its most severe challenges.
19. Ammar al-Hakim and ZUZ.
20. ZUZ, RN.
21. LSN.

Chapter 21

1. See Chapter 13 for a fuller assessment of the synergy argument.
2. For an extended treatment of issues involved in the US training programs of foreign forces, see Tecott (2021).
3. Qasim al-Ajari, the Iraqi National Security Advisor, in a May 2022 interview with the author, listed the US decapitation efforts as the major reason for the drastic decline in violence in 2007.
4. For a description of the group by one of its members, see Chalabi (2003).
5. Democratic Principles Working Group, "Iraqi Opposition Report on the Transition to Democracy," *Journal of Democracy* 14, no. 3 (July 2003): 14–29. The passage is from p. 15.
6. Author of *Republic of Fear* (1989), and *Cruelty and Silence: Tyranny, Uprising and the Arab World* (1993).
7. See Makiya (2003). This article was based on a speech given to the Heritage Foundation on October 3, 2002.
8. This lesson obviously relates to the observation above stating: "Counterinsurgent Failure: Clear, Hold, Build Alone as a Counterinsurgency Strategy." It might also be emphasized that if the most important dynamics in countering an insurgency are at the −2 and +2 levels, then the CHB strategy and its focus at +1 may have troubles accomplishing its goals.
9. For an extensive treatments of learning processes in the Iraq conflict, see Russell (2011) and Serena (2011).

Chapter 22

1. At the time of writing, spring of 2023, there was a small avalanche of articles reconsidering the US adventure in Iraq 20 years after the March 2003 invasion. Most of those articles concentrated on the tangled strategic logic of why the United States invaded Iraq in the first place. This book has left that discussion to others.
2. Personal communication with instructors at war colleges.
3. Neoconservatives advocated a muscular use of American military power to promote regime change as part of a transformative project.
4. See Ashford (2021) for summary of agreements and differences.
5. See Walt (2018). See the preface of that work for the summary statements in this paragraph.
6. McFate (2019, p. 130) refers to a Department of Defense report putting the number of contractor casualties at 1.8 to 4.5 times higher than military counterparts.
7. The Watson Institute summarizes: "No one knows with certainty how many people have been killed and wounded in Iraq since the 2003 United States invasion. However, we know that between 184,382 and 207,156 civilians have died from direct war related violence caused by the U.S., its allies, the Iraqi military and police, and opposition forces from the time of the invasion through October 2019." See https://watson.brown.edu/costsofwar/costs/human/civilians/iraqi.
8. Samuel Moyn (2021) makes an extended argument to this effect.

9. Wertheim (2023) argues that a primary reason for the invasion and occupation of Iraq was to demonstrate to the world that the United States was unquestionably globally dominant even in the wake of the 9/11 terrorist attacks on the US homeland.

10. Bacevich (2023) writes in the title of a *Foreign Affairs* article that "America Remains Trapped by False Dreams of Hegemony."

11. Many of the points and insights in this section follow from a research report by Zachary Burdette.

12. As Emma Ashford (2021) discusses, differences among members of the restraint school differ on the goals and necessary resources for an off-shore balancing strategy.

Chapter 23

1. Alan Kuperman is the leading source on this "moral hazard" problem. See Kuperman (2008).

2. See Raj Menon (2016) for an extended treatment of the problems and inconsistencies of humanitarian intervention.

3. Stephen Walt, a leading restraint advocate, describes the conditions necessary to justify genocide prevention (p. 289). These conditions include: "(1) the danger was imminent, (2) the anticipated costs to the United States were modest, (3) the ratio of foreign lives saved to U.S. lives risked was high, and (4) it was clear that intervention would not make things worse or lead to an open-ended commitment."

4. Much of this chapter has been gleaned from Petersen (2021).

5. See Ricks (2007, p. 234). Ricks is quoting Major Christopher Varhola, an Army Reserve civil affairs specialist, summarizing the position of a commanding officer early in the occupation.

6. Also see Lyall (2015) for a concise review of several major studies and their seemingly contradictory findings.

7. Personal experience, May 2022 and March 2023.

8. There is also the question of whether many drone pilots themselves can become conditioned to their job without significant psychological issues.

9. These figures are from US Multinational Force West (MNF-W), in Cordesman (2008).

10. Another community mobilization success story can be found in the US alliance with the Northern Tribes in Afghanistan during the original invasion. This alliance produced an unexpectedly swift rout of Taliban forces and was soon seen as a model.

11. As made clear in Chapter 11, in Anbar the Awakening was created largely through the agency of tribal leaders. They made the "flip" for their own strategic reasons.

12. As Colin Jackson has argued (2009), militaries are not geared toward dealing with situations that can become almost feudal in their complex local dynamics. Also, see Jackson's dissertation (2008) on counterinsurgency learning and the difficulties militaries experience if asked to change their doctrine to incorporate the feudal state-building dynamics of civil war.

13. For a broad discussion of proxy warfare and its problems, see Sara Plana (2021).

14. Several of the insights in this section are from a research report on homogenization written by Aidan Milliff.

15. Personal experience in interviews conducted in 2017–2018.

16. In the lead-up to the Russia-Ukraine war, when expectations of rapid Russian victory were common, some may have hoped for a de facto partition of the Russian-majority areas of the Donbas as the least costly solution.

17. For a brief summary of Staniland's thought, see Staniland (2018). For an extended treatment related to violence management, see Staniland (2021).

Appendix A

1. Guevara's *Guerrilla Warfare* can be seen as a complement to Mao, with a focus on organization and strategy specific to Latin America; as Mao's work is based largely on the war against Japanese occupation, Che Guevara's treatise is based largely on the Cuban Revolution.

2. This case study is based largely on Cable (1986) and Nagl (2002).

3. See Porch (2013) for a critique of Nagl (2005), in many respects.

4. As Krepenivich (2009, p. 290) goes on to write, "A sound strategy is one that leverages our asymmetric advantages to impose disproportionate costs upon the competition, making it unfeasible for our rivals to compete effectively."

Appendix B

1. Measured by Significant Acts of Violence (SIGACTS).
2. Lyall et al. (2013, p. 695) compare their data and methods to Beath et al. (2013). They also note that Beath et al. (2013) studied mainly Tajik and Hazara areas (6 of 10 districts of the sample); the majority Pashtun districts, the ones studied in Lyall et al. (2013), were far more violent on average.
3. Renard Sexton, "Aid as a Tool against Insurgency: Evidence from Contested and Controlled Territory in Afghanistan," *American Political Science Review* 110, no. 4 (November 2016): 731–749, https://doi.org/10.1017/S0003055416000356.
4. Neil Narang and Jessica A. Stanton, "A Strategic Logic of Attacking Aid Workers: Evidence from Violence in Afghanistan," *International Studies Quarterly* 61, no. 1 (March 1, 2017): 38–51, https://doi.org/10.1093/isq/sqw053.
5. The final number of observations in the analysis is lower because these data extend through 2012 but covariate data only cover 2011.
6. Benjamin Crost, Joseph H. Felter, and Patrick B. Johnston, "Conditional Cash Transfers, Civil Conflict and Insurgent Influence: Experimental Evidence from the Philippines," *Journal of Development Economics* 118 (January 2016): 171–182, https://doi.org/10.1016/j.jdev eco.2015.08.005.
7. Moreover, there was no statistically significant difference between municipalities with all villages receiving treatment and those with only half treated, which does raise the possibility that the program simply displaced violence to other villages rather than eliminating it.
8. Benjamin Crost, Joseph Felter, and Patrick Johnston, "Aid under Fire: Development Projects and Civil Conflict," *American Economic Review* 104, no. 6 (June 2014): 1833–1856, https://doi.org/10.1257/aer.104.6.1833.
9. Aditya Dasgupta, Kishore Gawande, and Devesh Kapur, "(When) Do Antipoverty Programs Reduce Violence? India's Rural Employment Guarantee and Maoist Conflict," *International Organization* 71, no. 3 (2017): 605–632, https://doi.org/10.1017/S0020818317000236.
10. Jason Lyall, Yang-Yang Zhou, and Kosuke Imai, "Can Economic Assistance Shape Combatant Support in Wartime? Experimental Evidence from Afghanistan," *American Political Science Review* 114, no. 1 (February 2020): 126–143, https://doi.org/10.1017/S000305541 9000698.
11. Lyall, Zhou, and Imai (2020, p. 127).
12. Jason Lyall, "Civilian Casualties, Humanitarian Aid, and Insurgent Violence in Civil Wars," *International Organization* 73, no. 4 (2019): 901–926, https://doi.org/10.1017/S002081831 9000262.
13. Daniel Silverman, "Too Late to Apologize? Collateral Damage, Post-Harm Compensation, and Insurgent Violence in Iraq," *International Organization* 74, no. 4 (2020): 853–871, https://doi.org/10.1017/S0020818320000193.
14. Oeindrila Dube and Juan F. Vargas, "Commodity Price Shocks and Civil Conflict: Evidence from Colombia," *The Review of Economic Studies* 80, no. 4 (October 1, 2013): 1384–1421, https://doi.org/10.1093/restud/rdt009.
15. Andrew B. Hall, Connor Huff, and Shiro Kuriwaki, "Wealth, Slaveownership, and Fighting for the Confederacy: An Empirical Study of the American Civil War," *American Political Science Review* 113, no. 3 (August 2019): 658–673, https://doi.org/10.1017/S0003055419000170.
16. Christopher Blattman and Jeannie Annan, "Can Employment Reduce Lawlessness and Rebellion? A Field Experiment with High-Risk Men in a Fragile State," *American Political Science Review* 110, no. 1 (February 2016): 1–17, https://doi.org/10.1017/S000305541 5000520.
17. Austin L. Wright, "Economic Shocks and Rebel Tactics," The Pearson Institute (2016).
18. Konstantin Sonin, Jarnickae Wilson, and Austin L. Wright, "Rebel Capacity and Combat Tactics," Becker Friedman Institute (2019).

19. Mara Redlich Revkin, "What Explains Taxation by Resource-Rich Rebels? Evidence from the Islamic State in Syria," *The Journal of Politics* 82, no. 2 (April 2020): 757–764, https://doi.org/10.1086/706597.

20. Ibid., p. 762.

21. See Table 7 in Kocher et al. (2011, p. 211).

22. Luke N. Condra and Austin L. Wright, "Civilians, Control, and Collaboration during Civil Conflict," *International Studies Quarterly* 63, no. 4 (December 1, 2019): 897–907, https://doi.org/10.1093/isq/sqz042.

23. Anna O. Pechenkina, Andrew W. Bausch, and Kiron K. Skinner, "How Do Civilians Attribute Blame for State Indiscriminate Violence?," *Journal of Peace Research* 56, no. 4 (July 2019): 545–558, https://doi.org/10.1177/0022343319829798.

24. Daniel Silverman, "What Shapes Civilian Beliefs about Violent Events? Experimental Evidence from Pakistan," *Journal of Conflict Resolution* 63, no. 6 (July 2019): 1460–1487, https://doi.org/10.1177/0022002718791676.

25. Konstantin Sonin and Austin Wright, "Information Operations Increase Civilian Security Cooperation," Becker Friedman Institute, 2019.

26. Sebastian Schutte, "Violence and Civilian Loyalties: Evidence from Afghanistan," *Journal of Conflict Resolution* 61, no. 8 (September 2017): 1595–1625, https://doi.org/10.1177/0022002715626249.

27. Jacob N. Shapiro and Nils B. Weidmann, "Is the Phone Mightier than the Sword? Cellphones and Insurgent Violence in Iraq," *International Organization* 69, no. 2 (2015): 247–274, https://doi.org/10.1017/S0020818314000423.

28. Andrew Shaver and Jacob N. Shapiro, "The Effect of Civilian Casualties on Wartime Informing: Evidence from the Iraq War," *Journal of Conflict Resolution*, March 10, 2021, 65, no. 7–8 (2021): 1337–1377, https://doi.org/10.1177/0022002721991627.

29. Austin Wright et al., "Civilian Abuse and Wartime Informing" (July 17, 2017).

30. Livia Isabella Schubiger, "State Violence and Wartime Civilian Agency: Evidence from Peru," *The Journal of Politics*, 83, no. 4 (2021): 1383–1398, https://doi.org/10.1086/711720.

31. Jason Lyall, "Does Indiscriminate Violence Incite Insurgent Attacks?: Evidence from Chechnya," *Journal of Conflict Resolution* 53, no. 3 (June 2009): 331–362, https://doi.org/10.1177/0022002708330881.

32. Evgeny Finkel, "The Phoenix Effect of State Repression: Jewish Resistance during the Holocaust," *American Political Science Review* 109, no. 2 (May 2015): 339–353, https://doi.org/10.1017/S000305541500009X.

33. Luke N. Condra et al., "The Logic of Insurgent Electoral Violence," *American Economic Review* 108, no. 11 (November 1, 2018): 3199–3231, https://doi.org/10.1257/aer.20170416.

34. In the Beath et al. (2013) study described in the previous section, only 3% of the participants claimed that their village had experienced an attack during the past year.

35. Jason Lyall, Yuki Shiraito, and Kosuke Imai, "Coethnic Bias and Wartime Informing," *The Journal of Politics* 77, no. 3 (July 2015): 833–848, https://doi.org/10.1086/681590.

36. Nils Hägerdal, "Ethnic Cleansing and the Politics of Restraint: Violence and Coexistence in the Lebanese Civil War," *Journal of Conflict Resolution* 63, no. 1 (January 2019): 59–84, https://doi.org/10.1177/0022002717721612.

37. Janet I. Lewis, "How Does Ethnic Rebellion Start?," *Comparative Political Studies* 50, no. 10 (September 2017): 1420–1450, https://doi.org/10.1177/0010414016672235.

38. Jennifer M. Larson and Janet I. Lewis, "Rumors, Kinship Networks, and Rebel Group Formation," *International Organization* 72, no. 4 (2018): 871–903, https://doi.org/10.1017/S0020818318000243.

39. Kanchan Chandra and Omar García-Ponce, "Why Ethnic Subaltern-Led Parties Crowd Out Armed Organizations: Explaining Maoist Violence in India," *World Politics* 71, no. 2 (April 2019): 367–416, https://doi.org/10.1017/S004388711800028X.

40. Daniel Corstange and Erin A. York, "Sectarian Framing in the Syrian Civil War," *American Journal of Political Science* 62, no. 2 (April 2018): 441–455, https://doi.org/10.1111/ajps.12348.

41. Güneş Murat Tezcür, "Ordinary People, Extraordinary Risks: Participation in an Ethnic Rebellion," *American Political Science Review* 110, no. 2 (May 2016): 247–264, https://doi.org/10.1017/S0003055416000150.

42. This paragraph is gleaned from Austin Long, "Deus Ex Machina? Problems in Using Mechanization to Explain Counterinsurgency Outcomes."

43. Ibid. Also, see Moyer (2011). Also see Smith and Toronto (2010).

44. Melissa Dell and Pablo Querubin, "Nation Building Through Foreign Intervention: Evidence from Discontinuities in Military Strategies," *The Quarterly Journal of Economics* 133, no. 2 (May 1, 2018): 701–764, https://doi.org/10.1093/qje/qjx037.

45. Matthew Nanes, "Police Integration and Support for Anti-Government Violence in Divided Societies: Evidence from Iraq," *Journal of Peace Research* 57, no. 2 (March 2020): 329–343, https://doi.org/10.1177/0022343319866901.

46. Mara E. Karlin, *Building Militaries in Fragile States: Challenges for the United States*, 1st edition (Philadelphia: University of Pennsylvania Press, 2018).

47. Ibid., p. 13.

48. Oeindrila Dube and Suresh Naidu, "Bases, Bullets, and Ballots: The Effect of US Military Aid on Political Conflict in Colombia," *The Journal of Politics* 77, no. 1 (January 2015): 249–267, https://doi.org/10.1086/679021.

49. Luke Abbs, Govinda Clayton, and Andrew Thomson, "The Ties That Bind: Ethnicity, Pro-Government Militia, and the Dynamics of Violence in Civil War," *Journal of Conflict Resolution* 64, no. 5 (May 2020): 903–932, https://doi.org/10.1177/0022002719883684.

50. Jason Lyall, *Divided Armies: Inequality and Battlefield Performance in Modern War* (Princeton, NJ: Princeton University Press, 2020).

51. Paul Staniland, "Militias, Ideology, and the State," *Journal of Conflict Resolution* 59, no. 5 (August 2015): 770–793, https://doi.org/10.1177/0022002715576749.

52. Brandon Bolte, "The Puzzle of Militia Containment in Civil War," *International Studies Quarterly* 65, no. 1 (March 8, 2021): 250–261, https://doi.org/10.1093/isq/sqab001.

53. Tobias Böhmelt and Govinda Clayton, "Auxiliary Force Structure: Paramilitary Forces and Progovernment Militias," *Comparative Political Studies* 51, no. 2 (February 2018): 197–237, https://doi.org/10.1177/0010414017699204.

54. Govinda Clayton and Andrew Thomson, "Civilianizing Civil Conflict: Civilian Defense Militias and the Logic of Violence in Intrastate Conflict," *International Studies Quarterly* 60, no. 3 (September 2016): 499–510, https://doi.org/10.1093/isq/sqv011.

55. Corinna Jentzsch, Stathis N. Kalyvas, and Livia Isabella Schubiger, "Militias in Civil Wars," *Journal of Conflict Resolution* 59, no. 5 (August 2015): 755–769, https://doi.org/10.1177/0022002715576753.

56. Matthew Adam Kocher, Adria K. Lawrence, and Nuno P. Monteiro, "Nationalism, Collaboration, and Resistance: France under Nazi Occupation," *International Security* 43, no. 2 (Fall 2018): 117–150, https://doi.org/10.1162/isec_a_00329.

57. Stefano Costalli and Andrea Ruggeri, "Indignation, Ideologies, and Armed Mobilization: Civil War in Italy, 1943–45," *International Security* 40, no. 2 (Fall 2015): 119–157, https://doi.org/10.1162/ISEC_a_00218.

58. Emily Kalah Gade, "Social Isolation and Repertoires of Resistance," *American Political Science Review* 114, no. 2 (May 2020): 309–325, https://doi.org/10.1017/S0003055420000015.

59. Anastasia Shesterinina, "Collective Threat Framing and Mobilization in Civil War," *American Political Science Review* 110, no. 3 (August 2016): 411–427, https://doi.org/10.1017/S0003055416000277.

60. Reed M. Wood and Jakana L. Thomas, "Women on the Frontline: Rebel Group Ideology and Women's Participation in Violent Rebellion," *Journal of Peace Research* 54, no. 1 (January 2017): 31–46, https://doi.org/10.1177/0022343316675025.

61. Sarah Elizabeth Parkinson, "Organizing Rebellion: Rethinking High-Risk Mobilization and Social Networks in War," *American Political Science Review* 107, no. 3 (August 2013): 418–432, https://doi.org/10.1017/S0003055413000208.

62. Laia Balcells, *Rivalry and Revenge: The Politics of Violence during Civil War* (Cambridge; New York: Cambridge University Press, 2017).

63. Megan A. Stewart, "Civil War as State-Making: Strategic Governance in Civil War," *International Organization* 72, no. 1 (2018): 205–226, https://doi.org/10.1017/S0020818317000418.

64. Adam G. Lichtenheld, "Explaining Population Displacement Strategies in Civil Wars: A Cross-National Analysis," *International Organization* 74, no. 2 (2020): 253–294, https://doi.org/10.1017/S0020818320000089.

65. Ben Oppenheim, Abbey Steele, Juan F. Vargas, and Michael Weintraub, "True Believers, Deserters, and Traitors: Who Leaves Insurgent Groups and Why," *Journal of Conflict Resolution* 59, no. 5 (August 2015): 794–823, https://doi.org/10.1177/0022002715576750.

66. Sabine Otto, "The Grass Is Always Greener? Armed Group Side Switching in Civil Wars," *Journal of Conflict Resolution* 62, no. 7 (August 2018): 1459–1488, https://doi.org/10.1177/0022002717693047.

67. Lee J. M. Seymour, "Why Factions Switch Sides in Civil Wars: Rivalry, Patronage, and Realignment in Sudan," *International Security* 39, no. 2 (Fall 2014): 92–131, https://doi.org/10.1162/ISEC_a_00179.

68. Enzo Nussio and Juan E. Ugarriza, "Why Rebels Stop Fighting: Organizational Decline and Desertion in Colombia's Insurgency," *International Security* 45, no. 4 (April 20, 2021): 167–203, https://doi.org/10.1162/isec_a_00406.

69. Patrick B. Johnston, "Does Decapitation Work? Assessing the Effectiveness of Leadership Targeting in Counterinsurgency Campaigns," *International Security* 36, no. 4 (Spring 2012): 47–79, https://doi.org/10.1162/ISEC_a_00076.

70. Joshua Eastin and Emily Kalah Gade, "Beheading the Hydra: Counterinsurgent Violence and Insurgent Attacks in Iraq," *Terrorism and Political Violence* 30, no. 3 (May 4, 2018): 384–407, https://doi.org/10.1080/09546553.2016.1167688.

71. Jacqueline L. Hazelton, "The 'Hearts and Minds' Fallacy: Violence, Coercion, and Success in Counterinsurgency Warfare," *International Security* 42, no. 1 (Summer 2017): 80–113, https://doi.org/10.1162/ISEC_a_00283.

72. Asfandyar Mir, "What Explains Counterterrorism Effectiveness? Evidence from the U.S. Drone War in Pakistan," *International Security* 43, no. 2 (Fall 2018): 45–83, https://doi.org/10.1162/isec_a_00331.

73. Christopher Blair, Michael C Horowitz, and Philip Potter, "Leadership Targeting and Militant Alliance Breakdown," *The Journal of Politics*, 84, no. 2 (2022): 923–943, https://doi.org/10.1086/715604.

REFERENCES

'Abd al-Jabbār, Fāliḥ, and Hosham Dawood, eds. *Tribes and Power: Nationalism and Ethnicity in the Middle East.* London: Saqi, 2003.

Abbs, Luke, Govinda Clayton, and Andrew Thomson. "The Ties That Bind: Ethnicity, Pro-Government Militia, and the Dynamics of Violence in Civil War." *Journal of Conflict Resolution* 64, no. 5 (2020): 903–932. https://doi.org/10.1177/0022002719883684.

Abdallah, A. "ISIS Kills 85 Civilians in Hawija." *Iraqi News,* August 6, 2016. https://www.iraqin ews.com/iraq-war/isis-kills-85-civilians-in-hawija/.

Abdulrazaq, Tallha, and Gareth Stansfield. "The Enemy Within: ISIS and the Conquest of Mosul." *Middle East Journal* 70, no. 4 (2016): 525–542. https://doi.org/10.3751/70.4.11.

Abdul-Zahra, Qassim, and Samya Kullab. "Thousands March in Large Show of Iraqi Paramilitary Force." *Associated Press,* June 26, 2021. https://apnews.com/article/islamic-state-group-middle-east-iraq-47d8e3d3e648f5d83ba33fe288c51e4a.

Adnan, Sinan, and Aaron Reese. "Beyond the Islamic State: Iraq's Sunni Insurgency." Middle East Security Report. Institute for the Study of War, October 2014. https://www.understanding war.org/report/beyond-islamic-state-iraqs-sunni-insurgency.

Adriaensens, Dirk. "Hawija: War Crimes, Iraqi Resistance and America's Weapons of Mass Destruction." *Global Research,* May 2, 2013. https://www.globalresearch.ca/hawija-war-cri mes-iraqi-resistance-and-americas-weapons-of-mass-destruction/5333689?pdf=5333689.

Alberts, Mike. "3rd Brigade and Tribal Leaders Make History in Hawija." Defense Video Imagery Distribution System, September 22, 2006. https://www.dvidshub.net/news/7863/3rd-brig ade-and-tribal-leaders-make-history-hawija.

Allison, Graham. "Defeating ISIS: With Whose Boots on the Ground?" *Atlantic,* 2014, sec. Global. https://www.theatlantic.com/international/archive/2014/10/defeating-isis-iran-united-states-syria/381944/.

Al-Nidawi, Omar. "The Growing Economic and Political Role of Iraq's PMF." Middle East Institute, May 21, 2019. https://www.mei.edu/publications/growing-economic-and-politi cal-role-iraqs-pmf.

Alshamary, Marsin. "Analysis: Iraqi Protesters Will Likely Push Forward Despite Violence." *PRI's The World,* February 7, 2020. https://www.belfercenter.org/publication/analysis-iraqi-pro testers-will-likely-push-forward-despite-violence.

Alshamary, Marsin. "Protestors and Civil Society Actors in Iraq: Between Reform and Revolution." Institute of Regional and International Studies, American University of Iraq, Sulaimani, December 2020. https://auis.edu.krd/iris/frontpage-slider-publications/protestors-and-civil-society-actors-iraq-between-reform-and-revolution.

Alshamary, Marsin R. "Prophets and Priests: Religious Leaders and Protest in Iraq." PhD Thesis, Massachusetts Institute of Technology, 2020.

Al-Tamimi, Aymenn Jawad. "Hashd Brigade Numbers Index." *Pundicity*, October 31, 2017. https://www.aymennjawad.org/2017/10/hashd-brigade-numbers-index.

Alwan, Hisham K., and Salam T. Jihad. "Iraq's Tigris River Yields Hundreds of Corpses." *ABC News*, October 7, 2006. https://abcnews.go.com/International/IraqCoverage/story?id=2539854&page=1.

Amos, Deborah. *Eclipse of the Sunnis: Power, Exile, and Upheaval in the Middle East.* New York: Public Affairs, 2010.

Anderson, Liam M., and Gareth R. V. Stansfield. *Crisis in Kirkuk: The Ethnopolitics of Conflict and Compromise*. National and Ethnic Conflict in the 21st Century. Philadelphia: University of Pennsylvania Press, 2009. https://doi.org/10.9783/9780812206043.

Anderson, Noel. "Competitive Intervention, Protracted Conflict, and the Global Prevalence of Civil War." *International Studies Quarterly* 63, no. 3 (2019): 692–706. https://doi.org/10.1093/isq/sqz037.

Arango, Tim. "Dozens Killed in Battles across Iraq as Sunnis Escalate Protests against Government." *New York Times*, April 23, 2013, sec. World. https://www.nytimes.com/2013/04/24/world/middleeast/clashes-at-sunni-protest-site-in-iraq.html.

Arango, Tim. "Uneasy Alliance Gives Insurgents an Edge in Iraq." *New York Times*, June 19, 2014, sec. World. https://www.nytimes.com/2014/06/19/world/middleeast/former-loyalists-of-saddam-hussein-crucial-in-helping-isis.html.

Arango, Tim, Suadad Al-Salhy, and Rick Gladstone. "Kurdish Fighters Take a Key Oil City as Militants Advance on Baghdad." *New York Times*, June 12, 2014, sec. World. https://www.nytimes.com/2014/06/13/world/middleeast/iraq.html.

Arraf, Jane. "After Iraqi Kurdish Independence Vote Backfires, 'I Do Not Regret It,' Says Barzani." *National Public Radio*, November 7, 2017, sec. Parallels. https://www.npr.org/sections/parallels/2017/11/07/562514981/after-iraqi-kurdish-independence-vote-backfires-i-do-not-regret-it-says-barzani.

Ashford, Emma. "Strategies of Restraint: Remaking America's Broken Foreign Policy." *Foreign Affairs*, September–October 2021, first published August 24, 2021. https://www.foreignaffairs.com/articles/united-states/2021-08-24/strategies-restraint.

Associated Press. "Shiite Powerhouse Al-Sistani Helped Shape Today's Iraq." *Associated Press*, March 6, 2021, sec. Ali al-Sistani. https://apnews.com/article/iraq-ali-al-sistani-pope-francis-saddam-hussein-59818e71b874766877b951f332bfeb8b.

Assyria TV. "Athra Kado, NPU: The Incident with Hashd Is Resolved." *Assyria TV*, July 15, 2017. https://www.assyriatv.org/2017/07/athra-kado-npu-incident-hashd-solved/.

Assyria TV. "KRG Prevents NPU Soldiers from Returning Back to the Nineveh Plains." *Assyria TV*, December 5, 2016. https://www.assyriatv.org/2016/12/krg-prevents-npu-soldiers-returning-back-nineveh-plains/.

Assyrian International News Agency. "Assyrians in Iraq to Unify Their Militias." *Assyrian International News Agency*, November 1, 2016. http://www.aina.org/news/20161101133731.htm.

Assyrian International News Agency. "KDP Closes Dohuk Office of the Assyrian Patriotic Party." *Assyrian International News Agency.*, November 4, 1999. http://www.aina.org/releases/appclose.htm.

Aziz, Sardar, and Andrew Cottey. "The Iraqi Kurdish Pershmerga: Military Reform and Nation-Building in a Divided Polity." *Defence Studies* 21, no. 2 (2021): 226–241. https://doi.org/10.1080/14702436.2021.1888644.

Bacevich, Andrew J. "The Reckoning That Wasn't." *Foreign Affairs*, March/April (2023), 6–21. https://www.foreignaffairs.com/united-states/andrew-bacevich-the-reckoning-that-wasnt-america-hegemony.

Bakr, Mera Jasm. "The War at Home: The Need for Internal Security Sector Reform in Iraqi Kurdistan." The Middle East Institute, July 2021. https://www.mei.edu/publications/war-home-need-internal-security-sector-reform-iraqi-kurdistan.

Balcells, Laia. *Rivalry and Revenge: The Politics of Violence during Civil War*. New York: Cambridge University Press, 2017.

Balcells, Laia. "Rivalry and Revenge: Violence against Civilians in Conventional Civil Wars." *International Studies Quarterly* 54, no. 2 (2010): 291–313. https://doi.org/10.1111/j.1468-2478.2010.00588.x.

Barter, Shane Joshua. "'Second-Order' Ethnic Minorities in Asian Secessionist Conflicts: Problems and Prospects." *Asian Ethnicity* 16, no. 2 (2015): 123–135. https://doi.org/10.1080/14631369.2015.1003687.

Beath, Andrew, Fotini Christia, and Ruben Enikolopov. "Winning Hearts and Minds through Development? Evidence from a Field Experiment in Afghanistan." Policy Research Working Paper; No. 6129. © World Bank, Washington, DC. http://hdl.handle.net/10986/11950 (2013).

Benjamen, Alda. *Assyrians in Modern Iraq: Negotiating Political and Cultural Space*. Cambridge: Cambridge University Press, 2022.

Bennett-Jones, Owen. "The Christian Militia Fighting IS." *BBC News*, April 10, 2016, sec. Magazine. https://www.bbc.com/news/magazine-35998716.

Berman, Eli, Michael Callen, Joseph H. Felter, and Jacob N. Shapiro. "Do Working Men Rebel? Insurgency and Unemployment in Afghanistan, Iraq, and the Philippines." *Journal of Conflict Resolution* 55, no. 4 (2011): 496–528. https://doi.org/10.1177/0022002710393920.

Berman, Eli, Jacob N. Shapiro, and Joseph H. Felter. "Can Hearts and Minds Be Bought? The Economics of Counterinsurgency in Iraq." NBER Working Paper, 2008.

Berman, Eli, Jacob N. Shapiro, and Joseph H. Felter. "Can Hearts and Minds Be Bought? The Economics of Counterinsurgency in Iraq." *Journal of Political Economy* 119, no. 4 (2011): 766–819. https://doi.org/10.1086/661983.

Biddle, Stephen. "Stabilizing Iraq from the Bottom Up: Statement Before the Committee on Foreign Relations." Statement Before the Committee on Foreign Relations at the United States Senate, April 2, 2008.

Biddle, Stephen, Jeffrey A. Friedman, and Jacob N. Shapiro. "Testing the Surge: Why Did Violence Decline in Iraq in 2007?" *International Security* 37, no. 1 (2012): 7–40. https://doi.org/10.1162/ISEC_a_00087.

Biden, Joseph. "Biden: Surge Success a Fantasy." November 28, 2007. https://justfacts.votesmart.org/public-statement/308002/biden-surge-success-a-fantasy#.X3jT-O0pBaQ.

Blair, Christopher W., Michael C. Horowitz, and Philip B. K. Potter. "Leadership Targeting and Militant Alliance Breakdown." *Journal of Politics* 84, no. 2 (2022): 923–943. https://doi.org/10.1086/715604.

Blair, Graeme, C. Christine Fair, Neil Malhotra, and Jacob N. Shapiro. "Poverty and Support for Militant Politics: Evidence from Pakistan." *American Journal of Political Science* 57, no. 1 (January 2013): 30–48. https://doi.org/10.1111/j.1540-5907.2012.00604.x.

Blattman, Christopher. *Why We Fight: The Roots of War and the Paths to Peace*. New York: Viking, 2022.

Blattman, Christopher, and Jeannie Annan. "Can Employment Reduce Lawlessness and Rebellion? A Field Experiment with High-Risk Men in a Fragile State." *American Political Science Review* 110, no. 1 (2016): 1–17. https://doi.org/10.1017/S0003055415000520.

Bodenhausen, Galen V., Lori A. Sheppard, and Geoffrey P. Kramer. "Negative Affect and Social Judgment: The Differential Impact of Anger and Sadness." *European Journal of Social Psychology* 24, no. 1 (1994): 45–62. https://doi.org/10.1002/ejsp.2420240104.

Böhmelt, Tobias, and Govinda Clayton. "Auxiliary Force Structure: Paramilitary Forces and Progovernment Militias." *Comparative Political Studies* 51, no. 2 (2018): 197–237. https://doi.org/10.1177/0010414017699204.

Bolger, Daniel P. *Why We Lost: A General's Inside Account of the Iraq and Afghanistan Wars*. Boston: Houghton Mifflin Harcourt, 2014.

Bolte, Brandon. "The Puzzle of Militia Containment in Civil War." *International Studies Quarterly* 65, no. 1 (2021): 250–261. https://doi.org/10.1093/isq/sqab001.

https://www.washingtonpost.com/opinions/2022/05/04/russia-ukraine-aggression-in-age-defensive-dominance/.

Boot, Max. "The Truth about Iraq's Casualty Count." *Wall Street Journal*, May 3, 2008, sec. Opinion. https://www.wsj.com/articles/SB120977505566564207.

Bosnian Book of the Dead. Research and Documentation Center in Sarajevo, 2013.

Boyle, Michael J. "Bargaining, Fear, and Denial: Explaining Violence against Civilians in Iraq 2004–2007." *Terrorism and Political Violence* 21, no. 2 (2009): 261–287. https://doi.org/10.1080/09546550902765565.

Burns, John F., and Jeffrey Gettleman. "Blasts at Shiite Ceremonies in Iraq Kill More than 140." *New York Times*, March 2, 2004, sec. World. https://www.nytimes.com/2004/03/02/intern ational/middleeast/blasts-at-shiite-ceremonies-in-iraq-kill-more-than.html.

Burton, Col., J. B. "ISW Interview with Col J. B. Burton, Commander of Dagger Brigade, Baghdad, Iraq." Interview by Kimberly Kagan, November 14, 2007. https://www.understandingwar.org/press-media/webcast/isw-interview-col-jb-burton-commander-dagger-brigade-bagh dad-iraq.

Byman, Daniel. *Al Qaeda, the Islamic State, and the Global Jihadist Movement: What Everyone Needs to Know*®. What Everyone Needs To Know. Oxford; New York: Oxford University Press, 2015.

Byman, Daniel L. "The Limits of Air Strikes When Fighting the Islamic State." Brookings Institution, 2016. https://www.brookings.edu/blog/markaz/2016/12/06/the-limits-of-air-strikes-when-fighting-the-islamic-state/.

Cable, Larry E. *Conflict of Myths: The Development of American Counterinsurgency Doctrine and the Vietnam War*. New York: University Press, 1986.

Cambanis, Thanassis, Dina Esfandiary, Sima Ghaddar, Michael Wahid Hanna, Aron Lund, and Renad Mansour. *Hybrid Actors: Armed Groups and State Fragmentation in the Middle East*. Washington, DC: Century Foundation Press, 2019.

Cancian, Matthew. "Untangling the Arab-Kurdish Web in Post-ISIL Northern Iraq." *Small Wars Journal*, 2016. https://smallwarsjournal.com/jrnl/art/untangling-the-arab-kurdish-web-in-post-isil-northern-iraq.

Carpenter, Ami C. *Community Resilience to Sectarian Violence in Baghdad*. Peace Psychology Book Series. New York: Springer-Verlag, 2014. https://doi.org/10.1007/978-1-4614-8812-5.

Cave, Damien. "Shiite's Tale: How Gulf with Sunnis Widened." *New York Times*, August 31, 2007. https://www.nytimes.com/2007/08/31/world/middleeast/31lawmaker.html.

CBS News. "Christians Reclaim Iraq Village from ISIS." *CBS News*, November 13, 2014. https://www.cbsnews.com/news/christian-iraq-village-kurdish-peshmerga-fighters-bakufa-isis/.

Cederman, Lars-Erik, Andreas Wimmer, and Brian Min. "Why Do Ethnic Groups Rebel? New Data and Analysis." *World Politics* 62, no. 1 (2010): 87–119. https://doi.org/10.1017/S0043887109990219.

Cetti-Roberts, Matt. "Inside the Christian Militias Defending the Nineveh Plains." *War Is Boring* (blog), March 26, 2015. https://medium.com/war-is-boring/inside-the-christian-militias-defending-the-nineveh-plains-fe4a10babeed.

Chalabi, Salem. "Transition to Democracy Report." *Journal of Democracy* 14, no. 3 (2003): 13–13. https://doi.org/10.1353/jod.2003.0048.

Chandra, Kanchan, and Omar García-Ponce. "Why Ethnic Subaltern-Led Parties Crowd Out Armed Organizations: Explaining Maoist Violence in India." *World Politics* 71, no. 2 (2019): 367–416. https://doi.org/10.1017/S004388711800028X.

Chapman, Dennis P. "Security Forces of the Kurdistan Regional Government." U.S. Army War College, 2009. https://apps.dtic.mil/sti/pdfs/ADA510826.pdf.

Chomani, Kamal. "Why Are Iraqi Kurds Fleeing to Europe?" *New Lines Magazine*, November 22, 2021. https://newlinesmag.com/reportage/why-are-iraqi-kurds-fleeing-to-europe/.

Christensen, Thomas J. "No New Cold War: Why US-China Strategic Competition will not be like the US-Soviet Cold War." Asian Institute for Policy Studies, 2020. https://en.asaninst.

org/contents/no-new-cold-war-why-us-china-strategic-competition-will-not-be-like-the-us-soviet-cold-war/.

Christia, Fotini. *Alliance Formation in Civil Wars.* Cambridge: Cambridge University Press, 2012.

Clayton, Govinda, and Andrew Thomson. "Civilianizing Civil Conflict: Civilian Defense Militias and the Logic of Violence in Intrastate Conflict." *International Studies Quarterly* 60, no. 3 (2016): 499–510. https://doi.org/10.1093/isq/sqv011.

Cockburn, Andrew. "Iraq's Oppressed Majority." *Smithsonian Magazine,* December 2003. https://www.smithsonianmag.com/history/iraqs-oppressed-majority-95250996/.

Cockburn, Patrick. *The Rise of the Islamic State: ISIS and the New Sunni Revolution.* London: Verso, 2015.

Cole, Juan. "The Iraqi Shiites: On the History of America's Would-Be Allies." *Boston Review,* October 1, 2003a. https://www.bostonreview.net/articles/juan-cole-iraqi-shiites-0/.

Cole, Juan. "The United States and Shi'ite Religious Factions in Post-Ba'thist Iraq." *Middle East Journal* 57, no. 4 (2003b): 543–66.

Condra, Luke N., James D. Long, Andrew C. Shaver, and Austin L. Wright. "The Logic of Insurgent Electoral Violence." *American Economic Review* 108, no. 11 (2018): 3199–3231. https://doi.org/10.1257/aer.20170416.

Condra, Luke N., and Jacob N. Shapiro. "Who Takes the Blame? The Strategic Effects of Collateral Damage." *American Journal of Political Science* 56, no. 1 (2012): 167–87. https://doi.org/10.1111/j.1540-5907.2011.00542.x.

Condra, Luke N., and Austin L. Wright. "Civilians, Control, and Collaboration during Civil Conflict." *International Studies Quarterly* 63, no. 4 (2019): 897–907. https://doi.org/10.1093/isq/sqz042.

Cook, Karen S., and Russell Hardin. "Norms of Cooperativeness and Networks of Trust." In *Social Norms,* edited by Michael Hechter and Karl-Dieter Opp, 327–347. New York: Russell Sage Foundation, 2001.

Cooper, Helene, Lara Jakes, Michael D. Shear, and Michael Crowley. "In Afghan Withdrawal, a Biden Doctrine Surfaces." *New York Times,* September 4, 2021, sec. U.S. https://www.nytimes.com/2021/09/04/us/politics/biden-doctrine-afghanistan-foreign-policy.html.

Cordesman, Anthony H. "Victory and Violence in Iraq." Center for Strategic and International Studies, 2008. https://www.csis.org/analysis/victory-and-violence-iraq.

Corstange, Daniel, and Erin A. York. "Sectarian Framing in the Syrian Civil War." *American Journal of Political Science* 62, no. 2 (2018): 441–455. https://doi.org/10.1111/ajps.12348.

Costalli, Stefano, and Francesco N. Moro. "The Dynamics of Violence in the Bosnian War: A Local-Level Quantitative Analysis." Occasional Papers No. 24. Università Degli Studi Di Siena Dipartimento Di Scienze Storiche, Giuridiche, Politiche E Sociali, 2010.

Costalli, Stefano, and Francesco Niccolò Moro. "Ethnicity and Strategy in the Bosnian Civil War: Explanations for the Severity of Violence in Bosnian Municipalities." *Journal of Peace Research* 49, no. 6 (2012): 801–815. https://doi.org/10.1177/0022343312453593.

Costalli, Stefano, and Andrea Ruggeri. "Indignation, Ideologies, and Armed Mobilization: Civil War in Italy, 1943–45." *International Security* 40, no. 2 (2015): 119–157. https://doi.org/10.1162/ISEC_a_00218.

Couch, Dick. *The Sheriff of Ramadi: Navy Seals and the Winning of al-Anbar.* Annapolis, MD: Naval Institute Press, 2013.

Courtois, Sébastien de. *Le nouveau défi des chrétiens d'Orient.* LATTES edition. Paris: LATTES, 2009.

Crost, Benjamin, Joseph H. Felter, and Patrick B. Johnston. "Conditional Cash Transfers, Civil Conflict and Insurgent Influence: Experimental Evidence from the Philippines." *Journal of Development Economics* 118 (2016): 171–182. https://doi.org/10.1016/j.jdeveco.2015.08.005.

Crost, Benjamin, Joseph Felter, and Patrick Johnston. "Aid under Fire: Development Projects and Civil Conflict." *American Economic Review* 104, no. 6 (2014): 1833–1856. https://doi.org/10.1257/aer.104.6.1833.

Daalder, Ivo H., and James M. Lindsay. "Last Best Hope." *Foreign Affairs*, July–August 2022. https://www.foreignaffairs.com/articles/world/2022-06-21/last-best-hope-better-world-order-west.

Dagher, Sam. "Iraq: Patrolling Baghdad's Dora Neighborhood, Where 'gators' Lurk." *Christian Science Monitor*, March 30, 2007. https://www.csmonitor.com/2007/0330/p01s03-woiq.html.

Dahir, Abdi Latif, and Falih Hassan. "A Top Aide to Saddam Hussein Is Reported Dead." *New York Times*, October 29, 2020, sec. World. https://www.nytimes.com/2020/10/29/world/middleeast/izzat-al-douri-saddam-hussein-iraq.html.

Damluji, Mona. "'Securing Democracy in Iraq': Sectarian Politics and Segregation in Baghdad, 2003–2007." *Traditional Dwellings and Settlements Review* 21, no. 2 (2010): 71–87.

Danner, Mark. "Taking Stock of the Forever War." *New York Times*, September 11, 2005. https://www.nytimes.com/2005/09/11/magazine/taking-stock-of-the-forever-war.html.

Daragahi, Borzou. "Sunni, Shiite Cleric Press for Calm." *Boston Globe*, September 17, 2005. http://archive.boston.com/news/world/middleeast/articles/2005/09/17/sunni_shiite_clerics_press_for_calm/.

Dasgupta, Aditya, Kishore Gawande, and Devesh Kapur. "(When) Do Antipoverty Programs Reduce Violence? India's Rural Employment Guarantee and Maoist Conflict." *International Organization* 71, no. 3 (2017): 605–632. https://doi.org/10.1017/S0020818317000236.

Dawood, Hosham. "The State-ization of the Tribe and the Tribalization of the State." In *Tribes and Power: Nationalism and Ethnicity in the Middle East*, edited by Fāliḥ 'Abd al-Jabbār and Hosham Dawod, 110–135. London: Saqi, 2003.

Dehghanpisheh, Babak. "How the Iraq War Changes U.S. Officers." *Newsweek*, March 15, 2008, sec. World. https://www.newsweek.com/how-iraq-war-changes-us-officers-83711.

Dell, Melissa, and Pablo Querubin. "Nation Building Through Foreign Intervention: Evidence from Discontinuities in Military Strategies." *Quarterly Journal of Economics* 133, no. 2 (2018): 701–764. https://doi.org/10.1093/qje/qjx037.

Dodge, Toby. "Iraq's Informal Consociationalism and Its Problems." *Studies in Ethnicity and Nationalism* 20, no. 2 (2020): 145–152. https://doi.org/10.1111/sena.12330.

Driscoll, Jesse. *Warlords and Coalition Politics in Post-Soviet States*. New York: Cambridge University Press, 2015.

Dube, Oeindrila, and Suresh Naidu. "Bases, Bullets, and Ballots: The Effect of US Military Aid on Political Conflict in Colombia." *Journal of Politics* 77, no. 1 (2015): 249–267. https://doi.org/10.1086/679021.

Dube, Oeindrila, and Juan Vargas. "Commodity Price Shocks and Civil Conflict: Evidence from Colombia." *Review of Economic Studies* 80, no. 4 (2013): 1384–1421. https://doi.org/10.1093/restud/rdt009.

Dury-Agri, Jessa Rose, Omer Kassim, and Patrick Martin. "Iraqi Security Forces and Popular Mobilization Forces: Orders of Battle." Institute for the Study of War, 2017. https://www.understandingwar.org/report/iraqi-security-forces-and-popular-mobilization-forces-orders-battle-0.

Eastin, Joshua, and Emily Kalah Gade. "Beheading the Hydra: Counterinsurgent Violence and Insurgent Attacks in Iraq." *Terrorism and Political Violence* 30, no. 3 (2018): 384–407. https://doi.org/10.1080/09546553.2016.1167688.

The Economist. "The Other Jerusalem." April 4, 2007. http://www.economist.com/node/8976641.

The Economist. October 31, 2015.

Elliot, D. J. "Training the Iraqi Police: From Ministry of the Interior Ad Hoc Paramilitaries to Professional Carabinerie." *FDD's Long War Journal*, July 3, 2007. https://www.longwarjournal.org/archives/2007/07/iraqi_national_polic.php.

Elster, Jon. "A Plea for Mechanisms." In *Social Mechanisms: An Analytical Approach to Social Theory*, edited by Peter Hedström and Richard Swedberg, 45–73. Studies in Rationality and Social Change. Cambridge; Cambridge University Press, 1998.

Elster, Jon. *Alchemies of the Mind: Rationality and the Emotions*. Cambridge: Cambridge University Press, 1999.

Eshoo, Anna. "Eshoo Statement on Iraqi Christians." Congresswoman Anna Eshoo, July 20, 2005. http://eshoo.house.gov/media/press-releases/eshoo-statement-iraqi-christians.

Eskander, Saad B. "Fayli Kurds of Baghdad and the Ba'ath Regime." In *The Kurds: Nationalism and Politics*, edited by Faleh A. Jabar and Hosham Dawood, 180–202. London: Saqi, 2006.

Everett, Burgess. "McCain: Russia is a Gas Station." *Politico*, March 26, 2014. https://www.politico.com/story/2014/03/john-mccain-russia-gas-station-105061.

Ezzeddine, Nancy, and Beatrice Noun. "Iraq and Lebanon's Tortuous Paths to Reform." Clingendael Institute, December 22, 2020. https://www.clingendael.org/publication/iraq-and-lebanons-tortuous-paths-reform.

Facebook. "ADM Illinois." Accessed April 6, 2022. https://www.facebook.com/ADMIllinois.

Felbab-Brown, Vanda. "Pitfalls of the Paramilitary Paradigm: The Iraqi State, Geopolitics, and Al-Hashd al-Shaabi." Policy Brief Series on the New Geopolitics. Brookings Institution, 2019. https://www.brookings.edu/research/pitfalls-of-the-paramilitary-paradigm-the-iraqi-state-geopolitics-and-al-hashd-al-shaabi/.

Felter, Joel, and Brian Fishman. "Iranian Strategy in Iraq: Politics and 'Other Means.'" Occasional Paper Series. Combating Terrorism Center at West Point, 2008.

Felter, Joseph H., and Brian Fishman. "Al-Qa'ida's Foreign Fighters in Iraq: A First Look at the Sinjar Records." Combating Terrorism Center at West Point, 2007. https://apps.dtic.mil/sti/citations/ADA474986.

Festinger, Leon. *A Theory of Cognitive Dissonance*. Stanford, CA: Stanford University Press, 1957.

Filkins, Dexter. "A Region Inflamed: Strategy; Tough New Tactics by U.S. Tighten Grip on Iraq Towns." *New York Times*, December 7, 2003. https://www.nytimes.com/2003/12/07/world/a-region-inflamed-strategy-tough-new-tactics-by-us-tighten-grip-on-iraq-towns.html.

Filkins, Dexter. *The Forever War*. New York: Alfred A. Knopf, 2008.

Finkel, Evgeny. "The Phoenix Effect of State Repression: Jewish Resistance during the Holocaust." *American Political Science Review* 109, no. 2 (2015): 339–353. https://doi.org/10.1017/S000305541500009X.

Fisher, Ian. "Dispute Rages over Attack That Killed 40 in Iraq Village." *New York Times*, May 22, 2004, sec. World. https://www.nytimes.com/2004/05/22/world/struggle-for-iraq-civilians-dispute-rages-over-attack-that-killed-40-iraq.html.

Flood, Derek Henry. "The Hard March to Mosul." *CTC Sentinel* 9, no. 8 (August 2016).

Flood, Derek Henry. "The Hawija Offensive: A Liberation Exposes Faultlines." *CTC Sentinel* 10, no. 9 (October 2017): 24–28.

Flynn, Michael T., Rich Juergens, and Thomas L. Cantrell. "Employing ISR SOF Best Practices." *Joint Force Quarterly* 50, no. 3 (2008): 56–61.

Franks, Tommy. *American Soldier*. New York: Regan Books, 2004.

Freedman, Lawrence, and David Boren. "'Safe Havens' for Kurds in Post-War Iraq." In *To Loose the Bands of Wickedness: International Intervention in Defence of Human Rights*, edited by Nigel S. Rodley, 43–92. London: Brassey's, 1992.

Gade, Emily Kalah. "Social Isolation and Repertoires of Resistance." *American Political Science Review* 114, no. 2 (2020): 309–325. https://doi.org/10.1017/S0003055420000015.

Gallagher, D., and G. Clore. "Effects of Fear and Anger on Judgments of Risk and Evaluations of Blame." Paper presented at annual meeting of the Midwestern Psychological Association, Chicago, 1985.

Galula, David. *Counterinsurgency Warfare: Theory and Practice*. Westport, CT: Praeger Security International, 1964.

Galula, David. "Pacification in Algeria, 1956–1958." Santa Monica, CA: Rand Corporation, 2006.

Gates, Scott, and Ragnhild Nordås. "Recruitment, Retention and Religion in Rebel Groups." American Political Science Association Annual Convention. Chicago, IL, 2013.

Gaughen, Patrick. "Backgrounder #13 Baghdad Neighborhood Project: Washash and Iskan." The Institute for the Study of War, 2007. https://www.understandingwar.org/sites/default/files/reports/Backgrounder13.pdf

Gerring, John. *Case Study Research: Principles and Practices.* New York: Cambridge University Press, 2006.

Gordon, Michael R., and Bernard E. Trainor. *The Endgame: The Inside Story of the Struggle for Iraq: From George W. Bush to Barack Obama.* Vintage Press, 2012.

Gordon, Michael R., and Duraid Adnan. "Iraqi Tribes to Take Lead in Falluja Fight, U.S. Says." *New York Times,* February 5, 2014, sec. World. https://www.nytimes.com/2014/02/06/world/middleeast/iraqi-army-to-cordon-off-falluja-before-tribes-try-to-retake-control-us-says.html.

Gould, Roger V. "Collective Action and Network Structure." *American Sociological Review* 58, no. 2 (1993): 182–196. https://doi.org/10.2307/2095965.

Government of Iraq, Ministry of the Interior. Constitution of Iraq (2016). http://www.iraqinationality.gov.iq/attach/iraqi_constitution.pdf.

Green, Daniel R., and William F. Mullen III. *Fallujah Redux: The Anbar Awakening and the Struggle with Al-Qaeda.* Annapolis, MD: Naval Institute Press, 2014.

Griswold, Eliza. "Is This the End of Christianity in the Middle East?" *New York Times Magazine,* July 22, 2015, sec. Magazine. https://www.nytimes.com/2015/07/26/magazine/is-this-the-end-of-christianity-in-the-middle-east.html.

Guardian Staff. "Iraq Minister Plays Down Bunker Torture Reports." *Guardian,* November 17, 2005, sec. World news. https://www.theguardian.com/world/2005/nov/17/iraq.usa1.

Gulick, John. "Baghdad: Portrait of a City in Physical and Cultural Change." *Journal of the American Institute of Planners* 33, no. 4 (1967): 246–255.

Gunter, Michael M. "The KDP-PUK Conflict in Northern Iraq." *Middle East Journal* 50, no. 2 (Spring 1996): 225–241.

Gurr, Ted. "A Causal Model of Civil Strife: A Comparative Analysis Using New Indices." *American Political Science Review* 62, no. 4 (1968): 1104–1124. https://doi.org/10.2307/1953907.

Haddad, Fanar. *Sectarianism in Iraq: Antagonistic Visions of Unity.* New York: Hurst, 2011.

Hagan, John, Joshua Kaiser, Anna Hanson, Jon R. Lindsay, Austin G. Long, Stephen Biddle, Jeffrey A. Friedman, and Jacob N. Shapiro. "Correspondence: Assessing the Synergy Thesis in Iraq." *International Security* 37, no. 4 (2013): 173–198. https://doi.org/10.1162/ISEC_c_00118.

Hagan, John, Joshua Kaiser, Daniel Rothenberg, Anna Hanson, and Patricia Parker. "Atrocity Victimization and the Costs of Economic Conflict Crimes in the Battle for Baghdad and Iraq." *European Journal of Criminology* 9, no. 5 (2012): 481–498. https://doi.org/10.1177/1477370812452087.

Hägerdal, Nils. "Ethnic Cleansing and the Politics of Restraint: Violence and Coexistence in the Lebanese Civil War." *Journal of Conflict Resolution* 63, no. 1 (2019): 59–84. https://doi.org/10.1177/0022002717721612.

Hall, Andrew B., Connor Huff, and Shiro Kuriwaki. "Wealth, Slaveownership, and Fighting for the Confederacy: An Empirical Study of the American Civil War." *American Political Science Review* 113, no. 3 (2019): 658–673. https://doi.org/10.1017/S0003055419000170.

Halperin, Eran. *Emotions in Conflict: Inhibitors and Facilitators of Peace Making.* New York and London: Routledge, 2015.

Hama, Hawre Hasan. "The Consequences of the Fragmented Military in Iraqi Kurdistan." *British Journal of Middle Eastern Studies* 48, no. 2 (2019): 331–346. https://doi.org/10.1080/13530194.2019.1582321.

Hanish, Shak. "Autonomy for Ethnic Minorities in Iraq: The Chaldo-Assyrian Case." *Digest of Middle East Studies* 20, no. 2 (2011): 161–177. https://doi.org/10.1111/j.1949-3606.2011.00090.x.

Hanna, Reine, and Gregory J. Kruczek. "Contested Control: The Future of Security in Iraq's Nineveh Plain." Assyrian Policy Institute, 2020. http://www.aina.org/reports/cctfositnp.pdf.

Hardin, Russell. *One for All: The Logic of Group Conflict*. Princeton, NJ: Princeton University Press, 1997. https://doi.org/10.1515/9781400821693.

Harris, Shane. "The Re-Baathification of Iraq." *Foreign Policy*, August 21, 2014. https://foreignpol icy.com/2014/08/21/the-re-baathification-of-iraq/.

Harris, Shane. *@War: The Rise of the Military-Internet Complex*. Boston: Houghton Mifflin Harcourt, 2014.

Hashim, Ahmed S. "Iraq's Chaos: Why the Insurgency Won't Go Away." *Boston Review*, November 1, 2004. https://www.bostonreview.net/articles/hashim-iraqs-chaos/.

Hashim, Ahmed S. *Iraq's Sunni Insurgency*. Adelphi Paper 402. Abingdon, UK: Routledge, 2009.

Hassan, Hussein D. "Iraq: Tribal Structure, Social, and Political Activities." Congressional Research Service Report for Congress, 2007.

Hawkins, John Michael. "The Costs of Artillery: Harassment and Interdiction Fire in the Vietnam War." Master's thesis, Texas A&M University, 2004. https://oaktrust.library.tamu.edu/han dle/1969.1/ETD-TAMU-2004-THESIS-H285.

Hazelton, Jacqueline L. "The 'Hearts and Minds' Fallacy: Violence, Coercion, and Success in Counterinsurgency Warfare." *International Security* 42, no. 1 (2017): 80–113. https://doi. org/10.1162/ISEC_a_00283.

Healy, Jack, and Namo Abdulla. "Iraqi Kurdistan, Known as Haven, Faces Unrest." *New York Times*, February 23, 2011, sec. World. https://www.nytimes.com/2011/02/24/world/middlee ast/24kurd.html.

Hechter, Michael, and Nika Kabiri. "Attaining Social Order in Iraq." In *Order, Conflict, and Violence*, edited by Stathis N. Kalyvas, Ian Shapiro, and Tarek Masoud, 43–74. Cambridge: Cambridge University Press, 2008. https://doi.org/10.1017/CBO9780511755903.

Hedstrom, Peter, and Richard Swedberg, eds. *Social Mechanisms: An Analytical Approach to Social Theory*. Studies in Rationality and Social Change. Cambridge: Cambridge University Press, 1998. https://doi.org/10.1017/CBO9780511663901.

Helfont, Samuel. *Compulsion in Religion: Saddam Hussein, Islam, and the Roots of Insurgencies in Iraq*. New York: Oxford University Press, 2018.

Hiltermann, Joost. "The 1988 Anfal Campaign in Iraqi Kurdistan." *Sciences Po, Mass Violence and Resistance Research Network*, 2008.

Hiltermann, Joost. "The Perils of a Post-ISIS Iraq." *Foreign Policy*, September 22, 2016. https:// foreignpolicy.com/2016/09/22/the-perils-of-a-post-isis-iraq/.

Horowitz, Donald L. *Ethnic Groups in Conflict*. Berkeley: University of California Press, 1985.

Huesing, Scott A. *Echo in Ramadi: The Firsthand Story of U.S. Marines in Iraq's Deadliest City*. Washington DC: Regnery History, 2018.

Human Rights Watch. "Iraq's Crime of Genocide: The Anfal Campaign Against the Kurds." A Middle East Watch Report, 1993. https://www.hrw.org/reports/pdfs/i/iraq/iraq.937/anfalfull.pdf.

Hussein, Rikar. "Christian Iraqi Forces Join Fight Against IS." *VOA*, February 8, 2016. https:// www.voanews.com/a/christian-iraqi-forces-join-fight-against-is/3181940.html.

International Crisis Group. "Averting an ISIS Resurgence in Iraq and Syria." *Crisis Group Middle East Report* No. 207, October 11, 2019. https://www.crisisgroup.org/middle-east-north-afr ica/eastern-mediterranean/syria/207-averting-isis-resurgence-iraq-and-syria.

International Crisis Group. "Fight or Flight: The Desperate Plight of Iraq's 'Generation 2000.'" *Crisis Group Middle East Report* No. 169, August 8, 2016. https://www.crisisgroup.org/mid dle-east-north-africa/gulf-and-arabian-peninsula/iraq/fight-or-flight-desperate-plight-iraq-s-generation-2000.

International Crisis Group. "Iraq and the Kurds: Confronting Withdrawal Fears." *Crisis Group Middle East Report* No. 103, 2011. https://www.crisisgroup.org/middle-east-north-africa/gulf-and-arabian-peninsula/iraq/iraq-and-kurds-confronting-withdrawal-fears.

International Crisis Group. "Iraq: Fixing Security in Kirkuk." *Crisis Group Middle East Report* No. 215, 2020. https://www.crisisgroup.org/middle-east-north-africa/gulf-and-arabian-penins ula/iraq/215-iraq-fixing-security-kirkuk.

International Crisis Group. "Make or Break: Iraq's Sunnis and the State." *Crisis Group Middle East Report* No. 144, August 14, 2013. https://www.crisisgroup.org/middle-east-north-africa/gulf-and-arabian-peninsula/iraq/make-or-break-iraq-s-sunnis-and-state.

International Crisis Group. "The Next Iraqi War? Sectarianism and Civil Conflict." *Crisis Group Middle East Report* No. 51, 2006. https://www.crisisgroup.org/middle-east-north-africa/gulf-and-arabian-peninsula/iraq/next-iraqi-war-sectarianism-and-civil-conflict.

International Crisis Group. "Iraq's Paramilitary Groups: The Challenge of Rebuilding a Functioning State." *Crisis Group Middle East Report,* July 30, 2018. https://www.crisisgroup.org/middle-east-north-africa/gulf-and-arabian-peninsula/iraq/188-iraqs-paramilitary-groups-challenge-rebuilding-functioning-state.

Jackson, C. F. "Fighting for Feudalism? Dilemmas of State Consolidation in Iraq and Afghanistan." New York: International Studies Association Annual Convention, 2009.

Jackson, Colin. "Government in a Box? Counter-Insurgency, State Building, and the Technocratic Conceit." In *The New Counter-Insurgency Era in Critical Perspective,* edited by Celeste Ward Gventer, David Martin Jones, and M. L. R. Smith, 82–110. Rethinking Political Violence Series. London: Palgrave Macmillan, 2014. https://doi.org/10.1057/9781137336941_5.

Jackson, Colin F. "Defeat in Victory: Organizational Learning Dysfunction in Counterinsurgency." PhD thesis, Massachusetts Institute of Technology, 2008.

Jakes, Lara. "After Backing Military Force in Past, U.S.A.I.D. Nominee Focuses on Deploying Soft Power." *New York Times,* April 13, 2021, sec. U.S. https://www.nytimes.com/2021/04/13/us/politics/samantha-power-biden.html.

Jentzsch, Corinna, Stathis N. Kalyvas, and Livia Isabella Schubiger. "Militias in Civil Wars." *Journal of Conflict Resolution* 59, no. 5 (2015): 755–769. https://doi.org/10.1177/0022002715576753.

Khan, Jesmeen. "The Iraqi Tribal Structure: Background and Influence on Counter-Terrorism." *Perspectives on Terrorism* 1, no. 1 (2010): 3–11.

Johnson, David E., M. Wade Markel, and Brian Shannon, "The 2008 Battle for Sadr City," RAND Occasional Paper, 2011.

Johnston, Patrick B. "Does Decapitation Work? Assessing the Effectiveness of Leadership Targeting in Counterinsurgency Campaigns." *International Security* 36, no. 4 (2012): 47–79. https://doi.org/10.1162/ISEC_a_00076.

Joost, Hiltermann. "The 1988 Anfal Campaign in Iraqi Kurdistan," *Online Encyclopedia of Mass Violence,* February 3, 2008. https://www.sciencespo.fr/mass-violence-war-massacre-resistance/en/document/1988-anfal-campaign-iraqi-kurdistan.html.

Jordan, David, James D. Kiras, David J. Lonsdale, Ian Speller, Christopher Tuck, and C. Dale Walton. *Understanding Modern Warfare.* Cambridge: Cambridge University Press, 2008.

Jordan, Jenna. "When Heads Roll: Assessing the Effectiveness of Leadership Decapitation." *Security Studies* 18, no. 4 (2009): 719–755. https://doi.org/10.1080/09636410903369068.

Kadhim, Abbas K. *Reclaiming Iraq: The 1920 Revolution and the Founding of the Modern State.* Austin: University of Texas Press, 2012.

Kalyvas, Stathis N. "Review of The New US Army/Marine Corps Counterinsurgency Field Manual." *Perspectives on Politics* 6, no. 2 (2008): 351–353.

Kalyvas, Stathis N. *The Logic of Violence in Civil War.* Cambridge: Cambridge University Press, 2006.

Kalyvas, Stathis N., and Nicholas Sambanis. "Bosnia's Civil War: Origins and Violence Dynamics." In *Understanding Civil War: Evidence and Analysis,* edited by Paul Collier and Nicholas Sambanis, Volume 2: *Europe, Central Asia, Other Regions,* 191–229. World Bank, 2005. https://doi.org/10.1596/978-0-8213-6049-1.

Kane, Sean. "Iraq's Disputed Territories: A View of the Political Horizon and Implications for U.S. Policy." United States Institute of Peace, 2011. https://www.usip.org/publications/2011/04/iraqs-disputed-territories.

Kaplan, Robert D. "Review of *Humane: How the United States Abandoned Peace and Reinvented War*, by Samuel Moyn." *New York Times*, September 14, 2021, sec. Books. https://www.nyti mes.com/2021/09/14/books/review/humane-samuel-moyn.html.

Karlin, Mara E. *Building Militaries in Fragile States: Challenges for the United States.* Philadelphia: University of Pennsylvania Press, 2018.

Karlin, Mara E. *The Inheritance: America's Military after Two Decades of War.* Washington, DC: Brookings Institution Press, 2022. https://doi.org/10.7864/j.ctv11hpt4s.

Kaufman, Stuart J. *Modern Hatreds: The Symbolic Politics of Ethnic War.* Cornell Studies in Security Affairs. Ithaca, NY: Cornell University Press, 2001.

Kaufmann, Chaim. "Intervention in Ethnic and Ideological Civil Wars: Why One Can Be Done and the Other Can't." *Security Studies* 6, no. 1 (1996a): 62–101. https://doi.org/10.1080/09636419608429300.

Kaufmann, Chaim. "Possible and Impossible Solutions to Ethnic Civil Wars." *International Security* 20, no. 4 (1996b): 136–175. https://doi.org/10.1162/isec.20.4.136.

Keaney, Thomas A. "Surveying Gulf War Air Power." *National Defense University*, 1993.

Keltner, Dacher, Phoebe C. Ellsworth, and Kari Edwards. "Beyond Simple Pessimism: Effects of Sadness and Anger on Social Perception." *Journal of Personality and Social Psychology* 64, no. 5 (1993): 740–752. https://doi.org/10.1037//0022-3514.64.5.740.

Khoury, Dina Rizk. *Iraq in Wartime: Soldiering, Martyrdom, and Remembrance.* New York: Cambridge University Press, 2013.

Kilcullen, David. *Counterinsurgency.* Oxford: Oxford University Press, 2010.

Kilcullen, David. *Out of the Mountains: The Coming Age of the Urban Guerrilla.* New York: Oxford University Press, 2013.

Kilcullen, David. *The Accidental Guerrilla: Fighting Small Wars in the Midst of a Big One.* Oxford: Oxford University Press, 2009.

Kilcullen, David. *The Dragons and the Snakes: How the Rest Learned to Fight the West.* New York: Oxford University Press, 2020.

King, Gary, Robert O. Keohane, and Sidney Verba. *Designing Social Inquiry: Scientific Inference in Qualitative Research.* Princeton, NJ: Princeton University Press, 1994.

Knarr, William. "The 2005 Iraqi Sunni Awakening: The Role of the Desert Protectors Program." Joint Special Operations University Report. Vol. 15–4. JSOU Report. MacDill Air Force Base, Florida: JSOU Press Florida, 2015. https://purl.fdlp.gov/GPO/gpo81733.

Knarr, William, Dale Alford, Mary Hawkins, David Graves, Jennifer Goodman, Matthew Bunn, Carolyn Leonard, et al. "Al Sahawa—The Awakening. Volume IV: Al Anbar Province, Area of Operations Topeka, Ramadi." Institute for Defense Analysis, Joint Advanced Warfighting Program, 2016. https://apps.dtic.mil/sti/citations/AD1019772.

Knights, Michael. "Saddam Hussein's Faithful Friend, the King of Clubs, Might Be the Key to Saving Iraq." *New Republic*, June 24, 2014. https://newrepublic.com/article/118356/izzat-ibrahim-al-douri-saddam-husseins-pal-key-stopping-isis.

Kocher, Matthew Adam, Adria K. Lawrence, and Nuno P. Monteiro. "Nationalism, Collaboration, and Resistance: France under Nazi Occupation." *International Security* 43, no. 2 (2018): 117–150. https://doi.org/10.1162/isec_a_00329.

Kocher, Matthew Adam, Thomas B. Pepinsky, and Stathis N. Kalyvas. "Aerial Bombing and Counterinsurgency in the Vietnam War." *American Journal of Political Science* 55, no. 2 (2011): 201–218. https://doi.org/10.1111/j.1540-5907.2010.00498.x.

Komer, Robert W. "Bureaucracy Does Its Thing: Institutional Constraints on U.S.-GVN Performance in Vietnam." Santa Monica, CA: RAND Corporation, 1972. https://www.rand.org/pubs/reports/R967.html.

Krepinevich, Andrew F. *7 Deadly Scenarios: A Military Futurist Explores War in the 21st Century.* New York: Bantam Books, 2009.

Krohley, Nicholas. *The Death of the Mehdi Army: The Rise, Fall, and Revival of Iraq's Most Powerful Militia.* London: Hurst, 2015.

Kruczek, Gregory J. "Christian (Second-Order) Minorities and the Struggle for the Homeland: The Assyrian Democratic Movement in Iraq and the Nineveh Plains Protection Units." *Journal of the Middle East and Africa* 12, no. 1 (2021): 93–121. https://doi.org/10.1080/21520 844.2021.1886521.

Kukis, Mark. "Ethnic Cleansing in a Baghdad Neighborhood?" *Time*, October 25, 2006a. https://content.time.com/time/world/article/0,8599,1550441,00.html.

Kukis, Mark. "Inside an Iraqi Battleground Neighborhood." *Time*, November 25, 2006b. https://content.time.com/time/world/article/0,8599,1562900,00.html.

Kukis, Mark. *Voices from Iraq: A People's History, 2003–2009*. New York: Columbia University Press, 2011.

Kuperman, Alan J. "The Moral Hazard of Humanitarian Intervention: Lessons from the Balkans." *International Studies Quarterly* 52, no. 1 (2008): 49–80. https://doi.org/10.1111/j.1468-2478.2007.00491.x.

Kurd Net Editorial Staff. "PUK and Gorran Sign Final Agreement in Iraqi Kurdistan." *Kurd Net—Ekurd.Net Daily News*, May 17, 2016. https://ekurd.net/puk-gorran-sign-agreem ent-2016-05-17.

Kurd Net Editorial Staff. "U.S.-Iraqi Kurdistan MOU Signed with Baghdad's Support and Approval." *Kurd Net—Ekurd.Net Daily News*, July 23, 2016. https://ekurd.net/us-kurdistan-deal-baghdad-2016-07-23.

Human Rights Watch. "The Kurdish Security Forces." Human Rights Watch, July 2007. https://www.hrw.org/reports/2007/kurdistan0707/5.htm.

Kurdistan Parliament, Iraq. "National Union Coalition MPs." Accessed April 22, 2023. https://www.parliament.krd/english/members-and-parties/parties/national-union-coalit ion-mps/.

Laitin, David D. *Hegemony and Culture: Politics and Religious Change among the Yoruba*. Chicago: University of Chicago Press, 1986.

Lamb, Christopher J., and Evan Munsing. *Secret Weapon High-Value Target Teams as an Organizational Innovation*. National Defense University, Center for Strategic Research Institute for National Strategic Studies, 2011.

Lambeth, Benjamin S. "Gradualism to a Fault." *Air Force Magazine*, March 26, 2021. https://www.airandspaceforces.com/article/gradualism-to-a-fault/.

Lamprecht, Peter. "Iraqi Gang Frees Kidnapped Christians." *Compass Direct News*, June 26, 2007. https://www.christianitytoday.com/news/2007/june/iraqi-gang-frees-kidnapped-christi ans.html.

Langer, Gary. "Concern in Iraq Peaks among Its Sunni Arabs, Sunni and Shia in Iraq: Where Things Stand." *ABC News Poll*, March 17, 2004a. https://abcnews.go.com/images/pdf/949 a2SunniShia.pdf.

Langer, Gary. "While Ambivalent about the War, Most Iraqis Report a Better Life, Iraq: Where Things Stand." *ABC News Poll*, March 15, 2004b. https://abcnews.go.com/images/pdf/949a1IraqPoll.pdf.

Larson, Jennifer M., and Janet I. Lewis. "Rumors, Kinship Networks, and Rebel Group Formation." *International Organization* 72, no. 4 (2018): 871–903. https://doi.org/10.1017/S00208 18318000243.

Lawrence, Quil. *Invisible Nation: How the Kurds' Quest for Statehood Is Shaping Iraq and the Middle East*. New York: Walker, 2008.

Leezenberg, Michiel. "Urbanization, Privatization, and Patronage: The Political Economy of Iraqi Kurdistan." In *The Kurds: Nationalism and Politics*, edited by Faleh A. Jabar and Hosham Dawood, 151–179. London: Saqi, 2006.

Lerner, Jennifer S., Roxana M. Gonzalez, Deborah A. Small, and Baruch Fischhoff. "Effects of Fear and Anger on Perceived Risks of Terrorism: A National Field Experiment." *Psychological Science* 14, no. 2 (2003): 144–150. https://doi.org/10.1111/1467-9280.01433.

Lerner, Jennifer S., and Dacher Keltner. "Beyond Valence: Toward a Model of Emotion-Specific Influences on Judgement and Choice." *Cognition & Emotion* 14, no. 4 (2000): 473–493.

Lerner, Jennifer S., and Dacher Keltner. "Fear, Anger, and Risk." *Journal of Personality and Social Psychology* 81, no. 1 (2001): 146–159. https://doi.org/10.1037/0022-3514.81.1.146.

Lewis, Janet I. "How Does Ethnic Rebellion Start?" *Comparative Political Studies* 50, no. 10 (2017): 1420–1450. https://doi.org/10.1177/0010414016672235.

Lichtenheld, Adam G. "Explaining Population Displacement Strategies in Civil Wars: A Cross-National Analysis." *International Organization* 74, no. 2 (2020): 253–294. https://doi.org/10.1017/S0020818320000089.

Lijphart, Arend. "Consociational Democracy." *World Politics* 21, no. 2 (1969): 207–225. https://doi.org/10.2307/2009820.

Lindner, Evelin. *Making Enemies: Humiliation and International Conflict*. Contemporary Psychology. Westport, CT: Praeger Security International, 2006.

Lindsay, Jon, and Roger D. Petersen. "Varieties of Insurgency and Counterinsurgency in Iraq, 2003–2009." *CIWAG Case Studies* 10 (2012). https://digital-commons.usnwc.edu/ciwag-case-studies/10.

Long, Austin. "The Anbar Awakening." *Survival* 50, no. 2 (2008): 67–94. https://doi.org/10.1080/00396330802034283.

Long, Austin. "Whack-a-Mole or Coup de Grace? Institutionalization and Leadership Targeting in Iraq and Afghanistan." *Security Studies* 23, no. 3 (2014): 471–512. https://doi.org/10.1080/09636412.2014.935229.

Long, Austin G. *The Soul of Armies: Counterinsurgency Doctrine and Military Culture in the US and UK*. Ithaca, NY: Cornell University Press, 2016.

Lyall, Jason. "Are Co-ethnics More Effective Counterinsurgents? Evidence from the Second Chechen War." *American Political Science Review* 104, no. 1 (2010): 1–20. https://doi.org/10.1017/S0003055409990323.

Lyall, Jason. "Civilian Casualties, Humanitarian Aid, and Insurgent Violence in Civil Wars." *International Organization* 73, no. 4 (2019): 901–926. https://doi.org/10.1017/S0020818319000262.

Lyall, Jason. *Divided Armies: Inequality and Battlefield Performance in Modern War*. Princeton Studies in International History and Politics. Princeton, NJ: Princeton University Press, 2020.

Lyall, Jason. "Does Indiscriminate Violence Incite Insurgent Attacks? Evidence from Chechnya." *Journal of Conflict Resolution* 53, no. 3 (2009): 331–362. https://doi.org/10.1177/0022002708330881.

Lyall, Jason. "Dynamic Coercion in Civil War: Evidence from Air Operations in Afghanistan," Unpublished paper.

Lyall, Jason. "Silver Bullet: Why Decapitation Strikes (Don't) Work." *Washington Post*, December 7, 2015. https://www.washingtonpost.com/news/monkey-cage/wp/2015/06/19/silver-bullet-why-decapitation-strikes-dont-work/.

Lyall, Jason, Graeme Blair, and Kosuke Imai. "Explaining Support for Combatants during Wartime: A Survey Experiment in Afghanistan." *American Political Science Review* 107, no. 4 (2013): 679–705. https://doi.org/10.1017/S0003055413000403.

Lyall, Jason, Yuki Shiraito, and Kosuke Imai. "Coethnic Bias and Wartime Informing." *Journal of Politics* 77, no. 3 (2015): 833–848. https://doi.org/10.1086/681590.

Lyall, Jason, and Isaiah Wilson. "Rage against the Machines: Explaining Outcomes in Counterinsurgency Wars." *International Organization* 63, no. 1 (Winter 2009): 67–106. https://doi.org/10.1017/S0020818309090031.

Lyall, Jason, Yang-Yang Zhou, and Kosuke Imai. "Can Economic Assistance Shape Combatant Support in Wartime? Experimental Evidence from Afghanistan." *American Political Science Review* 114, no. 1 (2020): 126–143. https://doi.org/10.1017/S0003055419000698.

Lynch, Marc. "Explaining the Awakening: Engagement, Publicity, and the Transformation of Iraqi Sunni Political Attitudes." *Security Studies* 20, no. 1 (2011): 36–72. https://doi.org/10.1080/09636412.2011.549017.

Makiya, Kanan. "A Model for Post-Saddam Iraq." *Journal of Democracy* 14, no. 3 (2003): 5–12. https://doi.org/10.1353/jod.2003.0056.

Makiya, Kanan. *Cruelty and Silence: Tyranny, Uprising and the Arab World*. New York: W. W. Norton, 1993.

Makiya, Kanan. *Republic of Fear: The Politics of Modern Iraq*. Berkeley: University of California Press, 1989.

Malik, Hamdi. "The Future of Iraq's Popular Mobilization Forces." Carnegie Endowment for International Peace, September 21, 2017. https://carnegieendowment.org/sada/73186.

Malik, Hamdi. "Pro-Sistani 'Popular Mobilization Units' Break with Pro-Iran Militias in Iraq." *Al-Monitor*, April 29, 2020. https://www.al-monitor.com/originals/2020/04/iraq-iran-pmu-sistani.html.

Malik, Hamdi. "The Still-Growing Threat of Iran's Chosen Proxy in Iraq." *War on the Rocks*, October 5, 2020. https://warontherocks.com/2020/10/the-still-growing-threat-of-irans-chosen-proxy-in-iraq/.

Mano, Haim. "Risk-Taking, Framing Effects, and Affect." *Organizational Behavior and Human Decision Processes* 57, no. 1 (1994): 38–58. https://doi.org/10.1006/obhd.1994.1003.

Mansour, Renad. "Networks of Power: The Popular Mobilization Forces and the State in Iraq." Chatham House Research Paper. Chatham House Middle East and North Africa Programme, 2021. https://www.chathamhouse.org/sites/default/files/2021-02/2021-02-25-networks-of-power-mansour.pdf.

Mansour, Renad. "The Popular Mobilisation Forces and the Balancing of Formal and Informal Power." *LSE Middle East Centre*, March 15, 2018. https://blogs.lse.ac.uk/mec/2018/03/15/the-popular-mobilisation-forces-and-the-balancing-of-formal-and-informal-power/.

Mao, Zedong. *On Guerrilla Warfare*. Praeger Publications in Russian History and World Communism. New York: Praeger, 1961.

Marks, Steven M., Thomas M. Meer, and Matthew T. Nilson. "Manhunting: A Methodology for Finding Persons of National Interest." Naval Postgraduate School, 2005.

McCauley, Clark. "Toward a Psychology of Humiliation in Asymmetric Conflict." *American Psychologist* 72, no. 3 (2017): 255–265. https://doi.org/10.1037/amp0000063.

McFate, Sean. *The New Rules of War: Victory in the Age of Durable Disorder*. New York: William Morrow, 2019.

McGrath, John J. "The Battle of Hawijah, April 7, 2004." In *Between The Rivers: Combat Action in Iraq, 2003–2005 [Illustrated Edition]*, edited by John J. McGrath, 1–18. Fort Leavenworth, KS: Combat Studies Institute Press, US Army Combined Arms Center, 2012.

McWilliams, Timothy S., and Kurtis P. Wheeler, eds. *Al-Anbar Awakening: From Insurgency to Counterinsurgency in Iraq, 2004–2009*, Volume I: *American Perspectives*. Marine Corps University Press, 2009.

McWilliams, Timothy S., and Kurtis P. Wheeler, eds. *Al-Anbar Awakening: From Insurgency to Counterinsurgency in Iraq, 2004–2009*, Volume II: *Iraqi Perspectives*. Marine Corps University Press, 2009.

Mearsheimer, John J. *The Tragedy of Great Power Politics*. New York: W. W. Norton, 2014.

Menon, Rajan. *The Conceit of Humanitarian Intervention*. New York: Oxford University Press, 2016.

Mir, Asfandyar. "What Explains Counterterrorism Effectiveness? Evidence from the U.S. Drone War in Pakistan." *International Security* 43, no. 2 (2018): 45–83. https://doi.org/10.1162/isec_a_00331.

Moïsi, Dominique. *The Geopolitics of Emotion: How Cultures of Fear, Humiliation, and Hope Are Reshaping the World*. Palatine, IL: Anchor Books, 2010.

Moloney, Ed. *Voices from the Grave: Two Men's War in Ireland*. London: Faber and Faber, 2010.

Monroe, Shelby. "How Do You Solve a Problem like Hawijah?," July 8, 2006. http://101dayswith101st.blogspot.com/2006/07/how-do-you-solve-problem-like-hawijah_08.html.

Morris, Loveday. "Investigation Finds 50,000 'Ghost' Soldiers in Iraqi Army, Prime Minister Says." *Washington Post*, November 30, 2014, sec. Middle East. https://www.washingtonpost.com/world/middle_east/investigation-finds-50000-ghost-soldiers-in-iraqi-army-prime-minister-says/2014/11/30/d8864d6c-78ab-11e4-9721-80b3d95a28a9_story.html.

Montgomery, Gary, and Timothy S. McWilliams. *Al-Anbar Awakening: From Insurgency to Counterinsurgency in Iraq, 2004-2009, Volume II, Iraqi Perspectives.* Quantico, VA: Marine Corps University Press, 2009.

Moyn, Samuel. *Humane: How the United States Abandoned Peace and Reinvented War.* New York: Farrar, Straus and Giroux, 2021.

Murray, Ben. "Hawijah: A Small City with Big Problems." *Stars and Stripes*, October 19, 2006. https://www.stripes.com/news/hawijah-a-small-city-with-big-problems-1.55657.

Nagl, John A. *Knife Fights: A Memoir of Modern War in Theory and Practice.* New York: Penguin Press, 2014.

Nagl, John A. *Learning to Eat Soup with a Knife: Counterinsurgency Lessons from Malaya and Vietnam.* Chicago: University of Chicago Press, 2002.

Nagle, John. "Consociationalism Is Dead! Long Live Zombie Power-Sharing." *Studies in Ethnicity and Nationalism* 20, no. 2 (2020): 137–144. https://doi.org/10.1111/sena.12329.

Nanes, Matthew. "Police Integration and Support for Anti-Government Violence in Divided Societies: Evidence from Iraq." *Journal of Peace Research* 57, no. 2 (2020): 329–343. https://doi.org/10.1177/0022343319866901.

Narang, Neil, and Jessica A. Stanton. "A Strategic Logic of Attacking Aid Workers: Evidence from Violence in Afghanistan." *International Studies Quarterly* 61, no. 1 (2017): 38–51. https://doi.org/10.1093/isq/sqw053.

Naylor, Sean. *Relentless Strike: The Secret History of Joint Special Operations Command.* New York: St. Martin's Press, 2015.

North, Douglass C., John Joseph Wallis, and Barry R. Weingast. *Violence and Social Orders: A Conceptual Framework for Interpreting Recorded Human History.* New York: Cambridge University Press, 2009. https://doi.org/10.1017/CBO9780511575839.

Nussio, Enzo, and Juan E. Ugarriza. "Why Rebels Stop Fighting: Organizational Decline and Desertion in Colombia's Insurgency." *International Security* 45, no. 4 (2021): 167–203. https://doi.org/10.1162/isec_a_00406.

O'Driscoll, Dylan, and Bahar Baser. "Independence Referendums and Nationalist Rhetoric: The Kurdistan Region of Iraq." *Third World Quarterly* 40, no. 11 (2019): 2016–2034. https://doi.org/10.1080/01436597.2019.1617631.

O'Hanlon, Michael E., and Ian S. Livingston. "Iraq Index." Brookings Institution, n.d. https://www.brookings.edu/iraq-index/.

Ollivant, Douglas A., and Erica Gaston. "The Problem with the Narrative of 'Proxy War' in Iraq." *War on the Rocks*, May 31, 2019. https://warontherocks.com/2019/05/the-problem-with-the-narrative-of-proxy-war-in-iraq/.

Ollivant, Douglas A., and Erica Gaston. "U.S.-Iran Proxy Competition in Iraq." New America, 2020. http://newamerica.org/international-security/reports/us-iran-proxy-competition-iraq/.

Olson, Mancur. *The Logic of Collective Action: Public Goods and the Theory of Groups.* Cambridge, MA: Harvard University Press, 1971.

Omestad, Thomas. "Vulnerable Iraqi Minorities Making Gains with USIP Help." United States Institute of Peace, December 26, 2012. https://www.usip.org/publications/2012/12/vulnerable-iraqi-minorities-making-gains-usip-help.

Oppel, Richard A., Jr., and Sabrina Tavernise. "Car Bombings in Iraq Kill 33, with Shiites as Targets." *New York Times*, May 24, 2005. https://www.nytimes.com/2005/05/24/world/middleeast/car-bombings-in-iraq-kill-33-with-shiites-as-targets.html.

Oppenheim, Ben, Abbey Steele, Juan F. Vargas, and Michael Weintraub. "True Believers, Deserters, and Traitors: Who Leaves Insurgent Groups and Why." *Journal of Conflict Resolution* 59, no. 5 (2015): 794–823. https://doi.org/10.1177/0022002715576750.

Otto, Sabine. "The Grass Is Always Greener? Armed Group Side Switching in Civil Wars." *Journal of Conflict Resolution* 62, no. 7 (2018): 1459–1488. https://doi.org/10.1177/0022002717693047.

Packer, George. "A New Theory of American Power: The United States Can—and Must—Wield Its Power for Good." *Atlantic*, November 21, 2022. https://www.theatlantic.com/magazine/archive/2022/12/american-foreign-policy-in-wartime/671899/.

Palani, Kamaran, Jaafar Khidir, Mark Dechesne, and Edwin Bakker. "The Development of Kurdistan's de Facto Statehood: Kurdistan's September 2017 Referendum for Independence." *Third World Quarterly* 40, no. 12 (2019): 2270–2288. https://doi.org/10.1080/01436 597.2019.1619452.

Parker, Ned. "The Conflict in Iraq: A Ministry of Fiefdoms." *Los Angeles Times*, July 30, 2007.

Parkinson, Sarah Elizabeth. "Organizing Rebellion: Rethinking High-Risk Mobilization and Social Networks in War." *American Political Science Review* 107, no. 3 (2013): 418–432. https://doi.org/10.1017/S0003055413000208.

Partlow, Joshua. "Mahdi Army, Not Al-Qaeda, Is Enemy No. 1 in Western Baghdad." *Washington Post*, July 16, 2007. http://www.washingtonpost.com/wpdyn/content/article/2007/07/15/AR2007071501248.html.

Patel, David S. "Ayatollahs on the Pareto Frontier: The Institutional Basis of Religious Authority in Iraq." Unpublished paper, 2005.

Patel, David S. "ISIS in Iraq: What We Get Wrong and Why 2015 Is Not 2007 Redux." Middle East Brief No. 87. Crown Center for Middle East Studies, 2015.

Patel, David S. "Order out of Chaos: Islam, Information, and the Rise and Fall of Social Orders in Iraq." Unpublished paper, October 12, 2017.

Pechenkina, Anna O., Andrew W. Bausch, and Kiron K. Skinner. "How Do Civilians Attribute Blame for State Indiscriminate Violence?" *Journal of Peace Research* 56, no. 4 (2019): 545–558. https://doi.org/10.1177/0022343319829798.

Perito, Robert M. "Iraq's Interior Ministry: Frustrating Reform." United States Institute of Peace, 2008. https://www.usip.org/publications/2008/05/iraqs-interior-ministry-frustrating-reform.

Petersen, Roger D. "The Future of American Military Intervention." *Horizons: Journal of International Relations and Sustainable Development*, no. 18 (2021): 180–195.

Petersen, Roger D. "Mechanisms and Structures in Comparisons." In *Critical Comparisons in Politics and Culture*, edited by John R. Bowen and Roger D. Petersen, 61–77. Cambridge: Cambridge University Press, 1999.

Petersen, Roger D. *Resistance and Rebellion: Lessons from Eastern Europe*. Studies in Rationality and Social Change. Cambridge: Cambridge University Press, 2001.

Petersen, Roger D. "Review of Timothy Andrews Sayle, Jeffery A. Engel, Hal Brands, and William Inboden. The Last Card: Inside George W. Bush's Decision to Surge in Iraq." H-Diplo Roundtable XXII-7, October 12, 2020. https://issforum.org/roundtables/PDF/Roundta ble-XXII-7.pdf.

Petersen, Roger D. *Western Intervention in the Balkans: The Strategic Use of Emotion in Conflict*. Cambridge Studies in Comparative Politics. New York: Cambridge University Press, 2011.

Petersen, Roger D., and Matthew Cancian. "Between Two Caesars: The Christians of Northern Iraq." *Providence* 10 (Winter 2018): 38–44.

Pittard, Dana J. H., and Wes J. Bryant. *Hunting the Caliphate: America's War on ISIS and the Dawn of the Strike Cell*. New York; Nashville: Post Hill Press, 2019.

Plana, Sara. "The Proxy Paradox: Explaining (Lack of) Over State-Sponsored Proxy Armed Groups." PhD thesis, Massachusetts Institute of Technology, 2021.

Pollack, Kenneth M. "The Middle East Abhors a Vacuum: America's Exit and the Coming Contest for Military Supremacy." *Foreign Affairs* 101, no. 3 (2022): 130–142.

Pond, Elizabeth. *Endgame in the Balkans: Regime Change, European Style*. Washington, DC: Brookings Institution Press, 2006.

Ponomarev, Sergey, and Tim Arango. "For Liberated Iraqi Christians, Still a Bleak Christmas." *New York Times*, December 23, 2016, sec. World. https://www.nytimes.com/2016/12/23/world/middleeast/for-liberated-iraqi-christians-still-a-bleak-christmas.html.

Popkin, Samuel Lewis. *The Rational Peasant: The Political Economy of Rural Society in Vietnam.* Berkeley: University of California Press, 1979.

Porch, Douglas. *Counterinsurgency: Exposing the Myths of the New Way of War.* New York: Cambridge University Press, 2013.

Posen, Barry. *The Sources of Military Doctrine: France, Britain, and Germany between the World Wars.* Cornell Studies in Security Affairs. Ithaca, NY: Cornell University Press, 1984.

Posen, Barry R. "Civil Wars and the Structure of World Power." *Daedalus* 146, no. 4 (2017): 167–179. https://doi.org/10.1162/DAED_a_00467.

Priest, Dana, and William M. Arkin. "'Top Secret America': A Look at the Military's Joint Special Operations Command." *Washington Post*, September 2, 2011, sec. National Security. https://www.washingtonpost.com/world/national-security/top-secret-america-a-look-at-the-militarys-joint-special-operations-command/2011/08/30/gIQAvYuAxJ_story.html.

Pring, Coralie. "Kurdistan Region of Iraq: Overview of Corruption and Anti-Corruption." Transparency International, 2015. https://knowledgehub.transparency.org/helpdesk/kurdistan-region-of-iraq-overview-of-corruption-and-anti-corruption.

Radin, Andrew. *Institution Building in Weak States: The Primacy of Local Politics.* Washington, DC: Georgetown University Press, 2020.

Radin, Andrew. "Politics as War by Other Means: The Limits of Foreign-Led State-Building after Civil Wars." PhD thesis, Massachusetts Institute of Technology, 2012.

Rasheed, Ahmed, and Tim Cocks. "Some Iraqi Fighters Desert Posts." *Reuters*, May 6, 2009, sec. World News. https://www.reuters.com/article/us-iraq-awakening-idUSTRE54544Q20090506.

Rathmell, Andrew, Olga Oliker, Terrence K. Kelly, David Brannan, and Keith Crane. "Developing Iraq's Security Sector: The Coalition Provisional Authority's Experience." Santa Monica, CA: RAND National Defense Research Institute, 2005. https://www.rand.org/pubs/monographs/MG365.html.

Rayburn, Joel D., Frank K. Sobchak, Jeanne F. Godfroy, Matthew D. Morton, James S. Powell, and Matthew M. Zais, eds. *The US Army in the Iraq War*, Volume 1: *Invasion— Insurgency—Civil War 2003–2006.* Carlisle, PA: United States Army War College Press, 2019.

Rayburn, Joel D., Frank K. Sobchak, Jeanne F. Godfroy, Matthew D. Morton, James S. Powell, and Matthew M. Zais, eds. *The US Army in the Iraq War*, Volume 2: *Surge and Withdrawal, 2007–2011.* Carlisle, PA: United States Army War College Press, 2019.

Reid, John. "Putin, Pretext, and the Dark Side of the 'Responsibility to Protect.'" *War on the Rocks*, May 27, 2022. https://warontherocks.com/2022/05/putin-pretext-and-the-dark-side-of-the-responsibility-to-protect/.

Revkin, Mara Redlich. "What Explains Taxation by Resource-Rich Rebels? Evidence from the Islamic State in Syria." *Journal of Politics* 82, no. 2 (2020): 757–764. https://doi.org/10.1086/706597.

Ricks, Thomas E. *Fiasco: The American Military Adventure in Iraq 2003–2005.* New York: Penguin Books, 2007.

Ricks, Thomas E. *The Gamble: General David Petraeus and the American Military Adventure in Iraq, 2006–2008.* New York: Penguin Press, 2009.

Roggio, Bill. "Sadr City Barrier 'A Magnet' for Mahdi Army Attacks." *FDD's Long War Journal*, May 2, 2008.

Roggio, Bill. "The Sunni Awakening." *FDD's Long War Journal*, May 3, 2007. https://www.longwarjournal.org/archives/2007/05/the_sunni_awakening.php.

Rosen, Nir. *Aftermath: Following the Bloodshed of America's Wars in the Muslim World.* New York: Nation Books, 2010.

Rosen, Nir. *In the Belly of the Green Bird: The Triumph of the Martyrs in Iraq.* New York: Free Press, 2006.

Rosen, Nir. *Life Under Muqtada: Inside Baghdad's Shiite Slums. National*, Abu Dhabi, June 14, 2008. http://alternet.org/waroniraq/8788?

Rosen, Nir. "The Great Divide: Nir Rosen Goes Inside Baghdad's Shiite Slums to Witness Life under Muqtada Al Sadr and His Mahdi Army." *National*, June 5, 2008. https://www.thenatio nalnews.com/world/mena/the-great-divide-1.230693.

Rothstein, Hy S. *Afghanistan and the Troubled Future of Unconventional Warfare*. Annapolis, MD: Naval Institute Press, 2006.

Rudaw. "Iran-Backed Party Secures Large Number of Minority Seats in Iraqi Parliament." *Rudaw*, October 14, 2021. https://www.rudaw.net/english/middleeast/iraq/14102021.

Rudaw English [@RudawEnglish]. "#BREAKING: Iraqi Forces Are Inside the Office of Najmaldin Karim, Governor of #Kirkuk City. #KurdistanBlockade." Tweet. *Twitter*, October 16, 2017. https://twitter.com/RudawEnglish/status/919940178000711686.

Rudolf, Inna. "The Sunnis of Iraq's 'Shia' Paramilitary Powerhouse." The Century Foundation, 2020. https://tcf.org/content/report/sunnis-iraqs-shia-paramilitary-powerhouse/.

Russell, James A. *Innovation, Transformation, and War: Counterinsurgency Operations in Anbar and Ninewa Provinces, Iraq, 2005–2007*. Stanford, CA: Stanford University Press, 2011.

Saadoun, Mustafa. "Shiite Factions Close to Sistani Move to Separate from Iran-Backed Militias." *Al-Monitor*, 2020. https://www.al-monitor.com/originals/2020/12/iraq-iran-pmu-sist ani.html.

Saouli, Adham. "Sectarianism and Political Order in Iraq and Lebanon." *Studies in Ethnicity and Nationalism* 19, no. 1 (2019): 67–87. https://doi.org/10.1111/sena.12291.

Sargsyan, Irena L., and Andrew Bennett. "Discursive Emotional Appeals in Sustaining Violent Social Movements in Iraq, 2003–11." *Security Studies* 25, no. 4 (2016): 608–645. https://doi.org/10.1080/09636412.2016.1220203.

Savage, Charlie, and Eric Schmitt. "Biden Approves Plan to Redeploy Several Hundred Ground Forces into Somalia." *New York Times*, May 16, 2022, sec. U.S. https://www.nytimes.com/2022/05/16/us/politics/biden-military-somalia.html.

Sayle, Timothy A., Jeffrey A. Engel, Hal Brands, and William Inboden, eds. *The Last Card: Inside George W. Bush's Decision to Surge in Iraq*. Ithaca, NY: Cornell University Press, 2019.

Scahill, Jeremy. *Dirty Wars: The World Is a Battlefield*. New York: Nation Books, 2014.

Schemm, P. "US Struggles with Baghdad Sectarian Turf Wars." *Macau Daily Times/Agence France-Presse*, June 14, 2007.

Schubiger, Livia Isabella. "State Violence and Wartime Civilian Agency: Evidence from Peru." *Journal of Politics* 83, no. 4 (2021): 1383–1398. https://doi.org/10.1086/711720.

Schutte, Sebastian. "Violence and Civilian Loyalties: Evidence from Afghanistan." *Journal of Conflict Resolution* 61, no. 8 (2017): 1595–1625. https://doi.org/10.1177/0022002715626249.

Schwalm, Tony. *The Guerrilla Factory: The Making of Special Forces Officers, the Green Berets*. New York: Free Press, 2012. https://www.simonandschuster.com/books/The-Guerrilla-Factory/Tony-Schwalm/9781451623611.

Schwartzstein, Peter. "The Perfect Recipe for Making Jihadis Was Developed in This Small Iraq Town." *Reuters*, April 22, 2016. https://qz.com/667051/the-perfect-recipe-for-making-jiha dis-was-developed-in-this-small-iraqi-town.

Schweitzer, Matthew. "The Battle to Repair Iraq's Social Fabric, Beyond Mosul's Front Lines." *World Politics Review* (blog), November 23, 2016. https://www.worldpoliticsreview.com/the-battle-to-repair-iraq-s-social-fabric-beyond-mosul-s-front-lines/.

Schwin, Payson, and Aaron Rupar. "Hagel on Escalation: 'The Most Dangerous Foreign Policy Blunder in This Country since Vietnam.'" *Think Progress*, January 11, 2007. https://archive.thinkprogress.org/hagel-on-escalation-the-most-dangerous-foreign-policy-blunder-in-this-country-since-vietnam-2c6cabb3d41e/.

Scott, James C. *The Moral Economy of the Peasant: Rebellion and Subsistence in Southeast Asia*. New Haven, CT: Yale University Press, 1976.

Searle, Thomas R. "Tribal Engagement in Anbar Province: The Critical Role of Special Operations Forces." *Joint Forces Quarterly* 50, no. 3rd Quarter (2008): 62–66.

"Security Situation in Baghdad: The Shia Militias." Public theme report. Finnish Immigration Service, Country Information Service, April 29, 2015.

Senanayake, Sumedha. "Committee Decision Increases Tensions in Kirkuk." *Radio Free Europe/Radio Liberty*, February 8, 2007, sec. Iraq. https://www.rferl.org/a/1074583.html.

Serena, Chad C. *A Revolution in Military Adaptation: The US Army in Iraq*. Washington, DC: Georgetown University Press, 2011.

Serena, Chad C. *It Takes More than a Network: The Iraqi Insurgency and Organizational Adaptation*. Stanford, CA: Stanford University Press, 2014.

Sexton, Renard. "Aid as a Tool against Insurgency: Evidence from Contested and Controlled Territory in Afghanistan." *American Political Science Review* 110, no. 4 (2016): 731–749. https://doi.org/10.1017/S0003055416000356.

Seymour, Lee JM. "Why Factions Switch Sides in Civil Wars: Rivalry, Patronage, and Realignment in Sudan." *International Security* 39, no. 2 (2014): 92–131. https://doi.org/10.1162/ISEC_a_00179.

Shadid, Anthony. *Night Draws Near: Iraq's People in the Shadow of America's War*. New York: Henry Holt, 2005.

Shanker, Thom. "Warning against Wars like Iraq and Afghanistan." *New York Times*, February 25, 2011, sec. World. https://www.nytimes.com/2011/02/26/world/26gates.html.

Shapiro, Jacob N., and Nils B. Weidmann. "Is the Phone Mightier than the Sword? Cellphones and Insurgent Violence in Iraq." *International Organization* 69, no. 2 (2015): 247–274. https://doi.org/10.1017/S0020818314000423.

Shapiro, Jacob N., and Nils B. Weidmann. "Talking about Killing: Cell Phones, Collective Action, and Insurgent Violence in Iraq." Unpublished manuscript. Princeton, NJ, 2011.

Shaver, Andrew, and Jacob N. Shapiro. "The Effect of Civilian Casualties on Wartime Informing: Evidence from the Iraq War." *Journal of Conflict Resolution* 65, no. 7–8 (2021): 1337–1377. https://doi.org/10.1177/0022002721991627.

Sherman, Matt. "Iraq's Little Armies." *New York Times*, March 8, 2006, sec. Opinion. https://www.nytimes.com/2006/03/08/opinion/iraqs-little-armies.html.

Sherman, Matthew. Interview with Matthew Sherman. Interview by *Frontline*, October 6, 2006. https://www.pbs.org/wgbh/pages/frontline/gangsofiraq/interviews/sherman.html.

Shesterinina, Anastasia. "Collective Threat Framing and Mobilization in Civil War." *American Political Science Review* 110, no. 3 (2016): 411–427. https://doi.org/10.1017/S0003055416000277.

Shultz, Richard H., Jr. *The Marines Take Anbar: The Four Year Fight Against al Qaeda*. Annapolis, MD: Naval Institute Press, 2013.

Silverman, Daniel. "Too Late to Apologize? Collateral Damage, Post-Harm Compensation, and Insurgent Violence in Iraq." *International Organization* 74, no. 4 (2020): 853–871. https://doi.org/10.1017/S0020818320000193.

Silverman, Daniel. "What Shapes Civilian Beliefs about Violent Events? Experimental Evidence from Pakistan." *Journal of Conflict Resolution* 63, no. 6 (2019): 1460–1487. https://doi.org/10.1177/0022002718791676.

Sjursen, Danny. "I Was Part of the Iraq War Surge. It Was a Disaster." *Nation*, May 9, 2017. https://www.thenation.com/article/archive/i-was-part-of-the-iraq-war-surge-it-was-an-utter-disaster/.

Skocpol, Theda. *States and Social Revolutions: A Comparative Analysis of France, Russia and China*. Cambridge: Cambridge University Press, 1979. https://doi.org/10.1017/CBO9780511815805.

Sky, Emma. *The Unraveling: High Hopes and Missed Opportunities in Iraq*. New York: Public Affairs, 2015.

Slaughter, Anne-Marie. "A New U.N. for a New Century." *Fordham Law Review* 74, no. 6 (2006): Article 1.

Smith, Niel, and Sean MacFarland. "Anbar Awakens: The Tipping Point." *Military Review* 88, no. 2 (April 2008): 41–52.

Snyder, Jack L. *The Ideology of the Offensive: Military Decision Making and the Disasters of 1914.* Cornell Studies in Security Affairs. Ithaca, NY: Cornell University Press, 1984. https://doi.org/10.7591/9780801468629.

Sonin, Konstantin, Jarnickae Wilson, and Austin Wright. "Rebel Capacity and Combat Tactics." BFI Working Paper. Becker Friedman Institute, 2019.

Sonin, Konstantin, and Austin L. Wright. "Information Operations Increase Civilian Security Cooperation." BFI Working Paper. Becker Friedman Institute, 2019.

Spencer, John. "Stealing the Enemy's Urban Advantage: The Battle of Sadr City." Modern War Institute at West Point, 2019. https://mwi.usma.edu/stealing-enemys-urban-advantage-battle-sadr-city/.

Spencer, Richard. "Iraq Crisis: The Streets of Erbil's Newly Christian Suburb Are Now Full of Helpless People." *Telegraph*, August 8, 2014. https://www.telegraph.co.uk/news/worldnews/middleeast/iraq/11022879/Iraq-crisis-The-streets-of-Erbils-newly-Christian-suburb-are-now-full-of-helpless-people.html.

Stanford's Center for International Security and Cooperation. "Mapping Militants." Accessed April 17, 2023. https://cisac.fsi.stanford.edu/mappingmilitants.

Staniland, Paul. "Between a Rock and a Hard Place: Insurgent Fratricide, Ethnic Defection, and the Rise of Pro-State Paramilitaries." *Journal of Conflict Resolution* 56, no. 1 (2012): 16–40. https://doi.org/10.1177/0022002711429681.

Staniland, Paul. "Militias, Ideology, and the State." *Journal of Conflict Resolution* 59, no. 5 (2015): 770–793. https://doi.org/10.1177/0022002715576749.

Staniland, Paul. *Networks of Rebellion: Explaining Insurgent Cohesion and Collapse.* Cornell Studies in Security Affairs. Ithaca, NY: Cornell University Press, 2014.

Staniland, Paul. "The U.S. Military is Trying to Manage Foreign Conflicts—Not Resolve Them. Here's Why." *Monkey Cage*, July 16, 2018.

Staniland, Paul. *Ordering Violence: Explaining Armed Group-State Relations from Conflict to Cooperation.* Ithaca, NY: Cornell University Press, 2021.

Stansfield, Gareth. "Finding a Dangerous Equilibrium: Internal Politics in Iraqi Kurdistan—Parties, Tribes, Religion, and Ethnicity Reconsidered." In *The Kurds: Nationalism and Politics,* edited by Faleh A. Jabar and Hosham Dawood, 258–76. London: Saqi, 2006.

Stern, Jessica. *Terror in the Name of God: Why Religious Militants Kill.* New York: Harper Collins, 2003.

Stewart, Megan A. "Civil War as State-Making: Strategic Governance in Civil War." *International Organization* 72, no. 1 (2018): 205–226. https://doi.org/10.1017/S0020818317000418.

Strayer, Joseph R. *On the Medieval Origins of the Modern State.* Princeton Classic Editions. Princeton, NJ: Princeton University Press, 1973. https://doi.org/10.1515/9781400828579.

Summers, Harry G. *On Strategy: The Vietnam War in Context.* Reissue edition. Novato, CA: Presidio Press, 1995.

Suny, Ron. "Why We Hate You: The Passions of National Identity and Ethnic Violence." Working Paper, Berkeley Program in Soviet and Post-Soviet Studies. Spring 2004.

Susman, Tina. "Two Baghdad Districts See No Decline in Sectarian 'Cleansing': Military Officials Say Violence Has Eased, but the Killings Continue." *Los Angeles Times*, August 12, 2007.

Taha, Amir. "Turning Ex-Combatants into Sadris: Explaining the Emergence of the Mahdi Army." *Middle Eastern Studies* 55, no. 3 (2019): 357–373. https://doi.org/10.1080/00263206.2018.1550078.

Tarrow, Sidney G., Charles Tilly, and Doug McAdam. *Dynamics of Contention.* Cambridge Studies in Contentious Politics. New York: Cambridge University Press, 2001.

Taylor, Brian D., and Roxana Botea. "Tilly Tally: War-Making and State-Making in the Contemporary Third World." *International Studies Review* 10, no. 1 (2008): 27–56. https://doi.org/10.1111/j.1468-2486.2008.00746.x.

Taylor, Kevin. "Postcards from Hell: A Two-Week Series about the Year-Long Tour of the Idaho 116th Brigade Combat Team." *Pacific Northwest Inlander*, May 24, 2006. https://www.inlander.com/news/postcards-from-hell-2128684.

Tecott, Rachel. "Targeted Killing: Thinking Through the Logic." *War on the Rocks*, September 28, 2016. https://warontherocks.com/2016/09/targeted-killing-thinking-through-the-logic/.

Tecott, Rachel Elizabeth. "The Cult of the Persuasive: The U.S. Military's Aversion to Coercion in Security Assistance." PhD thesis, Massachusetts Institute of Technology, 2021.

Tezcür, Güneş Murat. "Ordinary People, Extraordinary Risks: Participation in an Ethnic Rebellion." *American Political Science Review* 110, no. 2 (2016): 247–264. https://doi.org/10.1017/S0003055416000150.

The Economist. "The Other Jerusalem." April 4, 2007. http://www.economist.com/node/8976641.

The Economist. "One Step Back, Two Steps Forward." October 31, 2015. https://www.economist.com/middle-east-and-africa/2015/10/31/one-step-back-two-steps-forward.

Tilly, Charles. *Coercion, Capital, and European States, AD 990–1992*. Studies in Social Discontinuity. Cambridge, MA: Wiley-Blackwell, 1992.

Timmerman, Ken. "Kurdistan Minister—Rich Star, or Pawn?" *Newsmax*, May 1, 2008. https://www.newsmax.com/KenTimmerman/Kurdistan-minister/2008/05/01/id/337439/.

Todd, Lin, W. Patrick Lang, Jr., Albu Issa Tribe, R. Alan King, Andrea V. Jackson, Montgomery McFate, Ahmed S. Hashim, and Jeremy S. Harrington. "Iraq Tribal Study: Al-Anbar Governorate—The Albu Fahd Tribe, the Albu Mahal Tribe and the Albu Issa Tribe." Study Conducted under Contract with the Department of Defense, 2006.

Toft, Monica Duffy, and Yuri M. Zhukov. "Islamists and Nationalists: Rebel Motivation and Counterinsurgency in Russia's North Caucasus." *American Political Science Review* 109, no. 2 (2015): 222–238. https://doi.org/10.1017/S000305541500012X.

Toumaj, Amir. "Iraqi Popular Mobilization Forces Launch Operation Southwest of Mosul." *FDD's Long War Journal*, April 29, 2017. https://www.longwarjournal.org/archives/2017/04/iraqi-popular-mobilization-forces-launch-operation-southwest-of-mosul.php.

Tripp, Charles. *A History of Iraq*. 3rd edition. Cambridge: Cambridge University Press, 2010.

Tsebelis, George. *Nested Games: Rational Choice in Comparative Politics*. California Series on Social Choice and Political Economy. Berkeley: University of California Press, 1990.

Tucker, D., and C. J. Lamb. *Special Operations Forces*. New York: Columbia University Press, 2007.

Tversky, Amos, and Daniel Kahneman. "Loss Aversion in Riskless Choice: A Reference-Dependent Model." *Quarterly Journal of Economics* 106, no. 4 (1991): 1039–1061. https://doi.org/10.2307/2937956.

United States Department of State. "Country Reports on Terrorism 2017—Foreign Terrorist Organizations: Jaysh Rijal al-Tariq al-Naqshabandi (JRTN)," September 19, 2018. https://www.refworld.org/docid/5bcf1f3b21.html.

van den Toorn, Christine Mccaffray. "Internal Divides behind the Kurdistan Referendum." Carnegie Endowment for International Peace, 2017. https://carnegieendowment.org/sada/73359.

Urban, Mark. *Task Force Black: The Explosive True Story of the Secret Special Forces War in Iraq*. New York: Macmillan, 2011.

Verini, James. *They Will Have to Die Now: Mosul and the Fall of the Caliphate*. New York: W. W. Norton, 2019.

Volkan, Vamik. *Blood Lines: From Ethnic Pride to Ethnic Terrorism*. Boulder, CO: Westview Press, 1998.

Walt, Stephen M. *The Hell of Good Intentions: America's Foreign Policy Elite and the Decline of U.S. Primacy*. New York: Farrar, Straus and Giroux, 2018.

Washington Post. "Bloggers' Roundtable with Gen. Douglas M. Stone." September 18, 2007.

Wasser, Becca, Stacie L. Pettyjohn, Jeffrey Martini, Alexandra T. Evans, Karl P. Mueller, Nathaniel Edenfield, Gabrielle Tarini, Ryan Haberman, and Jalen Zeman. "The Air War against the Islamic State: The Role of Airpower in Operation Inherent Resolve." RAND Corporation, 2021. https://www.rand.org/pubs/research_reports/RRA388-1.html.

Watling, Jack. "The Shia Militias of Iraq." *Atlantic*, December 22, 2016, sec. Global. https://www.theatlantic.com/international/archive/2016/12/shia-militias-iraq-isis/510938/.

Weinstein, Jeremy M. *Inside Rebellion: The Politics of Insurgent Violence.* Cambridge: Cambridge University Press, 2007. https://mit.primo.exlibrisgroup.com/discovery/fulldisplay/cdi_webofscience_primary_000297985200014CitationCount/01MIT_INST:MIT.

Weiss, Michael, and Michael Pregent. "The U.S. Is Providing Air Cover for Ethnic Cleansing in Iraq." *Foreign Policy*, March 28, 2015. https://foreignpolicy.com/2015/03/28/the-united-states-is-providing-air-cover-for-ethnic-cleansing-in-iraq-shiite-militias-isis/.

Weiss, Thomas G. *Military-Civilian Interactions: Humanitarian Crises and the Responsibility to Protect.* New Millennium Books in International Studies. Lanham, MD: Rowman & Littlefield, 1999.

Wertheim, Stephen. "Iraq and the Pathologies of Primacy." *Foreign Affairs*, May–June, 2023. https://www.foreignaffairs.com/united-states/iraq-and-pathologies-primacy.

West, Bing. *The Strongest Tribe: War, Politics, and the Endgame in Iraq.* New York: Random House, 2009.

West, Ed. "Fighting Fire with Fire." *Catholic Herald* (blog), September 15, 2016. https://catholicherald.co.uk/fighting-fire-with-fire/.

Williams, Carol J., Paul Richter, and Laura King. "U.S. Faces Uncertain Task in Building Coalition against Islamic State." *Los Angeles Times*, September 12, 2014. https://www.latimes.com/world/middleeast/la-fg-us-international-coalition-20140911-story.html.

Williams, Noel. "Insights for Marine (and Beyond) Force Design from the Russo-Ukrainian War." *War on the Rocks*, March 31, 2022. https://warontherocks.com/2022/03/insights-for-marine-and-beyond-force-design-from-the-russo-ukrainian-war/.

Wilner, Alex S. "Targeted Killings in Afghanistan: Measuring Coercion and Deterrence in Counterterrorism and Counterinsurgency." *Studies in Conflict and Terrorism* 33, no. 4 (2010): 307–329. https://doi.org/10.1080/10576100903582543.

Wilson, Jamie. "US Voices Deep Regret for Baghdad Flag Incident." *Guardian*, August 14, 2003, sec. World news. https://www.theguardian.com/world/2003/aug/15/iraq.usa.

Wimmer, Andreas. *Nationalist Exclusion and Ethnic Conflict: Shadows of Modernity.* Cambridge, UK: Cambridge University Press, 2002.

Wing, Joel. "Musings on Iraq: Complete 2013 Kurdistan Regional Government Election Results." *Musings on Iraq*, October 9, 2013. http://musingsoniraq.blogspot.com/2013/10/complete-2013-kurdistan-regional.html.

Wong, Edward. "3 Car Bombs Go Off at Once in Northern Iraq, Killing 20." *New York Times*, June 8, 2005, sec. U.S. https://www.nytimes.com/2005/06/08/world/middleeast/3-car-bombs-go-off-at-once-in-northern-iraq-killing-20.html.

Wong, Edward, and Damien Cave. "Baghdad District Is a Model, but Only for Shiites." *New York Times*, May 22, 2007, sec. World. https://www.nytimes.com/2007/05/22/world/middleeast/22shiites.html.

Wood, Elisabeth Jean. *Insurgent Collective Action and War in El Salvador.* Cambridge, UK: Cambridge University Press, 2003.

Wood, Elisabeth Jean. "The Social Processes of Civil War: The Wartime Transformation of Social Networks." *Annual Review of Political Science* 11, no. 1 (2008): 539–561. https://doi.org/10.1146/annurev.polisci.8.082103.104832.

Wood, Reed M., and Jakana L. Thomas. "Women on the Frontline: Rebel Group Ideology and Women's Participation in Violent Rebellion." *Journal of Peace Research* 54, no. 1 (2017): 31–46. https://doi.org/10.1177/0022343316675025.

Worsnop, Alec. "Organization or Community? The Determinants of Insurgent Military Effectiveness." PhD thesis, Massachusetts Institute of Technology, 2016.

Wright, Austin L., Luke N. Condra, Jacob N. Shapiro, and Andrew C. Shaver. "Civilian Abuse and Wartime Informing." Working Paper, 2017. https://scholar.princeton.edu/sites/default/files/jns/files/wcss_17july2017.pdf.

Wright, David. "Vanishing History: Baghdad's Last 21 Jews." *ABC News Nightline*, January 30, 2004. https://abcnews.go.com/WNT/story?id=131496&page=1.

Wright, Timothy Flynn. "From Predator to Provider: The Role of Violence and Rules in Establishing Social Control." PhD thesis, Massachusetts Institute of Technology, 2018.

Yoshioka, Akiko. "Challenges for the Kurdistan Region: Disputed Territories and Kurdistani Identity." In *Iraq since the Invasion: People and Politics in a State of Conflict*, edited by Keiko Sakai and Philip Marfleet, 172–184. Abingdon, Oxon: Routledge, 2020 https://doi.org/10.4324/9780429201936.

Youash, Michael. "Creating a Nineveh Plain Local Police Force: Overcoming Ethno-Religious Minority Insecurity." Iraq Sustainable Democracy Project Policy Briefing. Iraq Sustainable Democracy Project, September 2007. http://www.iraqdemocracyproject.org/pdf/Minority%20Policing%20-%20policy%20brief.pdf.

Zucchino, David. "'Game Over.' Iraqi Forces See Beginning of the End for ISIS." *New York Times*, October 6, 2017, sec. World. https://www.nytimes.com/2017/10/06/world/middleeast/iraq-isis-hawija.html.

INDEX

For the benefit of digital users, indexed terms that span two pages (e.g., 52–53) may, on occasion, appear on only one of those pages.

Tables and figures are indicated by *t* and *f* following the page number